Government Structures in the U.S.A. and the Sovereign States of the Former U.S.S.R

Recent Titles in
Contributions in Political Science

The Kingfish and the Constitution: Huey Long, the First Amendment, and the Emergence of Modern Press Freedom in America
Richard C. Cortner

Unions and Public Policy: The New Economy, Law, and Democratic Politics
Lawrence G. Flood

U.S. Foreign and Strategic Policy in the Post-Cold War Era: A Geopolitical Perspective
Howard J. Wiarda, editor

Comparing State Polities: A Framework for Analyzing 100 Governments
Michael J. Sullivan III

Federalism and the Environment: Environmental Policymaking in Australia, Canada, and the United States
Kenneth M. Holland, F. L. Morton, and Brian Galligan, editors

Public Enterprise Management: International Case Studies
Ali Farazmand, editor

Mainstream(s) and Margins: Cultural Politics in the 90s
Michael Morgan and Susan Leggett, editors

The European Union, the United Nations, and the Revival of Confederal Governance
Frederick K. Lister

The Leviathan in the State Theory of Thomas Hobbes: Meaning and Failure of a Symbol
Carl Schmitt
Translated by George Schwab and Erna Hilfstein

On Ruins of Empire: Ethnicity and Nationalism in the Former Soviet Union
George Mirsky

Ethnoregional Conflict in Democracies: Mostly Ballots, Rarely Bullets
Saul Newman

Neocolonialism American Style, 1960–2000
William H. Blanchard

Government Structures in the U.S.A. and the Sovereign States of the Former U.S.S.R.

Power Allocation Among Central, Regional, and Local Governments

Edited by
JAMES E. HICKEY, JR.
and
ALEXEJ UGRINSKY

Prepared under the auspices of
Hofstra University

Contributions in Political Science, Number 357

GREENWOOD PRESS
Westport, Connecticut • London

Library of Congress Cataloging-in-Publication Data

Government structures in the U.S.A. and the sovereign states of the former U.S.S.R.: power allocation among central, regional, and local governments / edited by James E. Hickey, Jr. and Alexej Ugrinsky ; prepared under the auspices of Hofstra University.
p. cm.—(Contributions in political science, ISSN 0147-1066 ; no. 357)
Includes bibliographical references and index.
ISBN 0-313-29653-7 (alk. paper)
1. Comparative government. 2. Former Soviet republics—Politics and government. 3. United States—Politics and government. 4. Former Soviet republics—Economic conditions. 5. United States—Economic conditions. I. Hickey, James E. II. Ugrinsky, Alexej. III. Hofstra University. IV. Series.
JF51.G667 1996
320.3′0947—dc20 95-35685

British Library Cataloguing in Publication Data is available.

Library of Congress Catalog Card Number: 95-35685
ISBN: 0-313-29653-7
ISSN: 0147-1066

First published in 1996

Greenwood Press, 88 Post Road West, Westport, CT 06881
An imprint of Greenwood Publishing Group, Inc.

Printed in the United States of America

The paper used in this book complies with the Permanent Paper Standard issued by the National Information Standards Organization (Z39.48-1984).

10 9 8 7 6 5 4 3 2 1

Contents

Foreword

The genesis of this book was an extraordinary three-day conference held at Hofstra University School of Law during April 1992. The Conference—"Government Structures in the U.S.A. and the Sovereign States of the Former U.S.S.R.: Power Allocation Among Central, Regional and Local Governments"—was sponsored by the School of Law and was held in cooperation with a number of groups and organizations including the Russian Federation Permanent Mission to the United Nations and the Moscow Law Institute. The Conference involved over 100 scholars, government officials, public interest personnel and experts participating in over 20 substantive panels and sessions addressing the impact of relations among sovereign governments, subnational governments, and their citizens. The topics ranged from banking and budgets to education and human rights.

It is especially appropriate for a law school, such as Hofstra, to host such interdisciplinary events. It is law, when operating at its best, which stitches together the fabric of governance by binding up in a coherent way the many social, cultural and economic values reflected in local, regional, and state government arrangements. And it is critical that legal education work to equip every society's future lawyers to address those rearrangements in government articulately and with sophistication and sensitivity. It also is especially important that conferences take place in neutral fora such as academic institutions like Hofstra University.

This book provides valuable multidimensional insights into the political, policy, personal, and public interactions involved and should be of special interest to historians, politicians, lawyers, economists, teachers, and social scientists.

Stuart Rabinowitz
Dean, Hofstra School of Law
Alexander M. Bickel Distinguished Professor
of Communications Law

Preface

No question has more impact on people than government and the structure of government. The form of government and the exercise of government power directly affects individual and group rights of citizens, the correlative duties of government bodies, the allocation of energy and natural resources, the quality of the environment, the distribution of wealth, the nature of education, the expression of culture from language to religion, and the economic and political relations of states.

At the brink of the twenty-first century, the rationales for particular government structures are being actively and vigorously examined and reexamined as never before. That intense governance scrutiny has occurred in the 1990s in large part because of the end of the cold war, the demise of communism, the rise of democracy, the emergence of the global marketplace, the movement toward privatization, and the exponential increase in the amount and availability of information.

These factors have resulted in changes and calls for changes both in internal government arrangements among local, regional, and national governments and in external government relations among states.

Within states, people are questioning existing internal relationships among national government and subnational or local governments. These internal distributions of power involve fundamental questions of federalism in the broad sense. Recent challenges to distributions of government power are occurring with varying degrees of intensity around the world in such states as Canada, the former Czechoslovakia, Ethiopia, India, Italy, Mexico, Somalia, South Africa, the former Yugoslavia, as well as the former Soviet Union and the United States.

Externally, states are also altering their governmental relations with one another through the creation of what may be loosely termed international federal institutions charged with special or broad powers over the member states. This is especially reflected in evolving regional organizations like the European Union, the Commonwealth of Independent States, and the North American Free Trade Agreement.

This book presents an interdisciplinary, panoramic picture drawn by historians, comparative scholars, economists, bankers, political scientists, lawyers, and government officials of the struggle of the two great contrasting world powers (the U.S.S.R. and the U.S.A.) in the early 1990s to deal with questions of allocating government power. Both powers were, and are today, struggling to decide how best to distribute government power. The Soviet Union dramatically ceased to exist and was replaced by independent states loosely associated in a Commonwealth of Independent States. The United States at the same time was experiencing, and continues to experience, a movement to devolve federal power to the fifty states and thousands of local governments.

The interdisciplinary approach taken by this book on a specific set of issues represents the sort of new dialogue and broad base of information needed to analyze the form and effectiveness of government structures in the future. This book does not propose solutions so much as it affords an opportunity to appreciate the myriad perspectives by which one may approach solutions to governance. It also records some of the hopes, expectations, and reservations behind those perspectives.

James E. Hickey, Jr.

NOTE

I would like to thank Laura A. Mongelli and Joanna Balaskas for their competent and diligent work on this book.

Government Structures in the U.S.A. and the Sovereign States of the Former U.S.S.R

PART I

HISTORICAL PERSPECTIVES

Part I provides an historical context for the examination of government structures in the United States and in the states of the former U.S.S.R. that follows in the rest of the book. Any legal, political, cultural, or economic analyses of government in the U.S.A. and the sovereign states of the former U.S.S.R. need to take account of both historical similarities and differences in which federalism arises in each society. The historical notions of John Locke's popular sovereignty, which in many ways lies at the root of U.S. federalism concepts, are absent in the former U.S.S.R. By the same token, the propensity in the former U.S.S.R. for authoritarian systems of governments, first by the Russian tsars and later by the Communist Party, are unknown in U.S. experience.

The four chapters that comprise Part I understandably are oriented toward the governmental relationships among states of the former U.S.S.R. However, their content reveals much that is directly relevant to federalism issues pending in the U.S.A. as well.

John N. Hazard's chapter compares the constitutional processes in play in Philadelphia at the beginning of the U.S. republic with the problems of constitutional processes that are posed in the early 1990s in the former U.S.S.R. He recognizes that the political history of the former Soviet Union traditionally has preferred a central monopoly-of-power system over a pluralism-of-separate-authority approach. The chapter accurately questions whether the commitment of the Founders in Philadelphia to a federal system not bound by one ideology, a single property concept, or a one political party system is a useful model for the former U.S.S.R. in the 1990s, as some continue to assert.

Gordon Wood addresses the historical origins of American federalism. The absence of English or Crown authority and the dispersion of settlers geographically influenced greatly the emergence of strong local governments (towns and counties). Central government (state and federal) in the U.S.A. thus grew at the behest of local government units. Professor Wood points out that the present day sense of Americans of the intense localism and its importance in government is rooted in the historical experience surrounding the local authority embedded in the Articles of Confederation. With the end of the U.S.S.R. an analogous sort of sense of local autonomy that Professor Wood identifies in early American history can be seen in the local independence demonstrated by the new states of the former U.S.S.R. and by the local sub-national government units of the Russian Federation. Whether that intense localism will ever surrender a meaningful measure of authority to any future federal or confederative entity remains to be seen.

Mikhail Marchenko's paper concentrates on the historical considerations at play in the emerging governmental structures of the Russian Federation. He observes that principles of federalism historically have occupied a place in the political history of the Russian Empire. However, he also observes that those federalism principles have consistently tended to be suppressed by a strong bureaucratic centralism. Professor Marchenko correctly urges that both history and the multiethnic makeup of populations must be taken into serious account when shaping the new government structure of the Russian Federation. This observation by Professor Marchenko is also relevant in discussing any contractual and governmental functions of the Commonwealth of Independent States in the decades ahead.

Robert V. Daniels focuses on an important inherent historical difference between the societies of the U.S.A. and the former U.S.S.R.: multiculturalism in the former U.S.S.R. (as well as within Russia itself) is one of different ethnic cultures rooted to settled locations, while multiculturalism in the U.S.A. (with the exception of Native Americans) has been imported and dispersed in changing locations. Professor Daniels offers persuasively that this historical difference helps to explain the failure of federalism in Russia and the former Soviet Union, first with the establishment of the Soviet Empire and later with its collapse. This history reflects not the Soviet federalism that existed in the paper arrangements for governance over separate, settled cultures but in the reality of first a suppression of cultures and later of assertions of nationalism and rights of self-determination. It remains to be seen whether a commonwealth of independent states yet may provide a vehicle for some sort of economic federalism in the twenty-first century.

Thomas Earl Porter examines incipient federalism in tsarist imperial Russia at the end of the nineteenth and the beginning of the twentieth centuries. He sees federalist leanings in the reliance of the central imperial government on local governments to implement and administer the laws and policies of the Russian Empire. This reliance led, in Dr. Porter's view, to forms of local independence and self-governance, which in turn led to a quasi-federal system by the early twentieth century.

1

Political Structure and Power: Is Philadelphia a Model for Moscow?

John N. Hazard

Momentous events have transpired since this paper was completed. Following a coup on August 12, 1991, and the installation of an "interim" government, it became evident that President Mikhail Gorbachev was unable to convince the various republics of the U.S.S.R. that it was in their interest to form some type of "union." Tiring of the effort, the leaders of the Russian, Ukrainian, and Belarus Republics met in Minsk to make a new beginning.

On December 9, 1991 the press carried news of an agreement to form a Commonwealth of Independent States (CIS, or Commonwealth), with a coordinating center in Minsk.[1] The institutional structures were elaborated. The founders declared the U.S.S.R. as "ceasing its existence . . . as a subject of international law and geopolitical reality." The parties agreed to establish coordinating institutions to apply "principles . . . confirming our commitment to the goals and principles of the United Nations Charter, the Helsinki Final Act, and other documents from the Conference on Security and Cooperation in Europe." Additionally, they endorsed a bill of rights, augmenting a document that had been approved by the U.S.S.R. Congress of People's Deputies in Moscow as its last legislative act.[2]

After issuing the agreement, the parties invited other republics of what had been the U.S.S.R. to join the Commonwealth, and all did so except Georgia. Only the Baltic States, to which the Congress had granted independence at its last meeting, remained outside the Commonwealth. Georgia was expected to join the founders eventually.

An agreement was signed by the founders on December 21, 1991, to add an institutional structure to the Commonwealth.[3] It took the form of a proposal to establish coordinate institutions in the future, to be charged eventually with coordination of foreign policy, a common economic space, common European and Asian policy, a customs policy, common transport and communications policy, ecological security, environmental protection, immigration policy, and a crime-fighting goal. Most important, policy on nuclear weapons was to be coordinated by a Council of Heads of State. Disputes over interpretation of the agreements were to be resolved under procedures yet to be established. Beneath the Council of Heads of States was placed a Council of Heads of Government as an executive body.

In comparison with the structure formed at Philadelphia the Minsk-Alma Ata document provided a minimum of government structure. It was mindful of the European Economic Community, founded by the Treaty of Rome, in which the parties exhibited little desire to commit themselves permanently to a structure that might eventually command their obedience. Philadelphia was in no sense a model for Minsk. This was to be anticipated, considering the "baggage" carried with the founders from the past.

THE "BAGGAGE" INHERITED FROM THE PAST

The "baggage" of a century and more of Marxist thinking and the experience of the years following the Russian Revolution of 1917 weighs heavily, even in the 1990s, upon contemporary constitutional draftsmen. Although "class warfare" is no longer a slogan for guidance of policymakers, it was not long ago that entrepreneurs were thought to be masters of deception of the working class. Stalin's spokesman Andrei Vyshinsky expressed his distrust of Montesquieu's political structures. To Vyshinsky, "[t]he principle of the separation of powers was to strengthen the idea of class bourgeois power as power elevated above classes—popular sovereignty, supposed to distribute the functions of legislation and administration reasonably and impartially among diverse state organs."[4] In short, Vyshinsky declared "separation of powers" a fraud, designed to convince the masses that government was in their hands and not in the moneyed entrepreneurs.

Perhaps more potent than ideology had been experience. It is no secret to those who believed Lenin that he had little faith in the willingness of the masses to stay the long course required to create communism until they had mastered dialectical materialist thought. He offered guidance from those who had mastered the ages-long course taken by mankind through history. The lessons of the past had to be absorbed, as Marxists saw them. Not until this had happened would workers be content with the leavings from the tables of the rich. Fatter paychecks, not revolutionary change, would be the workers' goal.

With ideology and experience firmly rooted in consciousness the drafters, of the first Russian constitution of 1917 adopted the "assembly" system of government,[5] which provided no "separation of powers." To be sure there would be in addition to the assembly, from which total political power would issue, an executive and a judiciary, but neither was to be separated from the assembly.

This was manifested dramatically by the slogan of the time: "All Power to the Soviets."

This did not mean that the executive and the judiciary had no special place in the structures of the state. There was no formally constituted medieval monarch holding every function in his or her own hands. Power was to be lodged in the people as a whole: the executive and the judiciary performing functions assigned by the deputies establishing basic policy in the assembly. It was the assembly that expressed the "general will," revered by Jean-Jacques Rousseau as the personification of the people.

V. I. Lenin's 1917 structure, as embodied after formulating the first decrees in a constitution of 1918, created an executive chosen by the assembly members and made responsible to that body. So also the judiciary took form in a "people's court," formed by a Commissariat of Justice responsible to each provincial soviet.[6] Perhaps, unfortunately for a neat separation of functions, the executive came to the fore under Lenin's guidance. Although the 1918 constitution said clearly that the assembly was supreme, crisis conditions causing shortcuts were introduced in governmental practice. Lenin, as chair of the Council of People's Commissars ignored the Central Executive Committee of the Soviet when he thought himself imperiled.[7] To meet the perceived threat, he authorized, by early resolution, executive action. The Council of People's Commissars became, in fact, the power center of the new Russia.

As Lenin was the "father" of the revolution and a dynamic man who brooked no opposition to his planning, he soon took command. Proof of this fact is printed in the statute book, published as *Sobrani Uzakonenii*. This compendium intersperses the decrees of the Council of People's Commissars with the laws of the Soviet, suggesting that Lenin saw no reason to separate policy matters from executive decree.[8] Perhaps Lenin saw no reason to change hats when policy matters came to the fore.

Lenin's government structure functioned not only within the Russian Republic, for identical structures were formed in Ukraine, Belarussia, and Transcaucasus. In every region the assembly system was adopted, for Lenin's comrades in the republics functioning under the guidance of the Communist Party followed Lenin's models. This was so, even when the republics were brought together in a Union of Soviet Socialist Republics formed constitutionally in January 1923 under a treaty of union at the very end of December 1922.[9]

The forms of 1917, augmented to incorporate the federation, became the model that was to last for nearly 70 years within the U.S.S.R. There was no expression of a concept of "separation of powers" either in the republics or the federation.[10]

THE COMMUNIST PARTY'S ROLE

Rejection of Montesquieu was confirmed by an additional factor, namely the Communist Party, which emerged in a short time to establish a "one-party" state. Although Lenin had formed his government in November 1917 as a coalition of three parties, he soon had sufficient power to govern alone. By mid-1918, even those who had collaborated with the Bolsheviks could no longer support Lenin. The Socialist Revolutionaries became disgruntled as they watched the Bolsheviks moving toward centralized government, and the Menshevik Maximalists thought Lenin brutal in his treatment of the moderates. The Bolsheviks saw their opportunity and gave their coalition partners a nudge that was to drive them from the field, and by degrees even the state constitution was reformulated to reflect the reality of one-party governance.

Not until the death of Stalin in 1953, followed by the deaths of his successors, Nikita Khrushchev, Leonid Brezhnev, Konstantin Chernenko, and Yuri Andropov, was there the first glimmer of relaxation of Communist Party discipline. The first glimmer was introduced by the next successor, M. S. Gorbachev, proclaiming two new slogans, *glasnost* and *perestroika*. Discussion was introduced in both party and state agencies, and administrative structures were restructured in hopes of improving productivity.

Although these moves were momentous, they did not for some time alter the status of the Communist Party. It remained monolithic in structure, preserving its structure in both party rules and state law. Gorbachev's only change was to set aside restrictions on debate as they had been applied for decades under the rule of "democratic centralism" and to relax the hold established by Stalin on ministerial command over the directors of state enterprises. He made no change in the foundations of "socialism," defined in the constitution. State ownership of the principal means of production was unshakable.

This reverence for tradition meant that there was to be no "separation of powers" in the political system. Checks and balances on the party and the Soviet would be incompatible with the rule of the party. There was no semblance of the fear expressed by the "framers" of the United States Constitution in *The Federalist* prior to the constitutional convention of Philadelphia. The Americans wanted to restrain power through institutions, yet they also hoped to form a government capable of dynamic action, so as to avoid the errors perceived during the few years when the Articles of Confederation were in force.

Montesquieu's advocacy of "separation of powers appealed to James Madison as a means of combining dynamism with restraint of tyranny. He wanted to create a balance in the governing process. He and his like-minded colleagues thought it necessary to counter those of their critics who feared that "separation of powers" would create impotent government. He was quite clear that he was advocating a balance. He wrote, "the legislative, executive, and judiciary departments are by no means totally separate and distinct from each other."[11] He argued for checks and balances but not inaction.

CHECKS AND BALANCES IN CIS STRUCTURES

The drafters of a political structure for a Commonwealth of Independent States at Minsk and Alma Ata seem also to be searching for balance in government. Clearly, they want no resurrection of Stalin's terror, and equally clearly the framers of new structures want no centralized authority that can command from Moscow. This has been made clear with repudiation of President Gorbachev's plea for maintenance of "union" under a treaty binding the republics. Minsk is not a "capital" of the Commonwealth but a "coordinator." Committees are asked to formulate policies and create institutions thought capable of maintaining the essentials of economic power in a society long under central command and central economic planning. But beyond that minimum of coordination there is no legislature, no executive, and no judiciary. Every policy has to be initiated and executed in a conclave of equals. It is clear that the functions of government as traditionally conceived will be developed by the existing institutions in each republic capital. Only as these steps have been taken by each republic will there be coordination through negotiation at Minsk. Whatever develops in the process will seemingly be far less than has been achieved by the members of the European Community from Brussels.

Formal structures of government are only now in formulation. The Republic Assemblies, as Congresses of People's Deputies or Supreme Soviets, are meeting to draft new constitutions. The first to do so after the accord of Minsk was Kazakhstan.[12] Under date of December 16, 1991, its Supreme Soviet declared its determination to recognize the priority of individual rights and freedoms and a rule-of-law state. These principles are to be manifest in a political structure separating legislative, executive, and judicial authority. The legislative authority is to be exercised by the Supreme Soviet of the republic and the executive by the president of the republic who is the chief executive. Judicial authority is vested in the Supreme Court and the Superior Arbitration Court. The highest body of legal protection of the constitution shall be the Constitutional Court. In short, the model appears to be that of the presidential system adopted at the U.S. Constitutional Convention at Philadelphia, and developed since that time by amendment in accordance with the provisions of the Constitution. Additionally, there have been the interpretations of the Supreme Court, notably in the case of *Marbury v. Madison*.

The Kazakh Constitution is admittedly only a skeletal document to be developed over time, but the founding fathers appear to be searching for balance in government just as did the founding fathers in Philadelphia. Just how the legal structures will be developed must await the drafting of a new constitution, which is to be based on the short constitution and the Declaration of National Sovereignty of the Republic.

A draft of a constitution for the Russian Republic is even this very week of the Conference at Hofstra (week of April 6, 1992) before a Congress of People's Deputies of the republic. After a series of drafts, the constitutional committee seems to have reached agreement on general principles. In the draft dated March, 2, 1992,[13] a preamble states determination to affirm liberty and rights of man and a dignified life, to preserve state unity, civil peace and agreement, to regenerate society and to provide an unshakable democratic statehood of the Russian Federation. Article 3 declares sovereign power in the people and Article 5 declares democracy based on political and ideological diversity functioning within s multiple party system.

Article 7 introduces a commitment to maintain a market economy in sharp contrast with the state economy prescribed for the former U.S.S.R. Three subsections of Article 7 outline the concept of "social" market economy as freedom of enterprise and labor, diversity of ownership forms, equal conditions of legal protection, social benefit, and honest competition. The state is given a place in the regulation of economic life and maintenance of a social partnership between citizen and state, consumer and producer, employer and employee. Lest the thrust of the new approach to social relations be lost, the draft defines the "social state" as one seeking social justice, social services, and social safeguards. Evidently, the drafters feared that a market economy might reopen the gates to what are perceived as the harsh realities of capitalism with its unemployment, labor-management strife, and inflation.

The key to understanding of the new state seems to be its political structure. Article 6 makes it clear that the drafters have accepted Philadelphia's model—namely, that the functions of government will be performed by institutions that are powerful in their own right and independent. Montesquieu's slogan is encapsulated as the "separation of powers," just as it was in Philadelphia. As in Philadelphia, the goal of politics is to be "balanced" between the three "powers" of legislature, executive, and judiciary. The institutions defining these "powers" are described in traditional "separation of powers" language.

NO MORE IDEOLOGICAL SLANT

Students of constitutions promulgated in the U.S.S.R. and its republics, as well as republics in Eastern Europe generally, had come to identify the model with the ideology of "class warfare," in which preambles have been programmatic. There has always been a grand design to lead society toward a social structure called "communism." Although the expectation of early transition to a system in which the state would eventually wither away had been pushed farther and farther into the background, the structures designed to achieve this result were not abandoned. Society was expected to develop harmonious relationships in which "abundance" could be achieved.

This is not the place to develop this theme, for every member of this audience is aware of the ideology that has motivated policymakers in the years since 1917. The arresting feature of the new republic constitutions is the absence of ideology. It is as if Mr. Justice Oliver Wendell Holmes' dictum in the case of *Lochner v. New York* had been incorporated into Soviet law. In 1905 he wrote: "But a constitution is not intended to embody a particular economic theory, whether of paternalism and the organic relation of the citizen to the citizen to the state or of *laissez faire*. It is made for people of fundamentally different views."

In implementation of Holmes' goal the concept of "separation of powers" was conceived by the draftsmen of Philadelphia to make it difficult, if not impossible, to formulate a program to which citizens are obliged to adhere over the ages because one of another branch of government is powerless to influence state action. Pluralism in the evolution of policymaking has been thought to assure that dictators cannot seize the reigns of governance. Not only is pluralism enshrined in the first constitutions to emerge from drafters of constitutions in the CIS, but a second factor militates against monopoly of power—namely, that a system of market economy be enforced. No longer can the state monopolize production and gain thereby power over the formulation of policy.

One intriguing phrase appears in the Russian draft: the qualification of market economy by the adjective "social." What do the drafters imply by this adjective? Can it be that they hope to preserve for "socialism" something of the definition developed by a committee of social scientists in 1989, which they called a "new vision" of socialism? To the scholars the vision is that "priority must be given to the human being, his interests, and his needs."[14]

Although the committee chairman is no longer a policymaker, enough has been indicated in the literature of our time, to show that the state must be "humane." President Boris Yeltsin, in his speech of April 5, 1992, to the incoming Congress of People's Deputies, spoke of the need to preserve a strong executive in the new state structure, but his critics are fearful of lack of social protection. In all probability the peoples of Russia—and indeed of the CIS as a whole—will not tolerate leadership that ignores some of the social benefits that have come to be associated in the public mind with "socialism." Poverty, unemployment, and inflation are the "horsemen of the apocalypse"—just as they were in the last years of World War I—which unleashed the furies of the Russian Revolution.

The founders in Philadelphia anticipated that their form of government could meet the aspirations of their people because people would be bound to no ideology, no single property system, no single political party. Can it be expected that the Philadelphia model will prove as successful for the peoples of the East as it has been for the Americans?

NOTES

1. Text in translation: *New York Times*, December 10, 1991 A-19.

2. Text in *Izvestia*, September 7, 1991.

3. Text of Alma Ata accord, *New York Times*, December 23, 1991, A-10.

4. A. Y. Vyshinsky, *The Law of the Society State* (New York, 1948), 314.

5. *Ibid.*, 167, on the role of the Soviets. Karl Loewenstein popularized the system in Western literature as "the Assembly system of government."

6. See John N. Hazard, *Settling Disputes in Soviet Society* (New York, 1960), 6–9.

7. Russian Soviet Federated Socialist Republic (RSFSR) Constitution of 1918, executed July 10, 1919. For English translation see Aryeh L. Unger, *Constitutional Development in the U.S.S.R.: A Guide to the Soviet Constitution* (New York, 1982). 25–41. The RSFSR Central Executive Committee (CEC) transferred to the Council of People's Commissars (CPC) authority to act without prior reference to the CEC in the event that counterrevolutionary activity required such action. Resolution of November 20, 1917. The resolution was not printed in the official gazette (See SU, RSFSR, 1917–18). It was cited by James Bunyan and Harold Henry Fisher, *The Bolshevik Revolution, 1917–1918* (Stanford University Press, 1934), 189.

8. For the texts of such decrees, see SU, RSFSR, 1917–18. For examples of CPC decrees, see decrees on Press Censorship, State Monopoly of Publication of Advertisements and Notices, State Monopoly of Distribution of Agricultural Machines, Stop Payment of Dividends, Creation on Commissariats of Moslem and Jewish Affairs, Adoption of the Western Calendar, Nationalization of the Merchant Fleet, Creation of Labor Exchanges.

9. For the laws creating the constitutions of the non-Russian republics prior to the Treaty of Union, see *Istoriia Sovetskoi Konstitutsii (v Dokumentakh) 1917–1956* (Moscow, 1957). The text of the treaty between the RSFSR, the Ukrainian SSR, the Belorussian SSR, and the Transcausian SSR (including within it Georgia, Azerbaijan, and Armenia) signed on December 20, 1920, and proclaimed by the First Congress of Soviets of the U.S.S.R. is set forth on pp. 394–98.

10. For text of the U.S.S.R. Constitution of 1923–28, see English translation in Unger, *Constitutional Development*.

11. *The Federalist* (No. 47).

12. For text in English translation, see Parker School of Foreign and Comparative Law, Columbia University, Legal Materials, Russia and the Republics (Kazakhstan, 1). A full constitution was adopted by Kazakhstan on January 28, 1993. Vechernaya Alma-Ata, February 2, 1993, 2.

13. The text in Russian is published in *Argumenty I Fakti*, March 1992. Since this paper was written, the constitution of the Russian Republic expected to be adopted in 1992 remains in draft. In view of the continuing conflict between the Russian Republic Congress of People's Deputies and President Yeltsin, it seems unlikely that a new Russian Republic constitution will be adopted in the foreseeable future.

14. English translation of *Pravda*, July 14, 1989, 1, in *Current Digest of the Soviet Press*, Vol. 41, No. 31 (1989), 4–8.

2

The First National Constitution of the United States

Gordon S. Wood

There are some Americans today who actually believe that the Founding Fathers in 1787 got their ideas about federalism and the Constitution from the Iroquois Confederacy. I once thought that this peculiar notion was confined to the ranks of academic anthropologists, where it could do no harm. But I have since discovered that in October 1988 the United States House of Representatives and Senate passed resolutions recognizing "the contributions of the Iroquois Confederacy of Nations to the development of the United States Constitution." That grown people can believe in such a connection not only indicates the curious way scholarship and politics can get entangled in our culture but also suggests the appalling manner that otherwise educated people think about causality—about the way things come about.

The Iroquois and other Indians certainly made contributions to early American culture—many of them—but ideas about federalism and dividing political power were not among them. The Founding Fathers in 1787 did not have to borrow such political notions from the Iroquois. White Americans had their own long tradition of dividing up and parceling out power to draw on in the making of their Constitution.

The origins of American federalism go back at least to the early seventeenth-century English settlements. The early English migrants to America brought with them strong traditions of local and regional autonomy that conditions in the New World only reinforced and intensified. All the colonies in the seventeenth century experienced an acute localization of authority. Populations in both the Chesapeake and New England quickly dispersed—despite initial efforts to hold them together. The Virginia Company expected compact towns to develop, and it created four of these on paper. These boroughs would send burgesses to the colonial assembly—which is how the Virginia House of Burgesses got its name. But the scattering of settlers in private plantations undid these plans for towns, and before long, the central authorities were compelled to recognize the dispersion of settlement. Counties were soon created and these became the basic unit of local government and the basis of representation in the central government. The county courts combined within themselves various civil, criminal, ecclesiastical, admiralty, and administrative powers and jurisdictions that in England belonged to separate courts or political subdivisions. They assumed the power to deal with orphans, probate wills, collect taxes, regulate morals, supervise the militia, maintain prices, relieve the poor, issue land titles, license taverns, control the parish vestries, and enact by-laws. These local units thus concentrated power to an extent that the central government could scarcely match.

A similar dispersion and localization of authority took place in New England. Within three months of the Puritan landing in Massachusetts Bay in 1630, seven towns had been created in the area surrounding Boston. The New England town became the sole unit of local government, and, like the Chesapeake county court, it united within itself a host of powers that had been widely shared by different local institutions in England—those of the parish, borough, village, manor, and county.

Consequently, in New England as in the Chesapeake, local government gained a degree of autonomy and power that it had not had to the same extent in England. Not only was the presence of English or Crown authority at the outset practically nonexistent, leaving the various new colonies in the first half of the seventeenth century to fend for themselves, but the central government in each of the colonies themselves was weak. Everywhere officials struggled against the centrifugal forces at work, with varying degrees of success; but for the most part, the locus of power remained with the local authorities—whether the counties in the Chesapeake or the towns in New England.

It soon became evident that central authority not only existed at the behest or sufferance of the local units; it was often the creature of the local units. The colony of Connecticut, for example, was created in 1639 out of three independent towns—Hartford, Windsor, and Wethersfield—coming together and agreeing in written Fundamental Orders to form a superintending central government (which is why Connecticut today calls itself "the constitution state"). These Connecticut colonists had a clear sense they were creating something anew: unlike the English Crown, their central government was in no way the source of authority, but the consequence of it, the result of the parceling out of power from below. Joining with the town of New Haven in the 1660s only reinforced this view that authority was created by the bringing together of local power.

Rhode Island in the seventeenth century scarcely existed as a colony at all. It was in reality four towns, suspicious of one another, struggling to put together from below some sort of central authority; the towns could not even agree where the colony's government should meet, so they moved it from one town to another. Some towns in New England, like Springfield, Massachusetts, even existed for awhile independent of all superintending government. Given such experience it was easy, then, for the New England colonies to come together in 1643 to form the New England Confederacy to deal with common threats from the Dutch, French, and Indians. Already they were used to thinking about government as a consequence of the pooling together of power that was doled out by the local authorities.

Even the legislatures in each colony were effectively created from the bottom up, and the American colonists continued to think of representation in local terms—as an apportioning of local power upward to a central body. The representatives in the colonial legislatures—deputies and burgesses—spoke only for their local districts and sometimes acted as if they were ambassadors from their counties or towns to the central government. These counties or towns often bound their agents with instructions and sometimes refused to pay taxes if their agents had not been present when the tax was voted.

Throughout the entire colonial period, the central authorities—both the English Crown and the separate colonial governments—were always on the defensive, always trying to justify themselves in the face of this extreme localization of power. During the century from the 1660s to the 1760s, the English Crown was continually trying to gain control of the autonomous local units and reverse the powerful centrifugal forces at work in the American colonies. English bureaucrats in London were repeatedly concocting schemes for tightening up what seemed like an incredibly loose and decentralized empire. Sometimes they were supported by imperial-minded colonists such as Benjamin Franklin and Thomas Hutchinson, who in 1754 helped put together the Albany Plan of Union, uniting the colonies for military purposes. But such schemes ran too much against the deeply rooted localist traditions of the colonists and were continually frustrated. Finally, in the 1760s renewed efforts of the British government to reorganize and centralize the empire provoked colonial resistance and eventually rebellion.

In 1776 the colonies became 13 independent states, each of which had an acute sense of its autonomy; after all, except for Georgia, each of them had been in existence for at least nine decades and had developed its own peculiar historical traditions. It was natural for Americans in 1776, therefore, to think of their states and not the nation as the principal unit of government. Thus, at the time of independence, the United States of America had a literal and plural meaning that it has since lost. A man's "country" was his state; John Adams referred to the Massachusetts delegation to the Continental Congress in 1776 as "our embassy." The Declaration of Independence was a declaration of "thirteen united States of America," and it proclaimed that "as Free and Independent States they have full power to levy war, conclude peace, contract alliances, establish commerce, and do all the other acts and things which independent States may of right do." There was yet little national consciousness, and it was hard for Americans to think of themselves as a single people. The society was already ethnically diverse, with only half the people being English.

In light of these circumstances, we can better appreciate what a real achievement the first constitution of the United States was—the Articles of Confederation. The Articles were drawn up and approved by the Continental Congress in 1776–77, but they were not ratified by all the states until 1781, largely because of disputes over whether the states or the Confederation would control the western lands. Like the Americans' earlier experiments in federalism, this first constitution was the product of America's localist traditions, of the parcelling out of power from below.

Because the Articles lasted only a decade or so and because they have had to live in the shadow of the federal Constitution of 1787, the Confederation government they created has not had a very good reputation. It has, in fact, been continually derided for its weakness and its imbecility. It was in fact, as it declared, only a "league of friendship," the result of a sort of treaty among 13 independent states—something not all that different from the present European Community.

Weak as it may have been, however, in the context of the time and earlier American experience, the Confederation was actually a remarkable achievement. It was as strong and cohesive an alliance of independent sovereign states as had ever previously existed in history. It created a national community where none had existed before. Article 4 of this treaty or constitution, for example, granted the citizens of all the states equal privileges and immunities and permitted the free movement of all persons and goods between the states—provisions that the present European Community is still struggling to achieve.

Of course, Americans were willing to create such a relatively strong union because they were fighting for their independence against the greatest power on earth. Their unity was forged under wartime conditions. Because the Continental Congress began as an instrument of resistance, it was natural to think of the Confederation primarily as an instrument of war, a temporary union for the purpose of achieving independence.

Delegates at the Continental Congress in 1776–77 agreed fairly quickly to the powers to be granted to the Confederation—the powers to determine war and peace, conduct diplomacy and make treaties, regulate Indian affairs in territories outside the states, maintain a postal system, and act as court of last resort in disputes between the states. The Confederation had no power to tax or to regulate trade. All final lawmaking authority or sovereignty remained with the states.

Probably the best way to understand the Confederation is to see it as a substitute for the role the British Crown had played in the empire. Essentially the Congress was to take over the two traditional functions of royal authority—war and diplomacy. Like the Crown it would not levy taxes, regulate commerce, or make law. All it would do was make requests or recommendations to the states.

In short, the Confederation was not to be a government in its own right. John Adams called it a "diplomatic assembly," a collection of delegates or ambassadors from the 13 states. Each state, regardless of its size, had one vote. A two-thirds majority of nine states was required for major matters, including the making of treaties and the issuing and borrowing of money; a simple majority of seven states dealt with minor matters. To amend or change the Articles required the agreement of all the states.

For most Americans their individual state remained the political authority they most cared about. With the victory over the British at Yorktown in 1781 and the peace treaty recognizing American independence following in 1783, some Americans actually saw no further need for a central government. By December 1783 the Congress, in Thomas Jefferson's opinion, had lost much of its usefulness. He said that the constant session of Congress can not be necessary in time of peace. After clearing up the most urgent business the delegates should "separate and return to our respective states, leaving only a Committee of the states," and thus, "destroy the strange idea of their being a permanent body, which has unaccountably taken possession of the heads of their constituents, and occasions jealousies injurious to the public good." Actually, it was hard to think of the Congress as a permanent body simply because it kept moving about the country—from Philadelphia, to York, Pennsylvania, to Princeton, New Jersey, to Annapolis, Maryland, to New York City.

Congressional power, which had been substantial during the war years, now began precipitously to disintegrate, and delegates increasingly complained of the difficulty of gathering a quorum. The Congress could not gather a quorum even to ratify the treaty of peace with Great Britain on time. It had no money and could not even pay for the expense of sending the ratified treaty back to England; it took French money paid to a British ship captain to return the document to England.

By the mid-1780s more and more Americans complained of the weakness and the imbecility of the Confederation. Yet that perception was in large part a product of changes in the nature of the central government created by the Articles. The crises of the war, especially in 1779–80, had forced many American political leaders to rethink the character of the Confederation Congress. Because the Congress was much too large and divided, it was unable to act as a substitute or surrogate for the Crown as many in 1776–77 had assumed it would. To implement decisions and wage war, separate executive departments needed to be organized—departments of war, finance, and foreign affairs. When this was done in 1780–81, the Confederation began to resemble a regular government with its own ministries; it was becoming less an alliance of separate states and more a government in its own right. With the existence of separate executive departments, people began thinking of the Congress as a quasi-legislative body. If it were really a kind of legislature, then many concluded it ought to be able to exercise the powers that legislatures normally exercise—namely, the powers to tax, regulate commerce, and make law. Hence, many began urging that the Articles of Confederation be changed and that at least the powers to tax and regulate commerce be granted to the Congress. By the mid-1780s many Americans had new heightened expectations of what the institutions of their central government ought to do, and these new expectations made them increasingly dissatisfied with the weakness and incompetence of the Confederation.

By 1786–87 almost all American political leaders, including many of the later opponents of the Constitution drafted in 1787, were ready to reform or amend the Articles of Confederation, particularly by granting Congress the power to tax and to regulate trade. Since several attempts to amend the Articles by getting each state to agree had failed, more and more people were willing to use a convention of the states as the means of change. By 1787 this general willingness to reform the Articles gave some nationalistic-minded reformers like James Madison the opportunity to do more. Madison and some of his allies were determined not to reform the Articles but to scrap them altogether.

The Constitution that the Philadelphia Convention created in 1787 was very different from the Articles of Confederation. The new central government was not just the old Confederation with some additional powers. It was no longer a league or an alliance of sovereign states; it was government in its own right, a quasi-national government that was latently very powerful, as Americans of the twentieth century have increasingly discovered. Indeed, compared to many other federal governments in existence today, such as those of Canada or Germany, the United States has one of the most centralized in the world.

As powerful as the American federal government has become, however, and there is almost nothing today that it cannot do, it still operates in a culture that profoundly mistrusts distant central political power. The long tradition of local authority, rooted deep in the earliest experiences of the American people, still affects the character of American political life. Even today former Speaker of the House "Tip" (Thomas) O'Neill can say that "all American politics is local," and have everyone know what he means. Everyone has an acute sense that it is the American people in their separate localities that ultimately count and that any superior centralized authority set over them is a kind of temporary delegation from them. This intense sense of localism is not the product of human ingenuity or rational planning, and it cannot be fabricated out of reading a lot of books on federalism. It is the product of the historical experience and the daily lives of the American people.

3

The Russian Federation: History and Contemporaneity

Mikhail Marchenko

PRELIMINARY COMMENTS

A deep and thorough understanding of the current problems and the state of the Russian Federation inevitably presupposes at least a cursory look at its past—its inception and development—on the one hand, and, on the other hand, at its present and past through a comparison of the Russian Federation with other federations that have existed and still exist in parallel with it.

To avoid misunderstanding several preliminary remarks are in order about the problems under review. They primarily concern the concept, content, and purpose of federalism as a phenomenon. They also concern the application of federalism in the context of the Russian Federation as a component part of other federations that coexisted and very closely interacted with it for a long time.

The following view of the concept and content of the federal system and federalism, formulated by Richard Nathan and Erik Hoffmann (in Chapter 6) in the process of comparative research, could with certain reservations be adopted as a working conception. "Federalism is a form of government organization that tries to reconcile regional diversity with a certain level of collective unity and that does so in such a way that regional governments play an entirely concrete role."[1]

The reservations are essentially occasioned, first, by a certain degree of imprecision in the cited definition—it appears that federalism is not so much a "form of government organization" as it is, above all, a form of organization of the state itself and second, by the significant degree of abstractness of the cited definition. It would be more constructive and effective if it incorporated not only the most general theoretical calculations and principles, but also more concrete judgments that identify the given phenomenon more precisely.

The intention here is to indicate, if only in general outline, the basic generic features characteristic of all federal systems, the principles of their construction and functioning, and also their basic goals and tasks.

In particular, it appears axiomatic that any federal system acts as a unitary union state, consisting of two or more relatively independent states and state formations. Each of the states, as a subject of federation, has its own administrative-territorial divisions. In addition to federal organs, each has its own supreme organs of state authority and government, as well as judicial, law enforcement, health care, fiscal, and other organs. Each state has its own constitution and current legislation and may frequently have its own military formations and citizenship.[2]

The fundamental principles in the formation and functioning of the federal system, from the positions of which any system, including the Russian federal system, should be viewed and evaluated, are as follows: the voluntariness of the unification of states or state formations into a federation; the equality of subjects of federation regardless of the size of their territory, the size of their population, their economic potential; pluralism and democracy in relations between subjects of federation with one another and with citizens; the broad opportunity of citizens to participate actively and freely in federal and regional political processes; finally, the principle of legality and constitutionality, which means the strict, undeviating observance of ordinary and constitutional laws by the federation and subjects of the federation, by federal and all other organs and organizations, both in relations with one another and with citizens and party, trade unions, and other sociopolitical organs and organizations formed by them.

Those authors are unquestionably correct who believe that any federal system can be effective only if its activity is carried out within the strict framework of the constitution and current legislation, if the spheres of activity and the jurisdiction of central and state organs are clearly delineated, and if citizens' rights and liberties are strictly observed.[3] In this sense, one can only welcome the characterization of federalism as the "contractual repudiation of centralism," as the "structurally formalized dispersion of authority" among different state organs that are power centers of a sort, and as the "legal authority of which is guaranteed by the constitution."[4]

An examination of Russian Federalism begins from the premise that federalism must be viewed not so much from a formal legal position as from a phenomenon that exists in real life. All that the formal legal definition of federalism does is to make it easier to understand the nature of federalism in real life and actual practice and to determine whether or not it exists as an actual phenomenon.

Another premise for examination of Russian Federalism is that federalism is not a one-dimensional but a multidimensional phenomenon, that it is not only static, but dynamic as well. The multidimensionality of federalism refers to the existence of its various, more or less equally significant aspects. It also refers to its historical, political, legal or formal legal, social, fiscal, cultural, and ideological aspects.

Understanding of all those aspects unquestionably presupposes the use of the interdisciplinary research technique or approach and requires the joint efforts of jurists, political scientists, philosophers, historians, sociologists, and representatives of many other social sciences and disciplines. The efforts of not only the researchers of one country or state, but also of many other foreign countries, are also required. In this regard, we can only applaud the many years of efforts of both our own and foreign authors—so-called *Sovietologists* and *Kremlinologists*—to understand the essence, content, and real significance of the phenomenon that is called "Soviet pluralism" in the scientific literature.[5]

When federalism is discussed as a dynamic phenomenon, it not only is a phenomenon that is static at a given time, but it also is a phenomenon that is constantly developing and changing in connection with changes in the economic and sociopolitical conditions of societal life. Its existence in Russia and other countries is confirmed by the periodically changing nature of relations between the federation and its subjects. These relations are rigid, centralized, or decentralized to varying degrees in different periods of history. Thus, federalism, it appears, is not only a dynamic process but also a cyclical one.

Regardless of the country in which federalism is established and practiced—whether in the U.S.A., Russia, Germany or Canada—it does not exist only for itself, as an end in itself, but it is meaningful only when it serves society and the individual.

Researchers of federalism correctly write that it pursues at least five basic goal, among them the "reconciliation of unity and diversity"; protection against the tyranny of central government; the creation of conditions for the population's participation in the political process at several levels of authority; the creation of conditions for increasing the "effectiveness of government through regional competition"; and acting as a form or path "to stimulating innovative ideas in regional governments."[6]

Naturally, there are also other reasons for forming a federal system in a given country. Chief among them is all-round support for the free development of different nations and nationalities, the principles of pluralism and democratism, and guarantees of citizens' rights and liberties. It is specifically from these theoretical and practical political positions that all federalism, including "Russian federalism," should be evaluated.

DEVELOPMENT OF THE RUSSIAN FEDERATION

Historically, the Russian Federation was the first Soviet federation that originated soon after the October Revolution of 1917. It was legally formalized in the constitution of the Russian Socialist Federated Socialist Republic (RSFSR) of 1918. In December 1922 it, together with other republics—Ukraine, Belorussia, and the Transcaucasian Federation—formed a new federated state: the U.S.S.R.

The Russian Federation, according to its constitution, at present (April 1992) includes 16 autonomous republics, 5 autonomous oblasts, and 10 autonomous okrugs.

The Russian Federation was created as a result of the unification of the Russian nation, which comprises the majority of its population, with many other small nations such as Bashkir, Tatar, Mari, Mordovian, Chuvash, Udmurt, and Yakut.

Relations between federal organs and subjects of the Russian Federation have traditionally had and continue to have a very rigid, centralized base. The dominant principle in these relations until recently was so-called democratic centralism, but as a practical matter was essentially a bureaucratic centralism comprised of a strictly planned character, formal legality, and constitutionality. Many of these components retain their own, very considerable strength today as well. Accordingly, the federalism that exists in Russia, like the federalism that previously existed in the U.S.S.R., has been and continues to be manifested in real life in no other way than as unitarianism or formal legal federalism.

There are several characteristic features of Russian federalism that distinguish the Russian federal system from other federal systems. First, the components of the Russian federal system are autonomies rather than sovereign, de facto independent republic-states. They act as autonomous states (republics) and autonomous state formations (autonomous oblasts and okrugs) that nonetheless are to a significant degree dependent on the center. The Bashkir, Buryat, Dagestan, Kabardinian-Balkarian, Kalmyk, Karelian, Komi, Mordovian, Tatar, are examples of autonomous republics. According to the Russian constitution, the Adygey, Gorno-Altay, Jewish, Karachai-Cherkess, and Khakass are autonomous oblasts that are incorporated in large administrative-territorial units (krays). The Constitution also identifies okrugs—such as the Komi-Permyak, Koryak, Nenets, Khanty-Mansi, Chukchi, Evenki, and others—as autonomous subjects of the Russian Federation. Autonomous okrugs are also incorporated in administrative-territorial units: krays and oblasts. There have been changes in the status of certain subjects of the Russian Federation in recent years.[7]

According to the constitution of the RSFSR (in force in April 1992) and existing laws, autonomous republics, like autonomous oblasts and okrugs, possess quite broad powers from a legal point of view. Article 79 of the constitution states, for example, that an autonomous republic participates in the solution of questions that are the competences of the RSFSR, and secures the "integrated economic and social development of its territory." It "coordinates and oversees" the activity of enterprises, institutions, and organizations of republic subordination on questions that are in its jurisdiction. An autonomous republic" independently resolves questions in its jurisdiction" that are "outside the laws" of the Russian Federation. It has its own constitution, which "corresponds" to the Russian constitution, and which "takes into account the peculiarities of an autonomous republic." Russia's fundamental law also indicates that the "territory of an autonomous republic cannot be changed without its consent" (Article 80).

Constitutional legislation also vests autonomous oblasts and autonomous okrugs—subjects of the federation—with considerable powers.[8] It should, however, be noted that from the formation of the U.S.S.R. until the present (1992), these powers have for the most part been declared but not exercised. However, hasty or categorical conclusions should not be drawn from this, as sometimes happens in the literature, that the Russian Federation from the very moment of its formation was nothing more than a mere manifestation of the Russian people's "expansionism" and "colonialism" vis-à-vis other peoples. The groundlessness of such a conclusion becomes all the more evident if we recall that many peoples and nations living in Russian territory had no statehood of their own whatsoever before the federation was formed. Only when the Russian Federation formed did relations between the Russian nation and other nations (Tatar, Bashkir, Chuvash, Yakut, etc.) begin to develop on the basis of the autonomy of the latter.

The historical uniqueness of the Russian Federation consists, in addition to everything else, in the fact that it was initially proclaimed a federation, but its practical formation took place significantly later.[9] This meant that a number of nations and nationalities had the de jure and de facto possibility of creating their own national states or national state formations only after the RSFSR had been proclaimed. It should also be appreciated that 5 of the 15 union republics that existed as subjects of the U.S.S.R. originated from the RSFSR. Two of them—the Uzbek and Turkmen SSRs—originated immediately as union republics as a result of the establishment of national-state boundaries in Central Asia. The other three—the Tajik, Kazakh, and Kirghiz SSRs—upon gaining their autonomy were immediately transformed into union republics that were subjects of the U.S.S.R.[10]

What is the proposed solution to the question of subjects of the Russian Federation and its character in the draft of the new Russian constitution that is at present under discussion (April 1992)? How is the transformation of the predominantly formal legal Russian Federation into a de facto [federation] contemplated?

The legislature intends to address the problem of Russia's federal structure by three avenues. The first avenue is to replace previous subjects of federation-autonomies with new subjects—republics and lands "whose territories form the single territory of the Russian federation." It is presumed that the constitutional structure of republics and lands shall not contradict the Russian constitution. The territorial structure of republics and lands will incorporate "self-governing territorial communities" whose structure and function will be established by the corresponding constitutions of republics and lands. It is assumed that "any state recognizing Russia's constitution may be admitted to the Russian Federation" as a republic or land (Article 89, p. 4).

The second avenue is the more precise distribution of competences between the federation as a whole, on the one hand, and the above-named subjects of federation, on the other. In addition to the exclusive jurisdiction of the Russian Federation and its constituent subjects, their joint jurisdiction must be defined more precisely than was done in the past. According to the draft of the new Russian Constitution, the following are the joint competences of the Russian Federation, republics, and lands:

1. securing human and civil rights and liberties, legality and legal order, public safety
2. civil and commercial, labor, administrative, civil procedure, and administrative procedure legislation; copyright, patent, and publishing law; the protection of intellectual property
3. the judiciary, the legal profession, and the notariate
4. natural resources that are of general federal significance; natural resource utilization; the protection of the environment and of historical and cultural monuments; national parks, reservations, and reserves
5. child-rearing, education, science, and culture
6. health care and social security
7. citizenship of republics and lands
8. quarantine and combating natural disasters
9. state service

It is also provided that on a number of questions, the Russian Federation can promulgate principles of legislation on the basis of which republics and lands carry out legal regulation. Republics and lands can also promulgate laws on these questions if the federation has not exercised its legislative rights. If the laws of a republic or land and federal laws conflict, federal laws prevail.

Finally, the third avenue is not only the proclamation, but also the actual implementation of constitutional provisions concerning the status of subjects of the federation (republics and lands). Provision is accordingly made for certain economic, political, and legal guarantees that the status of new subjects of the Russian Federation—republics and lands—will be observed.

In particular, there are guarantees of the territorial integrity of subjects of the federation, the borders between which can be changed only on the basis of "treaties between them." Republics and lands are vested with quite a broad range of exclusive rights and freedoms. Their exclusive competences, for example, include:

1. the adoption and amendment of the constitution of a republic or land and oversight over its observance
2. the formation and organization of the activity of organs of power in a republic or land
3. legislative initiative in federal organs
4. participation in the formation and activity of the Supreme Soviet of the Russian Federation in accordance with the present constitution
5. economic, social, and cultural development programs of republics and lands
6. the budget of a republic or land; local taxes and duties; nonbudget funds
7. territorial division of republics or lands
8. international relations excepting those that are the exclusive competences of the Russian Federation
9. protection of the primordial habitat of minority peoples and ethnic communities; the creation of conditions for the national, economic, cultural, and linguistic development of all peoples
10. acts of civil status
11. decorations and honorary titles of republics or lands
12. other powers if they do not contradict the provisions of the present constitution.

Within the limits of their powers, republics and lands are entitled to conclude various agreements with one another that do not contradict the Russian constitution.

The draft of the new Russian Constitution also points to other guarantees of the observance of the legal status of subjects of the federation and the transformation of the present, to a significant degree, formal federation into a future "real" federation. Without becoming pessimistic, it should be noted that previous constitutions of the U.S.S.R. and RSFSR also contained many of the same or similar guarantees. This is readily apparent when one compares previous and current constitutional provisions. Obviously, it is not only and not even so much that rights, freedoms, and guarantees of their observance are proclaimed, as much as the degree of rigorousness with which they are observed in real life, in practice. The degree of practicability of the newly proclaimed rights will be shown by their practical implementation in the future.

PECULIARITIES OF THE RUSSIAN FEDERATION

A significant group of peculiarities of the Russian Federation in all stages of its formation and development is integrally connected with and, to a considerable degree, occasioned by the existence of other forms of Soviet federation in parallel with it within the framework of the former U.S.S.R.

The Russian Federation, as we know, was only one of three forms of Soviet federation. Besides it, there also existed two other forms of federation: the Union of Soviet Socialist Republics (U.S.S.R.) and the Transcaucasian Soviet Republic (TSR).

The TSR existed from March 1922 to December 1936 and incorporated three Soviet republics: Azerbaijan, Armenia, and Georgia. It was organized on a contractual basis. Sovereign states were its subjects. Each of them had its own supreme organs of state power and government, its own constitution.

The constitution of the Transcaucasian Federation was also adopted in December 1922. It consisted of two sections: the Declaration of the Formation of the TSR, and the Treaty on the Formation of the Transcausian Federation. The declaration indicated the basic goals andobjectives of uniting the republics into a federation. The treaty proper enunciated the basic provisions of the constitution of the TSR.

Each republic belonging to the TSR had the right to secede from the federation. The constitution linked the exercise of this right to the powers of the federation's highest organs of state power. Unilateral secession without regard to the opinion of other subjects (parts) of the federation was not permitted.

The TSR ceased to exist in December 1936. Each republic that had constituted the given form of Soviet federation independently became a part of the U.S.S.R. from that time.

The Union of Soviet Socialist Republics, as the next form of Soviet federation, originated in December 1922 and existed until December 1991. Its formation was based on a treaty concluded between four republics—two federations (RSFSR and TSR) and two unitary states (Ukraine and Belorussia). The U.S.S.R. was regarded a unitary union state with all the attendant intrastate and international consequences. Union republics remained subjects of the U.S.S.R. during the entire period of its existence.

Because the U.S.S.R., in addition to unitary states that were subjects of federation, also incorporated federal states that were subjects (of federation) until 1936—the RSFSR and the TSR—and after 1936, only the RSFSR, it is easy to see what a complex, multilevel, and largely contradictory system this form of Soviet federation presented. In the last 10–20 days of its existence, the U.S.S.R. numbered 35 national states—15 union and 20 autonomous republics—and also 18 national state formations—8 autonomous oblasts and 10 national okrugs.[11]

In what concrete way has the existence of other forms of Soviet federation influenced and been reflected in the Russian Federation? In what way was this expressed in the past and how can this be reflected in the Russian Federation at the present and in the future?

Speaking of the past, the constitution of the RSFSR almost completely reflected the political and legal mood, character, content, and purpose of the federation of the U.S.S.R. The formal-legal nature, the spirit of bureaucratism, excessive centralism, and de facto unitarianism constantly permeated not only the union federation, but the Russian Federation as well and there was little change with the abolition of the U.S.S.R. and its constitution. The central, formal-legal, and bureaucratic union link was automatically transformed into an analogous, republic link at the level of the Russian Federation.

In attempting to determine how the influence of other forms of Soviet federation, their experience of formation and functioning, are at present manifested or may be manifested in the future, it seems important to focus attention on the following four points.

First. Based on the example of the U.S.S.R. and TSR, the Russian Federation today—judging by the draft of its new constitution and other documents—has the intention and tendency to organize the interrelations of its subjects on a contractual rather than an autonomous basis. This is attested to, in particular, by the May 16, 1991, decrees of the RSFSR Supreme Soviet On Basic Principles of the National-State Organization of the RSFSR (On the Federal Contract), On the Procedure and Deadlines for Completing Work on the Draft of the Federal Contract, and similar acts.[12]

Previously, as we know, no provision was made for a contractual basis between subjects of the Russian Federation that were autonomies of various types. Only relations between subjects of the federation within the framework of the U.S.S.R. and TSR were organized on a contractual basis. The treaty forming the Transcaucasian Federation referred to the republics comprising it as none other than "contract republics." There was also frequent mention of them as "republics that are in the process of becoming contractual" (*dogovarivayushchiesya respubliki*) in official documents.

Relations between different union republics that were subjects of the U.S.S.R. were formally organized on the basis of contractual relations. The Treaty on the Formation of the U.S.S.R., signed on December 30, 1922, established in general outline the constitutional bases of organization of the given form of Soviet federation. It defined the supreme all-union organs of state power and government, their competences, and the procedure governing their formation. It established unitary union citizenship for the citizens of union republics. It defined the principles of budget relations between the U.S.S.R. and union republics.

Second. Based on the example of other forms of Soviet federation and its own experience dating back to the 1920s, the Russian Federation today, as a unitary state,tries to organize its relations on a contractual basis both inside and outside the nation, among former subjects of the union federation. This is most obviously attested to by such documents as treaties and agreements concluded by Russia with Belorussia, as well as with Ukraine and other member-states of the Commonwealth of Independent States. It is also evidenced by the repeated declarations, protocols, and decisions of heads of Commonwealth states and heads of the governments of Belorussia, Russia, and Ukraine On the Coordination of Economic Policy, On Coordination Institutions of the Commonwealth of Independent States, and so on.[13]

The experience of contractual relations from 1917 to 1922 is being widely used at the present time in the Russian Republic's practical relations with other former union republics. We refer, in particular, to such treaties and agreements as the Treaty Between the RSFSR and the Azerbaijan SSR on a Military-Economic Alliance (September 30, 1920), On the Workers' and Peasants' Treaty Between the RSFSR and Belorussia" (January 16, 1921). We also refer to a number of agreements concluded between the governments of the RSFSR and Azerbaijan SSR such as On the Unification of Food Policy, On the Unification of the Management of the Postal Service, the Telegraph, Telephone, and Radio-Telegraph, On Foreign Policy Questions (1920), and others.[14]

It should be emphasized in particular that the union treaties of republics during those years were the legal formalization of their military-economic alliances. They explicitly stated that republics conclude treaties out of an awareness of the need to unify their forces in the interests of defense and their economic organizational development.

Third. There is utilization of the practice of republics or federations borrowing legislative acts from one another. At the present time, the Russian Federation is widely using the legislation of the U.S.S.R.—that is, of a former union federation. Naturally, this is done with the proviso that union legislation not contradict republic legislation.

The analogous experience of the use of the legislation of one sovereign republic by another was widely known in Russia's relations with other states back in the 1920s. For example, the first constitutions of Azerbaijan, Armenia, Belorussia, Ukraine, and certain other republics were drafted and adopted on the basis of the principles and basic provisions of the RSFSR Constitution of 1918. The borrowing of normative acts extended not only to constitutional legislation, but also to current legislation as well. Thus, the RSFSR Criminal Code, the Statute on RSFSR Railroads, the RSFSR Labor Code, and other normative acts were put into effect by acts of the Ukrainian government on Ukrainian territory in the 1920s.[15]

Fourth. Following the example of former Soviet federations—the U.S.S.R. and TSR—that rejected subject-autonomies from the very beginning of their formation, the Russian Federation at the present time (as documents indicate) also intends to follow this path. As already stated, instead of subject-autonomies, the Russian Federation will be formed of subjects that are republics and lands.

The idea of Russia's total rejection of autonomies appears to be unquestionably fruitful and to a considerable degree overdue because even without this, autonomous republics such as the Tatar, Bashkir, Karelian, and others have already declared their independence and sovereignty, and have in fact rejected their official status as autonomies.

However, many questions remain open in the process: If not the status of an autonomy, then what kind of status? Will not the creation of several tens of new subjects of federation—republics and lands—lead to the increased instability and unwieldiness of the Russian state organization mechanism? How will such very heterogeneous subjects of federation as republics, on the one hand, and lands, on the other, combine and interact with one another? Is it indeed at all possible that their combination and effective interaction can be painless under the conditions of a federation?

After all, it should not be forgotten that in the process of the formation of the Russian Federation in 1918, the question of its incorporation of subjects of unequal status was already posed. It took the form of the so-called republic autonomization plan proposed by Joseph Stalin.[16] According to this plan, such "formations" as Poland, Ukraine, Finland, Turkestan, and the Kirghiz Kray, on the one hand, and the Crimea, Siberia, the Tatar-Bashkir territory, on the other, which were far from having the same political, national, and economic weight, should have been considered as equal subjects in the Russian Federation. In time this plan was rejected. It appears that we are now, 70 years later, trying to implement similar ideas by combining within the framework of a single federation such heterogeneous, disparate subjects as sovereign republics and lands.

PROSPECTS FOR THE FUTURE

In connection with the examination of the peculiarities and problems of development of the Russian Federation at the present time, it is natural to ask what the prospects are for its development in the future. What factors will promote and what factors will impede its development? Does not Russia—Boris Yeltsin's empire, as it is sometimes figuratively called—await the same sad end as that which befell the U.S.S.R.—Mikhail Gorbachev's empire—in the relatively recent past?

It is common knowledge that it is not only a risky but also a very thankless business to make political or other forecasts and to draw final conclusions. Therefore, without claiming the laurels of a political prophet or knowledge of the final truth, we shall merely confine ourselves to indicating the tendencies and factors that promote the preservation and development of the Russian Federation or, to the contrary, that impede its development.

Among the positive factors directed toward the preservation and the subequent strengthening of the Russian Federation are the following historical, cultural, and other ties traditionally forming between different nations and nationalities that live on Russian territory and that have their own statehood: the common spiritual and religious experience of many strata of society, ethnic groups, peoples, and nationalities; the quite precise and strict economic interconnection and interdependence of different regions, states, and state formations existing and functioning within Russia's framework; the existence of an official language—Russian—that was common to all strata of society of the Russian Federation, to all nations and nationalities (on a par with their mother tongue) for several decades; the democratization of various aspects of the internal life of Russian society and the state, of interstate federal ties; the faith that a considerable part of the population still has in the promise of Russian President Yeltsin to carry out radical economic and political reforms in the nation, to place relations between the Russian Federation as a whole, on the one hand, and its individual subjects, on the other, on a new, democratic basis.

Among the negative factors that are destabilizing the Russian Federation are the following: the influence of separatist and other similar tendencies that have led initially to the weakening and then to the ultimate disintegration of the U.S.S.R.; the intensification of fundamentalist and nationalistic influences in certain autonomous republics and regions; the increasingly frequent and open manifestation of left- and right-wing extremism in Russia in recent years; and manifestations of chauvinism, bureaucratism, and political dogmatism having a destabilizing influence.

Other socioeconomic and political factors are having a similar impact on the state of Russian society and its political and state system. Among them, for example, the weak social protection of the low-paid strata of society against skyrocketing inflation and prices in recent time; the significant pauperization of the majority of society as a result of the so-called liberalization of prices in January 1992; the growth of corruption in state structures; the weak professional preparation of many members of the Russian government and other newly appointed officials of different ranks after the putsch in August 1991; the growth of dissatisfaction among different strata of the nation's population with "unpopular" economic, financial, and other measures implemented by the government.

In addition to those factors, there are also other positive and negative factors that directly or indirectly affect the state of Russian society and the development of the Russian Federation. The level of development, tendencies, and fate of the Russian Federation ultimately will depend on which of them eventually win out and become dominant in the near future.

NOTES

1. Richard P. Nathan and Erik P. Hoffmann, "Contemporary Federalism: Comparative Perspectives," *Mezhdunarodnaya zhizn'*, No. 4, 1991, 35.

2. See *Yuridicheskiy entsiklopedicheskiy slovar'* (Encyclopedic Dictionary of Law) (Moscow, 1984), 394.

3. B. N. Topornin, "Constitutional Reform—the Path to a Law-Governed State," *Sovetskoye gosudarstvo i pravo*, 1990, 3–14.

4. D. J. Elazar, *Exploring Federation* (Tuscaloosa, Ala., 1987), 34–35.

5. See O. N. Chistyakov, *Stanovleniye Rossiyskoy Federatsii* (Formation of the Russian Federation) (Moscow, 1966); D. I. Zlatopol'skiy, *SSSR—Federativnoye gosudarstvo* (The U.S.S.R.—a Federated State) (Moscow, 1967).

6. Nathan and Hoffman, "Contemporary Federalism," 42.

7. See *Vedomosti S'yezda narodnykh deputatov RSFSR i Verkhovnogo Soveta RSFSR* (Gazette of the Congress of People's Deputies of the RSFSR and Verkhovnogo Soveta RSFSR), No. 16, 1991, 501.

8. *Konstitutsiya (Osnovnoy zakon) Rossiyskoy Sovetskoy Federativnoy Sotsialisticheskoy Respubliki* (Constitution [Fundamental Law] of the Russian Soviet Federated Socialist Republic) (Moscow, 1989), Articles 78–84.

9. O. N. Chistyakov, "The Formation of the Russian Federation (1917–1918), *Sovetskoye gosudarstvo i pravo,* No. 10, 1957, 7.

10. Zlatopol'skiy, *SSSR–Federativnoye*, 92.

11. Ibid., 56–57.

12. *Vedomosti . . . RSFSR*, 1991, No. 22. Articles 770, 772.

13. See *Izvestia*, December 9, 1991; December 23, 1991; January 17, 1992.

14. *S(vod) U(kazov) RSFSR* (Moscow) No. 85, 1920, 426.

15. *S(vod) U(kazov) Ukrainy* (Moscow), No. 36, 1922, Art. 553; No. 41, Art. 598; No. 52, Art. 751

16. See J. V. Stalin, *Sochineniia* (Works) Vol. 4 (Moscow, 1951), 69–71.

4

The Limits of Federalism and the Collapse of the U.S.S.R.

Robert V. Daniels

The collapse of the Communist Party of the Soviet Union and the liquidation of the Union itself in 1991 are generally regarded both in the former Soviet republics and in the West as triumphs of democracy and national self-determination. These views are at best oversimplifications.

Whatever other judgments one may make about it, the breakup of the Soviet Union was a failure of federalism. Federalism failed in two ways. First, the conception and experience of federalism in the Soviet Union were inadequate. Second, the circumstances challenging the federalist experiment of the era of perestroika might have overwhelmed even the best-conceived institutions of federalism.

The great impediment to successful federalism in the Soviet Union was at the same time the reason for the nominally federal structure of the communist regime—namely, the diverse ethnic makeup of the country. This multinational character of the Soviet Union was of course the legacy of centuries of expansion and conquest by the Russian Empire, extending from the subjugation of the Tatars in the sixteenth century and the seizure of part of Ukraine from Poland in the seventeenth century, to the occupation of Central Asia in the middle decades of the nineteenth century. Thus, the multiethnic character of the empire (and of the Soviet Union), based on peoples still living in their ancestral regions and using their respective languages, was quite different from the experience of the U.S.A., where different ethnic components migrated to North America (some—the Africans—involuntarily), and for the most part intermingled territorially and became assimilated linguistically into the English-speaking community. The only American equivalents of the Russian experience are the suppression of the Native Americans and the conquest of the Southwest from Mexico (and of Puerto Rico from Spain), incorporating settled ethnic groups who have more or less maintained their linguistic and cultural distinctiveness.

With modernization and the rise of national consciousness everywhere in the world by the beginning of the twentieth century, only the autocratic power of St. Petersburg kept the urge for self-determination among the non-Russian nationalities of the empire in check. Whenever the Russian center was weakened by revolutionary events or democratic reforms—in 1905, in 1917, and again under perestroika—the automatic response of the minorities was to strive for independence. To the minorities, democracy has meant above all the opportunity to escape from Russian rule, while this prospect in turn has raised doubts about democracy among the Russians if the outcome were to dismantle the empire and topple Russian from the ranks of the major world powers. Thus, the nationality question has been the Achilles' heel of democratic reform in the Russian Empire.

In contrast to the avowed centralism of the tsarist state, the Soviet regime attempted in its early years to come to terms with the multinational character of the country by adopting on paper a federal system of government. This was formalized in the establishment of the Union of Soviet Socialist Republics in 1922, with separate union republics corresponding more or less to the territories of the Russians and the major minorities, with so-called autonomous republics and lesser entities (mostly within the RSFSR) to recognize smaller minorities or those (like the Tatars) located in the interior of the country. However, all of these units, Russian and minority alike, were governed by the totally centralized dictatorship of the Communist Party, whose members running the union republics and other jurisdictions were appointed by and under the discipline of the party leadership in Moscow. Thus, the federal structure of the U.S.S.R., enshrined in the Stalin constitution, was an utter sham. It used to be said that newspapers were published in the Soviet Union in 140 different languages,but they all said the same thing.

Nevertheless, with the reforms of perestroika, the dummy federalism of the U.S.S.R. came to life. The union republics and the lesser nationality units became the political framework through which the forces of minority separatism were expressed. Another policy to accommodate minority identity was to categorize every Soviet citizen according to nationality and record this in the individual's internal passport. This ethnic concept of citizenship had potentially explosive consequences, like the federal structure of the union, once democratization released the expression of local identity.

One notion cultivated by the communist leadership is still taken for granted as people look back at the Soviet era. This is that the Soviet Union was a genuine multinational state, distinct from its Russian component. In fact, the center has always been a Russian center, under the empire, under the Soviet system, and today (1992). As far as the relations of power among the nationalities were concerned, the Soviet Union was only a refurbished form of the

Russian Empire. To be sure, the autocrat from 1929 to 1953, Joseph Stalin, was not a Russian but a Georgian, though Lenin accused him of harboring "the Great-Russian chauvinism of russified non-Russians." Stalin identified himself with the Russian majority, encouraged the revival of Russian nationalism from the 1930s on, promoted the russification of the minorities, and viciously purged minority leaders—even Communists—accused of "bourgeois nationalism."

In this context we cannot really speak of the "collapse" of the U.S.S.R. The Russian center is still intact. What has happened in the last couple of years has not been a "collapse" but rather a struggle for power at the center, and a weakening of the center's control over the non-Russian periphery. Both of these processes were evident in 1917 as well, and both have been intertwined, then and now. I will return to this question later on.

From the American point of view, the logical answer to the crisis of the Union was federalism. The federal answer seemed only to require breathing life into the old formal Soviet constitutional structure. Yet there were severe limits to what could be accomplished in this manner. On the one hand, the Soviet leadership lacked any real conception or experience of federalism as it should really function. On the other, the problems tearing the Soviet Union apart—above all the nationality problem—may well have been insurmountable for any federalist solution, leaving only the alternatives of breakup or renewed centralist despotism.

Russian history before the revolution offers no tradition of federalism unless one looks back to the feudalism that preceded the Mongol conquest in the thirteenth century. The entire modern history of Russia has been a record of central-ism; centralism became axiomatic for the survival of the Russian state in international competition, and remained no less so when the successes of the empire brought vast non-Russian regions into its compass. (The only qualification to this rule came in the 1860s with the introduction of the so-called *zemstva* and *dumy*—provincial and city councils whose powers were confined to the health-education-and-welfare sector of government.) In 1917, in reaction to the centralist tradition, the country experienced an orgy of decentralizing democracy in the Russian regions, as well as among the minorities. The communists' pyramid of local and provincial Soviets was initially a concession to this spirit, until it yielded to the overarching centralism of the Communist Party apparatus.

Nowhere in this experience, unfortunately, was there any awareness of the fundamental principle of federalism: the distribution of different powers among the various levels of government (not to be confused with the separation of powers among the legislative, executive, and judicial authorities at any level). Whenever a lower jurisdiction could assert its independence against the higher, as in 1917, and again after 1989, it would try to assert unlimited "sovereignty," lay claim to all public property within its boundaries, and defy all outside authority. Among the union republics after 1989, this attitude led to the so-called war of laws, as republics acted to suspend the application to their territory of Union legislation that was not to their taste. This recalled the so-called nullification controversy in the U.S.A. before the Civil War when several Southern states defied federal legislation infringing on their interests concerning slavery, the tariff, and "states' rights" in general. As the American example illustrates, the question of demarcating the powers of the federal and local authorities is not an easy one to answer. Yet a clear resolution is vital to the effective functioning of a federal system. And it was just such a clear resolution that was so conspicuously lacking in the Soviet experiment in federalism under perestroika. Neither the Union government nor the republics had any sense of the limits on their own authority imposed by sharing jurisdiction with the other level. Some of the trouble went back to the preperestroika regime and its failure to observe genuinely federalist practices in certain key areas, notably taxation and the judiciary. Executive functions were complicated by the distinction between all-Union ministries (heavy industry, transport, etc.), republic ministries (health, education, local industry), and Union-Republican ministries (finance, agriculture, the police, social services, and foreign affairs (Stalin's idea in 1945 to get more UN seats), where the ministry at the republic level functioned as a branch of the Union ministry—something like social welfare and employment security in American practice).

Over and above these limits in the Soviet tradition of federalism, the stresses released by political reform in the Soviet Union could well have overwhelmed any system of federalism. These were above all the forces of long-suppressed minority nationalism and separatism. But there were weaknesses in the structure of federalism that the Gorbachevian reformers inherited from their predecessors, weaknesses rooted in the origins of Soviet federalism as a system to accommodate the national minorities without compromising the power of the Russian center. The basis of the primary units, the union republics, was not a division into roughly equivalent territorial entities, as in American or German federalism, but ethnicity (as marked by language).

This left the Russian Republic as one entity overwhelming all the others. Any system of representation in a central government would either give the Russians domination (if by population) or diminish them absurdly (if by republic), though until Gorbachev's reforms this quandary was not felt because the Supreme Soviet in Moscow was representative (one house by population, the other by nationality) only pro forma. Matters would have been quite different if there were no parallel government of the Russian Republic in Moscow, and the Russian part of the country had been divided into regions—ten or twelve can readily be suggested, as some Russian constitutional theorists are suggesting today—roughly equivalent in power and importance to the non-Russian republics. Then there could have been no question of dissolving the Union government, even if certain non-Russian republics ultimately decided to secede.

The surge of minority nationalism after the electoral reforms of 1989 quickly altered the terms of the federalism question and made it rather one of confederation at best. To be sure, the semantic distinction of federation and confedera-tion is not that sharp in reality; there is a broad continuum of possible arrangements from the most limited local authority (in Britain, for instance) to the loosest links with the center (the Holy Roman Empire or the U.S.A. under the Articles of Confederation of 1777–87). But the demands posed by the non-Russian republics—separate currencies, separate military forces, independence from the legislative competence of the Union parliament—pushed the terms of the argument to the confederal extreme even before the August 1991 coup.

This direction was clear in the Union Treaty finally drawn up in March 1991 and accepted in principle in the Novo-Ogarevo Agreement of the "nine plus one" in April 1991. The treaty—the document that was scheduled to be formally signed the day after the August coup was launched—was intended to replace the coercive treaty of 1922 that created the U.S.S.R, and to provide the basis for a new Union constitution. Its language leaned heavily to the rights of the republics, "sovereign states" that "possess full state power" and "retain the right to the independent resolution of all questions of their development." But in the assignment of powers to the Union and the republics, the Union Treaty was so vague and confusing that it would be a nightmare for an American constitutional lawyer. The draft specified the logical Union responsibilities—defense, state security, foreign policy, communications, the space program—but promised the republics a share in formulating policy for all these areas, while putting the bulk of governmental responsibilities for the economy and social policy in the hands of "the U.S.S.R. . . . in conjunction with the republics." Then, as though to compensate, it declared, "Republic laws have supremacy on all questions, with the exception of those falling within the Union's jurisdiction." The new Constitutional Court was supposed to sort all this out if disputes arose.

The stakes in the struggle over federation or confederation were raised by the socialized character of the Soviet economy, where all industry and natural resources were state-owned. If the republics were to gain preeminent powers, this would include ownership of the economic assets within their borders. There was no clear formula to determine what properties, if any, should remain the domain of the Union government. Yet the Soviet economy was actually highly integrated and centralized, a system that would be—and in fact was—grievously disrupted by the independence of the republics. Generally speaking, within any economic entity, planned or market, that operates as an undivided whole, it is unrealistic to speak of significant economic powers for lower levels of government. This is equally true for the American federal system, where, states'-rights ideology to the contrary notwithstanding, states cannot exert economic power against nationwide business organizations or even tax them as they might wish. If, as the Soviet republics demanded, lower entities were to get real control over their respective economies, this doomed the functioning of the overall Soviet economy as a single unit.

Perhaps a distinctive line between federation and confederation is the right of a constituent entity to secede. To be sure, union republics had the right to secede under the Stalin constitution, but anyone who took it seriously was purged. The issue was forced by the new anticommunist Baltic governments that were elected democratically in 1990, and Gorbachev refused to face it squarely. He referred to a complex process of secession, subject to a Unionwide referendum, and made it clear that he would do anything within the terms of his democratized system—or even outside those terms—to prevent a republic from seceding. This attitude led him to order or condone military and economic action against separatists in Georgia in 1989 and in Lithuania in 1990 and again in early 1991. He responded to calls for "sovereignty" by alleging "fascistic tendencies," "superfragmentation and chaos," and "furious attempts to discredit the institutions of state power which embody the idea of a federal union state."[1] Alarm about the separatism that his own reforms had unleased was undoubtedly the major factor in Gorbachev's shift toward the party conservatives in the winter of 1990–91.

At Novo-Ogarevo, in the course of his zig-zag back toward reform, Gorbachev accepted language affirming the right of republics to secede or to become independent if they declined to sign the treaty.[2] Interestingly, the nine signatories at Novo-Ogarevo were the Slavic and Moslem republics where communists and excommunists remained in command even after the August coup; the six nonsigners were the non-Slavic-speaking European republics led (except for Moldova) by former anticommunist dissidents. In any case, the prospect of the actual or virtual dissolution of the Union pursuant to the treaty was anathema to the communist conservatives, and appeared as a major item on the agenda of the August plotters against Gorbachev: "the confrontation between nationalities and the chaos and anarchy that are threatening the lives and security of the citizens of the Soviet Union and the sovereignty, territorial integrity, freedom and independence of our fatherland. . . . a mortal danger threatens our homeland . . . , the breakup of the state."[3] But even at the end, Gorbachev himself was unreconciled to the breakup of the Union. "I support the preservation of the union state and the integrity of this country," he said in his resignation statement on December 25th. "Developments took a different course. The policy prevailed of dismembering this country and disuniting the state, which is something I cannot subscribe to."[4]

The survival of the Union, dubious enough between the pressures of minority separatism and the weakness of any conception of federalism, was further threatened after 1990 by the emergence of purely political considerations. These involved two elements—one institutional and the other personal. The institutional element was the existence of the huge Russian Republic, the main body of the Union with its capital in Moscow like the capital of the Union as a whole. As long as the governments of the union republics, Russia included, were mere appendages of the Russian-dominated Communist Party, this division created no problem. But once Gorbachev implemented the reforms of democratization in 1989, the potential existed for what Lenin called "dual power" in Moscow and an automatic struggle for power between the Union and Russian governments.

The potential institutional conflict quickly became a personal political contest as the former Moscow party secretary Boris Yeltsin returned from the political wilderness to challenge his former leader Gorbachev. Yeltsin had been brought into the new Gorbachev leadership in 1985 to clean up the notoriously corrupt party organization in the City of Moscow, but in so doing, he aroused the ire of party conservatives. In June 1987, in one of his many tactical retreats to appease the conservatives, Gorbachev allowed Yeltsin to be passed over for promotion to full member of the Politburo. This crucial event, overlooked in virtually all accounts of the Yeltsin-Gorbachev rivalry, accounts for Yeltsin's defiance of Gorbachev in the fall of 1987 and in turn Gorbachev's humiliation of his former lieutenant. Yeltsin has repeatedly referred back to 1987 as the point when Gorbachev "began to go wrong" and "began . . . deceiving the people."[5] The record since that time suggests a firm determination on Yeltsin's part to settle scores. Yet, in the spirit of his new democratization program, Gorbachev had to leave Yeltsin free to speak out and to run for a seat in the new Congress of People's Deputies in March 1989, which he won triumphantly as a voice for accelera-ted reform. A year later, after the series of more fully democratic elections in the union republics, the radical reformers advanced Yeltsin as a candidate for the chairmanship of the newly democratized Supreme Soviet of the Russian Republic. Gorbachev campaigned vehemently against him, but took no steps contrary to his own new constitution to stop his rival.

Once in command of the Russian Republic, Yeltsin worked consistently to undermine Gorbachev's power as president of the Union. His approach was simple: to support the calls for "sovereignty" on the part of all the union republics, including his own, thereby curbing the authority of the Union government and enhancing the authority of his own rival regime in Moscow. It did not matter that for Russia to be "sovereign" against itself was a patent absurdity. Russian "sovereignty" within the old structure of the Union could only mean Russian nonsovereignty over the other republics. The real question was which Russian government, under which Russian leader, would prevail. To win, Yeltsin was willing to pay the price, for the time being, of dissolving the authority of the Russian center exercised by Gorbachev's Union government. This process was under way well before the August coup, and directly underlay the final collapse of Union authority that followed the coup attempt.

Following the August coup, Yeltsin moved relentlessly to liquidate the

Union government while Gorbachev tried to salvage its ebbing life by reviving his project of a Union Treaty. The decisive undoing of this hope was the matter of taxation where—still lacking the idea of a federal division of authority—revenues had been transferred to the republics, who were then supposed to share Union expenses, including the armed forces. Literally bankrupt, Gorbachev was helpless to resist Yeltsin's physical takeover of Union government ministries and assets, even the Kremlin itself. Finally came the Minsk Agreement of 8 December of Russia, Ukraine, and Belarus to declare the Soviet Union dissolved. This was a coup d'état, no less than the communist coup of October 1917, technically preempting the rights of the nine other remaining members of the Union, though in fact none of them objected.

There is a curious parallel between the events of 1917 that brought the communist regime into being, and the events of 1991 that put an end to it. Alexander Kerensky's Provisional Government faced the Bolshevik-controlled Petrograd Soviet in a situation of dual power, just as Gorbachev's union government faced Yeltsin's Russian government and the radical reformers. Before the Bolsheviks ever acted, Kerensky had lost virtually all popular confidence as support drained away to the left and to the right—just as Gorbachev's support had drained away. There is even a parallel between the August coup, crippling Gorbachev politically, and the abortive right-wing coup led by the chief of staff, General Lavr Kornilov, in August 1917, which was equally damaging to Kerensky. After the coup attempt it was as easy for Yeltsin to step in as it had been for Lenin, when, as the latter said, he found power lying in the streets and picked it up.

Ironically, once Yeltsin had disposed of Gorbachev and the Union, he found himself face to face with the same urges and problems. Under the umbrella of the Commonwealth of Independent States he hoped to maintain some semblance of Russian influence over the former union, with emphasis on the minimal features of a confederation—namely, the military, the currency, and foreign relations. He took it as a matter of course that the Russian government should inherit the position of the Soviet Union in international matters, including embassies abroad, treaty obligations, and the UN Security Council seat. Yet he had gone so far in advancing the sovereignty of the republics against Gorbachev that there was no restraining them now, certainly not Ukraine with its assertion of complete economic independence and its claim on an independent share of the Commonwealth's armed forces. At the same time, Yeltsin was confronted within the Russian Federation with a series of separatist movements among the smaller minorities—notably the Tatars and the Chechen-Ingush—analogous to those that had challenged Gorbachev in the union at large. Toward these movements within the Russian Federation, Yeltsin has proved so far to be an even more adamant centralist than Gorbachev (though not enough to satisfy the Russian nationalists in his entourage, led by Vice-President Aleksandr Rutskoi). His Federation Treaty between the Russian government and its subordinate minority units, the autonomous republics, has run into all the problems that Gorbachev's Union Treaty encountered.

Yeltsin's position after the breakup of the Union lends some credence to the notion that his embrace of sovereignty for the Union republics was as much a matter of expediency as of principle. Nor has he consistently observed the principles of federalism in dealing with the Russian provinces under his rule, though in many cases they had also asserted powers of local self-government well before the coup. He responded immediately to the August coup by dispatching his personal representatives to the Russian provinces to impose his authority over the local communists who, ironically, hoped to use their "states' rights" to survive politically. Unfortunately, Yeltsin's methods remind the historian of the manner in which Stalin built his apparatus of personal power in the 1920s.

By all logic, the circumstances of the Soviet Union in 1991 cried for a federal solution. Genuine federalism, made possible by the dismantling of the Communist Party dictatorship, would have given the minorities full scope for cultural self-expression. At the same time, it could have avoided the divisive concept of citizenship based on ethnicity rather than territory, a principle that implied second-class citizenship for the subminorities present in every ethnic subdivision because of the historic mixing of nationalities. Federalism could have maintained the Unionwide economy without adding to the country's economic woes by placing barriers among the highly interdependent regions. It would have allowed institutions of democratic logical administration to be fashioned more gradually and more constructively. It would have avoided the unnerving problems of dividing the Soviet armed forces while trying to maintain some form of responsible control over the nuclear weapons stockpile, and it would have preserved the Soviet Union, despite all its problems, as a more influential and less troublesome power on the international scene.

Yet the obstacles to successful federalism were daunting, given the urges of long-suppressed nationalism colliding with the old habits of centralism, as well as the defects in the federal structure that the reformers inherited. More statesmanship in all quarters might have made a difference. If Gorbachev had been more flexible toward the nationalities at an earlier point in perestroika, if Yeltsin had not chosen to use the Russian Republic as a weapon against Gorbachev, if some of the excommunist leaders in the other republics had not yielded to the political pressure to outdo former dissident nationalists, the federal—or confederal—union might have been preserved, at least with its essential powers in defense, money matters, and foreign relations. In the absence of these might-have-beens, the democratized Union was a lost cause, and the individual Soviet republics were left to cope with each other and with the outside world under very unpromising circumstances.

NOTES

1. M. S. Gorbachev, *Report to the Supreme Soviet*, November 16, 1990.
2. *Izvestia*, April 25, 1991.
3. Appeal to the Soviet People by the State Committee on the State of Emergency in the U.S.S.R., *Pravda* and *Izvestia*, August 20, 1991.
4. Text in *The New York Times*, December 26, 1991.
5. *Newsweek*, December 30, 1991, 21; John Morrison, *Boris Yeltsin: From Bolshevik to Democrat* (London and New York, 1991), 290.

5

Incipient Federalism in Late Imperial Russia

Thomas Earl Porter

The proliferation of independent groups and informal political associations over the last half decade in Russia has reawakened scholarly interest in the late tsarist era. Historians and social scientists are searching for meaningful parallels, for a "usable past" between social and political change in contemporary Russia on the one hand, and on the other, the revolution of westernization that was launched by the era of great reforms in the 1860s but finally aborted in 1917. Is there historical precedent for the political liberalization now under way in the former Soviet Union? More important, does the outburst of initiative across that land belie the image held in the West of a citizenry singularly lacking in habits of enterprise, independence, and self-government due to centuries of autocracy and bureaucracy—suggesting that it may be tapping deeper wellsprings of autonomy in that culture than previously imagined? If so, we need to reexamine the past in order to clarify these historical nuances; to suggest, in other words, that the contemporary manifestations of public identity have deep roots that survived three-quarters of a century of communism.

Modern Russian history began with the emancipation of the serfs in 1861. Russia finally started to move away from its medieval society of orders to one where, theoretically at least, all of its citizens were equal before the law. Russia's inept performance in the Crimean War had served to convince the tsar and his ministers of the need for modernization. In the West this had led to social and economic problems whose resolution had required the active participation of society in national affairs. In late Imperial Russia it would also lead to the development of a public sphere, which would provide for the emergence of a civil society; these are necessary preconditions for the devolution of governing authority that characterizes a federal state.

This remarkable renovation of Russia's sociopolitical order would not be completed until shortly before the outbreak of World War I. However, the tsarist government had immediately recognized the need to devise a new system of governance in order to replace the landlords' lost authority. Tsar Alexander II created the institutions of local self-government (*zemstva*), hoping to form a single, integrated bureaucratic apparatus from which it would be possible to mobilize Russia's resources and thus make it easier to provide for the defense of the nation and the welfare of its people.

The chief architect of the *zemstvo* statute of January 1, 1862, was Minister of the Interior P. A. Valuev. His principal concern was to maintain the primacy of the bureaucracy (and in particular his own ministry) and to stifle the requests made by society for more autonomy and jurisdiction in local affairs. Valuev wanted to ensure that the role allotted to society would be minimal. He considered the *zemstva* to be

> only a special organ of one and the same state power and from it receives its rights and authority; the *zemstvo* institutions, having their place in the state organism, are not able to exist outside of it, and, equally with other institutions, are subject to those general conditions and to that general guidance which are established by the central authority.[1]

Valuev was a proponent of the state theory of self-government. According to this theory, local government takes on the administration of particular state functions because they are believed to be best able to fulfill these state responsibilities. There is no independent activity by the organs of local self-government; there is merely a deconcentration of power wherein the state bureaucracy retains control but assigns specific functions to these bodies. Local society simply serves to implement state policies. However, many of the noble landlords who stood for election subscribed to the societal theory of self-government. These men drew distinctions between state affairs and local interests. They thought that society's interests, which were generally economic in nature, should be distinguished from the essentially political interests of the state. In other words, the *zemstva* should be an independent institution standing outside of the governmental apparatus. These *zemstva* activists (*zemtsy*) called for a devolution of governing authority.

The *zemstva* were established in the provinces and counties of the empire. These institutions consisted of an assembly (which was to have decision-making powers) elected for a three-year term and an executive board to implement policies. The statute defined the duties of the *zemstva* as the management of "local economic welfare and needs" with 14 different areas of jurisdiction.[2] Of crucial import to the development of political pluralism was the prohibition on inter*zemstvo* contacts; Article 3 limited the activity of the *zemstva* to the boundaries of the province or county. This restriction would be instrumental in fueling the conflict between state and society; it was designed to ensure that the *zemstva* would have no lateral contacts between themselves and would, therefore, be only a link in the administrative chain that stretched from St. Petersburg to the countryside.

But it was the statute's nebulous language that first caused the friction between state and society. Some responsibilities were transferred in their entirety to the *zemstva* for management, while other duties remained under the aegis of the state with the *zemstva* acting as the government's agent. The *zemstva* were given the authority "to look after" the development of trade and industry, but only allowed the opportunity "to cooperate" with the government in preventing cattle diseases and preserving crops from destruction by insects. They were also granted the right to participate . . . mainly in economic terms" in the management of public health and education. This vague language left the *zemtsy* to wonder what the limits of participation and cooperation were. Valuev's intention to utilize the *zemstva* merely as an extension of the bureaucratic apparatus is made evident by the statute's requirement that they assist "in the fulfillment of demands which might be placed upon them by the civil and military administration."

More important, however, was the fact that the elective principle was inaugurated. In keeping with the emancipation's intention of making the peasants "free rural inhabitants," the elections for the *zemstva* were based on the type of property held and not on the estate to which the voter had formerly belonged. All males over the age of 25 who held (1) private rural property, (2) private urban property, or (3) allotment land (land granted to the communes upon emancipation in order to prevent the peasantry from falling into peonage) were eligible to vote in one of these three *curiae*. Peasants who held private rural property were allowed to vote in the first *curia*. This gave further legal sanction to the peasants' new status in society; Russia was emerging from its society of orders to a nation composed of socioeconomic classes with all of its citizens equal before the law.

The *zemtsy* soon realized that the prohibition on inter*zemstvo* contacts would adversely affect their ostensibly legitimate efforts "to manage local economic welfare and needs." They understood that the massive problems that beset Russia could not be solved without the active participation of society. This gave rise to the movement for the coordination of their activities and the transformation of the *zemstva* into independent organs of local self-government. Many bureaucrats viewed this effort as an attempt to impinge upon their prerogatives. In the years following the establishment of the *zemstva*, the mutual distrust between the *zemtsy* and the bureaucrats was exacerbated by a series of conflicts over *zemstva* jurisdiction and the authoritarian attitudes of the provincial governors.

In addition, many zemstvo called for the "crowning of the edifice" with an all-Russian *zemstvo*. This political body would be the equivalent of a national representative assembly. While this paper is concerned with the development of the *zemstva* into independent organs of local self-government that would serve to transform Russia into a quasi-federal state by the early twentieth century, the ultimately successful endeavors of society both to manage local affairs without state interference and to obtain a voice in national political life illustrate well the development of political pluralism in late Imperial Russia.

The struggle between the state and society continued unabated for the next four decades. In 1866 the Senate reaffirmed the prohibition contained in the statute on inter*zemstvo* contacts.[3] In December of the same year provincial governors were given the right to refuse to confirm in office any persons elected by the assemblies but considered "unreliable" by the authorities.[4] Clashes also occurred over the issue of taxation powers. The statute had granted only limited tax powers to the *zemstva*, the result of Valuev's intention to hold down their revenues and thus force them to be dependent on government largesse.

Another decree promulgated on June 13, 1867 was designed to bring the *zemstva* more fully under state control. The law gave the chairmen of the *zemstva* assemblies sweeping new powers. These included the right to exclude topics from the agenda that were considered to be outside of *zemstvo* competence.[5] The chairmen would henceforth be held responsible for the conduct of the delegates and the content of their proposals. This law in effect made the chairmen governmental representatives, thus realizing the bureaucracy's long-standing goal of manifesting its presence on the local level.

The government, did, however, occasionally allow regional congresses to convene in order to deal with pressing problems. During the Russo-Turkish War of 1877, the regime allowed several provincial *zemstva* to act jointly in order to succor the wounded. In December 1880 a congress met in Kharkov to discuss measures to be taken to combat a diphtheria outbreak; in February 1881 another congress was allowed to meet in Odessa because of the need to take steps to alleviate damage caused by an infestation of crop-damaging beetles.[6] These problems were of such great magnitude that they knew no boundaries and interregional cooperation was necessary to guarantee the maximum efficiency of operations.

The government wanted to ensure that it retained its control over the *zemstva* and sought to integrate them more fully into the bureaucratic apparatus. The assassination of Tsar Alexander II in 1881 had brought his deeply conservative son to the throne. A new *zemstvo* statute was issued on June 12, 1890. The imperial decree that accompanied the introduction of the statute underscored the regime's intention merely to deconcentrate governing powers; it explained that the 1864 statute had been modified so that the *zemstva* "in proper unity with other governmental institutions could carry out with greater success the important state business entrusted to them."[7]

The revised statute underscored this point. Article 1 of the 1864 statute had defined the duties of the *zemstva* to be "the management of local economic welfare and needs." The corresponding article in the 1890 statute read simply "local welfare and needs." The word "economic" had been dropped because proponents of *zemstvo* independence had argued that economic interests did not come under the purview of the state and that inter*zemstvo* contacts were necessary to address effectively Russia's economic needs.

Article 118 stipulated that all members of the *zemstvo* executive boards at the county and provincial levels had to be confirmed in office; all members of the executive boards and county executive board chairmen had to be approved by the governor of the province; the chairmen of the provincial executive boards had to be confirmed by the minister of the interior. Article 119 of the statute provided for the appointment of chairmen by the minister himself if those men who had been chosen by the assemblies were not confirmed in office a second time. Finally, the government's intention to force the *zemstva* to be simply organs of state administration was shown by the requirement of Article 124, which declared that all members of executive boards were to be considered in the state's service.[8]

Of even more significance was the fact that the 1890 statute abolished the "nonclass" character of the *zemstvo* and curtailed the elective principle insofar as the peasantry was concerned. The new law was designed to once again make the nobility into a bulwark for the regime and to freeze the sociopolitical evolution that was occurring as a result of the government's modernization drive. Ironically, the autocracy would continue to espouse its outdated ideals and extoll the virtues of the nobility while pursuing an industrialization process that would fundamentally alter Russian society.

Since the nobility was no longer tied to the autocracy through the former symbiotic relationship that characterized the old regime, many noblemen would continue to press for an extension of their right to participate in the governance of the nation. They were joined by members of Russia's burgeoning entrepreneurial class. After Tsar Nicholas II's accession to the throne in 1894, another wave of agitation for the creation of a national representative body and more authority for the *zemstva* swept over Russia. Nicholas dismissed these pleas as being "senseless dreams." The *zemtsy* were led by Dmitrii Shipov, chairman of the Moscow provincial *zemstvo* board, who understood that some type of national organization was necessary for the successful defense of society's rights and the independence of local self-government.[9] He presided over a series of informal meetings attended by like-minded *zemtsy* who called for the end of governmental supervision over their activities, the extension of *zemstvo* jurisdiction to all local needs, and, most important, "the right to contact one another as well as to hold all-*zemstvo* congresses of representatives."[10]

The reactionary minister of internal affairs, V. K. Plehve, had duly noted the *zemtsy*'s demands and thought the congresses little more than a conspiracy against the throne. He felt that neither the Russian people in general nor the educated circles in particular were sufficiently well-trained to be allowed to govern their country or even to take an extensive part in the government . . . the most efficient way to ensure the future peaceful and systematic development of Russia would be to perfect the State machinery.[11]

Shipov and the other *zemtsy* immediately offered their services to the nation. They met in Moscow to form a united *zemstvo* union in order to render assistance to the troops. Representatives from 11 provinces attended. In order to alleviate the regime's misgivings about joint *zemstvo* activity, it was decided that each province would independently organize medical detachments that would be funded exclusively by their own *zemstvo* assembly. General guidelines and recommendations as to the type of equipment and supplies that would be needed in the Far East were drawn up by the General *Zemstvo* Organization's (Obshchezemskaia Organizatsiia) headquarters in Moscow. However, Plehve immediately issued a circular to his minions in which he ordered them to block any meetings that took place without prior written permission.[12]

Plehve also refused to confirm Shipov's recent reelection as chairman of the Moscow provincial *zemstvo* board. This was a direct response to Shipov's continuing efforts to defend the independence of local self-government and to form an interregional *zemstvo* union. Plehve admitted this in an interview with Shipov:

I consider your activity harmful . . . in the political sense. When one speaks about political harmfulness . . . one usually has in mind political unreliability, conspirative revolutionary activity, etc. In your case, however, this does not even arise. I consider your activity harmful in the political sense because you consistently strive for the widening of the competence and sphere of activity of the public institutions and for the establishment of an organization which would bring about the unification of the activities of *zemstvo* institutions in various provinces.[13]

Society was shocked when its well-intentioned relief efforts were thwarted by the bureaucracy. State and society were on a collision course. One young officer bitterly asked:

Is not every spontaneous action doomed? Is there any room left for conscious patriotism? Has not even the humble attempt of the self-governing assemblies to unite in helping the sick and wounded been denounced as criminal, and forbidden by Plehve? What wonder, then, if the outward manifestations of our patriotism are not like those of other nations? How can it be otherwise, as long as real patriots are treated as traitors, while traitors are proclaimed patriots?[14]

At this point the *zemtsy* decided "to turn personally and directly to the tsar."[15] Prince George E. L'vov, who would be Russia's first prime minister after the collapse of the monarchy and thus represent the final victory of society over the state, met with Nicholas II. The union was subsequently granted permission to proceed with its humanitarian endeavors. During the period from May 27, 1904 through September 1, 1905, the General *Zemstvo* Organization accepted 50,835 soldiers for medical treatment. It also provided hot meals to another 389,579 men.[16] In order to pay for these operations, society raised the stupendous sum of 2,080,894 rubles.[17]

In his treatise *Democracy in America*, Alexis de Tocqueville asseverated that voluntary associations and institutions of local self-government serve both to limit the power of the central authority and to promote the development of civil society. Voluntary associations such as the General *Zemstvo* Organization exemplify the ideals of public service and philanthropy, while independent organs of local self-government provide for citizen participation in governance; they are both essential components of the public sphere. Tocqueville also noted the close and multiple ties between them: "Civil associations pave the way for political ones, but on the other hand, the art of political association singularly develops and improves this technique for civil purpose."[18]

Peter Stolypin, Russia's last great statesman, encouraged this independent activity and strove mightily to reinvigorate the *zemstva* and to extend their powers. He markedly curtailed government supervision of the organs of local self-government and removed the restrictions on *zemstvo* taxation powers. He cooperated fully with the General *Zemstvo* Organization, allowing it to operate independently in the areas of famine relief, peasant resettlement, and other philanthropic endeavors. Combined with the other remarkable developments in Russia's socioeconomic life, such as the Stolypin land reforms (which Lenin rightly feared), the proliferation of cooperatives, and the myriad other informal groups and independent organizations that sprouted up in the economic, social, cultural, and religious spheres, Russia saw the emergence of a civil society that, but for World War I, would have led ultimately to a Western-style pluralistic state with a delimitation of the central authority's power and a devolution of governing responsibilities to the provinces.

During the years following the revolution of 1905, Russian society succeeded in freeing itself from the grasp of the monistic state. By 1914 the *zemstva* had an annual budget of 347 million rubles, of which 30% was spent on public education, 26% on medical assistance, 7% on road building, another 7% on administrative overhead, 6.3% on economic and agricultural programs, and only 5% on expenditures for government institutions.[19]

But just as the stresses and strains of modern warfare had inaugurated the era of reforms after Crimea and the semiconstitutional monarchy after the Russo-Japanese fiasco, the Great War could also have brought further political concessions. The increasing irrelevance of the regime was laid bare during this conflict; once again, Russian society demonstrated its vitality as the federated General *Zemstvo* Organization was replaced by the dynamic, centralized, All-Russian Union of *Zemstvos* (Vserossiiskii Zemskii Soiuz). This organization, again led by Prince L'vov, along with the other voluntary associations established by Russia's increasingly civic-minded entrepreneurial and professional class, virtually ran the war effort.

Many of the tsar's ministers and counselors also recognized that the last vestiges of autocracy would soon be eliminated. Several ministers joined in with the demands of the Duma, which called for further reforms in order to complete Russia's political transformation. But society's victory over the state, symbolized by Prince L'vov's assumption of the position of prime minister in the provisional government, proved ephemeral when the pleas of Russia's peasant majority went unheeded. The establishment of independent organs of local self-government, coupled with the proliferation of voluntary associations in the cultural, social, economic, and religious spheres leads one to the conclusion that Russia was in fact developing a public sphere. The Russian people are now looking for evidence of the emergence of a civil society in the years preceding the detour down the long road to nowhere. What we may well be witnessing in the 1990s is a recrudescence of pre-Soviet patterns of public initiative that were suspended by the Bolshevik takeover of 1917. Federalism, a form of decentralized governance that requires public activity and society's autonomy from the state, was incipient in late Imperial Russia, and the emergence of a new civil society in Russia suggests that a multi-centered, federated state will rise like a phoenix from the ashes of the old Soviet regime.

NOTES

1. Quoted in V. V. Garmiza, *Podgotovka zemskoi reformy, 1864 q* (Moscow, 1957), 203.

2. *Polnoe Sobranie Zakonov Rossiiskol Imperii Sobranie Vtoroe* (St. Petersburg, 1876), XXXIX, #40457, January 1, 1864.

3. B. B. Veselovskii, *Istoriia zemstva na sorok let* (St. Petersburg, 1911), vol. 3, 126–27.

4. Garmiza, *Podgotovka,* 251.

5. *PSZRI Vtoroe*, XLII, 44690, June 13, 1867.

6. Veselovskii, *Istoriia*, 248.

7. *PSZRI Tret'e*, X, #6922, June 12, 1890. 7.

8. Ibid., #6927.

9. D. N. Shipov, *Vospominaniia i dumy o perezhitom* (Moscow: S. P. Yakovleva, 1918), 57–58.

10. George Fischer, *Russian Liberalism from Gentry to Intelligentsia* (Cambridge, MA: Harvard University Press, 1958), 128–29.

11. V. I. Gurko, *Features and Figures of the Past* (Stanford, CA: Stanford University Press, 1939), 109.

12. Veselovskii, *Istoriia,* 592.

13. Shipov, *Vospominaniia,* 234.

14. Paul Miliukov, *Russia and Its Crisis* (New York: Collier Books, 1906), 221.

15. T. I. Polner, *Zhiznennyi put' Kniazia G. E. L'vova* (Paris, 1932), 66.

16. *Obshchezemskaia Organizatsiia na Dal'nem Vostoke* (Moscow: Gorodskaia Tipografiia, 1909), 66.

17. Ibid., 451.

18. Alexis de Tocqueville, *Democracy in America*, ed. Phillips Bradley (New York: Vintage Press, 1945), 2: 114–23.

19. Sergei Pushkarev, *Self-Government and Freedom in Russia* (Boulder, CO: Westview Press, 1988), 58.

PART II

A COMPARATIVE OVERVIEW

Part II brings together a selection of papers that introduce questions of government structure in a comparative way. The inherent tensions in governmental authority between state sovereignty and the right of self-determination arise in a variety of contexts in the U.S.A. and the states of the former U.S.S.R. as well as around the world. This section addresses in a comparative way governance questions not only in the U.S.A. and the states of the former U.S.S.R. but also in other countries and regions around the world in recognition that any useful comparison of the U.S.A. and the states of the former U.S.S.R. ultimately should be viewed in a global, comparative context.

Erik P. Hoffmann and Richard P. Nathan use the U.S. federal system as a model to illustrate their view that it is the relationship of a central government to diverse *regions* that is the key to analyzing any system of power sharing among government structures (in the U.S.A. between the federal government and the states). Among the comparative lessons for the states of the former U.S.S.R. that the U.S. model provides, according to Hoffmann and Nathan, are the need to weigh the economic, cultural, and political effects of changing government structures in Russia and in the CIS Here, a *regional* government structure may be needed to bridge any gaps between central and local authority.

Sarah F. Liebschutz and Barbara Jancar-Webster examine American federalism, both its success and its appeal for a government structure for the states of the former U.S.S.R., and conclude persuasively, however, that it is not a political framework that is readily transferable to the former U.S.S.R. The reasons offered for this conclusion revolve around insightful explorations of the proposition that the very factors that give "resilience and solidity to the U.S. federal system are absent in the Soviet case."

Vladimir A. Saveliev's paper focuses on the foreign policy aspects of government structures from Russian and CIS perspectives. He insightfully identifies issues that are the object of discussion and resolution in the states of the former U.S.S.R. and in the U.S.A. today as much as they were in 1992. He correctly identifies the umbrella under which specific foreign policy issues are formulated for Russia as the revival of the Russian state (including a resolution of the socioeconomic crises) and the agreement of the world community (especially Western states including the U.S.A.) on the appropriate prerequisites for full participation of Russia and the CIS as members of the world community. This, of course, requires a resolution of the foreign policies of Western states (including the U.S.A.) about the form and content of the relations they want with the states of the former U.S.S.R. and the CIS

Helen Ostrovidova expands the comparative inquiries of government structures in two ways: first by focusing on state sovereignty and by comparing sovereignty theories in the context of the emergence of the former Yugoslavia and the former U.S.S.R. from single, communist states to several independent states moving toward democracy. Dr. Ostrovidova traces the historical, cultural, and political realities behind assertions of statehood and sovereignty by the republics of the former Yugoslavia and the former U.S.S.R. Dr. Ostrovidova draws on those comparisons to identify lessons that may be relevant to Asian communist states like China and Vietnam that are beginning to experience similar pressures toward capitalism, democracy, and regional self-determination and independence.

6

Modern Federalism: Comparative Perspectives and Lessons for the Commonwealth of Independent States and Russia

Richard P. Nathan and Erik P. Hoffmann

COMPARATIVE PERSPECTIVES

There are a wide variety of federal systems in the world today, and none can claim to be the best under all circumstances. Certain kinds of political behavior and institutions are useful in most or many situations, but the theory of federalism is not settled and widely agreed upon. Although more than one-third of the world's countries have employed federal ideas and structures, the last comprehensive comparison of federal governments was published over 30 years ago.

The approach used in our research rejects theories that emphasize the centralizing, legalistic, or amorphous character of federal systems. We view federalism as a governmental form that seeks to reconcile regional diversity with a level of collective unity and does so in a way that gives a distinctive role and identity to *regional* governments. We see federalism as a sharing of power in which citizens relate to two governments, each with consequential rights and responsibilities. Inevitably, a degree of tension exists between the central and regional governments over the scope of the federal compact, the boundaries of shared governmental powers, and the relationship of governmental bodies to the citizenry. Existing federal systems vary greatly in how they deal with these tensions, producing diverse patterns and results.

We believe a federal system must be grounded on a democratic pluralist polity that enables citizens to participate in the national and regional political processes. Most successful federal relationships operate under a written constitution that obligates and restrains popularly elected central and regional leaders, involves elected representatives in the constitutional amendatory process, and protects the spiritual and material freedoms of the individual.

Political power must be dispersed vertically among the central, regional, and local institutions, and horizontally among the legislative, executive, and judicial branches of government in all arenas. Each institution and branch has the authority to make final decisions on certain issues and to influence decisions on many other issues in overlapping spheres of jurisdiction.

The legitimacy of these governmental bodies is buttressed by the national and subnational constitutions, and their effectiveness is enhanced by elected deputies responsible to national and subnational constituencies. Such bodies empower national officials to resolve general and collective issues and subnational officials to resolve specific and particularistic issues. Thus, federal structures help to guard against the tyranny of the top leader, the few, or the many.

Modern federalism is rooted in the experience of the United States, the oldest federal system. Using the United States as our model, we see the states as having a substantial role and identity along *six dimensions*:

The *historical/cultural* dimension, which refers to the states' capacity to generate important loyalties in people's minds and to provide routes of access into national and regional politics. This point is especially important in countries in which real or pseudo-federalism is grounded in differences in culture and language, as was the case in the former Soviet Union and former Yugoslavia and is in Switzerland, India, Brazil, and, to a lesser extent, Canada, and other countries.

The *political/constitutional* dimension, which refers to the extent of the states' authority to determine, organize, and control their own political structure (including their own constitutions, major political institutions, and boundaries). This dimension requires us to consider the power of the central government to influence the structure and operations of state and local political institutions and the boundaries of state and local governmental units. It also requires consideration of the constitutional and legal machinery available to define and redefine the federal balance over time. This balance may involve the roles, powers, and activities of a supreme or constitutional court and the amendatory process for the national constitution.

The *fiscal* dimension, which refers to the extent to which states can set and levy their own taxes, as well as the tax-collection role of the central government and the terms or mechanisms for redistribution of central government revenues to the states. A major variable under this heading is the financial dependence of the regional governments on the central government.

The *programmatic* dimension, which refers to the functional areas of government (e.g., public safety, education, health, natural resources, transportation) in which the states have exclusive or predominant responsibility and the nature of these responsibilities (e.g., the regulation of insurance, marriage and divorce, criminal law and corrections, and aspects of business activity, professional conduct, and occupational licensing). The role of the states in areas often considered the responsibility of the central government, such as in international economic policy and trade, is of increasing importance.

The regional governments' *representation/participation in the central government*, which involves the representation of regional officials in national institutions and the participation of regional officials in the formulation and implementation of national policies. In some countries, regional governments are represented directly by officials elected for this purpose in the upper house of the national legislature, which may have special authority over matters related to center-periphery relations. Other countries provide for a defined role for regional chief executives in national policymaking (as in a regional premiers' conference with specified powers). Elsewhere this role is institutionalized but more informal (as in the U.S. National Governors' Association and Russia's embryonic Council of Heads of Republics and the Union of Governors). The obligations of the central government to regional governments, often constitutionally guaranteed, are of particular significance in legitimizing regional representation and participation in national politics.

The role of regional governments in the *supervision of local governments*, which includes the authority of regional governments to determine the form, function, and finances of local governments, and to determine whether and how local officials are selected (e.g., elected or appointed). Also important under this heading is the extent to which the central government directly or indirectly controls local governmental affairs, bypassing regional governments on matters affecting the policies, finances, and administration of local government.

At its roots, this conceptual framework embodies an assumption that federalism exists in structural, behavioral, historical, and cultural terms as *a distinct political form*. Five principal aims can be derived from the history of feder-alism in the United States and other countries. Federalism is designed to reconcile unity and diversity, to protect against abuses and arbitrariness by the central government; to enhance participation by citizens in the political process within and between various organs of government; to increase the policy-making and administrative efficiency of government through regional competition; and to stimulate innovative socioeconomic, scientific-technological, and cultural-educational policies by regional governments.

In a federal system the central government does not inexorably gain or lose power vis-à-vis the regional governments. The distribution of power tends to be *cyclical*. For example, the U.S. states have become more assertive when the role of government as a whole is reduced in society. In these conservative periods—the 1880s, 1920s, and 1980s—activist state governments were initiators and innovators. In more liberal periods, the successful experiments of activist states were generalized throughout the country by national governmental action that substantially expanded governmental prerogatives and spending in all arenas. The histories of Australia, Canada, and other federal countries reflect this cyclical pattern.

We distinguish two basic patterns regarding the origins of federalism. One is fueled by centripetal forces and concerns, involving the adoption of the federal form to *integrate* a polity. The second is centrifugal, involving the adoption of federal features to avoid *disintegration*. The cases we know best from the history of federalism are basically of the first variety. They are federal systems set up to integrate previously more separate political communities. This is the experience of the United States, Australia, and Canada—all former British colonies that cover large land masses. The same may ultimately occur in the European Community. If one applies our six dimensions of "federalness" to the European Community, one observes considerable movement toward political arrangements that fit this theoretical framework.

In the current period, there are several cases in which federalism is under close scrutiny as a way to curtail political disintegration and fragmentation. Federalism has been discussed as a solution for ethnic conflict in Cyprus and the Sudan. Federal arrangements have been considered in Spain to reduce tensions among different ethnic groups. And federal principles are at the core of most reformist and centrist thinking about the future of Russia.

But some countries and potential multinational federations have experienced strong centrifugal forces. For example, the rise of Czech and Slovak nationalism aborted the new federal republic, the federal structure of Yugoslavia broke apart with much bloodshed, federalism was rejected as a means of preserving the Soviet Union, and federalism was not initially considered as a unifying principle for the sovereign states of the former Soviet Union.

Of the 15 former republics of the Soviet Union, 12 have formed a loose though increasingly viable *con*federation. Azerbaijan joined the Commonwealth of Independent States in September 1993, anticipating that Russia would support the new Azerbaijani government under former communist Gaidar Aliev against domestic rivals and in the losing territorial battle with neighboring Armenia. Georgia joined the CIS in October 1993, hoping that Russian armed forces would stop assisting separatists in Abkhazia and would help stabilize the new Georgian government under former Soviet Foreign Minister Eduard Shevardnadze against internal adversaries as well. It is not inconceivable that the Baltic countries will eventually ask to join the CIS—especially Lithuania, because its economy is the least developed and some former communist officials enjoy considerable public support.

The leaders of all CIS states strongly backed President Boris Yeltsin in his two-year struggle with the Supreme Soviet, because top parliamentary leaders and Vice President Aleksandr Rutskoi openly called for the resurrection of the Soviet Union, thereby threatening the sovereignty of the newly independent states. Also, the countries of the CIS have made progress in resolving their most serious disputes—control of nuclear weapons and ownership of the Black Sea Fleet—and they have begun cooperative efforts in fields such as commerce, interstate banking, energy pricing, rail transportation, higher education, ethnic peacekeeping, boundary disputes, open borders, and the rights of Russians living in the "near abroad." But there is still no agreement on the basic institutions or distribution of power in the fledgling confederation.

Internally, the successor countries of the Soviet Union differ widely in their aspirations and initiatives to move from a one-party to a multiparty structure, from a centralized to a market economy, and from the suppression to the expression of national identities. Especially important are the efforts to create a democratic and stable federal order in Russia. But here, too, fissiparous tendencies are powerful. The struggle among the national executive, legislative, and judicial branches of government gave considerable leeway to all republic, provincial, and local governments. In their competition for power and legitimacy, central institutions courted regional bodies with promises of even greater political and economic rights. Also, the spectacle of stalemate and ineffectualness at the center prompted many local leaders to press wide-ranging demands on national officials or to try to take their locality's fate into their own hands. None of these problems was resolved by the October 1993 insurrection and bloodshed in Moscow. It is to be hoped that the first national parliament to be elected in the post-Soviet period, together with a new national constitution and compatible republic constitutions, will help to establish policymaking procedures and policies that reduce violent conflict and obstructionism and that foster cooperative problem-solving among the different levels and branches of the Russian government.

LESSONS FOR THE COMMONWEALTH OF INDEPENDENT STATES AND RUSSIA

Creating new institutions for the Commonwealth of Independent States and for a confederal or federal system in Russia, giving them stability and legitimacy, and empowering them to cope with the economic and ethnic turmoil of the 1990s are challenges of unprecedented complexity and risk. Virtually all of the former Union republics and many of the new republics, provinces, and regions have sizable and mixed ethnic minorities. Some of the other territories have concentrations of enormous real and potential economic wealth, and a few have abundant nuclear or conventional weapons. Thus, the introduction of commonwealth, confederal, or federal forms can mitigate *or* exacerbate ethnic hostilities and local economic ambitions.

We wish that American and West European experience could be easily imported or copied to speed the democratization of post-Soviet policymaking procedures and policies. But Western political, economic, legal, and information cultures are very different from those in the former Soviet Union. Indeed, some important Western concepts cannot be found in the Russian language, and others are difficult to comprehend even in the present-day context. For example, the concepts of "privacy" and "liability" do not have Russian counterparts; "effectiveness" and "efficiency" cannot be distinguished and compared; "compromise" has lingering pejorative implications; "constitution" has authoritarian connotations left over from the Soviet period; "parliament" has only recently been used to describe the Supreme Soviet and sometimes with irony; and "separation of powers" and "checks and balances" do not connote the *sharing* of responsibilities and the *protection* of civil rights as in the West. Understanding the normative and technical ramifications of such concepts—to say nothing of the concepts of "political pluralism," "market economy," "rule of law," and "civil society"—is of immediate practical significance to all citizens of the former Soviet Union.

What can the CIS learn from the experience of other modern commonwealths and confederations, and how can Russia create a modern confederal or federal system? A first lesson from the comparative analysis we have done so far is that national governments must acknowledge that regional governments have basic constitutional rights and responsibilities, which national and regional governmental branches must jointly safeguard. But it is not always possible or desirable to enumerate these rights and responsibilities fully and unambiguously in national and regional constitutions. The sharing of power in a democracy is based on many formal laws and informal traditions, and it presumes conflict, competition, coalitions, and comity. Overlapping spheres of authority and redundancy are deliberate, and they generate pressures for destructive or constructive change—and sometimes gridlock. Also, divided sovereignty can accelerate centrifugal or centripetal social forces, perhaps especially in a period of declining economic growth and productivity and increasing ethnic pride and rivalry. On the one hand, federal forms may facilitate the peaceful reconciliation of national and regional interests and may even be essential to a polity's survival. On the other hand, political parties and interest groups may use federalist and confederalist ideas to promote separatism, economic protectionism, and virulent forms of nationalism. Hence, national and regional governments must balance flexibility and clarity in stipulating their mutual obligations. And this balance must help to institutionalize competition as well as cooperation and a duality of competencies, and also a division of labor.

A second lesson is that federal institutions and practices must be deemed legitimate and that to gain such legitimacy their basic features must be understandable to the citizenry. Short constitutional documents with general concepts are far superior to long documents with detailed prescriptions as mechanisms for mobilizing popular support and for adapting fundamental principles to changing domestic and international conditions. Firmness and lucidity about political principles and policymaking procedures, together with elasticity and terseness—even vagueness—about the substance and implementation of public policies, must somehow be combined. But concise documents gain legitimacy only if there is widespread public acceptance of the process by which they were created and ratified, as well as widespread confidence in the national and regional leaders' will and capability to fulfill their reciprocal commitments. Otherwise, a brief document will lack legitimacy and do no more than justify the current priorities of central officials and the existing political order—be it reactionary, conservative, reformist, or radical. Additional key sources of legitimacy are free, frequent, and direct elections; relatively stable and effective intergovernmental relationships; equitable representation of ethnic and other particularistic interests; honest and able legislators and administrators, independent judges and lawyers; regional and local officials' responsibility and responsiveness to their own constituents; economic opportunity for individuals and the protection of their political rights and civil liberties; and laws that limit the power of the rulers as well as the ruled—all of which are fostered by federal arrangements and by the tolerant political culture that undergirds them.

A third lesson for the CIS and Russia, from a comparative viewpoint, is that the economic elements of commonwealth, confederation, or federalism are critically important. Centralized planning and management of key spheres of the national and republic economies are compatible with a modern federal system, as the experience of the European Community is demonstrating. Especially in the fields of monetary and fiscal policy, there are even stronger incentives for economic unity among the former countries of the Soviet Union and among the 21 republics (including defiant Chechnya) and 68 other administrative units of Russia. Also, it may be mutually beneficial for new economic policymaking and coordinating bodies of the CIS and Russia to reestablish selected production and distribution networks destroyed during the disintegration of the Soviet Union.

For the immediate future at least, the highly centralized legacy of the Soviet economy will be difficult to overcome (e.g., about 500 Soviet factories located in all 15 republics were the sole producers of items not manufactured elsewhere in the U.S.S.R.). Of course, huge amounts of property can no longer be controlled by a single political party, a gigantic military-industrial complex cannot be isolated from civilian research and development, and a security-police apparatus cannot be empowered to intervene at will in all business and personal activities. But it will take enlightened national, regional, and local political leaders to help entrepreneurs regenerate the economies of the Soviet Union's successor countries and to ground these economies on fundamentally new principles. Among these principles are privatization, conversion, mutual interest, multiple markets and sources of supply, tax-collecting powers for regional and local governments, and participation in the world economy as a producer of technologically sophisticated manufactured goods—not merely as a provider of raw materials.

A fourth lesson is that the devolution of power from central authorities does not necessarily improve the quality of life of all citizens. Newly empowered republic and provincial leaders can be more aggressive toward their neighbors and more repressive of indigenous minorities than national leaders. Ironically, the weakening or replacement of national officials (e.g., elected presidents and parliamentary deputies) and the withdrawal or co-optation of their local representatives (e.g., armed forces and security-police personnel) can heighten ethnic tensions and human rights violations. But national policymaking and coordinating bodies can play a constructive role in arbitrating subnational conflicts and in reducing bloodshed, discrimination, and deprivation. For example, the U.S. Supreme Court has used its constitutional power and the president his political, budgetary, and even military powers to promote racial equality in the states. The administrative and judicial branches of the federal government have focused on voting and civil rights as well as educational and economic opportunities. Federal tax revenues pay for national programs like Medicaid and welfare or are allocated to the states through entitlement programs.

For another example, the policy of glasnost and the disintegration of the Communist Party enabled Soviet citizens to vent their pent-up animosities toward different ethnic groups. Dozens of interethnic conflicts intensified as political and economic expectations rose dramatically. But many popularly elected presidents and legislators are promoting ethnic harmony within and among the newly sovereign countries of the former Soviet Union. With the ominous examples of Yugoslavia and Nagorno-Karabakh before them, political leaders of the CIS and Russia have abundant incentives to resist demagoguery and encourage tolerance. Indeed, more and more leaders of the Soviet Union's successor countries are looking to Russia's president and asking for support against indigenous separatist movements energized by ethnic identity or animosity. And more and more Russian regional leaders of administrative units based on ethnicity, as well as their counterparts representing territories, are negotiating with Moscow primarily to further the economic interests of their localities.

A final lesson from a comparative perspective is that the sharing of power among central, regional, and local governments must be tailored to political, economic, and social realities. The world's federal systems differ widely in their levels of political democratization, economic modernization, and social stratification. New federal mechanisms in the CIS and Russia could not miraculously eliminate authoritarian political-administrative and cultural-ideological legacies of the tsars and commissars, nor could federalism quickly resolve fundamental socioeconomic and environmental-ecological dilemmas bequeathed by the Soviet Union. However, federal forms in diverse countries have enhanced the political and spiritual freedom of individuals, aggregated competing interests, facilitated economic development, and curbed ethnic rivalries—all at the same time. Because the world's societies are learning more about themselves and others, because economies are becoming more and more marketized and interconnected, and because polities are increasingly helping or hindering one another's development, the federal idea has considerable potential to spur the democratization of domestic and international relations.

Our view is that the most important lessons for the CIS may be learned from the newest federal system—the European Community—and the most important lessons for Russia from the oldest federal system—the United States. Initial concerns of the CIS include defense, commerce, transportation, and the movement of workers across borders—all of which have been dealt with by the new entities of the European Community. Immediate challenges to Russia are the establishment of collaborative relationships among the national executive, legislative, and judicial branches and of federal arrangements based on a civic culture and new laws helping to create a market economy that is integrated into the world economy. Taxation powers, investment priorities, privatization, conversion, environmental clean-up legislation, and the rights and responsibilities of dual citizenship are much more pressing issues for Russia than for the CIS.

But the unique characteristics of the former Soviet Union must always be kept in mind. European federalism is not evolving in a region dominated for over 70 years by a unitary one-party system or Stalinist dictatorship and debilitated by a highly centralized, militarized, and autarkic economy. American federalism did not emerge in a society without any tradition of the separation of church and state, the rule of law, and the value of the individual. Also, Russia's 21 "sovereign" republics contain only some 30% of the country's territory and 15% of its population and enjoy much greater independence from Moscow than larger and richer regions. Almost all of these republics have their own draft constitutions and most of these regions do not, producing a distinctive problem for writers of Russia's Constitution. To complicate matters further, over 80% of Russia's population is ethnic Russian, but over 50% of Russia's territory and over 50% of its most valuable natural resources are under the jurisdiction of non-Russian ethnic groups, most of which are outnumbered by Russians in their own regions. And over 70% of the regional governmental bodies supported the August 1991 putsch against Mikhail Gorbachev, the indirectly elected president of the Soviet Union, and Boris Yeltsin, the popularly elected president of Russia. It is not surprising, then, that many of Russia's regional leaders and councils continued to resist a strong chief executive, who called for radical economic reforms that rewarded initiative and performance, and instead supported the increasingly conservative and reactionary legislature, which called for gradual economic changes that preserved traditional local power structures and citizens' job security and purchasing power.

Clearly, the CIS and Russia must develop novel confederal or federal forms and may not be able to borrow or adapt much from the experience of other confederal or federal systems. It is worthwhile for Russian specialists to study labor-market practices in the European Community or U.S. state constitutions, but for suggestive purposes only. Economic and defense policymaking in the CIS and state-building, marketization, and conversion in Russia are unprecedented challenges.

Charles Krauthammer asked in 1990 whether the future will bring "the federation of different peoples into superpolitical structures" or "the breakup of such polyglot structures as the Soviet Union into their ethnic elements?" He forcefully affirmed:

> In the age of the fax and the fiber-optic cable, federation is the future. But federation works only under the condition of freedom. Otherwise what passes for federation is really colonialism. It may be that in a postcolonial world, confederal states require divorce before reconciliation. There are really benefits to confederation, as Europe is in the process of demonstrating. But people are hardly likely to appreciate these benefits until they can choose them freely. . . . Federalism does more than nurture democracy. It may be the only force capable of taming that great nemesis of the 20th century, nationalism. As Europe has discovered after two world wars, sovereignty is not all it is cracked up to be. But those who have never had it may be skeptical about such a judgment. They may need a taste of the fruit, before giving it up for a higher good ("Blest Be the Ties That Bind," *Time*, August 13, 1990, 76).

Whether the disintegration of the Soviet Union will be followed by the disintegration of the CIS and Russia remains to be seen. The CIS's political leaders are still disputing the contours of a fragile new commonwealth, and they are devoting little attention to its institutional and constitutional bases. Moreover, top Russian executive, legislative, and judicial officials are debating the merits of alternative federal orders, and many subnational territories in Russia are demanding autonomy to advance their ethnic and especially economic interests. Furthermore, the nascent Commonwealth and the emergent federal structures inside its major country are interacting in unpredictable ways and are producing novel alliances. So did the simultaneous efforts to forge a Union Treaty for the preservation of the Soviet Union and a federal system for the liberalization of Russia during the two years before the August 1991 putsch. To be sure, the experience of the European Community and diverse federal countries includes abundant mistakes to avoid and accomplishments to emulate. But the mistakes and accomplishments of others must be creatively interpreted and implemented in the truly unique, extraordinarily complex, highly politicized, increasingly interdependent, and rapidly changing conditions in the former Soviet Union and the world. A formidable challenge indeed—especially for President Yeltsin and for other Russians trying to create a democratic and stable Russian federal system and a peaceful and prosperous Russia within the CIS and international community.

7

American and Soviet Perspectives on Federalism: A Cross-National Analysis

Sarah F. Liebschutz and
Barbara Jancar-Webster

Is America a model for the world? Americans of all stripes have been preoccupied with this question virtually since the founding of the American nation. Recent tumultuous events surrounding the breakup of the Soviet Union have heightened its relevance. A succinct and sage response to the question was offered by Ted Robert Gurr at the 1991 Annual Meeting of the American Political Science Association. After reviewing empirical evidence that would logically lead to a negative answer, he concluded that "the appeal of the American myth to people emerging from authoritarian societies is far more powerful than any critical arguments I can muster."[1] The crux of the appeal? "*The belief that in America anything is possible.*"[2] That optimism encompasses not only economic and social spheres, but also political institutions.

The central characteristic of the American political system is federalism. Defined by Daniel Elazar most simply as "*self-rule plus shared rule,*"[3] federalism appears to satisfy "the need for people and polities to unite for common purposes yet remain separate to preserve their respective identities."[4] As a *political principle*, federalism emphasizes "the consensual basis of the polity and the importance of liberty in the constitution and maintenance of democratic republics."[5] As an *organizing principle*, federalism has two requisites: (1) that powers are divided between national and regional governments; and (2) that the powers of the regional governments are "consequential."[6]

The American federal system—"a centralized national government modified with provisions to preserve the states"[7]—has been much admired for its 200-year viability. The bases for that viability—unbroken, with one notable exception—however, require examination. As we shall show, the factors that explain the maintenance of federalism in the United States, rooted as they are in historical experience, reinforced by political socialization, and expressed by bargaining between the states and the central government, are not necessarily applicable to other political systems. In particular, we shall show that the American federal framework, despite its considerable appeal for amicable resolution of the contentious ethnic, religious, ideological, and linguistic cleavages that inundate Russia and the other newly independent states of the former Soviet Union, is not transferrable.

AMERICAN FEDERALISM: CHARACTERISTICS

It is our rock and our redeemer, the civil religion of a society that has no state church. It is a unifying symbol as powerful in our diverse Republic as the queen in a monarchy. For a restless people, it is the prime source of stability, of certainty.[8]

So was the United States Constitution celebrated on the occasion of its 200th anniversary.

The Constitutional Convention of 1787 that forged the American federal structure reflected the consensual desire of the 13 original states to "hold the nation together as an independent and effective nation-state."[9] International weakness and domestic economic concerns of the new nation were motivating factors.

There was special concern for the country's international position. Competition among the states for foreign commerce allowed the European powers to play the states off against each other.[10] At the same time, well-to-do Americans—in particular the New England merchants and southern planters—were troubled by the influence that "radical" forces exercised in the Continental Congress and in the governments of several of the states.[11]

Despite the consensus among the 55 delegates to the Constitutional Convention of 1787 that fundamental flaws in the Articles of Confederation—of which "political strife, international embarrassment, national weakness, and local rebellion"[12] were symbols—needed to be rectified, the Constitution, itself, was forged in controversy. Its purposes, at base, were contradictory: *to create a central government with sufficient power to "secure liberty and preserve the Union,"*[13] and *to limit that power, with its potential for abuses of liberty.*[14] These cross-purposes were resolved in a series of compromises about the division of powers between the national government and the states. The careful division that was proposed was intended to reassure opponents like Patrick Henry and George Mason of Virginia, who argued that a new central government, "however hemmed in, would lead to tyranny."[15]

The Constitution, ratified in 1788, contains a threefold division of powers—the institutional specification of the American federal system. Powers are delegated to the national government, reserved to the states, and denied to both the national government and the states. Powers exclusive to the national government, James Madison wrote, were "few and defined," and intended to be exercised "principally on external objects such as war, peace, negotiation, and foreign commerce."[16] Powers reserved to the states, described as "numerous and indefinite," were intended to "extend to all the objects which, in the ordinary course of affairs, concern the lives, liberties and properties of the people, and the internal order, improvement and prosperity of the state."[17] To counteract criticisms that the national government would "squint toward monarchy,"[18] Madison argued that the powers delegated to the national government would be much less frequently called into play than those reserved to the states. The third division denied some powers, generally to safeguard individual rights, to both the national and state governments.

For all of its symbolism as stability and certainty, however, the American Constitution (and the American federal state that it created) has been, "through all its history, subject to ferocious argument and controversy."[19] Such controversy swirled around ratification of the Constitution in 1787, was ignited into a Civil War less than a century later, and continues to the present day as provisions of the Constitution are tested in the courts. Yet, in spite of—or perhaps because of—these disputes centering on federalism as political and organizing principle, "the system has worked to a remarkable degree as the framers hoped."[20]

AMERICAN FEDERALISM: FACTORS PROMOTING MAINTENANCE

What explains the endurance of the American federal system for more than 200 years? Many explanations have been advanced, from the Supreme Court's role as umpire of federalism[21] to the highly decentralized nature of political parties in America.[22] Here, we suggest the usefulness of three more generic explanations: (1) *high levels of identification by Americans with the nation*; (2) *a well developed national economic system*; and (3) *consensus among citizens and elites about the viability of federalism*.

Identification with the Nation

What makes a nation a nation? The answer turns on shared traditions and culture, shared history, and/or a common language. Harold James, author of a text on German identity, suggests that national identity depends "on the application of imagination to formulate, and indeed even sometimes invent, all of these common features."[23] But he adds that if such "identity lies in political and institutional arrangements, there is no need to be preoccupied with the search for an elusive national character."[24]

For Americans, national pride and national character are inextricably linked to governmental and political arrangements. An empirical examination of political culture by Gabriel Almond and Sidney Verba some 30 years ago found high levels of spontaneously expressed American national pride. In response to a question about the sources of national pride,

> eighty-five percent of American respondents [surveyed in 1960] cited some feature of the American government or political tradition—the Constitution, political freedom, democracy, and the like—as compared with 46 percent for the British, 7 percent for the Germans, 3 percent for the Italians, and 30 percent for the Mexicans.[25]

More recent analyses of identification of Americans with the nation reinforce the Almond and Verba findings. Bruce Campbell, for example, asserted boldly in a 1979 text: "One of the most unshakable elements of the American political culture is the sense we have of belonging."[26]

> Very few people doubt their basic political identity; when you fill out an application for a job or a passport, you just *know* what to put in the box labeled nationality. From an historical perspective, this unquestioned sense of national identity is tied to the fact that, with one major exception, our political experience over the past 200 years has been as a single identifiable political entity."[27]

The primacy of national over regional identification is a key component of American national identification. Seymour Martin Lipset, who has compared two neighboring federal systems, concludes that provincial loyalties are much more important for Canadians than are loyalties to states for Americans. In fact, Lipset explains his inability to locate any surveys comparing American regional or national loyalty as "testimony to the improbability of asking Americans to choose between state and nation."[28] Even absent such data, however, he hazards the not unreasonable guess that "Americans faced with a similar choice would opt for the nation over the state by a larger majority than their neighbors."[29] "Canada," he concludes, "is more decentralized politically and more regional culturally, the United States more national on both counts, and the people and intellectuals of each reflect the differences."[30]

A second component of national identity, at least in credo, is its primacy over individual characteristics. As expressed by President Franklin D. Roosevelt, when he authorized the creation in 1943 of a special army unit, "for loyal American citizens of Japanese descent": "The principle on which this country was founded and by which it has always been governed is that Americanism is a matter of mind and heart; Americanism is not, and never was, a matter of race or ancestry."[31]

The strength of American national identity certainly does not imply similar experiences of Americans as citizens. Judith Shklar, in fact, argues that "American citizenship as nationality has its own history of exclusions and inclusions."[32]

America has not marched single file down a single straight liberal highway as both the lamenters and the celebrators of its political life have claimed, either in despair or in complacency. What has been continuous is a series of conflicts arising from enduring anti-liberal dispositions that have regularly asserted themselves, often very successfully, against the promise of equal political rights contained in the Declaration of Independence and its successors, the three Civil War amendments.

It is because slavery, racism, nativism, and sexism, often institutionalized in exclusionary and discriminatory laws and practices, have been and still are arrayed against the officially accepted claims of equal citizenship that there is a real pattern to be discerned in the tortuous development of American ideas of citizenship.[33]

Shklar concludes that in "voting and earning, two of the most elementary and essential components . . . of a society committed to political equality and to the principle of inclusion,"[34] American citizenship has not yet been fulfilled.

Despite this sobering reality, loyalty to the nation as well as to the ideal of national citizenship remain strong among Americans.

The Single Market

A well-developed, highly integrated national economy is the second factor that reinforces American federalism. The Constitution founders could not have foreseen "the vast market with an industrial base that was second only to Britain in the nineteenth century, and second to none since then."[35] They were, however, keenly aware that the separate boundaries, separate laws, and separate traditions of the states under the Articles of Confederation created "numerous impediments between the different parts of the Confederacy."[36] The straightforward clause in the Constitution (Article I, Section 8) granting Congress the power to "regulate commerce with foreign Nations and among the several States" became "the charter of . . . the most powerful economy on earth."[37]

From the beginning, the national government played a key role in fostering free enterprise and the unimpeded flow of commerce among the states. In the nineteenth century, the national government used several approaches to stimulate the growth of the economy. They included *public works* (e.g., roads and canals), *tariffs* (to promote domestic business by raising the price of imported goods) and *subsidies* (e.g., grants of cash and land, and low-cost land sales).[38] A seminal Supreme Court decision in 1824 established the supremacy of the national government in all matters involving interstate commerce, by asserting that states could not pass laws to interrupt the free flow of commerce among them.[39]

By the time of the outbreak of the Civil War, in 1860, "commerce surged between the states . . . with regions specializing in what they could do best."[40]

Southern states supplied the nation with tobacco and cotton; the plains states contributed grain and livestock; southern New England textiles and textile machinery; the mid-Atlantic states, boots, shoes, glass, and metal making. Capital and labor also moved easily across borders.[41]

America's industrialization proceeded by reliance on the commerce clause "to unify an immense market and thus fuel the nation's extraordinary growth."[42] In contrast to Japan and Europe, where, as Robert Reich notes, centralized bureaucracies presided "to overcome the vestiges of feudal privilege and guild restrictions . . . , the Federal government employed [at the end of the nineteenth century] fewer civilians than the Pennsylvania Railroad."[43]

Integration of the national economy as well as the "taming of the excesses of capitalism"[44] continued apace in the twentieth century. The Federal Reserve System, with 12 district banks reflecting the nation's geographic diversity, was established in 1913 to regulate the banking industry. The national government's role as arbiter of the economy was extended in the first half of the twentieth century by laws designed to restrain monopolies and terminate price-fixing practices, to regulate sales of securities, and to establish collective bargaining; and in the latter half of this century, to "protect consumers from unsafe products, minority groups from private discrimination, and all citizens from environmental pollution . . . [and to] stabilize the economy."[45]

Clearly the national government's role was fundamental to the development of a highly integrated economy. Such centralizing actions pursuant to the commerce clause, however, might seem to undermine a basic principle of federalism—the retention of *consequential* powers by the regional governments. Yet the interdependent states individually retained, and continue to retain, many consequential economic powers—powers to tax, to regulate business within their borders, to enter into regional compacts with other states, and to implement, in ways that reflect their own bargaining prowess vis-à-vis Washington, intergovernmental grants-in-aid intended to advance manpower and other national policies.[46] These facts all reinforce a consensus that federalism remains viable.

Federalism: The Ties That Bind

Federalism is not easy to define, to understand, or to explain. Its aims—to achieve national unity while preserving diversity—are inherently ambiguous and lead to tensions between national and state governments. What is the extent of support for continuation of this ambiguous, tension-inducing system in the United States?

Many important changes have occurred in the American political culture over the past four decades. "Americans . . . are more cynical about politicians, less confident in their institutions, and more politically sophisticated."[47] Yet the American public continues to indicate high levels of support for existing federalist political arrangements. For example, 80 percent of respondents in a 1976 national survey stated they were "proud of many things about our form of government"; and 47 percent responded that "no change was needed in our form of government."[48] More recently, a 1990 national survey commissioned by the Advisory Commission on Intergovernmental Relations found that relative confidence in national, state, and local governments to effectively handle problems depends on the nature of the problem. For example, the national government is most trusted to "provide services to immigrants and attract foreign investment"; state governments, to "maintain highways and bridges."[49] More mixed levels of trust were expressed for such problems as health care for the disabled, poor, and elderly; child care; and job training, where service responsibilities are shared by national, state, and local governments.

Why, in view of the well-documented increased skepticism toward government, has support for federalist governing arrangements remained intact? One line of explanation, from a political socialization perspective, is that dissatisfaction has been focused "on specific policies and the individuals responsible for those policies rather than on the institutions themselves."[50] Public outrage, for example, at the Watergate scandal that led to the resignation of President Richard Nixon in 1974 or the Iran-Contra affair during the 1980s was not linked to demands for basic structural changes in the federal system.

A second line of explanation, from an empirical, historical perspective, is that the federal system is dynamic, able to adapt successfully to changing circumstances. Morton Grodzins, Daniel Elazar, and Samuel Beer have explicated the cooperative, evolutionary nature of federalism as a "tool for solving problems over time."[51] Others have argued a cyclical paradigm. Richard Nathan posits that in conservative periods, the states tend to be more prominent; in liberal periods, there is "an accretion of the role of the central government."[52] Empirical analyses of the responsive bargaining of states to the policies of retrenchment and decentralization under the Reagan administration in the 1980s lend considerable support, as well, to this dynamic perspective on federalism.[53]

In sum, federalism continues to enjoy the fundamental support of Americans as the best alternative to provide "self-rule plus shared rule." In fact, there seem to be no viable alternatives for governing the nation.

A FEDERALIST SOLUTION: APPLICABILITY TO THE FORMER LANDS OF THE U.S.S.R.

The very factors that have given resilience and solidity to the U.S. federal system are absent in the Soviet case. Until the explosion of ethnic feeling released by *glasnost*, the significance of the Soviet nationality question was stressed by relatively few Western scholars specialized in the issue.[54] In study after study on the Soviet Union in the 1960s, 1970s, and 1980s, ethnic differences were not considered a major source of tension,[55] despite the extraordinary dissident activity among the Crimean Tatars and other ethnic minorities.[56] Yet, aside from its communist single-party command form of rule, the central feature of the Soviet Union has been the multinational multiethnic federal state.

In the 1979 census,[57] 104 different nationalities and ethnic groups were identified within the territory of the Soviet Union, including 36 Muslim or partly Muslim groups, with a combined population of 50 million. Russians accounted for 52.4% of the population, Ukrainians 16.1%, and the dominant Muslim groups about 15%.[58] The nationality of Soviet citizens is written in their passports and is carried with them throughout their whole lives. They may change their nationality, if they so desire at those times when the passport is renewed, but they cannot say they have no nationality. By contrast, ethnic divisions in the United States tend to be grouped into large general categories: black, Asian, Hispanic, Native American, white. Nationality in the U.S. passport is automatically American. Employers may not ask the ethnic origin of prospective employees. In the United States, everything is done to obscure national origin. In the Soviet Union, national origin was emphasized.

In the United States, federalism is based on territoriality. Ethnicity is a matter of civil rights, not states' rights. The principle of ethnic territorially adopted by the Soviet regime meant that most of the national populations live in a national "homeland." Each major nationality has its union republic, which was declared "sovereign" in the 1936 and 1977 Constitutions. The smaller ethnic groups have their autonomous republic or autonomous province (oblast). However, the borders of the union republics were arbitrarily drawn in the 1920s. Extensive forced, planned, and voluntary migration has resulted in a veritable smorgasbord of ethnic groups in every republic, comparable to the results of inner migration in the United States. About 18 percent of all Russians live outside the Russian Republic. Some 14% of all Ukrainians, 34% of all Armenians, and 19% of all Azerbaijanis live outside their respective republics. Kazakhs and Kirghiz are not yet the majority ethnic groups in their republics, while the Crimean Tatars are only now returning under very arbitrary regulations to the peninsula from which Stalin forcibly evicted them during World War II.

All of the groups have been subjected to intensive indoctrination. Communist propaganda extolled the eternal friendship of the peoples of the U.S.S.R. and radiantly smiling young Uzbek women in native dress exchanged greetings of "*mir i druzhba*" with the ingenuous tourist.

After only two years of *perestroika*, Alma-Ata erupted yet another time in ethnic violence, and the peoples of the Caucasus, shouting slogans of national independence, demanded the settling of old national scores. Nationalist fever spread to the Baltic Republics, which, in 1990, declared independence, and swiftly engulfed Ukraine, Moldavia, and the republics of Central Asia. In August 1991, hopes for a new Union Treaty were shattered by an attempted right-wing coup that brought about the dissolution of the U.S.S.R.

Why did disintegration happen so quickly and why has the federalist idea been so poorly received among the peoples of the former Soviet Union? What is the prognosis for federation in the future? The answers to these questions lie in the negative application of the three factors that were successful in the American case.

Identification with the Center

The Soviet Union was the last of the European colonial empires, heir to imperial Russia. The formation of the Russian Empire began toward the end of the fourteenth century when the Russian grand duke of Moscow united the adjoining Russian lands and began to extend his borders north, south, east, and west. In the sixteenth and seventeenth centuries, the Russian tsars conquered the lands south to the Crimea[59] and east to the Pacific.[60] Expansion continued until the end of the nineteenth century.[61] In 1881 the Russians signed an agreement with the British delineating the southern borders of the empire between Turkistan and Afghanistan, and in 1900 occupied the Pamirs in what is today Tajikistan.[62]

Three attributes of this expansion relate directly to the inability of the non-Russian populations to identify with the central power. First, unlike the westward movement of the United States, the Russians were unable to annihilate the indigenous populations. They were forced to subjugate them. Russian immigration, encouraged by the Crown, became Russian colonization. Like the other great colonial empires, tsardom made good use of the old Roman principle *divide et impera* and cultural imperialism. Tsar Nicholas I initiated the policy of "official nationality," defining the peoples who could be recognized as Russian as professing the three principles of autocracy, Orthodoxy, and Russian nationality. Russian nationality was a Slavophile term denoting adherence to Russian culture and the Russian language. Those who did not meet the requirements of official nationality were termed *inorodsty* (aliens). Included in the first group were the Slav peoples, Belorussians, Great Russians, Ukrainians, and Poles. "Aliens" were virtually all the other ethnic groups. In keeping with these divisions, the name "Rossia" supplanted the medieval term for Russia, "Rus," and inferred the cultural dominance of Great Russianism throughout the empire. The new Soviet person is the modern version of the official Tsarist "national."[63]

Second, the Russian expansion came directly into contact not only with peoples who had equal military skills and technology, but at one time had great cultures and empires of their own. Primary among these should be mentioned the kingdoms of Lithuania and Poland, the Georgians and Armenians, and the numerous khanates deriving from the Mongol conquest. In the fifteenth century, the capital of Tamerlane's empire, Samarkand, was a monument to science and learning. For two centuries the more backward Russians were subjected to the Tatar yoke from which they were able to extricate themselves less by military prowess than by the disintegration of Mongol rule.

Third, the Russian Empire was born from a clash of religions and cultures. The Russian, Spanish, and Balkan peoples constitute the three European Christian nations to experience a long period of Muslim domination. Similar to Spain, the grand princes of Moscow fashioned a new Christian power center on the decaying authority of the Muslim Tatars. After Constantinople was captured by the Muslim Turks, Tsar Ivan III named Moscow the Third Rome and imparted to Russian Orthodoxy a messianism that became one of the cornerstones of the Russian Empire.[64] Subsequent Russian Christian expansion came inexorably into conflict with the Islamicized descendents of the Mongol hordes.[65] Today, Islam is once again resurgent and the new independent republics of Central Asia are turning south to their Muslim roots.

In the western part of the Russian Empire, Christianity was split into different sects, many of these directly related to ethnic or national identity. Lithuania and the Russian-occupied part of Poland were Catholic. Latvia and Estonia were predominantly Lutheran. In Ukraine were German Baptist, Mennonite, and other Protestant sects. The Armenian and Georgian Churches are among the oldest organized Christian sects in the world.

The Soviet state inherited the ethnic and religious cleavages of the Tsarist Empire. Lenin branded Russia "the prison house of nations," arguing that "a people who oppresses another people cannot itself be free."[66] But one of the fundamental tenets of Marxism was that the working man had no country. In Lenin's view, national differences were exploited by the bourgeoisie to detract from the central issue of the class struggle. Lenin's underestimation of the force of the nationalist issue resulted in a paradoxical policy. The non-Russian nationalities had the theoretical right to secede from the empire. But the Russian centrist tradition was to be continued in the Soviet state under a new socioeconomic order, which would express "the unity of the workers of all nations."[67]

Stalin, like Lenin, held that the end of capitalism would spell the end of nationalism. Since the proletariat was the most progressive class, only the proletariat had the right to decide the question of self-determination.[68] Stalin coined the phrase "bourgeois in form, socialist in content." Under Soviet conditions, nations might retain their "bourgeois territorial shape," but in the "dictatorship of the proletariat," these would be subsumed under the larger Soviet state.

The rapid disintegration of the Russian Empire bears a strong comparison with the breakup of the Soviet Union today. On November 15, 1917, Lenin promulgated the Declaration of the Rights of the Peoples of Russia. The document condemned ethnic oppression, proclaimed the right to self-determination, and called for "a voluntary and honorable union of the peoples of Russia."[69] Most of the non-Russian nationalities promptly seceded and during 1917–20 attempted to establish independent states. However, then, like today, serious problems arose. The Russian minority opposed independence. Lenin saw the economic advantages of a large state slipping away from him. The so-called civil war was at once a war between Russians for control of the new colonial order and a war between the Russians and the non-Russian nationalities. One by one the Red Army reconquered the non-Russian states. By 1921, Russian military forces had reimposed centralized rule, at great economic and social cost, on all the former lands of the tsar. Only Finland, Poland, and the Baltic republics succeeded in preserving independence.

The ferocity of the civil war meant there was not going to be a happy "union of equal peoples."[70] Soviet power might be strong enough to reconquer the Russian Empire but not strong enough to rule without local support. Step by step, the Bolsheviks created a multinational federation ruled from a strong center.[71] The final acquisitions, the three Baltic republics and Moldavia, were forcibly incorporated during World War II.[72]

Federation attached the union republics to Moscow through the instruments of a centralized government, economy, and single political party, but it did not win the minds of the population. For this task Lenin devised a policy of "indigenization" or *korenizatsia*. Each republic would have its republican political and economic structure and its own national language, literature, and schools. *Korenizatsia*'s main objective was to enable Communism to take "root" (*koren'*) among the various ethnic groups through the penetration of the Communist Party and the implementation of the party program. An aspect of *korenizatsia* unique to Central Asia was *khudzum*, or "attack" on female seclusion. The emancipation of women, it was hoped, would mobilize women to the communist cause and transform the Muslim family into a family supportive of the new social order. Muslim tradition proved highly resistant, and at the end of the 1920s, the program was abandoned.[73]

Stalin attempted to reverse Lenin's policy through one of the most ruthless uses of violence in the twentieth century. The liquidation of the Ukrainian intelligentsia and the deliberately induced famine have been well documented by Robert Conquest.[74] Less known is the uprooting and forced resettlement of the Kazakh nomads and the death of 1.5 to 2 million of those people from famine and murder.[75] During World War II, Stalin deported seven whole nationalities from their territories and dissolved their republics, because they allegedly aided the Germans. Nikita Khrushchev is reported to have said that the Ukrainians avoided facing a second genocide during the war because they were too numerous to deport. Only in the past year has return to the homeland and recovery of national autonomy become possible for all the millions deported, with the exception of the North Caucasus peoples who were allowed to return earlier.[76]

Non-Russian national identity was further depressed through a comprehensive socialization process dedicated to turning all citizens of the U.S.S.R. into Soviet citizens and to force them into abandoning those nationality traits and characteristics that would not merge with the prescribed image of the proper Soviet citizen. In the 1920s, the process was part of *korenizatsia*. Khrushchev's propagandists made much of the "coming together of the peoples" (*blizhenie narodov*). Under Leonid Brezhnev, the emphasis shifted to *slianie*, or merging. From childhood on, the mass media drummed home the correct attributes of the Soviet citizen: obedience to authority, love of communism and the motherland (U.S.S.R.), and the gradual merging together of ethnic differences. This image was reinforced by the use of Russian as the major language of communication between nationalities, enforced censorship over what could and could not be published about the history of the non-Russian peoples, the settlement of Russians in the non-Russian territories, and the propagation of Russified European values as the Soviet norm. Censorship made a nonevent of national resistance. Under Khrushchev, state persecution of religious believers and national leaders began anew. The word "dissident" was coined to describe those who risked their lives trying to make Khrushchev act on his liberal statements and adhere to the Soviet constitution.

The 1977 Brezhnev Constitution celebrated the consolidation of friendship between the U.S.S.R.'s nations and nationalities,[77] and the equality and "fraternal cooperation between the various ethnic groups" (Preamble). A highly centralized federalist structure was given legal substance, while at the same time further circumscribing the union republics' areas of choice.[78]

The Soviet record, then, is a mixed one. On the one hand, there is a history of coerced mobilization, mass genocide, deportation, and systematic terror against expressions of nationalism and religious belief, to a degree unequaled in modern history. On the other hand, under Soviet rule, each ethnic group was assured its own language and government, limited as the use of each was. There was no officially designated language of communication for the Union as a whole, and the fact that Russian became ipso facto the language of trans-Union commerce, while national languages were confined to the local level, contributed to anti-Russian resentments and probably hastened the collapse of the imperial system.

If nationalism in the European part of the Soviet Union originated in the nineteenth century, nationalism in the Central Asian republics is a twentieth-century phenomenon. Soviet power forcibly settled the nomads onto collective farms and into cities. Soviet power set borders where formerly there were none, and Soviet power prescribed a local language and alphabet where Arabic and Mongol-Turkic dialects had prevailed. By the 1960s, Western scholars were noting the resurgence of Islam and the formation of national consciousness in the region.[79] Today, each of the Muslim republics is asserting its own unique identity,[80] while ethnic groups within the republics compete for power.

The Soviet attempt to form a Soviet citizen in the American pattern, with uniform values and identity with the Soviet center, produced a mixed result. The twin Soviet policies of persecution and limited national territorial assertion helped create an almost universal Soviet mind-set or *weltanshauung* while, at the same time, sustaining personal identification with local nationality traditions and values. National self-assertion was well under way before Gorbachev. *Glasnost* completed the process with the erosion of the credibility and validity of Soviet power. *Homo sovieticus* was the first victim of the demythologization of Communism.

The Single Command Market

The three-century existence of the Russian-Soviet state forged a degree of political and economic interdependence among its constituent nationalities, but economic interdependence remained colonial in orientation, directed toward the center from the periphery. Three observations may be made of this pattern of development that has obscured the content and scope of interdependence and contributed to ethnic tensions.

The first observation concerns the historically uneven development of industry within the lands of the U.S.S.R. Kievan Rus was built on the north-south trade between the northern Slavic tribes near the Baltic and the Byzantine Empire. The Mongol conquest shifted population, economic activity, and political power to the northeast. The thirteenth and fourteenth centuries saw the flowering of the great trading states Novgorod and Pskov exploiting the wealth of the Russian forests in furs, wax, and honey and serving as intermediary stops on the great trade routes leading to the ports along the Baltic, and hence to England and Flanders.[81] The success of Moscow may be attributed in large part to its central location at the headwaters of the Oka, Volga, Don, and Dnieper Rivers.[82]

Economic trends in the seventeenth century reflected Russia's continuing preoccupation with the Mongols. Much of domestic production went to feed and arm the army. A new commercial code expanded private enterprises and both Russian and European entrepreneurs were quick to take advantage of it.[83]

A copper smelter and processing center was started in the Urals,[84] but industry, mining, and metallurgy remained close to Moscow. Siberia opened up a vast realm of furs, the most important element in foreign trade in pre-Petrine Russia. Russian settlers followed the Russian military line, penetrating ever further into the southern steppe despite continuous struggles with the Crimean Tatars and Central Asian nomads.

In the eighteenth century, iron-smelting and copper processing enterprises had become well established in the Urals due to the active involvement of the state in industrial development. Canals were built. The south sent its agricultural products to the north, the countryside was able to provide the cities with grain. Russian foreign trade tripled in the course of the reign of Catherine the Great.

The first half of the nineteenth century saw the beginnings of a market economy, but internal trade remained largely within the European sector. Excess grain produced on the large estates enabled Russia to export grain via the Black Sea ports. The fastest growing industry was the new Russian cotton industry based on processing cotton from the recently acquired lands of Central Asia.

During the second half of the nineteenth century, the tempo of industrialization increased. As in previous centuries, industrial development was distinguished by its localization and state involvement, and followed the traditional thrust of the Russian economy west and south. Of eight basic industrial regions, only three were outside European Russia.[85]

The pattern of development in the nineteenth century ensured that virtually everything produced in Central Asia was consumed in Russia. In contrast to the United States, the railroad did not contribute to equal economic opportunity. By opening the region to the Russian merchant, the railroad helped transform southern Central Asia into a cotton-growing and raw-materials colony that relied on Russian industry for all manufactured goods.

At mid-nineteenth century, the industries of Central Asia were concentrated in the Uzbek and Tajik areas, and were centered on the production of silk and cotton that were brought to Russia on caravans that crossed the desert two or three times yearly. The introduction of an American-type cotton gin in the 1880s and the construction of the Orenburg Tashkent Railroad substantially increased the amount of cotton sent to Russia.[86] Improved transportation also helped expand the mining of minerals begun in the seventeenth century in the Altai Mountains. Most of the nonferrous metallurgical mines, as well as the coal mines exploited under Soviet rule, began operation in the nineteenth century. In the 1870s, oil operations were begun on the northwest shore of the Caspian Sea. Foreign entrepreneurs were particularly active in the area, with Americans mining the coalfields of Ekibastuz and the lead and zinc mines at what is now Leninogorsk. World War I gave impetus to extractive activities. But agriculture products remained the basis of the Central Asian economy.[87]

Soviet rule continued tsarist policy. Central planning and heightened state involvement were superimposed upon state ownership and preoccupation with defense. Major industry was kept concentrated in European Russia and Ukraine. Industrial development in Central Asia remained minor until necessity forced the Russians' hand during World War II. Uzbekistan became a one-crop economy. Kazakh industrial growth did not pick up until the 1930s, when Soviet planners concentrated on the mining industry to the exclusion of other branches. World War II accelerated the development of industries neces-sary for defense.[88] Since World War II, the expansion of communications and transportation has facilitated the growth of the iron and steel industry and the exploitation of the republic's vast mineral resources. However, these developments brought little benefit to the people of the area, as local growth has been sharply curtailed by the lack of water.

In 1985 the Central Asian economy still exhibited the typical colonial pattern: The profits and products of the region went to the Russian administrators; agriculture was left to the *inorodsty*. Even Central Asia's natural gas was sent to European Russia, as was the natural gas from Iran and Afghanistan, which entered the U.S.S.R. through the region. The area did not contribute even a quarter of all-Union industrial production.[89]

A second factor in economic interdependence is the break that central planning exerted on economic development. The absence of a free economy meant no free circulation of capital, goods, or labor. Whatever passed back and forth between the republics was distributed by Moscow, from Moscow. Central planning set prices, distributed labor and materials, bailed out inefficient factories. The principle of rational division of labor created regional and branch monopolies. Uzbekistan is a tragic case in point. During the 1960s, Soviet planners insisted on the expansion of cotton production in Uzbekistan, and demanded the end of the practice of setting aside fallow fields planted to alfalfa. Production was to be increased through an increase in fertilizers. Although cotton production did increase into the 1970s, the results of overuse of pesticides and fertilizers proved to be catastrophic in terms of human health.[90]

In the need to access scarce supplies held by the monopolies and to bypass the gaps and lags in the central distribution, the enterprises in the different republics developed broad pseudo-economic exchange networks based on the time-honored custom of *blat* (payoffs), out-and-out corruption, black marketeering, and direct barter. Many of the leaders of the new republics most certainly did not appreciate how interdependent their economies were until the central distribution broke down. The market for Ukrainian sugar is Russia, not the European Community. When Ukraine stopped sending sugar to Russia, the Russians were forced to go without sugar. If the Baltic republics cannot buy their fuel from Russia, they have no other supplier readily at hand. Because it can no longer get oil through the pipeline from St. Petersburg at ruble prices,

Estonia must continue making fuel from its vast oil shale reserves. The pollution generated by this dirty refining process could be a major factor preventing the country's joining the Common Market.

The drive to conclude interrepublican economic agreements that started well before the August putsch and ended in the creation of the Commonwealth of Independent States was aimed at forestalling economic fragmentation and the collapse of republican economies. When these agreements proved unable to maintain the old system after the abolition of the Communist Party, economic disintegration progressed rapidly. The European republics placed unrealistic hopes in Western assistance, while the Central Asian republics turned south to find help in reclaiming their devastated economies.

A final factor contributing to fragmentation has been the very size of the economic and environmental catastrophes visited on the republics by the central government. Chernobyl, the Kola and Yamal Peninsulas, and the Aral Sea are the most visible.[91]

Economic and environmental catastrophes have affected living standards in all the republics, but nowhere more than in Central Asia. Between 1960 and 1979, despite a doubling or more in personal income in the Central Asian republics, incomes still remained below the national average and only 80% of personal income earned in the Baltic Republics.[92] The Soviet effort to improve income equality across the regions was foiled by population demographics and inadequacies in the social security and social welfare systems, as well as in the very low level of pay in the agricultural sector. The disparities between the European and Central Asian standards of living served to heighten identification with local nationalism. The higher rate of population increase in Central Asia most certainly has been responsible for the increase in rural unemployment. Overpopulation, a low rate of geographic mobility, and lack of opportunity also increased the trend toward private agriculture with attendant disastrous consequences on the environment. Poverty and unemployment were as much responsible for the violent riots in the Ferghana Valley as were real or perceived ethnic grievances.

Thus, while historically there has been economic interaction between the constituent peoples of the Soviet Union, this interaction contributed to an increase rather than a decrease in nationality identification. What might have happened if central planning and Soviet-style socialism had not been imposed is pure speculation. Without a market mechanism, no substantive economic interdependence could develop. When the central distribution collapsed, the informal pseudo-economic modes of exchange in their turn could only encourage economic disintegration through a sharp rise in inter-enterprise indebtedness.

Nationalism: The Ties That Bind

Finally, the recognition of mutual interdependence has been obscured by the availability for the first time of viable political alternatives to the historic imperial centralized state. Probably few today within the territory of the former Soviet Union see the central government as a solution to their problems. Glasnost revealed how deep rooted the problems were and how connected with policies emanating from Moscow. Virtually every republic sees economic reform in terms of political reform within a sovereign republican framework. The European republics look to the West for democratic models. In the Caucasus, nationalism has priority over any other consideration. In Central Asia, the re-creation of the Muslim *umma* may prove to be as compelling an alternative as federation or republican independence.

In all the republics, national identity not only survived the years of communist rule, but throve under it. Those peoples who were forcibly incorporated into the U.S.S.R. during World War II, retained vivid memories of their earlier freedom.[93] In the Gorbachev era, the Baltic republics took the lead in the movement for national independence and in developing popular front tactics. The casual tourist to Georgia and Armenia in the 1960s and 1970s was immediately made aware of national history. By the 1980s, both Georgians and Armenians would talk openly with foreigners about independence. Under Gorbachev, the Caucasus exploded in violent nationalist clashes, fomented with doubt by politicians eager to exploit frustration born of years of suppression, national deportations, and Russification to maintain themselves in power. The central authorities contributed to the violence by arresting the leaders of the Nagorno-Karabakh annexation movement and by refusing to allow legal prosecution of the officers suspected in organizing the killing of innocent demonstrators in Tbilisi in 1988 by elements of the Soviet armed forces.[94]

The national tragedy of the 1930s gave birth in the 1960s to a new generation of Ukrainian nationalists. Brezhnev found these so threatening that he purged them. In the 1970s, the Kremlin's fears of resurgent Ukrainian nationalism led to the further purge of Peter Shelest, First Party secretary of the Ukrainian SSR, and to the sentencing to forced labor of Mykola Rudenka and Oleksii Tykhyi, founders of the Ukrainian Helsinki Watch Group, for their role in monitoring civil rights abuses in Ukraine.[95] Chernobyl was the supreme nationalist catalyst in the Gorbachev period. The disaster proved to Ukrainians that the Soviet central power was a threat to their very survival, and brought together a loose coalition of opposition forces in a movement called Rukh, which put on the mantle of Ukrainian nationalism.[96]

Acculturation and assimilation had progressed farthest in Belorussia. But the spread of unofficial groups in the first years of *glasnost* coupled with Moscow's cavalier attitude toward the republic's enormous damages incurred by the Chernobyl disaster rekindled national feeling. In February 1989, 50,000 rallied in Minsk to form the Renewal: Belorussian Popular Front for *Perestroika*.[97]

Cultural identity in Central Asia survived through two media: tribal patronage and religion. Clan and tribal consciousness became even stronger during the Soviet era through the fusion of tribal structure with party structure. Conditions were ripe for corruption and Mafia-like organizations on a wide scale in Kazakhstan, Kirghizia, and Turkistan. In Uzbekistan, the cotton barons were eulogized as exemplary Soviet managers, until their leader, Akhamdzhan Adylov, was brought to justice in 1984.[98] As fear of central power disappeared, republican leaders refused to cede to central party demands for reform. Where the center did impose change, as in Uzbekistan, there was no change in the level of lawlessness and corruption. Tribalism persists in the black market gangs and in the hold the Communist Party retains over politics despite democratization.

Religion also did not succumb to Soviet rule. Probably Islam proved better at adapting to Soviet conditions than its Christian counterparts. Throughout Central Asia, Islamic leaders assented to Soviet rule and urged their followers to join Soviet organizations. As Muslims became joiners, these organizations underwent a profound transformation, ceasing to be vehicles of Soviet socialization and encouraging identification with Islamic values.[99] Under Gorbachev, the Islamic practices learned in secret in the Soviet era came out in the open. Mosques reopened and public profession of faith came back in full strength. Equally important, everywhere in Cantral Asia, Islamic parties are on the rise. The conclusion of the Islamic variant of the Common Market in 1992 and the special agreements reached between the Islamic republics suggests that the old *umma* may indeed be returning in modern economic form.[100]

The alternatives open to the republics assures a virtual unanimous rejection of the continuation of the Soviet Union, even in its most modified form of a commonwealth of sovereign republics. Outside pressures, not domestic politics, may forge a new reality from the former Soviet economic space. The pressures within are for increased fragmentation, regardless of whether such fragmentation is in an ethnic group's interest or not. Years of oppression and lack of contact with the outside world have fostered an almost paranoic parochialism where all who do not belong to the tribe or ethnic group by definition are suspect. Equally important, regional leaders, virtually all of whom are former communists, feel compelled to exploit latent nationalist feelings to secure their hold on power.

CONCLUSION

We see then that the values that support the American federation are virtually absent from the Soviet Union. There is no identification with a federal concept similar to that which the word "American" implies. Past economic practices reinforced rather than overcame regional economic disparities. Under communist rule, central economic policy had as one of its principal aims the perpetuation of republican dependency on the center, rather than the promotion of interrepublican interdependence. Finally, as *glasnost* revealed the full extent of the terror, persecution, economic mismanagement, corruption, and environmental disaster perpetrated in the name of socialism, nationalism and republican independence became an ever more attractive solution.

What then is the future of this former imperial giant? National independence has become a source of rising ethnic tension. There are severe ethnic disagreements within republics, most notably in Georgia, Azerbaijan, Moldova, Kazakhstan, Uzbekistan, and the Russian Republic itself. In every population, the proportion of Russians is high. Russian protest prompted the Soviet federal solution in the 1920s. Russian backlash today could prompt the reimposition of dictatorship. Many Russians indeed agree that authoritarianism is the only way to a reformed economy and a free market, citing the Chilean and Korean experience. Finally, there is the question of borders, such as those between Russia and Ukraine, and Russia and Kazakhstan, that discourages any thought of peaceful settlement. A Yugoslav-type civil war cannot be ruled out.

It is an exercise in futility to point out that the markets for the 15 republics reside in the old borders of the Soviet Union and economic agreement is in everyone's best interest. The Ukrainian-Russian dispute over the Black Sea Fleet is symptomatic of the overriding concern of each republican leadership to wrest what it believes to be its rightful share from the union carcass.

Economic prosperity and political stability remain far in the future for the peoples of the former Soviet Union. In the last analysis, what produced a stable federal solution in the United States was the freedom of each state and the people in that state to make their own decisions. This freedom engendered a willingness to compromise. Unless that freedom is given to the former Soviet republics and their peoples, history would suggest that there will be no stability unless it be authoritarian. There is no example in history of a country that succeeded in creating a truly federal system from a highly centralized state without some kind of upheaval as catalyst. The present suggests that the breakup of the old Russian empire into ever smaller and smaller parts will continue, as the successors to the old *nomenklatura* fight over the spoils. Only increasingly harsher economic reality will force the now independent leaderships to recognize of their own free will the need for some kind of common, perhaps confederal solution.[101] That moment seems to recede ever farther into the distance with every passing day.

NOTES

1. Ted Robert Gurr, "America as a Model for the World: A Skeptical View," *PS* 24 (December 1991): 666.

2. Ibid.

3. Daniel J. Elazar, *Exploring Federalism* (Tuscaloosa: University of Alabama Press, 1987), 12.

4. Ibid., 33.

5. Ibid., 6

6. For elaboration of these requisites, see Sarah F. Liebschutz, *Bargaining Under Federalism* (Albany: SUNY Press, 1991), 12–14.

7. William H. Riker, *The Development of American Federalism* (Norwood, MA: Kluwart, 1987), 30.

8. Anthony Lewis, "An Ingenious Structure," *The New York Times Magazine*, September 19, 1987, 39.

9. Theodore J. Lowi and Benjamin Ginsberg, *American Government: Freedom and Power* (New York: W. W. Norton, 1990), 35.

10. "At one point during the winter of 1786–87, John Adams of Massachusetts, a leader in the independence struggle, was sent to negotiate a treaty with the British, one that would cover disputes left over from the war. The British government responded that, since the United States, under the Articles of Confederation, was unable to enforce existing treaties, it would negotiate with each of the thirteen states separately." Ibid.

11. See Ibid., 36, for elaboration of these points.

12. Ibid., 37.

13. Alexander Hamilton, "Number 1," in James Madison, Alexander Hamilton, and John Jay, *The Federalist Papers* (New York: Penguin, 1987), 89.

14. See James Madison, "Number 51," in Ibid., 319.

15. Lewis, "An Ingenious Structure," 39.

16. Madison, "Number 45," in Madison, Hamilton, and Jay, *The Federalist Papers*, 296.

17. Ibid.

18. Ibid.

19. Ibid.

20. Lewis, "An Ingenious Structure," 39.

21. See Archibald Cox, *The Court and the Constitution* (Boston, MA: Houghton Mifflin, 1987).

22. See Riker, *The Development of American Federalism*.

23. Harold James, *A German Identity: 1770–1990* (New York: Routledge, 1989), 8.

24. Ibid., 9.

25. Gabriel A. Almond and Sidney Verba, *The Civic Culture* (Boston: Little, Brown, 1960), 64–68.

26. Bruce A. Campbell, *The American Electorate: Attitudes and Actions* (New York: Holt, Rhinehart and Winston, 1979), 76.

27. Ibid.

28. Seymour Martin Lipset, *Continental Divide: The Values and Institutions of the United States and Canada* (New York: Routledge, 1990), 210.

29. Ibid., 211.

30. Ibid.

31. Cited in "The Hidden Heroes," *The New York Times*, December 7, 1991, 27.

32. Judith N. Shklar, *American Citizenship: The Quest for Inclusion* (Cambridge, MA: Harvard University Press, 1991), 4.

33. Ibid., 13–14.

34. Ibid., 101.

35. Lowi and Ginsberg, *American Government*, 662–63.

36. Hamilton, "Federalist Number 22," in Madison, Hamilton, and Jay, *The Federalist Papers*, 177–78. Robert Reich writes that "New York put duties on goods en route to Connecticut. Connecticut retaliated in kind, taxing commerce from New York. James Madison likened New Jersey, whose goods had to flow through New York and Philadelphia, to a 'cask tapped at both ends.'" Robert B. Reich, "The Expanding Economic Vista," *The New York Times Magazine*, September 13, 1987, 55.

37. Reich, in Ibid., 54.

38. Lowi and Ginsberg, *American Government*, 663–64.

39. *Gibbons v. Ogden*, 9 Wheaton 1.

40. Reich, "The Expanding Economic Vista," 54.

41. Ibid.

42. Ibid., 55.

43. Ibid.

44. Ibid.

45. Ibid.

46. See Liebschutz, *Bargaining Under Federalism*, 37–38, 125–34 for elaboration of these points.

47. Alan Abramowitz, "The United States: Political Cultures Under Stress," in Gabriel Almond and Sidney Verba, eds., *The Civic Culture Revisited* (Boston: Little, Brown, 1980), 203.

48. These survey items were contained in the 1972 and 1976 National Election Studies by the Center for Political Studies of the University of Michigan.

49. Advisory Commission on Intergovernmental Relations, *Changing Public Attitudes on Governments and Taxes: 1990* (Washington, D.C.: ACIR, 1990), 8.

50. Abramowitz, "The United States," 203.

51. See Richard P. Nathan and Fred Doolittle, *Reagan and the States* (Princeton, NJ: Princeton University Press, 1987), 358–87.

52. Ibid., 362. See also Mavis Mann Reeves, "State Activism as a Balance in Preserving Federalism," *Journal of State Government* 62 (January–February 1989): 20–24.

53. See Nathan and Doolittle, *Reagan and the States*, for empirical evidence of responses by nine states, and Liebschutz, *Bargaining Under Federalism*, Chapters 9 and 10 for analyses of bargaining by the New York State government and nonprofit organizations.

54. Among the more prominent scholars should be mentioned Edward Allworth, Jeremy Azrael, Alexandre Bennigsen, Helene Carrere d'Encausse, Robert Conquest, Robert Freedman, Martha Brill Olcott, Richard Pipes, Ronald Suny, and Geoffrey Wheeler. For a summary of the problem as related to religious dissent, see Barbara Jancar, "Religious Dissent in the U.S.S.R.," in Rudolf Tokes, ed., *Dissent in the U.S.S.R.: Politics, Ideology & People* (Baltimore: Johns Hopkins University Press, 1975), 190–230.

55. The titles are too many to list. Three examples follow: In his otherwise excellent analysis of the Soviet Constitution of 1977, Robert Sharlet makes no mention of the wider powers extended to the Union republics and no mention of the nationality issue at all. (Robert Sharlet, *The New Soviet Constitution of 1977: Analysis and Text* [Brunswick, OH: Kings Court Communications, 1978]). Another case in point is Stephen White, *Political Culture and Soviet Politics* (New York: St. Martin's Press, 1979), 144–54. On the basis of increased knowledge of Russian among the national minorities, White argues the "virtual assimilation" of the non-Russian ethnic groups. Noted Swedish economist Anders Aslund provides no discussion whatsoever of the disparities in development between the Soviet east and west, or north and south in his recent study of Soviet economic reform. (Anders Aslund, *Gorbachev's Struggle for Economic Reform: The Soviet Reform Process, 1985–1988* [Ithaca, NY: Cornell University Press, 1989]).

56. For the story of the Crimean Tatars and the nationality dissidents, see Robert Conquest, *The Nation Killers* (New York: Praeger, 1970), and Peter Reddaway, *Uncensored Russia* (London: George Allen & Unwin, 1972).

57. *Naselenie SSSR, Podannym Vsesoiouznoi perepisi naseleniia 1979 goda* (Moscow: Politizdat, 1980).

58. In the first Soviet census in 1926, 200 different peoples or ethnic groups were registered. Soviet ethnographer Viktor Kozlov explains the decrease in number of groups by a process of ethnic consolidation, the development of "more precise ethnic terminology and a clearer demarcation of peoples from ethnic subdivisions." (Viktor Kozlov, "The Peoples of the Soviet Union," in Teodor Shanin, ed., *The Second World* (Bloomington: Indiana University Press, 1988), 17 and 216.

59. By the end of the fifteenth century, the Russians held the northwest part of the Central Volga region, and extended their control over all the lands within the Novgorod sphere of influence, as well as lands seized from Lithuania. In the mid-sixteenth century, the Russians extended their borders east and southeast, occupying the whole length of the Volga River and penetrating beyond the Urals into Siberia. Expansion into Siberia continued in the seventeenth century.

60. Cossack troops reached the Pacific in 1640 and shortly thereafter collided with Chinese forces. The Treaty of Nerchinsk assigned to the Chinese land later known as the Far Eastern Territory, which came into Russian hands only in 1858 and 1860.

61. In the first half of the nineteenth century, Russia annexed Bessarabia and a large part of the Caucasus. In the middle of the nineteenth century, it annexed Finland and more of Poland. The extension of control over Central Asia took up a large part of the century. By 1850, a significant stretch of Kazakhstan up to the Aral Sea and the Chu and Issyk-Kul Rivers had been annexed. In 1885 Tashkent fell. In 1873, the Russians forced their protectorates on the historic khanates of Bukhar and Khiva. In the next ten years, they captured the rest of Turkistan.

62. A standard text on the history of Russia is Nicholas V. Riasonovsky, *A History of Russia*, 4th ed. (New York: Oxford University Press, 1984). The reader is also referred to Alexandre Bennigsen and S. Enders Wimbush, *Muslims of the Soviet Empire, A Guide* (Bloomington: Indiana University Press, 1986), 5–12; Arthur E. Adams, Ian M. Matley, and William O. McCagg, *An Atlas of Russian and East European History* (New York: Frederick A. Praeger, 1966); Geoffrey Wheeler, *The Modern History of Soviet Central Asia* (New York: Frederick A. Praeger, 1964).

63. For a discussion of Tsar Nicholas I's policy of official nationality, see Nicholas V. Riasanovsky, *Nicholas I and Official Nationality in Russia, 1825–1855* (Berkeley: University of California Press, 1961). Maksudov and Taubman develop Russian-Soviet linkages on nationality in Sergei Maksudov and William Taubman, "Russian-Soviet Nationality Policy and Foreign Policy: A Historical Overview of the Linkage between Them," in Michael Mandelbaum, ed., *The Rise of Nations in the Soviet Union: American Foreign Policy & the Disintegration of the U.S.S.R.* (New York: Council on Foreign Relations, 1991), 15–43.

64. In 1314 Islam became the official religion of the Golden Horde.

65. Riasonovsky, *Official Nationality*, 77–96.

66. V. I. Lenin, *Pol'noe sobranie sochinenii*, 5th ed. (Moscow: Politizdat, 1961), XXVI, 108.

67. V. I. Lenin, *Selected Works*, Vol. I (New York: Progress Publishers, 1967), 652.

68. I. V. Stalin, *Sochineniia* (Moscow: Politizdat, 1946), 313–14.

69. As cited in Kozlov, "The Peoples of the Soviet Union," 29–30.

70. Ibid.

71. In July 1918 a Russian Socialist Federated Soviet Republic (RSFSR) was proclaimed. In 1921 the Russian, Ukrainian, and Belorussian Soviet Republics formally entered into treaty relationships governing military and economic affairs. On February 22, 1922, the non-Russian Soviet republics along with the Far Eastern Republic signed a protocol authorizing the RSFSR to represent them at the Genoa Conference. In November 1922 the Far Eastern Republic was liquidated and annexed by the RSFSR. The Union of Soviet Socialist Republics came into being on December 30, 1922, composed of four republics: the RSFSR, the Ukrainian SSR, the Belorussian SSR, and the Transcaucasian Socialist Federated Soviet Republic. In 1923 the RSFSR organized two new soviet people's republics, Khorezm and Bukhara. From these were created two new union republics in October 1924, Uzbek and Turkmen. In December 1929, the Tajik autonomous SSR was separated from Uzbek and became a union republic in its own right. See Richard Pipe's now classic account of the formation of the U.S.S.R. in his *The Formation of the Soviet Union: Communism and Nationalism, 1917–1923* (Cambridge, MA: Harvard University Press, 1954).

72. With the adoption of the 1936 "Stalin" constitution, the number of republics rose to 11. The Transcaucasian Federation was broken up into the union republics of Georgia, Armenia, and Azerbaijan, and the Kazakh and Kirghiz Autonomus Republics were elevated to union status. Soviet victories in World War II added four more republics: Estonia, Latvia, Lithuania, and Moldavia (the old Tsarist Bessarabia). For a brief summary of the creation of the Soviet republics, see John S. Reshetar, Jr. *The Soviet Polity: Government and Politics in the U.S.S.R.*, 3rd ed. (New York: Harper & Row, 1989), 17–19.

73. The struggle against established social customs was accompanied by mass demonstrations where women tore off the veil in public. The program had a high social cost. Women were driven from their homes and, with nowhere to go, committed suicide in large numbers. Irate husbands murdered their insubordinate wives. See Barbara Jancar, *Women under Communism (*Baltimore: Johns Hopkins University Press, 1978), 59–60; Gregory J. Massell, *The Surrogate Proletariat* (Princeton, NJ: Princeton University Press, 1974).

74. Robert Conquest, *Harvest of Sorrow: Soviet Collectivization and the Terror-Famine* (New York: Oxford University Press, 1986).

75. Martha Brill Olcott, *The Kazakhs* (Stanford, CA: Hoover Institution Press, 1987), 176–98.

76. These included over 450,000 Volga Germans (1941), 140,000 Crimean Tatars (1944), and Muslim peoples of the North Caucausus, including 318,000 Chechens (1944), 75,000 Ingush (1944), and lesser numbers of Balkar, Karachi, and Kalmyks (1944). The Crimean Tatars and Volga Germans were not allowed to return. On November 30, 1945, the Crimean AAR was formally abolished and the territory renamed the Crimean oblast of the RSFSR. On February 19, 1954, it became part of the Ukrainian SSR. The Muslims of the North Caucasus were allowed to return. In 1957, upon order from Khrushchev, the Karachai-Cherkass Autonomous Oblast and the Kabardino-Balkar ASSR were reformed within the territory of the RSFSR. For further details on the deportations, see Robert Conquest, *The Soviet Deportation of Nationalities* (London: Macmillan, and New York: St. Martin's Press, 1960).

77. Under Brezhnev, the nationality problem was said to have been solved. Official data indicated that between 1959 and 1979, mixed marriages grew slowly. The highest percentage occurred in Latvia, and the lowest in Armenia. In Central Asia, mixed marriages mostly occurred between indigenous men and Russian women. For discussion, see Helene Carrere d'Encausse, *Decline of an Empire* (New York: Newsweek Books, 1979), 249–53; Kozlov, "The Peoples of the Soviet Union," 188–204; and Ethel Dunn and Stephen P. Dunn, "Ethnic Intermarriage as an Indicator of Cultural Convergence in Soviet Central Asia," in Edward Allworth, ed., *The Nationality Question in Soviet Central Asia* (New York: Praeger Publishers, 1973), 45–58.

78. Article 3 spelled out the principle of democratic centralism and Article 6, the leading role of the Communist Party. These principles guaranteed the centralist character of the Soviet federation. In terms of the specific relation of the Union republics to the center, Article 45 provided for the opportunity to study in the native language in secondary school, but not in higher education. The republics' right to secede is explicitly guaranteed (Article 72) and they are called "sovereign" socialist states (Article 76), with sovereign rights (Article 81). However, the territory of the U.S.S.R. is described as "unitary" and includes the Union republics, while sovereignty is ascribed to the whole territory of the U.S.S.R., not its constituent parts (Article 75). Article 74 ensures that Union law prevails over republican law.

79. See, in particular, Alexandre Bennigsen and Chantal Lemercier-Quelquejay, *Islam in the Soviet Union* (New York: Frederick A. Praeger, 1967); Carrere d'Encausse, *Decline of an Empire*; and Allworth, *The Nationality Question*, 61–175.

80. The Tajiks are reaffirming their Iranian roots, the Uzbeks recall the empire of Tamerlane, and the Kazakhs are claiming a continuous Kazakh presence in the steppes north and east of the Syr Darya River to the current RSFSR border.

81. Riasonovsky, *A History of Russia*, 83–84. The rise of Moscovy was principally to the south and west, because the Mongols continued to block expansion to the east. Ivan III absorbed Novgorod and Tver and established single rule in the Russian territories, marking the beginning of full Russian independence (ibid., 104).

82. Ibid., 109–13.

83. Foreign trade received an impetus with relations established with the English and the Dutch.

84. Ibid., 184.

85. The eight regions were the Moscow region, the St. Petersburg region, the Polish region, the south Ukrainian region (coal, iron ore, chemical products), the Urals (iron, nonferrous metals, minerals) the Baku sector (oil), the Southwestern region (beet sugar), and Transcaspia (manganese, coal). (Riasanovsky, *A History of Russia*, 425).

86. Cotton deliveries increased from 8,000 tons in 1870 to 354,000 tons in 1915 (Ian Murray Matley, "Industrialization," in Edward Allworth, ed., *Central Asia: A Century of Russian Rule* [New York: Columbia University Press, 1967], 310).

87. Ibid., 329–30.

88. From 1922 to 1928, efforts were made to restore industry to the pre–World War I level. By World War II, a cotton textile industry was in existence with a large textile mill in Tashkent. In 1940 nitrogen fertilizer was being produced by an electrochemical works at Chirchiq. The revitilization of industry was especially difficult in Kazakhstan because of the lack of transport. The mines and the lead plant in Ekibastuz, the Ridder lead mines, and the Spasskii copper plant had to be closed during the 1920s.

89. A steel complex was built near Karaganda. Coal production increased. In 1937 a chromium deposit, believed to be one of the largest in the world, was discovered near Aktybinsk and a ferro alloys plant was built to exploit it. In all, Kazakhstan contributed about 67% of the molybdenum, 50% of the cooper and 80-90% of the lead produced in the Soviet Union during the war (ibid., 341).

90. (a) In 1975 the European part of the Soviet Union, including the Baltics, produced 75% of total electric energy, 70% of the ferrous metallurgy, 87% of total chemicals and petrochemicals, 86% of all machine building, 82% of all light industry, and 81% of all food processing. By contrast, Central Asia did not produce even 10% of the balance. (Boris Z. Rumer, *Soviet Central Asia: "A Tragic Experiment"* [Boston: Unwin Hymen, 1989], 43.)

(b) Ibid., 68–83. In some grain-growing areas of Kirghizia, DDT exceeds the permissible norms by up to 45 times! (Gosudarstvennyi komitet SSSR po okhrane prorody [State Committee SSSR for Environmental Protection], *Gosudarstvennyi doklad: Sost aianie prirodnoi sredy i prirodookhrannaya deiatel'nost' v SSSR v 1989 godu* [State Report on the State of the Environment and Environmental Protection Activities in the U.S.S.R. for 1989] [Moscow: Gosudarstvennyi komitet SSSR po okhrane prirody, 1990], 59.)

91. For an excellent report on the Aral Sea, see V. M. Kotlyakov, "The Aral Sea Basin: A Critical Environmental Zone", *Environment*, 33, 1 (January/February 1991), 4–9, 36–38. The Soviet government and central ministries planned to remedy the water scarcity problem by diverting the waters of the Ob south. Reaction among Siberian writers and scientists was very strong, as was that of the world scientific community. In the face of national and international criticism, and severe budget shortfall, Gorbachev cancelled the plan. The breakup of the union probably has done more to finish the idea than any other previous action. For a discussion of the river diversion project, see Barbara Jancar, *Environmental Management in the Soviet Union and Yugoslavia: Structure and Regulation in a Communist One-Party Federal State* (Durham, NC: Duke University Press, 1987), Chapter Five. See also Rumer, *Soviet Central Asia*, 85–104.

92. Alistair McAuley, *Economic Welfare in the Soviet Union: Poverty, Living Standards and Inequality* (Madison: University of Wisconsin Press, 1979), 109–14.

93. A recent and comprehensive study of Lithuania since 1960 is Thomas A. Oleszczuk, *Political Justice in the USSR: Dissent and Repression in Lithuania,*

1969–1987 (Boulder, CO: East European Monographs, distributed by Columbia University Press, 1988).

94. The Armenians became the first nation to come forward on a nationality platform with their demands for the incorporation of Nagorno-Karabakh into Armenia. The Georgians followed the Armenian example. Protests over the building of the Caucasian railway through some of the most beautiful scenery in the Caucasus forced abandonment of the plan. The November 1988 "massacre," when the Soviet troops opened fire on a student demonstration in Tbilisi, was deliberately organized to protest Moscow's removal of the right of secession from the Soviet Constitution. For the army's defense of its actions in the Caucasus, see *Epitsentr: Armiia v Zakavkazskikh sobytiiakh 1988 goda* (Epicenter: The Army in the Transcaucasus Events of 1988) (Moscow: Voennoie izdatel'stvo, 1990).

95. See Peter J. S. Duncan, "Ukrainians," in Graham Smith, ed., *The Nationalities Question in the Soviet Union* (London: Longman, 1990), 98–100.

96. The plan to expand nuclear power in the Ukraine united the cultural opposition, scientists, and a broad public determined to close down nuclear power totally in the republic. An analysis of the composition of "Rukh" may be found in David Marples, "A Sociological Survey of 'Rukh'," *Report from the U.S.S.R.*, 2, 2 (January 12, 1990), 18–20.

97. For accounts of the Belorussian "workers' rebellion," see Kathleen Mihailisko; "The Workers' Rebellion in Belorussia," *Report from the U.S.S.R.*, 3, 17, 21–5, and "Workers and Soviet Power: Notes from Minsk," *Report from the U.S.S.R.*, 3, 27 (July 5, 1991), 15–21.

98. In Kazakhstan, Dinmukhamed Kunaev surrounded himself with people from his own tribe. Members of specific individual clans predominated in the Kirghiz and Turkmen Party Central Committes. Adylov's personal life was one of wealth and property: thoroughbred horses and a harem. Those who opposed him were thrown into underground prisons and tortured. Women were whipped in front of their husbands. Old men allegedly bowed when he passed by, exclaiming "Allah is great." In Uzbekistan, organized crime defied Moscow's efforts to uproot it. Between 1983 and 1987 hundreds of leading Uzbek officials were tried. Arrests led all the way up to the Uzbek Central Committee. But the scandal reached the top echelons of the Soviet Communist Party. For details of Adylov's lifestyle and Central Asian corruption, see Rumer, *Soviet Central Asia*, 144–57.

99. Carrere d'Encausse, *Decline of an Empire*, 245–47.

100. There has been much discussion in the press about the role of Islam and the rise of Islamic parties in Central Asia. During the last days of peristroika, Radio Liberty carried short articles on the subject. The reader is referred to the following: Azade-Ayse Rorlich, "Islam in Kirgizia: The Making of 'Thinking Believers,'" *Report from the U.S.S.R.*, 2, 19 (May 11, 1990), 21–22; Paul Goble, "The New Mufti of Alma-Ata," *Report from the U.S.S.R.*, 2, 25 (June 22, 1990), 20–21; James Critchlow, "Ties with Turkey: A Lifeline for Central Asians," *Report from the U.S.S.R.*, 3, 6 (February 8, 1991), 19–21. More recently, Central Asia has been the focus of renewed foreign policy initiatives by Pakistan, Iran, and Turkey. ("Pakistan, Looking North," *Economist*, February 22–28, 1992: 57; "Islam resumes its march," *Economist*, April 4–10, 1992: 53–58; "Choosing partners," *Economist*, April 25–May 1, 1992: 60; "With him, chaos,"

Economist, May 9–15, 1992: 84.) For a brief report on the agreement between the Central Asian republics, see *Nezavisimaya gazeta*, April 24, 1992, 1.

101. For a discussion on this point, see "Paspad 'ruble-vogo prostranstva'" (The Disintegration of the Ruble Area), *Dielovye liud'i* (Business World), 3, 21 (March 1992): 20–21.

8

Reconstruction in the U.S.S.R. and the Experience of the West

Vladimir A. Saveliev

The logic of social reforms in Russia once again revives the age-old debate as to whether Western social reform experience is applicable to our traditions and reality (and if so, in what way and in what forms). As we look at the discussion "Russia and the West" today, can we become a part of Western civilization, or must we seek our own entirely distinct political and economic identity?

Obviously, neither Russia's prerevolutionary past nor the present features of the West should be approached uncritically. There is something to be learned from both but neither by itself can be a model that can be recklessly copied without regard to Russia's concrete historical conditions.

The specific character of Russia today (April 1992) is probably, above all, the specific character of a political system, of a political regime that was established in the name of "building socialism in one country." It is the fusion of the state with the sole party and hence the statization of the ruling party and the partyization of the state. The totalitarian "party-state" monster, despite the erosion of the political, economic, and ideological monopoly of the Communist Party of the Soviet Union (CPSU), permeates many pores of our social life even today.

The weaknesses of the model of statehood that was adopted after October 1917, in simple terms, is about whether democracy can even be attained through dictatorship. Why was it that not only in our country, in Russia, but in all countries that were formerly called "peoples' democracies" or the "socialist common-wealth," moral monsters or political pygmies with tragic regularity climbed the summit of power? When did the conceptual dictatorship of the proletariat become a dictatorship in Stalin's name, a dictatorship of the bureaucratic apparatus crowned with the virtually unlimited power of one person—a kind of "socialist monarchy"? It is hardly possible to give an unequivocal answer to this question. Naturally, this did not happen in the blink of an eye, in one hour or one day. It was quite a long process and it was not Stalin's figure alone that gave it a monstrous, inhumane, repressive character.

Curiously, warnings in the past about possible distortions, abuses, and terror were heard from both supporters and opponents of socialist ideals. I. S. Aksakov wrote—in assessing the prospects of a rigid, hierarchical, one-party socialist model in a country that was midway between a developed and an underdeveloped country—that "the equality the socialists dream about is something in the nature of barracks equality and the soldierly sameness the brass sees, but is not living, free equality."[1]

Long before the October Revolution, A. I. Gertsen expressed his apprehensions concerning the "all-absorbing monster of centralization. Before it, particularity wilted and was obliterated; the individual blanched and vanished." Understanding the threat of the alienation of he individual, Gertsen reflected in "Letters from France and Italy":

> social upheavals are never ready before the struggle; what is ready is the rejection of the old; struggle is what really gives birth to social ideas; it turns them from abstractions into living things, from theory into institutions. The proletariat will measure by the yardstick by which it has been measured. Communism's awakening will be stormy, terrible, bloody, unjust, and swift. Amidst the thunder and lightning, the glow of burning palaces, the ruins of factories and offices, there will appear new commandments and coarsely outlined features of the new symbol of faith. They will combine in thousands of ways with historical life; but no matter how they combine, it is socialism that will for the most part call the tune; present state life with its civilization will perish or, as Proudhon courteously phrased it, will be liquidated. Do you feel sorry for civilization? I do too. But the masses, to which it has given nothing but tears, need, ignorance, and humiliation, are not sorry for it.[2]

The paradox of the socialist revolution in Russia was that during the civil war—despite the bitter fighting, the executions and tribunals, the Cheka and grain requisitioning by force—for a certain period of time (in the view of certain strata and groups, and not only those that were directly associated with socialist goals), there continued to exist a relatively democratic system, albeit only in a few respects, but one that was positively different from the Romanov dynasty. This was in a divided country where there was mass emigration, where some citizens were deprived of their political rights, and where other citizens were unable to exercise the rights that were proclaimed. There indeed really was a time without censorship and passports (even though opposition newspapers had long ago been banned), when one could freely travel abroad (even though for many, this became compulsory and even forcible). General party meetings were essentially in the nature of open forums, where even the most urgent problems were openly discussed.

The Soviets were proclaimed to be the main argument in favor of the new proletarian democratism. However, both the Soviets—the core of the political system—and the system itself as a whole underwent a metamorphosis in the first years of their existence, not so much as a reincorporation of the old system but as the formalization and the not yet completed incorporation of the new system. As a result, the interests of the leaders prevailed over the interests of the masses, the gulf between them constantly widened, and the former slogans and ideals of the October Revolution diverged more and more from the actual situation. Of course, society did not cease to develop, the people worked and built, but it is strange, if you think about it, that this movement was "higher and higher." To paraphrase the well-known saying about Bismarck, it can be said that the Soviet Union under Stalin became a great power, but the people became small. (Of course, Russia was a great power even before the revolution, but the economic tempo and successes of "socialist construction" are today more and more disputed as painful hypertrophy, to say nothing of the colossal human losses due to collectivization and industrialization that were integrally connected with the Gulag.) Democracy shrank to the point where it was the exclusive arbitrary power of one person who reaffirmed the truth of the old saying: "Power corrupts, and absolute power corrupts absolutely."

Generations of revolutionaries sang: "We'll destroy the old world to its foundation, then build a new world of our own." The problem was just what should be considered the "foundation." After all, should not something be left as the social, political, and economic base? Historically, it was specifically Stalin and those closest to him—who always called themselves "true Leninists"—who always determined how much of the past should be destroyed and how much should be preserved. One gets the impression that the Stalinist elite destroyed the initial, primitively socialist structures, and moved from bourgeois-democratic to feudal-monarchistic and even slave-owning structures. The forced labor of prisoners, the practice of tying peasants to the land, the absence of civil rights and liberties, the only party as the "order of knights" (sword-bearers)—to list all the attributes of the prebourgeois mentality (*doburzhuaznost'*) would take more than a single line. They formed a new foundation, the cult of personality (a euphemism that was bashfully used after the Twenty-second Congress of the CPSU to define the deified personification of individual/one-man power combining political and spiritual hegemony and the roles of Louis XIV and the Pope).

The great scholar V. I. Vernadskiy, who was active in the Constitutional Democratic Party, made a precise diagnosis in his diary in 1941:

> The major failures of our authorities are the result of the weakening of their cultural level: the average level of communists—both morally and intellectually—is lower than the level of noncommunists. It declined greatly in recent years: the party's best people who made the revolution, the country's best people were in prison, in exile, and have been executed. . . . The flower of the nation has been overshadowed by wheeler-dealers and career-minded lackeys. . . . Contrary to the principles that guided our revolution, we, a totalitarian state, are in a collision of [Eastern and Western] worlds.[3]

B. Slutskiy in his own way figuratively characterized institutions that have forgotten the working person in whose name and in whose behalf they were created.

I walked on and on,
And saw before me
His palaces and factories,
The tall, towering buildings,
The checkered squares,
Everything that Stalin built.
The building of socialism is complete,
Now, let's settle it with people.[4]

The peoples of Russia were punished for their conceit as pioneers, for believing in the exclusiveness of their path under the leadership of the "wisest of the wisest leaders of peoples of all eras." (It is noteworthy that even expressions of dedication were borrowed from monarchs and clergymen, while the ascetic vocabulary of the early revolutionary leadership was mostly and deliberately forgotten.) The people received a bureaucratic Moloch instead of democracy.

Sadly, this is our distinctive trait. What is to be done about it? Obviously, the rational vector of development is not to place any more hope whatsoever in the "exclusiveness" that has already brought the country to the point of desperation. Not to recognize this means that it only remains to agree to the variant of the military coup or the "iron heel." Thus, we must follow the general civilizational path without further inventing a communist bicycle with square wheels, be it in the form of the "leading role of the CPSU" or the "plan-regulated market economy."

Thus, the first task is to rid ourselves of the pernicious political monopoly of one party that in seven-plus decades has not succeeded in proving its exclusive right to true justice and prosperity. One involuntarily recalls the giganto-pithecus—an extinct ancestor of Homo sapiens. Despite its considerable size and strength, this being was unable to adapt to life in an extremely competitive environment. And it died out, proving that in nature dead-end lines of development are possible even for "nearly" human beings.

One also frequently hears the thesis that only the CPSU can be an organizing and consolidating force under the present difficult conditions. This is doubtful on the basis of practical observations of how party bureaucrats resist the transformation of their own party and on the basis of simple analogies. Why are certain circles, no matter what they call themselves—conservative communists, advocates of socialist choice, the orthodox, and fundamentalists like N. Andreyev, and so on—again insisting on exclusiveness? Just where are other examples of reforms that have been carried out by a party with a monopoly on power? For example, revolutions in England and the U.S.A. in the past and more recent reforms in Portugal, Spain, Chile, and other countries, came off without parties of "consolidationist leaders"? (It is important to note that in the destatization process, in the process of making the transition from totalitarianism to democracy, we should obviously follow not so much the path of developed Western democracies like the U.S.A., Great Britain, or France, but the relatively recent experience of Portugal or Spain, which joined the ranks of democratic countries in the 1970s and 1980s.)

The less our hopes are set on our exclusive intercultural "Eurasianness" and pioneering spirit, the less suffering and deprivation will be inflicted on our people. Russia was a "second echelon" country in the development of capitalism and followed the lead of Germany and Japan rather than the path of Great Britain, France, or the U.S.A. Russia was always noted for emphasizing the role of the state and for monopolism in industry and agriculture (but not in politics), even before the bolsheviks came to power. While claiming to be the successors to Greco-Latin civilization, we nevertheless did not fully experience the Reformation, the Renaissance, and the Age of Enlightenment. Nevertheless, no one in the world has ever built a modern civilized society by emphasizing exclusiveness, by ignoring the general rules of the world community.

The fact that many forms of the political process are in inverse order and upside down can hardly be attributed solely to our historical uniqueness. This is more likely the result of specific features of contemporary political structures and of even the subjective factor, when reforms are made to fit obsolete structures or even specific political leaders. No law-governed state can exist without the principle of constitutionalism, without solid constitutional principles. But how do we learn constitutionality? Other countries initially adopt a Fundamental Law (even in the most critical times), and then, on the new legal foundation, elect organs of power, including the head of state, executive power, and so on. But we institute presidential rule, and then start thinking about how to create a new constitution instead of the one that was adopted during the worst times of stagnation.

It now develops that the historical dispute about the fate of Russia has still not been resolved, that our country (with regard to democratization) is by no means exceptional as it was previously thought to be. We painfully, with the groans of great-power chauvinists about the general "trampling of graves" or, to the contrary, necrophilia, are slowly but surely ridding ourselves of the haughty conceit of pioneers of "proletarian justice." Moreover, the appeal to native roots is more natural than it is for Russian reformers to appeal to the experience of German or Swedish reformers or for workers to appeal to the conceptions of British Labourites. (However, we are fortunately once more beginning to learn much that is positive in foreign countries. The lessons of Tsar Peter I and the results of the population poll on changing the name of Leningrad to St. Petersburg were by no means accidental.)

Obviously, ideological and social diversity is first of all reflected (at present, not preprogrammed by order of CPSU rayon [district] committees) in representative organs at all levels, not so much through factions of "traditional" organizations (trade unions; the Academy of Sciences; the army; professional organizations of composers, artists, and others; rich landowners; and more) as through the personification of the election process, of the previously depersonalized, lost individual. Today, everyone has his or her own perestroika, even though it naturally agrees to a certain extent with the interests of concrete social groups and strata. And if an election campaign is inclined to emphasize individuality, the imperative of successful parliamentary activity is the creation of alliances, factions, and coalitions with the aim of attaining a victorious and therefore effective majority. The voting of members of any party should not by any means be preprogrammed to be unanimous. Interest groups—ecologists, the energy complex, military-industrial circles, regional groups, rich landowners, and others—will inevitably be affirmed. It is no secret that some of these "interests" are already on the march, are becoming organized in committees and commissions, and are developing their proposals and the tactics for implementing them. Considering the realities of a society that is becoming fragmented and politicized, every new party (Russia still has fewer than the 159–200 parties that exist in Georgia, but you can no longer count Russia's parties on the fingers of both hands) must approach the struggle for votes, voters, and deputies more seriously from the standpoint of realpolitik. Russians are becoming accustomed to dissidence on various questions and are appreciating the need for difficult compromises as the norm rather than as an anomaly in political life. In a phrase, we should learn "*e pluribus unum*," the well-known Latin saying that was adopted not by chance as a motto at the dawn of the U.S.A.

Naturally, democratic principles extend not only to internal or social policy, but are also applicable to Russia's foreign and military policy. International relations and military affairs must unquestionably remain the province of the central state. While supporting everything positive in foreign policy after 1985 (the appeal to the principles of the new political thinking, the withdrawal of Soviet forces from Afghanistan, noninterference in the reform process in East European countries, the unification of Germany, increased glasnost on military-political issues), democratic forces must at the same time develop their own vision of the future of international relations connected with the general liberalization process.

Liberalization in the economic sphere is characterized by the decline of the regulatory role of the state (deregulation) and the emphasis on market relations, by the intensification of international economic relations, and, in the political area, by the abandonment of totalitarian and authoritarian state structures for more democratic, pluralistic structures.

The liberalization process naturally also has foreign political consequences. The foreign policy of the corresponding countries becomes more open and takes into account the interdependence of the modern world, but is also less predictable or more precisely loses its former single-dimensionality since a more varied conglomerate of political and economic forces and interests is beginning to participate in its formation. Liberalization has consequences that cannot be assessed merely by a "plus" or "minus" sign. It includes the increased dependence on foreign creditors and suppliers of progressive technology, the development of centrifugal and even separatist tendencies in political systems of states, the infringement of the interests of previously affirmed political and economic elites, and the accelerated erosion of traditional political cultures.

Nevertheless, attempts to halt liberalization, whether it begins from above or below, are usually unsuccessful. (Only Iran could probably be cited as the rare exception [not indisputable and obvious in all respects] in recent years.)

At any rate, liberalization appreciably alters the entire international system in which the economically prosperous great powers are playing a larger part, the significance of the purely military component is diminishing, and international organizations (especially the United Nations and the Group of Seven) are growing in importance. Since the liberalization process has become much more dynamic with the inclusion of the U.S.S.R. and East European countries in recent years, the analysis of this process also becomes more urgent.

Deideologization, destatization, demilitarization, deimperialization, and the elimination of the party's monopoly on international relations must become the foreign policy principles of the renewed Russian state.

Today's fragile, interconnected, multipolar, interdependent world, confronted by global problems that cannot be solved in isolation, exclusively within the framework of sovereign states (controlling the production and testing of nuclear arms, overseeing the safety of nuclear energy, protecting the environment, combating terrorism and human rights violations, securing the international division of labor and specialization, regulating world trade and international finance) urgently requires that the traditional, confrontational, black-and-white view of existing socioeconomic systems as "socialist" and "capitalist" be abandoned. The attempt to overcome the division of the world into military blocs means rejecting the slogan of building and supporting world socialism and forgetting the idea of dividing the world into two camps. These are the specific features of deideologization and deimperialization.

The transition to a truly new foreign policy means establishing democratic civilian control (up to and including the appointment of a civilian politician as minister of defense) over the hitherto largely uncontrolled military-industrial complex in our country; the radical reduction of the military budget; the real, accelerated conversion of defense branches of military production; and the termination of ideologically motivated military aid throughout the entire world.

The army urgently needs democratic reform in depth to reduce the size of the general staff, to eliminate inhumane internal norms, and to raise professionalism and increase social protection for service personnel. Our society must truly demilitarize in the shortest possible time.

Personnel changes ("departyization") must also affect both the military and the foreign policy apparatus. In no modern country is military and foreign political leadership formed, as it is in Russia, along partisan lines, frequently without regard to experience and competence, and to the detriment of truly professional diplomatic and military personnel. The past and present failures in foreign and military affairs indicates that the "partyocracy" should quit foreign policy and the army.

Without political pluralism reinforced by economic pluralism (above all, the diversity and equality of different forms of property), the reform of the political system in our country is doomed to founder. As a result, the government pyramid could well revert either to oligarchical totalitarianism (à la Brezhnev, which expressed the compromise of opinions in the leadership of the party apparatus) or to dormant Stalin-type totalitarianism under which one all-powerful ruler—a socialist dictator—calls the tune. This will at best be a kind of "partyocratic" monarchy. And instead of a society living within the law on the principles of autonomy and self-government, there will continue to be a pseudopolitical order under the control of a fused party-state. Therefore, the democratization of society, its transformation on the basis of constitutional democratic principles, is impossible if we do not shed the illusions that prosperity and development are the product of three "monos": political monopolism, monocentrism of state and party power, and monolithic socialist like-mindedness.

NOTES

1. I. S. Aksakov, *Collected Works* (Sobraniye sochineniy) (Moscow, 1891), Vol. 2, 88.
2. A. I. Gertsen, *Utopian Socialism in Russia* (Utopicheskiy sotsializm v Rossii) (Moscow, 1985), 121–22.
3. V. I. Vernadskiy, *Literaturnaya Gazeta*, March 16, 1988, 13.
4. B. Slutskiy, *Novyy mir*, 1987, No. 10, 175.

9

A Comparative Analysis of Theories of Sovereignty in the Former U.S.S.R. and Yugoslavia

Helen Ostrovidova

The world community is carefully watching the development of the political situation in the former socialist world. In December 1991, the U.S.S.R. was declared to be dead. Another socialist state—Yugoslavia—is the next to disintegrate. The crash of communist ideology and its political regimes, deep economic crisis, demise of administrative structures of government, and the growing anxiety of the international community—all serve as a background for the political disintegration of these two former communist states.

The ideological basis of this disintegration is the principle of sovereignty. But the public's attitude—nationally and internationally—to this principle is very different. There is in the former U.S.S.R. nostalgia about past unity and power, but more often there is the fear of the possibility of the beginning of a civil war or of its escalation (as in Yugoslavia).

However, sympathy was the domineering attitude toward "the struggle for sovereignty"—especially at its initial stage. Public opinion associates the reaching of independence with the victory of democratic forces over conservative ones. And though reaching sovereignty doesn't always mean a victory over the conservative center and vice versa, sovereignty is often used to keep local conservatism and potential totalitarism on the periphery; it is this sympathy that is a dominant attitude of the international community in regard to the problem of the demise of the U.S.S.R. and Yugoslavia.

And so it is very logical to ask why is independence good? What are the roots of the sympathy toward people fighting for independence against the center? Maybe because the struggle for sovereignty is considered by people to be a struggle of oppressed people against oppressors. Traditionally, Soviet, Yugoslavian, and international propaganda have strived to create a very good image of such a struggle. The general approach considers the domination of a powerful core over a weak periphery as evil, but victims among local people who are being provoked by nationalistic leaders for a "struggle for freedom" are shown to be heroes.

The events in the U.S.S.R. at the beginning of the 1990s gave extra arguments in favor of this approach. After the crash of "social ideals" in Gorbachev's Soviet Union, the Soviet metropolis as the center appeared to become a stronghold of conservatism and an evil against which it was necessary to fight under the banner of sovereignization. And, to some extent, it was true. Gorbachev's center became conservative and afraid of radical reforms. Gorbachev's team could not win the game for "smooth reforms."

It immediately became clear that "the fair struggle for national revival" has many negative features and tragic consequences. Public opinion has already changed.

"We don't need an old Union"—the people say—"but some kind of a new one should be kept." However, as December 1991 showed in the U.S.S.R., it was too late. A similar situation occurred in Yugoslavia. At the first stage of confrontation, Slovenia proposed to create a confederation with limited functions of central organs. Croatia supported the idea but Serbia was against it. At the next stage of conflict, Serbia was ready to accept Slovenia's formula but it was already late. Any variant of confederation became impossible.

So what can be the main trends of the sovereignization process in the two former socialist states? What can be the international consequences of sovereignizations? What lessons can be learned from Eastern Europe by socialist Asia and its regional neighbors? The answer to these questions requires looking at the problems of the roots, of the presuppositions, and of the future of the idea of sovereignization in the former U.S.S.R. and Yugoslavia.

ROOTS OF THE UNITY

It is reasonable to sympathize with the nation demanding sovereignty if we look at the history of the nations as the permanent confrontation between metropolis and periphery. And if the situation in the society is bad, it is an opportunity to accuse a conservative metropolis of all the national misfortune and troubles.

However, there can be another look at the history. Let us consider not the dictates of the center (in the U.S.S.R., Russian; in Yugoslavia, Serbian), but the party-bureaucratic structure that helped to rule huge territories and was a basis for the former unity of the two countries. It is true that the party-bureaucratic apparatus can stop or greatly change any progressive decision of the leaders of the country. But, on the other hand, this apparatus provides conservative stability of economy and politics that is very healthy for society at the time of intensive reforms.

In the former socialist countries, the center-periphery relations were built so that rather stable vertical connective structures between national leaders and the center allowed the center to conduct a general policy on the national periphery; but on the other hand, nationalistic bureaucracy could pursue with formal loyalty to the center its own dictatorial ambitions toward local populations. That is why it is very natural that the weakening of central control was in interest of the nationalistic apparatus.

A very important feature of the situation in the U.S.S.R. was the fact that the unity of the country had been guaranteed not by law, but by the practice of vertical subordination within the framework of party discipline. The practice of appointment of local leaders from the Center provided deep dependence of the local bureaucracy on the Center. This dependence was strengthened by the inclusion of Soviet territories into a single economic and military structure.

The power of the Moscow party center over national republic leaders was the political basis of the unity of the U.S.S.R. Dependence of the local bureaucracy on central authorities in the nomination of cadres and administrative questions was the administrative basis of the unity. The economic basis was a planned economy that gave priority to construction of monopolistic industrial complexes within the limits of the all-Union division of labor. The united military forces, the united system of national security, and frontier guards being subordinate to the center was the military basis of the unity.

In Ukraine and Belorussia (republics which historically were closer to the center), the style of administrative and political life of the republics was very similar to the Moscow center. In Muslim republics with their own strong historical traditions, nationalistic bureaucrats had to adjust their political and administrative styles of leadership to Moscow standards. In the Baltic republics, Moscow established its administrative style by sending its political leaders from the Russian center and by increasing the Russian population. The unity of the centralized party-bureaucratic rule of the country was the integrated basis of the unity of the U.S.S.R. It replaced a former tsarist system of control that existed before 1917.

At first glance the situation in Yugoslavia is very different. All Yugoslavian republics were approximately equal in size of population and territory, so there was not a real center. There were confrontations between economic leaders, between the economic centers of Slovenia and Croatia, and the political-administrative center of Serbia.

Yet the same party-bureaucracy connections were the basis of the unity of the country. The specific features of these connections were determined by a specifically Yugoslavian model of "socialistic self-government." According to the Constitution of 1974, there were six centers in Yugoslavia, as many as there were republics. It meant that formally every country could be called a confederation. It also meant that Yugoslavian "democratic socialism" was formally opposed to Soviet totalitarianism. However, the Yugoslavian confederation did not weaken the party-bureaucratic power. Furthermore, this confederation's principle of self-government played the role of a mine under the pavement of totalitarianism Yugoslavian statehood.

GROUNDS FOR SOVEREIGNTY

The crash of socialist totalitarianism in the U.S.S.R. and Yugoslavia undermined the main basis of the party control over the life of the republics. The administrative-bureaucratic roots of unity were abolished. The idea of sovereignization began to find more and more followers. But what are the grounds for the ideology and practice of sovereignization?

Natural-Geographic Grounds

Natural geographic grounds include such factors as unity of territory, language, historical fate, and others allowing the international community to consider a state independent. It is important to say that there is no precise grouping of such factors, and their existence can be only one of the factors to pose the question of sovereignization. From this point of view, it is probable that all the Soviet and Yugoslavian republics have the right to pose the sovereignization question.

Historic-Political Grounds

For many centuries the empire of the Russian tsar extended its territory by conquering other nations and lands that did not have a statehood. And although there are many discussions about the history of the former Soviet republics, it is more or less clear that historically neither Ukraine, nor Belorussia, nor Moldavia, nor the Muslim republics ever existed as independent states within the present frontiers. Only the Baltic republics and to some extent Georgia can pretend to restore independence. All others can only establish independence by declaring to be liberated from the Moscow authorities.

In Yugoslavia, the historical grounds for sovereignization are different. The union of Serbia, Croatia, and Slovenia at the beginning of the twentieth century was a voluntary one. It was concluded between independent states, and so it is quite correct to talk about a restoration of statehood of these three republics. But the question of sovereignty of the three other Yugoslavian republics is more complicated. Thus, in Yugoslavia, the question of sovereignization is not one of liberation from the power of the center but more one of annulment of old agreements.

Social-Economic Grounds

In the U.S.S.R., it is the Russian economy that is the basis for the all-Union division of labor, and so the economic troubles in other republics are strictly linked with the economic situation in Russia. Hence, nationalistic governments formally have a right to critize Moscow for "bad work," for "an unjust division of rights and responsibilities" in questions of production and distribution of national income. And partly it is true because the command-administrative system made local economies absolutely dependent upon decisions of the Center. And it is not by chance that the most developed Soviet republics—the Baltic ones, whose level is two to three times above that of the Muslim republics—put the question of gaining sovereignty above all others.

A similar situation exists in Yugoslavia. Slovenia and Croatia, whose economic level exceeds by ten times that of the others, became pioneers in the struggle for independence.

Thus, economic crisis and the hope to overcome it without pressure from the center and the desire to help less developed "brothers" are real grounds for sovereignization motives.

The Bolshevik Heritage

The grounds for independence about which we are going to talk now are contrary to those just mentioned; they have a more speculative than objective character. But in real policy this is not less important.

Starting his perestroika, Gorbachev slowly but truly eliminated from society many elements of Stalinist and Leninist theory and practice: the ruling role of the party, Marxist ideology, centralized plan economy, and class struggle inside and outside the country. However, Gorbachev could not do anything with one of the most hypocritcal parts of Bolshevik heritage—the national policy. The farce of the Lenin-Stalin approach to the national problem was, in fact, that Bolshevism declared the principle of national independence and sovereignty to be the main principle of the constitution, and at the same time created strong political reprisal mechanisms to prevent anybody from using this right. So, from a pragmatic point of view, neither for Stalin nor for his successors was there a problem of preserving the unity of the U.S.S.R. Any sign of an attempt to use a constitutional right for independence was declared to be an anti-Soviet, antisocialist activity with all the practical consequences.

However, this constitutional hypocrisy, like any other kind of hypocrisy, is a very dangerous trap. As soon as centralized party-administrative control over the country had weakened, the national bureaucracy immediately used a constitutional opportunity to pose the question of independence. And now we can only regret that Gorbachev could not finish the Leninist heritage more consistently, including this "fake" right for nations that had never before dared to pose the question of sovereignization in accordance with the Soviet constitution.

Traditional Mentality

In traditional societies like Russia or Yugoslavia or the Muslim republics, a rule of law is very weak. Historically, the Russian Orthodox Church and Russian politicians and philosophers never accepted a leading role of law above the state authority. They never accepted the sovereignty of law because power and authority derived from God, but law was made by people.

During the Bolshevik era, this approach was strengthened. In reality, the police and all courts and prosecutors were subordinated to the party authorities in the U.S.S.R., as in all socialist countries. Members of the Central Committee, for example, could not be convicted. Kim Il Sung of North Korea once expressed the socialist attitude to the law very clearly: "What does it mean a law? It is made by people, so people can change it." So, to change a constitution or not to follow its rules and regulations in legally gaining independence is very natural for socialist states. In Yugoslavia, for example, the Constitution of 1974 was the sixth constitution.

So, from a mental point of view, the division of the country in many pieces is not something unusual if people in power want it. Constitutional procedure is not something to pay attention to.

Interests of the National Bureaucracy

It is difficult to argue that a trend toward a maximum independence from higher power structures and toward a concentration of maximum power in its own hands is a logical feature of activity of all types of the bureaucracy. This logical tendency permanently carries a potential for independence. But this "bureaucratic independence" does not create guarantees for the real freedom of the people. More often it just helps to concentrate more power in the hands of local leaders.

It is also important to keep in mind the aims of Eastern Slavic peoples and Asian peoples, who traditionally do not give priority to the individual in state versus individual relations models.

So the aspiration of local bureaucracy for strengthening its own power in the national republics in the face of a weakening of the central power structure is one of the most important grounds for posing the question of sovereignization. In gaining independence, local bureaucracy sees a chance to defend itself from unpredictable political and economic decisions of the center, and to satisfy "presidential ambitions" of young nationalistic leaders and to strengthen its own position within a legal or black-market private economy.

The Yeltsin-Gorbachev Conflict

All of the above-mentioned grounds for sovereignization are very important, but none of them would work if there was no political leader who could want to use them in his or her political interests. And, because of the strong dominance of the center, such a leader could not appear in small Soviet republics that were always afraid of the center's pressure. It's enough to remember the very shy attempts of the Baltic republics to pose the question of sovereignty at the first stage of perestroika, from 1985 to 1989.

Boris Yeltsin became such a leader. But the Russian president did not begin to use the idea of Russian independence as the start of his political activity. Sovereignization became a main goal of Yeltsin's policy only in the third stage of his struggle against Gorbachev. Yeltsin had lost two first rounds of the fight—losing first his position in the Politburo, and then being unable to get a place in the Parliament of the U.S.S.R.

In the third round Yeltsin used the weakest point of Gorbachev's system: constitutional "double-think." Yeltsin used constitutional interpretation of independence contrary to its content. And the farce of the Soviet constitution became absolutely clear: There were, indeed, two or more presidents in one state. Finally, Yeltsin won beautifully, though rather toughly, his game against Gorbachev after the failed August 1991 coup and the creation of the Commonwealth of Independence States in December 1991. But, by winning, Yeltsin placed himself in Gorbachev's position. Many autonomous Russian republics began to ask for independence using the "double-think" of the Russian Constitution, which is similar to the Constitution of the U.S.S.R., which proclaimed a right for independence. But Yeltsin's advantage now is that he does not have a strong and popular political enemy like Gorbachev had in Yeltsin.

In reality, the sovereignization movement in the U.S.S.R. started at the time when Yeltsin began to use the idea of the independence of Russia against Gorbachev's political leadership. We can see similar tendencies in Yugoslavia. A post-Tito political system under which a central bureaucracy changed its leader every year, choosing from the leaders of the nationalistic bureaucracy that could not exist for long without conflicts. Controversial attitudes toward private property initiated a first conflict between Serbian leaders and leaders of Slovenia and Croatia. This conflict soon turned into a civil war. Because of an approximate equality of military and political power of Serbia and Croatia, the military confrontation could take a long time without an absolute victory to either side.

So, for the purpose of this analysis, it is important to state that both in the former U.S.S.R. and in Yugoslavia, the idea of independence and sovereignty was used by one group of politicians—former patriots—against another group in the postcommunism power struggle. And all other grounds for independence were used basically as arguments in this struggle for personal power.

OBJECTIONS

There can be rather reasonable objections to this interpretation of the roots of the sovereignization movement. This movement reflects, among other things, the waking-up of national self-consciousness, the people's demands to respect their national rules, and their will to be masters of their land. These objections present other views on political development, giving a more important role in history, not to individuals but to "objective regularities." These views say that the sovereignization movement reveals a will of the masses to be independent.

But what does it mean "to reveal a will" of the masses? Is it not just another example of the Bolshevik heritage? We think that the will of the masses can be revealed only in democratic society—that is, in a society based upon the middle class of educated and financially independent people. By "educated people" we mean those who can ask questions about their political and economic life and independently find the answers.

In socialist or postsocialist societies there are no different kinds of people because 90% of the population are bureaucrats working in offices or at state-owned plants or state-owned collective farms or department stores. There are no free agents or businesspeople—there are only people working for the state.

Thus, in the U.S.S.R. or in Yugoslavia, the concept of the masses will not be a true one. However, it can be used by politicians in their power games. In socialist countries the idea of independence is not born among ordinary people, but it is introduced to them by political circles. If people enjoy a free and good life, they usually do not care about the nation's independence and sovereignization problems. But in a time full of troubles, in postcommunist economies, people are used to implementing these ideas into practice in the interest of the leader.

CONCEPTS OF SOVEREIGNTY

Paradoxically, none of the Soviet or Yugoslavian 43 republics have a well-developed concept of sovereignty if independence is viewed as an objective process. Questions of independence and transitions from interrepublic relations within the union to interrepublic relations of sovereign states remain unanswered. For example, how should democracy be protected? How should the influence of local administrative and religious conservatives be limited? However, if the sovereignization movement is first of all a political power game rather than an objective process, political leaders naturally will think about their tactical goals and not about sovereignty concepts.

National concepts of sovereignty can be defined only by analyzing practical moves of the republics and their reaction to most important events flanked by the problems of independence. These concepts can be compared through attitudes to private property and socialist ideas, the readiness to participate in some kind of new confederation or union of former Soviet republics, and the main goals and means of achieving the sovereignty.

First, the three Baltic republics whose sovereignty was immediately accepted by the international community should be distinguished. From the beginning, these republics were for full sovereignty and against participation in any new unions that could be built to replace the old U.S.S.R. The basis for their concept of full sovereignty was the fact that these three republics, as we have mentioned, were reacquiring their independence, not gaining a new one. So the Baltic republics refused to sign an economic agreement in October 1991 that could have become—as Gorbachev had hoped—a basis for a new Union.

Georgia's position is in many aspects very close to the Baltic republics' concept of full sovereignty. But it was changed after a successful military coup in January 1992 when Georgia joined the Commonwealth of Independent States, though nobody can say for sure or for how long.

All other republics signed an economic agreement in October 1991 and, until the creation of the CIS in December, shared a so-called concept of limited sovereignty. The reason for this position was not the fact that these republics terribly needed to preserve economic links with the center. The Baltic republics were not afraid to lose those links. The problem was that these (non-Baltic) republics did not reacquire their sovereignty but were getting it anew. So the local bureaucracy that had grown with the firm support from the center became afraid to lose this support and, as a result, to lose its political power. Such approaches were strong in the Muslim republics of Asia and Belorussia. Ukraine and Azerbaijan, which had in their Azerbaijan history a kind of restricted independence and rather huge natural resources, have a very weak desire to keep old linkages between republics in any new form.

The Armenian variant is another type of limited sovereignty concept. The difficult geopolitical location of Armenia and the continuing war against Azerbaijan induced Armenian leaders to look for a union with the former Center to protect their nationalistic country leadership. Armenia hopes to use Russian pressure on Azerbaijan in its own favor.

All the republics may be divided into some groups in accordance with the main goals they want to achieve by pushing the sovereignization process. The Baltic republics wanted to break off all linkages with the Bolshevik heritage and use independence for economic growth and political self-realization.

Leaders of Uzbekistam, Turkmenia, Azerbaijan, and Tajikistan concentrated on preserving the existing bureaucratic structures, simply changing the communist ideology for a nationalist one. So it is not accidental that these republics viewed very negatively Russia's attempts to start economic reform without coordination with other republics.

The final crash of the command-distribution economic system created new dangers for the remaining administrative structures in Muslim republics. Kyrgyzstan stands a little bit apart, proclaiming free market and democracy principles. But it is very unlikely that Kyrgyz president Askar Akaevich Akaev can keep his position for a long time under pressure from the nationalist bureaucracy and Muslim groups. Georgian, Armenian, and Moldovan (Moldavian) sovereignty concepts are close to this group of countries. Belorussian sovereignty can be determined as a passive variant. It seems that Belorussian bureaucrats declared their independence by inertia following the main trend of the U.S.S.R's disintegration and now do not know exactly what to do with it. Maybe this is the reason why Minsk was chosen as the capital of the CIS.

Concepts in Ukraine and Kazakhstan are very different from the above. These republics are territorially the largest after Russia—18% of the population of the former U.S.S.R. lives here, and 17% of the (old) Union's national income is produced in Ukraine. These two republics are in a special geopolitical situation. They are in the center of Eastern Europe and Middle Asia, and they possess strategic nuclear weapons. This determines their specific role after the collapse of the U.S.S.R. The ambitions of Ukrainian and especially Kazakh leaders seem to be very dangerous to regional security. Their desire to play military roles in the power game with Russia and the other republics gives rise to serious tension in relations between these republics and Russia. Thus, the concepts of sovereignty in these republics can be characterized as ambitious and striving for regional leadership.

The difference in sovereignty concepts predetermined the tactics of the republics during their negotiations with Russia. At the end of 1991 supporters of limited sovereignty concepts continued their move to full sovereignty. Republics that had gained full sovereignty began to look for establishment of normal interstate relations with Russia. The fate of the Asian republics depends upon the forms of development of the sovereignization process in Kazakhstan, upon how their relations with Russia will develop, and upon what the policy of the Muslim Middle East countries will be. It is reasonable to expect reorientation for the Middle East of Soviet Muslim republics if their relations with Russia meet many difficulties. However, this reorientation will become a permanent tendency only after postcommunist regimes in Soviet Asian republics are changed into regimes whose supporters represent the growing interests of Muslim religious groups. Of course, if there was no free Kazakhstan—as is logical from the historic point of view—if Kazakhstan was a part of Russian territory, Russia could preserve its influence upon four other Muslim republics: Kyrgyzstan, Tajikistan, Uzbekistan, and Turkmenistan. But now the Khazan republic pretends to be a leader of a new possible union of five Muslim Asian states.

All the republics can be divided into three groups by means and methods of gaining sovereignty. The first group includes the Baltic republics, which consistently used political methods of gaining independence. Georgia and Moldova used more aggressive means. All other republics used the situation in the U.S.S.R. after August 1991 and, it is possible to say, have gotten sovereignty as a present, in a "natural way."

We can see some analogies in Yugoslavia, Slovenia, and Croatia, which have fought for their independence. Macedonia, Bosnia, and Hertzegovina are waiting for their chances. Slovenia and Croatia are also using independence rhetoric in trying to obtain support from abroad.

A common conclusion is as follows: Absence of developed concepts of sovereignty can be considered as one more confirmation of the artificiality of the problem of sovereignization and of the attempts to use this problem to support bureaucratic ambitions of nationalistic leaders.

IS IT POSSIBLE TO STOP DISINTEGRATION?

The reason for the breakdown is not an independence movement, but the collapse of the socialist administrative-distribution system, which was a result of Gorbachev's perestroika. Sovereignization can only help to accelerate disintegration.

Thus, signing of any kind of economic agreements between members of the former U.S.S.R. does not mean much because it cannot stop the collapse of the administrative socialist economy. Nor can it help to develop a new variant of integration of market economies of independent states, because these new states do not have the precondition for such a cooperation—that is, private producers. For that reason, Gorbachev's attempt to form an economic union in October 1991 was no more than a political game to preserve power in the hands of the central bureaucracy.

Opponents of disintegration also claim that without some kind of cooperation, republics can neither overcome economic difficulties nor get economic aid from Western countries, which need guarantees of political stability to increase their assistance to former member republics of the U.S.S.R. or Yugoslavia. To some extent these arguments are serious, but they cannot outweigh the interests of the local bureaucracy trying to achieve maximal independence from the central bureaucracy.

International pressures will have an effect only with direct interference into domestic affairs. But the world is not yet ready for such an operation.

The disintegration of the U.S.S.R. cannot be stopped. The creation of the CIS means the end of the power of central bureaucracy. But it also means that the local bureaucracy still hopes to use former economic and political relations to strengthen its own power.

THE MEANING OF THE CREATION OF THE COMMONWEALTH OF INDEPENDENT STATES

First, the elimination of the U.S.S.R., in spite of Gorbachev's objections, meant the end of the Gorbachev-Yeltsin conflict. Russian President Yeltsin took revenge against Gorbachev for his losses in the final stages of the conflict.

Second, the CIS agreement confirmed that Russia had succeeded to international rights and obligations of the former U.S.S.R. Russia "inherited" the U.S.S.R.'s place on the UN Security Council. Control over nuclear weapons manifested Russia's intention to honor all international agreements. Russian President Yeltsin, with the demise of the Soviet Union presidency, at the same time has manifested effectively the leading role of Russia in the post-U.S.S.R. period.

Third, the signing of the CIS agreement guaranteed to the leaders of other republics their political ambitions. All republics now consider themselves equal independent states. What these leaders need now is international recognition.

Fourth, discussions during the CIS agreement-signing showed the remaining large differences in national conceptions of independence. The Slavic republics became founders of the Commonwealth: Russia and Ukraine as potential leaders, Belorussia as the last and the smallest (3.6% of the U.S.S.R. population, and 3.8% of GNP) slavic republic. Kazakhstan also was nominally one of the founders of the CIS, in exchange for a Russian promise not to pursue any Northern Kazakh territory, which historically belonged to Russia and was given to Kazakhstan only in Stalin's time. Kazakhstan's primary role was to host the Alma-Ata meetings during which the CIS agreement was finally concluded. Azerbaijhan and Armenia used their participation in the CIS to prevent the other side from gaining an advantage in their military/political conflict. The Baltic republics ignored the CIS following their line for full independence. The four Muslim republics joined the CIS without any hesitation. They see in the CIS an opportunity to use in any way the remaining potential of the former Union, and they do not see any danger from the national bureaucracy of the no-longer-existing political center in Moscow. The Georgian position is unclear because of the military coup in January and its uncertain consequences. But it is very probable that Georgia, being afraid to stay face-to-face with economic chaos and Islamic encirclement, will try to use some kind of cooperation with the CIS to its favor.

Fifth, the creation of the CIS can have an influence on the dynamics of the political struggle in Yugoslavia, and on the attitude of the international community toward the Yugoslavian situation.

Sixth, the creation of the CIS is very important from the point of view of developing tendencies of national sovereignty. The CIS is a new but not a final stage of the sovereignization movement. The problem is that the CIS means nothing for the economic integration of republics of the former U.S.S.R. It does not create a new market economy basis for a commonwealth. The latter can be established only as a result of energetic economic reforms, recognition of private property, and limiting monopolization and "partyocratization" of the economy. The Commonwealth cannot restore an old administrative-command system of economic unity because the administrative basis of Soviet society is now a thing of the past.

It is very likely that market-type reforms in the economy of the different republics will occur at different paces. Historical traditions, mentality, and understanding of which model of state-to-individual relations (with a stress on state or on Individual) is more efficient differ greatly in the Slavic, Muslim, and Baltic republics. There is also no chance of following the examples and experiences of the European Community, or even the former Comecon experience, in the framework of the CIS.

The economic development and creation of some type of market economy in the republics of the former U.S.S.R. will be conducted with cooperation among these republics and their regional neighbors. Factors of cultural, geographic, and ethnic unity will push republics to give priority to a new regional integration instead of trying to restore in some new form the U.S.S.R. Perhaps only Russia will have global economic and political interests to pursue. All other republics will be more or less regionally oriented. For example, Uzbekistan has already declared a Turkish variant of development as a model for itself and it is now intensifying economic links with Turkey. Kazakhstan more likely will choose a Chinese variant of develop-ment and will try to make limited market reforms while at the same time keeping power in the hands of the former "partyocracy" (but without socialist phraseology, which has been replaced by nationalistic phraseology).

By contrast, the economic interests of Ukraine and Belorussia are oriented toward Europe, and Moldova is planning to unite with Romania.

For the reasons stated above, it is likely that the CIS will not be a stable and efficient union, and it is very unlikely to exist for a long time. The elimination by the republics of the power of the center and of Gorbachev also meant the loss of a mechanism with which they could coordinate their activity. As a result, future crises will be faced by republics alone or in some new and different regional union. The disintegration of the former U.S.S.R. and the lack of success of the CIS will likely lead to new conflicts and instability.

The former republics will develop into independent participants in international relations and will establish their own bilateral and multilateral relations with other independent states. At first glance this situation brings new problems to the international community. But there are two important advantages: first, the situation in the former U.S.S.R. becomes clearer, and this clarity gives hope for future stability; second, the United Nations and the international community can increase their roles in regulating national conflicts between the former Soviet republics when such conflicts stop being domestic ones and turn into international ones.

For Russia, this situation is very important for several reasons. First, Russia would like to avoid a repetition of the U.S.S.R.'s disintegration within the Russian federal republic, which includes some autonomous republics striving for their own independence, like Chechen-Ingush. Second, Russia desires to develop discreet relations with new states and to establish Russia as the successor to the international rights and obligations of the former U.S.S.R. Third, Russia wants to try to adjust economic reforms to a national conflicts situation solved with the assistance of the international community. Fourth, Russia considers it important to take a hard policy toward those republics whose military and political ambitions become too dangerous for the East European and Asian situations.

The Yugoslavian problem is very different from the Russian situation. There cannot be a successor to the role of the former federation in the face of one of the republics. It also makes more difficult the task of regulating relations between the new Yugoslavian states and the international community. And the European community may be ready to invest some money in the stabilization of a region which is geographically close to the center of Europe and where political and economic compromises are possible. (One investment could be the creation of a "Fund for the Restoration of Yugoslavia," using part of the debt owed by the former Yugoslavia to the European Community.)

CONCLUSION: LESSONS FOR ASIA

Comparison of the Soviet and Yugoslavian approaches to sovereignization helps one to see some common points. (These points can also be applied to Asian socialist states that, like China or Vietnam, are also facing the problem of preserving the unity of their respective countries.)

1. An administrative system of production and distribution of national income was a basis of the unity of the former U.S.S.R. and of Yugoslavia. Starting with perestroika, the deconstruction of the administrative command system led to a disintegration of the unions irrespective of whether it was totalitarian (U.S.S.R.) or self-governing (Yugoslavia).

2. It is impossible to prevent disintegration with citizen appeals, political negotiations, or military force.

3. Ambitious nationalistic leaders try to use disintegration and ideas of

independence in their power struggle, involving many ordinary people, speculating on their national feelings, and sometimes pushing these people to sacrifice their lives for nationalistic ideals.

4. Disintegration leads to regional and global political destabilization.

5. Western countries and the international community failed to create a mechanism of constructive influence on internal conflicts, but their neutral position can undoubtedly be considered an effective one. Yet, after the judicial disintegration of the U.S.S.R., national conflicts stopped being an internal concern of Moscow leaders and became international ones, opening the doors for the interference of the United Nations and the international community.

The lessons for Asia are several. First, the internal political situation and socialist administrative systems in China and Vietnam are similar to the U.S.S.R and Yugoslavia. Second, the collapse of socialism in China, Vietnam, and North Korea can lead to disintegration of these states, to the growth of nationalism, and to the appearance at the political stage of new ambitious nationalistic leaders. Third, the preservation of socialist regimes in China, Vietnam, and North Korea could provide some kind of regional stability, though there are serious impediments in the way of the creation of a market economy throughout Asia. At the same time, the international and Asian communities are not yet ready to react positively to the collapse of Asian socialism. It may be reasonable from the security point of view to foster such political processes in Asian socialist countries that could lead to a deconstruction of Asian socialism. Will it not have very difficult consequences for which other countries may not yet be ready? Fourth, democratic and market-economy countries should do their best to have a positive influence on Asian socialism. Here, there is a need both for a good system of coordination and cooperation of activities in relations with the remaining Asian socialist countries, and for the creation of a working mechanism to eliminate the negative consequences of possible disintegration of Asian socialist countries. During the process of sovereignization, many Muslim republics of the former U.S.S.R. can follow the old socialist line under nationalistic banners. Kazakhstan, for example, is discussing variants of making up some kind of new regional union, including Mongolia, North West China, and the Burjat territories of Russia. And if Nursultan Abishevich Nazarbaev's regime (in Kazakhstan) succeeds eco-nomically, its political ambitions can only grow.

Finally, it is important to stress a rather "questionable" thesis: a conservative or even a stagnation stability in socialist Asia is more favorable to regional stability than the new examples of collapse of socialism, at least until civilized nations create an efficient system of reaction to all kinds of unrest and instability in former or remaining socialist states.

PART III

GOVERNMENT POWER AND ACCOUNTABILITY

When the United States Constitution was written over two hundred years ago, its founders recognized the importance of the separation of powers among the various branches and levels of government. The lines of separation, however, are not always clearly defined by the Constitution, and conflicts arise over the proper allocation of power. Part III examines the various conflicts that arise in the division of power in governmental structures of the United States and in the former U.S.S.R. The analysis in Part III also relates to any future economic or political integration of North America begun under the North American Free Trade Agreement (NAFTA) or the former U.S.S.R. states as attempted through the CIS.

The paper by Senior Judge Hans A. Linde discusses the development of the federal and state court systems in the United States. It first identifies three characteristics of the American judicial system that are more important than any others: the nature of litigation, differences in state and federal jurisdiction, and the selection and tenure of judges. The paper explains the primary role that the judiciary plays in the government and observes that, while judicial review of the constitutionality of laws is perhaps the most well-known feature of the judiciary, it is in actuality seldom used. Instead, most of the issues facing federal courts are constitutional questions that do not involve the judicial review of laws. Rather, courts spend the bulk of their time ensuring that constitutional procedures have been followed and that individual rights are safeguarded. The paper examines the historical and institutional foundations of judicial power and lists several factors that contribute both to the judicial heritage of the United States and to deference to a court's decision. The paper concludes by correctly asserting that the court is better suited to enforce the Constitution's negative guarantees against governmental abuse rather than to pursue affirmative social programs that might displace both the democratic decision-making process and the accountability of the legislature for budgeting public resources.

Martha A. Field's paper analyzes the role of the United States' dual-court system. It observes that the United States has a very-well-developed federal system that on the one hand provides an accessible forum for those issues that would best be heard in a federal court, but that often leads to jurisdictional confusion, inefficiency, and expense. The paper suggests that in a federal system perhaps only one level of courts might be needed unless overlapping jurisdiction is eliminated. The paper questions the appropriate extent of judicial activism (the extent to which a court should substitute its own policy judgments for those of Congress or the president) in interpreting the Constitution or statutes) by comparing two major areas in which the Supreme Court has utilized judicial activism: the protection of established economic interests during the 1930s, and the protection of individual rights during the 1960s–1980s. The paper concludes that limiting judicial activism by defining specifically both the judicial role and individual rights is possible but probably undesirable because it also limits adaptability to changing circumstances, which is needed for an enduring Constitution.

Catherine Thérèse Clarke's paper addresses the issue of constitutional interpretivism as it relates to the then new Russian Constitution, particularly in the area of criminal procedure. She expresses the concern that the criminal procedure provisions may be inadequate to protect individual rights. She fears that the vagueness of the provisions will encourage unabashed judicial activism, which will lead to the evisceration of the protections provided in the Constitution. This concern is engendered by what she sees as the role that judicial constitutional noninterpretivism played in diluting the search and seizure provisions of the U.S. Constitution, which now has 14 judicially created exceptions. The paper suggests that to avoid the danger of judicial activism and the eventual erosion of individual rights, more standards must be explicitly provided in the language of the Russian Constitution itself. The Constitution's foundation for the various criminal codes of the several republics will be strengthened if the protections given to individuals are made more explicit.

The paper authored by Yurii S. Shemshuchenko addresses the relationship between the president of Ukraine and the other branches of government. The paper concludes that the president's ultimate responsibility is to coordinate the activities of the differing authorities and to ensure that the balance between the branches of government is maintained.

Susan W. Tiefenbrun's article discusses U.S. state and local government involvement in the area of foreign affairs and the associated problem of a federal government speaking with "two voices" in foreign affairs. Although the Founding Fathers wanted uniformity to govern international affairs, the U.S. Constitution does not provide for a central foreign affairs power per se in the federal government. Although it is the consensus today that the federal government has the sole foreign affairs power, the paper observes that state governments continue to engage in foreign affairs activities without federal government objection (for example, state-imposed investment restrictions on U.S. companies abroad, sister city relationships, state trade missions, divestment or procurement legislation, Buy-American laws, and import quotas). The paper concludes that state involvement ought to be allowed as long as a state's action does not affect the federal government's ability to speak with one voice.

Marat A. Sarsembayev's commentary discusses the international law personality of Kazakhstan and the Central Asian republics, both prior to and immediately after the breakup of the Soviet Union. As members of the Soviet Union, the republics were formally recognized to be subjects of international law. In reality, however, the republics' international law personalities were subsumed into that of the Soviet Union, depriving the republics of the benefits that are supposed to accompany international recognition. The republics did not have any individual diplomats or embassies, and their ability to sign treaties and enter international organizations was virtually nonexistent. For example, the Soviet Union was a signatory to more than 15,000 treaties or agreements, while Kazakhstan and the Central Asian republics were collectively signatories to only 50 treaties until 1991. However, with the fall of communism and the collapse of the Soviet Union, the republics have finally been able to assert their international law personality. For example, Kazakhstan swiftly established diplomatic relations with more than 30 countries and entered into more than 60 treaties. Furthermore, Kirghizstan, Tajikistan, Turkmenistan, Uzbekistan, and Kazakhstan have all become members of the United Nations. The author applauds these results as being just the beginning of the republics' long and fruitful involvement in international relations.

The article by W. Gary Vause discusses the division of powers between the Russian Federation and the independent republics related to foreign trade and investment. In March 1992, 18 of the 20 republics of the Russian Federation signed the Federation Treaty. The treaty gave exclusive jurisdiction over foreign relations to the Russian Federation itself, while still recognizing the independence of the individual republics. The treaty's goal was to reverse the traditionally isolationist role that the Soviet Union has played in world economics and to liberalize economic relations between the new Russian Federation and the rest of the world by increasing international and foreign investment. However, the central-planning and protectionist vestiges of the old Soviet regime have left the new republics in poor economic health. The author suggests priorities for the republics: to join the General Agreement on Tariffs and Trade (GATT), to acquire advanced technology, to implement fiscal and monetary reforms, and to restructure the trade infrastructure within each state. To induce foreigners to invest in the Russian Federation, certain problem areas must be addressed: financing, quality control, labor and employment issues, intellectual property protection, dispute resolution, and a reduction in the bureaucratic framework. Lastly, privatization efforts must continue and improve before a large-scale foreign involvement will flow.

10

Judicial Power in the United States

Hans A. Linde

THE AMERICAN JUDICIARY

Federalism implies two levels of government independently empowered to make and administer laws on behalf of the same citizens within the same territory. An important aspect of federal systems is whether these laws also are applied by separate courts.

The system of courts in the United States is easy to describe, but its operation is complex and difficult in practice. When making comparisons, a simple institutional description of a society's courts can be seriously misleading without also considering for what functions the society relies on general laws rather than discretionary authority.

Like most developed economies, the American economy rests on transactions among private parties under general laws without direct participation or intervention by government officials. It relies on private pursuit of civil damages or other judicial remedies for harm suffered from violations of law, which are separate from official enforcement of criminal law and administrative regulations. Therefore, the main focus of the American legal profession is much more on civil law, including actual or potential litigation, than it is in less developed or substantially socialized economies.

Unlike many federal systems, however, the United States historically left to the states the basic criminal and civil laws governing property, contracts, noncontractual duties (torts, fiduciary duties, restitution), and family relations, as well as independent power to impose taxes and regulations. National regulatory laws and taxes assume the existence of basic state civil and criminal laws, even when Congress superimposes national regulation of labor relations, financial institutions, environmental standards, or civil rights.

Separate judicial systems in the 50 states, the District of Columbia, the Commonwealth of Puerto Rico, and in other territories administer the great bulk of the caseload. A single state like California has more judges trying vastly more cases than the entire federal judiciary. Fewer than one case in a thousand is tried in a federal court. The United States Constitution specified the existence and jurisdiction of a Supreme Court of the United States, but it left the establishment of lower federal courts to Congress. For most of the nineteenth century, the United States functioned with a modest number of federal judges deciding limited classes of cases.

After two centuries, the federal and state judicial systems have taken similar forms. Each relies on one or two layers of trial judges and, with a few exceptions, a general appellate court and a Supreme Court. (A few courts specialize in functions such as review of taxes, patents, or criminal appeals.) Three other characteristics are more important than this bare table of organization. One is the shared assumptions about the nature of litigation. A second is the difference in state and federal jurisdiction apart from any difference in applicable law. The third is the selection and tenure of the judges.

Litigation

American courts and procedure are built on the model of jury trials, even though in practice these are now the small minority of cases. The model requires a sharp separation of issues of law from issues of fact, both at trial and on appeal. It presupposes presentation of witnesses and arguments by opposing lawyers, casting the judge primarily as a passive umpire who presides over the proceeding, rules on motions, and instructs jurors on the law, but does not attend the jury's deliberation. Elaborate rules govern what evidence may be admitted. In criminal cases, this adversary model allows for the plea bargains followed by negotiated guilty pleas, with no trial, that make American criminal caseloads possible. Because the jury model leaves little room for multijudge trials of the kind known in European courts, facts in nonjury trials are found by a single judge.

In most cases, appellate courts review only the issue of whether the trial judge made a significant legal error. If so, the case must be sent back to be tried over. Appellate courts do not take new evidence and are bound by facts found in the trial court, unless a finding is not supported by substantial evidence. The rules are less strict in equity cases and others that historically were never tried before juries; there, a trial judge often takes a more active role, and the appellate court may reach a contrary decision on the evidence. But appeals depend on a transcription or recording of what took place in the trial court, and they generally decide only issues argued by the parties' advocates.

Jurisdiction

In state courts, jurisdiction depends on whether a case has sufficient connection with persons or events in the state, and whether the defendant has been properly called to appear in the case. To enter the federal courts, which exist in every state, a case must qualify either by the characteristics of the legal issue—a "federal question" is one "arising under the Constitution or laws of the United States" as distinct from state laws—or by the characteristics of the parties, if the parties include the United States, or if they are citizens of different states or nations and their dispute concerns more than $50,000. Even the U. S. Supreme Court cannot review the many state court decisions that fall outside these criteria, and in practice the Supreme Court does not review federal cases based only on diversity of citizenship.

It is an error to assume that federal courts administer federal law and state courts administer state law, though this is true of criminal prosecutions. In principle, the substantive law in civil cases is the same whether a case is tried in a federal or a state court. State courts are bound by any federal law that applies to the case, and federal courts are bound to follow the decisions of the highest state court on issues of state law.

Nonetheless, the coexistence of federal and state courts allows complicated and time-consuming jurisdictional maneuvers to get a case into one's preferred court. Both sets of courts must cope with the decentralization of laws and regulations among more than 50 entities, inviting disputes over the law applicable to a case. The structure has great strengths in securing both local autonomy and national standards. But with an appellate process that cannot correct most trial court errors without a new trial, the American judicial system is the world's most complex and doubtless the most expensive. It is not the most suitable model to emulate in any but the richest federation.

The Judges

Most descriptions of the power and independence of American judges describe only the relatively small number of federal judges, who are appointed for life by the president with the consent of the Senate. The vastly more numerous state judges are appointed or elected for terms of various length under diverse systems in the separate states. Some are elected under party labels, more are elected in nonpartisan elections, many are initially pointed, but face periodic retention or rejection votes on an election ballot. Governors, like presidents, make most judicial appointments from members of their own political parties, but in most states political partisanship plays no further role. Popular election doubtless can inhibit some judges from making unpopular decisions, but it does not reduce their power or their independence in relation to the other branches of government. That independence has other sources.

An American trial judge has power in part because each judge acts alone and most appeals are limited to errors of law. In part, judges have power because state (but not federal) civil law rests on common law and state governments have little taste for systematic civil lawmaking. Most importantly, as in the English courts, trial judges generally come from extensive prior law practice in civil or criminal litigation. American legal education prepares students to represent clients, not to administer a bureaucracy. Judges appointed or elected from private law practice do not think of themselves as joining the government, and neither does the government. Young lawyers do not enter judicial service as a form of civil service career, as in many European models. They do not qualify by taking examinations. American government lacks ministries of justice, and judges cannot be temporarily assigned to prosecutorial or governmental tasks or reassigned to different courts. This is part of the constitutional separation between the branches that is common to the states and the United States. Rare exceptions like Justice Robert Jackson's acceptance of a role in prosecuting German war crimes and Chief Justice Earl Warren's in investigating the assassination of President Kennedy were criticized as a misuse of their judicial prestige.

Judges drawn from private practice come with no special allegiance to the government. Their experience, like their law school education, has been to protect private rights, often against government officials. Even if a judge's experience was in government, this shared professional orientation as much as any legal or ideological principles secures American judges' sense of independent responsibility.

THE JUDICIAL ROLE IN GOVERNMENT

The most famous feature of the American legal system is the power of courts to hold laws invalid under the state or federal constitutions. This, however, is the least frequent form of judicial control of official acts.

Courts every day are asked to enforce or to set aside administrative acts ranging from local occupational licenses, building permits, or employment decisions, to nationwide regulations of entire industries. These cases usually involve compliance with statutes and administrative procedures, and they are heard by the ordinary courts that hear civil and criminal cases, not in special administrative courts. Normally there is no need to question the statute's constitutional validity.

Second, courts routinely apply and enforce constitutional procedures that do not involve the validity of a law. The state and federal bills of rights specify many guarantees in criminal and civil cases that need no further legislation.

The most famous, and controversial, enforcement of these guarantees has been the rule, since the 1960s, that prosecutors cannot use evidence obtained by an unlawful search or seizure, or without proper warnings before taking a suspect's statements.

Third, federal statutes enacted in the 1870s, following the Civil War, as well as the constitutional writ of *habeas corpus*, provide judicial remedies when officials violate federal guarantees of individual rights. These three forms of review account for the great bulk of judicial control of official acts; only a small fraction concerns the validity of laws.

Judicial power to review statutes for constitutionality is no longer unique. In Europe it has been assigned to special constitutional courts. That model was originally designed to maintain constitutional government by adjudicating disputes directly between legislative and executive institutions (something American courts rarely do), and the model has been adapted to maintain individual rights and international obligations.

In contrast, every American court must consider a constitutional claim whenever necessary to decide a case before the court. The lowliest municipal court may have to decide whether a state statute or an act of Congress is unconstitutional, although such a decision is unlikely to be the final word.

For the first hundred years the U.S. Supreme Court used judicial review mainly as an instrument of federalism, setting aside the acts of states so as to protect the national market and private enterprise. State courts also reviewed state economic regulations under their state constitutions. Extensive use of judicial review to protect civil rights and liberties under the state and federal bills of rights began only in the 1930s.

As already mentioned, enforcement of constitutional rights in the law enforcement process rarely involves judicial review of laws. Courts themselves are responsible for following constitutional procedures of open courts and jury trials, upon specific charges, with rights to legal counsel, to call witnesses and to confront opposing witnesses, to refuse to testify against oneself, and due process generally. These guarantees of fair trials have been in the state and federal bills of rights for more than two centuries, before the growth of full-time police forces, and they have no exception for crimes against national security; indeed, there are special restraints on prosecutions for treason. But courts long were reluctant in criminal cases to review police abuses, such as unlawful arrests or detentions, interrogations, or searches and seizures.

American law enforcement is extremely decentralized even within each state, and most prosecutors are locally elected. This itself is a major safeguard against totalitarian government. But neither the courts nor prosecutors have direct supervision or disciplinary authority over the police. Ultimately the U.S. Supreme Court recognized that if law enforcement was to comply at least with those standards imposed on all states, persons accused of crimes must be able to resist noncompliance in defending their individual cases, even if this defeats some prosecutions.

ROOTS OF JUDICIAL POWER

Why do American courts, often a single judge, assume the power to confront prosecutors, police officials, and legislative and political leaders with confidence that a court's order will be obeyed? This was not always so; Chief Justice Roger Taney had no such confidence in confronting an order of President Abraham Lincoln. But a president in office a century later could not doubt the obligation to enforce a court's desegregation order against a resisting state governor, even when the president disliked the order.

Some institutional reasons have already been mentioned. Governments in the United States cannot dismiss and replace judges, as sometimes happens elsewhere, nor can they reduce their salaries. The courts, not the executive branch, prepare and submit the courts' budgets. Thus judges are protected against retribution by other officials, though not against angry voters in states where judges need to be reelected. And judges may punish noncomplying persons for contempt of court, even if they are officials.

Reciting legal rules, however, does not explain why a judge's orders are followed. The courts' power has deep historical, cultural, and political roots. Individuals and whole communities may long resist change in customs like racial segregation or school prayer. But for officials., especially the highest officials, defiance of a court order today would carry an unacceptable political price.

Judicial Prestige

The singular position of common law judges goes back three centuries and more. Many judges then and now are considered worthy of full biographies, and the most famous names have entered the English and American cultural traditions. The high judges of the royal courts dealt with other political leaders as equals because they knew them as equals, a role later illustrated on the U.S. Supreme Court by such chief justices as Taney (a former attorney general and secretary of the Treasury), Charles Evans Hughes (governor of New York, secretary of state, and presidential nominee), and William Howard Taft (a former president). Sir Edward Coke had been a ferocious attorney general for Queen Elizabeth; to find a Russian analogue to Chief Justice Coke's later death-defying defense of the common law courts against James I, one might imagine Andrei Vishinsky as a judge turning against Leonid Brezhnev. Less dramatically, Lord Mansfield, not Parliament, created much of commercial law, and common law judges like Oliver Wendell Holmes, Jr., of Massachusetts and Benjamin N. Cardozo of New York (before they became federal justices) are the patron saints of American jurisprudence.

Paradoxical as it may seem to some, the strength of American courts also rests on the common law tradition of signed opinions rather than one anonymous, ostensibly unanimous opinion for the court, and on each judge's right to publish a concurring or dissenting position. Issues of great, often constitutional, importance are publicly debated in deciding specific cases. The courts could hardly attract former senators, governors, legislators, attorneys general, and law professors without the freedom to explain views that a majority opinion has not adopted. Although judges had higher visibility when there were only a few of them, today's numerous and less-known judges still inherit some of their predecessor's public stature.

Professional Expectations

The judges' independence and confidence in their authority are bred in the preparation and experience of the American legal profession. A developed economy depends on independent, impartial, professional courts, and these in turn demand mutual confidence in the honesty, integrity, and knowledge of judges and lawyers. This is not a special American virtue; in the heterogeneous American court system, some participants fall short of norms maintained in other developed judiciaries. Judicial elections do not always produce the best qualified judges, and they create a need to win campaign support and financial contributors. But any direct communication with a judge about a pending case or particular issue from the government, a political organization, or any other party outside the prescribed judicial procedures is unlawful. The judge would be obliged to report such a communication and might also be disqualified from continuing with the case.

Other facts support the independent power of courts. American law students are trained with a view of representing clients, sometimes public but mostly private. They expect both to deal with and to fight officials. American lawyers are educated to see every question in an adversarial, dialectic context of arguments and counterarguments, particularly against government agencies, to the point where they find it hard to think of law divorced from judicial opinions. Legislative institutions, in contrast, are comparatively weak. Professional bar associations maintain relationships with the courts, and many lawyers are active in local governments and nonprofit organizations. Judges drawn from private practice, in turn, think of the advocates who appear before them as their former colleagues, and vice versa. Moreover, the private economy pays well for legal services at the level of competence that it also needs on its courts, particularly on the federal courts. This assures judges of a comfortable salary, not as high as in a good private practice, but better than other public officials.

Courts and Policy

One effect of strong courts is that all kinds of policy disputes, particularly about civil liability, are taken to court before the losing side turns to legislators for change. The last 30 years have left many Americans with the impression that courts can deal with all injustices and harmful policies by common law (as in the expansion of tort in product liability, employment, and noneconomic injuries) or in the name of the Constitution. But despite their independence, courts rarely stray far from the dominant beliefs of their times and places, not because they fear retribution from government, but because most share these beliefs. After the Supreme Court's constitutional breakthroughs during Chief Justice Warren's era in matters of race, religion, sex, and criminal procedure, most cases on the rights of women and minorities in employment and public services now apply statutes passed by Congress and state legislatures, not the Constitution.

Courts are better suited to enforce the constitutions' negative guarantees against governmental abuse than to secure the many affirmative social programs that are promised in constitutions of other nations (and some American states) and that require spending and other positive actions by governments. Beyond policing unconstitutional inequality in such programs, judges are reluctant to displace democratic decisions and accountability for budgeting public resources. Yet if such constitutional promises are unenforceable, law-conscious Americans do not see them as real "rights." In the American tradition, the ideas that constitutional provisions are rights against government and these rights are enforceable by independent courts go hand in hand.

11

The Role of the Courts in the Federal System of the United States

Martha A. Field

It is a great honor to participate in this distinguished Conference. My assignment is to discuss the role of courts in the U.S. political system. I will not draw many comparative analogies with the systems of the sovereign states of the former Soviet Union, but I will discuss features about the role courts have played here that would seem relevant to other nations or confederations embarked upon developing a federal system.

The first and foremost role of the national courts in our federal system is to interpret and enforce national law. The federal judiciary, headed by the United States Supreme Court, is the branch that makes federal law supreme, enforcing it against states and adjudicating when state laws are in violation of federal constitutional or statutory law. The federal judiciary has played this role rather successfully over the course of our history, even though it has aptly been called "the least dangerous branch," having neither military nor monetary resources of its own. Its success has been made possible by acquiescence and sometimes active cooperation of the executive and legislative branches of government.[1]

Our national courts pass on the meaning of national law but do not review what *state* law means. They decide whether state law is *permissible* under the federal Constitution, but as long as it is within constitutional limits, the state and its courts have the last word on interpretation of state law. To us this system seems almost axiomatic—almost inherent to federalism. But it is worth noting that it is not a universal feature of federalism. In Canada's federal system, provincial law is much less clearly separated from national law and its meaning is subject to review by the Supreme Court of Canada.

The separateness of state law in this country has another consequence that is of particular relevance today. States cannot have laws that contradict federal law or the federal Constitution, but they are permitted to create bodies of state statutory or constitutional law that protect rights *more* broadly than the U.S. Constitution does. Our commentator Judge Hans Linde has been a leader in this movement for state courts to use state constitutions more actively to create independent, supplementary bodies of state constitutional law, and this is a much more important part of our constitutional jurisprudence today than it was 25 years ago.

The comparison with Canada raises another question about our system: Is it really worthwhile to have two fully developed court systems—state and federal—as we do? Our Constitution requires the establishment of a Supreme Court, which reviews cases coming to it from both state and federal courts. The Constitution allows but does not require Congress to establish lower federal courts, but Congress always has relied upon lower federal courts with broad categories of jurisdiction. Much of their jurisdiction is concurrent with the state courts, and the parties then have the right to select the forum—or one of the parties does.

In comparison with the United States, Canada has a much less developed federal court system. One result is many fewer jurisdictional complications. In the United States, well-developed federal court systems are important to the enforcement of federal supremacy. There is more litigation than one Supreme Court can handle; if there is to be federal input in cases the Supreme Court does not hear, and if there is to be federal court input on factual findings, which are so often crucial to the determination of important issues, then there must be lower federal courts.[2] And the federal court judiciary has consistently been a respected and distinguished group of jurists in our history.

There is also reason to support the well-developed state court systems that we have in every state. It is one important part of the autonomy that remains with states and that makes them significant units of government, as the Constitution requires.[3]

But for all its advantages,[4] the dual system has its costs. The relationship between state and federal jurisdiction is extremely confusing. Very complicated doctrines have grown up about which court should go forward and which should hold back. Sometimes both systems adjudicate a dispute, and the issue becomes whose judgment counts. Sometimes instead, years are spent determining which is the proper forum to proceed, during which time *neither* hears the case. Indeed, the jurisdictional doctrines are sometimes even used for the purpose of delay by litigants and even by courts avoiding troublesome decisions. Needless to say, such a system is expensive and inefficient. These costs are sufficiently serious that another country starting out could well conclude it would be preferable either to rely on courts only on one level or else to demarcate relatively clear lines between the two levels of courts and eliminate overlapping jurisdiction. In the United States, federal supremacy and judicial supremacy have been intertwined. Our Constitution (unlike the Constitution of the new Russian Federation) does not explicitly provide for judicial supremacy, but it was established early in our history in the famous decision in *Marbury v. Madison*.[5] The judiciary does not always exercise this power of review in the same fashion, however.

One of the most difficult questions for our system is the appropriate extent of judicial activism, the extent to which courts should generously construe our Constitution even though that entails enforcing their own views over those of state judges and legislators and over coordinate branches of government. This issue has long been at the center of our constitutional debate and is one on which the courts have differed radically over the years. It is also an issue on which our Supreme Court today may be in the course of changing its stance.

On one level, all agree that the judiciary should not intervene whenever a court has a policy disagreement with state or federal legislatures. Even the Supreme Court is not the arbiter of appropriate policy. Congress and state legislatures adjudicate government policy; they are the branch representatives of and responsive to the people. Their notions of policy are to govern, not those of nine appointed, tenured, and usually aged justices.

But how can the justices enforce the Constitution and still stay away from their notions of policy—still defer to the legislative judgment? That is the dilemma. Indeed, the same dilemma seems to lurk at least as a possibility in the proposed Russian Federation Constitution, because it both recognizes judicial supremacy and guarantees substantial rights to the people.

Our courts seem to be resolving the dilemma by sorting out subject matter areas along a spectrum ranging from those in which deference to the legislature is appropriate within very broad limits, to those in which much less deference to legislative majorities applies. There are some subjects on which the judiciary is sometimes accused of abdicating its role as supreme decision maker.[6] On occasion, the Supreme Court has ruled that some other decision maker is appropriate concerning a particular issue or set of issues. Some issues are best decided by another branch of government. Some issues are best left to individuals with no government regulation or control.

As an example of the former kind of issue—that the Court has decided is committed to another branch of government—the Supreme Court has adopted the position that issues concerning the federal-state balance are better left to Congress. The most persuasive advocate of this position is our commentator Dean Choper.[7] This type of analysis arises in cases where states complain that Congress has trespassed upon their powers—cases we might refer to as Tenth Amendment cases. State interests are represented in Congress.[8] It is better for them to work out the balance than to have close judicial supervision.

Perhaps this arguable abdication to Congress is partly related to political question concerns—to a fear that courts may not be listened to if they readily insert themselves in the tugs of war between other arms of government. The Court has sometimes responded in such a pragmatic fashion. For one example, during the Vietnam conflict, it had several opportunities to pass upon its legality as an undeclared war. It and most lower courts declined to decide the question, calling it a political question, even though young men who were being made to fight in the war against their will had challenged the war's legality in what might be seen as classic individual rights litigation.

But in the cases involving the distribution of legislative powers between federal and state governments, the Court has not acted primarily out of avoidance but has relied upon affirmative reasons that Congress is the more appropriate decision maker. Its basic position is that Congress can and will reach a satisfactory balance and that politics is at least a good way of deciding the appropriate balance as judicial reasoning would be. The judiciary seems thereby to give up a piece of its supremacy, but *it* is the body that decides what and when, and it also retains power to change its mind.

Moreover, current doctrine does not totally eliminate judicial oversight, even though allocation of subjects for federal and state lawmaking is primarily for Congress. Courts will still intervene if needed to protect the existence of states as significant units of government, to prevent the obliteration of states, and to protect the essentials of a federal system. But as long as there are two significant levels of government, the *courts* will not interfere to decide which subjects must be left to states as opposed to the national government. That decision is for Congress.

The areas where the Court has deferred and the areas where the Court has exercised substantial protection of private interests against legislatures have both changed over time. For example, the Court has sometimes recognized the Tenth Amendment as protecting some areas of lawmaking from invasion by the national government.[9] Moreover, since the early 1960s, we have been experiencing an era of judicial activism on behalf of individual rights. The "right to privacy" branch of that development began a quarter century ago with *Griswold v. Connecticut*.[10] There the Court held that married persons were permitted to make their own decisions about birth control and that a Connecticut statute criminalizing their use of birth control was unconstitutional. It so ruled even though no wording of the Constitution appeared to address this issue. Accordingly, the Court was hard pressed to explain why its holding was not usurpation of a legislative judgment. It was sensitive to the issue because judges interposing their own values had received a bad name during the first three and a half decades of this century. During that era, our courts had used guarantees like due process and equal protection[11] to protect liberty of contract against government encroachment. Courts had used that notion to invalidate government regulation of maximum hours and minimum wages and other matters clearly recognized today as appropriate subjects of legislation.

The Court's interference with social and economic reform made it very unpopular during this period. It changed its tune in 1937 after President Franklin Roosevelt's threat to pack the Court with more progressive justices.[12] But this era of judicial activism on behalf of established economic interests

—known as the *Lochner* era for one of its more notorious cases[13]—had discredited judicial activism and broad readings of the vague language of the Fourteenth Amendment's due process and equal protection clauses.

Nonetheless, in *Griswold v. Connecticut*, the Supreme Court launched an era of recognizing areas of individual decision-making in which states should not interfere. *Griswold* opened the door with an extremely uncontroversial subject—the use of contraception by married couples. But the right of privacy it recognized became more controversial as extended to single people and to subjects that are themselves controversial, like abortion. Despite the strong disagreement over many of these subjects today, there is much more consensus that there are core situations in which this right of individual decision-making—sometimes called the right of privacy—does apply. Examples might be the right to marry, to marry a person of one's own choosing, to practice birth control, to refuse unwanted medical treatment, to have children, or to choose one's living companions. This right of privacy also includes some other questions concerning lifestyle that cannot be dictated by government even though they are not listed in the Constitution.

In recognizing such areas, the Court in *Griswold* was hard pressed, and has been since, to explain how its new judicial activism—on behalf of individual decision making and later on behalf of equality[14]—was any different from the discredited activism on behalf of economic interests that *Lochner* had stood for. It has adopted the explanation, first, that certain protected freedoms never were intended to be subject to majority will and also that there exists particular need for judicial protection of "discrete and insular minorities"—groups historically discriminated against and not represented in the political process, so that it falls to the judiciary, enforcing the Constitution's guarantees of autonomy and equality, to protect their rights.

If there is a justification for the judicial activism of the 1960s–80s but not that of the *Lochner* period, it lies in this dichotomy between economic and individual rights, although the line is sometimes a difficult one to draw.[15] It lies in the greater ability of legislators to protect the one rather than the other. (It is the same concept of representation in the political process that serves to allocate the appropriate decision-making here that was used to reinforce *congressional* decision-making in the federal-state balance or Tenth Amendment cases.) But the question now on the agenda in American constitutional law is whether the two categories—economic and individual rights—*are* to be treated differently or whether instead judicial scrutiny on behalf of individual rights will go the same way as *Lochner* did. The current (mid-1990s) Supreme Court is fast retreating from the protection of individual decision making under the rubric of "right to privacy," and from a strict view of the Constitution's equality guarantees.[16] Will the period of individual rights—represented primarily by the Warren and Burger Courts of the mid-1950s to 1980s—come to be seen as much of an aberration as the *Lochner* era that preceded it? Will both be deemed to represent judicial arrogation of legislative choices—judicial overreading of federal constitutional guarantees?

Some of us hope that the distinction between individual economic protections will continue to be recognized and that the judicial protection of individual privacy and equality rights will continue. But whether it will is in some doubt. And the resolution depends upon decisions to be made by the U.S. Supreme Court, some of which may occur soon.

These questions of the degree of judicial activism to some extent are inherent in any system with judicial supremacy. They may be reduced somewhat but not eliminated by greater specificity in defining both the judicial role and the scope of rights. Canada, for example, learned from the U.S. experience in this respect. Provisions in the Canadian Constitution specifically address and answer several difficult issues that have arisen under our equal protection clause and that would be implicated in the equality guarantees Canada adopted—issues concerning the meaning of discrimination, affirmative action, de facto discrimination, and gender discrimination, for example. One impetus may have been disagreement with the conclusions our courts had reached, for the approaches Canada adopted differ considerably from our judge-made rules. Similarly, the proposed Constitution of the new Russian Federation is far more specific in enumerating citizens' rights than the U.S. Constitution is.

But, of course, a constitution cannot be too specific and neither of those documents is. With greater specificity, a constitution could ameliorate problems of judicial activism perhaps, but with great specificity, it would also lose that constitution's ability to adapt as well as to direct. And the ability to adapt—which we in the United States accomplish largely through the discretion of the federal judiciary—is one requirement for an enduring constitution.

NOTES

1. The power of the courts is only to say what the law is. James Madison was fearful, at the time of the Constitution's framing, that this system would prove too weak to assure national supremacy over state and regional loyalty and sought instead a national veto on all state laws, but dual lawmaking and dual court systems carried the day. See letter from James Madison to George Washington (Apr. 16, 1787), in 9 *Papers of Madison* at 383–84 (Robert Rutland et al., eds., 1962); letter from James Madison to Thomas Jefferson (Oct. 24, 1787), in 10 *Papers of Madison* at 109–14 (Robert Rutland, et al., eds., 1962); Charles F. Hobson, "The Negative on State Laws: James Madison, the Constitution, and the Crisis of Republican Government," 3 *William & Mary Quarterly* 215 (1979); and Jack N. Rakove, "The Madisonian Moment," 55 *University of Chicago Law Review* 473 (1988). The U.S. Supreme Court's oversight contributes *both* to uniformity of interpretation of national norms and to their enforcement over

conflicting state laws.

2. The Supreme Court renders decisions after argument in approximately 140 cases per year: 120 in 1990, 139 in 1989, 143 in 1988, 142 in 1987. "The Supreme Court: 1990 Term: Leading Cases: IV. The Statistics," 105 *Harvard Law Review* 419 (1991); "The Supreme Court: 1989 Term: Leading Cases: IV. The Statistics," 104 *Harvard Law Review* 129, 359 (1989); "The Supreme Court: 1988 Term: Leading Cases: IV. The Statistics," 103 *Harvard Law Review* 137, 394 (1988); "The Supreme Court: 1987 Term: Leading Cases: IV. The Statistics," 102 *Harvard Law Review* 143, 350 (1988).

3. *Garcia v. San Antonio Metro. Transit Auth.* 469 U.S. 528, 548, 556 (1985) (quoting *New York v. United States*, 329 U.S. 572, 583 (1946); Martha A. Field, "*Garcia v. San Antonio Metropolitan Transit Authority*: The Demise of a Misguided Doctrine," 99 *Harvard Law Review* 84, 110–14 (1985).

4. See, e.g., Robert M. Cover, "The Uses of Jurisdictional Redundancy: Interests in Ideology, and Innovation," 22 *William & Mary Law Review* 639 (1981).

5. 5 U.S. 137 (1803).

6. William Van Alstyne, "The Second Death of Federalism," 83 *Michigan Law Review* 1709 (1985).

7. See Dean Choper, "The Scope of National Power Vis-a-Vis the States: The Dispensability of Judicial Review," 86 *Yale Law Journal* 1552, 1561–65 (1977).

8. For a critique of this approach, see Field, *supra* note 3, at 106–10.

9. See, e.g., *Willson v. Black Bird Creek Marsh Co.*, 27 U.S. 245 (1829) and *Child Labor Tax Case*, 259 U.S. 20 (1922). Compare *Tarble's Case*, 80 U.S. 397 (1871) (apparently recognizing separate sphere for federal and state government authority).

10. 381 U.S. 479 (1965). The equal protection branch began eleven years earlier in *Brown v. Board of Education* (Brown I), 347 U.S. 483 (1954).

11. It also prohibited some state legislation under the contracts clause, and limited federal legislation by restrictive definitions of the commerce power. See, e.g., *Morehead v. New York ex rel. Tipaldo*, 289 U.S. 587 (1936) (holding that New York minimum wage statute for women was invalid); and *Hammer v. Dagenhart*, 247 U.S. 251 (1918) (invalidating congressional child labor statute).

12. William Lasser, *The Limits of Judicial Power: The Supreme Court in American Politics* (1988).

13. 198 U.S. 45 (1905).

14. The case that opened the era of strict equal protection is *Brown v. Board of Education*, decided 11 years before *Griswold*. But it was not until after substantive due process had started to develop that the breadth of the new equal protection became clear when strict equal protection analysis was applied to a wide range of subjects, even those having nothing to do with race. See, e.g., *Eisenstadt v. Baird*, 405 U.S. 438 (1972) (statute prohibiting distribution of contraceptives to unmarried persons); *Craig v. Boren*, 429 U.S. 190 (1976) (gender differential in statute governing sale of alcohol); and *Caban v. Mohammed*, 441 U.S. 390 (1979) (gender-based distinction in adoption statute).

15. For example, is an ordinance denying the right to run a laundry on the basis of race or ethnicity a violation of economic rights or individual rights, or both? See *Yick Wo v. Hopkins*, 118 U.S. 356 (1886).

16. See, for example, *Michael H. v. Gerald D.*, 499 U.S. 984, 111 S.Ct. 1645 (1991) (reduction of equal protection scrutiny); *Cruzan v. Director, Missouri Dept. of Health*,

497 U.S. 261, 110 S.Ct. 2841 (1990) (Scalia, J., concurring) (questioning applicability of substantive due process in contrast to its recognition by the other justices); and *Webster v. Reproductive Health Servs.*, 492 U.S. 480 (1989) (limiting scope of substantive due process).

12

Constitutional Interpretivism and Criminal Procedure in the Russian Federation Constitution

Catherine Thérèse Clarke

The Russian Constitutional Commission, headed officially by President Boris Yeltsin and directed by First Secretary Oleg G. Rumyantsev, is the official entity charged with drafting a new constitution that will establish a new federal government for the former U.S.S.R. The newly drafted Russian Federation Constitution, if ratified,[1] will change history and the lives of over 147 million people.[2] One of the framers described the importance of the federation's new Constitution:

> [t]he four previous Soviet Constitutions were not a foundation for rule of law. They were ideological texts. Our [new] constitution is intended as a civil contract among individuals. Each constitutional phrase has to be a stable basis for laws, for protection of the individual. And that, for all their pretty words, was never in our Soviet constitutions.[3]

The Russian Federation draft Constitution reflects a substantial effort to provide more than "pretty words." The drafters intend for the Constitution to build a strong and profound reformation of the rule of law that will protect individual liberties and redefine federalism in the Russian Federation. Once a constitution is adopted, those charged with the momentous job of interpreting and applying the constitutional mandates may benefit from considering other countries' constitutional experiences. Perhaps the U.S. Constitutional experience will also be instructive. While the Constitutional Court will interpret the new constitutional language, it is critical that the various republics, krays, oblasts, and okrugs participate in the structuring of the new government and, at the same time, establish their own constitutional foundations.

One area of the law that exemplifies the constant struggle to interpret the express words of the U.S. Constitution is that of the Fourth Amendment.[4]

There are three reasons why the Fourth Amendment experience can be instructive to other countries engaged in the process of constitution drafting and subsequent judicial interpretation. First, this area is of universal importance for individuals because it concerns the safety and privacy in one's home, belongings, and physical person. Second, a pivotal element of a truly free society, regardless of cultural or religious barriers, is the right to be free from unreasonable governmental searches and seizures. Third, it is an area where the duality of judicial concerns is obvious: the duty to support law enforcement efforts versus the obligation to protect individual rights. Consequently, the unique American constitutional obfuscations in the Fourth Amendment area may serve as friendly guideposts to assist judges, lawyers, and government institutions charged with enforcing the new constitutional rule of law in the Russian Federation and associated republics.[5] Moreover, the U.S. Fourth Amendment search and seizure jurisprudence best exemplifies the U.S. Supreme Court's perpetual effort to interpret express constitutional language in light of twentieth-century problems.

This chapter begins with an overview of the federalist structure within the Russian Federation Constitutional Commission's proposed Constitution, with emphasis on the role of the judiciary. A general discussion of the scholarly debate over judicial methods of U.S. constitutional interpretivism follows. Next, the paper will narrow its focus by drawing a comparison between the current judicial interpretation of the U.S. Fourth Amendment and select provisions of the Commission's proposed Constitution. Several U.S. scholars claim that the Fourth Amendment has been eviscerated due to judges' narrowing interpretations of constitutional liberties, perhaps attributable to escalating crime rates and perceived ineffectiveness of law enforcement efforts.[6] The paper suggests that the express constitutional language in the Russian Federation proposed draft may be more narrowly defined to increase the burden upon the government agents in justifying their search and seizure activities rather than placing the burden on the individual appearing in a court of law. The paper concludes that the Republics (member states, krays, oblasts, or okrugs) within the federal system adopt separate constitutions that extend the Federation's constitutional protections depending on the unique geographic, religious, racial, and cultural concerns. Both the U.S. and Russian Federation constitutional provisions aim to protect individual rights against unlawful searches and seizures in a federalist system. Although some U.S. constitutional jurisprudence in this area has become "mired in confusion and contradiction,"[7] this background may serve to elucidate the future rule of law in Russia, particularly because for both countries "[t]he life of the law has not been logic: it has been experience."[8]

FEDERALISM AND GOVERNING STRUCTURES IN THE PROPOSED RUSSIAN FEDERATION CONSTITUTION

The proposed Russian Federation document resembles the U.S. Constitution in that it establishes democratic institutions such as private ownership, a market economy, and social, economic, and cultural rights.[9] The proposed Constitution, however, enumerates the rights of citizens in greater detail than the U.S. Constitution. For example, it contains provisions for the right to work,[10] the right to safe working conditions,[11] the right to free medical services,[12] and the right to a free education.[13]

The draft reflects contemporary societal concerns, such as the affirmative obligation placed on citizens to protect the environment;[14] and historical concerns, such as the provision that provides equal protection for ex-convicts.[15] The proposed draft is more progressive than the U.S. Constitution in that it expressly extends equal rights to both men and women.[16]

Arguably, the most significant provisions within the proposed Constitution are those relating to the federal government structure and the separation of powers.[17] The draft resembles the U.S. constitutional structure by establishing a presidency[18] and a two-house legislature.[19] The Parliament, which includes both houses similar to the U.S. Congress, is responsible for promulgating "laws on the affairs pertaining to the powers of the Federation."[20] More important, the interpretation of these laws and the new Constitution has been allocated to independent courts with the power of judicial review to strike down unconstitutional laws.[21]

The Russian Federation consists of national and regional state entities that have equal constitutional and legal rights within the republic's lands and federal territories.[22] The federal government has exclusive jurisdiction over such areas as foreign policy, natural resources, armed forces, currency, and citizenship.[23] Plenary powers, however, have been mandated for provincial and local governments for national and regional areas of regulation outside of the scope of federal jurisdiction.[24] Both governments have concurrent authority over the areas of environmental protection, sciences, health services, human rights, labor, and civil and criminal law and procedure.[25] In addition to the Russian Federation Constitution, it is expected that each republic will promulgate separate constitutions to recognize the independent status of each republic or member state, validate the integrity of the federal system, establish independence in the sphere of the reserved powers, and promote human rights.

More important, the judicial system in the Constitutional Commission's proposed draft will consist of the Supreme Court of the Russian Federation, the Constitutional Court, federal courts, republican courts, and the federal territory and local courts.[26] The Constitutional Court has been expressly authorized to protect the constitutional structure,[27] to decide constitutionality of laws or edicts of the president, to decide constitutional law disputes between the

Russian Federation and the republics, and, among other express powers, to issue conclusions on cases in which the Russian Federation president is accused of violating the constitution or the laws.[28] The judiciary system is primarily responsible for enforcing constitutional protections, particularly in the area of criminal procedure.

General criminal procedure protections are expressly stated throughout the Commission's draft Constitution. The criminal codes of the various republics cannot violate those fundamental constitutional rights and principles prescribed in the federal constitution.[29] Instead, the enumerated constitutional criminal procedure provisions in the proposed draft are the foundation upon which the other codified rights and responsibilities of the Republic Criminal Codes are based.[30] That the constitutional rights be stated unequivocally in the Russian Federation Constitution is imperative; and those charged with interpreting these provisions must do so cautiously to avoid the erosion that has occurred in parts of the U.S. Constitution.

CONSTITUTIONAL INTERPRETIVISM

The doctrinal debates on constitutional interpretation and the role of the judiciary are critical in American constitutional jurisprudence.[31] In American constitutional jurisprudence, few words carry such import as those in *Marbury v. Madison*[32] establishing the power of judicial review:

> It is emphatically the province and the duty of the judicial department to say what the law is. Those who apply the rule to particular cases, must of necessity expound and interpret that rule. If two laws conflict with each other, the courts must decide on the operation of each. So if a law be in opposition to the constitution; if both the law and the constitution apply to a particular case, so that the court must either decide that case conformably to the law, disregarding the constitution; or conformably to the constitution, disregarding the law; the court must determine which of these conflicting rules governs the case. This is of the very essence of judicial duty. If then, the courts are to regard the constitution, and *the constitution is superior to any ordinary act of the legislature, the constitution, and not such ordinary act, must govern the case to which they both apply.*[33]

Thus, in *Marbury*, the judiciary delegated to itself through a judicial opinion, the authority to interpret the U.S. Constitution. At the risk of serious oversimplification of complex constitutional theories of interpretation, it is fair to state that two general approaches have developed: (1) interpretivism and (2) noninterpretivism. Interpretivist judges confine themselves to enforcing norms that are expressly stated, or are obviously implicit, in the written Constitution.[34] There are other categories and subcategories of interpretivists, including originalists,[35] neorealists,[36] structuralists, strict textualists, and strict intentionalists, to name a few. Admittedly, almost all modes of constitutional decision making involve some form and degree of interpretation.[37] Noninterpretivist judges, in contrast, "go beyond that set of references and enforce norms that cannot be discovered within the four corners of the document."[38] The complications that have arisen in American constitutional jurisprudence include an ongoing debate about the role of the judiciary in interpreting the U.S. Constitution, and the propriety of judicial activism in creating the law of the land through appellate opinions, not legislative acts. As Robert Bork wrote:

> Whatever line-drawing must be done starts from a solid base, the guarantee of freedom of speech, of freedom from unreasonable searches and seizures, and the like. By contrast, the judge-created phrases specify no particular freedom, but merely assure us, in sonorous phrases, that they, the judges, will know what freedoms are required when the time comes.[39]

Legal scholars express prudential concerns that according to the separation of powers doctrine, judges should interpret the law, not make the law, which some argue is a constitutionally based mandate.[40] Individual liberties, particularly the right to privacy, have created the most fervent debate on the role of the American judiciary in constitutional interpretation. Depending on the political makeup of the courts, this judicial activism may limit protections rather than afford the intended protections to individuals.[41] Constitutional interpretivism changes with the conservative and liberal shifting of the Supreme Court. Particularly in the Warren Court era,[42] the U.S. Supreme Court was criticized for exercising unbridled judicial power.[43] The 1973 abortion decision of *Roe v. Wade*[44] is the "clearest example of noninterpretivist reasoning [in] four decades,"[45] and may represent the peak of the expansion of the U.S. Bill of Rights. Since 1973, the Court has taken an interpretivist approach in severely curtailing the holding of *Roe v. Wade* and, in the future, may adopt a strict interpretivist approach to overrule *Roe*.[46] These judicial undulations from an interpretivist to noninterpretivist approach within separate provisions reduce predictability in the court system, occasionally provoke hostility from the public, and force state or national legislative rejoinders.

THE ALLOCATION OF POWER FOR THE PROTECTION OF INDIVIDUAL LIBERTIES

Some respected American scholars advocate that it is not the judiciary's role in interpreting the U.S. Constitution to secure individual rights and liberties, but to focus instead on the federalist structure of government.[47] One constitutional scholar perceives a detrimental pattern in the United States by jurists and scholars to visualize constitutional values primarily in terms of individuals' rights and to undervalue judicial protection of principles that allocate decision-making responsibilities among governmental units. . . . To see the purposes of judicial review almost entirely in terms of securing individual rights is to invert the priorities of the framers and ultimately to trivialize the Constitution. The framers' political theory was immediately concerned with organization, not individuals.[48]

Other scholars maintain that the judiciary should protect their political power to preserve individual rights, and refrain from debates about governmental theory and judicial enforcement of structural values.[49]

Separating powers among the branches and creating strong state and national governments in a compatible federalist structure is a major concern of the Russian Federation.[50] Nevertheless, the protection of individual rights is the paramount concern of the Russian framers. For example, the Russian Constitution Article 1.3(1) states that the "supreme value is [the] human being, his/her life, his/her honor, dignity, and freedom, personal sanctity, natural and inalienable rights."[51] In addition, the proposed draft mandates that individuals may exercise their rights, and that the state is an instrument to preserve and protect these individual liberties.[52]

INDIVIDUAL LIBERTIES IN THE AREA OF CONSTITUTIONAL CRIMINAL PROCEDURE

The new Russian Constitution provides several articles that pertain to the protection of individual liberties. Specifically, the criminal procedure articles focus on individual liberties and away from structural organization, principles of power allocation, and theories of structural values.[53] The proposed Constitution includes important ideological proclamations concerning individual rights in the federation. The U.S. constitutional criminal procedure provisions and the role of U.S. courts is instructive to the future Russian Federation's ability to protect rights at the arrest, investigation, trial, and punishment stages of the judicial process.

The criminal procedure provisions in the new Russian Constitution delegate broad authority to the courts by stating that the rights shall be enforced "by law"[54] without further clarification.[55] It is striking that no article in this draft Constitution closely resembles the language of the Fourth Amendment of the U.S. Constitution.[56] Article 2.3.2 is the closest provision to the Fourth Amendment of the U.S. Constitution. It provides:

The Russian Federation prohibits interference with private and family life. Everybody has protection from arbitrary encroachment on personal and family life on the part of the state, society, and individuals. Personal correspondence, telephone conversations and other information must remain secret. Infringement on [a] person's honor and reputation is illegal. Collection, storage, and dissemination of the personal information without permission of the affected person are permitted only in cases defined by law and with certain procedural order. Secrets of correspondence, telephone conversations and telegraph messages are protected by law.[57]

Another article of the proposed Russian Federation Constitution reflects the warrant requirement for search and seizure of the U.S. Fourth Amendment; it states that the "[h]ome is sacred. Nobody[58] has the right to search [the] home against the will of its residents or to violate [the] sanctity of the dwelling. It may be done only in cases prescribed by law." Subsection two further states that "[t]he search warrant is issued upon the decision of [the] court." The vagueness of these provisions compared to the detail of the other articles of the Russian Constitution is noteworthy.[59]

These protections against unlawful searches and seizures are stated with even greater vagueness than the Fourth Amendment protections enumerated in the U.S. Constitution. By comparison, the Fourth Amendment of the U.S. Constitution establishes "[t]he right of the people to be secure in their persons, houses, papers, and effects, against unreasonable searches and seizures."[60] The major concern of the framers of the U.S. Constitution was to establish specific procedures[61] for the issuance of warrants[62] to avoid abuses that had occurred in England.[63] The framers of the Russian Constitution should analyze these provisions in light of the difficulties of interpretation and the impact of judicial activism that has occurred in American Fourth Amendment jurisprudence.

JUDICIAL INTERPRETATION AND THE EVISCERATED WARRANT REQUIREMENT OF THE FOURTH AMENDMENT OF THE U.S. CONSTITUTION

The danger of placing unbridled authority in the courts is a legitimate concern that has been documented in the jurisprudence on the warrant requirement of the Fourth Amendment in the U.S. Constitution. These once-cherished protections have been eviscerated[64] as the exceptions have swallowed the rule. Although the U.S. Supreme Court, in dicta, often acknowledges a preference for the police to secure warrants before a search and seizure, this is a rhetorical rather than a substantive protection.[65] Today, there are over 14 judicially created exceptions to the Fourth Amendment warrant requirement.[66] Because of the authority placed in the courts by the Fourth Amendment, the American judiciary has interpreted and confused those Fourth Amendment constitutional protections that once firmly established protections for individual privacy and liberties against unreasonable government intrusion.[67]

These same dangers exist in the proposed Russian Constitution. The new Russian Federation and the framers of the Constitution should be forewarned that total delegation of authority to the courts to issue warrants and protect individual liberties may result in unabashed judicial activism. In the Fourth Amendment area it is obvious that the U.S. Supreme Court has traditionally taken a noninterpretivist approach. When reviewing the constitutionality of a search and seizure, judges have adopted different approaches, but the norm is to consider whether the search and seizure is reasonable. As one scholar commented on the current approach of the Supreme Court: "Chief Justice Rehnquist . . . interprets *reasonableness as separate from the warrant requirement, and his view predominates the present majority. This view denies the essence of fourth amendment protections.*"[68]

In practice, the individual charged with a crime in the U.S. criminal courts carries an inordinately heavy burden, despite the alleged presumption of innocence. For example, warrantless arrests are the norm rather than the exception. At the subsequent motion to suppress hearing, the individual typically carries the unwieldy burden of establishing the unreasonableness of the police conduct, when the prosecutor need only show that the search and seizure fits (or even resembles) one of the 14 exceptions to the warrant requirement. Particularly in a time when crime permeates daily life in the United States, establishing that police conduct was "reasonable" under the Fourth Amendment is a facile task for any prosecutor.

THE NEW RUSSIAN FEDERATION CONSTITUTION SHOULD ESTABLISH EXPRESS CONSTITUTIONAL STANDARDS AND BURDENS OF PROOF TO BETTER PROTECT INDIVIDUAL RIGHTS

The broad language as it currently appears in the Russian Constitution leaves the right to be free from unreasonable searches and seizures subject to the shifting of an interpretivist or noninterpretivist judiciary. The danger is that in the area of the Fourth Amendment, the Supreme Court of the United States has used an essentially noninterpretivist construction of these explicit protections.[69] To avoid this erosion and protect against arbitrary and unreasonable searches and seizures, the Russian constitutional language could direct the courts in interpretation, and guide regional and local legislatures charged with drafting criminal codes. That is, more standards must be provided in the Articles of the proposed Russian Constitution. The constitutional standards must be stated unequivocally to provide a minimum foundation for constitutional protections and guidance by which the central, regional, and local legislatures will revise the criminal codes; after all, the Russian Constitution shall be the supreme law of the republic.[70] If the *Marbury v. Madison*[71] doctrine establishing the power of judicial review is ratified as it appears in Article 5.7.8 (allocating authority to the Constitutional court), then the Russian Constitution will be "superior to any ordinary act of the legislature."

One solution for dealing with search and seizures (and arrests)[72] would have the constitution state that searches and arrests pursuant to a *warrant* are presumptively reasonable and more important, that warrantless searches and seizures are "*presumptively unreasonable*."[73] "Law enforcement officers should be permitted to rebut this presumption only by the strongest showing of inability to obtain a warrant."[74] A judge will determine if this presumption has been rebutted on a case-by-case basis.[75] The standard for establishing that the warrantless search and seizure was reasonable should be by clear and convincing evidence. If the government meets this burden, then the defendant would be allowed to present evidence in a motion to suppress that the search was unreasonable in light of the circumstances. If the government has not overcome the burden of "presumptively unreasonable," then the court must exclude the evidence from the court pursuant to Article 2.6.2(6) because "[e]vidence obtained illegally has no legal effect."[76]

For example, a revised version of Article 2.3.4 of the Russian Constitution could be the following:

1. [The] home is sacred. Nobody has the right to search [a] home against the will of its residents or to violate [the] sanctity of the dwelling. It may be done only in cases prescribed by law.
2. The search warrant is issued upon the decision of the court.
3. Warrantless searches are presumptively unreasonable. The government may rebut this presumption by showing that the search and seizure was reasonable based upon clear and convincing evidence. The defendant shall then have an opportunity to establish its unreasonableness in view of the totality of the circumstances. The court shall determine on a case-by-case basis if the evidence is sufficient to rebut this presumption of unreasonableness.

This constitutional language will avoid the pitfalls and erosions of constitutional protections that have occurred in the past 20 years in American Fourth Amendment jurisprudence.

The presumptively unreasonable standard has several benefits:[77] it reinforces the preference for warrants (except in exigent circumstances); provides a bright-line for police, judges, prosecutors and the public; encourages law enforcement officials to secure warrants and obey the express constitutional mandates; encourages judicial intervention at the early stages of investigation; and emphasizes substance, based on the framers' intent, while it preserves constitutional procedure in searches and seizures.[78]

This approach does not further either the interpretivist or noninterpretivist approaches to judicial constitutional interpretation. It merely places the burden on the parties to prove their case, while at the same time reinforcing critical individual liberties. "While the nature of government intrusions may differ today, the need for protection against them remains essential."[79]

THE ROLE OF STATE AND REPUBLIC CONSTITUTIONS IN PROTECTING INDIVIDUAL RIGHTS IN A FEDERALIST SYSTEM

Another indispensable consideration for the drafters working to establish an effective constitutional structure is that of each republic's Constitution in relation to the Russian Federation's new Constitution. In the United States, each state has adopted a separate state constitution, which often resembles the federal Constitution. These state constitutions are portentous in terms of individual liberties. State courts are the final interpreters of state constitutions and, in so doing, may grant individuals *more* rights pursuant to the state constitution than the rights guaranteed by the U.S. Constitution.[80]

In the future, state or republic laws will likely differ from Russian Federation law, and state courts may find different rights within state constitutions, but this is wholly consistent with a federalist system.[81] As long as the state courts base the decisions on interpretations of state law and the state constitution, it will not violate basic principles of federal law. In the future, it will be crucial for the courts of any of the Russian Federation republics to defer to that republic's own constitution, and establish the limits of that republic's government within that constitutional structure.[82]

There is an additional danger that a republic will infringe upon a national right; thus, it is also imperative that there be an avenue of recourse to the equivalent of a separate federal court, the Constitutional Court, or protection by the National Assembly or Duma. Constitutional law will become a complex "shared enterprise"[83] between the republics and the Commonwealth; however, the republics should remain faithful to their constitutions. As Judge Hans A. Linde so eloquently wrote regarding the U.S. state and federal constitutional dichotomy:

> Fidelity to a constitution does not mean narrow literalism. . . . [F]idelity to a constitution means at least to identify what clause is said to invalidate the challenged law, to read what one interprets, and to explain it in terms that will apply beyond the case at issue, not to substitute phrases that have no analogue in the state's charter. It means to respect the ordinary lawmaking processes and withhold premature constitutional judgments, but it also means not to assume uncritically that government can overcome the limits set for it by a constitutional guarantee whenever a court believes that the government's purpose is more important, merely because this is how the Supreme Court has redefined federal doctrine.[84]

The republics of the Commonwealth, particularly when protecting individual liberties, should strive to remain faithful to the republics' constitutions, define their constitutional parameters, and, in appropriate circumstances, postpone actual constitutional decisions until other branches have spoken.

CONCLUSION

The new Russian Federation Constitution is intended to be a contract among individuals and the federation.[85] However, words mean little without enforcement power. As discussed, there are alternative approaches to enforcement of constitutional rights; however, the greatest responsibility falls upon the Russian Constitutional Court, which yields significant power. By allocating interpretative authority to the courts through broad constitutional language in the areas of individual liberties, without specific constitutionally based standards to apply, the adopters are risking judicial activism and judicial lawmaking that may run contrary to the original intent. This ongoing criticism of the American judiciary arises particularly in the realm of the right to privacy and Fourth Amendment jurisprudence. Whether an interpretivist approach or noninterpretivist approach is adopted by the future Russian Constitutional Court, it is critical to give clear meaning to the individual liberty provisions in these very early stages of developing the rule of law. The role of the republics and local governing authorities will be critical to the future enforcement of individual constitutional protections. Among the many obstacles facing the republics of the former Soviet Union, the current constitutional predicament is whether the three branches of government can establish credibility with the people; or whether the populace's confidence in the federalist system and the new Constitution will dissipate, as it has with the four prior Constitutions of the Russian Federation.

NOTES

1. In 1990 the Russian Parliament declared independence from the Soviet Union. The Parliament thereafter formed the Russian Federation Constitutional Commission to draft a new constitution. The Commission, made up of 107 Parliament deputies, formed a group of 15 who were charged with the responsibility of drafting a new noncommunist constitution. This group was chaired by First Secretary Oleg Rumyantsev. Delegates in the Russian Parliament have blocked the two-thirds vote needed to enact the new Russian Federation Constitution.

2. The Soviet Union encompasses one-sixth of the total land area on earth. In traveling between the western to the eastern borders, one passes through 11 of the earth's 24 time zones. The Russian Republic contains two-thirds of the land area and approximately one-half of the population of the country.

3. Remnick, "'We, the People,' From the Russian," *Washington Post National Weekly Edition*, September 10–16, 1990, 11.

4. "The right of the people to be secure in their persons, houses, papers and effects, against unreasonable searches and seizures, shall not be violated, and no Warrants shall issue, but upon probable cause, supported by Oath or affirmation, and particularly describing the place to be searched, and the persons or things to be seized." U.S. Constitution (hereinafter U.S. Const.), Amendment IV.

5. Analyzing constitutional theories of the United States will aid in evaluating the express language and future applications of the new Russian Federation Constitution, particularly considering the current U.S. doctrinal debates on constitutional interpretation and the role of the judiciary. See e.g., Robert L. Clinton, *Marbury vs. Madison and Judical Review* (1989); Vincent Blasi, *Law and Liberalism in the 1980s* (1991).

6. See *infra* notes 64–68 and accompanying text.

7. Phyllis T. Bookspan, "Reworking the Warrant Requirement: Resuscitating the Fourth Amendment," 44 *Vanderbilt Law Review* 473, 475 (1991). See *id.* at note 4 (citing Craig M. Bradley, "Two Models of the Fourth Amendment Warrant Clause," 83 *Michigan Law Review* 1468 (1985); Lloyd L. Weinreb, "Generalities of the Fourth Amendement," 42 *Utah Law Review* 47, 49 (1974) (stating that the Fourth Amendment doctrine is unstable and unconvincing). See *infra* notes 64–69 and accompanying text.

8. Oliver Wendell Holmes, Jr., *The Common Law* (1881).

9. For example, the draft Constitution of the Russian Federation (hereinafter Russian Const.) includes: Art. 1.2, Democracy; Art. 1.4, Political pluralism; Art. 1.7, The Social market economy; Art. 1.9, The Federal structure; Art. 2.3, Civil rights; Art. 2.5, Social, economic, and cultural rights; Art. 3.1, Ownership, labor, and business ventures; Art 3.2, Marriage and family; Art. 3.3, The sciences, education training, and culture.

10. Russian Const. Art. 2.5.1 provides: "Everybody has the right to work, that is to freely use his/her capabilities to work, as well as a free choice of profession, occupation, and place of employment in accordance with his/her professional training."

11. Russian Const. Art. 2.5.3 states in pertinent part: "[t]he Russian Federation guarantees everybody fair and favorable working conditions including fair and equal payment for the labor of equal value without any discrimination."

12. Russian Const. Art. 2.5.6. provides: "Citizens of the Russian Federation are entitled to obtain both free and profit based skilled medical services. [The] law prescribes the rules of realization of this right."

13. Russian Const. Art. 2.5.5. states: "Everybody is guaranteed free basic education within the state educational institutions. The basic education is universal. Further education is encouraged, and it is available in its various forms depending on the person's capabilities."

14. Russian Const. Art. 2.7.2.

15. Russian Const. Art. 2.1.3(1) provides: "Citizens of the Russian Federation within its territory are guaranteed equal rights and liberties regardless of their race, nationality, language, social origin, ownership status, and position, residency, attitude to religion, party membership, as well as former incarceration for criminal activity."

16. Russian Const. Art. 2.1.3(2) ("man and woman have equal rights and liberties").

17. See Russian Const. Art. 1.5.

18. See Russian Const. Ch. 5.3A.

19. The two houses in Parliament are the Federal Council and the Council of Peoples' Representatives. See Russian Const. Art. 5.2.1A(2). Both chambers are elected

simultaneously for a four-year term. Russian Const. Art. 5.2.1A(3).

20. Russian Const. Art. 5.2.3A(1). The Parliament has been given express authority to elect and remove the Parliamentary Commissioner on human rights. *Id.* 5.2.3(A)(4).

21. See generally Russian Const. Ch. 5.7, The Judiciary Power. The power of the judiciary belongs solely to the courts, "and shall be conducted in through [*sic*] the constitutional, civil, criminal, and administrative judiciary processes." Russian Const. Art. 5.7.2. See also Art. 5.7.8 (enumerating the specific powers of the Constitutional Court in order to protect the Constitution).

22. Russian Const. Art. 4.1.1. The Constitution affirmatively states that the "Russian Federation is a republic. It has the supreme right to handle both its territory and national wealth. It independently defines and executes its domestic and foreign policy, it adopts its Constitutions and its laws bearing the supremacy over its territory. The state sovereignty of the Russian federation is indivisible and inseparable."

23. Russian Const. Art. 4.2. See also Russian Const. Ch. 7.3, On the Federal Structure, and Ch. 7.4, On the System of State Power.

24. Russian Const. Art. 4.2.6–4.2.7. "Republics themselves solve their internal problems. Within their territories they have all legislative, executive, and judicial authority. It applies to the part which the present Constitution does not link to the authority of the Federation." Russian Const. Art. 1.9(2).

25. Russian Const. Art. 4.2.3. (specifies the areas where joint authority is shared by the Russian Federation and the Republics).

26. Russian Const. Art. 5.7.6.

27. *Id.* 5.7.8(1).

28. Russian Const. art. 5.7.8(1) 1–5.

29. The criminal codes may define criminal conduct in greater detail and establish the procedures for detention, arrest, and other critical criminal law and procedure issues.

30. This does not mean that the states and legislative bodies do not have an important role to play in establishing and enforcing the criminal procedure laws. However, it does mean that the Russian Federation Constitution should state clearly those protections that are important to maintaining individual liberty, as well as allocating decision-making authority among other branches of government.

31. Clinton, *Marbury v. Madison and Judicial Review, supra* note 5; Blasi, *Law and Liberalism in the 1980s, supra* note 5.

32. *Marbury v. Madison*, 5 U.S. (1 Cranch) 137 (1803).

33. *Id.* (emphasis added).

34. John H. Ely, *Democracy and Distrust* 1, 341 (1980).

35. For an excellent discussion of "originalism" and the various camps of constitutional interpretation see Paul Brest, "The Misconceived Quest for the Original Understanding," 60 *Boston University Law Review* 204 (1980). "By Originalism, I mean the familiar approach to constitutional adjudication that accords binding authority to the text of the Constitution or the intention of its adopters." *Id.* (footnote omitted). Originalists claim that the benefits of this approach are that the decision makers are constrained and there is ongoing consistency in interpretation. *Id.* Brest explores a variety of concepts and modes of interpretation such as: textualism and the plain meaning rule; intentionalism and the ascertainment of the intentions of the adopters; and, strict and moderate originalism. *Id.* at 205–35. See also, Antonin Scalia, "Originalism: The Lesser Evil," 57 *Cincinnati Law Review* 849 (1989).

36. See e.g., Alexander M. Bickel, *The Least Dangerous Branch* (1962). For example, in comparing the neorealists' method of interpretation to the literalists' approach, Bickel wrote: "The neorealists, I have mentioned, have most curiously married themselves to the present generation of literalists, for whom, as for their ancestors, the beginning and the end of judicial review are both to be found in the text of the Constitution." *Id.* at 84. In commenting upon the Supreme Court, he adds that "Justice Black and his 'activist' brethren are far from professing the exercise of any will of their own. They take sides, to be sure, but they unblushingly admit only to taking the side of the constitutional text." *Id.* at 85.

37. "The differences lie in what is being interpreted, and I [Brest] use the term 'originalism' to describe the interpretation of text and original history as distinguished, for example, from the interpretation of precedents and social values." Brest, "*supra* note 35, n. 1.

38. *Id.*

39. Robert H. Bork, *The Tempting of America, the Political Seduction of the Law* 118 (1990).

40. Consistent with this opinion, the Supreme Court stated that actions that are "essentially legislative in purpose and effect" must meet the express constitutional requirements of bicameralism and presentment of Article I. See U.S. Const. Art. I, § 7. "Essentially legislative" actions are those that alter the "legal rights, duties and relations of persons." *Immigration and Naturalization Service v. Chadha*, 462 U.S. 919 (1983) holding that a one-house legislative veto provision is unconstitutional because it is legislative in purpose and effect, and does not satisfy the express Article I requirements of bicameralism and presentment).

41 Russian Const. Art. 2.3.4(2) ("search warrant issued upon the decision of the court").

42. The Warren Court, the period in which Earl Warren was chief justice of the Supreme Court from 1954 to 1969, is regarded as having expanded the Bill of Rights. Members of the Court who favored broader individual rights included Thurgood Marshall, William Brennan, Hugo Black, and William O. Douglas.

43. For example, Former Justice William Brennan has been called "a respected and unapologetic practitioner of judicial power and imaginative constitutional analysis when the issues involve individuals' rights." Robert F. Nagel, *Constitutional Cultures* 60 (1989).

44. *Roe v. Wade*, 410 U.S. 113 (1973).

45. Ely, *supra* note 34, at 2–3.

46. The line of cases (as listed in reverse chronological order) heading in the interpretivist direction includes, but is not limited to: *Planned Parenthood of Southeastern Pennsylvania v. Casey*, 112 S.Ct. 2791 (1992) (narrowly reaffirming *Roe*'s holding recognizing the woman's right to choose a previability abortion, but affirming numerous state regulations as long as they did not impose an "undue burden" on the woman's right to choose; spousal notification held as unconstitutional because it imposed an undue burden); *Rust v. Sullivan*, 111 S.Ct. 1759 (1991) (upholding the prohibition of Title X funding of abortion counseling, referral and activities advocating abortion as a method of family planning); *Hodgson v. Minnesota*, 110 S.Ct. 2926 (1990) (upholding Minnesota statute requiring notice to both parents before a minor could have an abortion when combined with a judicial bypass provision, as well as a 48-hour waiting period); *Ohio v. Akron Center for Reproductive Health*, 110 S.Ct. 2792 (1990)

(upholding judicial bypass procedure in Ohio statutes requiring parental notice for minor to have abortion); *Webster v. Reproductive Health Serv's*, 109 S.Ct. 3040 (1989) (upholding Missouri statutes requiring preabortion viability tests); *Thornburgh v. American College of Obstetricians and Gynecologists*, 476 U.S. 747 (1986) (upholding informed consent provisions of Pennsylvania abortion statute); *Akron v. Akron Center for Reproductive Health*, 462 U.S. 416 (1983) (reaffirming the state's compelling interest in health regulation at the end of the first trimester); *H.L. v. Matheson*, 450 U.S. 398 (1981) (upholding Utah statute requiring a physician to notify the parents of unemancipated dependent minor of her upcoming abortion); *Harris v. McRae*, 448 U.S. 297 (1980) (establishing that Title VII does not obligate a state to fund medically necessary abortions); *Maher v. Roe*, 432 U.S. 464 (1977) (upholding Connecticut's distinction between use of Medicaid funds for medically necessary abortions, and elective abortions); *Planned Parenthood v. Danforth*, 428 U.S. 52 (1976) (disallowing spousal and parental consent provisions in Missouri abortion statute). Roe may be overruled as unconstitutional based on interpretivist reasoning that the right to an abortion is not provided for expressly in the language of the U.S. Constitution; and that the substantive due process protections can no longer be interpreted by the judiciary to include this right. The U.S. Supreme Court is likely to continue reestablishing the federalist structure by deferring to the state legislatures for abortion regulations.

47. See, e.g., Nagel, *supra* note 43, at 64.

48. *Id.* This view is supported by the fact that the Bill of Rights was not ratified until three years after ratification of the U.S. Constitution (December 15, 1791) and was originally interpreted to restrain only the federal government. See Bernard Schwartz, *A Documentary History of the Bill of Rights* 627 (1971). The American Constitution framers' "most important contributions had to do with principles of power allocation—with the blending and separation of power among the branches of government and with the bold effort to create a strong national government while maintaining strong state governments." *Id.* at 64.

49. Jesse H. Choper, *Judicial Review and the National Political Process: A Functional Reconsideration of the Role of the Supreme Court* (1980). The political process should decide structural principles surrounding the separation of powers and those subjects that are proper for congressional legislation. Jesse H. Choper, "The Scope of National Power Vis-à-Vis the States: The Dispensability of Judicial Review," 86 *Yale Law Journal* 1552 (1977).

50. In sweeping language the constitutional drafters stated that the "Russian state is based on the separation of powers: legislative, executive, judiciary," which also includes the separation of authority of the Russian Federation, its republics, and local governments. Russian Const. Art. 1.5(1). Moreover, this draft states that "[i]n accordance with the principle of separation of powers, state bodies act individually within the framework of their power, they interact and counterbalance each other." *Id.* It is unclear how a violation of this broad principle of separation of powers will be reviewed and corrected. Presumably, it will be the judiciary that will assume this role as in the United States.

51. Russian Const. Art. 1.3(1). This statement, establishing individual rights, appears in section one of the Russian Federation Constitution. The allocation of authority and federalism principles are established in later articles. See also *supra* note 3 and accompanying text (Oleg Rumyantsev's statement).

52. Russian Const. Art. 1.3(3) provides that: "[w]ithin the law, each citizen exercises his/her rights individually in accordance with the principle 'everything that is not prohibited by law is permitted.' The state serves both to man and to the society, it protects and guarantees human and citizen's rights as well as democratic constitutional system, law and order."

53. Nagel, *supra* note 43, at 65. Critical of the American judiciary's emphasis on securing individual liberties, Nagel states that "[i]n adopting a viewpoint and a vocabulary that focuses on individuals, modern judges and scholars have tended to shut themselves off from full participation in the great debates about governmental theory begun by the framers." *Id.*

54. Russian Const. Art. 2.3.2 provides that certain rights are "protected by law." Article 2.3.4. states that search of a home "may be done only in cases prescribed by law."

55. Several unanswered questions remain. For example, is the law that enforces these rights the law of the Russian Federation, or the criminal codes and laws of regional and local governments?

56. See *supra* note 4.

57. Russian Const. Art. 2.3.2.

58. It is unclear whether this would include only state actors or includes all people who search a home without lawful consent of the owners. By contrast, the U.S. Constitution Bill of Rights protects only against state action, not the actions of private individuals. More important, it is unclear what qualifies as a "home" or a "dwelling"—or if there is a difference between the two terms. It is important to note that the Russian concept of "home" and "dwelling" (flat) are *not* directly analogous to the traditional U.S. conception of these terms.

59. See *supra* notes 11–29 and accompanying text.

60. U.S. Const. Amend IV.

61. These procedures are probable cause, and an oath or affirmation before a neutral and detached magistrate. *Id.*

62. H. Richard Uviller, "Reasonability and the Fourth Amendment: A (Belated) Farewell to Justice Potter Stewart," 25 *Criminal Law Bulletin* 29, 32–33 (1989) (footnote omitted).

63. Bookspan, *supra* note 7, at 516–19 (discussing the history of the core fourth amendment protections that were intended by the framers to protect against King George's soldiers who relied on general warrants and writs of assistance to ransack houses, papers, and personal effects of the citizenry).

64. See, e.g., Silas J. Wasserstrom, "The Incredible Shrinking Fourth Amendment," 21 *American Criminal Law Review* 257, 259 (1984). Bookspan, *supra* note 7, at 473, 474–81, 516–19.

65. See *United States v. Ventresca*, 380 U.S. 102–105 (1965) (citations omitted); *Illinois v. Gates*, 462 U.S. 213 (1983) (attempting to encourage recourse to the warrant procedure); *Terry v. Ohio*, 392 U.S. 1 (1968). See also Y. Kamisar, W. LaFave, and J. Israel, *Basic Criminal Procedure* 207 (7th ed. 1990) (citations omitted).

The Supreme Court has long expressed a strong preference for searches made pursuant to a search warrant. . . . But this is far from being an accurate portrayal of current law or practice; the fact of the matter is that a great majority of police seizures and searches are made and upheld notwithstanding the absence of a warrant.

Id.

66. *Skinner v. Railway Labor Executives' Ass'n*, 489 U.S. 602 (1989) (emergency accident exception); *New York v. Burger*, 482 U.S. 691 (1987) (regulated industries exception); *United States v. Leon*, 468 U.S. 897 (1984) (good-faith exception to the exclusionary rule); *Segura v. United States*, 468 U.S. 796 (1984) (exigent circumstances exception to the warrant requirement); *Michigan v. Long*, 463 U.S. 1032 (1983) (protective search of car interior without a warrant was constitutional where the officers had a reasonable belief that the suspect posed a danger or possessed weapons in the immediate area); *United States v. Ross*, 456 U.S. 798 (1982) (warrantless search of entire car and any containers was constitutional as long as the search was reasonably contemporaneous to the arrest based on the automobile exception to the warrant requirement); *New York v. Belton*, 453 U.S. 454 (1981) (search incident to a lawful arrest in a car may be of the entire interior of the car, including clothing within the car, but excluding the trunk); *United States v. Ceccolini*, 435 U.S. 268 (1978) (independent source exception); *Camara v. Municipal Court*, 387 U.S. 523 (1976) (administrative exception); *United States v. Martinez-Fuerte*, 428 U.S. 543 (1976) (no warrant needed to set up a fixed checkpoint to curb the flow of illegal aliens); *Schneckloth v. Bustamonte*, 412 U.S. 218 (1973) (voluntary consent search of premises does not require a warrant); *Almeida-Sanchez v. United States*, 413 U.S. 266 (1973) (border stop and search of a car without a warrant is constitutional if based on probable cause or consent); *Coolidge v. New Hampshire*, 403 U.S. 443 (1971) ("plain view" doctrine as exception to warrant requirement); *Chimel v. California*, 395 U.S. 752 (1969) (warrantless search incident to a valid custodial arrest constitutional if in the immediate vicinity or "grabbable area"); *Terry v. Ohio*, 392 U.S. 1 (1968) ("stop and frisk" exception to the warrant requirement).

67. See, e.g., *Horton v. California*, 496 U.S. 128 (1990). The Fourth Amendment has a particularity requirement that "no warrants shall issue, but upon probable cause . . . and *particularly describing the place to be searched.*" U.S. Const. Amend. IV (emphasis added). The most recent judicial interpretation of this particularity requirement was in *Horton*, where the Supreme Court effectively nullified the particularity requirement of the U.S. Constitution. Pursuant to the "plain view" doctrine, to justify a warrantless search and seizure, the Court had held that the seizure may be lawful if the law enforcement official was: (1) legitimately on the premises; (2) discovered evidence inadvertently; and (3) it was immediately apparent that evidence or instrumentalities of a crime was before them. *Coolidge v. New Hampshire*, 403 U.S. 443 (1971). See also *United States v. Espinoza*, 826 F.2d 317, 318 (5th Cir. 1987) (requiring the inadvertence element [#2] to preserve the particularity requirement of the Fourth Amendment). In *Horton* the Supreme Court, in interpreting the Fourth Amendment, held that "even though inadvertence is a characteristic of the most legitimate 'plain view' seizures, it is not a necessary condition" to protect against violations of the particularity requirement. *Horton*, 496 U.S. at 131.

68. Bookspan, *supra* note 7, at 473, 519 (footnote omitted).

69. Laurence A. Benner, "Diminishing Expectations of Privacy in the Rehnquist Court," 22 *John Marshall Law Review* 825 (1989); Note, "*Murray v. United States*: The Emasculation of the Fourth Amendment Warrant Clause," 10 *Pace Law Review* 167

(1990). See *supra* note 66 (discussing the numerous exceptions to the warrant requirement.

70. Russian Const. Art. 1.6 provides in pertinent part: "The Constitution of the Russian Federation is the Supreme Law of the [R]epublic. Any law and legal rules contradicting the Constitution are not legally valid." The Preamble of the draft Russian Federation Constitution also declares that the Constitution is "The Principal law of our society and our state."

71. *Marbury v. Madison*, 5 U.S. (1 Cranch) 137 (1803).

72. Russian Const. Art. 2.3.3(1) provides that: "[e]verybody has the right to be free and for personal immunity. Arrest and incarceration are permitted exceptionally upon decision of the courts." Russian Const. Art. 2.2.2(2) is similar to the U.S. Constitutional prohibition against cruel and unusual punishment. It states: "[N]obody may be subjected to tortures or cruel and humiliating treatment, as well as to be subjected to medical and scientific experiments without the person's consent."

73. The Supreme Court has used this language on occasion. See e.g., *Horton v. California*, 496 U.S. 128 (1990). Bookspan, *supra* note 7, at 473, 514–29 (discussing that the "reasonableness" standard commonly used by the courts today and the per se approach as an appropriate protection for the warrant requirement). However, see *supra* note 65 explaining the evisceration of the warrant requirement so that warrantless search and seizures are presumptively unreasonable in theory only.

74. *Id.* at 515. "As stated by Justice Robert Jackson, officers acting as their own magistrate must be able to justify a warrantless search by demonstrating some real immediate and serious consequences if they had applied for a warrant before acting." *Id.* (footnote and citation omitted).

75. *Id.* at 516. Professor Bookspan states that two critical assumptions underlie this presumptively unreasonable test: (1) "that the core of the fourth amendment is its requirement that no warrants shall issue, but upon probable cause," and (2) "that a reasonable search is one executed with a valid warrant except in very limited circumstances." *Id.* The author then explains both of these underlying principles and concludes with a discussion of the benefits of the presumptively unreasonable test. *Id.*

76. Russian Const. Art. 2.6.2(6) is the equivalent of the judicially created exclusionary rule in the United States. See *Mapp v. Ohio*, 367 U.S. 643 (1961); *Weeks v. United States*, 232 U.S. 383 (1914).

77. Bookspan, *supra* note 7, at 528.

78. *Id.* at 529.

> It recognizes the language, intent, and transcendence of the Framers of the Constitution. It does not demand that the Framers rule our constitutional jurisprudence from the grave, but rather that we respect the continued integral importance of warrants to the protections inherent in the Fourth Amendment. It counterattacks the passion of the moment—as reflected in the reasonableness analysis—and reflects more deeply held moral principles about the integrity of persons, the value of privacy, and the foundation of our government.

Id.

79. *Id.* at 518.

80. See, e.g., *PruneYard Shopping Center v. Robbins*, 447 U.S. 74 (1980) (upholding a state constitutional expansion of rights to free speech and association beyond U.S. Constitutional rights). See also "Developments in the Law—The

Interpretation of State Constitutional Rights," 95 *Harvard Law Review* 1324 (1982); Brennan, "State Constitutions and the Protection of Individual Rights," 90 *Harvard Law Review* 489 (1977); Howard, "State Courts and Constitutional Rights in the Day of the Burger Court," 62 *Virginia Law Review* 873 (1976).

81.

> Not everything in a constitution is important, and much that people would call fundamental is found in laws, not in constitutions. State laws can and do differ on highly charged issues of life and death, of sexual and family relations, and courts also may divine different answers in state constitutions. That is the essence of federalism.

Hans A. Linde, "Are Constitutions Common Law?" 34 *Arizona Law Review*, 215, 228 (1992).

82. Alternative means to provide an enforcement mechanism for individual constitutional rights in the Russian Federation may exist. In order to limit the government actors in search and seizures, there could be a legal form of recourse for those whose rights have been violated. For example, the use of civil juries may be initiated to remedy constitutional violations committed against individuals by the government. In the 1700s, the American colonists distrusted the federal governing body and authorized civilian participation in adjudication. A civil jury, akin to the present-day grand jury system, would review alleged violations of constitutional rights by government agents. These civil juries would consistently monitor governmental conduct (or misconduct) in search and seizures. Consequently, active citizen participation in the governing process through civil juries may cultivate public confidence and understanding of constitutional rights, and improve government accountability in the criminal justice system.

83. *Id.* at 228.

84. *Id.* at 228–29.

85. "Each constitutional phrase has to be a stable basis for laws, for protection of the individual." Statements of Oleg Rumyantsev, quoted in Remnick, *supra* note 3, at 11.

13

The "President" and State Authorities in Ukraine

Yurii S. Shemshuchenko

Ukraine elected the first president in its history—L. M. Kravchuk—at the end of 1991. Ukrainians linked their hopes for the resolution of economic and political problems and for the strengthening of legal order in the republic to the establishment of the presidency. But the president will hardly be able to improve the situation by himself. Much also depends on other organs of the independent Ukrainian state and on the correct definition of the place and role of the president in the general system of state authorities. This chapter discusses the impact of the separation of powers on the legislative, executive, and judicial branches.

THE PRESIDENT AND THE LEGISLATIVE BRANCH

In accordance with the Constitution of Ukraine, the president is the republic's highest official and chief of the republic's executive branch. His relations with the Ukrainian Supreme Soviet are governed by the constitutional provision that the Supreme Soviet is the highest collegial organ of state power that exercises legislative and control functions and is empowered to decide all questions in republic life without exception. The president and his powers are constitutionally limited to a certain range of issues. The president guarantees the rights and liberties of citizens, Ukraine's state sovereignty, and the observance of the Constitution and the republic's laws. He also represents Ukraine in interstate and international relations. He takes necessary measures to secure the republic's defensive capability, state security, and territorial integrity, and makes decisions both on the declaration of war, on total and partial mobilization on republic territory, and on the introduction of martial law in individual localities in Ukraine. He conducts negotiations and signs interstate and international treaties; decides questions pertaining to the admission to and release from Ukrainian citizenship; and declares individual localities in Ukraine to be economic disaster areas.

The president of Ukraine delivers messages to the people of the republic and submits annual reports on the execution of his socioeconomic and other programs, on the situation in Ukraine, to the Supreme Soviet. The Supreme Soviet, by a majority of votes of the total number of people's deputies, is entitled to demand that the president issue a special report on key issues in the life of the state.

Laws passed by the Supreme Soviet take precedence over presidential ukases. The latter must be promulgated on the basis of and in fulfillment of the Constitution and laws of Ukraine, and must also be within the limits of powers conferred on the president. Presidential ukases are not normative in nature. But these limits are not always observed. U.S.S.R. President Gorbachev and Russian President Yeltsin, for example, induced their respective parliaments to delegate to the President legislative powers in certain areas (management of the national economy, price formation, strengthening of the legal order, etc.). This is a deviation from the separation of powers, and contains the danger that the president might usurp the functions of parliament.

The president of Ukraine may not be a people's deputy but he has certain legal options to influence the character of legislative activity of the republic's Supreme Soviet by participating in its work and by exercising the legislative initiative of the pocket veto. But here, too, the Supreme Soviet has the last word. Thus, in the process of signing a law, the president of Ukraine must within two weeks return it together with his objections to the Supreme Soviet so that it may be discussed and voted on once again. If a majority of the Supreme Soviet reaffirms its earlier decision, the law is considered to have passed.

The president of Ukraine is elected to a five-year term by the republic's population on the basis of universal, equal, and direct suffrage. The president enjoys the right of immunity, but the Ukrainian Supreme Soviet may call an all-Ukraine referendum on the stoppage of the president's powers prior to the expiration of the term of office at the initiative of the republic's citizens (at least 3 million citizens are entitled to participate in the referendum). In addition, if the president violates the Constitution and the laws of Ukraine, he may be removed from his post by the Ukrainian Supreme Soviet based on the conclusion of the republic's Constitutional Court. Ukrainian legislation does not confer on the president any rights pertaining to the early termination of the powers of the Ukrainian Supreme Soviet. Nor has Ukraine adopted the legislative norm of a number of Western countries empowering the president to dissolve parliament.

Relations between the president and the Ukrainian Supreme Soviet are thus structured in such a way as to ensure the completeness of the legislative and oversight functions of the latter and to provide guarantees against the usurpation of unlimited authority to abuse power by the president.

THE PRESIDENT AND THE EXECUTIVE BRANCH

The Ukrainian state can be called neither a parliamentary nor a presidential republic. The model of presidential authority here is similar to but not identical with the French model. This model reflects the national peculiarities and the idea of subordination of the system of government in form of the presidency to Soviets of People's Deputies. Such specific symbiosis suggests the development of a special parliamentary-presidential form of government in Ukraine.

In important respects, the president stands above the government organizational system. The establishment of the presidency in Ukraine was primarily occasioned by the need to strengthen the executive branch, without which it would be impossible to bring order to social relations. As the chief of the executive branch, the president heads the entire state administration. But the president is not an organizational part of this system.

In the sphere of state government, the president of Ukraine, first, directs the activity of the republic's Cabinet of Ministers; second, directs the activity of lower organs of state government either directly or through the Cabinet of Ministers; third, directly resolves administrative problems within presidential competency; and, fourth, oversees the activity of the state administration at all levels.

The president of Ukraine submits to the republic Supreme Soviet candidates for the post of prime minister and, if necessary, suggests removal from that post. With the consent of the Supreme Soviet, the president appoints the ministers of defense, internal affairs, foreign affairs, finance, justice, and a number of other officials. Other members of the Ukrainian Cabinet of Ministers are appointed and dismissed at the behest of the prime minister.

The president of Ukraine has the right to rescind decrees and orders of the republic's Cabinet of Ministers, the government of the Crimean Autonomous Republic, the acts of ministries and other subordinate organs of executive committees of local Soviets of People's Deputies.

However, the president of Ukraine is still not exercising these powers sufficiently. The "war of laws" is continuing in the republic, and many local organs of power and government lay claim to their own sovereignty and do not properly carry out the ukases of the president and the laws of the state. This situation is fraught with further complications. After all, it is well known that economic successes are unattainable without a well-organized government and the appropriate legal order.

There are also problems in the nature of relations in the Supreme Soviet-

President-Cabinet of Ministers system. The cabinet is responsible for its activity both to the president, who is the chief of the executive branch, and to the republic's Supreme Soviet. The government has the specific obligation to submit programs for solving various problems to Parliament for its scrutiny and to report on its work. The Ukrainian Supreme Soviet may express its lack of confidence in individual members of the Cabinet of Ministers or in the Cabinet of Ministers as a whole, which will require their resignation. This can be done independently of the president's position on a given question.

THE PRESIDENT AND THE JUDICIAL BRANCH

The independence of the courts defines the relations between the judiciary and the presidency in Ukraine. According to the republic's Constitution, no one, including the president, may interfere with the administration of justice by the courts. The president has the right to pardon persons sentenced by Ukrainian courts. The question of empowering the president to appoint people's court judges is also under discussion. The present procedure, under which rayon/city people's judges are elected by oblast and Kiev City Soviets of People's Deputies, respectively, contradicts the separation of legislative and judicial powers, and places judges in a de facto state of dependence on the organs that elect them.

The Ukrainian Constitutional Court is vested with the function of overseeing the legality of presidential ukases. If this court finds that presidential ukases contradict the Constitution and the laws of Ukraine, they are declared invalid.

According to the new Law on the Office of the Ukrainian Procurator General (General'naya prokuratura Ukrainy), it oversees the legality of court rulings and sentences as well as of acts adopted by ministries and departments/agencies, and by local organs of state government. The Office of the Ukrainian Procurator General is the republic's independent organ for overseeing issues of legality. In the process of drafting the new Constitution of Ukraine, there was heated debate concerning the place of the procurator in the system of state authority. Two basic approaches were discussed: First, preserving the autonomy of the procuracy, with the procurator general being approved by the republic's Supreme Soviet; second, including the procuracy in the system of judicial organs and limiting its functions exclusively to supporting court indictments. In my view, the first of these points of view is preferable. The procurator general is at present needed as an autonomous organ for strengthening legality and legal order. After all, its protests result in more than 10,000 unlawful acts by organs of government and several thousand court sentences and rulings being rescinded in the republic every year. Suits by procurators recover millions of rubles in damages caused by the unlawful actions of officials.

Those who advocate including the procurator in the judicial system refer to foreign experience. But it, too, varies. According to the Spanish Constitution of 1978, for example, the procurator is autonomous and its functions are similar to those of the Soviet procurator. In countries where the procurator is under the courts, there are other systems of state organs, such as administrative courts, attorneys, ombudsmen, and so on, that oversee the state of legality. Differentiation in levels of legal culture or sophistication should not be underestimated. All this speaks in favor of an autonomous procuracy in the system of state authority in Ukraine.

What has been said in this chapter suggests that the Ukrainian presidency is an institution of power that is new to Ukrainian sovereign statehood. The appointment of the president of Ukraine as chief of state is the result of the concerted efforts of legislative, executive-administrative, and law enforcement organs. Naturally, this is a complex and important task and cannot be avoided. Only through concerted efforts can Ukraine attain an optimally functioning power mechanism and the necessary balance of its constituent elements. The future will show how equal the president is to this task.

14

State and Federal Foreign Affairs Power in the United States

Susan W. Tiefenbrun

The Constitution of the United States has placed control of foreign affairs in the hands of the federal government in order to preserve a sense of national unity. However, an increase in state involvement in foreign affairs and a proliferation of state and local laws affecting foreign policy are at variance with the constitutionally mandated federal foreign affairs power. The purpose of this paper is to investigate the legal and policy implications relevant to the increase in state and local government involvement in foreign affairs.

We shall examine briefly the historical purposes for the constitutional centralization of governmental power in foreign affairs and provide evidence of the development of state and local activities governing foreign affairs. We shall then examine the constitutional and legal constraints on state and local involvement in foreign affairs and contrast these to constitutionally permissible state and local activities. We shall propose criteria for judging cases in which states' activities encroach on the federal foreign affairs power. Finally, we shall present arguments for and against state involvement in foreign affairs in order to better understand the policy issues underlying the conflict between state and federal power.

HISTORICAL PERSPECTIVE OF THE FEDERAL FOREIGN AFFAIRS POWER

One of the main purposes of the Constitution was to place control of foreign affairs in the hands of the federal government.[1] James Madison in 1788 wrote in *The Federalist*: "If we are to be one nation in any respect, it clearly ought to be in respect to other nations."[2] Historically, the centralization of governmental power in foreign affairs began to evolve even before the Constitution was ratified in 1789.[3] Our nation began in 1776 as "United Colonies," "Free and Independent States" under the Declaration of Independence. It then developed into a "firm league of friendship" under the Articles of Confederation in 1781.[4] The abandonment of the Articles of Confederation and the call for a constitutional convention were motivated partially by the weakness of the new union on the international scene.[5] The Articles of Confederation provided only for the loose cooperation of 13 otherwise independent republics; standing alone without the support of a strong central government, these republics were vulnerable to domestic and foreign attacks. The Constitution attempted to rectify the drawbacks of the weak confederation by granting increased powers to the central government and by prohibiting certain activities by the states in the area of foreign affairs and defense. Thus, the nation became a "more perfect union" created by the people under the Constitution in 1789.[6]

FOREIGN AFFAIRS POWER IN THE CONSTITUTION

The new Constitution that replaced the Articles of Confederation increased the power of the central government in matters of foreign affairs. But only a general outline of a centralized "foreign affairs power" was actually written into the Constitution. It took more than 200 years to determine the extent of the central government's foreign affairs power.

The Constitution allocates specific powers to the national government with respect to foreign affairs.[7] For example, the national government has authority over duties and tariffs, foreign commerce, immigration, foreign exchange rates, piracy, offenses against laws of other nations, and the power to declare war. The president has executive power, and as commander in chief of the nation, he has the authority to declare war with the consent of Congress, enter into treaties, and recognize other nations. The supremacy clause establishes the federal preemption doctrine, which provides that nonfederal entities may not take action that is inconsistent with federal policy.

Although early writings about the Constitution[8] clearly indicate that the Founding Fathers intended national uniformity to govern international affairs, neither the Articles of Confederation nor the Constitition provides for a central "foreign affairs power."[9] Nevertheless, it is clear that the United States must act "as a single nation in the world community."[10] Stated differently, "The Federal Government must speak with one voice when regulating commercial relations with foreign governments."[11]

Only as late as the twentieth century did the United States Supreme Court hold that a general foreign affairs power resided in the national government, and no part of this power was reserved to the states under the Tenth Amendment.[12]

Although the consensus today is that the central government alone may directly exercise power in foreign affairs[13] there is evidence to support the belief that many states and local governments are participating in foreign affairs today.[14] Criticism is mounting because of the seizure by the states of the federal foreign affairs power. "Foreign policy must be made in Washington and not in the citizens' backyards."[15]

Historically, treaties[16] and international agreements[17] are recognized as superior over state laws. Congressional legislation on foreign affairs supersedes state law. State rulings based on customary international law raise questions and are subject to review by the Supreme Court. Conflicts between state action and the federal government's exercise of its foreign affairs powers are resolved in favor of the federal government under the supremacy clause pursuant to the doctrine of federal preemption.[18] Criticizing the development of states' power in the area of foreign affairs, one reporter commented: "The national interest demands that local interference in foreign and defense policy be curtailed before the federal government finds itself hamstrung by hundreds of would-be secretaries of state touting their own parochial agendas."[19]

EVIDENCE OF CURRENT STATE INVOLVEMENT IN FOREIGN AFFAIRS

State and local governments are involved in many types of activities having international ramifications. For example, state, county, and municipal governments have passed resolutions and referendums relating to foreign affairs. In 1990 some states passed investment restrictions to force U.S. companies operating in Northern Ireland to reform their hiring practices toward Roman Catholics.[20] Over 830 cities and other municipal governments have established official "sister city" relationships with over 1,270 cities and communities in 90 other countries[21] in order to encourage trade and favor cultural exchange. In 1970, 13 states adopted laws designed to prevent businesses from participating in the Arab boycott of Israel. Almost every state has sent trade missions to other countries in order to encourage exports and foreign direct investment. Over 28 cities and communities in the United States have declared themselves "sanctuaries" for refugees from Central America. In the early 1960s some cities tried to ban the sale of goods manufactured in communist countries. Some 23 states have enacted various kinds of divestment or procurement legislation directed at South Africa's apartheid policies. The European Economic Community has complained bitterly about some American states that have actually passed Buy-American laws affecting public procurement practices that run afoul of the GATT Procurement Code.[22] States have erected barriers to international financial services.[23] Some states have declared nuclear-free zones. Other states impose agricultural import quotas and customs user fees that act as nontariff barriers. Atypical state taxing methods may impact on international trade agreements.[24]

CONSTITUTIONAL CONSTRAINTS ON STATE INVOLVEMENT IN FOREIGN AFFAIRS

In each of the examples above, the state has asserted its unauthorized power over foreign affairs and encroached upon the federal foreign affairs power. Nevertheless, there has been surprisingly little, if any, reaction to preemption by the states of constitutionally mandated federal power.[25]

It is a matter of broad principle that the federal government is the sole representative of the United States in its dealings with other foreign nations.[26] The Constitution expressly or impliedly bars many state and local activities that might encroach on the federal foreign affairs powers. For example, states are forbidden to make treaties, or engage in war (unless they are invaded).[27] States may make "agreements and compacts" only with the consent of Congress.[28] States cannot engage in relations with other governments or exchange ambassadors, and they may not negotiate with other foreign governments on matters of U.S. foreign policy.[29] Article VI of the Constitution provides that laws and treaties of the United States are "supreme laws of the land" and preempt state law. International agreements, federal determinations and interpretations of "customary international law" and probably executive acts that are within the president's authority also preempt state law.[30] No state, without the consent of Congress, may lay imposts, duties, or tariffs on imports or exports.[31] State regulations or taxes are invalid if they burden interstate or foreign commerce.[32] In such a case, an extensive inquiry will be made when analyzing claims arising under the foreign commerce clause, and the court will ask whether the state or local law prevents the federal government from "speaking with one voice" when regulating commercial relations with foreign governments.[33]

CASE LAW IN DEFENSE OF FEDERAL FOREIGN AFFAIRS POWER

Zschernig vs. Miller[34] confirmed a sweeping and exclusive foreign affairs power in the federal government. In 1968 the Supreme Court held that the Constitution bars an "intrusion by the State into the field of foreign affairs which the Constitution entrusts to the President and the Congress."[35] *Zschernig* is a unique case that has never been overruled and in which the Supreme Court clearly states that there is a "dormant" foreign relations power doctrine.[36]

In *Zschernig*, the Oregon Court applied a state "Iron Curtain" probate statute and denied an East German resident his inheritance because he failed to prove that he would receive the benefit and use of the inheritance "without confiscation" and that Americans would have a right to reciprocal inheritance in his country.[37] Justice William O. Douglas in *Zschernig* looked into the way the reciprocity statutes were applied and found that detailed inquiries would have to be made by the probate courts into the kind of government that existed in the foreign land, the administration of the foreign law, the credibility of the foreign diplomatic statements, and the existence of a right to receive funds in that foreign land. Justice Douglas reasoned that such inquiries could indirectly affect foreign countries and cause embarrassment to our nation's foreign relations.[38] The Oregon state probate statute was, therefore, held invalid because it unduly interfered with the conduct of foreign relations.

CONSTITUTIONALLY PERMISSIBLE STATE AND LOCAL INVOLVEMENT

Throughout our history we have seen that Americans are profoundly opposed to political overcentralization and to the extended authority of the national government.[39] Americans have been reluctant to cede state and local control to the federal government; some are even convinced that state and local governments can implement programs and policies better than the federal government. But state and local interference in foreign policy is not appropriate to the American system of federalism if it prevents America from speaking with one voice and standing as a unified and strong federation.

State Activity Having Incidental Effect

Certain state activities that have only an indirect effect on foreign affairs are permissible. State and local laws may apply to foreign and U.S. nationals, companies, and properties otherwise subject to state and local laws, unless these laws are expressly or impliedly precluded by the Constitution or preempted by Congress or the executive, even if these state and local laws have some international consequences.[40] If the state action has only "some incidental or indirect effect on foreign countries,"[41] the action is permissible.

Cultural Exchanges, Missions, Investment Offices

States may make certain kinds of agreements with foreign governments without the consent of Congress, except as preempted by Congress or the executive.[42] For example, states may engage in cultural, educational, or goodwill exchanges with foreign countries. States may send trade or investment promotion missions to foreign countries. States may establish investment offices in foreign countries. These do not appear to be constitutionally barred.

Congressional or Presidential Authorization

State action that has been authorized by Congress or the president is permissible, even if it encroaches on federal authority over foreign relations.[43]

States' Rights to Publicize Views on Foreign Affairs

Resolutions urging arms control or dealing with issues of foreign policy and that are intended to raise public consciousness are permissible and, if made by private citizens, are protected by First Amendment guarantees of freedom of speech.

CRITERIA FOR JUDGING CASES OF STATE ENCROACHMENT ON FEDERAL POWER

Even though the foreign affairs power resides exclusively in the central government, a state may act on matters affecting foreign affairs if the state law also falls within an area of state authority. To determine whether state laws and judicial decisions are preempted by the exclusive foreign affairs powers of the federal government, a court must (1) determine whether the state law falls within the realm of acceptable state authority given to it by the Tenth Amendment of the Constitution; (2) determine whether and the degree to which the state's activity affects foreign affairs; and (3) balance the value of achieving national uniformity against the value of giving effect to local decision making.[44]

ARGUMENTS AGAINST STATE INVOLVEMENT IN FOREIGN AFFAIRS

United We Stand, Divided We Fall

Should state and local governments conduct foreign-related activities? Should Congress and the president preempt these activities? Some argue that state and local involvement in foreign policy is contrary to the American system of federalism. In its posture toward other nations, the United States must be united and speak as one nation. On issues as vital to national security as foreign afffairs, our nation must speak with one voice in a unified, strong manner.

State Involvement May Be Offensive

States publicly disagreeing with administration policy may undermine our nation's credibility. State activities may also frustrate national policy or cause offense to foreign nations.

State Involvement Is Inconsistent with Democracy

State and local involvement in foreign affairs is inconsistent with our democratic tradition, which assumes that foreign policy will be determined and implemented by the president and Congress elected by the nation as a whole.[45] This issue came up in many cases during the Vietnam War, and they turned on whether municipal governments had authority to adopt initiatives, resolutions, and referendums on foreign policy.[46]

States Lack Knowledge

Some argue that state and local governments are ill-equipped to make reasoned public judgements about international issues because they lack information and expertise.

ARGUMENTS FOR STATE INVOLVEMENT IN FOREIGN AFFAIRS

Living Law

One of the most compelling arguments for state involvement in foreign affairs is that American law is a living, organic body of laws that reflects changes in American society. State involvement in foreign affairs allows American politics to adapt to a changing world where the demarcation between national and state governments is less clear than it was when our republic was founded and when the Constitution was written and adopted.

State Activities Have No Significant Detrimental Effect

Since most state involvments in foreign affairs such as the creation of sister cities, trade and export programs, and trade missions have a beneficial impact on international affairs, they should be allowed. Nuclear freeze and test ban initiatives are intended only to influence our own government policy and do not detrimentally affect our foreign policy. Some argue that divestment measures in South Africa are designed to influence citizens in the United States and not affect foreign governments.

State Involvement Strengthens Democracy

State involvement in foreign affairs touches the very core of our democratic principles and strengthens our democracy. State involvement in foreign affairs allows a citizen's voice to be heard among those of the masses as government looms large in its global authority. Dissent should not be stifled,[47] even if it causes our nation to appear less unified to other nations of the world. What we may lose in the appearance of unity, we gain in our credibility as a democratic nation imbued with the principles of free speech and committed to the protection of individual rights.

No Expertise Required in Certain Foreign Affairs Issues

The establishment of sister cities does not need the kind of expertise associated with foreign policy or international affairs. Moreover, state involvement in foreign affairs actually promotes innovative ideas in these areas that would otherwise be left to experts.

CONCLUSION

We must evaluate state and local involvement in foreign affairs in order to determine whether this activity will have an incidental or indirect effect on foreign countries and whether it will detrimentally interfere with our nation's foreign relations. The creation of sister cities and cultural exchange programs does not raise constitutional issues or cause negative effects. But procurement legislation, Buy-American Laws, and antiapartheid divestment policies directed at specific foreign policies may be deemed a constitutionally prohibited boycott or embargo. State and local governments should take responsibility for ensuring that their laws and involvement in foreign affairs stay within constitutionally permissible grounds. But if state involvement in foreign affairs provides an avenue for dissent and raises the consciousness of the people, this benefit must be balanced against the potentially negative effect of the perception of American disharmony in the international arena.

The republic of the United States was born in 1789. In 1992 the concept of federal supremacy over foreign affairs may be in need of modification in order to adapt to the changing world. With advancement in communication, foreign policy today includes many issues such as trade, jobs abroad, environmental activity, cultural and educational programs, and human rights. Thus it seems reasonable to encourage our individual citizens, states, and local governments to participate actively in the implementation of foreign policies that affect their lives. State involvement in foreign affairs should be permissible as long as the state activity does not significantly damage the goal of our federal government to speak for the nation as a whole and with one voice.

It is time to contemplate a new federalism that encourages state and local involvement in certain foreign affairs matters. Federal deregulation, federal budget cutbacks, and pressure from constituents have forced states to assume responsibility for what once were perceived as exclusively "federal" issues. Political action committees are forming everywhere and their influence is pervasive. Special interest groups are growing at an unprecedented rate. Grassroots advocacy has proven to be quite effective in protecting and advancing the interests of states and local entities on such issues as hazardous waste disposal, international trade, clean air and water, banking, and workplace safety—that is, traditional federal issues.[48] Such a new federalism would have the beneficial effect of encouraging the ordinary reasonable citizen to participate in foreign policy by actively engaging in local government.

NOTES

1. L. Henkin, *Foreign Affairs and the Constitution* 227 (1972) (hereinafter referred to as Henkin). See also Bilder, "The Role of States and Cities in Foreign Relations," 83 *American Journal of International Law* 821 (October 1989) (hereinafter referred to as Bilder).

2. *The Federalist* No. 42, at 279 (J. Madison) (J. Cooke ed., 1961).

3. Maier, "Preemption of State Law: A Recommended Analysis," 83 *American Journal of International Law* 832 (October, 1989) (hereinafter referred to as Maier).

4. *Id.*, at 832.

5. Spiro, "Taking Foreign Policy Away from the Feds," 11, 1 *The Washington Quarterly* 191 (Winter 1988) (page 42 on Lexis) (hereinafter referred to as Spiro).

6. Maier, *supra* note 3, at 832.

7. See, e.g., U.S. Const. Art. I, § 8, cls. 1 (duties and imposts); Art. I, § 8, cls. 3 (foreign commerce); Art. I, § 8, cls. 4 (immigration); Art. I, § 8, cls. 5 (foreign exchange rates); Art. I, § 8, cls. 10 (piracy, offenses against the law of nations); Art. I, § 8, cls. 11 (declaration of war); Art. II, § 1, cls. 1 (executive power); Art. II, § 2, cls. 1 (commander

in chief); Art. II, § 2, cls. 2 (treaty power, recognition power); Art. VI, cls. 2 (Supremacy Clause).

8. *The Federalist* No. 80, at 112–114 (with an introduction by Edward Gaylord Bourne) (Washington, D.C.: Dunne, 1901).

9. Maier, *supra* note 3, at 832.

10. Henkin, *supra* note 1, at 15–16.

11. *Michelin Tire Corp. vs. Wages*, 423 U.S. 276, 285 (1976).

12. *United States vs. Curtiss-Wright Export Corp.*, 299 U.S. 304, 316 (1936); compare *Missouri vs. Holland*, 262 U.S. 416, 433 (1920).

13. Maier, *supra* note 3, at 833.

14. Bilder, *supra* note 1, at 821.

15. Spiro, *supra* note 5, at 191.

16. *Ware vs. Hylton*, 3 U.S. (3 Dall.) 199, 236–37 (1796).

17. *United States vs. Belmont*, 301 U.S. 324, 331 (1937).

18. *Restatement (Third) of Foreign Relations Law of the United States* @ 1 Reporters' Note 5 (1987) (hereinafter referred to as Restatement), at 112 (2). See Maier, *supra* note 3, at 833.

19. Spiro, *supra* note 5, at 191, 202–3.

20. See Spiro, *supra* note 5, at 191, 193 for examples of nonbinding resolutions passed by state or local legislative bodies or by referendum.

21. Bilder, *supra* note 1, at 822.

22. The European Economic Community has issued a report on U.S. trade barriers caused by state regulation. Thirty-seven states under the Buy-American Act grant preferences to state suppliers. This violates the GATT Procurement Code. "EC Report on U.S. Trade Barriers," 7, 17 *International Trade Reporter*, 598 (April 25, 1990). A more recent report in the 8, 1 *International Trade Reporter* 17 (January 2, 1991) insisted that state and local governments be covered under the GATT Procurement Code.

23. The McCarran-Ferguson Act leaves the regulation of insurance activities to the states. A foreign company must obtain a separate license to operate in each state. Some states impose special capital and deposit requirements for non-U.S. insurers, and this requirement violates GATT and its principles of reciprocity.

24. California's unitary tax method imposes an income tax on profit earned abroad. This method impairs the unified voice of the federal government according to Mr. Smith of the *Wall Street Journal* (February 23, 1983).

25. Bilder, *supra* note 1, at 824.

26. *Id.* See *United States vs. Curtiss-Wright Export Corp.*, 299 U.S. 304, 318 (1936).

27. Bilder, *supra* note 1, at 824. U.S. Const. art. I, § 10.

28. *Id.*

29. Bilder, *supra* note 1, at 824. See *Curtiss-Wright*, 299 U.S. at 316.

30. See Bilder, *supra* note 1, at 824.

31. U.S. Const. art. 1, § 8, cls. 3. See *Michelin Tire Corp. vs. Wages*, 423 U.S. 276 (1976).

32. See Bilder, *supra* note 1, at 824.

33. *Japan Line Ltd. vs. County of L.A.*, 441 U.S. 434, 449 (1979), quoting *Michelin Tire*, 423 U.S. at 285.

34. *Zschernig vs. Miller*, 389 U.S. 429, *reh'g denied*, 390 U.S. 974 (1968).
35. *Zschernig vs. Miller*, 389 U.S. at 432.
36. See Bilder, *supra* note 1, at 825.
37. *Id.* at 821.
38. *Zschernig*, 389 U.S. at 434–35.
39. See Spiro, *supra* note 5, at 191.
40. See Henkin, *supra* note 1, at 476–77, n. 51.
41. *Clark vs. Allen*, 331 U.S., at 517.
42. See Restatement, *supra* note 18.
43. See Henkin, *supra* note 1, at 241.
44. See Maier, *supra* note 3, at 834.
45. Bilder, *supra* note 1, at 827. Compare Spiro, *supra* note 5, at 191-92.
46. *Farley vs. Healey*, 67 Cal. 2d 325, 431 P.2d 650, 62 Cal. Reporter 26 (1967). This issue came up more recently during the Persian Gulf War.
47. See Bilder, *supra* note 1, at 829.
48. Markowitz, "On the Homefront," *Public Relations Journal* 14 (June 1986).

15

Delineation of Foreign Policy Powers Within the Framework of the Soviet Confederation (Based on Materials of Kazakhstan and Central Asian States)

Marat A. Sarsembayev

The Union of Soviet Socialist Republics ceased to exist after the putsch of August 19–21, 1991. Several republics (Ukraine, Uzbekistan, Kyrgyzstan, and certain others) declared their independence, and the Congress of People's Deputies itself declared the disintegration of the old Union. However, the former republics were not opposed to the formation of a new Union.

In this connection, it makes sense to compare the text of the most recent variant of the Union Treaty, which was published on the eve of the putsch, with recent political realities. This comparison will also help to differentiate more clearly the foreign policy powers of the new Union and its members.

This Union Treaty was a compromise between republics and Moscow. It was for this reason that the draft Union Treaty transferred many functions to the competence of the Union and devoted much attention to the initial joint competence of the Union and republics.

The Union Treaty followed a confederation form rather than a federalist form. A federation is a union in which the state subjects of federation enjoy minimum internal and foreign policy powers. Under a confederation each constituent state is an autonomous, sovereign state, that creates several coordinating (not subordinating) central organs for the realization of common tasks.

I think that some examples of common tasks in the transitional period could include joint defense (the control over nuclear buttons would then remain in reliable hands), the protection of common borders, the resolution of customs problems, and the payment of common foreign debts (these have accumulated to no less than $75 billion).

In the incipient Soviet confederation, foreign policy powers must be delineated between the Union and its members in such a way that member-states could carry out their own foreign policy activity, without asking Moscow and without coordinating their foreign policy actions with Moscow. At the same time, member-states could carry out the international obligations that they have assumed on the basis of foreign policy programs coordinated with one another. The function of the Council of Ministers of Foreign Affairs of the U.S.S.R. and republics and other organs of the Union should not be a directing function, but should be confined to giving republics every assistance in the exercise of their foreign political and economic powers.

The draft of the Union Treaty attempts to delineate foreign policy powers in such a way that Moscow will retain significant foreign policy control at the expense of the power of the republics.

Under the Union Treaty, the republics are not full-fledged, equal subjects of international law—a fact that detracts from the status of the republics as sovereign, independent states.

Even though the seventh provision of Section I of the "Basic Principles" of the treaty proclaims that "states forming the Union are entirely equal members of the international community," the phrases that follow strip the words "entirely equal" of their value. Let us reflect on the meaning of the phrase that states participating in the treaty "are entitled to establish direct diplomatic and consular ties and trade relations with foreign states." The words "ties and trade relations" convey a lack of desire by the republics to have the right to establish formal diplomatic and consular relations with foreign countries. The draft treaty should read: "They [member-states] establish direct diplomatic and consular relations with foreign states." "Ties" are erratic; "relations" indicate constancy and stability.

The Treaty suggests that sovereign state-republics exchange fully authorized representations (*predstavitel'stva)* with sovereign foreign states. From the text of the treaty, it is not clear whether representations are meant in the sphere of trade or in the sphere of diplomatic and consular relations. What kind of foreign state entering relations with a sovereign state-republic would wish to exchange only fully authorized representations (*polnomochnyye predstavitel'stva*) but not diplomatic relations? This revolutionary Bolshevik innovation in the sphere of diplomacy has disappeared without a trace.

Today, it is fashionable to criticize the Stalin and Brezhnev Constitutions. And yet it was these totalitarian fundamental laws that clearly spoke of and continue to speak of the right of republics to exchange specifically diplomatic and consular representatives. The right of republics (referred to in the treaty) to exchange fully authorized representations is therefore a step backward compared even with the Stalin and Brezhnev Constitutions. Even if the intent was to give the nation a federally structured state system, the right of a republic to exchange diplomatic and consular representatives should not have been infringed. While the republics could not affect such an exchange in practice, this right should not be taken away. Otherwise, the status of a republic as a sovereign state, as an entirely equal subject of international law, as an entirely equal member of the international community, will logically be called into question. The treaty should therefore read that member-states "exchange diplomatic, consular, and trade representations with them [foreign countries]."

Participation in the activity of international organizations was an integral element of the international legal personality (*pravosub'yektnost'*) of a republic. Such a right is indicated in the text of the treaty. However, when compared with the Declaration of State Sovereignty of the Kazakh SSR, for example, the treaty is silent on the right of republics to participate in the United Nations. Kazakhstan could be a member of the UN even in a federal structure. This could be seen on the basis of the example of Ukraine and Belorussia.

While foreign policy powers of republics are casually mentioned in the Union Treaty, the new Confederative Treaty should devote individual articles to every power of a member-state in the sphere of foreign policy.

An examination of the foreign policy powers of the Union and republics in their historical and contemporary aspects demonstrates the delineation of the foreign policy powers of the Confederative Union and the member-states comprising it. During the entire communist U.S.S.R. period (1922–1991), the authority to establish embassies, consulates, and trade representations was the absolute exclusive province of the Union. In 1991 the U.S.S.R. had 117 diplomatic and 68 consular representations in operation in foreign countries, and except for Ukraine and Belorussia, which had permanent representations at the UN, the republics had none. According to official doctrine, this bias (*perekos*) not only does not infringe the foreign policy interests of republics, but even promotes the rational satisfaction of these interests. This is reflected in the participation by representatives of various republics and peoples of the U.S.S.R. in the activity of these overseas organs of U.S.S.R. foreign relations. These embassies are indeed staffed, in particular, by representatives of indigenous peoples of Kazakhstan and Central Asia. But they are few. With the exception of Ch. Aytmatov, at the present time there are no top-level Soviet diplomats from Central Asia or Kazakhstan.

The Presidium of the U.S.S.R. Supreme Soviet had the right to appoint and recall diplomatic representatives of the U.S.S.R. to foreign states and international organizations. Between 1954 and the middle of March 1990, the Presidium of the U.S.S.R. Supreme Soviet appointed 856 ambassadors extraordinary and plenipotentiary to foreign states. The representation of the republics of Kazakhstan and Central Asia took the form of 16 appointments or 1.8% of the total number. For the various republics, this appears as follows: 8 appointments from the Uzbek S.S.R. (0.9%), 3 appointments from the Tajik S.S.R. (0.3%), 2 appointments from the Kazakh S.S.R. (0.3%), 1 appointment from the Turkmen S.S.R. (0.6%), and 1 appointment from the Kirghiz S.S.R. (0.16%).

The states of Central Asia and Kazakhstan will now determine the number and kind of representations they wish to establish in which countries. For example, the number of embassies may remain the same while the structure of Soviet embassies, consulates, and trade representations will change. They could consist of official representatives of republics, with the head of the embassy chosen from their number. In another variant, representatives of several members of the confederation could form one embassy in a given foreign state. In a third variant, each member of the confederation could have its own independent embassy or consulate. It is indisputable, however, that there will be diplomatic and consular representations of foreign states in the capitals of members of the confederation.

Under the old, federalist Union, the power to conclude international treaties belonged almost entirely to the Union. Of the more than 15,000 treaties and agreements signed by the Soviet Union as of 1991, five republics of Central Asia and Kazakhstan accounted for approximately 50 agreements or 0.004% of the total number of U.S.S.R. treaties. A considerable number of the republics' international treaties was signed during the years of perestroika, and, moreover, the signings were frequently contrary to the center's wishes.

Republics that were independent states have been working to correct this bias since August 1991. In accordance with the Declaration of State Sovereignty and the Declaration of Independence, states in the region of Kazakhstan and Central Asia will themselves conclude international treaties in different spheres of activity on the basis of their needs. Naturally, practically all treaties will be concluded by the region's states themselves. If states that are republics of the former federative Union sign a Confederative Treaty, the given organ may sign international treaties, but it will do so only with agreement of all members of the confederation. The possibility of signing treaties with European and similar economic communities is not excluded. In any event, the confederation's competence in the area of treaties will be very limited.

The U.S.S.R. is a member of hundreds of international organizations, but the republics of Central Asia and Kazakhstan did not belong to any international intergovernmental organizations except for the Afro-Asian Organization of Economic Cooperation, in whose work all republics of Central Asia and Kazakhstan participated in the 1960s. Representatives of Central Asian republics occasionally attended sessions of the Organization for the Solidarity of Asian and African Peoples. But these organizations belonged and still belong to the category of international nongovernmental organizations. The delineation of powers in this sphere was also in favor of the Union but not the republics.

At the same time, the republics participated to a certain degree in the activity of international intergovernmental organizations through delegations formed by the Union. As a part of all-Union delegations, representatives of the region's republics participated in the work of the UN and its specialized institutions at different times.

Thus, Kazakh S.S.R. Foreign Affairs Minister T. T. Tazhibayev took part in the work of the 5th, 10th, and 11th sessions of the UN General Assembly as part of the official U.S.S.R. delegation. As a representative of the U.S.S.R., Tazhibayev took part in the discussion of the question of "non-self-governing territories" at all three sessions of the General Assembly's Fourth Committee.

As part of the all-Union delegations to the 5th, 7th, 8th, 9th, 18th, and 20th sessions of the UN General Assembly, A. Kh. Babakhodzhayev, A. M. Kuchkarov, and G. S. Sultanov, who were Uzbek S.S.R. foreign affairs ministers at different times, also discussed the question of non-self-governing territories and international trusteeship. Kirghiz S.S.R. foreign affairs minister spoke twice at the 13th session of the UN General Assembly, where he took part in the discussion of the meaning of the right of self-determination and in the discussion of the question of human rights violations. Kazakh S.S.R. Foreign Affairs Ministers M. I. Isinaliyev and A. Kh. Arystanbekova took part in subsequent UN General Assembly sessions.

Union republics of Central Asia and Kazakhstan participated not only in the activity of official UN organs, but also of regional organizations of the world institution. Thus, representatives of the Uzbek S.S.R. took part in the 10th (Uzbek S.S.R. Minister of Culture A. M. Kuchkarov), 13th (Deputy Chairman of Uzbek S.S.R. Gosplan G. U. Aliyev), 17th (Chairman of Uzbek S.S.R. Gosplan S. K. Ziyadullayev), and 19th, 25th, and 26th (Uzbek S.S.R. deputy foreign affairs minister) sessions of the UN Economic Commission for Asia and the Far East. The Kazakh S.S.R. foreign affairs minister took part in the 41st session of the UN Economic and Social Commission for Asia and the Pacific.

Under the Confederative Union, the question of membership by all republics comprising the Union of Republics, including Kazakhstan and Central Asia, in the United Nations Organization, in its specialized institutions, and in other international organizations, ought to be raised. States comprising the Confederative Union ought to become members of the UN General Assembly, and the U.S.S.R. ought to remain a permanent member of the UN Security Council.

It is no secret that the nation's economy, including the regional economy, has disintegrated. In this connection, the region's states are in dire need of international credits. The region's states might do well to proclaim themselves developing states in order to obtain credits on preferential terms from the International Monetary Fund and other international financial and credit organizations.

The examination of the question of delineating foreign policy powers between central and republic authorities also raises the question of delineating these foreign policy powers between republic and local authorities. Local Soviets in the postwar period (roughly since the 1960s) were integrated into the mechanism of state foreign relations, which established contacts between cities, oblasts, and union republics with the same political and territorial units in foreign states. This found expression in the exchange of delegations; in the organization of friendship days, weeks, and festivals; in film festivals; and such. For example, the executive committee of the Dushanbe City Soviet of People's Deputies has close contacts with local organs in the city of Sanaa (Yemen) and the same can be said about relations between local government in the cities of Bishkek (Kyrgyzstan) and Ouagadougou (Upper Volta [Burkina Faso]), Tashkent (Uzbekistan) and Seattle (USA), Tripoli (Libya), Tunis (Tunisia), Dushanbe (Tajikistan) and Lusaka (Zambia), Alma-Ata (Kazakh SSR) and Modena (Italy), Brazzaville (People's Republic of Congo) and Rennes (France).

Republic local state organs in the region can also sign acts of an international law nature in their own name. Upon the arrival in Alma-Ata of a delegation from the Republic of Afghanistan province of Kandahar, a protocol was signed at the Alma-Ata Oblast Executive Committee establishing direct patronage and goodwill relations between Alma-Ata Oblast and the province of Kandahar. In 1987, relations between Kazakhstan, the Central Asian republics, and Afghanistan entered a new stage in which the foundation was laid for direct contacts between Chimkent Oblast and Kabul, between Karaganda Oblast and Uruzgan, between Tashkent Oblast and Samangan, between Samarkand Oblast and Baghlan, between Surkhandarya Oblast and Balkh, between Kurgan-Tyube Oblast and Herat, between Chardzhou Oblast and Faryab. They are engaged in direct relations in different spheres of activity. Since 1973, the Tashkent City Soviet has maintained ties with local authorities of the American city of Seattle. In 1982 these sister cities issued a Declaration for Peace and Averting the Nuclear Threat in which they expressed deep concern in the name of their residents over the continuing growth of stockpiles of nuclear arms.

Eight cities in the region have sister city relations with 17 cities in the world, which is 0.35 and 0.4% compared with the U.S.S.R. (200 Soviet cities maintain ties with 400 cities in different countries). This is evidence of the weak participation of the region's republics in the sister city movement. At the same time, cities in the region could use this form of international relations as a means of securing direct ties between enterprises in their city with enterprises in sister cities, which could find expression in a separate agreement.

All this activity, organized by executive committees of local Soviets of People's Deputies and coordinated by higher organs of member-states, could, to a significant degree, promote the further development of relations of friendship, mutual aid, and cooperation of peoples in the region's republics with other peoples on the globe.

Of course, local authorities have been guided and should be guided by treaties and agreements of central organs of states of Central Asia and Kazakhstan. They perform a predominantly executive role. Central organs of republics should publish legislation defining the role and place of local organs in republic foreign political and economic activity, render them assistance, and exercise general oversight.

In the final analysis, the foreign policy powers of the Confederative Union and member-states should be delineated in the favor of member-states.

REFERENCES

"The collegium of the U.S.S.R. Ministry of Foreign Affairs Announced Its Self-Dissolution." *Izvestia*, September 11, 1991.

Diplomaticheskiy slovar'. V 3-kh tomakh (Dictionary of Diplomacy in 3 Volumes) (Moscow, 1984–86).

Kazakhstanskaya pravda, Alma-Ata, September 17, 1987.

The personal archives of Kazakh S.S.R. Foreign Affairs Minister T. T. Tazhibayev.

Pravda Vostoka, Tashkent, November 4, 1987.

SSSR i strany Afriki. 1946–1962. Dokumenty i materialy (The U.S.S.R. and African Countries. 1946–1962), Vol. 1 (Moscow: Gospolitizdat, 1963), 299–319, 327–54.

"The Treaty on the Union of Sovereign States," *Izvestia*, August 16, 1991.

"The Union Ministry of Foreign Affairs: Reorganization on the March," *Izvestia*, September 24, 1991.

16

International Trade and Investment Relations Under the Federation Treaty

W. Gary Vause

INTRODUCTION

During the early 1990s, the world witnessed the largest bankruptcy proceeding in history as remnants of the former Soviet Union attempted to save the pieces of the empire through drastic restructuring. While "external creditors" already had staked their claims, the citizenry of the former Soviet Union (the "internal creditors") attempted to work out an agreement for the continued administration of the government enterprise.[1]

In the context of this internal turmoil, President Boris N. Yeltsin faced a critical Congress of People's Deputies during the second week of April 1992. To his credit, he was able to address the Congress armed with a major political accomplishment: a new federal treaty designed to form the basis for the new post-Soviet Russian state.[2] This essay analyzes events through early spring 1992, and discusses the effect of those events on the Russian Federation's competitive position in international economic relations. The principal focus is on the division of powers under the Federation Treaty between the central government and local governments within the federation.[3]

On March 31, 1992, 18 of the 20 republics of the Russian Federation signed the Federation Treaty.[4] The two exceptions were Tarstan (Tatar Republic) and Checheno-Ingushetia (Chechnia). More than 80 government leaders participated in the signing ceremony, representing various levels of administration throughout the federation, including autonomous republics, regions, districts, and the cities of Moscow and St. Petersburg.

The treaty not only clarified the relationship between Moscow's central government and Russia's local authorities, it also granted those local authorities more political and economic autonomy, including shared power over natural resources. Apparently, however, those concessions were not enough to satisfy all the regions. It had been clear since March 14, 1992, when the draft treaty originally was initialled, that the Chechen-Ingush and Tatar republics would not sign the treaty. This was a significant loss of support, for those predominantly Muslim republics are both rich in oil resources.

While forming a treaty consensus within the former Soviet Union, Yeltsin's government simultaneously was making progress on the international front. On the same day the treaty was signed, the International Monetary Fund (IMF) announced that it had endorsed Russia's economic reform plan, thus paving the way for the central government in Moscow to receive up to $4 billion dollars in IMF aid during the following year.[5] This would put Russia under the virtual stewardship of the IMF, requiring it to meet certain conditions, such as stringent targets to control the inflation rate and budget deficit. This major step brought Russia to the brink of IMF membership, which was considered critical to the integration of the Russian economy into the world trading system.

The following day, April 1st, U.S. President George Bush and German Chancellor Helmut Kohl announced a $24 billion, one-year program of financial aid to support the region's move toward a democratic, free-market economy.[6] The United States pledged a contribution to this package that totaled nearly $4.5 billion.

These historic events attest to the dramatic changes in East-West relations following the end of the Cold War. The events of early 1992 are evidence of the dynamic transition from the Cold War's strategic-military orientation toward an improved climate of economic relations, based upon mutually beneficial trade and investment relations. Nevertheless, the last vestiges of the Cold War policy of containment could still be seen in the U.S. reluctance to make massive economic development grants to the former Soviet Union. This reluctance transcended the limitations of America's recessionary economy; Russia was still considered a threat so long as it continued to maintain formidable tactical and strategic forces.

The announcement by the Russian military leadership on April 2, 1992, that it would pursue an entirely new defensive military policy, contrary to its traditional offensive policy, augured well for improved economic relations between Russia and the United States. It was no coincidence that President Bush announced during the same week that he would approve almost $4.5 billion as part of the $24 billion allied aid package.

Despite the hopeful signs that political barriers to normal economic relations could be dissolved, it nevertheless remained clear that other substantial barriers to improved trade and investment relations between the United States and the former Soviet Union would persist. The following analysis will give special attention to selected issues that continue to pose barriers to a more constructive economic engagement between the United States and the Russian Federation.

TRADE AND COMMERCE

Generally, the treaty vests exclusive jurisdiction over "the Russian Federation's foreign economic relations" in the central government of the federation.[7] However, it also provides that

> the republics in the Russian Federation are independent participants in international and foreign economic relations, agreements with other republics, krays, oblasts, and autonomous formations of the Russian Federation, if this does not contradict the Constitution and laws of the Russian Federation and this treaty. The coordination of international and foreign economic relations of the republics in the Russian Federation is carried out by federal bodies of state power of the Russian Federation, together with the republics in the Russian Federation.[8]

The treaty provides that the federal government shall have authority over "federal conflict law."[9] In the event of a dispute over the authority of federal lawmakers and republican lawmakers, such disputes are to be resolved by the Constitutional Court of the Russian Federation.[10]

Protectionism

Traditionally, a high degree of protectionism existed in all communist states. This problem was particularly acute in the Soviet Union, where protectionism was virtually institutionalized. Lenin's foreign economic policy was extremely protectionist, and was carried out in the Soviet Union not so much by a traditional tariff approach, but through the government's total monopoly on foreign trade.

So long as the Soviet Union was willing to conduct trade from a relatively isolated posture, trading primarily with members of the Council for Mutual Economic Assistance (COMECON), it could afford to maintain such extreme protectionist practices toward the noncommunist world. The result, of course, was that the Soviet Union was left behind while other nations, including other communist nations such as China, initiated modernization programs that were fueled by foreign capital, technology, know-how, and investment.

It was not until the late 1980s that Soviet leadership began to acknowledge the importance of involvement in foreign competitive markets. The uneasy match of free market economic principles with central planning proved to be too difficult even for Gorbachev. The unsuccessful coup that ultimately forced the issue, and ironically led to the demise of the political vitality of both Gorbachev and the Communist Party, was a consequence of Gorbachev's failure to decisively press forward with reforms.[11] It was only by abandonment of Gorbachev's "half-loaf" approach to economic change that major reform efforts could be credibly pursued.

By 1992 it appeared that the solution seemed to lie in a comprehensive, federally driven policy of reform, coupled with ample discretion for the exercise of local initiative. In adopting that approach, the new Federation Treaty attempted a modest emulation of the European Community model. It placed within the jurisdiction of central federal authorities the "establishment of juridical bases for a single market; financial, currency, credit, and customs regulation."[12] While Russia had the ability to forge an economic union among its member regions, however, it faced a more difficult challenge in merging with the international, market-economy trading system. Nowhere was that challenge more pronounced than in Russia's aspiration for full participation in the General Agreement on Tariffs and Trade (GATT).

Admission to GATT

The parties to GATT negotiating rounds traditionally have focused on the reduction of tariffs and other trade barriers in an effort to liberalize world trade. Because the Russian Federation is not a member of GATT, it does not enjoy GATT's most-favored-nation status or its protections from discriminatory tariffs by GATT signatory nations.

The Soviet Union has exhibited ambivalence about GATT in the past. The U.S. Commerce Department proposed that the Soviet Union join GATT in 1973, but the Soviet Union declined. In 1982 and 1986, the Soviet Union expressed its desire to join, but was rejected by GATT's largely Western membership.

The West's reluctance to admit the Soviet Union to GATT was based on more than just Cold War enmity. The difficulty of meshing a market system with a centrally planned economy appeared too formidable a task for GATT's predominately market economy membership. The lack of a free market economy in the Soviet Union drew specific objections, such as the high level of Soviet subsidies to domestic industries engaged in export trade and the pervasive protectionist barriers against imports.

After its application for membership was rebuffed in 1986, the Soviet Union pursued a domestic agenda for reform in its foreign trade structure. It simultaneously made GATT membership a major policy objective. In recent years, the momentum has increased to admit Russia to GATT.

Technology Transfers

The states that formerly comprised the Soviet Union continue to have critical needs for advanced technology. A principal motivation for opening their markets to foreign joint ventures is to attract such advanced technology and know-how from the West. However, the Cold War freeze on high technology transfers from the West to the Soviet Union had not yet fully thawed by the early 1990s. This was especially true regarding U.S. technology transfers to the Soviet Union.

The U.S. trade controls for national security purposes are found principally in the Export Administration Act (EAA) of 1979, as amended,[13] and the Export Administration Regulations.[14] A goal of the EAA legislation is:

> (A) to restrict the export of goods and technology which could make a significant contribution to the military potential of any other country or combination of countries which would prove detrimental to the national security of the United States; and
>
> (B) to restrict the export of goods and technology where necessary to further significantly the foreign policy of the United States or to fulfill its declared international obligations.[15]

These goals are accomplished through export controls consistent with specific criteria established by Congress. This complex legislation vests considerable discretion in the executive branch, and was intended to be used sparingly to minimize harm to American businesses while protecting national interests. The president is authorized to prohibit the exportation of any articles subject to the jurisdiction of the U.S.A. or exported by any person subject to the jurisdiction of the U.S.A.[16] Presidential authority is delegated to the Department of Commerce, and the department's most effective restraint is found in the licensing requirements.

The U.S. government announced in March 1992 that it would defend even more aggressively the shortened "core list" of controlled exports established by members of the Coordinating Committee on Multilateral Export Controls (COCOM).[17] Even if an individual country (e.g., Russia) could prove to the president that it was no longer a military threat to the United States, there still was concern that high technology exports with possible military applications might be transshipped from the original destination to other regions that might pose a threat to U.S. interests. To the extent the new Russian Federation could exercise strong federal powers to control such transshipment, it thereby could enhance the federation's eligibility to receive imports of high technology from the West.

In an unprecedented show of cooperation, the former Soviet republics of Russia, Ukraine, Belarus, and Kazakhstan began to work closely with U.S. officials to create new export control regimes designed to prevent the spread of weapons of mass destruction. Russia was most successful in early efforts to establish such a regime. The work toward an agreement between the United States and 26 other countries (including Russia) to prevent the spread of nuclear-weapons-related goods and technology provided a powerful incentive for further cooperative efforts regarding military-sensitive, high technology products. Without such an export control regime in place, however, the U.S.

government understandably would be slow to ease limits on high technology exports to Russia and other members of the former Soviet Union.[18]

Fiscal and Monetary Reforms

Economic conditions had badly deteriorated in Russia by spring 1992.[19] One of the most serious crises facing Russia and other states of the former Soviet Union was the sharp drop in hard currency income. In a relatively short period, the Soviet Union moved from the world's largest oil producer to a country that expected to have virtually no oil exports by the end of 1992.[20] The continuing failure of the Soviet Union to generate hard currency earnings through the sale of oil, gold, and other products accelerated the collapse of the region's economy.

A major Russian objective has been the establishment of a convertible currency. This goal is intimately linked to the abolition of the centralized allocation of resources and the establishment of a decentralized, market-oriented economy. To these ends, the Federation Treaty provides that "financial, currency, credit, and money issues" are among those matters within the exclusive jurisdiction of the Federation.[21]

The new economic program of the Russian government basically has been grounded upon a standard economic stabilization approach, reflecting the goals of liberalizing economic relations with other countries, lifting price controls, balancing the budget, adhering to strict financial and credit policies, and implementing tax reform measures.[22]

Russia's agreement with the IMF cleared the way for the creation of a ruble stabilization fund, a critical step in controlling the inflation rate. Additionally, Western financial aid and the rescheduling of debt payments significantly increased the prospects for currency convertibility and market reform.

On March 2, 1992, Yegor Gaidar, finance minister and chief architect of the Russian Federation's market reforms, presented an updated economic reform package to Parliament. The reform program was designed to allow foreign investors who earned ruble profits to export those profits, using the floating market rate after April 20, 1992. The chief motivation of the reformers was facilitation of Russia's entry into the IMF.[23]

The Trade Infrastructure

By the late 1980s, the Soviets had instituted major internal organizational changes to carry out new foreign economic policies to encourage increased international trade and investment. Although considerable decentralization already had been achieved with respect to foreign trading authority, significant problems remained.

On February 24, 1992, President Yeltsin issued a decree that split the powerful Ministry of Economics and Finance into two separate entities, the Finance Ministry and the Ministry of Economics. The decree also created a new Ministry of Foreign Economic Relations. Deputy Prime Minister Yegor Gaidar, chief architect of the reform program, was selected as head of the Finance Ministry. Yeltsin's former chief deputy, Andrei Nechayev, was selected as the new minister of economics. The Ministry of Foreign Economic Relations replaced the State Committee on Foreign Economic Relations. The former state committee head, Pyotr Aven, was selected to head the new Foreign Economic Relations Ministry.

Both Aven and Gaidar are well schooled in Western business practices. Many of the new appointees, known in some quarters as the "young Turks" of the Yeltsin administration, were prominent pro-reform advocates and quickly became targets of the conservative elements in the Congress.

Another key agency in the restructuring process was the Committee on Foreign Investment, originally formed in December 1991. It was headed by Leonid Grigorev, coauthor of the ill-fated "500 days" reform package announced in the fall of 1990. The Committee on Foreign Investment adopted the following goals:

- Formulation of a strategy for attracting foreign capital
- Registration of joint ventures
- Drafting of legislation on foreign investment and oversight of compliance
- Working with the State Committee for Management of State Property (responsibility for privatization) and issuance of licenses for foreign participation
- Evaluation of large-scale foreign investment projects, including defense conversion[24]

On February 15, 1992, the Russian government hired the Wall Street firm of Goldman, Sachs & Co. to assist the Committee on Foreign Investment in attracting foreign investors.[25] However, it was obvious that a great deal needed to be done before that goal could be realized. Among other things, a reliable and transparent legal infrastructure was needed before foreign trading partners could confidentially identify those entities in federation states that have the power to make enforceable trade contracts. Moreover, it was clear that the bureaucracy needed further streamlining to eliminate the burdens of rivalry, turf protection, and lack of coordination among government ministries.

FOREIGN INVESTMENT

Investment in the Soviet Union was viewed for many years as an unattractive alternative for most Western businesses. Major causes for disenchantment included the anti-Western attitudes of the Soviet government and the inadequate guarantees and protections from the government. However, the official Soviet attitude began to change with the gradual thaw in East-West relations.

On January 13, 1987, the Council of Ministers of the U.S.S.R. passed a decree establishing the Foreign Joint Venture Law,[26] which represented a significant departure from the traditional hostility toward foreign capital operating on Soviet soil. On the same day, the Presidium of the U.S.S.R. Supreme Soviet passed an implementing edict,[27] which authorized foreign investment in the Soviet Union for the first time since 1930 (when the Soviets canceled all foreign joint ventures).

Following on the heels of major political changes, a new foreign investment law was passed in July 1991.[28] In what came to be known as the "war of the laws," the republics also passed their own foreign investment enabling legislation.[29] The fact that the republics were able to seize the initiative in an area of such national importance reflected the declining strength of the central government.

Obviously, to the extent each state or local governmental entity exercises independent sovereign power, the foreign investors' attention will shift to the appeasement of local authorities. Unless a doctrine of "federal preemption" is applied, a morass of conflicting local rules can quickly stifle the viability of foreign investment projects. The following discussion treats some of the critical issues that must be addressed as federal (or republican) foreign investment laws are promulgated and administered.

Negotiations and Formation of the Venture

Due to an undeveloped legal infrastructure and the current climate of political disorder, investment in many of the republics will be an exercise in faith and creativity. There are a multitude of challenges that must be faced by any foreign investor. Such challenges include the tasks of securing business licenses, complying with special operational rules, negotiating tax rates, satisfying safety standards, complying with environmental and consumer protection requirements, sourcing raw materials, establishing reliable suppliers, and a host of other issues.

Financing U.S. Investment

Prior to the collapse of the Soviet Union, the United States already had completed a number of rounds of negotiations with the U.S.S.R. on a bilateral investment treaty. By early 1992, the Overseas Private Investment Corporation

(OPIC) was nearing agreement to support U.S. investments in Russia with direct loans, loan guarantees, and political risk insurance. The plans were to set a coverage limit for Russia of $500 to $600 million dollars.[30]

Quality Control

The reputation for poor-quality workmanship and poor worker performance in the Soviet Union likely will continue to haunt efforts to revitalize the economy through trade and foreign investment for some time to come. Although quality control ultimately will be a matter of local responsibility, the new Federation Treaty provides that the federal government and the republics share joint jurisdiction with regard to issues of education and training.[31] The federal government should take the initiative in promoting quality control through national education and training programs.

Labor and Employment Issues

Labor matters also are within the joint jurisdiction of the federation and the republics under the new treaty.[32] For generations, Soviet workers have taken job security for granted, leading some commentators to observe that communism in the Soviet Union created the "iron borscht bowl of guaranteed employment and all its attendant disincentives for productivity."[33]

It is likely Soviet workers will continue to have difficulty adapting to profit-oriented enterprises. Disputes over discipline are bound to be frequent in foreign investment enterprises. Because such matters as employee discipline are deeply rooted in local concerns, it may be expected that the federal government and local authorities will have numerous clashes over the division of responsibility in their joint management of this sensitive issue.

If the experience in the People's Republic of China can be used by analogy, the central (federal) authority likely will promote broader discretion for enterprise management in matters of labor discipline, while local authorities will be more paternalistic and protective of workers. Thus, while the federal law may be attractive to foreign investors, the local "operational codes" may in fact pose barriers to enforcement of enterprise disciplinary rules.

The Bureaucratic Maze

The entrenched and lethargic bureaucracy was one of the most formidable challenges Gorbachev confronted during his tenure. The bureaucracy will likely continue to pose a problem for foreign investors as former bureaucrats remain in positions of power in the new federal system. The Soviet Union had a history of notorious discrepancies between the paper promises of the central government and the bureaucratic realities at the local level. Such discrepancies can pose traps for the unwary, and those traps likely will not be fully discovered until after the foreign investment has been made.

To a certain extent, strengthened discipline and better education of the bureaucracy may help. In the long term, however, the bureaucracy simply must assimilate new notions about the rule of law and privatization, a task that will not be accomplished easily.

Conditions for Foreign Workers and Staff

A common complaint among foreign investors in communist and former communist countries has been that living conditions for foreign expatriates are inadequate, inconvenient, and often inordinately expensive. Pricing policy is a matter within the stated jurisdiction of the federal authorities.[34] Again, these matters likely will be resolved at the local level, if resolved at all. Part of the solution lies in the improvement of the infrastructure.

Infrastructural Issues

Foreign investors will find in most areas of the former Soviet Union a pervasive problem of inadequate infrastructure. In theory, at least, the federal authorities have considerable power to resolve infrastructural issues. The Federation Treaty provides that federal authorities shall have jurisdiction over federal funds for regional development:[35] federal transport, railways, information, communications, and federal energy and nuclear systems.[36]

Intellectual Property Protection

The Soviet Union has made significant, although yet inadequate, strides in the protection of intellectual property. The new Federation Treaty vests in the federal government authority over "juridical regulation of intellectual property."[37]

Dispute Resolution

Arbitration under the Soviet *Arbitrazh* generally has been respected by foreign investors. The new Federation Treaty vests jurisdiction in the federal government over "the judicial system; the procuracy; criminal, criminal procedure, and criminal sentencing legislation; amnesties and pardons; civil, civil procedure, and *arbitration procedure legislation*; juridical regulation of intellectual property."[38] The treaty also vests jurisdiction in the federal authorities over federal conflict law.[39]

Taxing Powers

The treaty vests in the federal government authority over "*federal* taxes and dues,"[40] presumably leaving considerable revenue powers to local taxing authorities.

Natural Resources, Raw Materials Sourcing

The treaty decentralizes authority over the control of natural resources and the environment. Article II provides that the federation and the republics shall have *joint* jurisdiction over "the utilization of natural resources, the protection of the environment, and ensuring ecological safety; specially protected natural areas; the protection of historical and cultural monuments."[41] Article III further provides:

> Questions of the possession, use, and disposal of land, its mineral resources, water, and other natural resources, are settled on the basis of the legislation of the Russian Federation and the legislation of the republics in the Russian Federation. The status of federal natural resources is defined in accordance with the mutual accord of the federal bodies of state power of the Russian Federation and the bodies of state power of the republics of the Russian Federation.[42]

PRIVATIZATION

The process of privatization in the Russian Federation clearly has implications for its foreign economic relations. A series of laws enacted in the U.S.S.R. since 1989 established the legal framework for privatization in the Russian Republic.[43]

One of the early laws enacted by the Supreme Soviet of the U.S.S.R. in the move toward a market economy was the Cooperatives Law, enacted on May 26, 1988, and subsequently amended in 1989 and 1990.[44] On November 23, 1989, the Leasing Law was enacted.[45] On February 28, 1990, the Supreme Soviet enacted the Land Law.[46] The Property Law was enacted on March 6, 1990.[47] The Law on Enterprises was adopted on June 4, 1990.[48] On June 19, 1990, the Regulations Governing Joint-Stock and limited-liability companies were promulgated.[49] On August 8, 1990, the Council of Ministers passed the Resolution on Small Enterprises.[50] On December 10, 1990, the Supreme Soviet of the U.S.S.R. promulgated a new Investment Law.[51] On July 1, 1991, a new Privatization Law was enacted by the Supreme Soviet.[52]

Despite this rapidly evolving legal framework, the privatization process appears to be bogged down in bureaucratic inertia. This is true in part because it is a highly complex process, but also because there is a shortage of knowledgeable personnel who can expedite the new process of privatization.

Despite efforts by the government to codify legal rules, prospective foreign investors continue to express concerns over such matters as employee rights and foreign ownership issues in privatized firms. Overall, the role of foreign investors in the privatization process is still unclear,[53] and it is unlikely that American firms will rush to participate in Russia's privatization process in the near future.

CONCLUSION

Extrication from the economic morass left by the Soviet Union's collapse likely will prove to be the challenge of the century for Russia and the other republics. As is the case in most bankruptcies, considerable sacrifice will be expected and old ways of doing business must be changed. As may be seen from the abbreviated list of concerns discussed above, mere tinkering with the details will not suffice; a major sea change in the social and political economy is essential.

The new Federation Treaty of spring 1992 was an important, although inconclusive, step toward meaningful reform. Many problems were unresolved by the treaty, however, and new issues were raised. One thing is certain—a massive commitment to reform is essential to place the former states of the Soviet Union on a sound economic foundation. It remains to be seen whether the surviving political system is up to the task.

NOTES

1. See Jude Wanniski, "The Future of Russian Capitalism," *Foreign Affairs*, Spring 1992, at 17, 19.

2. The Russian Federal Treaty, English trans. published in FBIS-SOV-92-051 (Mar. 16, 1992) [hereinafter *Treaty*]. See Steven Erlanger, "Most Pieces of Russia Agree to Coalesce, For Now," *The New York Times*, April 1, 1992, at A8.

3. The treaty is to become a part (an independent section) of the Constitution of the Russian Federation after it is approved by the Congress of People's Deputies of the Russian Federation. *Treaty, supra* note 2, at Article VIII.

4. Last-minute negotiations made possible the signing of the treaty by repre-

sentatives of Bashkir, the most populous of the autonomous republics.

5. Steven Greenhouse, "I.M.F. Endorses Russian Plan for Economy, Clearing Way for Aid and for Membership," *The New York Times*, April 1, 1992, at A1.

6. Andrew Rosenthal, "Aid to Russia; Bush and Kohl Unveil Plan for Seven Nations to Contribute $24 Billion Dollars in Aid For Russia," *The New York Times*, April 2, 1992, at A1.

7. Treaty, *supra* note 2, at Article I(k).

8. *Ibid.*

9. *Ibid.* at Article I (o).

10. *Ibid.* at Article VI(2).

11. See W. Gary Vause, "The Coming End of Perestroika's Golden Age of Law Reform," 20 *Stetson Law Review* 201 (1990).

12. *Treaty, supra* note 2, at Article 1(g).

13. 50 U.S.C. app. § 2401–2420 (1988).

14. 15 C.F.R. § 730–799 (1993).

15. 50 U.S.C. app. § 2402 (2) (A-B) (1988).

16. 50 U.S.C. app. § 2402 (1982 & Supp. III 1985).

17. "U.S. Will Defend Aggressively COCOM's Core List of Controlled High-Tech Exports," 9 *International Trade Report* (Bureau of National Affairs [BNA]) 483 (March 18, 1992).

18. "U.S. Official Reports Progress in Helping Ex-Soviet Union Establish Export Controls," 9 *International Trade Report* (BNA) 482 (March 18, 1992).

19. Robert S. Strauss, the U.S. ambassador to Russia, declared on March 11, 1992, that "economic chaos" exists in the Soviet Union and the situation is worsening. "Ambassador Strauss Calls Situation in Former Soviet Union 'Chaotic,'" 9 *International Trade Report* (BNA) 495 (March 18, 1992).

20. "Hard-Currency Shortfall Seen Speeding Economic Decline of Former Soviet Union," 9 *International Trade Report* (BNA) 414 (March 4, 1992).

21. Treaty, *supra* note 2 at Article 1(g).

22. "Western Aid, Rescheduling Seen Affecting Ruble Convertibility, Russian Reform," 9 *International Trade Report* (BNA) 405 (March 4, 1992).

23. "Russian Economic Reform Plan Aims for Swift Entry into IMF," 9 *International Trade Report* (BNA) 460 (March 11, 1992).

24. "Russia's Yeltsin Reworks Economic Team, Sets Up Foreign Economic Relations Agency," 9 *International Trade Report* (BNA) 403 (March 4, 1992).

25. *Ibid.*

26. The January 13, 1987, Council of Ministers decree On Procedures for the Creation and Operation in the U.S.S.R. of Joint Enterprises in Which Soviet Organizations and Firms from Capitalist and Developing Countries are Partners was first published in *Pravda*: "In the U.S.S.R. Council of Ministers," *Pravda*, January 27, 1987, at 2 (Eng. ed., Associated Publishers, Inc.). In the United States, the Bureau of National Affairs published an English translation of the Council's decree: "Soviet Council of Ministers Decision on Joint Ventures with Western Firms," 4 *International Trade Report* (BNA) 358–61 (March 11, 1987). An English translation of the Council's decree also was published by the American Society of International Law: "Union of Soviet Socialist Republics: Decree on Joint Enterprises with Western and Developing Countries," 26 *International Legal Materials* 749 (1987) [hereinafter Soviet Joint

Venture Law]. See generally Russell H. Carpenter, Jr., and Bradford L. Smith, "U.S.-Soviet Joint Ventures: A New Opening in the East," 43 *Business Lawyer* 79 (1987); Kelly Ross, "Recent Developments, Foreign Investment: New Soviet Joint Venture Law," 28 *Harvard International Law Journal* 473 (1987).

27. The English translation of the January 13, 1987, Supreme Soviet edict On Questions Connected with the Creation of the Territory of the U.S.S.R. and the Activity of Joint Enterprises, International Associations, and Organizations with the Participation of Soviet and Foreign Organizations, Firms, and Agencies of Administration is published by the American Society of International Law: "Union of Soviet Socialist Republics: Edict Concerning Taxation of Joint Enterprises in the Soviet Union and Dispute Settlement," 26 *International Legal Materials* 759 (1987).

28."The Fundamentals of Legislation on Foreign Investment in the U.S.S.R," *Izvestia*, July 24, 1991 (enacted July 5, 1991) [hereinafter Foreign Investment Law].

29. See, for example, Law of Russian Soviet Federative Socialist Republic on Foreign Invetment in the RSFSR, published in "The Most Important Documents of the Month," collection of government documents, July 1991.

30. "U.S. to Conclude Trade Agreements with Ex-Soviet Republics, Offer Firm Support," 9 *International Trade Report* (BNA) 352, 353 (February 26, 1992).

31. Treaty, *supra* note 2, at Article II(d).

32. *Ibid.*

33. Joseph Pattison and Martin Klingenberg, "Soviet Announcement Should Stir Interest of U.S. Corporations," *Legal Times*, March 2, 1987, at 12.

34. *Treaty*, *supra* note 2, at Article I(g).

35. *Ibid.* at Article I(h).

36. *Ibid.* at Article I(i).

37. *Ibid.* at Article I(n).

38. *Ibid.* (emphasis added).

39. *Ibid.* at Article I(o).

40. *Ibid.* at Article I(h) (emphasis added).

41. *Ibid.* at Article II(c).

42. *Ibid.* at Article III(3).

43. For an excellent treatment of the privatization issue, see Olga Floroff and Susan Tiefenbrun, "A Legal Framework for Soviet Privatization," 18 *Pepperdine Law Review* 849 (1991).

44. Law of the Union of Soviet Socialist Republics on Cooperatives in the U.S.S.R., 22 Vedomosti SSSR, item 355 (1988), reprinted in *Izvestia* (Novosti trans. with Coudert Brothers unofficial trans. of amendments) (enacted by the Supreme Soviet of the U.S.S.R. on May 26, 1988, and amended October 16, 1989, and June 6, 1990).

45. The Fundamental Legislation of the Union of Soviet Socialist Republics and the Union Republics on Leasehold, 25 Vedomosti SSSR, item 481 (unofficial trans. 1989).

46. The Fundamentals of Law on Land Ownership, 10 Vedomosti SSSR, item 129 (1990), reprinted in Olga Floroff and Susan Tiefenbrun, "New Fundamentals of Law on Land Ownership," 4 *New York International Law Review* 92, 94–106 (1991).

47. Law of the Union of Soviet Socialist Republics on Property in the U.S.S.R., 11 Vedomosti SSSR, item 164 (1990), reprinted in 42 *Current Digest of the Soviet Press*, No. 12 (1990).

48. Union of Soviet Socialsit Republics "Law on Enterprises in the U.S.S.R."

Izvestia, June 12, 1990, reprinted in *National Affairs*, June 20, 1990, at 58–60.

49. Regulations Governing Joint-Stock and Limited-Liability Companies, 2 Biull. Norm. Akt. SSSR, item 590 (1991) [hereinafter Joint-Stock and Limited-Liability Companies Regulations]. It should be noted that Resolution No. 590 also enacted Regulations Governing Securities.

50. Resolution No. 790 of the Council of Ministers of the U.S.S.R. of August 8, 1990, On Measures to Encourage the Establishment and Development of Small Enterprises, Buill. Norm. Akt. SSSR, item 790 (1990, reprinted in *Ekonomicheskii Zhurnal*, No. 33, August 1990 (Novosti trans.)

51. The Fundamentals of Legislation on Investment in the U.S.S.R., 51 Vedomosti SSSR, item 790 (Asset trans. 1990).

52. "The Law of the Soviet Socialist Republic on the Fundamental Principles of Statization and Privatization of Enterprises" (1991), reprinted in *Izvestia and Sovetskaia Rossiia*, August 8, 1991, at 1.

53. "Foreign Participation in Privatizing Russian Economy Likely To Be 'Very Limited,'" 9 *International Trade Report* (BNA) 358 (February 26, 1992).

PART IV

STATE AND LOCAL GOVERNMENT

"Creeping" federalism is a phenomenon experienced by most stable federal government structures over the long term, interspersed with spasms of federal deregulation and decentralization. The instability of government structures in the former U.S.S.R. has led to sovereign independence by former U.S.S.R. republics and claims to autonomy by local geographic governmental units within the Russian Federation. Even the U.S.A. recently has been in a cycle of deregulation (airlines, education, trucking, utilities, etc.) with state and local governments bearing a greater portion of the governmental budget burdens than they have in the past.

Richard Briffault's paper succinctly makes the case that the last three decades document the federalization of state and local political processes in the U.S.A. This trend has evolved in direct reflection of the national commitment to federal protection of individual and minority group participation in the political process. The paper concentrates on the two most important aspects of participation: one man-one vote and minority group representation in government.

The paper by Philip Grossman and Priya Rajagopalan addresses the dissolution of the U.S.S.R. and the fiscal issues that may yet dictate a meaningful role for a centralized CIS or other governmental unit. The paper examines specifically the cost and benefits of having local or former republic independent states now bear the burden of taxing and spending powers. The paper asserts that administrative inefficiencies and economic waste of 15 separate fiscal entities of the 15 former republics may yet create some fiscally efficient role for the CIS in the decades ahead.

Lyudmila M. Simonova's paper suggests that local and regional governments within the Russian Federation must stimulate free enterprise and economic growth, especially in the energy sector, while at the same time both safe-guarding favorable conditions for the daily lives of the population and finding workable answers to the existing and anticipated environmental crises. The paper focuses on the large energy enterprises of the Tyumen region to suggest that effective development of organized free enterprise requires a measure of central government coordination and influence.

Alexei I. Ivandaev's paper examines the market problems facing the local governments in autonomous territories of the Russian Federation.

Irina A. Vekshina's paper uses Siberia to illustrate the relation of local and regional governments to the central government during the period of perestroika. The paper optimistically observes that during perestroika the local and regional government structures became distinct from the command and control central government structure and that a rather unique federal power sharing arrangement evolved not only in Russia and Siberia but also in several other former republics of the former U.S.S.R.

Gennadii N. Chebotarev's paper recounts the deterioration of living conditions in Russian autonomous territories and calls for increased self-government, especially for the Northern territories.

17

Federalism in Political Structure and Power: The New Role of Federal Law in Constraining Political Processes in American State and Local Governments

Richard Briffault

A central element of American federalism is the power of the states to define their own internal political structures. The Constitution of 1787 did not prescribe rules concerning state political structure. Instead, it assumed state autonomy and built on state decisions concerning state representative institutions and state electorates in creating the national government. Members of the House of Representatives are elected "by the People of the several States," with the electors in each state to have "the qualifications requisite for electors of the most numerous branch of the state legislature."[1] Senators were originally chosen by state legislatures;[2] when the Constitution was amended to provide for the direct election of senators, the electorate for the Senate, like the House, was that "of the most numerous branch of the State legislatures."[3] The president is selected by electors appointed by the states "in such manner as the legislature thereof may direct."[4]

Free to design their own institutions of political power, the states have over two centuries experimented considerably. Some state political decisions—such as the definition of their electorates, or requirements that parties nominate candidates through primaries—have direct ramifications for national politics. Other state political actions—such as unicameral legislatures,[5] the election of judges and cabinet officers whose federal counterparts are appointed,[6] the election of local legislatures at large rather than from districts, or the provision for direct citizen law making through referenda or ballot initiatives[7]—are departures from the national "model" of government structure that have altered state and local politics without directly affecting the national government.

Over the last 30 years, however, the balance of federalism in the regulation of the political process has changed significantly. Through a combination of developments—constitutional amendments, congressional enactments, and

Supreme Court decisions—state and local political processes have been, to a large degree, federalized. Political participation in state and local government has become a fundamental *federal* right. This, in turn, has involved federal institutions in the definition of the contours of that right, with the result that many state laws have been invalidated and many state political institutions profoundly altered. The definition of the state and local electorate, the structure of state and local legislatures, access to the ballot for candidates for state and local offices,[8] the regulation of state political parties,[9] and campaign finance practices in state and local elections[10] are now shaped by federal statutes and constitutional doctrines.

These federal interventions have proceeded from an evolving commitment to federal protection of the rights of individuals and minority groups to full participation in state and local political processes. The most important sources of that commitment, explored in this paper, are the new concept of a federally protected right to vote; the "one person, one vote" doctrine; and the emerging concept that racial and ethnic minority voters have a protected interest in minority group representation.

THE RIGHT TO VOTE

Traditionally, qualifications for voting in state and local elections were a state, not a federal, matter. This position was well-illustrated in *Minor v. Happersett*,[11] an 1874 Supreme Court decision concerning a challenge to Missouri's denial of the vote to women. The plaintiff's claim to the franchise, notwithstanding her sex, rested on the recently ratified Fourteenth Amendment, which provided that "all persons born or naturalized in the United States and subject to the jurisdiction thereof" are "citizens of the United States and of the State wherein they reside." She contended that this provision made her a citizen of the United States and of her state, and, thus, she was entitled to vote. The Supreme Court agreed that she was, indeed, a citizen, but ruled that her citizen status had no consequence for her claim to the franchise.

The Court found that the federal Constitution, with one exception, had nothing at all to say about the right to vote. The suffrage was left entirely to the states, which could impose whatever qualifications they deemed appropriate. The one exception—the Fifteenth Amendment—proved the rule, since, the Court reasoned, there would have been no need for a special constitutional provision prohibiting the states from denying the franchise on grounds of race or previous condition of servitude if the Constitution, either by its original provisions or the Fourteenth Amendment, had otherwise treated the right to vote as an element of citizenship. The right to vote was simply not in the federal Constitution.

Although *Minor*'s specific ruling denying the franchise to women was overturned by the Nineteenth Amendment in 1920, its rejection of a general federal constitutional protection of the right to vote continued past 1960. Apart from the criteria specifically proscribed by the Fifteenth and Nineteenth Amendments—race and gender—the states could determine the qualifications for the franchise. Many states conditioned the suffrage on payment of a poll tax; adopted property ownership or property tax payment requirements for voting on bond issues; or imposed literacy tests, "good moral character" rules, lengthy durational residency requirements, and sundry other restrictions. The Supreme Court expressly sanctioned some of these restrictions;[12] the rest were implicit in *Minor*'s disavowal of any general constitutional interest in the state and local franchise.

During the course of the 1960s, however, the constitutional analysis of the state and local vote underwent a revolution, and by the early 1970s all of these qualifications had been invalidated. The right to vote was pronounced a fundamental federal constitutional right, and state laws limiting the franchise were subjected to strict and exacting judicial scrutiny. The franchise became virtually a presumptive right of adult resident citizens.

The change in constitutional doctrine was most dramatically evidenced by *Harper v. Virginia Board of Elections*[13] and *Kramer v. Union Free School District.*[14] *Harper*, decided in 1966, considered a Fourteenth Amendment challenge to Virginia's $1.50 poll tax for voting in state and local elections. In an early harbinger of increased federal interest in voting, the Twenty-fourth Amendment had been adopted two years before. It barred the denial of the vote in federal elections for nonpayment of the poll tax, but was silent as to the use of the poll tax in state elections. On the theory of *Minor*, the Twenty-fourth Amendment should actually have supported Virginia's poll tax, since if the Fourteenth Amendment proscribed the poll tax there would have been no need for another amendment. In any event, under *Minor* there was no constitutional protection of the vote in state elections; indeed, three decades earlier the Supreme Court had sustained a poll tax requirement.[15]

Harper, however, struck down the poll tax. In so doing, it set forth the contours of current federal doctrines concerning the right to vote. Although the Court first noted that "the right to vote in state elections is nowhere expressly mentioned"[16] in the Constitution, it found that voting is nonetheless a "fundamental" right because it is "preservative" of all other political and civil rights. There is no federally secured right to vote in state and local elections, but "once the franchise is granted to the electorate, lines may not be drawn that are inconsistent with the Equal Protection Clause of the Fourteenth Amendment."[17] Any state classification that restricts the vote "must be closely scrutinized and carefully confined."[18] As wealth "is not germane to one's ability to participate intelligently in the electoral process,"[19] the poll tax was unconstitutional. Subsequently, building on *Harper*, the Court invalidated state laws that limited the right to vote on municipal bond issues to property owners or property taxpayers.[20]

The Court went further three years later in *Kramer*. That case involved a challenge to a New York law that limited the franchise in school board elections to owners or renters of taxable real property and parents of children enrolled in local public schools. The school board, as the Court noted, is an office that need not be elective at all and in some cities in New York State was filled by appointment, not election.[21] Moreover, since both renters and parents could vote, the franchise restriction did not discriminate on the basis on wealth. Nor was the restriction the result of bias against an excluded group or person. The poll tax was notorious for its use in disenfranchising blacks, but the plaintiff in *Kramer* was a childless adult who lived in his parents' home, not a member of any victimized class. Further, the state's voting qualifications were arguably germane to the purpose of the election. School districts are funded out of a specific local revenue source—the property tax—and provide a single service, the education of local children. The state law limited the franchise to those who paid the local tax (property owners and renters, who pay the tax indirectly) and to those whose children consumed the district's services. Nevertheless, the Court held that the restriction failed the exacting judicial scrutiny that restrictions on the franchise must receive.

To survive strict judicial scrutiny, a state must demonstrate that the restriction is narrowly tailored to promote a compelling state interest. The state asserted a compelling interest in limiting the electorate to those persons "primarily interested" in school affairs. Without determining whether a state could so limit the electorate, the Court found that the state's restriction was insufficiently precise to attain that goal since it excluded the plaintiff, who was "interested in and affected by school board decisions."[22] Given the plaintiff's lack of a direct stake in school board decisions, the Court's action indicated an expansive notion of those "affected" by public decisions and entitled to vote in the elections for public officials.

Kramer was highly significant in two ways. First, by treating the right to vote as virtually presumptive once the state decides to make a particular public office elective, the case set the tone for subsequent decisions concerning the rights of individuals to participate in the political process. Voting and related political activity were treated as fundamental rights, despite the lack of any specific constitutional reference. Second, by imposing strict scrutiny and, in particular, by requiring that classifications be narrowly tailored to meet even a legitimate state goal, *Kramer* doomed many other suffrage restrictions.[23] Most significantly in terms of the number of people enfranchised, *Kramer* led to the invalidation of most durational residency requirements.[24] Apart from citizenship, current residency in the jurisdiction, and minimum age, few state restrictions on the franchise can now pass constitutional challenge.[25]

The only exemption from the general rule of strict scrutiny, and invalidation, of limitations on the vote appears to be certain special districts, such as irrigation and flood control districts. The Supreme Court has determined that given the limited function of those districts, and the fact that they primarily provide services for land rather than people, the states may treat such districts like business enterprises rather than political entities, so that strict scrutiny of limitations on the franchise will not be applied.[26]

Congress has also played a role in extending federal protection to the franchise in state and local elections. Congress, like the Supreme Court, has sought to expand opportunities for political participation at state and local levels. One major congressional action was the adoption, followed by state ratification, of the Twenty-sixth Amendment in 1971 that lowered the voting age to 18. But Congress' principal instrument in this area has been the Voting Rights Act, adopted in 1965 and subsequently amended. Although enacted out of a concern to provide effective federal remedies against racial discrimination in voting, the act goes well beyond race.

The most dramatic feature of the act in terms of redefining the state and local electorate is its ban on literacy tests. Prior to the adoption of the act, the Supreme Court had sustained state literacy tests in general, and in *Harper* the Court had implied that a literacy test, unlike a wealth test, could be germane to the right to vote. Specific applications of the literacy test, however, had been invalidated when it could be demonstrated that a test was used to effectuate racial discrimination. In the act, Congress found that literacy tests were frequently used for invidious racial reasons and that requiring proof of a discriminatory purpose on a case-by-case basis imposed heavy burdens on black plaintiffs. So the act simply outlawed such tests, initially in certain jurisdictions where low voter turnout implied that the tests had been used invidiously, and, after 1970, on a nationwide basis. Subsequent amendments to the act also provided for the protection of access to the ballot for the disabled, language minorities, servicemen, and Americans living overseas.

Congress is currently considering a further drastic alteration of federal-state relations in the process of enfranchisement. The proposed Voter Registration Act of 1991 would set national standards for the registration of voters. Many voting rights activists and political scientists have repeatedly condemned state registration procedures—particularly the requirement of registration at a time well in advance of election day, and the requirement of reregistration after moving or failing to vote—as erecting high administrative hurdles for many individuals, particularly the poor, the less-educated, and minorities. The act would facilitate registration by requiring the states to adopt a uniform national application for registration to vote by mail; to include voter registration applications in motor vehicle driver's license applications; and to provide for voter registration at public assistance, unemployment compensation, and other welfare agency offices.

Although the act would apply to registration for voting for federal elections only—which, pursuant to the original understanding of 1787, is handled by the states—it presumably would affect registration for state elections too, since cost considerations would presumably militate against maintaining two sets of registration procedures. Even as a legislative proposal yet to be enacted, the act is symbolic of the current balance of federalism with respect to the right to vote. The act would treat federal and state elections separately, and continue to assume that state governments will take responsibility for setting voter qualifications—for federal as well as state elections. Yet, the act also indicates a well-grounded belief that to protect and expand the opportunities for individual political participation the federal government ought to adopt uniform national rules instead of continuing to leave such matters to the states.

LEGISLATIVE APPORTIONMENT

From 1787 to 1964, the structure of state and local legislatures was entirely a matter of state determination. In many states representation was based on political subdivisions rather than population. Some states followed the federal "model," with representation in the upper house of the state legislature based on county units, and representation in the lower house involving one representative for each county, with the rest of the representatives allocated to counties according to population. This generally favored rural areas over urban areas, although the patterns of representation sometimes simply reflected historical and geographic boundaries rather than any particular bias. This situation was utterly transformed by the Supreme Court's "one person, one vote" decisions of 1964, which held that the equal protection clause of the Fourteenth Amendment requires that state legislative districts be substantially equal in population.

Three principal themes run through the "one person, one vote" decisions. First, representative government means government by majority rule. The majority of the people in each state must be able to elect a majority in each house of the legislature. Apportionment schemes that reduce popular majorities to legislative minorities are a violation of a basic principle of self-government.

Second, deviations from the equal population standard are a violation of the individual rights of those people who are placed in oversized districts. Proceeding from the concept of voting in state elections as a "fundamental" right, even though not specifically mentioned in the constitution, the Court reasoned that the right to vote entails the right to an "equally weighted" vote. To allow a small number of voters and a large number of voters each to elect a single legislative representative means that one set of votes "counts" for more than another set of votes. This is a denial of the equal protection of the laws for residents of the larger district. So long as cities and counties have different populations, the states may not base state legislative representation on political subdivisions. Equal population is the dominant rule; respect for political subdivision lines may play only an interstitial role in choosing among apportionment plans that give substantial weight to population.[27]

Third, these principles are binding national rules, not mere political arguments that particular states can opt to adopt or reject. This is partly for pragmatic reasons. Since legislative apportionment is typically undertaken by incumbent legislators, they will be inclined to draw legislative lines that reinforce the status quo that first elected them rather than vindicate principles of majority rule and individual rights. A constitutional standard is necessary so that courts may hold the incumbents to account.

Moreover, these rules are constitutional as a matter of principle. They are a mandatory norm for state governments because voting and representation are "fundamental"—they transcend federalism concerns. States may not deviate from them regardless of local history, geography, population, or political heritage, or even when a majority of the state's voters have authorized such a departure. The fundamental status of the right to vote has made "one person, one vote" fundamental as well. Although states and localities may consider other distinctive group interests in the composition of their legislatures, they may do so only *after* the basic requirement of substantial population equality—the "one ground rule"[28] for the structure of legislatures—has been met. In particular, minority interests cannot be protected through overrepresentation (compared to what population would dictate) in the legislature.

The Supreme Court's "one person, one vote" decisions, which have been extended to all general-purpose representative bodies including local legislatures,[29] have had particular implications for government in metropolitan areas. Metropolitan areas in the United States are notoriously fragmented among dozens, and sometimes hundreds, of competing local jurisdictions of widely divergent areas, populations, wealth, needs, and administrative capabilities.[30] Efforts to promote metropolitan consolidation have been blocked by smaller local units that seek to preserve their distinctive identities and interests and fear being swallowed up in larger metropolitan entities. One solution might be federative arrangements in which metropolitan governments are composed out of the local units, with existing municipalities playing a formal role in regional governance. To the extent that such a "federation" would give the residents of some local units a greater voice in the metropolitan government than their numbers alone would warrant, "one person, one vote" would appear to preclude such arrangements.[31] Indeed, the Supreme Court recently invalidated the voting rules of the Board of Estimate of the City of New York—the City itself the result of a late-nineteenth-century consolidation—because its "one borough, one vote" rule overrepresented the residents of the city's smallest, most distinctive borough, even though a majority of the votes on the Board were cast by representatives of a majority of the city's population.[32]

MINORITY RIGHTS

A third major impetus to federal alteration of state and local political arrangements has been the protection of racial and ethnic minority rights. This has been an area of long-standing federal concern. As previously noted, the first major federal initiative in the area of state voting was the constitutional ban on racial discrimination in voting, adopted in 1870. For nearly a century after the Fifteenth Amendment's adoption, however, its principle was more ignored than honored. Through mechanisms both subtle and bold the Southern states—where, until the middle of the twentieth century, most blacks lived—effectively disenfranchised their black populations. Federal enforcement of the Fifteenth Amendment was limited, and, although the Supreme Court invalidated the most blatant devices for evading the ban on racial discrimination,[33] Southern ingenuity in developing techniques for resisting black registration efforts rendered the Fifteenth Amendment largely ineffective.

The Voting Rights Act of 1965 largely transformed this situation, with an unprecedented federal legislative and administrative involvement in voting, displacing state laws in a number of Southern states. The act provided that in any state or county that used a literacy test or similar "qualification or prerequisite to voting or standard, practice, or procedure," for voter registration, and that had a turnout in the 1964 presidential election 12 percentage points below the national average, those tests and qualifications were suspended; federal examiners could be dispatched to enroll qualified voters; federal poll-watchers could be appointed; and federal criminal and civil penalties would be imposed on those who would interfere with the vote. Most dramatically, in order to prevent the implementation of new discriminatory techniques, no jurisdiction falling within the "coverage" formula could adopt any new voting rule or alter any existing rule without "preclearance" from the federal Department of Justice. The Supreme Court sustained the act against claims that it violated principles of federalism.[34]

The "preclearance" requirement continues to entail significant Justice Department review of state and local political practices. With the extension of the act in 1975 to include discrimination against language minority groups, and the expansion of the "trigger" for preclearance to include low voter turnout in the 1968 and 1972 presidential elections, the "covered jurisdictions" now include nine states, and counties in eight other states, including many outside the South.[35] The definition of a voting "standard, practice, or procedure" has also been interpreted expansively by the Justice Department and the Supreme Court to include municipal annexations,[36] reapportionment,[37] changing an office from elective to appointive,[38] and the relocation of polling places. All these actions require federal preclearance in covered jurisdictions.

Moreover, although the original impetus behind the Voting Rights Act was to enforce the right of black individuals to register and vote, Congress, the

Department of Justice, and the Supreme Court have recognized that minority voters, even when fully enfranchised, may not receive "fair and effective representation" if they are unable to elect candidates of their choice. Typically, this will result from the interplay of two factors: racially polarized voting, in which whites will not support minority candidates; and electoral devices that minimize or eliminate minority-dominated electoral units. Such "vote dilution" may be due to racial gerrymandering.[39] But, increasingly, federal attention has focused on other mechanisms, such as multimember districts for state legislative elections and at-large elections for city legislatures that, although not discriminatory on their face, make it difficult for minority groups to elect their own representatives.

In a multimember or at-large setting, the same jurisdiction-wide majority has the potential to control all the legislative seats. Where there is racially polarized voting, this means that a geographically concentrated minority, which might have constituted a majority in one or more single-member districts and won some seats, may be unable to win any elections at the jurisdiction-wide level and, thus, may be entirely denied any legislative seats.

The Supreme Court has refused to pronounce multimember districts or at-large elections unconstitutional per se, even on a showing that minorities have been unable to elect their own representatives, but the Court has been willing to invalidate such mechanisms when they are combined with other indicia of racial discrimination or result in lack of electoral success for minorities.[40] The Department of Justice has determined that a state or local effort to switch from single-member to multimember or at-large districts is subject to preclearance under the Voting Rights Act, and such preclearance will rarely be granted.[41] In addition, in 1982 Congress amended the Voting Rights Act to make it easier for minority plaintiffs to challenge existing, and long-standing, multimember or at-large systems without having to prove racially invidious intent. Although the 1982 amendment is vague with respect to the elements of proof in a vote dilution case, the Supreme Court interpreted it to permit the finding of a statutory violation largely on a showing of minority underrepresentation in a setting of racially polarized voting.[42]

As a result of Justice Department enforcement actions and private plaintiff suits under the amended statute, multimember and at-large election systems have been successfully challenged in many jurisdictions with minority population concentrations. Indeed, this form of legislative structure appears headed for extinction, to be replaced by legislatures organized into single-member districts, with those district lines frequently drawn to maximize the number of minority representatives. In effect, although both the Supreme Court and Congress have disavowed any right to minority proportional representation, some norm of minority proportional representation, or at least a presumption that something is seriously amiss when minorities are under-represented in state and local legislatures, appears to have emerged over the last decade.

Some have criticized this development. Unlike disenfranchisement or gerrymandering, at-large and multimember districts may be adopted for "good government" reasons. At one time, at-large elections were considered a reform, permitting the election of officials who would advance the interests of the city as a whole and not parochial neighborhood concerns (although this position has been subject to the criticism that at-large councils typically are dominated by downtown business groups). Multimember districts are sometimes attempts to meet the dictates of "one person, one vote" while continuing to use political subdivision lines as units of legislative representation.

Even from the perspective of minority representation, some have argued that minorities actually might enjoy greater political influence when they are a part of the constituencies of a larger number of legislators—albeit white legislators —rather than concentrated in minority districts. Others contend that the very attention to the representation of minority groups as groups, through the invalidation of multimember or at-large districts and the race-conscious line-drawing of the resulting single-member districts, creates a divisive racial component to legislative representation.[43]

Proponents of the federal attack on minority vote dilution counter that the predicate for any successful dilution claim is racially polarized voting—evidence both that minority voters would have only limited ability to influence officials responsive to white electorates and that there already is a divisive racial component to local politics. Increasing the number of minority representatives is an antidote to a history of racial exclusion and may be necessary to ensure that minority voters are treated, and seen to be treated, as full members of state and local polities.

Beyond the wisdom or defects of the vote dilution is its significance in understanding the current place of federalism in shaping state and local political structure and power. The vote dilution doctrine is both (1) a logical outgrowth of the redefinition of the right to vote in state and local elections as a fundamental *federal* right and the concomitant theory that the right to vote implies a right to "equally weighted" votes, and (2) a dramatic alteration in the traditional allocation of power with respect to state and local government structure.

As state and local legislators already know, the days when state and local electoral qualifications and the organization of state and local political institutions were primarily, if not exclusively, a matter for state and local determination are long gone. Each decennial reapportionment sends a sharp signal that the federal constitutional and statutory commitment to protecting individual political participation and the emerging concern for minority group representation impose strong federal—judicial, legislative, and, through Justice Department preclearance, executive—constraints on state and local political structures and, especially, the design of state and local representative institutions.

NOTES

1. Art. I., Sec. 2, cl. 1.
2. Art. I., Sec. 3, cl. 1.
3. Amdt. XVII, cl. 1.
4. Art. II., Sec. 1, cl. 2.
5. Nebraska currently is the only state that has a unicameral legislature.
6. In most states, the attorney general and a chief fiscal officer—treasurer or controller—are independently elected, not appointed by the governor. Another commonly elected cabinet official is the chief state education officer.
7. Most states require voter approval before the state may issue debt. J. Maxwell and J. Aronson, *Financing State and Local Governments* 207–8 (3rd ed. 1977). Half the states allow a relatively small group of citizens to suspend the operation of any new law pending its submission and approval by voters in a referendum. D. Magleby, *Voting in Ballot Propositions in the United States* 38–39 (1984). Almost two dozen states allow citizens to initiate legislation directly by drafting proposals and placing them on the ballot where, if a requisite majority of the voters approve, they may become law. See *id.*
8. See, e.g., *Williams v. Rhodes*, 393 U.S. 24 (1968); *Lubin v. Panish*, 415 U.S. 709 (1974).
9. See, e.g., *Eu v. San Francisco County Democratic Central Committee*, 109 S. Ct. 1013 (1989).
10. See, e.g., *Citizens Against Rent Control v. City of Berkeley*, 454 U.S. 290 (1981).
11. 88 U.S. 162 (1974).
12. See, e.g., *Breedlove v. Suttles*, 302 U.S. 277 (1937) (upholding the poll tax); *Lassiter v. Northampton Election Board*, 360 U.S. 45 (1959) (upholding literacy test).
13. 383 U.S. 663 (1966).
14. 395 U.S. 621 (1969).
15. *Breedlove v. Suttles*, 302 U.S. 277 (1937).
16. *Harper v. Virginia Board of Elections*, 383 U.S. 663, 665 (1966).
17. *Id.*
18. *Id.* at 670.
19. *Id.* at 669.
20. See *Cipriano v. City of Houma*, 395 U.S. 701 (1969) (revenue bonds); *City of Phoenix v. Kolodziejski*, 399 U.S. 204 (1970); *Hill v. Stone*, 421 U.S. 289 (requirement of separate approvals of both total electorate and property taxpayers invalidated).
21. 395 U.S. at 629.
22. 395 U.S. at 632 and n. 15.
23. In the area of public education, *Kramer* recently led to the invalidation of an Illinois plan for the decentralization of the governance of the Chicago schools to the neighborhood level, where the legislation vested primary electoral authority in neighborhood *parents*, rather than neighborhood *residents*. See *Fumarolo v. Chicago Board of Education*, 566 N.E. 2d 1283 (Ill. 1990).

24. *Dunn v. Blumstein*, 405 U.S. 330 (1972).

25. The principal remaining restriction is conviction of a felony. In *Richardson v. Ramirez*, 418 U.S. 24 (1974), the Supreme Court found express constitutional authorization for such a restriction in language in the Fourteenth Amendment permitting states to deny the franchise "for participation in rebellion, or other crime."

26. See, e.g., *Ball v. James*, 451 U.S. 355 (1981); *Salyer Land Co. v. Tulare Lake Basin Water Storage Dist.*, 410 U.S. 719 (1973).

27. See e.g., *Mahan v. Howell*, 410 U.S. 315 (1973) (permitting modest deviation from perfectly equal state legislative districts in order to accommodate political subdivision lines); *Abate v. Mundt*, 403 U.S. 182 (1971) (similar accommodation of subdivision lines in local legislature apportioned primarily according to population).

28. *Avery v. Midland County*, 390 U.S. 474, 485 (1968).

29. *Id.*

30. See, e.g., G. Weiher, *The Fractured Metropolis: Political Fragmentation and Metropolitan Segregation* (1991); J. Harrigan, *Political Change in the Metropolis* (4th ed. 1989); G. Miller, *Cities by Contract: The Politics of Municipal Incorporation* (1981).

31. See, e.g., *Hadley v. Junior College District of Metropolitan Kansas City*, 397 U.S. 50 (1970). See also *Cunningham v. Municipality of Metropolitan Seattle*, 751 F. Supp. 885 (W.D. Wash. 1990).

32. *Board of Esimate v. Morris*, 109 S.Ct. 1433 (1989).

33. See, e.g., *Guinn v. United States*, 238 U.S. 347 (1915) (invalidating Louisiana law that exempted from burdensome registration requirements only those persons who had been entitled to vote in 1867, and their sons and grandsons); *Smith v. Allwright*, 321 U.S. 649 (1944) (invalidating Texas white primary); *Gomillion v. Lightfoot*, 364 U.S. 339 (1960) (invalidating Alabama racial gerrymander); *Louisiana v. United States*, 380 U.S. 145 (1965) (invalidating literacy test administered in order to disenfranchise blacks).

34. *South Carolina v. Katzenbach*, 383 U.S. 301 (1966).

35. The covered states are Alabama, Alaska, Georgia, Louisiana, Mississippi, South Carolina, Texas, and Virginia. One or more counties in California, Florida, Michigan, New Hampshire, New York, North Carolina, and South Dakota are "covered jurisdictions." 28 C.F.R. pt. 51 App.

36. *Perkins v. Matthews*, 400 U.S. 379 (1971).

37. *City of Rome v. United States*, 446 U.S. 156 (1980).

38. *Allen v. State Board of Elections*, 393 U.S. 544 (1969).

39. See, e.g., *Gomillion v. Lightfoot*, 364 U.S. 339 (1960).

40. See, e.g., *Rogers v. Lodge*, 458 U.S. 618 (1982); *White v. Regester*, 412 U.S. 755 (1973); *Whitcomb v. Chavis*, 403 U.S. 124 (1971).

41. See, e.g., *City of Rome v. United States*, 446 U.S. 156 (1980).

42. *Thornburg v. Gingles*, 478 U.S. 30 (1986).

43. See, e.g., A. Thernstrom, *Whose Votes Count?* (1987).

18

Decentralization Costs and Benefits: Designing a Federal State

Philip J. Grossman and Priya Rajagopalan

Over the past few months, the Soviet Union has begun the transformation from a highly centralized state to a highly decentralized state. Complete dissolution of the union is a distinct possibility. Many of the 15 republics making up the Soviet Union have declared their independence from the central government.[1] These declarations have, however, been tempered by the recognition that complete independence is not immediately feasible. It is recognized by even the most independently minded republics that economic ties will continue to bind the republics to the Union, at least for the short run.

Given that the Soviet Union will continue to exist as both a political and an economic entity for the foreseeable future, this reformulation of the Soviet federation will require a new power-sharing agreement between the republics and the central government. Clearly, this will involve decentralization of control over taxing and spending powers. This need not, and should not, imply complete emasculation of the central government. The question that must be answered is, which fiscal prerogatives should remain with the central government and which should devolve to the republics?

To shed some light on this issue, this paper considers the costs and benefits of decentralization of government taxing and spending powers. The prescriptions of the conventional theory of federalism are contrasted with those of the "Leviathan" models of government. The paper also reviews the empirical evidence from tests of the Leviathan theory.

ADVANTAGES OF A FEDERAL STATE

Economists have long recognized the economic advantages of a federal system of government (see, for example, Tiebout 1956). Tiebout considers a system of local jurisdictions whose governments provide goods and services. The benefits are received, and taxes to support each government are paid, only by residents in the jurisdiction. If the citizens are able and willing to move from one jurisdiction to another, then, Tiebout argues, the jurisdictions will compete among themselves for the residency of the citizens.

The various jurisdictions will each offer bundles of goods and services, considered to be of value to current and prospective citizens, at the lowest possible tax price. Those communities that are most responsive to citizen demands will experience immigration and growth in their size, while those that fail to satisfy citizen demands will experience emigration and declining jurisdiction size.[2] (It is assumed that citizens are free to move among the various jurisdictions and that the costs of doing so are insignificant.) With a sufficiently large number of jurisdictions, the range of preferences held by citizens (i.e. high tax/high service, low tax/low service, high level of education services/low quality roads, etc.) can be satisfied. Essentially, Tiebout's federal system of government serves as a competitive marketplace for local government goods and services, analogous to the competitive marketplace for private goods, where the consumer shops among competing sellers and chooses the one that offers the product/price combination he or she likes best.[3]

Consumers' preferences will be less well met if they are uniformly served by a single, centralized government. Those whose preferred bundle of goods and services differs from that provided by the government will be dissatisfied. Their choice is restricted in both "voice" and "exit." Only those with preferences close to those of the median voter will be reasonably satisfied.[4] Those whose preferences differ dramatically from the preferences of the median voter cannot rectify the situation by migrating to an alternative community, since none exists.

THE CONVENTIONAL LITERATURE

The conventional literature's acceptance of Tiebout's prescription for a highly decentralized federal system of government is not unconditional. The benefits of decentralization carry costs, which may require that governments, to efficiently provide their goods and services, be larger in size than envisioned by Tiebout.

A focus of the conventional literature has been the cost of "spillovers" arising from excessive decentralization (see Oates 1972; Olson 1969; and Stigler 1965, for example). Costs arise from the spatial nature of the externalities generated by some of the goods provided by governments. If the benefits or costs associated with government-provided goods are not confined within the geographic boundaries of the providing government, a spillover, or spatial externality, occurs. If the cost of a government service is partially borne by nonresidents, residents will tend to underestimate the true social cost of the good and demand a level of provision beyond the efficient level. Alternatively, the benefits of a government service may be partially received by nonresidents. Residents will tend to underestimate the true social benefits of the good and demand a level of provision below the efficient level.

To internalize these spatial externalities and permit efficient provision of government goods requires "perfect correspondence" (Oates 1972) or "fiscal equivalence" (Olson 1969). Each good is provided by a government whose geographic boundaries encompassed fully all parties who benefit or who bear costs from the provision of the good. The difficulty is that the extent of spillover is not the same for all government goods. For example, the benefit spillovers from a hospital emergency room may be contained within a different sized geographic area than the benefit spillovers from a fire station, police station, public museum, highway system, or nuclear defense system. As the extent of spillovers varies across goods, so does the size of government best suited to internalize the externalities generated.

The Tiebout model also takes no consideration of the decision-making costs that are incurred by citizens in such a system. With so many governments, there may be excessive duplication of administrative services and little opportunity to exploit economies of scale in government administration. Compliance costs may also be considerable. The time and expense to citizens of remaining informed and of participating in the democratic process could be considerable. In light of spatial externalities and decision-making costs, the optimal federal structure may not be a Tiebout-style system. Internalizing spillovers and reducing decision-making costs may require less decentralized provision of goods and services than that implied by the Tiebout model. Goods and services requiring similar sized governments might be centralized into single government units. Increasing centralization will, however, limit the range of options available to citizens and may result in governments too large to allow for uniformity in preferences.

An alternative, as well as a possible complement, to greater centralization is intergovernmental grants. Short of "perfect correspondence," there will be spillovers. To internalize any remaining spillovers, a system of matching conditional grants is suggested (Breton 1965).[5] In cases of benefit spillovers, the lower-level government's provision of a good will be less than the efficient level. The higher-level government can encourage higher levels of provision by conditioning grants to the recipient government's spending levels on the targeted good. Furthermore, as the higher-level government finances the grants from taxes collected over a broader base than that which finances the lower-level government's expenditures, nonresidents who benefit from the externality-causing good end up contributing to its cost.

THE LEVIATHAN MODEL OF FEDERALISM

While the costs involved with decentralization are recognized by the Leviathan literature, it is argued that there is a cost to greater centralization that is too little recognized by the conventional literature. This is the increased potential for fiscal exploitation (Brennan and Buchanan 1980, 181). The disagreement between the Leviathan and conventional literatures regarding the potential for fiscal exploitation is founded upon the differing underlying assumptions of the two models.

This conventional theory is premised upon a government that is a benevolent despot that will implement efficiency-enhancing policies. The Leviathan literature argues that the conventional theory of federalism offers no basis for a division of governmental powers (Brennan and Buchanan 1980, 174). Given this benevolent despot assumption, there is no upper limit to the size of a governmental unit. All goods and services could be provided by a centralized despot. Local goods, in varying service levels, could be provided with appropriately decentralized administration.

If the agents of government could be relied upon to be benevolent and altruistic, seeking to further the social interest, then the monopoly position of a centralized despot would not harm society's well-being. The interests of the government agents and of society at large would be one and the same and the general public need not fear the acts of its government.

To support an argument for a federal system, government must be assumed to be something less than a benevolent despot. If government agents are not totally benevolent and totally altruistic, and are instead the egoists that economic theory assumes them to be in their private-sector dealings, then the interests of government need not coincide with the social interest. The acts of egoist government agents may be directed by the same motivations that direct their private-sector dealings—the advancement of their own private interest without regard to their impact on the well-being of society. In such cases, society may best be served by constraining government agents in their actions to insure that the agents' interests more closely correspond to the interests of society.

The Leviathan government, in its simplest form, is assumed to be a monopoly government whose objective is the maximization of revenue for its discretionary use. Government is not inherently benevolent, but rather is indifferent and possibly even malevolent, and is not effectively constrained by democratic processes. Although it is not suggested that government necessarily acts in this manner, this worst-case scenario is justified by arguing that "there are inherent tendencies in the structure of government to push it toward that sort of behavior implied in the monopolistic model, tendencies that may emerge in settings where constraints are wholly absent."[6]

Use of this model allows for the examination of the effectiveness of the constraints society might wish to impose upon a currently benevolent government to insure that government's interest continues to correspond with society's. One might believe that, in general, government agents have society's best interest in mind. However, one would be inclined to rest easier if it is known that, in fact, the interests of government agents were made identical to society's interests by the constraints placed on their actions and by incentives they face. The ability of the Leviathan government to maximize revenue is assumed to be limited only by the constitutional constraints placed upon its actions.[7] Possible constraints can be grouped into three categories:

1. constraints on allowable tax bases (e.g. limiting government to taxes on wages and salaries or forbidding debt financing);
2. constraints on the structure of the tax rates imposed on allowed tax bases (e.g. permitting progressive taxes only); and
3. constraints placed on government's monopoly position (e.g. imposing a federal rather than unitary system of government).

In the first two cases, the constraints directly affect the maximum revenue government can collect. In the third case, the constraint has an impact on both revenue collected and, perhaps more important, on the proportion of revenue that must be spent on general benefit goods and services—that is, it imposes limits on government's discretionary use of its revenue.

The Leviathan derives its power from its monopoly position. The advantage of a federal state over a unitary state is that this power is dispersed over a number of governments. This power sharing introduces the potential for competition. To the extent that this competition flourishes, revenue constraints are imposed on government and its Leviathan characteristics held in check.

The Tiebout model illustrates the benefit of federalism to constrain the Leviathan. A mobile citizenry in a federal system of competing subnational jurisdictions serves to limit (1) the revenues collected by the local governments, and (2) the proportion of revenues that is devoted to the purposes of government agents rather than spent on goods and services of general benefit. To see this, consider two jurisdictions where the governments offer the same level and range of goods and services. Citizens of both jurisdictions have identical incomes and tastes. If the proportion of the first government's revenues spent on general benefit goods is less than that for the second, it must raise a larger amount of revenue from its citizenry than does the second government.

For citizens living in the first jurisdiction the cost of government goods they receive is greater than if they resided in jurisdiction two. There, they would receive the same level of goods, at a lower tax price. Technically, their "fiscal residual"—the difference between the tax price they pay and the value of the publicly provided goods they receive—in jurisdiction two is greater than in jurisdiction one. If citizens are completely and freely mobile, citizens of jurisdiction one will "vote with their feet" and migrate to jurisdiction two.

Government one is then faced with two choices. It can reduce the revenues collected while increasing the proportion of revenue that goes to general benefit goods. In this way, it betters or exceeds the performance of jurisdiction two. The second choice is to cease to exist.

In a system of many local jurisdictions, no government is able to exploit its citizenry—that is, to do other than maximize their fiscal residual. Any attempt to exploit causes instantaneous and complete migration to another jurisdiction, one with a nonexploitive government. Though the tax/service bundles offered by governments might differ, no government is able to exact a surplus from its citizenry. Each is forced to provide its bundle of services at the lowest tax price possible or face fiscal extinction. Thus, though the level of taxation and expenditures might differ across jurisdictions, this reflects differences in tastes. Importantly, the share of revenue spent on goods and services is constant across all jurisdictions and is the minimum necessary to finance the goods and services.

Tiebout emphasized two reasons why this fiscal competition may be muted—limited tax/service bundle choice and restricted mobility—while Brennan and Buchanan added a third, intergovernmental collusion.

Number of Communities

Tiebout assumed a large number of jurisdictions offering a competing range of tax/service bundles. If, however, the number of local jurisdictions is limited, then the range of tax/service bundle choices will also be limited. In such a case, citizens that do not find an offered tax/service bundle that reflects their preferences will choose the jurisdiction that comes closest. The limited range of tax/service bundles creates an opportunity for fiscal exploitation by government. Furthermore, a fewer number of jurisdictions increases the greater the possibility of interjurisdictional collusion for the purpose of fiscal exploitation. The collusion issue is discussed more fully below.

Mobility

A vitally important requirement is the mobility of the citizenry. If citizens are immobile, either because of a limited range of jurisdictional choices, high moving costs, locational rents earned by economic resources, or simple locational preferences, the efficiency of federalism as a means of limiting the fiscal exploitation on the part of government is reduced. If people are unable or unwilling to move, the competitive pressures on government to maximize the percentage of collected revenues spent on general benefit goods and services are lessened.

Intergovernmental Collusion

Though Brennan and Buchanan argue that a federal system of government offers the potential of a constrained Leviathan, they recognize that governments seek ways to circumvent the fiscal discipline imposed by competitive federalism. They argue that "within a constitutionally designed federal structure, one would predict that there would be constant pressure by competitive lower-level governments to secure institutional rearrangements that would moderate competitive pressures."[8]

Such agreements might take the form of lower-level governments agreeing among themselves on a common tax rate and tax base. This approach might be unstable as there is no effective enforcement mechanism. An alternative and more stable tax cartel would involve the central government levying a uniform tax across all jurisdictions, sharing the revenues with the lower-level governments. This tax cartel takes the form of lower-level governments ceding to the central government taxing powers previously held by only the lower-level governments or shared by all governments. The central government, now in a monopoly position with respect to the relevant tax base, can levy the revenue-maximizing tax rate. It can collect more than the sum of revenues that could be collected by the individual lower-level governments. The revenue is then shared, with each lower-level government receiving at least what it collected under the competitive regime. The additional revenue collected is shared among the central government and the lower-level governments. The lower-level governments' total share is received in the form of intergovernmental grants.

EMPIRICAL TESTS OF THE LEVIATHAN HYPOTHESES

Attempts to empirically test the implications of the Leviathan model have largely focused on the hypothesis that the size and growth of government is a function of the degree to which government power is centralized. Increased centralization increases a government's monopoly power and thereby its ability to appropriate to itself a greater share of the income generated by the economy.[9] Attention has also been directed to the hypothesis that governments will collude among themselves to moderate the competitive pressures of a federal system. Governments will try to establish a more uniform "tax price" system across all jurisdictions. In return for ceding taxing powers to the central government, subnational governments will receive in return intergovernmental grants.

One of the earliest tests of the decentralization hypothesis was performed by Oates (1985), who measured fiscal decentralization in the United States as the concentration of state and local revenue and expenditure powers at the state level. He found insignificant evidence to support the decentralization hypothesis. Nelson (1986) also found no support for the same proposition. However, in a later paper Nelson (1987) found that greater "fragmentation," measured as population per multifunction government, is associated with lower levels of public spending. Zax (1989) found that both greater decentralization and greater fragmentation at the county level of government contributes to smaller government. Joulfaian and Marlow (1990) presented additional findings that decentralization and fragmentation contribute to smaller government size.

Marlow (1988), questioning the results of Oates (1985) and Nelson (1987), claims that they tested the decentralization hypothesis for only a part of total public activity (state and local vs. federal, state, and local). By ignoring the federal government, a major component of the government activity is excluded. He also claims that measuring centralization as the rate of tax receipts to tax expenditures results in the underestimation of the total impact of government. After taking the above points into consideration, Marlow, using time-series data for the United States, finds an inverse relationship between decentralization and government size.

Grossman (1989, 1992) and Grossman and West (1994) tested the companion collusion hypothesis. Grossman considered the United States and Australia, respectively. His evidence for the United States is consistent with Marlow's findings on decentralization. On the collusion issue, the results are consistent with the argument that intergovernmental grants enable governments to evade the discipline of fiscal federalism. In the study of Australia, Grossman found that decentralization had no effect on the size of the Australian public sector. However, the fiscal dependence of state governments on the Australian Commonwealth is positively related to the size of the public sector—findings consistent with those for the United States. Grossman and West examined data for Canada. Their evidence indicated an inverse correlation between fiscal decentralization and the total share of the Canadian government in gross national product. On a disaggregated level, the federal government's share in GNP declined, while the shares of the provincial and local governments actually increased with decentralization. Increased intergovernmental grants were positively correlated with total Canadian government size as well as with the size of each separate level of government. That is to say each government appeared to increase in size when the degree of collusion increases.

CONCLUSION

Decentralization of government's taxing and spending powers can better enable government to respond to the differing preferences of a heterogeneous population. A system of local jurisdictions offering a variety of tax/service bundles can serve as a competitive marketplace in which citizens shop for their utility-maximizing bundle.

These advantages, however, come at a cost. Decentralization, to an extent necessary to satisfy the full range of citizen preferences, may mean inefficient provision of government goods. The population benefiting from government provision of a good may exceed the population of the providing government. Unable to capture the full benefits and unable to impose a share of the cost on benefiting nonresidents, governments are likely to underprovide a good. Furthermore, such a decentralized system may incur both excessive administrative costs, due to duplication and unexploited economies of scale, and excessive compliance costs. Reducing these costs may require greater centralization than is consistent with fully satisfying the preferences of the heterogeneous population.

Efficient provision of government goods and the reduction of decision-making costs requires greater centralization of government powers. This is not a problem if it is assumed that government will act in the general interest; if government is a benevolent despot.

If, instead, government is comprised of self-interested individuals, then the actions of government may not advance the general interest and, in fact, could work against it. In this case, greater centralization increases the risk of greater fiscal exploitation of the public by government. Increased decentralization and the fiscal competition it introduces can serve to constrain the exploitive tendencies of a self-interested government.

These benefits and costs of greater decentralization must be considered by the Soviet Union as it studies what form of federal structure to adopt. It must weigh the risk of fiscal exploitation, a risk that Soviet history suggests is not insignificant, against the potential efficiency gains of greater centralization.

NOTES

1. Of the 15 republics, 11 have declared their independence. To date, only the independence of the three Baltic republics has been recognized by the central government.

2. An implicit assumption is that governments can cease to exist due to lack of economic viability. Likewise, new governments can form at will. It is also assumed that there is an optimal size to a jurisdiction defined by the characteristics of the goods and services provided.

3. In addition, a federal system of government enhances the ballot box pressures already inherent in a two-party political system. For example, popular changes adopted in one jurisdiction may spill over to another, not due to migration, but rather to perceived political pressures. The sitting party in the second jurisdiction may feel compelled to adopt the policy of the first jurisdiction to forestall its opposition from using the policy as an issue in a subsequent election.

4. This assumes tax/expenditure bundles are determined by majority voting.

5. Matching unconditional grants are all that will be necessary if taxes are benefit taxes. If taxes are other than benefit taxes, then unconditional grants will also be necessary. Due to space limitations, benefit taxes will be assumed and the discussion will focus on matching conditional grants.

6. Brennan and Buchanan (1980), 16.

7. It is argued that voting is unable to effectively constrain the Leviathan. See Brennan and Buchanan (1980, 20–23).

8. *Ibid.*, 182.

9. It has been hypothesized, nevertheless, that increased decentralization could result in a higher level of government expenditure. Quoting the economic historian John Wallace, Oates (1985, 749) suggests that "since individuals have more control over public decisions at the local than at the state or national level, they will wish to empower the public sector with a wider range of functions and responsibility where these activities are carried out at more localized levels of government." See Grossman and West (1994) for a criticism of this hypothesis.

REFERENCES

Brennan, Geoffrey, and Buchanan, James M. *The Power to Tax: Analytical Foundations of a Fiscal Constitution*. Cambridge: Cambridge University Press, 1980.

Breton, Albert. "A Theory of Government Grants." *Canadian Journal of Economics and Political Science* 31 (May 1965): 175–87.

Grossman, Philip J. "Fiscal Decentralization and Government Size: An Extension." *Public Choice* 62 (July 1989): 63–69.

———. "Fiscal Decentralization and Public Sector Size in Australia." *Economic Record* 68 (September 1992): 240–46.

Grossman, Philip J., and West, Edwin G. "Federalism and the Growth of Government Revisited." *Public Choice* 79, Nos. 1–2 (April 1994).

Joulfaian, David, and Marlow, Michael L. "Government Size and Decentralization: Evidence from Disaggregated Data." *Southern Economic Journal* 56 (April 1990): 1094–102.

Marlow, Michael L. "Fiscal Decentralization and Government Size." *Public Choice* 56 (March 1988): 259–70.

Nelson, Michael A. "An Empirical Analysis of State and Local Tax Structure in the Context of the Leviathan Model of Government." *Public Choice* 49 (1986): 283–94.

———. "Searching for Leviathan: Comment and Extension." *American Economic Review* 77 (March 1987): 198–204.

Oates, Wallace. *Fiscal Federalism*. New York: Harcourt Brace Jovanovich, 1972.

———. "Searching for Leviathan: An Empirical Study." *American Economic Review* 75 (September 1985): 748–57.

Olson, Mancur. "The Principle of 'Fiscal Equivalence': The Division of Responsibilities Among Different Levels of Government." *American Economic Review* 49 (May 1969): 479–87.

Stigler, George J. "The Tenable Range of Functions of Local Government." In *Private Wants and Public Needs*, 167–76. Edited by Edmund S. Phelps. New York: W. W. Norton, 1965.

Tiebout, Charles. "A Pure Theory of Local Public Expenditure." *Journal of Political Economy* 64 (October 1956): 416–24.

Zax, Jeffery S. "Is There a Leviathan in Your Neighborhood?" *American Economic Review* 79 (June 1989): 560–67.

19

Municipal Strategy for Developing Regional Free Enterprise in Siberia

Lyudmila M. Simonova

The search for a way out of Russia's economic crisis at a time when virtually all types of resources are scarce compels the Russian government to look to the only economic resource it still has at its disposal: the business activity of its population. "If Rome was saved by geese," notes Russian premier I. Silyayev, "Russia will be saved by free enterprise." The most important task of central and local authorities at the present time is to ensure the appropriate conditions and guarantees for its development.

On the other hand, the initial functioning of the new economic structures has shown that the principal danger to Russian entrepreneurs is presented by factors not so much of an economic as a political order, especially by the opposition and incompetence of the authorities at all levels. The purely economic task of finding a way out of the crisis and of rehabilitating the economy is accordingly closely tied to the political reform of management structures at all levels and to the distribution of authority between them. Moreover, as sociological polls show, the local authorities are the source of the majority of the population's "crisis of confidence." Efforts by local self-government organs at the regional level must therefore invariably be accompanied by the definition of the directions of reform of these organs themselves, as well as the directions of reform of the relations between them and the central organs of government, and of the redistribution of authority between them. We shall demonstrate this on the basis of the example of Tyumen Oblast (region) in Siberia.

Tyumen Oblast is the nation's largest agricultural and industrial region. It produces over 300 million tons of oil and almost 600 billion cubic meters of natural gas, which account for 30 percent of the nation's hard-currency earnings. The region's agricultural output was estimated in 1991 at 1,345 million rubles. Its national income was four times higher than the national average.

However, the oil and gas industry is in economic crisis. Its fixed capital assets, which it imported two or three decades ago, have become unfit for use and cannot be replaced because of the lack of hard currency and centralized capital investments. Forecasts indicate a sharp drop in oil production and a decline in oil exports in the latter half of the 1990s. The lack of investment resources perpetuates the region's specialization as a producer of natural resources and deprives it of the prospect for effecting the structural perestroika of its economy.

In addition, social and ecological problems have become particularly acute. These problems are reflected in the precipitous decline of a number of indicators of the living standard of the population of Western Siberia compared with other regions. The progressive degradation of native industries, the disappearance of indigenous nationalities of the North, and the destruction of their natural habitat have been the consequence of Moscow's "colonial" policy toward the region.

Political crises in Moscow and at the local level have added to the socioeconomic and ecological crises. Thus, contradictions caused by the redistribution of authority between the oblast Soviet and the Soviets of its two constituent okrugs (districts)—the Yamal-Nenets and Khanty-Mansi okrugs —ultimately led to the growth of separatism. As a result, one of the okrugs was removed from the oblast and was designated the Yamal-Nenets Autonomous Republic. The conflict at the local level was accompanied by the "paralysis" of Moscow's authority connected with the redistribution of authority between all-Union and republic government organs, which precluded any guarantee that they could resolve the region's economic, social, and ecological problems. The development of a strategy for the development of the region based on the region's own forces, and especially on the development of free enterprise and on the initiation of business activity as basic conditions to its economic rebirth, therefore became vitally important for Tyumen Oblast. This concept aims at the attainment of the following major goals:

- satisfying the national economy's need for sources of energy
- securing favorable conditions for the daily life of the population of the region, including the indigenous nationalities of the North
- structural perestroika of the regional economy
- overcoming the ecological crisis

The attainment of these goals requires the formation of a favorable environment for the development of the oblast's free enterprise potential and the existence of certain political, legal, and economic conditions.

The clash between the rights of all-Union and local government bodies to dispose of the resources and goods produced in the region led to the unwarranted concentration of authority at the highest level, to the de facto lack of rights of local Soviets, notwithstanding the proclaimed "expansion of the independence" of the latter in the Law on Property in the U.S.S.R.

The region's "drama" consists of the impossibility of agreeing with the "rules of the game" that are dictated by Moscow, on the one hand, and of rejecting them entirely, on the other. This is because the degree of centralization of management of the oil and gas branch as the basic branch in the nation's fuel-energy complex is higher than in other branches, and because, for the most part, it specifically represents the region's economy. This is exacerbated by narrow branch specialization and hence by the limited maneuverability of the economy, which is traditionally tightly bound to the centralized material-technical supply system. What is more, the lessening of the degree of centralization of the region's management may lead both to uncontrolled development of free enterprise and to spontaneous privatization, accompanied by the real danger that the region's resources may be sold off and its production potential squandered. The traditional "solution" to the cumulative problems does not produce a positive effect and serves to consolidate the existing system of management.

It has been proposed that some of Moscow's authority be delegated to a lower, regional level, to a newly created state government organ directly subordinate to the government, to a so-called regional ministry whose functions would include the direction and coordination of the activity of all management agencies in the oil and gas, geological, and construction branches.

This is a typical administrative "half-measure" for decentralizing management and shifting emphasis from the "branch" to the "territory" and for creating an interbranch management body. Most important, the partial delegation contradicts the goals of creating a free enterprise type of economy.

The transfer of enterprises of the West Siberian Oil and Gas Complex (ZSNGK) to the jurisdiction of the RSFSR, whose government views the extractive branches as a "trump card on the road to the twenty-first century," proved to be the solution to the conflict between the region and Moscow. The Russian government is currently examining a package of documents—which would confer the status of special economic zone on Tyumen Oblast—that contains a complex of proposals on expanding the region's economic rights, revising prices of sources of energy, transforming the structure of the regional economy, improving the population's life, and on resolving ecological problems.

Those proposals that concern the expansion of the region's economic freedoms are essentially elements of the mechanism for realizing the property rights of peoples living in the area to minerals and raw materials and for introducing the principle of payment to exploit natural resources. Organizationally, this can be represented in the form of two parallel regional structures: a committee for the management of natural resources and a natural resources fund that would include representatives of all federal agencies on a parity basis at both oblast and okrug levels.

The given management structures, similar to those indicated in the Law, On the Privatization of State and Municipal Enterprises in the RSFSR, would have the oblast committee for the management of property and the property fund (1) evaluate the resource potential and the magnitude and level of reserves, classify them, make an expert assessment of them, lease out plots of land, estimate rent and lease payments, and so on; and (2) organize sales, collect rent payments, and distribute them among all federal agencies and other parties.

Delegation of part of the rights of mineral ownership to the regional level creates the economic basis of the formation and development of free enterprise potential. The major source here will be revenues from oil and gas—the region's principal product—from which regional funds can be formed for financing the most promising regional programs for:

- liquidating and averting adverse ecological consequences
- renewing and supporting native industries and indigenous nationalities of the North
- structural perestroika and diversification of the economy, supporting the development of self-propelling, dynamic branches of industry of the region on the basis of renewable natural resources and the creation of compensatory and supplementary production

The result of these programs will be to concentrate investment resources required for reviving and expanding the scale of free enterprise in the region, and the requisite economic environment.

The strategy to develop free enterprise in the region in this part envisages the following directions:

1. Realizing the principle of payment for all types of natural resource utilization in accordance with the Law on Minerals in the RSFSR that is currently being drafted.
2. Providing for the exercise of the right of regional management agencies to independently sell part (from 10 to 30%) of the product overseas and elsewhere.
3. Vesting oblast and okrug Soviets and enterprises with the right to license products for export in order to concentrate hard currency earnings at the local level.
4. Changing prices on sources of energy (for example, from 60 rubles a ton on oil to 200 rubles a ton; from 52 rubles per cubic meter on natural gas to 100 rubles, taking the rent component into account).
5. Making an economic valuation and classification of the resource potential; determining and grading the economically substantiated level of rent payments; ascertaining ways of collecting the latter and forming a regional committee for resource management to this end.
6. Forming a special commercial structure—the regional natural resources fund—whose income in the form of special regional funds is viewed as the principal source of future ecological and social programs and programs for the structural

perestroika of the economy, in order to collect part of the rent payments in the region and distribute them among federal agencies.

Consequently, the requisite concentration of start-up capital for the development of free enterprise in the region will be attained and the local budget will be regulated at all levels. However, free enterprise is presently insignificant. It is operating at a deficit, and the potential for financial maneuvering is limited. Notwithstanding the proclaimed independence of Soviets to form, execute, and oversee local budgets, these rights remain a fiction because the basic norms governing the formation of revenues are articulated by republican bodies.

This is also why all the region's hidden reserves and potential for developing free enterprise in the oblast should be mobilized to the maximum. In particular, ways of concentrating monies in nonbudget accounts should include the collection of fines for polluting the environment, part of the funds resulting from lotteries conducted for this purpose, proceeds from the sale of ownerless and confiscated property, and voluntary contributions from citizens and organizations.

It is also necessary to develop the free enterprise activity of the Soviets themselves at various levels, with the aim of augmenting the budget. Commercial organizations like the Center for the Support of Small Business, for example, or a university-assisted innovation center, the creation of which was previously proposed by us at Tyumen University, should be set up under the Soviets. It is also possible to organize a center providing temporary credit relating to the issuance of stocks and credit for top-priority social regional programs, as well as personnel training services, commercial material-technical supply brokerages, and so on.

Thus, an administration for supporting free enterprise and new economic structures is at present operating on a commercial basis under the Tyumen Oblispolkom (Oblast Executive Committee). It registers new enterprises and provides consulting services. The Ispolkom (Executive Committee) can also earn hard currency by acting as the founder of joint ventures involving foreign capital.

However, the current, entirely progressive legal norms do not give us the desired revival of free enterprise activity in Tyumen. Such revival has been realized in a deformed or crippled form and have not led to economic growth. The reason for this failure lies in the priority given to the regulation of legal relations to the detriment of economic relations.

In the proposed conception, emphasis specifically is placed on the economic category of property and on the realization of the regional population's right to own the minerals and natural resources in that region. The enumerated economic steps will make it possible to achieve several things:

- to open the region's economy to the maximum
- to raise Tyumen Oblast's export potential
- to ensure the possibility of its self-financing with hard currency
- to import foreign capital to branches of the regional economy that have the highest priority
- to accumulate investment resources and increase investment activity

Those steps in their aggregate also will ensure the starting potential for the development of free enterprise and for expanding its scale.

However, not just any kind of free enterprise is acceptable. The specific nature of the ZSNGK, the need for structural perestroika and the diversification of its economy, for the creation of self-propelling and supplementary production, dictate the need only for "organized free enterprise" with strong centralization, with the active intervention and oversight of the local Soviets, and with purposeful state investment policy—all the more so because it is specifically this kind of free enterprise that becomes more important during the present period of transition.

Proceeding from the economic realities and the traditions of management in the ZSNGK, it seems that the strategy of developing a regional free enterprise system should give priority to "collective free enterprise" based on large economic systems.

In Western market economies, small and medium-sized enterprises, some of which form the foundation for the prolonged and gradual growth to large firms "from below," are as a rule firmly entrenched in the role of free enterprise "incubators." In Tyumen Oblast, however, enterprises in this sector are still relatively few, have been in operation a relatively short time, and are skating on very thin ice. Large enterprises, on the other hand, exist in practically finished form. They define the "face" of the region, they have many years of experience interacting with management structures, their behavior is controlled, and they reflect the general trend in regional development quite completely. In our view, this is specifically why large economic forms should be viewed as self-propelled drivers of the development of regional free enterprise (business concerns, commercial and investment banks, state branch holding companies, etc.). They can finance significant regional scientific-technical and marketing programs, and support small business. At the same time, because they have interrepublic influence, they can economically unify and, finally, "reconcile" numerous national markets with one another.

However, notwithstanding the enumerated advantages, they will probably be effective only if they interact closely with small business, the directions of whose development should be the subject of a special program.

The next stage in formulating the strategy of development of regional free enterprise is the definition of the principal spheres of free enterprise activity and the most important "addressees" of investment. They are first of all branches that are based on the use of renewable natural resources (timber, peat, etc.). In this sector, like the traditional sector—oil and gas extraction—large economic structures will continue to be of predominant importance.

The sphere of small business is above all virtually undeveloped production and social infrastructures, where an early return can be realized just by accelerating the turnover of social capital. Small business may respond to agriculture that is in need of investment. Small business is connected with guaranteeing proper life conditions of the population of the region—the local economy; traditional crafts of small nationalities of the North, and such, for the reconstruction of which one can recommend the use of preferential taxation, regional orders, preferential (reduced) credit rates, and other economic instruments.

Today, free enterprise structures in the oblast are forming spontaneously and with an obvious lag. Brokerage rather than production activity remains the most attractive sphere to entrepreneurs: the "stake" is primarily on the scarcity of resources. Financial tyranny by banks and financial institutions toward new structures and the unprofessional, poorly trained makeup of Soviets at all levels make themselves felt.

The total lack of information and the lack of development of the informational structure are also a serious obstacle to the development of free enterprise in Tyumen Oblast. It was, therefore, not by chance that quite vigorous free enterprise activity initially developed in spheres with a higher degree of information support (for example, the commercialization of the Komsomol, the CPSU, and other social organizations).

In particular there is a need for the patient generation of the very "figure of an entrepreneur": the prolonged cultivation of a special entrepreneurial culture, a specific system of values in society, which unfortunately is beyond the purview of this article. In the process of implementing the strategy set out above, one should strive for a "critical mass" of conditions and stimuli for the development of interregional free enterprise, after which the strategy should be modified as needed through adaptation.

Only a person with the right to buy, own and sell property can guarantee the maintenance of political stability and simultaneously the economic rebirth of society. The development of free enterprise is therefore the most important task of the central and local authorities. This cannot be achieved without reforming the authority structures proper, without redistributing authority between them. The basic aspect of municipal strategy is to create the necessary prerequisites to the development of free enterprise: political (the transition to the jurisdiction of the RSFSR), legal (conferral of the status of a special economic zone on Tyumen Oblast), and economic. The economic part of the strategy presupposes the development of a mechanism for realizing the regional population's rights of ownership of minerals and natural resources, which is expressed in the expansion of concrete economic freedoms. Realization of the latter will make the region capital-redundant, will raise the level of investment activity. All this combined will ensure the start-up potential for the development of free enterprise and the expansion of its scale.

The need to coordinate free enterprise activity with macroeconomic goals generated the choice of such a type of free enterprise as highly centralized, "organized free enterprise" based on large economic structures, but with the support of small business. The maximum use of the region's mobilizing potential and the free enterprise of the municipal authorities proper serve as an additional "injection" of free enterprise activity.

The formulation of a strategy for developing free enterprise in Tyumen Oblast also presupposes the definition of the basic spheres of free enterprise activity (with the identification of priorities) and directions of development of the "free enterprise sphere."

20

The Struggle for Power Allocation Between the Central Government in Moscow and the Administration of the Tyumen Region

Alexei I. Ivandaev

A coup d'état in 1991 resulted in strengthening the powers of the presidential government in Russia and the creation of a new system of executive power accountable to the president. Executive-instructive functions of the government in regions, areas, and autonomous areas were given to administrative leaders, appointed by the president and accountable to him (Decree of President Yeltsin of August 22, 1991: On some Aspects of Executive Power Activities in the Russian Federation). In order to coordinate activities of executive power structures, special representatives of the president were appointed by him (Decree of President Yeltsin of August 24, 1991: On Representatives of the Russian Federation President in Regions and Areas of the Russian Federation).

Rapid changes of the political and economic situations after the coup d'état and the disintegration of the U.S.S.R. into separate independent states resulted in the need to develop a new Constitution of the Russian Federation, as well as a federal treaty and other new laws needed to solve the problems of switching the country to a market economy. Weaknesses of the existing code of laws and regulations (i.e., absence of any laws about private property, external economic activities, natural resources, etc.) resulted in significant difficulties for the government and contributed to enacting numerous and ineffective presidential decrees and governmental orders. Lack of experience in business activities and in usage of new laws, as well as underdevelopment of precedent rights, resulted in additional difficulties.

In this situation the struggle for power between the federal government and the local governments in autonomous republics, regions, and areas appeared to be closely connected with the fight of the people, living in the respective territories, for their rights. This is especially true for the republics and regions located in the immense Siberian territory. Here the local population fights against the colonial politics of the central government and demands a fair compensation for the extensive unregulated development of Siberia natural resources. Many regions, areas, and even autonomous areas applied to the Russian parliament with the demand to decentralize the system of ruling and to consider their rights equal with the rights of autonomous republics. Federal (and even local, when we speak about okrugs inside local areas) powers have to see in these demands tendencies of separatism and even pretensions to destroy the Russian state, taking them very painfully after such a fast disintegration of the U.S.S.R. As for the local powers, they fight mainly for their economic rights concerning the use of territorial property and natural resources and not just for their political rights in the federation. For example, Khanty-Mansi and Yamal-Nenets autonomous okrugs, which belong to the Tyumen area, use the flag of national autonomy, fighting for their own territorial interests and the interests of local oil workers.

The tension of the situation could be decreased by a proper federal treaty, but the draft of such a treaty has now been transformed into the draft of the agreement On Allocation of Power Between Federal Authorities of the Russian Federation and Local Authorities of Republics, Regions, Areas, Autonomous Areas, and Autonomous Okrugs in the Russian Federation, which the Parliament of Russia proposed to local authorities. This document had been primarily prepared to secure the existing inequality of territories by the hands of local authorities and practically canceled everything positive concerning the state hierarchy in the new constitution draft.

Hopes about the disintegration of central rule, which should have been a result of the division of the U.S.S.R. into independent states, did not come true for Russia. Newly created Russian ministries took on most of the old administrative functions of the former Soviet ministries. Despite the global changes and decentralization of supply, the new Russian center, for the most part, retained the old administrative functions. In this situation, the struggle of local governments for the economic and political independence of their territories became, in essence, struggle for survival.

The fight between the administration of the Tyumen region and the central Russian government is very specific because this region is the biggest oil-rich area in the country and it is socially and economically underdeveloped. Tyumen, the capital city of the region, is one of the dirtiest and most uncomfortable cities in Siberia and in all of Russia. Workers in the crude oil industry of the Tyumen area live in awful conditions compared to their colleagues abroad, and to most of the Russian population. Tens of thousands of Tyumen oil workers still live in temporary houses that are not equipped with any utilities. No more than 69% of the oil workers in the region have proper housing, which is 12.4% less than the number for the oil workers in other areas of the country. And it is despite the fact that two-thirds of the Russian crude oil comes from the Tyumen region and 368.8 million tons of crude oil were extracted there in 1980—more than in any other country in the world. It is also despite the fact that crude oil exports from the U.S.S.R. in several years were more than 170 million tons, and even in 1990 were around 100 million tons.

Tyumen's crude oil did not make the people in the region rich. The standard of living in this oil capital is lower than in the capital of any other region in the country. Tyumen is 62nd in the republic in housing development, 67th in development of schools and hospitals, 74th in telephones. Crude oil from the Tyumen region did not enrich either the country or its oil and gas industry.

Today, the industry is falling apart. The volumes of drilling and crude oil extraction are declining. The shortage of machinery, spare parts, and workers has left some oil wells unused. The decline of the interfield pipelines means that some of the oil fields will soon become unusable because most of the bigger pipelines are in dire need of replacement. Liberalization of wholesale and retail prices on consumer goods and agricultural products, together with state-fixed crude oil prices, has resulted in this near-death condition of the oil industry. Production of crude oil in 1990 dropped by 30 million tons comparing to 1989, and in 1991 it was reduced by an additional 50 million tons. That is almost a 20 percent reduction in two years. A further decrease in production is expected mainly because of the lack of technical resources and materials.

At the request of the Tyumen regional administration, several groups of scientists and specialists developed a set of recommendations regarding the actions necessary for the Western Siberian oil and gas industry to function normally. These recommendations had been discussed at the regional and federal levels, and at the meetings with Russian President Boris Yeltsin. These heated discussions and the struggle of interests resulted in a special decree No. 122 of President Yeltsin of September 19, 1991: On the Development of the Tyumen Region. This decree was targeted toward solving social, economic, and ecological problems of the region, resolving its national and territorial problems, and developing the oil and gas industry in the Tyumen area.

The decree states that the cornerstone of the economic revival of the Tyumen region has to be the united "Program of the development of the region and the regional crude oil and gas industry." Control over the execution of this program should be performed by the administration of the program. The administration has to be formed by the Council of Ministers of Russia, together with the Tyumen regional government and the governments of Khanty-Mansi and Yamal-Nenets okrugs. The administration has the following rights:

- to approve technical and economic drafts for reconnoitering and exploitation of the oil fields,
- to give permissions to conduct the above mentioned work,
- to form and freely use products and resources funds equal to the value of 10 percent of oil, gas, and other commodities produced in the region.

In order for the program to work, the decree assigned to the Council of Ministers, together with the Tyumen regional government, the function of defining the status of the program and its administration and of founding the program's fund with the investors represented by the Council of the Ministers of the Russian Federation, Tyumen *oblispolkom*, oil and gas companies, and other Russian and foreign investors. Moreover, the decree stated that the crude oil and wood export quotas for the Tyumen region, issued by the Council of Ministers of Russia, have to be distributed under agreements with the administration of the program and regional and okrug executive powers. The Russian Council of Ministers was ordered to distribute during the fourth quarter of 1991 sufficient financial means in hard currency among the Tyumen region, Khanty-Mansi and Yamal-Nenets okrug administrations needed to solve the most pressing social and economic problems.

These points are only the most important components of the decree. This rather extensive decree ordered federal executive staff to take extraordinary measures to pull the region and its strategically important oil and gas industry out of the crisis. However, it took almost two months for the Russian Council of Ministers to adapt Resolution No. 591: About Urgent Measures for Solving Social and Economic Problems of the Tyumen Region and Khanty-Mansi and Yamal-Nenets Okrugs. In addition to the measures stated in Yeltsin's decree, this resolution allowed the Tyumen regional government, Khanty-Mansi and Yamal-Nenets okrug administrations, and the administration of the program to conduct tenders for foreign companies to participate in the development of the region's natural resources. The Council of Ministers did not specify the organization that will have the executive powers (e.g., administration of the program); that is why Resolution No. 591 led to further struggle between regional, okrug, and program administrations.

The rest of the resolution of the Russian government was made similar to previous joint resolutions of the Central Party Committee and the Council of Ministers of the U.S.S.R. binding to "consider," "propose," "work out," "prepare," and so on.

This resolution only made the main points of the presidential decree more detailed and readdressed them to numerous ministries and departments for execution without indication of concrete executives. Only one decision of the government reflected in this resolution contributed to the change of the political and economic situation in the Tyumen region. This was the cancellation (from the October 1, 1991 decree) of limitations on the use of consumption funds of enterprises and organizations, and (from the January 1, 1992 decree) the cancellation of the upper limits of wages for the calculation of regional and Northern increases to salaries.

It must be emphasized that in the struggle for power between the federal government and regional administration, there has always existed a striving to be able to set quotas, to give out crude oil drilling and export licenses, and to be able to draw foreign investments into the local oil and gas industry. Last year, authorities issued licenses to export 150 million tons of crude oil while it was planned to export only 60 million tons. It is not necessary to explain how profitable it can be to purchase a ton of crude oil at the government-set price of 70 rubles, or even at the market price of 1,000–2,000 rubles, and, when the dollar exchange rate is 1:130–170, sell it for $120.00. One can only guess about the bribes to get respective licenses. Not in vain, Vice Prime Minister E. Gaidar pointed out in his interview with *Izvestiya* that the oil and gas industry is "one of the most criminogenic spheres of power."

In order to eliminate the existing situation and to provide economic sovereignty, the Russian government passed Resolution No. 7 of November 15, 1993: On Regulations of Deliveries of Crude Oil and Oil-based Products Out of the Russian Federation. In this resolution, the government assigned the function of making and distributing quotas on crude oil and oil-based product exports to the Ministries of Economy and Finance, and Fuel and Energy. The resolution states that the quotas can be given only to the manufacturers themselves, excluding export deliveries for the Russian state needs. A ten-day period was set for a revision and possible renewal of all of the earlier issued licenses. The expiration date for the renewed licenses was set at December 31, 1991.

Through this resolution, the government limited exports of crude oil and oil-based products from December 1, 1991, to the quotas set by the ministers of Economy and Finance, and Fuel and Energy, to account for the Russian state needs. Therefore, the Russian government had used the oil industry as the trump card in its political game with the states of the Commonwealth of Independent States (CIS). Negotiations about trading and export of crude oil now began to be conducted behind the backs of the oil producers, as well as behind the backs of administrations of the oil-rich regions. At the end of October 1991, Vice Prime Minister E. Gaidar made an attempt to steer the oil industry away from the free market by suppressing the privatization process and turning the existing oil and gas producers into holding companies with 100 percent state property.

The issues of socioeconomic development of the Tyumen region and recovery of the oil and gas industry were widely discussed in central and local press. When Tyumen started the fight for its territorial rights and received approval from the president in terms of the decree of September 19, 1991, the administration tried to make cardinal changes in the ways of using natural resources, taking into account interests of the territories and the population. The main goal of these changes was to create a relationship between the producers and the territories under which people living in these territories would receive a fair compensation for the extraction of natural resources and the adverse consequences of extraction would be addressed. These changes seemed unacceptable to the federal government, which still retained rudiments of centralist and totalitarian style. This and other privileges that resulted from the president's decree put the Tyumen region into a "one against all" situation. Even though steps taken by the administration of the region were formally approved by the president, a campaign opposing regional administration actions, and especially opposing the head of administration Yu. Shafranik, was initiated.

The further outcome of the struggle mainly depended upon the support of the regional group of Russian Federation people's deputies. At the meeting of the head of administration with the deputies, which took place on January 11, 1992, it was noted that in spite of the crucial economic situation in the region and in its oil and gas industry, the problem of financing of the regional industry in 1992 had not yet been solved, and 10 percent of the extracted crude oil to form the regional fund of resources was still not given. The attention had been brought to intrigues behind the scene connected with the interests of the Moscow crude oil stock exchange, the position of Ukraine, an idea to include the Tyumen region into the Ural Republic, and others. Deputies decided to try to explain to the government the catastrophic situation in the crude oil industry once more, and presented the issue about responsibility of the government, which did not fulfill the decree of president to the proper committee of the Supreme Council. The fact that the situation was very critical was underlined by the deputies from Tyumen, who proposed to go on a hunger strike on January 15, 1992, during the Parliament session.

The struggle for power continued during the meetings of the top economic executives of the region with members of the government, especially with Minister of Fuel and Energy V. Lopuhin. Nevertheless, the participants agreed that only an immediate execution of the president's decree of September 19, together with providing the actual crude oil quotas, can liquidate the catastrophic situation in the region. Disintegration of the industry can be prevented if the Russian government will turn its face toward the people of the region. The participants of these discussions stated that the president has to make a new ruling.

Continuing his struggle for power against the federal administration, the leader of the Tyumen regional government, Yu. Shafranik, wrote a letter to Yeltsin with a suggestion to specify a number of points regarding the decree of September 19, namely:

- to clearly separate the functions of the republican administration with the functions of the administration of the program to use natural resources. The function of approving the technical and economic drafts about reconnoitering and exploitation of the resources shoud be transferred from the territorial committee of the Council of Ministers of the Russian Federation—for example, to the West Siberian Geological Committee.
- to specify the order of issuing and distributing crude oil and wood quotas, underlining that they should be issued by the Council of Ministers and distributed

by the administration of the program in the frameworks of the agreements with its territorial committees and local governments of the region and its autonomous okrugs.

- to consider 10% of the production of the oil and wood industries to be a natural resources usage fee to the administration of the program.
- to define and fix for a period not less than ten years the volumes of oil and gas quotas. Set the export quota to no less than 50% of the resources kept by the administration of the program.
- to give the administration of the program the right to export part of the volume of the wide fraction of light hydrocarbons and oil gas, which is not used inside the country, for a period of no less than 15–20 years.

On January 24, 1992, the meeting called by President Yeltsin was to decide, for the most part, the fate of the region. The results of this meeting were in favor of the people of the Tyumen region. The quota of free trade of the products of local manufacturers was changed from 10 to 35 percent. A number of other key issues were resolved as well.

A significant contribution to the struggle of the regional administration with the central government for power, and a shift of the oil and gas industry onto the free market base, were made by the Russian-American Seminar for Investment in Western Siberian Oil and Gas Complex, as well as the Congress of the Oil Industry Men of the Commonwealth of Independent States. These events took place in Tyumen in January-February 1992, and became significant turning points in different directions of the struggle between the local and federal governments.

At a meeting at the office of the Russian president on January 24, the following agreements led to the creation of the new Decree No. 93 of February 17, 1992: On Urgent Measures to Stabilize the Situation in the Oil and Gas Industry of the Republic. This decree allowed the local executive powers to buy up to 10% of the total volume of the extracted crude oil and gas to form territorial resources and sell up to 40% of it to the buyers inside the country at free market prices. It also allowed executives to make contracts to deliver crude oil for export in limits of the territorial resources funds and as defined by the regional quotas.

A resolution was adapted that specified additional measures needed to normalize the state of the oil and gas industry. As a whole, this decree and resolution achieve the goals set by the administration of the Tyumen region in its fight for power against the federal government.

It should be pointed out that when the U.S.S.R. still existed, a similar power struggle took place between the Soviet and republican ministers. Due to the slow decision-making progress, that struggle led to further crisis in the oil and gas industry as well.

It should be emphasized that last year's fight for power was essentially a fight for economic independence and territorial wholeness of the region. The regional administration was victorious for the most part, but it is, of course, too early to close the book on this subject.

21

Elements of Federalism in Relations Between Regional and Local Authority During the Perestroika Period in the U.S.S.R. (as Exemplified by Siberia)

Irina A. Vekshina

To establish such a system for the given people—with its geography, history, traditions, and psychology—that would lead to its flowering, not its degeneration.

A. I. Solzhenitsyn
(*Rebuilding Russia*)

The state-regional organization of the U.S.S.R. has been and continues to be one of the most complex, multi-level systems in the world. Its vast expanses and the specific structural features of the system of Soviets left their mark on the territorial organization of state authority.

The state (*gosudarstvennyy)* level is the highest level of organization. There are three types of states: the U.S.S.R., the union republic, and the republic within a union republic (in the RSFSR). The middle—regional—level is represented by krays (territories),[1] oblasts (regions),[2] and autonomous oblasts and autonomous okrugs (areas).[3] The lowest—local—level includes rayons (districts), cities, settlements (*poselki)*, village Soviets (*sel'sovety*),[4] and city rayons (*rayony v gorodakh*). This level also has its own hierarchy. Rayons combine settlements, village Soviets, and cities of rayon jurisdiction (*goroda rayonnogo podchineniya)*; the largest cities are divided into rayons and incorporate settlements and village Soviets.

Notwithstanding the great complexity of state-regional organization, the system has three principal levels: the state, the region, and the territory that is to be self-governing (*samoupravlyayemaya territoriya*). The practice of state structure (*gosudarstvennoe stroitel'stvo*) shows that each of these three levels has its own inviolable administrative territories. In other words, the division of powers also exists at the territorial level. Authority is divided into national, regional, and local. Under these conditions, it is very important to find a model of interrelations between regional and local authority that will make it possible to combine the solution of national, regional, and local problems effectively.

The system formed by the state, the region, and the territory that is to be self-governing is not the only model. This is evidenced, in particular, by the experience of the U.S.A. If one looks elsewhere in the world for analogs of the state-territorial organization of the U.S.S.R.,[5] it is structurally similar to the system in the Federal Republic of Germany (FRG). The FRG also has five levels of government: federal, provincial, regional, district and urban, and communal. However, comparison of the nature of relations between regional and local authority in the U.S.S.R. and the FRG reveals significant differences. The history of state-territorial organization in the U.S.S.R. and the practice of recent years attest to the special path of development of relations between regional and local authority in the Soviet nation.

The complex system of state-territorial organization in the preperestroika period was strictly centralized. Soviet power was based on the so-called principle of democratic centralism.[6] This has been manifested in the existence of managerial interrelationships from the bottom to the top in the system of Soviets of People's Deputies.[7] Both official and scientific circles rejected the concept of local Soviets as organs of local self-government. Attempts to analyze local organs of power in this aspect were criticized, and local self-government was treated as a phenomenon that was exclusively characteristic of a bourgeois state.

Under the erstwhile doctrine, relations between regional and local organs of power were hierarchically structured. Cities and rayons were to a considerable degree governed not by the Soviets of the given areas, but rather through higher kray and oblast Soviets and their organs of government. According to the law, kray and oblast organs of power were classified among local Soviets at the higher level. They also possessed all the basic authority to govern a region and its constituent territories. Mandatory decisions (*obyazatel' nyye k ispolneniyu resheniya*) were the principal juridical form in which kray and oblast Soviets directed organs of power subordinate to them. As organs of government, kray and oblast Soviets could within the framework of their competence opt to vest lower Soviets with any kind of authority and obligate them to perform any task. Lower Soviets in krays and oblasts performed only routine functions and had no opportunity to participate in the actual government of a kray or oblast.

Because of the inflexibility of government, the remoteness of actual power from the places where it was wielded, and the lack of rights of lower-level organs of power, the old system of interrelations between regional and local authority was highly inefficient.

The perestroika process inaugurated the decentralization of government, the affirmation of institutions of local self-government, and the introduction of a new type of relations at the regional level.

The Law of the U.S.S.R. on the General Principles of Local Self-Government and Local Economy in the U.S.S.R.[8] for the first time identified kray and oblast Soviets and local organs of power belonging to these systems as two relatively independent power structures.

Under the law, village, settlement, rayon, city, and city rayon Soviets are classified as Soviets at the primary level (*pervichnyy uroven'*) of local self-government. It is specifically these Soviets that are empowered to (self-)govern the region of their jurisdiction and to independently resolve all issues of local significance.

Kray and oblast Soviets have been assigned a new role as centers for coordinating and regulating local policy. Their principal functions include: organizing economic and sociocultural services for rayons and cities on a contractual basis (*na dogovornykh nachalakh*), implementing interregional measures, providing financial assistance to balance local budgets in instances specified by law, providing methodological assistance, and securing legality in local self-government.

While offering a new model of interrelations based on coordination and cooperation, the all-Union law merely presents a general scheme of relations between regional and local authority. Soviet republics are now faced with the task of making the scheme more concrete and of finding mechanisms for introducing the new model.

This task was addressed under special conditions. The severance of old governance ties (*upravlencheskiye svyazi*) was accompanied by the rapid development of centrifugal regional tendencies, by the creation of "appanage principalities" (*udel'nyye knyazhestva*) all the way down to the lowest regional level. The local level passed its own "laws" that conflicted with the legislation and decisions of higher-level Soviets. However, the impossibility of political and economic reform in a chaotic, uncoordinated regime very soon became apparent. The appropriate response was consolidation—this time on a new conceptual base. The country's unique socioeconomic and political situation and the remoteness of regional and local authority from central authority created favorable soil for the development in the U.S.S.R. of a hitherto atypical phenomenon: the appearance of elements of federalism in relations between regional and local authority. This process was made possible by the previous experience and traditions of federalism in the U.S.S.R.

Federalism was based on a broad interpretion of federation from the first years of Soviet power. The dominant conception of federation was that it was a form of state organization, a complex idea consisting of state organizations possessing legally defined autonomy. As a result, from the very beginning of federalism in the Soviet state, there were two types of Soviet federation: an autonomous federation[9] and a federation uniting union republics on the basis of agreement between them.[10] Traditional ideas about federation are currently being reexamined. The narrow view of federation as a union of sovereign republics (states) is becoming more and more popular in political and scientific circles. Even now, autonomous republics are being transformed into republics in the RSFSR[11] and an agreement with the same conceptual base as the All-Union Treaty is being drafted.

Notwithstanding the rejection of the concept of a truncated (*usechennaya*) autonomous federation, state-regional entities created with its help have retained their practical significance. The democratization and decentralization of government and increased regional autonomy have revealed broad opportunities for using intermediate forms at the regional level between the federation and the centralized state.

The former relations between the state and autonomous organizations could be characterized as relations with elements of federalism. The advantage of introducing the given model at the level of the interaction between regional and local authority as well is obvious from the standpoint of Soviet reality. First of all, given the weak state of democratic institutions, such a model makes it possible to prevent the restoration of the old command-based system of administrative management once and for all. The new model will make it possible to overcome the relations of mistrust that exist today between regional and local authorities and that are a serious impediment to creative activity. Finally, it can be instrumental in most consistently coupling the traditions of state organization to the ideas of expanding the autonomy and independence of the regions that are to be self-governing.

Before trying to identify the basic elements of federal relations, I consider it important to define the nature of regional and local organs of power. The separation of regional organs of power from the system of local Soviets as the primary link of organs of state power appears to be the most correct. The result is the creation of an ideal construction for introducing elements of federal relations. On the one hand, there is state power in the form of regional organs of power, while on the other hand, there are Soviets of regions that are to be self-governing as an autonomous branch of local authority. This type of relation has now been affirmed in the RSFSR. Unlike other republics that have regions (*regiony*), in Russia the Law of the RSFSR on Local Self-Government in the RSFSR[12] removes kray and oblast Soviets from the category of local Soviets and defines them as organs of state power at the primary level. Rayon, city, settlement, and village Soviets of People's Deputies are classified as organs of local power.

Even though the existence of two independent branches of power within the framework of the region creates favorable soil for the formation of elements of federal relations, in practice they may be introduced to varying degrees. It is, therefore, very important to determine which elements of federal relations are basic to the creation of a new model of relations. I believe that two groups of elements of federal relations can be established.

The first group is connected with the right of a region's constituent territories to independence. The following rights to territorial organs of power that are to be self-governing are the basic features of autonomy: the right to make their own laws, to independently establish the types and structures of organs of local self-government, to define the boundaries of a territory that is to be self-governing, and to possess their own symbols and attributes of power. At the present time, only the last of these rights is realized to a sufficient degree.

Local organs have had the right to make their own laws since the first years of Soviet power. But it hardly would have been possible to say before, that the existence of this right was evidence of elements of federal relations. The latter is true only when the local Soviets are vested with the right to adopt their own charters of local self-government.

It made no sense to adopt charters during the period of strict management relations, because the legal bases of the activity of the local Soviets were written into law, into government acts, and into the decisions of higher organs of power and government. With the passage of the Law of the U.S.S.R. on General Principles of Local Self-Government and the Local Economy in the U.S.S.R., local organs of power were empowered to formulate their activity in legal terms. The first acts were called decrees on organs of local power and government.[13] However, their content was significantly broader than their name. They not only established the organizational bases of the activity of organs of local self-government and differentiated the jurisdiction of Soviets and their organs, but also defined the economic and budget-financial system of local self-government, and interrelations with enterprises, organizations, and other agents of local self-government.

It was important to legislatively formalize the initial experience of issuing charters on local self-government, thereby juridically recognizing charters as special acts within the legislative system. This task was resolved for the first time in the Law of the RSFSR on Local Self-Government in the RSFSR, Article 5 of which indicates the right of local Soviets to adopt charters on local self-government. Unfortunately, the Russian law did not fully recognize the right of local Soviets to adopt constituent acts and placed their lawmaking activity under the control of higher Soviets. This RSFSR law provides for the registration of charters on local self-government by higher organs of state power.

The registration procedure hardly seems to be necessary or fair, especially if local organs of power are presumed to have their own independent legislative spheres. Russian law empowers kray and oblast Soviets to rescind decisions by local organs of power and government if they contradict legislation, which is entirely sufficient for reacting to unlawful charters. Even more progressive from these standpoints are laws of other republics where, even though the right of local organs of power to adopt charters on local self-government is not mentioned, such legislation is also not prohibited.

The right to independently determine the types and structure of a Soviet's organs is also highly contradictory in current legislation. During the period of rigid managerial interrelationships, the types and structure of organs were written in detail into laws and acts of the government of the U.S.S.R. and the republics. The structure and personnel of local Soviets were formed on the basis of detailed lists of types of Soviet organs, inflexible salary schedules, and wage funds handed down from above. Article 6 of the U.S.S.R. Law on General Principles of Local Self-Government and Local Economy specified the right of local Soviets to independently determine the structure and staff of their organs, but did not as yet address the right to an independent determination of their types. Further steps toward autonomy may be expected of republic laws.

Fundamentally different approaches have been found in republic legislation. The first laws on local self-government regulated types of organs of authority and government quite strictly.[14] Especially categorical in this respect was the Law of the Ukrainian S.S.R. on Local Soviets of People's Deputies in the Ukrainian S.S.R. and Local Self-Government[15] that defined the structure and types of organs down to the level of departments (*otdely*) and administrations (*upravleniya*) of local executive authority. The variant chosen in the Law of the RSFSR on Local Self-Government in the RSFSR strikes the author as the most preferable. It indicates only the existence of two branches of power: representative, in the person of the Soviets, and executive, in the person of the administration. The formation of the structure and types of Soviet and administrative organs is left to the discretion of the local organs themselves.

The most urgent problem in the development of the autonomy of local organs of power is the acquisition of the right to define administrative-territorial organization within the framework of territories that are to be self-governing. Previous legislation gave broad powers to kray and oblast Soviets and deprived lower Soviets of any rights in this sphere.[16]

At the present time, there is only the hint of reform in this direction. The republics are drafting laws on administrative-territorial organization. In my view, the reduction of the autonomy of local authority to its logical end should presuppose the following expansion of the rights of local Soviets in this sphere. First, it should be legally recognized that regional organs of power are not entitled to establish boundaries of territories that are to be self-governing without taking the opinion of local Soviets into account. Second, it is important that local Soviets be given the right to determine the administrative-territorial divisions and boundaries of territories that are to be self-governing themselves. In this respect, the most recent legislation has already expanded the rights of local Soviets. Thus, the Law of the RSFSR on Local Self-Government in the RSFSR gave city Soviets the right to form administrative-territorial units within a city as they see fit.[17]

The realization of the idea of independence of the local Soviets creates preconditions for their broad use of a special legal form—agreements—in their interrelations with regional organs of power.

Both regional organs of power and local Soviets have an interest in concluding agreements. The special interest that local Soviets have in concluding agreements with kray, oblast, and other regional organs of power is connected with guaranteeing the independence of territories that are to be self-governing. For kray, oblast, and other regional organs of power, the conclusion of agreements with local Soviets makes it possible to stabilize regional government and to increase its influence on the activity of the local Soviets in the interests of the region in general. The principal questions that organs of power are interested in covering in the agreements are: the redistribution of the power to govern a subordinate territory, mutual obligations in the coordination of legally significant actions, the differentiation and transfer of objects of property, and coordination of the policy of socioeconomic development.

The initial experience of forming relations based on agreements has shown that such relations develop on a multivariant basis. At the present time, there are at least three approaches to the use of the agreement form.

First is the conclusion of individual agreements with regional organs of power by specific local Soviets. If this approach to the regulation of relations is used, the road to consolidation and the resolution of contradictions will be long and irrational. Since local Soviets today lack the experience and a sufficiently good legal and information base, it can be assumed with a considerable degree of probability that the draft agreements prepared by them will include many imperfect, legally flawed acts. Hence, there is the great danger that the adoption of these drafts will be a prolonged process. For example, coordination of the agreement between the Novokuznetsk City Soviet and the Kemerovo Oblast Soviet of People's Deputies has dragged on for more than a year. Considering the fact that there are 17 rayon and 20 city Soviets in Kemerovo Oblast, it is difficult to even imagine how long it might take the Kemerovo Oblast Soviet to conclude agreements with all city and rayon Soviets in the oblast.

Another, more rational, approach is the development and adoption of model agreements with local Soviets in the region by regional organs of power. It would then be possible to expect shorter opinion coordination procedures. In Siberia, the Altay kray has such experience in providing legal support in the drafting of agreements. By its decision of December 27, 1990, the Altay kray Soviet adopted a model agreement on the redistribution of powers between kray and rayon Soviets of people's deputies.

Finally, the most rational way is to conclude a single general agreement between the regional organ of power and the local Soviets of a region that would resolve all basic questions relating to the distribution of authority and spheres and objects of influence in a region. Such an approach does not preclude the possibility of concluding individual agreements—both in general and on individual points—with local Soviets that have expressed their agreement with the content of the general agreement and its individual articles. In my view, it is specifically the third approach that is most promising as the basis for forming elements of federal relations at the level of the region-territory that is to be self-governing. As regards individual agreements, they can evidently be widely used in individual directions and spheres of government.

The second group of elements of federal relations is connected with the development of the status of agents (*sub"yekty*) participating in regional government on the part of local organs of power. The Soviets had no *de facto* rights in this respect in the preperestroika period. Today, there is every reason to affirm the development of the legal status (*pravosub"yektnost'*) of local Soviets as agents of regional government. This can be seen in the example of Kemerovo Oblast.

The decree adopted by the Kemerovo Oblast Soviet on November 17, 1990, by the oblast Soviet devoted an entire section to the question of involving local Soviets in oblast government. The Soviet gave city, rayon, settlement, and village Soviets—as agents of oblast government—the right to initiate legislation, to submit projects to the oblast Soviet, to propose holding extraordinary sessions of the oblast Soviet, to make proposals on the agenda of oblast Soviet sessions, and on conducting oblast referenda on the most important issues. Soviet and administrative officials were allowed to participate on a consultative, nonvoting basis in the work of the respective organs of the oblast Soviet and the oblast administration. The empowerment of oblast Soviets to suspend decisions of oblast Soviet organs if they contradict existing legislation or infringe upon the lawful rights and interests of the population living on the territory of the local Soviets up to and including the reversal of a decision of the Oblast Soviet itself is of interest.

The decree on the Kemerovo Oblast Soviet for the first time made provision for the creation of a special organ: the Congress of Representatives of Oblast Soviets (one deputy from each Soviet). This Congress was founded for the purpose of involving local organs of power in the discussion of questions pertaining to the joint resolution of regional problems, to the demarcation of jurisdiction between the oblast Soviet and oblast local Soviets, to forms of participation of oblast Soviets in securing the balanced economic and social development of the oblast, and other key issues of regional significance. At the first meeting of the Congress on March 1, 1991, representatives of oblast Soviets discussed avenues of land reform in the region and adopted a special resolution based on the discussion.[18]

The Congress of Representatives of Oblast Soviets is only one form of Soviet representation at the regional level. Other forms of representation may include regional bicameral organs of power currently proposed by scholars and laypersons, where one chamber will be formed from representatives of regional local Soviets (e.g., will be made up of representatives of rayon and city Soviets). Committees of representatives of local Soviet officials under kray and oblast Soviets and the kray and oblast administration are another possible form. The currently discussed draft Law of the RSFSR on Kray and Oblast Government indicates the formation of a kray or oblast Soviet, half of which is made up of people's deputies elected by the population of a kray or oblast in territorial electoral districts and persons elected by rayon and city Soviets at sessions of city and rayon Soviets as a variant.[19] While it is difficult to say which forms will become the principal forms in the future, it can already be said that the representation institution is developing in small forms. Conferences (*soveshchaniya*) of representatives of local Soviets are functioning under chairpersons of kray and oblast Soviets, conferences of heads of the local administration are operating under kray and oblast administrative leaders, and representations of leaders of organs of local Soviets and the local administration are forming under the respective organs of kray and oblast Soviets and the kray and oblast administration.

The consolidation of Soviets based on the development of elements of federal relations is a process that complicates the structures and functions of government and that demands additional time and expenditures. But its unquestionable merit is its orientation toward attaining accord and trust in the region, toward the unification of the efforts of local and regional authorities in the resolution of common problems of development of the region and its territories in people's interests. It is for this very reason that the author of this article believes that the use of elements of federalism at the level of the region or territory that is to be self-governing within given limits is promising not only for the U.S.S.R. but also for other states, as well with due regard to their particular historical and national development.

NOTES

1. Krays exist in only one republic, the RSFSR. The difference between a kray and an oblast is that a kray usually incorporates an autonomous oblast. Of the six krays that exist in the RSFSR, only one—Primor'ye—does not have an autonomous oblast.

2. Oblasts exist in seven republics: RSFSR, Ukrainian S.S.R., Belorussia, Uzbekistan, Kazakhstan, Kyrgyzstan, and Turkmenia. New regional formations are coming into existence at the present time. Moldavia, for example, has created *Zhudetsy* (Districts [Russ.: *Uyezdy*]) that basically resemble administratrive districts in the Federal Republic of Germany. This article focuses primarily on the most common regional formations, krays and oblasts.

3. Autonomous okrugs exist only in the RSFSR.

4. In some republics, village Soviets are referred to by different names: Stanitsy, Apilinki, Auly, Kishlaki, and such.

5. The reference is to the organization of the U.S.S.R. according to U.S.S.R. constitutional legislation in effect on September 1, 1991.

6. Special scientific studies devoted to the principle of democratic centralism based on the activity of the Soviets have been published. See, for example, V. I. Vasil'ev, *Demokraticheskiy Tsentralizm v Sisteme Sovetov* (Democratic Centralism in the Soviet System) (Moscow: Yuridlit, 1973).

7. The 1997 Constitution of the U.S.S.R. defined Soviets of People's Deputies as a unified system. Article 39 stated: "Soviets of People's Deputies—the U.S.S.R. Supreme Soviet, Supreme Soviets of union republics, Supreme Soviets of autonomous republics, Kray and Oblast Soviets of People's Deputies, Soviets of People's Deputies of autonomous Oblasts and autonomous Okrugs, rayon, city, and rayon-in-city, settlement and village Soviets of People's Deputies—comprise a unified system of organs of state power."

8. See *Vedomosti S"yezda narodnykh deputatov i Verkhovnogo Soveta SSSR* (Official Gazette of the Congress of People's Deputies and the U.S.S.R. Supreme Soviet), No. 16 (1990): 267.

9. According to the 1978 Constitution of the RSFSR, 16 autonomous republics, 5 autonomous Oblasts, and 10 autonomous Okrugs were subjects of federation (*sub"yekty federatsii*) in the RSFSR.

10. The federation was based on the All-Union Treaty of 1922.

11. At the present time, there is only one autonomous oblast—the Jewish Autonomous Oblast—left in the RSFSR. See the July 3, 1991 Law on Amendments and Supplements to the Constitution (Fundamental Law) of the RSFSR in connection with the transformation of autonomous oblasts into Soviet Socialist Republics as part of the RSFSR.

12. See the July 6, 1991 Law of the RSFSR on Local Self-Government in the RSFSR (No. 1551-1).

13. See, for example, Decree on an Organ of Local Self-Government at the Primary Level in the City of Maardu. Decision of the Maardu City Soviet of People's Deputies on September 12, 1990, Tallin-Maardu; Decree on the Kemerovo Oblast Soviet of People's Deputies. Decision of the Kemerovo Oblast Soviet dated November 17, 1990.

14. See, for example, the February 12, 1990 Law of the Lithuanian S.S.R. on Principles of Local Self-Government (*Sovetskaya Litva*, March 2, 1990); Latvian S.S.R. laws On Urban Self-Government (February 15, 1990); On Rayon Self-Government (February 15, 1990); On Volost' (small rural district) Self-Government (February 15, 1990) (*Sovetskaya Latviya*, February 28, March 3, March 6, 1990).

15. The December 7, 1990, Law of the Ukrainian S.S.R. on Local Soviets of People's Deputies in the Ukrainian S.S.R. and Local Self-Government (*Industrial'noye Zaporozh'ye*, December 12, 1990).

16. Thus, in the RSFSR, in accordance with the Statute on the Procedure for Resolving Questions of Administrative-Territorial Organization in the RSFSR, rayons, cities, and city rayons are formed and abolished, and rayon administrative centers are established and relocated by the Presidium of the RSFSR Supreme Soviet at the behest of the executive committees of krays, oblasts, and cities (cities of republic subordination); and village Soviets are formed, abolished and merged, and their administrative centers are established and relocated by the executive committees of kray and oblast Soviets at the behest of executive committees of lower Soviets of People's Deputies. August 17, 1982, Ukase of the Presidium of the RSFSR Supreme Soviet (Vedomosti Verkhovnogo Soveta RSFSR, No. 34, 1982, Art. 1271).

17. RSFSR law only temporarily requires the agreement of city rayon Soviets to the liquidation of rayons by a city Soviet pending expiration of the term of office of incumbent rayon Soviets (lit. rayon Soviets of the present convocation).

18. See *Kuzbass*, March 1, 1991, for the materials of the congress.

19. See the Draft Law of the RSFSR on Kray and Oblast Government in the RSFSR (edited by professors G. V. Barabashev and K. F. Sheremet).

22

Local Government and the Socioeconomic Development of Indigenous Northern Populations in Siberia

Gennadii N. Chebotarev

There are two autonomous okrugs (territories): Khanty-Mansi and Yamal-Nenets. The Khanty, Mansi, Nenetses, Komis, Selkups, and other minorities making up 1.7 percent of the total population are now living in their territories. The intensive development of natural resources (primarily oil and gas) has resulted in the deterioration of the natives' living conditions, and has decreased their numbers. For example, in 1970, 19,800 people lived in the Khanty-Mansi Autonomous Okrug and now only 18,000 live there.

The causes of the population decrease are migration, assimilation, and depopulation. The life span of the Nenetses in Yamal in the 1970s fluctuated from 45 to 55 years. The aborigines have a high morbidity rate from tuberculosis and gastrointestinal diseases. There are serious problems in education, in national culture development, in providing employment for the natives, and in environmental protection (the latter being most acute).

While inspecting the Ob flood lands in the Nizhnevartovsk and Surgut oil industry districts, it was found that the amounts of petroleum products in the water and ground there greatly exceeded the maximum permissible concentration. Pollution and other negative results of economic activities has contributed to a loss in fish catch in the Khanty-Mansi Okrug of nearly 10–12,000 tons. To compensate for the loss, the fishing industry needs a great amount of funds.

The economic development of the Northern territories was usually carried out without any scientific basis, and without taking into account the social, economic, and ecological consequences of development. (Development plans often contradicted the traditional way of living of the indigenous peoples.) The deer pasture areas and the number of deer decreased and the number of unprofitable farms involving traditional trades increased.

State regulation of the socioeconomic and political development of the Northern minorities must improve to prevent further deterioration in the living conditions of the natives. Establishing property rights in land in the traditional native territories can play an important role in the recognition of other rights conferred by the Convention of the International Labor Organization about indigenous peoples living in tribes in independent countries. If development problems are solved, the customs and traditions of the people could be revived, the natural resources could be more sensibly exploited, and the region's ecology stabilized.

One of the most important steps in realizing those aims is to set up special territories of natural conditons and to define the system of land tenure through the local Soviets.

The Tyumen Regional Soviet of People's Deputies, for example, established the order of allotment and confiscation of native lands for other than economic activities. The lands can be allotted and confiscated according to the results of a referendum among the aborigines and ethnic groups by consent with the appropriate Soviets of People's Deputies.

A statute on tribal lands in the area was adopted at the session of the Khanty-Mansi District Soviet of People's Deputies. Tribal lands within the territories of the priority land usage are as a rule allotted according to the decision of the local Soviet of People's Deputies (SPD). The allotments are given as rent-free estates. It had been drafted by a group of lawyers and scientists at Tyumen University. The assignment of lands to the community, tribes, and families of the Northern peoples acknowledges rights to land, mineral wealth, pastures, forests, and rivers, with a view to restoring the number of people, their culture, and national trades.

The statute regulates the use of natural resources for such national trades as hunting, fishing, reindeer-breeding, farming, and mushroom and berry picking. It asserts the right to free enterprise and the right to dispose of these products of trade. The statute regulates allotments for industrial needs and entry to the tribal lands. It also contains protection regulations.

Under the statute, those who cause damage, for example, by taking illegal possession of the land, or by misusing natural resources, must pay for the damages, including lost profits. The owner or the local administrative bodies defending the owner's interests and the public procurator have the right to bring a court action to recover damages.

The regulation of relations among the aborigines is primarily to establish legal rules and requisites for the Northern minorities to have an opportunity to develop and preserve their traditions and national culture, and to solve political problems on their own. The peoples of the North must have self-government and independence to extend their political and legal rights to guarantee their future existence. Today, many questions of vital importance are settled locally in the district or settlement, at the community assemblies or the elders' seatings, and not in the okrug or region organizations or in the ministry.

Self-governing for the Northern peoples is problematic. The north of the Tyumen region is mainly rural, where there are more than a hundred national settlements each with village SPDs. However, the native deputies of the village Soviets make up less than 10–12% of the representatives in the Soviets. They are even fewer in the settlement district and town Soviets.

Thus, new efficient structures of local authorities must be formed in population centers of the Northern aboriginal peoples—the Khants, Mansis, Nenetses, and other ethnic groups. New governing structures could be formed of national settlement SPDs or other local bodies and the native self-governing bodies of the particular territory.

The national village/settlement SPDs will represent the first territorial level of local government, which organizes the people to solve local problems. The solutions will take into account local peculiarities and interests of the people in accord with the law and material and financial resources. The national village and settlement SPDs could be formed either on the basis of existing village or settlement Soviets, or from the districts and village Soviet areas designated by the Elders' Council that have assured representation of aboriginal groups.

The national village/settlement SPDs must reflect the results of a referendum of the majority of the population living in the traditional places of the Northern minorities within the territory of the newly formed Soviet. According to the results of the referendum, national village/settlement SPDs could be formed when more than half of the people voted for the Soviet, even if the natives do not make the majority of the population. The decision to form a new village/settlement SPD according to the results of the referendum should be considered at the session of the district SPD of the area. The district SPD could establish the territorial borders of the national village/settlement SPD by agreement with the aboriginal communities, and by taking into account the tribal lands within the traditional territories.

National village/settlement Soviets represent local bodies in their areas. The local administration will be the directing body of the area, with the *starosta* (the village elder) elected by secret native ballot. As a rule, the *starosta* appoints the administration members from the aboriginal people.

The national Soviet must have wide powers to implement a Russian program of development of the Northern aboriginal peoples. The session of the national village/settlement Soviet, by itself, may exercise the following powers:

- to establish the exclusive right to exploit biological resources, fishing and hunting lands, and deer pastures on the territory of the Soviet
- to establish, within the transition to the market period, privileges for Northern minorities, sovkhozes, kolkhozes, enterprises, and organizations dealing with the national trades, to propose to the district Soviet to reserve the native territories not alienated for industrial exploitation or vice-versa, and to approve native land allotments

- to give permission to enterprise and traditional trades for the minor peoples living on the territory of the reservation by consent with the okrug and district Soviets
- to give permission to hunt and fish for food by any unforbidden tackles in all the water reservoirs except pools for spawning all year round
- to reserve jobs for aborigines
- to permit forestry based on the forest inventory by consent with the okrug Soviet and the Ministry of Forestry of the Russian Federation
- to consider and approve building projects
- to give proxies granted by the laws of the Russian Federation

Other questions not falling under the competence of the national village/settlement Soviet can be resolved by the local administration.

According to the statute of the Russian Federation, About the Local Self-government, the Soviet can be elected or dismissed by a decision taken by a corresponding Soviet or a referendum. In that case, other organs of self-government are authorized. In the national settlements, the Elders' Council can represent such organs. Taking into consideration the historical traditions, the local self-government experience, and the right of the Northern aborigines to foster their originality, it is necessary to offer all facilities for reviving community activities.

The community is a voluntary union of citizens, families, and tribes living a traditional way of life and united by the necessity of the common usage of natural resources. The highest authority of the community is a *skhod* (gathering), which chooses the head and the Community Council (for large communities) as the executive organs.

In national settlements, the Elders' Councils are convened to draw in the representatives of the Northern minorities for solving state and local problems. The Elders are, as a rule, elected from the aboriginal people at the gatherings of the villagers. According to the decision of the village SPD, these councils can function as the directing bodies.

Thus, the improvement of self-government structures will strengthen the economic and political independence of the Northern minorities and will focus the efforts of the local authorities on solving the most urgent vitally important problems of the aboriginal peoples.

PART V

COMMUNICATION AND NEWS

The ability of members of society to communicate with one another and to have access to news may influence greatly the government structure that evolves. By the same token, government regulation or control may either encourage or discourage communication and news access. Communication in a society (local, state, regional, or global) today may range from television (public, private, and cable), radio, and print (newspapers, magazines, and books) to computer (networks, programs, and databases). These traditional and innovative forms of communication are nowhere present, fostered, and protected to the degree, variety, and access that they are in the U.S.A. At the same time, nowhere has access and content of communication been more controlled than in the former U.S.S.R.

The U.S. Constitution safeguards news-gathering publication and access explicitly through the First Amendment's guarantee of freedom of expression to an extent unknown in other countries. The news media rely primarily on private sources (newspapers, television, and computer services) augmented slightly by nonprofit public sources (for example, the Public Broadcasting System [PBS]). Prior to the breakup of the U.S.S.R., news, as a matter of government structure, was gathered, packaged, and disseminated exclusively by state organs (TASS, *Pravda*, *Izvestia*, etc.).

Communication and news both in the U.S.A. and in the former U.S.S.R. are subject to great changes in the immediate decades ahead both technically, caused by development in satellites, computers, and information highways, and structurally, caused by the new world order and the emerging global economy.

Thomas W. Hazlett's paper addresses the difficult relationship of the U.S. government's regulation, deregulation, and reregulation of the cable television industry. His analysis focuses on such problems associated with reliance on the economic marketplace to provide communication as the tendency toward a natural monopoly and the related dangers for free and complete access to information that that tendency brings. He correctly urges the states of the former U.S.S.R. as they evolve into democracies and private market economies to be aware of the "mixed performance" of the U.S.A. in efficiently and effectively facilitating communication.

Stephen Hess in his paper relates the news media in the U.S.A. to federalism in the important area of the coverage of government. He observes the dominance in news coverage of the federal government over state and local governments. He notes on the one hand the growing shift in government authority and responsibility from the federal government to state and local governments, and on the other hand the failure of the news media to reflect that shift in coverage. He calls for the news media to shift the focus of its coverage accordingly.

23

Federal Preemption of Local Regulation of Cable Television

Thomas W. Hazlett

MEDIA, PUBLIC OPINION, AND GOVERNMENT STRUCTURES: WHY CABLE REGULATION?

It seems almost suicidal, on a panel advertising such exciting issues as the media and public opinion, to focus on the intellectual depressant: government structures. Even more life threatening is to introduce a very particular history of a very particular industry: the cable television sector. Hence, my death-defying talk on this panel is billed, "Federal Preemption of Local Regulation of Cable Television."

Before you suggest that your doctor assign this paper to patients allergic to the traditional painkillers, let me make a desperate pitch for why this may be an illuminating and, possibly, even entertaining foray. First, the development of cable television, now well into its fifth decade in the U.S.A., illustrates some highly typical tussles between the various levels of government. Local, state, and federal governments have all been involved in promoting—or retarding—the growth of cable television.[1] Second, these regulatory battles have involved fundamental First Amendment, freedom of the press, dimensions. Often these have involved implicit or explicit attempts to use the evolving technologies of on-line television to inform, explore, or otherwise impact public opinion. Third, in excavating the actual history of the U.S. regulation of the cable TV market, we might focus our discussion on government regulation with far greater precision. Distinct from theoretical argumentation, where the "public interest" is promoted in an abstract future sterilized with the author's own unspecified antiseptic, the track record of regulatory institutions offers an essential "reality check" on the models of the visionary.

These very American lessons regarding regulation of the electronic press, learned the good old-fashioned way—by hugely fouling things up—may allow our visitors from the East to gain important insights that travel nicely. I will attempt, however, to be modest in my goals. Recently, the Nobel Laureate in Economics, Milton Friedman, remarked that the best form of aid we could extend Eastern Europeans seeking our assistance would be to direct the U.S. State Department to deny entry visas to any individual from such lands coming to America in search of economic or political advice. I can see from the attendance here that either Professor Friedman's aid plan has not yet been implemented, or our State Department computers need reprogramming. But, given that you have come all this way, I think you should stick around to at least learn something from our failures. And, when you do, please be generous; *share* those insights with us.

U.S. CABLE TELEVISION: A QUICK OVERVIEW

Before proceeding, I will explain the concept and technology of cable television for those who may be unfamiliar with it. The traditional way of receiving video channels on a TV set has been via 6 MHz signals transmitted through the air. These are received either by a television set's built-in antenna, or by affixing an aerial out a window or on a rooftop.[2] Beginning in the United States in 1948, areas that could not receive adequate over-the-air TV broadcasts, due to their remote locations or hilly terrain, began to be wired with copper coaxial cables. These were attached to large antennas atop nearby mountains or microwave receiving stations, which allowed distant signals to be imported. Broadcast TV channels were gradually made available to those beyond the broadcast contours by this patchwork system of, in essence, "antenna extenders."

Owing to improvements in electronics associated with cable television transmission, channel capacities began to grow. The early cable systems transported just three to five channels; by the 1960s these expanded to 12 channels. In the 1970s, state-of-the-art cable capacity increased to 35 channels; by 1980, 54 channels became standard. Today, recently built (or rebuilt) systems routinely carry 70 channels, and soon cheap fiber optics and digital compression techniques will push cable into the 100-500 channel world.

These channels are filled with a variety of viewing fare: local off-air broadcast signals, satellite networks produced specifically for cable, premium movie channels, and programming produced by community members or the local cable operator. The cable consumer is first offered a basic cable package: in 1990 this was priced at (a national average) $17.31 and featured 32 channels (including retransmitted broadcast channels and such cable networks as CNN, ESPN, and the Discovery Channel). In addition, the customer may subscribe to premium movie services (such as HBO or Showtime); in 1990, these averaged $10.38 each. Approximately 95% of the U.S. public is now passed by a cable and may, therefore, subscribe; of these, about 62% do. Total industry revenue in 1991 was $21.3 billion; this breaks down to $29.93 per month for the typical cable subscriber.

THE FIGHT FOR CABLE JURISDICTION

Cable television regulation has passed through three distinctive regimes, and now appears headed for a fourth.[3] From about 1948 to 1960, cable was left alone by both local and federal regulators; the Federal Communications Commission (FCC) specifically rejected (on three different occasions) staff requests to impose common carrier requirements on the medium. From about 1960 to 1975, however, the FCC reversed this laissez-faire policy, and vigorously imposed rules controlling virtually every element of the business. Content restrictions, for instance, severely limited what types of programs cable operators could offer. The regulatory rationale behind these rules was that cable firms were not to hurt broadcast television audiences, which would, in turn, undermine FCC ability to license broadcasters "in the public interest."

In about 1975 we entered a period of deregulation: federal impediments to cable competition were dropped.[4] With this newfound freedom to compete for audience share, cable firms made a mad dash to wire cable-hungry U.S. cities: What awaited them were smiling city bureaucrats. With scores of firms competing for lucrative municipal cable franchises, franchises that the cities jealously guarded as monopoly awards (see Hazlett 1986), city officials alertly discovered they could extract generous contributions on behalf of their city treasuries, political allies, campaign war chests, and influential friends simply by "auctioning" to the highest *political* bidder.[5] This was the age when the term "rent-a-citizen" became de rigueur within the cable industry; to have any chance of securing a major cable franchise, a bidding firm was careful to distribute equity shares in the future venture among the community's most persuasive movers and shakers. It was a very profitable time to be a retired city councilman, a respected community activist, or a City Hall lobbyist noted for your clout.

While this process was wracked by corruption, the largest social costs were incurred by the delays that long-debated franchise awards pushed onto consumers, and by the inefficient cross-subsidies that the local politicians demanded. The delay in cable franchising is legendary in New York City, for instance. When Manhattan was one of the very first urban areas wired for cable in the late 1960s, the Lindsay administration excitedly appointed experts and commissions to plan for the coming new video technology of tomorrow. Such experts envisioned a "brave new world." Unfortunately, they forgot—for nearly 20 years—to get the rest of New York City wired. That job is just now being completed.

The wasted resources exhausted by government-mandated programming has been similarly disastrous. In 1990, over $250 million was expended by cable systems nationwide for what is called "public access, local origination" programming (Continental 1990, ii), or 38 cents per subscriber per month. This is the paradigmatic cross-subsidy provided by cable systems to gain political support for a monopoly franchise award. From audience ratings used by cable operators to determine the imputed value of alternative channel lineups, we may estimate the consumer value generated by this (forced) investment. Assuming that all U.S. cable systems provide both a public access and a local origination channel, average audience shares are worth just 4 cents per month per subscriber.[6] In other words, using the revealed preference of television viewers themselves, 90% of this annual expenditure—or about $225 million per year—is lost, a casualty of local government regulation.

As is typical in other markets, the current era of cable "deregulation" has been herky-jerky. While the federal government has stripped away the anticable rules and even preempted localities on the question of rate regulation in the 1984 Cable Act, cities have been more or less allowed to deter competition via monopoly franchises. So we have the public policy nightmare; protected monopolies, without price regulation, as well as government-mandated requirements that cable companies spend millions on local networks that nobody wants to watch. In light of this, one might almost assume that the long delays in franchising were a good thing.

Given widespread dissatisfaction with the state of our cable affairs, Congress and the FCC are now grappling with various schemes to *reregulate* the cable television industry. A bill to allow cities to once again control the price of basic cable has passed one or the other house in Congress in each of the past two years. Those who have studied our actual experiment in local rate regulation, however, have seen that city regulators did not use that power to keep rates low, but rather to extract payments for favored constituencies. (This evidence strongly emerged when I studied the California experience with a state deregulation of cable rates in 1979 [Hazlett 1991].) The proof of this pudding is that cable reregulation is strongly supported by the National Association of Broadcasters—the competitors to cable TV who have no interest in effectively lowering cable rates and further dissipating their falling audience shares (see NAB 1990).

The central problem with local control of cable television franchising is that each municipal government must make a choice between greater competition—which would lower prices and speed-up service—and monopoly—which maximizes the demand for a license itself. Under the competitive scenario, consumers realize broad gains; under the latter, targeted interest groups, including incumbent city council members themselves, can pocket high returns. The evidence indicates that the lure of the latter is very hard for any government to resist and special interests with large per capita payoffs tend to dominate general interests.

In cable, this paradigm has played out on both local and federal levels. Locally, companies that seek competitive cable franchises are routinely denied permission to risk their own capital by city governments that recite public interest themes in order to protect the private interests with which they ally. Nationally, cable was suppressed for 15 years or more precisely due to influential industry incumbents: broadcasters requested that their markets be protected from cable competition and the FCC meekly obliged, going so far as to conjure a public interest veneer for the scheme. This policy resulted in Americans being denied the great range of choice available on cable television today.

The intellectual craftsmen who molded the anticable rules of the 1960s and 1970s argued that only if the broadcast market was shielded from potential wireline rivals could the FCC force TV broadcasters to air programs that were in the "public interest." Such fare was defined as (1) local, and (2) covering controversial issues from a balanced perspective. The verdict on this regulatory scheme has now been rendered by history: The Federal Communications Commission was notoriously unsuccessful in promoting either over the broadcast airwaves, and it is only in the age of cable that either local programs or controversial news and opinion shows are commercially viable. Local programs are ideally suited to cable televison because the cable signal is so tightly confined. In a recent article, the *National Journal* noted that despite being under no obligation to sell time to political candidates, cable television has become the perfect medium for reaching voters:

> Cable TV sales representatives argue that cable is "geoefficient" and that politicians can use it to inexpensively target their message to the most receptive voters. Because they serve jurisdictions smaller than major metropolitan areas, cable operators say, it's now possible for politicians—especially House candidates—who have found television advertising too expensive to sell themselves on TV.[7]

Ironically, today it is only over cable—on unlicensed, unregulated networks that have no obligation to broadcast controversial issues or operate in "the public interest"—that one finds the range of opinion represented by CNN's lineup of the *Capitol Gang*, the *Jesse Jackson Show*, *Evans & Novak*, *Crossfire*, *Crier & Company*, *Sonia Live*, or *Larry King Live*. Other unlicensed cable networks—C-Span I, C-Span II, the Monitor Channel, CNBC, Discovery, and A&E—now offer similar outpourings of public affairs programs from all over the sociopolitical landscape. When the government ostensibly protected the public from excessive competition and mandated that the "public interest" be served on licensed TV, the American public was actually denied the very choices that now, at long last, realize the stated objectives of the old "public interest" standard. Regulation did not fail in *theory*, it failed in *fact*. Deregulation did not succeed in *theory*, it succeeded in *fact*. Government regulation starved the public consumer of news, information, and entertainment and market competition brought home the bacon.

WHEN FEDERAL PREEMPTION MAKES SENSE

The failed experiments with cable regulation at both the local and federal levels provide some general lessons. While the federal deregulation of the 1975–84 period did, indeed, free up cable to compete with broadcasters, it failed to allow cable to compete more with itself, with the result that Americans are now (unless they are lucky enough to live in Allentown, Pennsylvania; Montgomery, Alabama; or Waldport, Oregon) held hostage to the prices and programs offered by a monopoly cable supplier. This has constrained the benefits of this advanced technology, as well as constricted the range of opinion expressed by the local system news shows.

The problems with local licensing, therefore, are twofold: local regulators will be predisposed in favor of monopoly awards, owing to lobbying cost biases long recognized in the public choice and political science literatures, and government licensing of a local medium of expression will predictably chill free speech. Of course, the self-interest of incumbents (both on the city council and in the cable TV market) would be perfectly willing to trade off editorial discretion for a secured interest in a monopoly license, but the fundamental values of the First Amendment reject such an approach.[8] Hence, strong and reinforcing forces reliably operate upon City Hall to restrict entry into the cable market subject to the watchful eye of the local political authority. Such a scenario should bring smiles to cable investors, local politicians, and old party apparatchiks everywhere.

It does not do much for consumers, market competition, technical innovation, or freedom of expression. These may be considered important social goals. To give them a fighting chance in this political world, one should design the federal-local structure quite differently: federal preemption of local regulation on a rule generally binding upon all governments (a constitutional freedom of speech provision). You may recall that we have such a thing in our Bill of Rights. This nicely binds the federal government and it has been used to undermine local monopolies. In at least four U.S. federal cases, courts have thrown out monopoly franchises as a violation of the free press rights of excluded "electronic publishers."[9] This is precisely the sort of federal preemption that is warranted: imposing deeply important, broadly applied rules of social policy that are crafted out of deference to fundamental liberties.

The incentive to create local monopolies is doubly strong in cable, imbued as it is with the output of a communications medium, but it is a likely outcome in any sector where service is geographically determined. For instance, the eminent American jurist Archibald Cox (former U.S. solicitor general and Harvard University professor of law emeritus), has written that the single most important Supreme Court case in U.S. history was *Fulton Steamship* (1809). This decision struck down the State of New York's attempt to establish a monopoly steamship service for Robert Fulton, inventor of this transport mode. Professor Cox opines that, in the absence of such a ruling, each state would have had the incentive to restrict entry into a variety of services.[10] The development of free trade and travel among the states has been so important to the ultimate economic emergence of the United States, according to Cox, that this single decision looms in greater importance to our social health than even the classic civil rights decisions of the Warren Court (Cox 1987).

While both Democrats and Republicans in the U.S.A. have enjoyed the opportunity to regulate cable television at the local level (Democrats because it is regulation, Republicans because it is local), the resultant monopoly market structure has served both consumer welfare and civil liberties very poorly. Cable systems ought to compete on price, service, and quality. A 1990 survey by the FCC found that cable systems that did compete head to head priced basic cable service 34% less than monopolies on a per channel basis (FCC 1990). Not surprisingly, competitive markets inspire news reports that cable service—a national bane and a common butt of late-night TV jokes—is excellent.[11]

But it is the underlying values of the First Amendment that are most endangered by cable monopolies. As an advanced system of communications able to deliver scores, and soon hundreds, of video channels to eager consumers, the ability of cable televison to "publish" news, information, and entertainment services is unchallenged. Particularly at a local political level, where so often the watchful eye of the national press is impossibly overmatched by the scope and detail of events, cable television possesses a unique opportunity for monitoring our democratic institutions. So long as cable companies generate large profits via monopoly market shares awarded by local officials, one need not have access to a crystal ball to conclude that local political reporting on cable will be minimal, tame, and apologetic.

The opportunity to avert this shamefully undemocratic civility may still not have passed in the United States, where threads of the First Amendment still survive in the regulated cable markets, and where new competitors to cable—including wireless multichannel television and the growing fiber optic networks of the telephone industry—promise to disrupt old political equilibria. But it has surely not passed for those who get to begin their societies anew, to plan for freedom, and to erect countermeasures designed to deflect the natural political tendency to protect the established and to forestall the new. This is the challenge of any dynamic society. The U.S.A.'s mixed performance should make the states of the former U.S.S.R. respectfully apprehensive as to the degree of difficulty in building truly liberal institutions, as well as better informed—and perhaps even motivated—to be able to attempt this worthwhile endeavor. The great part of joining the family of dynamic nations, albeit as the youngest and tenderest offspring, is the privilege of participating in such daunting missions; the troubling aspect is that such effort has now become their duty.

NOTES

1. My brief analysis is confined here to the key tension between local and federal regulation. For a more complete discussion that includes the role of state regulation, the reader is referred to Copple (1991).

2. This receiving device is, of course, connected to the TV monitor via a copper wire.

3. Hence, I titled a recent paper of mine on this subject, "The Unregulation, Regulation, Deregulation, and Reregulation of Cable Television" (Hazlett, 1990b).

4. Some were eliminated "voluntarily" by the FCC; others were dismantled as per federal court decisions, which became less deferential to FCC regulation during this period.

5. The term "auction" is not used here to denote a competitive bidding procedure wherein the franchising authority awards the license to the highest dollar bid. Rather, a winner is selected by which vector of city fees and off-budget payments (including cross-subsidies, stock grants, campaign donations, "public interest" funding, etc.) are highest valued. The term has actually been used by federal courts to describe the municipal franchising process (see Ninth Circuit opinion in *Preferred v. Los Angeles* [1985]).

6. From the "Channel Valuation Model" given in *Marketing New Media* (Carmel, CA.: Paul Kagan & Associates; January 15, 1990, 2). This model is based upon a linear division of the basic cable rate (set at $19.13/subscriber/month) by viewing share of each cable channel (including retransmitted broadcast channels).

7. Jerry Hagstrom, "Ad Attack," *National Journal* (April 4, 1992), 813.

8. See Ithiel Pool (1983) and Lucas Powe, Jr. (1987) for two excellent book-length analyses concerning First Amendment problems with government licensing.

9. These cases are *Group W. v. Santa Cruz (1985)*; *Pacific West v. Sacramento* (1987); *Century Federal v. Palo Alto* (1988); and *Preferred Communications v. Los Angeles* (1990).

10. This is true particularly for transportation services, where if the state limits entry, close substitutes in other jurisdictions are unavailable. Cable television is a geographically sensitive consumer product in this sense; it is very costly to travel (or move) to another area simply to obtain more competitive service.

11. See John Barnes, "Why Cable Costs Too Much," *Washington Monthly* (June 1989), 12–17; John Merline, "How to Get Better Cable TV at Lower Prices," *Consumers' Research* (May 1990), 10–17; John Emshwiller, "Cable Entrepreneurs Take

on Entrenched Competitors," *Wall Street Journal* (July 12, 1990); Mark Lewyn and Julie Amparano Lopez, "More Choice for Cable TV?" *Business Week* (May 13, 1991).

REFERENCES

"Comments of Continental Cablevision." *In the Matter of Competition, Rate Deregulation and the Commission's Policies Relating to the Provison of Cable Television Service.* Federal Communications Commission, MM Docket No. 89-600, March 1, 1990.

Copple, Robert F. 1991. "Cable Television and the Allocation of Regulatory Power: A Study of Demarcation and Roles," *Federal Communications Law Journal* 44(1) (December): 1–172.

Cox, Archibald. 1967. *The Court and the Constitution*. Houghton-Mifflin.

FCC. 1990. "Report in the Matter of Competition, Rate Deregulation and the Commission's Policies Relating to the Provision of Cable Television Service." Federal Communications Commission, MM Docket No. 89-600, July 26.

Hazlett, Thomas W. 1986. "Private Monopoly and the Public Interest: An Economic Analysis of the Cable Television Franchise." *University of Pennsylvania Law Review* 134 (July): 1335–1409.

———. 1989. "Cabling America: Economic Forces in a Political World." In C. Veljanovski, ed., *Freedom in Broadcasting*. London: Institute of Economic Affairs, 208–23.

———. 1990a. "Duopolistic Competition in Cable Television: Implications for Public Policy," *Yale Journal on Regulation VII* (Winter): 65–119.

———. 1990b. "The Unregulation, Regulation, Deregulation, and Reregulation of Cable Television." Paper presented at the Western Economics Association Annual Meetings (San Diego, July).

———. 1991. "The Demand to Regulate Franchise Monopoly: Evidence from CATV Rate Deregulation in California." *Economic Inquiry* 29 (April): 275–96.

NAB. 1990. "Comments of the National Association of Broadcasters in the Matter of Competition, Rate Deregulation and the Commission's Policies Relating to the Provision of Cable Television Service." Federal Communications Commission, MM Docket No. 89-600, March 1.

Pool, Ithiel de Sola. 1983. *Technologies of Freedom*. Cambridge, MA.: Harvard University Press.

Powe, Lucas, Jr. 1987. *American Broadcasting and the First Amendment*. Berkeley: University of California Press.

24

Levels of the Game: Federalism and the American News System

Stephen Hess

In May 1987, the United States Information Agency opened an exhibition in Moscow called "Information USA." It was to tour the Soviet Union for 18 months, 10,000 people a day lined up to get in, and each, on entering, was given a magazine, resembling a newsweekly, to help explain what they were about to see. I had the opportunity to contribute a short history of the U.S. news media in which I thought it would be helpful to begin with some data on how my country was drenched in information.

My assignment is to relate the U.S. media system to federalism. But again, for the record, I think it is appropriate to recap the reach of the media—with some updated figures—that we will then deconstruct by level of government.

The media in America form two strands that have peacefully coexisted since the eighteenth century: a vastly dominant commercial segment, expected to rise or fall on the operators' ability to make a profit, and collectively offering tremendous diversity to the buying public; and a much smaller but significant noncommercial segment, in which almost every shade of opinion is represented by its own publications, from the liberal *Nation* through the conservative *National Review*.

Americans today can choose from nearly 11,000 periodicals published in the United States. (A typical drugstore around the corner from my office in downtown Washington, DC, displays 260 different magazines.) In broadcasting, too, choices have proliferated with the increase in radio and TV stations and channels. Virtually every American has at least one television set (91 million households, with 60 million homes having more than one set), and those sets receive broadcasts from 1,092 local commercial TV stations as well as 350 noncommercial stations (often affiliated with a university). Over 55% of American homes subscribe to cable TV systems typically having a capacity of 30–53 channels.

With some 541 million radio sets in use, the average number per household is more than five. Americans can listen to more than 11,000 radio stations, most of which are locally owned and independently programmed. Many specialize in various types of popular music, but there are 449 stations devoted exclusively to news.

These figures are important not only to show the extent of media saturation, but because polling data suggest that Americans get most of their news from television: 40 million watch the weekday evening news on ABC, CBS, and NBC combined; 3 million watch the nightly news program of noncommercial PBS, which is supported by a mix of government and private donations; and 800,000 watch CNN's prime cable news program.

At the same time, evidence shows that voters—the most politically aware part of the population—are more likely to be newspaper readers. About 1,600 newspapers publish daily in the U.S.A. with a combined circulation of 62 million, as well as 7,500 weekly newspapers whose total circulation is 53 million.

In the 1950s and 1960s there was also a flourishing radical "underground press" in most major cities, and, while most of these newspapers died with the Vietnam War, their place has often been taken by the "alternative" weekly, more directed to the coverage of lifestyles than to politics. In addition, there are city papers aimed at specialized audiences, foreign language readers, blacks, gays, and others. Moreover, as Phyllis Kaniss points out, "With major technological breakthroughs in production, like offset printing and computer typesetting, many small-scale entrepreneurs are finding they are able to start weekly papers with a relatively small capital investment."[1]

Despite this substantial supply of information, the thesis of this paper is that one level of government in the United States gets shortchanged. While the national media (network TV, newsweekly magazines, and certain elite newspapers) concentrate on international and national news, the local media (TV stations and most newspapers) concentrate on city-level news, and news of state government often gets overlooked. There are reasons why this happens, of course, which I will review. But the information loss becomes increasingly serious as the actions of state government become more and more important in our lives.

Scholars seem to have ignored this area of investigation since the work of William T. Gormley, Jr., in the mid-1970s.[2] Although there have been several anecdotal accounts of this phenomenon,[3] only one piece of recent research—to the best of my knowledge—specifically sets out to measure the level of coverage of state government. Tracy Westen and Beth Givens (see Tables II.4 and III.1 at the end of this chapter) took soundings in California in 1987. Other research for other purposes, however, sheds light on the subject. For instance, there is a body of data, originally associated with the work of Leon Sigal, that identifies sources quoted in stories.[4] When rank-ordered by whether these persons are officials of foreign, national, or state and local governments, the information suggests a hierarchy in newspaper stories. Similarly, Kaniss' research (Table II.1) and my research (Table II.2) were designed to chart other types of news, local and congressional respectively. Still, since all the results point in the same direction, I feel reasonably secure in my conclusions.

Network TV is a medium of national/international news (Tables I.1, I.2). Of the 50 top network stories of 1991, in terms of minutes, 20 were international, including 9 of the first 10. The other top story, according to the *Tyndall Report*, was the Clarence Thomas confirmation fight. The highest-ranked story with a local angle—Los Angeles police beating up Rodney King—was in 13th place with 138 minutes (compared, for example, with 314 minutes on Kurdish refugees).[5]

David Morgan's 1975 data on "political news" in New York State newspapers also suggest the top-down focus of news in the *New York Times* as contrasted with ten less prestigious papers. Some 40% of the *Times* coverage was international, whereas the next highest figure was 25% for *Newsday*, the Long Island daily; the average of 11 newspapers being 18.7%. The *New York Times*, on the other hand, had the lowest state news percentage (11.6) while the 11-paper average was 21%. Leo Bogart's 1982 data (Table IV.2) show that as papers get larger they have more international news and less state and local news. Thus in papers of 24 pages or less, 58% of the total news is state and local news, 23% is international news; when papers expand to 61 pages or more, the figure for state and local news drops to 44% and rises to 34% for international news.

On network TV the absence of stories about state and local government is the result of trying to appeal to a national audience—an item from a state legislature might occasionally be aired to reflect a national trend or report a bizarre incident, but could not be expected to be of much interest to viewers in other states. The national/international character of news in larger newspapers, however, presumably is meant to attract a more cosmopolitan readership or, perhaps, simply reflects more cosmopolitan editors.

Local TV news broadcasts are designed to have the broadest possible appeal. They have 6 million more viewers than the network news. The geographic distribution of where the stories come from can be seen in the percentages from Kaniss' 1990 survey of three Philadelphia stations: international 2, national 9, state 31, local 58. In other words, the locale of news produced by local stations is the mirror image of news coming from the national networks.

But when stories on local TV programs are rank-ordered by content, the percentage distribution for government/political stories in my 1987-88 survey is somewhat different: international 13, national 47, state 17, local 23. There is more international and national news (usually produced by the networks with whom the stations are affiliated) of a government/political nature; state and local stories are much more often about other subjects, such as crime and natural disasters. Again, as in the case of newspapers, stations in major markets air much more international news and much less local news than stations in small markets (Table I.3). The one study of all-news radio (Table III.1) shows a pattern similar to that of local TV, yet with a heavier emphasis on national stories. This is probably because such news comes from wire services and is therefore cheaper than staff-produced state and local material. Notably, in all surveys the percentage of state news is smaller than local news.

State governments, unfortunately, have often made themselves a difficult target for observation by news organizations and others. At best, only 19 of the 50 states have their capitals in their major city. (I say "at best" because there could be dispute over Cheyenne or Casper, Wyoming.) Indeed, I doubt that most Americans could identify the capitals of Kentucky (Frankfort) or Nevada (Carson City). In some cases—Springfield, Illinois, and Jefferson City, Missouri, as examples—the capitals were deliberately placed at the center of the state, certainly a justifiable reason when traversing the rutted roads of nineteenth-century America. Still, Illinois and Missouri state governments would get more attention if their capitals were located in Chicago and St. Louis. The history of siting the seats of government has a certain charm: Tallahassee, Florida, was chosen, in part, because it was as far away from Indians and swampland as possible. As far as I know, no state capital was chosen so as to be close to journalists.

We should not conclude that merely relocating the capital will automatically refocus attention on state government. Karl T. Kurtz, of the National Conference of State Legislatures, in 1990 contrasted newspaper coverage of legislatures in Colorado and Utah, two Rocky Mountain states, with capitals in their principal cities (Denver and Salt Lake City). He faulted coverage in Colorado, praised coverage in Utah, concluding that the differences were "due to varying civic cultures and the competitive and financial circumstance of the major newspapers."[6] On the other hand, there has not been an out-of-town TV bureau in Sacramento, California, since 1988. It is hard to imagine California government getting less media attention if its capital were in Los Angeles or San Francisco.

Another factor that works against creating news bureaus in state capitals, particularly for TV stations, is that many state legislatures are part-time enterprises. Only eight states in 1988 were considered to have full-time legislatures comparable in operational terms to the U.S. Congress. There are still seven states in which the legislatures do not even meet in annual sessions.

Local TV news programs also are probably less likely to cover state government if their stations' markets are in more than one state. (This has been shown to be true for reporting on U.S. senators.)[7] In a state like New Hampshire, for instance, the northern part of the state gets its television from Maine and the state's more populous south gets most of its television from Boston.[8]

But, I think, the primary reason why the states have received the least media attention is that they are the most artificial unit of the federal system. Beyond the original colonies, a few states with natural boundaries, and the two states that had been independent nations (Texas and Hawaii), most states look like boxes, designed by surveyors and authorized by politicians (which they were). Patriotism is usually defined by nationhood; cities reflect our economic and social being. What of states? I suspect (without supporting data) that if you ask a Chicagoan where he's from, he'd say Chicago, not Illinois—or a Detroiter would not say Michigan. There are some special exceptions: Texans! New Yorkers! In the words of political scientists M. Kent Jennings and Harmon Zeigler,

> the states are caught between the immediacy of the local system and the glamour and importance of the national and international systems. . . . Too remote to stimulate much participation by their citizens, and too big to make extensive participation possible anyway, these units intermediate between city and nation are probably destined for a kind of limbo of quasi-democracy.[9]

The problem with this quite accurate assessment, published in 1970, is that things have changed. According to Denis P. Doyle and Terry W. Hartle, writing in 1985, "The last two years have witnessed the greatest and most concentrated surge of educational reform in the nation's history. . . . Indeed, the most surprising aspect of the 'tidal wave of reform' is that it came from state governments."[10] According to Carl E. Van Horn, writing in 1989,

> Important new policy initiatives have come from the states in a broad range of policy areas—natural resources and energy policy, human services and health care, economic development and education, and business and insurance regulation. State governments are deeply engaged in issues that affect state residents on a daily basis—the quality of schools, the supply of water, and the condition of roads and waterways, for example. States are also tackling some of the nation's most difficult problems—surrogate motherhood, the care and treatment of the medically indigent, drug abuse in the public schools, teenage pregnancy, pay equity, the liability insurance crisis, and the right to die.[11]

And, writes David S. Broder, "Congress and the president have continually laid new responsibilities on the states, while reducing the flow of federal aid. . . . In the current recession [1992], states are making horrendous budget choices—cutting assistance to the poor, choking off support to education, delaying transportation projects, neglecting environmental needs—and raising taxes."[12]

Surely it is time for American news organizations to reassess the attention they pay to that increasingly significant level of government between nation and city.

SURVEYS OF MEDIA, BY LEVELS OF GOVERNMENT REPORTED
(Percent)

I. National Television

1. 1985–86: ABC, CBS, NBC

International	24
National	67
State	5
Local	4

Adapted from Dan Berkowitz, "TV News Sources and News Channels," *Journalism Quarterly*, Vol. 64 (1987), 511; 2.5 hours of network broadcasting, identifying the "source affiliations" in stories.

2. 1976: ABC, CBS, NBC

National	96.8
State	1.9
Local	1.3

Adapted from Doris A. Graber, *Mass Media and American Politics*, 3d ed. (Washington, DC: CQ Press, 1989), 88; reflects "frequency of mention" of stories about government/politics.

II. Local Television

1. 1990: 3 Philadelphia stations

International	2
National	9
State	31
Local	58

Adapted from Phyllis Kaniss, *Making Local News* (Chicago: University of Chicago, 1991), 127; a two-week sample of WCAU, WPVI, and KYW. This table reflects "newstime by geographic area," and excludes suburban, regional, and other city categories.

2. 1987–88: 57 stations in 35 cities

International	13
National	47
State	17
Local	23

Adapted from data prepared for Stephen Hess, *Live from Capitol Hill!* (Washington, DC: Brookings, 1991), 139; the table reflects government/political stories from these cities: Los Angeles (KABC, KNBC, KNXT), San Francisco (KRON), Boston (WNEV, WCVB), Detroit (WDIV, WJBK), Cleveland (WEWS, WJKW, WKYC), Pittsburgh (WPXI), Minneapolis (WCCO, KARE), Atlanta (WAGA), Seattle (KIRO, KING, KSTW), Baltimore (WMAR, WJZ, WBAL), Sacramento (KCRA, KXTV, KOVR), Cincinnati (WLWT), Milwaukee (WITI), Greenville, SC (WYFF), Salt Lake City (KSL), Dayton, OH (WHIO), Albany, NY (WTEN, WNYT), Charlottesville, VA (WVIR), Richmond, VA (WWBT), Wichita, KS (KAKE), Roanoke, VA (WDBJ, WSLS), Lynchburg, VA (WSET), Syracuse, NY (WSTM, WIXT), Green Bay, WI (WFRV, WBAY), Omaha, NE (WOWT), Rochester, NY (WROC, WHEC, WOKR), Harrisburg, IL (WSIL), Paducah, KY (WPSD), Champaign, IL (WCIA, WICD, WAND), Lexington, KY (WLEX), South Bend, IN (WNDU, WSBT), Springfield, MA (WGGB), Washington, NC (WITN), Ft. Myers, FL (WINK), and Grand Junction, CO (WREY).

3. 1987–88: Stations in large and small markets

	large (1–25)	small (71–186)
International	21.1	7.5
National	51.9	32.5
State	12.0	20.0
Local	15.0	40.0

Adapted from Hess, 141.

4. 1987: 10 California stations

International	4.2
National	26.5
State	20.6
Local	48.8

Adapted from Tracy Westen and Beth Givens, *The California Channel* (Los Angeles: Center for Responsive Government, 1989), 47; a survey of eight days of "Issues" from Fresno (KFSN, KSEE), Los Angeles (KABC, KNBC), Sacramento (KCRA, KXTV), San Diego (KGTV, KFMB), and San Francisco (KGO, KPIX).

5. 1985-86: 5 Indiana stations

International	0
National	16
State	30
Local	54

Adapted from Berkowitz; 3.5 hours from Indianapolis and Terre Haute, identifying the "source application" in stories.

6. 1976: 2 Chicago stations

National	76.6
State	9.3
Local	14.2

Adapted from Graber; CBS and ABC affiliate stations, reflecting the "frequency of mention" of stories about government/ politics.

III. All-News Radio

1. 1987: 5 California stations

International	5.0
National	42.9
State	15.5
Local	36.6

Adapted from Westen and Givens, 49; from Fresno (KMJ), Los Angeles (KNX), Sacramento (KFBK), San Diego (KSDO), and San Francisco (KGO).

IV. Newspapers

1. 1971, 1977, 1982: 300 papers

	1971	1977	1982
International	34.2	28.4	24.2
National	23.2	15.8	19.4
State & Local	42.6	55.9	56.5

Adapted from Leo Bogart, *Press and Public,* 2d ed. (Hillsdale, NJ: Lawrence Erlbaum Associates, 1989), 213.

2. 1982: Small and large papers

	Number of pages	
	24 or less	61 or more
International	22.6	34.3
National	19.2	21.6
State & Local	58.2	44.1

Adapted from Bogart, 218.

3. 1979–80: 4 North Carolina papers

International	0.8
National	32.9
State	30.8
Local	35.5

Adapted from Jane Delano Brown and others, "Invisible Power," *Journalism Quarterly*, Vol. 64 (1987), 49; 12 days of *Charlotte Observer*, *Asheville Citizen*, *Fayetteville Observer*, and *Raleigh News and Observer*, identifying "source affiliation."

4. 1979–80: *New York Times*, *Washington Post*

International	20.3
National	59.0
State	9.9
Local	10.8

Adapted from Brown and others, 49; 12 days, "source affiliation."

5. 1975: 9 New York papers

International	21.0
National	44.6
State	15.8
Local	18.6

Adapted from David Morgan, *The Capitol Press Corps* (Westport, CT: Greenwood, 1978), 21; 3-week survey of "political news" in *Adirondack Enterprise*, *Binghamton Sun-Bulletin*, *Buffalo News*, *Newsday*, *New York Daily News*, *New York Times*, *Syracuse Herald-Journal*, *Syracuse Post-Standard*, and *Watertown Times*.

6. 1973–74: 149 papers

International	3.5
National	5.0
State	3.5
Local	88.0

Adapted from Dan Drew and G. Cleveland Wilhoit, "Newshole Allocation Policies of American Daily Newspapers," *Journalism Quarterly*, Vol. 53 (Fall 1976), 435; estimates of managing editors.

NOTES

1. Phyllis Kaniss, *Making Local News* (Chicago: University of Chicago Press, 1991), 155.

2. See William T. Gormley, "Television Coverage of State Government," *Public Opinion Quarterly*, Vol. 42, No. 3 (Fall 1978), 354–59, and "Coverage of State Government in the Mass Media," *State Government*, Vol. 52 (Spring 1979), 46–51.

3. See Neal Koch, "Television Turns Its Back on the Statehouse," *Channels* (April 1989), 12; Rick Kushman, "Tuning Out the Capitol," *California Journal* (May 1989), 221–23; and Rob Gurwitt, "In the Capitol Pressroom, the Old Boys Call It a Day," *Governing* (July 1990), 27–30.

4. See Leon V. Sigal, *Reporters and Officials* (Boston: DC Heath, 1973).

5. *Tyndall Report*, Vol. 4, No. 10 (January 1992) (published by ADT Research, 135 Rivington St., New York, NY 10002); also see "1991—The Year in Review," *Media Monitor*, Vol. 6, No. 1 (January 1992) (published by Center for Media and Public Affairs, 2101 L St., NW, Washington, DC 20037).

6. See Karl T. Kurtz, "The Public Standing of the Legislature," a paper prepared for an Eagleton Institute of Politics Symposium (April 1990).

7. See Charles Stewart III and Mark Reynolds, "Television Markets and U.S. Senate Elections," *Legislative Studies Quarterly*, Vol. 15, No. 4 (November 1990), 495–523.

8. See David Von Drehle, "Patchwork of Surprising Complexity: A Tale of 4 Distinct New Hampshires," *Washington Post*, February 16, 1992, A33.

9. M. Kent Jennings and Harmon Zeigler, "The Salience of American State Politics," *American Political Science Review*, Vol. 64 (June 1970), 524.

10. Denis P. Doyle and Terry W. Hartle, *Excellence in Education: The States Take Charge* (Washington, DC: American Enterprise Institute, 1985), 1.

11. Carl E. Van Horn, *The State of the States* (Washington, DC: CQ Press, 1989), 7.

12. David S. Broder, "The Governors in '92," *Washington Post*, January 15, 1992, A23.

PART VI

ENERGY AND THE ENVIRONMENT

The production of energy (from oil, coal, natural gas, enriched uranium, and such alternative energy sources as the sun, wind, and geothermal energy) historically has been the engine for economic growth in both the United States and the former U.S.S.R. Those natural resources are converted to essential electricity, heat, and mechanical energy, which are used to manufacture goods, to transport goods to market, and to provide light, warmth,. and cooling for businesses and homes. Those energy sources and their products will continue to be just as critical to the sustained domestic economic growth and competitiveness of both the U.S.A. and the states of the former U.S.S.R. in the emerging global economy as they have been in the past. However, the production and use of energy in the future will be increasingly constrained by the demand to avoid the adverse consequences of inefficiency in the energy fuel cycle (from production to end use). Those consequences, of course, are experienced in the form of air, water, and land pollution within states, within regions, and in global commons such as the atmosphere and the oceans.

A critical question for all governments in the twenty-first century will be to determine the best government structure to produce energy efficiently in ways that minimize domestic and international environmental consequences and that maximize economic wealth. The issue underlying the papers in Part VI is whether a central command and control structure, or a decentralized market control structure, or some structure in between will provide the most suitable governmental answer for the U.S.A. and states of the former U.S.S.R. to accommodate sustained economic development in an environment that is safe and healthy in the decades ahead.

Oleg S. Kolbasov soberly observes that the future government structure to deal with the environment in the Russian Federation in the wake of the dissolution of the U.S.S.R. into 15 independent states has been a "minimal" effort. Currently, environmental protection and use of natural resources is governed jointly by Moscow and the member-units of the federation, much as it was in the former U.S.S.R. but with heightened contests over sovereignty, budgets, and applicable law—all of which are taking place in the context of privatization, high inflation, and exploitation by new "businessmen" and criminals.

Lee P. Breckenridge analyzes the developing trend in U.S. environmental law toward decentralization of environmental and natural resource governmental authority. Her paper makes an interesting analogy to modern scientific chaos theory. She concludes that there exists in the U.S.A. a "fractal federalism" constantly being adjusted by local, state, and federal levels of government. Those adjustments provide a sort of dynamic intergovernmental interaction that will operate in an emerging global marketplace concerned about global environmental problems.

Svetlana N. Kravchenko analyzes the international, regional, and local government structures to address the environment by the newly independent state of Ukraine. She rightly observes that Ukraine has unique environmental and governmental problems to address in the years ahead. Environmentally, it must address the consequences of the Chernobyl disaster and severe industrial pollution of the air and water. Internationally, the Ukrainian government must deal with its regional relationships on environmental matters with both European neighbors and the states of the former U.S.S.R. Domestically, Ukraine faces intragovernmental problems of national and local governments and unique problems of autonomy in the Crimea and elsewhere. Kravchenko's paper helpfully reviews the initial legislative attempts by Ukraine to address these problems and stresses the urgency to act effectively immediately, before many of the adverse effects of excessive resource and industrial exploitation produce irreversible effects.

Yuri Tunitsia argues passionately for special ecological constitutions for Ukraine and for the world community that would provide a classic command and control system of ecological banks, courts, and police. He sensibly observes that any such constitutional mechanisms must accommodate the special problems of privatization, economic conversion of defense industries to a new world order, and the imbedding of environmental costs in the price of goods and services.

James E. Hickey, Jr. examines the tensions that exist in the allocation of government authority over the electric industry in the U.S.A. The continuing conflict between the states and the federal government, Professor Hickey observes, has resulted in the demise of the U.S. nuclear power industry, expensive and excessive litigation over electric pricing authority of states and the federal government, and harm to international relations with the neighboring countries of Canada and Mexico as a result of domestic energy and environmental regulatory decisions. Professor Hickey implies that there may be elements of a command and control federal authority over electric production and use that the states of the former U.S.S.R. ought to preserve rather than jettison in the conversion to market economies.

Finally, Victoria Yegorova analyzes energy policy for an independent Ukraine with an emphasis on the revitalization of the coal industry, now that the Chernobyl disaster has made nuclear power less attractive as a viable political, environmental, or financial option. This revitalization, she argues, will assure Ukraine of needed energy independence for economic development, will reduce dependence on Russian natural gas, but will also increase the dangers of further exacerbating air pollution. Yegorova urges that such a revitalization will require coordinated government regulation and policy at local, regional (especially in the coal-rich Donbass region), and national levels to increase domestic energy production with the least possible environmental consequences.

25

Reform of Federalism and Ecological Security

Oleg S. Kolbasov

The process of political restructuring started in 1985 and developed under the slogan to destroy entirely the federal center of the Union of Soviet Socialist Republics, and, hailed by inhabitants, came to an end in 1991 by the complete destruction of the federal state. The Soviet Union disappeared. Instead of 15 former union republics, 15 independent states were formed. One federal center was replaced by 15 new centers.

Most of the former union republics became unitary states. The Russian Federation was retained as a federal state with the same federal principles as were applicable before. The federal structure of the state today includes the following units: 21 republics within the Russian Federation (RF), 1 autonomous region, 10 autonomous districts, 6 areas, 49 districts, some 2,000 regions, over 3,000 cities and other settlements, and 23,000 rural communes. Each level has its legislative and administrative authorities, whereas the federal power tends to be strengthened. At the federal level, more than 100 state entities are vested with important administrative powers. In addition to the president of the RF with its office, there is the Parliament (1,068 people's deputies) with its personnel, government comprising more than 30 ministries and departments, three federal courts (constitutional, general, and arbitration), and the procurator's office. Today, for large numbers of people (150 million inhabitants in the territory of 17 million square km), the federal structures in Moscow remain the same center as was the center of the former Soviet Union.

The same historic factors that contributed to the destruction of the Soviet Union are still acting in relation to the Russian Federation. Desperate efforts are now being taken to prevent the destruction of the Russian Federation. The so-called Federal Agreement was signed, as a matter of urgency, by representatives of the privileged and unequal member-units of the federation—by republics within the RF (except for the Republics of Tatary and Chechnia), an autonomous region, by autonomous districts, areas, regions, and by the cities of Moscow and St. Petersburg.

The Federal agreement leads the practice back to the model of the legislative structure of the former U.S.S.R. The Federal agreement divides competence between the federation and state bodies of the member-units of the federation. It establishes two categories of powers: (1) exclusive powers of the federal bodies of the RF, and (2) joint powers of the federal bodies and those of member-units of the federation. Regulation of nature use, environmental protection, and ecological security is covered by joint powers of the federation and member-units of the federation. Joint powers means that the federation adopts the framework legislation—fundamentals of legislation and member-units of the federation—laws, and other normative acts in accord with the federal fundamentals.

At the same time, tendencies that caused the destruction of the Soviet Union are still active: wars of sovereignties, of laws, of budgets, and an ever-increasing disruption of economic, scientific, cultural, and other social contacts and links. All this is developing in the background of high inflation, of dividing and plundering of the public wealth, of quick enrichment by a handful of so-called businessmen and sincere cheats, of an increase in crime, and of the fall of morals.

Under such conditions, the task to ensure ecological security is decided on a minimum level. The leaders of the State are taking intensive efforts in two directions in order not to lose control over the run of events in the field of environmental protection: (1) in a legislative sphere, and (2) in the sphere of creating administrative structures.

The most important event in the legislative sphere was the adoption of the RF Act on Protection of the Natural Environment (the Environment Act), which was enacted by the Parliament on December 19, 1992, and entered into force on March 3, 1992, on the day of its official publication in the newspaper *Russiyskaya Gazeta*.

The Environment Act reflects a comprehensive approach to regulating all types of environmental protection, including preventive control over industrial and other anthropogenic impacts on the natural environment, environmental impact assessment, use of economic regulatory instruments in the interests of environmental protection, regulation of individual behavior and organizations in emergency ecological situations, and protection of special natural areas and objects. A separate chapter of the act concerns the right of individuals to a healthy and favorable natural environment. Much attention is attached to ecological standard-setting and ecological requirements applicable to those spheres of human life where the strongest anthropogenic pressures on nature emerge. Certainly, provision is made for liability measures and compensation.

The Environment Act does not regulate use of natural resources. Specialized resource-oriented laws are adopted for this end. For example, on April 25,

1991, the Parliament approved the Land Code of the RF, which explicitly regulates land ownership and land use relations, registration, and protection of various categories of lands. On February 21, 1992, the RF Parliament passed the Act on Subsoil, which defines in detail the legal regime of mineral deposits, sets conditions and procedures to grant use to national and foreign companies, and establishes procedures to control activities. Fundamentals of Forest Legislation were adopted in March 1993. Drafts of similar acts applicable to water resources, wildlife, and specially protected areas and objects are now under preparation. In addition, numerous administrative acts, presidential decrees, governmental decrees, and various rules, regulations, and instructions are being issued.

The most important administrative event in this sphere was the creation in November 1991 of the Ministry of Ecology and Natural Resources of the Russian Federation, which replaced the former Ministry of Ecology and Nature Use of the Republic and absorbed the former U.S.S.R. Ministry of Nature Use and Environmental Protection.

The Ministry of Ecology and Natural Resources was the central federal entity responsible for state administration in the field of environmental protection and regulation of natural resource use. It conducted environmental impact assessments of projects, registered and assessed all types of natural resources, arranged for environmental scientific research, prepared and introduced into practice economic instruments that encourage prevention and control of harmful impacts on the natural environment, supervised compliance with environmental requirements, and handled violations.

In September 1992 the Ministry of Ecology and Natural Resources was reorganized into the Ministry of the Environment and Natural Resources. In the process, it lost its powers to control and regulate nature use. The state ecological administration was disintegrated.

At the federal level, in addition to the Ministry of the Environment and Natural Resources, there are a number of committees, including the following: Sanitary and Epidemiological Control; Land Resources; Subsoil; Fishing; Water Economy; Forest Economy; Control of Nuclear and Radiological Security; Civil Defense; Emergency Situations and Elimination of Consequences of Natural Disasters; and Social Security of Citizens and Rehabilitation of Areas Affected by Chernobyl and Other Radiological Accidents.

Curiously, these legal and administrative measures that were intended to regulate environmental protection and use of natural resources do not create sufficient guarantees for ecological security. A lot of external conditions exist that weaken the influence of environmental law from a general negative political, economic, and social atmosphere. One such condition is reflected in the practical loss by the center of its abilities to govern territories. For environmental protection, this loss of governance means that republic, district, regional and local committees for environmental protection and use of natural resources are financed and materially supported from the funds and reserves of the republics, districts, and regions, and are therefore dependent on republic and local governments. Many suppose that under such conditions the federal government becomes an excessive and unnecessary structure. This has certainly negatively influenced official discipline.

A contractual form of cooperation between the central and local environmental departments has turned out to be ineffective when federal budgeting is unavailable because implementation of contractual obligations need financial and material support, which is lacking.

An extra-high level of inflation that the contemporary generation of people face causes not only material difficulties but also social indifference, and demoralizes the population.

Inflation negatively and directly influences the administrative system. All the previously established funds for environmental protection measures have turned out to be insufficient. Recently, fixed permanent rates of payments for the use of natural resources and pollution of the environment became too low in the face of inflation, as the amounts of payments for ecological funding counted on the basis of such rates effectively declined. The system of penalties for environmental offenses provided for by the Criminal and Administrative Codes is practically paralyzed. The same is true for the system of compensation for destruction of the natural environment and illegal harm to natural objects, which is based on the previously developed methodological approaches for counting the volume of environmental damage.

Notably, the risk of industrial accidents has grown; as about 70% of the main productive sources became physically outdated and cannot be modernized in a short time (equipment, pipelines, regulating devices, transportation communications, energy supply systems, waste treatment constructions, devices for control, and technological defense). The risk of accidents also has grown due to weakening of production and discipline of workers and middle-level technical personnel at enterprises.

Intensified and uncontrolled market relations and new possibilities for uncontrolled export of products, materials, raw materials, and other wealth have caused an unprecedented rise in plundering of natural resources. It mainly concerns hydrocarbon energy minerals, ferrous and nonferrous metals, timber, fish resources of the economic zone of the RF, valuable plant life, and wildlife resources.

At the same time, under conditions of the so-called free market and the general aspiration to become rich, modern businessmen are reluctant to fulfill environmental protection obligations and to grant money for environmental protection aims. The programs of low-waste and wasteless technologies, construction of waste treatment facilities, rehabilitation of destroyed landscapes, and the like are not implemented. The state authorities are physically unable to control execution of environmental programs. They do not have sufficient punitive means and cannot change the run of events in a positive direction.

Under conditions of the present federal reform, the importance of cooperation in environmental protection with former union republics grows. Recognizing this fact and taking into consideration the natural geographic and socioeconomic links among the former republics, some of which (Azerbaijan, Armenia, Belarus, Kazakhstan, Kyrgyzstan, Moldova, Russian Federation, Tajikistan, Turkmenistan, and Uzbekistan) signed the Agreement on Cooperation in Ecology and Evnironmental Protection on February 8, 1992, in Moscow.

The parties to the agreement assumed mutual obligations to conduct a coordinated ecological policy and, to this end, to take joint actions for adopting legislation for developing and implementing practical programs for using coordinated methods when assessing impacts of economic activities on the environment for creating and supporting an interstate ecological database system and other procedures. To implement these obligations, the parties agreed to found an Interstate Ecological Council and an Interstate Ecological Fund under it.

It is clear that the reform of federal relations in the former U.S.S.R., together with varying adverse consequences, have resulted in the weakening of the ecological security of the country. And it is doubtful whether it is possible to resume the level of environmental protection that existed before perestroika (restructuring).

26

Fractal Federalism: Evolving National-State Relations in U.S. Environmental Law

Lee P. Breckenridge

The national environmental legislation of the 1970s in the United States brought sweeping changes to governmental mechanisms for addressing environmental problems. Under laws enacted through the mid-1960s, states largely retained independent authority to regulate pollution and to address other environmental matters within their borders as they saw fit, while the national government played a secondary, though growing, role.[1] By 1970, however, attention had shifted to the national government for solutions to many of the pressing environmental problems facing the country.

The inadequacies of state law in coping with the widening environmental impacts of an increasingly industrialized and environmentally destructive economy had become apparent. State agencies lacked adequate funding, expertise, and legal powers. Transboundary water and air pollution conspicuously eluded the control of state authorities. Competition among states for private investments also appeared to undermine the resolve of state authorities to take action on environmental issues (U.S. Senate 1982, 38–43; Butler 1982).

The Clean Air Act Amendments of 1970,[2] the Federal Water Pollution Control Act Amendments of 1972,[3] the Resource Conservation and Recovery Act of 1976,[4] and the Comprehensive Environmental Response, Compensation and Liability Act of 1980,[5] with a host of other national environmental statutes,[6] marked a decade of strong centralization of authority. The specific arrangements between federal and state governments varied among the different statutes, from preemption of state authority to joint administration of programs. Most of the new laws did not wholly override state laws, but drew state environmental protection programs into the service of centrally articulated national goals.

This paper first highlights some key legal requirements of national environmental programs that induced state legislatures and administrative agencies to fall in step with new central-government mandates, and to promulgate and revise state requirements to imitate national laws and regulations. The paper goes on to show, however, that while hierarchical federal-state relationships characterized the development phases of these national programs, the new laws also planted the seeds of more complex interactions among state and federal governments. Some important statutory provisions have not only allowed state leadership and innovation, but have strengthened state authority and expanded the effect of state requirements through incorporation into national law.

The final section of the paper draws an analogy between the complex mechanisms of national-state relations and the turbulent patterns found in nature that are described in modern chaos theory in the language of "fractal" geometry. The paper suggests that nonlinear and evolving interactions are an important feature of U.S. environmental law, and that further elaboration of feedback mechanisms in legal arrangements among different scales of government is needed in order to address unresolved environmental problems, such as global warming and nonpoint source pollution. While near-parallel, mutually adjusting regulation by multiple levels of government may seem chaotic at times, a pattern of dynamic interaction through defined procedures may provide the most workable approach to interconnected local, regional, national, and international environmental phenomena.

HIERARCHICAL BEGINNINGS OF THE NATIONAL ENVIRONMENTAL PROGRAMS OF THE 1970s

The effect of many of the new environmental protection statutes of the 1970s was to push the creation of similar smaller-scale state programs, molded on a federal template and responsive to federal directives. The air pollution, water pollution, and hazardous waste management programs illustrate how federal law shaped state law to meet national objectives.[7]

The Clean Air Act, Clean Water Act, and Resource Conservation and Recovery Act (RCRA) all purport to recognize state autonomy by allowing states to choose whether to administer designated portions of a national regulatory program. A state may agree to implement a program meeting federal specifications, and receive federal funding in return. Or it may refuse to act in accordance with federal requirements, leaving the United States Environmental Protection Agency (EPA) to administer the program directly.

Although these laws grant the states an apparent choice, the arrangements do not in fact leave the states much discretion. As one writer has noted:

> Indeed, one might argue that the opportunity afforded the states to operate some of these programs is more of an effort to conscript them into federal service than it is an

acknowledgement of their autonomy. . . . The tendency of these developments is to turn the states into regional offices of the federal government (Pedersen 1982, 3, 6).

For example, under the Clean Water Act a state may administer the federal water pollution permit program through state law, if its laws and regulations meet federal approval. To obtain this approval, state requirements must ensure compliance with EPA's nationally uniform technology-based effluent limitations, and the state's enforcement authority and public participation procedures must also meet federal specifications.[8] Even after the EPA issues program approval, administrative activities remain subject to federal oversight. The state must transmit copies of permit applications and proposed agency decisions to the EPA for review.[9] The EPA may deny or withdraw program approval if the state program proves inadequate,[10] and may administer the program directly.[11] While a state may develop its own water quality goals for different waterways, even these are subject to EPA review.[12]

The Clean Air Act is likewise structured to induce state adherence to a federal model. State Implementation Plans (SIPs) for achieving federally established National Ambient Air Quality Standards (NAAQS) must meet numerous requirements governing procedures and standard-setting, in order to gain EPA approval.[13] State administration of an approved air pollution program is subject to ongoing EPA supervision and authority to call for plan revisions.[14] For states without federally approved programs, the EPA administrator must issue and administer federal regulations in the form of a Federal Implementation Plan.[15] The amendments to the Clean Air Act in 1990 have imposed additional requirements governing federal approval and oversight of state permitting programs.[16]

RCRA similarly establishes a national hazardous waste management program that is delegated to the states through EPA authorization.[17] To gain approval, a state program must be "equivalent to," and "consistent with," the EPA-administered program, and it must provide for "adequate" enforcement.[18] The states' duplication of a federal model is nowhere more apparent than in the RCRA program. EPA regulations and policies governing authorization and review of state activities under this law have been particularly detailed and inflexible. The line-by-line review of state laws and regulations by EPA, despite state agency protests against federal heavy-handedness, has typically resulted in the verbatim iteration of federal standards in state regulations (Paddock 1990, 20–22; Keystone Center 1989, 6–8; Isaac 1989, 50–58).

The extent of the federal direction and oversight of state programs can be discerned not only in the language, but also in the structure of state programs. Many state agencies now replicate the structure of the U.S. EPA, dividing responsibilities among administrative offices according to the lines of the federal laws and the federal bureaucracy (Rabe 1986, 23–24, 30–32).

State compliance with federal directives has been driven not simply by the prospect of direct EPA intervention in state affairs, but also by the availability of federal funding to implement the national mandate. States have relied heavily upon federal funds to carry out their responsibilities in implementing federal programs. As one state official observed in 1982,

> the federal dollar has become an absolutely essential ingredient in the development of state environmental protection. . . . In effect, the growth in size and associated responsibility of these programs during the past "decade of the environment" [the 1970s] has been almost entirely supported by the infusion of new federal dollars (Eichbaum 1982, 27).[19]

The percentage of state environmental budgets attributable to federal funding declined through the 1980s, but the federal contribution has remained significant (NGA 1989, 1–3; Paddock 1990, 36).

Not all of the national laws contain such inflexible state authorization requirements as the Clean Air Act, the Clean Water Act, and RCRA. The Comprehensive Environmental Response, Compensation and Liability Act (CERCLA), for instance, does not require federal authorization of state programs, but the funding procedures in this statute have nonetheless encouraged states to mimic the federal program in their own laws. Federal funds are not available to accomplish remedial action at hazardous waste sites unless the state pays part of the costs and agrees to cover subsequent operation and maintenance activities.[20] CERCLA also allows the EPA to contract with state agencies to accomplish cleanup actions in accordance with federal requirements.[21]

One effect of CERCLA, therefore, has been to encourage states to adopt parallel "superfund" laws for the sake of participating in the federal cleanup program. While there is considerable variation in the structure and details of state programs, an EPA-sponsored study in 1990 found that many states had enacted laws "in the image of CERCLA" with parallel provisions for enforcement authority, site priority listing, and remedy selection. All but one state had established a cleanup fund, and the majority reported that they used EPA guidelines in setting cleanup standards (U.S. EPA 1990b, 6, 32).

In sum, as the national environmental programs were implemented during the 1970s and early 1980s, the most apparent pattern in federal-state relations was the federal government's dominant, supervisory role and the states' conformity to the federal lead.[22] The federal government established environmental goals, issued standards, granted funding, and audited compliance with federal mandates, while the states set about the tasks of implementation, through programs structured to meet federal approval.

STATE INITIATIVES, REGIONAL COALITIONS, AND FEDERAL RESPONSES

To view the states as mere agents of the federal government, however, would underestimate the states' capacities for leadership, and would overlook those aspects of national environmental legislation that have, over time, strengthened state agencies and boosted the effectiveness of state law. The replication, at the state level, of central environmental agencies like the EPA, and of federal-style laws and regulations, was only the first step in a longer, interactive process, not a one-time shift to a static federal-state hierarchy. What emerged from the initial phases of the federal programs were stronger, more powerful, and more expert state environmental programs, capable of considerable influence and innovation. These state programs, in turn, have challenged and influenced the national agenda.

While Congress, acting under the commerce clause of the United States Constitution, has sweeping powers to preempt state action and to intrude on traditional areas of state environmental control,[23] most national environmental legislation has left room for state initiatives going beyond mere implementation of federal directives (Strohbehn 1982, 10–11). The Clean Water Act and RCRA both explicitly provide that states may impose their own, more stringent requirements, although states may not adopt or enforce standards that are less strict than those established nationally.[24] Similarly, the Clean Air Act generally allows more stringent state regulation, although state controls over fuels and motor vehicle emissions are limited.[25] CERCLA, meanwhile, provides simply that the federal law shall not "be construed or interpreted as preempting any State from imposing any additional liability or requirements with respect to the release of hazardous substances."[26]

Through these policies that avoid preemption of state law, national environmental legislation has allowed the expansion of state authority in ways that have produced a growing complexity of interactions among the federal and state governments. While not all states have stepped far beyond the roles assigned under the federal programs, some states have shown ever-increasing leadership in environmental matters. As a report by the National Association of Attorneys General asserted in 1989, "there has been a quiet revolution in which, with little fanfare, the states have reemerged as major players" (NAAG 1989, 1). Going well beyond existing federal legislation, states have launched a diverse array of environmental initiatives in areas such as pollution prevention and integrated environmental management, sometimes departing in important and innovative ways from the structure of federal programs (NAAG 1989; Rabe 1986, 51–65; U.S. EPA 1990a, 67–72, 111–17, 130–39, 254–62, 535–44, 594–603, 713–19)

The proliferation of state environmental initiatives over the past ten years has justified the well-known characterization of the states as the laboratories of a federal system.[27] As they have undertaken an ever-broadening range of new projects, and have argued for a less hierarchical relationship with the federal government, state officials themselves have frequently noted the states' expertise and leadership, their ability to be imaginative and innovative in the development of environmental programs, their responsiveness to local conditions and concerns, and their ability to move quickly from concept to implementation (Eichbaum 1982, 25–28; Cole 1987, 8, 14–15). The National Association of Attorneys General, urging changes in federal-state relationships in a 1989 report, characterized the states' role in environmental protection this way:

> States can often move more quickly, more boldly, and more imaginatively than can the federal government. As the testing laboratories of democracy, they offer our best hope for solutions to the unprecedented environmental problems that states are facing on a daily basis. Perhaps most important, states are much more accountable and responsive to the public than are the federal agencies in Washington, DC (NAAG 1989, 2).

Increasingly sophisticated coordination and clearinghouse activities of state-sponsored organizations—such as the Council of State Governments (COSG), the National Association of Attorneys General (NAAG), the National Governors' Association (NGA), the associations of state air pollution, water pollution and waste management officials,[28] the four regional environmental enforcement projects,[29] the Coastal States Organization (CSO), and the Northeast States for Coordinated Air Use Management (NESCAUM)—have enhanced the dissemination of ideas among states. Conferences, newsletters, reports and joint projects have fostered the formation of coalitions, the coordination of enforcement efforts, and the replication of legislative and regulatory models. Such joint initiatives have in turn influenced national environmental decision making.[30]

The northeastern states' efforts to control transboundary air pollution provide one prominent example of state leadership that has shaped environmental law and administrative policy on a national scale, despite provisions in the federal Clean Air Act limiting the states' authority over fuels and automobiles. The history of those efforts illustrates the increasingly interactive nature of the sometimes collaborative, sometimes confrontational, federal-state relationship in the environmental arena.

The Northeastern states gained an early sense of shared purpose through joint efforts to obtain more stringent limits on the sulfur oxide pollution emitted by coal-fired plants in the Midwest.[31] The states' long advocacy of strict national measures to control "acid rain" brought tangible results only in 1990, when Congress amended the Clean Air Act to impose extensive new national controls on sulfur oxide emissions from coal-fired plants.[32] Meanwhile, however, the states built on their successes in organizing regional action by tackling another pressing air pollution problem, ground-level ozone, the primary component of photochemical smog.[33]

Eight Northeastern states[34] joined to form the Northeast States for Coordinated Air Use Management in order to develop regional plans for addressing shared air pollution problems. Relying on NESCAUM's data analysis and preparation of model legislation and regulations, officials of the NESCAUM states in 1987 agreed to control ozone formation by limiting the evaporative characteristics of gasoline sold in the summertime. Citing the EPA's long-standing failure to develop nationwide controls on gasoline volatility, the states agreed to work toward a regional solution through parallel regulations promulgated separately in each NESCAUM state.[35]

Despite strong opposition from the oil industry[36] and initial resistance to the states' proposals by EPA,[37] the regulations eventually took effect under federal law with EPA approval, replacing less stringent requirements that EPA had promulgated in the interim.[38] The limitations imposed in the northeastern states' pilot regulations subsequently gained federal statutory effect through the Clean Air Act amendments in 1990, which adopted the more stringent standards as a requirement applicable to all areas in the country other than those that have officially "attained" the national ozone standards.[39]

More recently, Northeastern states joined with Mid-Atlantic states and the District of Columbia, pledging to seek state-by-state adoption of California's pollution requirements for new automobiles.[40] The innovative California Low Emissions Vehicle Program is more stringent than the Federal Tier I Motor Vehicle Control Program, which EPA administers under the Clean Air Act.[41] While federal law generally precludes state control of emissions from new automobiles, it has preserved the ability of states in "nonattainment" areas to adopt California's requirements, instead of those developed by the federal government.[42] If the Eastern states go forward as planned, a large fraction of the U.S. population will live in areas governed by emissions rules developed in California, not in Washington, DC.

These examples from the air pollution field illustrate the increasingly strong state leadership in the formulation of new requirements, and, in a reversal of roles, the manner in which the states have paved the way for new national policies, rather than merely following a federal lead. The expansion of the states' role is not simply a matter of newfound state initiative, however. Federal law itself boosts state authority in important ways.

THE EXTENSION AND MAGNIFICATION OF STATE ENVIRONMENTAL AUTHORITY THROUGH INCORPORATION INTO FEDERAL LAW

Some national laws have gone beyond avoiding preemption of state law, and have given states authority that they would not have had without congressional action. National environmental laws have extended the reach of state powers by incorporating state standards into federal law in three main ways: by treating state standards as federal requirements; by subjecting federal facilities and federal activities to state regulation and enforcement; and by establishing protocols that give state standards transboundary authority through operation of federal law. These procedures collectively magnify the effect of state requirements, including those that are more stringent than federal law would otherwise impose.

The Clean Water Act provides particularly clear-cut examples of all these mechanisms. The statute requires water pollution discharges to meet not only the federal requirements that EPA develops, but more stringent requirements developed under state law, as well.[43] This means that the EPA must include state law requirements in federal water pollution control permits.[44] By a process of statutory and administrative transformation, the state standards become federal standards, enforceable in federal courts by EPA or by anyone else who has standing to sue under the federal citizens' suit provision.[45] Somewhat similar provisions of the Clean Air Act establish the federal enforceability of any state air pollution requirements that are part of an EPA-approved State Implementation Plan.[46]

Other provisions of the Clean Water Act waive the sovereign immunity of the United States, stating that federal facilities and federal activities must comply not only with federal law, but also with state and local water pollution control requirements.[47] The Clean Air Act, RCRA, and CERCLA likewise give states authority over federal installations and federal activities through waivers of sovereign immunity.[48] The effect of these provisions is to subject a wide range of federal actions to direct state control.

State "certification" provisions further expand the scope of state authority over activities licensed by the federal government. The Clean Water Act states that no federal agency may issue a permit (under the Clean Water Act or any other act) if the state where a proposed activity will occur denies a certification that the activity will meet state water pollution requirements.[49] Analogously, CERCLA and the Coastal Zone Management Act both require modification of federal activities to meet state standards, through state review and notification procedures that are somewhat similar to the Clean Water Act certification process.[50]

Transboundary pollution provisions also extend the powers of states to address pollution originating outside their borders. Such provisions have been a special source of controversy, as state and federal government agencies have disagreed about the interpretation of pertinent statutory language. The Clean Water Act provisions, for example, were the subject of lengthy litigation among Arkansas, Oklahoma, and the EPA, in a case involving transboundary pollution from a sewage treatment plant in Arkansas. EPA has construed the statute to require the EPA administrator, upon notice from a downstream state, to impose permit conditions on upstream dischargers to ensure compliance with downstream water quality requirements.[51] In an opinion that relied heavily on judicial deference to federal agency discretion, the U.S. Supreme Court ruled that the EPA acted within its authority under the Clean Water Act in construing and applying Oklahoma's standards to an Arkansas discharge.[52]

The state voice protecting local environmental interests from transboundary impacts has gained influence through recent congressional action altering national administrative processes. Both the Clean Air Act and the Coastal Zone Management Act were amended in 1990, following years of state litigation against the federal government for failure to translate state environmental requirements into national requirements under existing law.[53] The amended transboundary requirements in both acts now define states' authority more clearly, and afford broader protection from environmental impacts originating outside a state's borders.[54]

All of these legal mechanisms undermine the image of federal-state hierarchy. By subjecting federal activities to state oversight, and federal standards to state reformulation, national environmental laws in important respects have served rather than dictated state environmental agendas.

THE "FRACTAL" CHARACTERISTICS OF INTERGOVERNMENTAL RELATIONSHIPS UNDER U.S. ENVIRONMENTAL LAW

Although federal-state relations under U.S. environmental laws have many lingering hierarchical aspects, the increasingly dynamic—some might say chaotic—character of federal-state relationships under these laws is striking. Federal measures have spawned state programs mirroring a federal profile, but states in turn have developed and expanded their programs, eventually shaping the federal agenda according to the states' own models. National laws and regulations have been in part responsible for their own alteration, since they have encouraged state initiatives in various ways, and have drawn the results of state innovation back into the processes of federal standard-setting. Divergences at different scales of government have persisted through long periods of confrontation and litigation, but statutory and administrative approaches have also emerged for integrating views at different levels of government into unified outcomes.

Certainly, the complexities of such interactions cannot be adequately captured in any hierarchical framework or linear diagram. To describe current trends demands an emphasis on the sometimes turbulent processes of decision making, on the creative tension of similar but differing views, and on the feedback of ideas and information from one scale of government to another, rather than on the identification of any fixed structure or set of standards.

A useful analogy may be found in the dynamic patterns of turbulent natural phenomena—patterns that are now described in contemporary chaos theory through the language of "fractal" geometry (Jurgens, Peitgen & Saupe 1990, 60). The following aspects of fractals seem particularly apt in the present context: self-similarity at different scales, magnification of small effects through repeated iteration (or feedback loops), and interrelatedness of events at all scales (Briggs and Peat 1989, 93–112; Gleick 1987). The U.S. environmental laws discussed above manifest analogous characteristics. They provide for replication of legislative and regulatory models at different scales, feedback of ideas and information among various governmental entities, and continuing mutual adjustment of goals and standards developed by different levels of government.

The legal mechanisms that accomplish these interactions under existing environmental law warrant special attention as the United States moves to address particularly difficult, unsolved environmental issues. The most problematic environmental questions facing the country are national and even international in scope, but originate in highly specific and diverse local conditions. Carbon dioxide emissions cause worldwide climate change, but emanate from practices that vary widely from one human community and geographical setting to another. Maintaining species diversity is a matter of international concern, but depends on protecting an endless variety of microenvironments. Pollution of oceans affects fisheries resources of international importance, yet the control of contaminated runoff can be achieved only through site-specific modification of land-use practices.

The task of addressing these complex environmental problems cannot be accomplished through any single, fixed set of central-government requirements. The challenge is to integrate governmental actions occurring on different political scales, in order to address interrelated local, regional, and global environmental phenomena. The difficulties of doing so are compounded by a lack of scientific information sufficient to trace all of the relevant environmental interconnections.

Jessica Tuchman Mathews (1989, 176), speaking of the need for a new model of international lawmaking to address environmental problems, has written: "The present model is static: years of negotiation leading to a final product. The new model will have to be fluid, allowing a rolling process of intermediate or self-adjusting agreements that respond quickly to growing scientific understanding."

Similar comments might be addressed to the interactions among national, state, and local governments. Legal mechanisms are needed for readily integrating environmental information, policies, and standards from one scale of government into the requirements of the others. The mechanisms currently found in U.S. environmental law for incorporating changing provisions of federal and state programs, each into the other, offer some useful paradigms.

NOTES

1. Congress enacted a series of national laws in the 1950s and 1960s to address aid and water pollution issues, but these laws emphasized technical assistance to states and municipalities, and their effect was limited. The shift in the federal approach, from the 1950s to the 1970s, is discussed in Paddock 1990, 7–12; U.S. Senate 1982, 7–30.

2. Pub. L. No. 91-604, 84 Stat. 1676 (codified as amended at 42 U.S.C. §§ 7401–7671q [1988 & Supp. III 1991]).

3. Pub. L. No. 92-500, 86 Stat. 816 (codified as amended, Clean Water Act, 33 U.S.C. §§ 1251 to 1387 [1988 & Supp. III 1991]).

4. Pub. L. No. 94-580, 90 Stat. 2795 (codified as amended at 42 U.S.C. §§ 6901–6992k [1988]).

5. Pub. L. No. 96-510, 94 Stat. 2767 (codified as amended at 42 U.S.C. §§ 9601–9675 [1988]).

6. The decade also saw enactment of many other national environmental statutes, in addition to these four legislative pillars of the national pollution control effort. The new laws of the 1970s included the Federal Insecticide, Fungicide, and Rodenticice Act, Pub. L. No. 92-516, 86 Stat. 973 (codified as amended at 7 U.S.C. §§ 136–136y [1988 & Supp. III 1991]); the Toxic Substances Control Act, Pub. L. 94-469, 90 Stat. 2051 (codified as amended at 15 U.S.C. §§ 2601 to 2671 [1988 & Supp. III 1991]); the Coastal Zone Management Act of 1972, Pub. L. 92-583, 86 Stat. 1280 (codified as amended at 16 U.S.C. §§ 1451 to 1464 [1988 & Supp. III 1991]); the Endangered Species Act of 1973, Pub. L. 93-205, 87 Stat. 884 (codified as amended at 16 U.S.C. §§ 1531 to 1544 [1988]); the Surface Mining Control and Reclamation Act of 1977, Pub. L. 95-87, 91 Stat. 447 (codified as amended at 30 U.S.C. §§ 1201 to 1211, 1231 to 1328 [1988 & Supp. III 1991]); the Marine Protection, Research, and Sanctuaries Act of 1972, Pub. L. 92-532, 86 Stat. 1052 (codified as amended at 33 U.S.C. §§ 1401 to 1445 [1988 & Supp. III 1991]); and the Safe Drinking Water Act of 1974, Pub. L. No. 93-523, 88 Stat. 1660 (codified as amended at 42 U.S.C. §§ 300f to 300j [1988]).

7. For a comprehensive legal analysis of the justifications and strategies for the federal government's conscription of state resources in the service of national environmental programs, and of the potential constitutional impediments to such centralization, see Stewart 1977.

8. 33 U.S.C. § 1342 (b).

9. 33 U.S.C. § 1342 (d).

10. 33 U.S.C. § 1342 (c) (3).

11. 33 U.S.C. § 1342 (a).

12. 33 U.S.C. § 1313; *Mississippi Commission on Natural Resources v. Costle*, 625 F. 2d 1269 (5th Cir. 1980) (upholding EPA's refusal to approve the Mississippi water quality standard for dissolved oxygen, and its promulgation of a substitute federal standard).

13. 42 U.S.C. § 7410.

14. 42 U.S.C. § 7410 (k) (5).

15. 42 U.S.C. § 7410 (c).

16. 42 U.S.C. §§ 7661–7661f.

17. For a more detailed legal analysis of issues in federal-state relations during the initial phases of the RCRA program, see Florini 1982.

18. 42 U.S.C. 6926 (b).

19. The report of a survey on sources of funds for state environmental programs, conducted jointly by the National Governors' Association Committee on Energy and Environment, the State and Territorial Air Pollution Program Administrators, the Association of State and Interstate Water Pollution Control Administrators, and the Association of State and Territorial Solid Waste Management Officials, shows the state dependence on federal funding as of 1982 (Curtis and Creedon 1982).

20. 42 U.S.C. § 9604 (c) (3).

21. 42 U.S.C. § 9604 (d).

22. Writing in 1982, one commentator characterized federal-state relations this way:

> Although today states carry the great day-to-day burden of . . . [government activity to protect the environment], a perception evolved early in the 1970s that the routine would be done by states only after forceful prodding from the federal government and that otherwise little progress could be anticipated as a result of state action. . . . States are perceived as having reluctantly assumed their responsibilities in response to the carrot and stick of the federal government (Eichbaum 1982, 26).

23. *E.g., International Paper Co. v. Ouellette*, 479 U.S. 481 (1987) (addressing extent of preemption under the Clean Water Act); *Hodel v. Virginia Surface Mining and Reclamation Association*, 452 U.S. 264 (1981) and *Hodel v. Indiana*, 452 U.S. 314 (1981) (upholding the constitutionality of the Surface Mining Control and Reclamation Act of 1977).

24. 33 U.S.C. § 1370; 42 U.S.C. § 6929.

25. 42 U.S.C. § 7416. See also *Union Electric Co. v. EPA*, 427 U.S. 246 (1976) (concluding that EPA does not have statutory authority to reject a State Implementation Plan that surpasses minimum federal requirements).

26. 42 U.S.C. § 9614. While the avoidance of sweeping preemption characterizes most environmental legislation, some provisions do preclude the exercise of state authority. For example, the Toxic Substances Control Act, 15 U.S.C. § 2617 (a) (2), prohibits parallel state regulation of toxic chemicals.

27. *New York State Ice Co. v. Liebmann*, 285 U.S. 262, 311 (1932) Brandeis, J., dissenting) ("It is one of the happy incidents of the federal system that a single courageous State may, if its citizens choose, serve as a laboratory; and try novel social and economic experiments without risk to the rest of the country").

28. State and Territorial Air Pollution Program Administrators (STAPPA), Association of State and Territorial Solid Waste Management Officials (ASTSWMO), and Association of State and Interstate Water Pollution Control Administrators (ASIWPCA).

29. Northeast Hazardous Waste Project, Western States Hazardous Waste Project, Midwest Environmental Enforcement Association, and Southern Environmental Enforcement Network (SEEN).

30. Linda Tarr-Whelan, of the National Center for Policy Alternatives, has termed the momentum developed through state leadership and coalition-building "progressive federalism."

> Our states are initiating national domestic policy by creating and then duplicating solutions for pressing problems. Pressure is meanwhile building for a national floor. When a critical mass is achieved, state action pushes the federal debate. The legislation that results gives states grat flexibility and requires implementation by them, not federal agencies. That flexibility starts the next cycle" (Tarr-Whelan 1988, 3).

31. Through the 1980s the Northeastern states, sometimes joined by the Canadian Province of Ontario, pursued lawsuits against the federal government, seeking implementation of the Clean Air Act to control the interstate and international air pollution resulting in acid rain. For example, *Connecticut v. EPA*, 656 F.2d 902 (2d Cir. 1981); *State of New York v. Administrator, United States EPA*, 710 F.2d 1200 (6th Cir. 1983); *New York v. EPA*. 716 F. 2d 440 (7th Cir. 1983); *State of New York v. United States EPA*, 852 F.2d 574 (D.C. Cir. 1988); *Environmental Defense Fund v. EPA*, 870 F.2d 892 (2d Cir. 1989); *Her Majesty the Queen in Right of Ontario v. United States EPA*, 912 F.2d 1525 (D.C. Cir. 1990). The coalition of states carried their interests to Congress, as the court actions failed to produce administrative changes under existing law.

32. 42 U.S.C. §§ 7651–7651o.

33. Ground-level ozone results from the reaction of volatile organic compounds, nitrogen oxides, and other chemicals in the presence of high temperatures and sunlight. It is a regional problem on the East Coast of the United States because prevailing winds transport the mixed pollution from vehicles and industries long distances, across state borders, from southwest to northeast.

34. New York, New Jersey, New Hampshire, Maine, Rhode Island, Connecticut, Vermont, and Massachusetts.

35. "Northeast Group Backs Volatility Rules; Would Affect Gasoline Sold in Warm Months," 17 *Environment Reporter* 1827 (1987); "Improved EPA Vehicle Test Procedures Would Help Curb Ozone Pollution, Group Says," 19 *Environment Reporter* 693 (1988); "New Jersey Nears Final Action on Rule to Require Reduced Gasoline Volatility," 19 *Environment Reporter* 1226 (1988).

36. *American Petroleum Institute v. Jorling*, 710 F. Supp. 421 (N.D.N.Y. 1989) (contesting New York's regulations); "States' Rules on Gasoline are Resisted," *The New York Times*, March 6, 1989, D1.

37. When the EPA failed to act on the states' proposed amendments to their State Implementation Plans, delaying the effect of the state regulations under federal law, the Commonwealth of Massachusetts sued the EPA, seeking a court order requiring EPA to act. *Massachusetts v. Reilly*, Civil Action No. 89-0403-WD (D. Mass.). The EPA subsequently announced its approvals of the states' SIP amendments, before the case was heard. See also, "How the Northeast Asserted Itself on Smog," *The New York Times*, June 11, 1989, 5.

38. The states' regulations established limits of 9.0 psi (pounds per square inch) Reid Vapor Pressure (RVP) (a measure of the volatility of the gasoline). The EPA issued national regulations imposing a less stringent requirement 10.5 psi, RVP, for the northeastern states. (54 Fed. Reg. 11,868 [1989]). The effect of this federal action was to preempt the stricter state standards in the absence of EPA approval of the states' regulations. See 42 U.S.C. 7545 (c)(4). EPA subsequently granted its approval (54 Fed. Reg. 19, 173, 23, 650, 25, 572, 26, 030 [1989]).

39. 42 U.S.C. § 7545 (h).

40. "9 States in East Plan to Restrict Pollution by Cars," *The New York Times*, October 30, 1991, A1. The endeavor is further described in Massachusetts Department of Environmental Protection, Bureau of Waste Prevention, Division of Air Quality Control, *Background Document for Proposed Amendments to 310 CMR 7.00 et seq.* (September 1991). The NESCAUM states had already taken steps toward adopting

California standards, under a memorandum of understanding signed in 1989. See "Northeast States Move to Restrict Pollution by Cars," *The New York Times*, August 11, 1989, A1; "Report Says Northeast States Could Benefit from Adoption of California Tailpipe Program," 20 *Environment Reporter* 153 (1989); "Northeast Officials Evaluating Adoption of California Vehicle Emission Standards," 19 *Environment Reporter* 1905 (1989).

41. 42 U.S.C. § 7521(g).

42. 42 U.S.C. § 7507.

43. 33 U.S.C. § 1311(b)(1)(C).

44. 33 U.S.C. § 1342(a).

45. 33 U.S.C. § 1319 (EPA authority); 33 U.S.C. § 1365(a) (citizen suit provisions).

46. 42 U.S.C. §§ 7413(a), 7604(a).

47. 33 U.S.C. § 1323.

48. 42 U.S.C. § 7418; 42 U.S.C. § 6961 (1988); 42 U.S.C. §9620(a)(1).

49. 33 U.S.C. § 1341(a), (d). EPA itself has urged states to take stronger control of wetlands protection, and of U.S. Army Corps of Engineers permitting decisions in particular, through state water quality certifications (U.S. EPA 1989). For a particularly intriguing example of the effect of a state's denial of certification on applicable federal law, see *United States v. Marathon Development Corp.*, 867 F.2d 96 (1st Cir. 1989). The court held that a defendant in a criminal prosecution for wetlands filling could not claim that his activities had been authorized under a "nationwide permit" issued by the U.S. Army Corps of Engineers, because the Commonwealth of Massachusetts had prevented the permit from taking effect in the state through refusal to grant a water quality certification.

50. CERCLA provides that federal remedial measures at hazardous waste sites must comply with "applicable or relevant and appropriate requirements" that the state identifies under state law. 42 U.S.C. § 9621(d)(2). The Coastal Zone Management Act requires federal agency activities "affecting" a state's coastal zone to be "consistent with" state coastal zone management requirements that are part of a federally approved coastal zone management plan; offshore oil drilling leases, in particular, are subject to a special procedure for obtaining state concurrence with the determination of "consistency." 16 U.S.C. § 1456(c).

51. 33 U.S.C. § 1341(a); 40 C.F.R. § 122.4(d) (1991). These provisions pertain to federally issued permits, not to state permits issued under a delegated program.

52. *Arkansas v. Oklahoma*, 112 S.Ct. 1046 (1992). Oklahoma agreed with the EPA's general approach, but disagreed with EPA's conclusions about the permit terms required by the Oklahoma standards. Arkansas, meanwhile, protested the incorporation of Oklahoma standards in the permit. In reviewing EPA's action, the U.S. Supreme Court sidestepped the question of whether the statute required EPA to adopt interpretation that it chose, but upheld the agency's interpretation of the law and its issuance of the permit as reasonable in the face of both states' objections.

53. See note 31 above, and *Secretary of the Interior v. California*, 464 U.S. 412 (1984).

54. The 1990 Clean Air Act amendments broadened the states' ability to obtain stricter control in upwind states' State Implementaton Plans. See 42 U.S.C. § 7410(a)(2)(D) (establishing SIP requirements); 42 U.S.C. § 7426 (requirements for stationary sources with transboundary impacts); 42 U.S.C. §§ 7506a and 7511c (authorizing creation of interstate transport commissions). The Coastal Zone Manage-

ment Act also in essence gave enhanced authority to state coastal zone management requirements, by including within their purview any federal activities "affecting" the coastal zone that take place outside state boundaries. 16 U.S.C. § 1456(c).

27

Federalism and Problems of Environmental Protection in Sovereign Ukraine

Svetlana N. Kravchenko

A starting point for discussion of environmental protection in Ukraine is federalism. The term "federalism" is used sufficiently often in science and implies not only the theory of federative states but different forms of functions between states and regional unions deprived of the state nature. Federalism is the principle of connection between the whole and the parts in the territorial and political organization of the state and the idea of compromise among all state and local interests.

The federal system of the U.S.A., established by the Constitution of 1787, is appraised by American and European researchers as a perfect theoretical model of a federative state. But literal transference of this model to Europe, including Ukraine, is possible only by taking into account historical, economic, social, and cultural features of development of European countries and Ukraine.

One of the American state system's godfathers, Thomas Jefferson, wrote: "My general idea comes to the foundation here of a single nation in the sphere of international politics and of separate nations in the sphere of all purely home affairs." He supposed that national problems can be adequately solved in terms of stimulation of development of self-governmental principles.

The evolution of the American federal system led to the increase of the role of harmonious cooperation between federal and local bodies (the concept of "creative federalism" by President Lyndon Johnson, President Richard Nixon's "new federalism," and President Jimmy Carter's "new partnership").

As you know, the Soviet Union as a federative state ceased to exist as a result of deep internal socioeconomic and political changes and the development of national consciousness in the former republics that were, in truth, conventional administrative localities of the former U.S.S.R.

On August 24, 1991, Ukraine proclaimed the Act of Independence and became a sovereign state. This process was completed by a national referendum, by the election of the first Ukrainian president, and by the recognition of Ukraine by more than 100 countries as a sovereign state and a participant of international relations.

In accordance with the Declaration of State Sovereignty of Ukraine adopted by the Supreme Soviet on June 16, 1990, Ukraine determines on its territory the order of nature protection and natural resources use, the norms of ecological safety, limits and payments for natural resources use, and sanctions for environmental damage, and establishes the state and local bodies of management in the sphere of environmental protection.

The draft Constitution of Ukraine provides a unitary state in which all legislative power will be vested in a two-chamber Parliament consisting of the People's Council and the Council of Regional Representatives. The problem of regional self-government, of local autonomy, and of the foundation of new regional bodies is still being discussed. It is possible that in Ukraine there will be eight to ten territorial autonomies that are based on economic and ethnic unity.

Crimea is an autonomous component part of Ukraine, which became an autonomous republic after the referendum at which 93 percent of its population voted for the renewal of an autonomy within Ukraine.

In time the problem of a federative system in Ukraine may arise. However, it probably will be only in the context of the state sovereignty of the whole Ukraine and not of separate regions, lands, or other localities. These territorial units will be provided with the status of autonomy in the sphere of legislative, executive and legal powers. The present task is to establish an indivisible Ukraine as a sovereign state, with developed self-governmental bodies at the regional level.

The power allocation among central, regional, and local government is a very important and practical problem in the sphere of environmental protection and natural resources use. For example, the Lviv regional government has decided to build a water pipeline. In accord with the new Land Code of Ukraine (adopted in December 1990), the power of regional government has diminished, but the competence of local governments—village and settlement Soviets—has enlarged. The village and settlement Soviets have to give their consent to building the water pipeline. But the populace of these villages and settlements disagrees because the water would disappear from their wells. The village and settlement Soviets have not consented to the water pipeline's building, so it remains uncompleted. As a result, Lviv is experiencing an acute lack of water. Water is supplied to houses only during a few hours a day.

In making Ukraine a sovereign state, many problems have arisen, including the following: interstate cooperation in various branches; harmonization of Ukrainian national legislation with the international law; participation in the international organizations; execution of international treatments (in which

Ukraine takes part); and protection of the Ukraine environment.

Ukraine has signed the Treaty on Economic Cooperation with the former republics of the disintegrated U.S.S.R., but it has not signed the Interstate Ecological Treaty. Ukraine has concluded treaties with Russia, Belorussia, and Kazakhstan on mutually beneficial and equal collaboration, not only in different branches of the national economy, but also in the sphere of environmental protection, including prevention of transboundary pollution and creation of an international system of ecological safety.

Until recently, environmental protection and natural resource use were regulated by the Union and republican legislation. Since Ukrainian independence, the regulation of all questions dealing with environmental protection and natural resources is vested exclusively in Ukraine. The Ukrainian Parliament and the Environmental Protection Ministry (established in May 1991) are developing a Ukrainian national environmental law. National environmental legislation will be renewed, supplemented, and coordinated with the Ukrainian Law on Protection of the Environment dated June 1991. For example, during the next five years, there are plans to work out 200 legislative and other normative acts of Ukraine, which will regulate environmental protection and natural resource usage.

The Law on Protection of the Environment is the basic legislation for environmental protection. The law regards environmental protection, rational use of natural resources, and environmental security as general conditions for the stable economic and social development of Ukraine.

Until the law was passed, economic purposes were basic and very often were achieved through damaging nature. The law consolidates the principle of significantly valid concordance of environmental, economic, and social interests when it declares that "priority of environmental security requirements, the compulsory observance of environmental standards, norms and limits while realizing economic, executive, legislative and other activities."

The law stipulates special kinds of nature use and payment for environmental pollution, as well as compensation for damages connected with violation of environmental legislation. That stipulation is aimed at perfecting the economic mechanism of optimum use of natural resources.

The law uses a combination of stimulation and responsibility to promote concordance of economic and ecological interests. It grants tax privileges for enterprises, organizations, and citizens that develop measures for environmental protection and for rational uses of natural resources. Privilege credits are also given to develop environmental measures. Public environmental funds are obtained from taxes.

Before the Law all natural resources on the territory of Ukraine were an object of the Union property. Now, according to Article 4, natural resources of Ukraine belong to the Ukrainian people, who have the right to possess, use, and govern them. This is a very important condition of Ukrainian state formation.

In the Ukrainian Law on Forms of Property, adopted on January 30, 1992, which appears in the new edition of the Land Code of Ukraine, three forms of land property—state, collective, and private—have been established. Citizens of Ukraine now may own a plot of land with natural resources on it.

Ukrainian peoples' sovereignty in the sphere of environmental protection and natural resource use is translated into reality both directly by referendum and through the Ukrainian state power bodies. On behalf of the Ukrainian people, management is conducted by the Supreme Soviet of Ukraine. For the first time, the Ukrainian Law on Protection of the Environment confirms the right to safety for human life and a healthy environment. This right is guaranteed by public hearings of legislative projects, by glasnost in the environmental decision-making process, and by citizens' rights to obtain accurate information on environmental situations. Citizens have the right to know, through participating in public environmental activities, how environmental projects affect their own health. The law confirms the court defense of the right to safety, life, and a healthy environment, and to compensation for damages caused by any breach of environmental law.

These individual rights correspond to duties to protect nature, to use natural resources rationally, and not to breach the environmental rights of other people. The law prohibits the construction and operation of enterprises or other facilities that do not meet environmental standards. The activity of enterprises that violate environmental law may be temporarily stopped or even canceled by the Cabinet of Ministers, regardless of the form of property involved.

Environmental standards regulate protection for plants, use of mineral fertilizers and toxic substances, and the location and development of popu-lated areas and military facilities.

For the first time, legal definitions are given for environmental catastrophes and increased ecologically dangerous environmental situation zones. More detailed regulation of the legal status of these zones is under consideration in a separate act.

The Ukrainian Environmental Protection Act envisages criminal, administrative, civil, and discipline responsibility for the following transgressions:

- breach of an individual right for safe environment
- breach of environmental standards
- violation of fulfillment of a state environmental examination requirements
- nonexecution of state environmental control bodies order
- excessive one-time waste disposal
- breach of conservancy areas
- denials of full and trustworthy information about an environmental situation
- falsification or withholding of environmental information.

The problem with the law and other Ukrainian environmentally related legislation is not its content but the lack of application and enforcement.

Among the reasons for failure to carry out the laws on the books are the following:

- environmental measures are not profitable because they are expensive and do not immediately produce needed revenue
- environmental legislation is not perfect
- businessmen and law-and-order bodies do not care enough about the environment
- the principle of obligatory punishment for environmental offenses is not observed
- environmental awareness is at a low level.

Financing environmental protection measures, which already had been insufficient, has been reduced further from 1% to 0.4% of the GNP of Ukraine. As a result, the ecological situation in the Ukraine is dangerous and grave and is severely compounded by the Chernobyl disaster, the largest accident in the history of atomic energy use. Losses from this disaster up to the year 2000 will amount to between 180 and 250 billion rubles without including the losses of life. By comparison, in the U.S.A., such expenses after the accident at the Three Mile Island atomic station were estimated at $135 million dollars.

Five regions of Ukraine were exposed to radioactive pollution from Chernobyl, and a high level of disease is observed there (respiratory diseases, diseases of the blood and endocrine system, different breaches of immunity, pregnancy, mental derangement, and others). In many regions that were exposed to radioactive pollution, concentrations of nitrates repeatedly exceed the maximum permitted.

Another prime reason for the dangerous ecological situation in Ukraine is intensive and concentrated exploitation of natural resources by industrial enterprises. Every year, 20 million tons of industrial discharges go into the atmosphere—more than 1 billion cubic meters of harmful materials are ejected into the rivers, 1.5 billion cubic meters of solid wastes are accumulated in dumps. Previously, Ukraine occupied 2.7% of the former Soviet Union, produced 20% of the U.S.S.R.'s national product, and received 25% of its industrial pollution.

Under the conditions of domination of the centralized command and control administrative system in the former Soviet Union, for decades the Ukrainian economy had been directed with disregard for the objective needs of its people and without a proper evaluation of economic capabilities of individual regions. As a result, one of the most ecologically polluted economies, oversaturated by chemical, metallurgical, and mining production facilities with obsolete technologies, has been formed.

Some 118 million hectares of black soil are eroded. This has never happened during 5,000 years of history of Ukrainian agriculture. Thousands of rivers have perished. The Black Sea and Sea of Asov are degraded because of water pollution. The Carpathian Mountains have lost half of their forests. There is a water deficit in a number of Ukrainian cities, and air pollution exceeds environmental quality standards.

If Ukraine does not take extraordinary measures today to improve the environment, it will be too late tomorrow for the irreversible processes of natural degradation will have started.

In the final analysis, environmental law can and must play an important role in the improvement of the environment in Ukraine. In fact, the environment—the seas, rivers, air, wildlife—know no boundaries. Environmental problems become global and must be solved by norms superimposed on national law by international law and by collaboration among different countries in the sphere of environmental protection.

28

Ecological Federalism in the Context of Regional and World Development

Yuri Tunitsia

The reason for the collapse of the Soviet Union and Yugoslavia, two large European federations, was that the purpose for their creation was not a necessity of life. That purpose did not reflect the vital interests of nations that were forcibly drawn into artificial, exceedingly ideologized totalitarian federal states. Possibly this is the very reason for the existence of today's very acute problem of keeping the Russian Federation itself from collapse.

The causes for this are clear: the East European "socialist" countries were created mainly by means of dictatorship, not through voluntary unification as a federation. Dictatorship was the basis of the official theory of socialism. An important 1915 work by V. I. Lenin entitled "On the Slogan of the United States of Europe" states:

> Unevenness of economic and political development is an absolute law of capitalism. It follows that a victory of socialism is possible initially in a few or even one separate capitalist country. After its victory, the proletariat of this country, having expropriated capitalists and organized socialist production, would rise *against* the other, capitalist world, drawing in oppressed classes of other countries, exciting uprisings against capitalists in these countries, even coming out with military force if necessary against exploiter classes and their states. The political form of the society where the proletariat wins by way of overthrowing the bourgeoisie will be a democratic republic that is progressively centralizing the force of the proletariat of a given nation or nations fighting against states that have not gone over to socialism. Annihilation of classes without dictatorship of the oppressed class, the proletariat, is impossible. Free unification of nations under socialism without more or less stubborn struggle of socialist republics with states lagging behind is impossible.[1]

The ideological struggle of the U.S.S.R. with states "lagging behind" went on for more than 70 years. That struggle involved great expenses and losses from both sides. Finally, ideological barriers have fallen. An absolute majority of the world countries, with the exception of a few, have freed themselves from political dogmas. Fundamental reasons for confrontation have disappeared. A time has come to jointly solve problems of survival and social and economic development. Suddenly, everyone on this planet has become closer to each other. Even though the planet is not united in solving many global problems of today's world, it is much closer to unity and to understanding those problems than it used to be.

Problems of protection and improvement of the natural living environment, of rational use and reproduction of natural resources (that is, ecological problems) are among priority problems that require immediate solution by common efforts. Environmental protection and rational use of natural resources are an integral part of economic and social development. This was pointed out in the address of the International Commission for the Environment and Development prepared under the leadership of G. H. Brundtland.[2] In 1987, this address was approved by the General Assembly of the United Nations. "Regional Strategy for Environmental Protection and Rational Utilization of Natural Resources in Member Countries of the European Economic Commission for the Period up to the Year 2000 and Later," adopted in 1988, is based on the same conception of fundamental unity of natural environment and development. The strategy of the European Community agrees with the World Strategy for Nature Protection announced in 1980, which also consists of stable development while ensuring protection of natural resources.

The topicality of federalism problems that are being considered today is based on the fact that a number of new independent states that used to be members of the U.S.S.R. will build their state systems on federal principles. This applies to Russia, Ukraine, Georgia, and some other states, which is going to raise many new questions. In addition, the problem of purposeful ecological federalism is objectively put on the agenda along with the traditional classic federalism.

The term "ecological federalism" itself has not been encountered until recently. The issue of state, intergovernmental, and public organizations, along with unions, associations, political parties, and other bodies joining efforts to protect and improve the environment as a factor of economic and social development has undoubtedly been in existence for a long time.

Even though the science of nature preservation and practical measures in this specific area of human activity have a long history, ecological federalism is essentially a phenomenon of the twentieth century. In 1913, at the First International Congress on Issues of Nature Preservation in Switzerland, the issue of ecological federalism was raised, subconsciously, for the first time. This event may be viewed as the aspiration of nature defenders of that time to combine their efforts for the cause of preservation of separate species of living organisms, plants, and separate components of nature on Earth. Later, in 1922 the International Council for Bird Preservation was created in London. In 1923, the International Association for Nature Preservation began to function in Paris. In 1930, the International Hunters Association also was founded in Paris. In 1948, in Switzerland, a new nongovernmental federation, the Inter-national Union for Nature Protection was formed—later renamed the International Union for the Conservation of Nature and Natural Resources (IUCN). Today it comprises more than 300 national, governmental, and public organizations from 90 countries. A specialized international body, the United Nations Environmental Program (UNEP), headquartered in Nairobi, Kenya, has been functioning since 1973, along with many other international ecological organizations.

It is very important today that processes of transition to sustainable development (regional and global) should be under common control of all countries of the world. The community of human needs demands creation of an efficient intergovernmental system that, while respecting the democratic principle of consent, would at the same time recognize the unity of our planet and the need for common coordinated actions in the preservation of our natural living environment.

The experience accumulated by the world society for 20 years from the United Nations Conference on the Human Environment of 1972 (Sweden) to the 1992 United Nations Conference on Environment and Development (Brazil) supports a movement to a higher organizational level of ecological federalism. In the past 30 years, many important environmental documents have been adopted that ought now to become equally binding, like the World Strategy for Nature Preservation (1980) and the Regional Strategy for Environmental Protection and Rational Utilization of Natural Resources of the EEC Member Countries (1988).

The problem of ecological federalism is a general problem of our time. It will remain a topical problem for a long time. Common ecological problems exist in all countries. Regardless of political system, state system, or the level of economic development of a country, ecological problems cannot be solved by any one country acting alone. The common ecological space, intercommunication, and interdependency of different components of the natural environment (even in geographically distant regions) demand consolidation of efforts for common solutions to protect and improve the natural living environment. Ecological federalism is an objective process of creation, functioning, and perfection of various governmental, intergovernmental, and nongovernmental (political, public, scientific, production-and-commercial, etc.) associations with the object of purposefully solving the problems of nature preservation, rational use, and reproduction of natural resources on both regional and global scales. All other political, social, ideological, and economic issues are subsidiary to the fundamental question involved in ecological federalism, which is the survival of humankind.

It is thus necessary to draft a World Ecological Constitution as the main law of contemporary international society, provisions of which should be mandatory for every country with no exceptions. In fact, basic conceptual provisions of the future World Ecological Constitution have been already developed. They are included in Section 12 of the report of the International Commission for the Environment and Development and in Annex 1 to this report.[3] The World Ecological Constitution should be adopted by the UN General Assembly after broad discussion of its draft.

According to the World Ecological Constitution, an international executive body under the aegis of the United Nations should be created. It could be called the World Ecological Confederation. The main tasks of such a body should be the control of adherence to the ecoconstitution's requirements and coordination of activities of national and international organizations in the area of preservation of the natural living environment and social and economic development. Satisfactory performance of the World Ecological Confederation's functions should be secured by International Ecological Police, which, using modern technical means for monitoring the natural living environment, will continuously control the condition of the natural environment on our planet. Ecological violations discovered by International Ecopolice should be considered by the specially created International Ecological Court. And finally, there should be established an International Ecological Bank, which will receive fines for ecological violations and funds from other sources, as well as finance priority measures on natural environment preservation and provide help to underdeveloped countries for special purposes. Similar federal ecological bodies should be created in different areas of the world (for instance, a European Ecological Confederation) and in every separate country.

For example, there were proposals in Ukraine to draft and adopt an Ecological Constitution (or Ecological Code) as the principal law to define the main principles and requirements for both commercial activity and nature preservation on its territory. In addition, proposals were also made to draft and adopt a set of direct nature preservation laws that would enable a plaintiff direct access to court that would establish an arbitration body and an Office of the public prosecutor. In Ukraine, an Ecological Code should be developed to define provisions of the Declaration of State Sovereignty of Ukraine, to agree with provisions of the future Constitution, and to comprise ecological requirements mandatory for all laws and other directive documents. All laws adopted earlier should also be brought into compliance with an Ecological Code. Only then may a real solution to acute interdependent ecological and economic problems be meaningfully addressed. An Ecological Code for Ukraine should not be voluminous and should reflect at least those legal regulations that are recommended by the UN General Assembly for all of its member countries.

These regulations include the principal right of all people to have a natural environment favorable for living and economic development. The correlative duties of the state would include the following:

- to ensure preservation and rational use of the environment and natural resources in the interests of the present and future generations
- to support ecosystems and processes necessary for the functioning of the biosphere
- to preserve biological diversity and follow principles that ensure steady optimal productivity when using natural resources and ecosystems
- to establish rules for environmental protection (this is exactly the purpose of a purely nature protection legislation)
- to monitor changes in the quality of the environment and in the use of natural resources and to publish monitoring data
- to make preliminary ecological estimates and demand their observance when carrying out new types of activities
- to provide timely information on possible effects of commercial activities on the environment, while granting all citizens equal rights to protect their lives in administrative bodies and courts
- to ensure that preservation of the environment is considered an integral part of planning and of all the activities in the area of economic development
- to show goodwill and to cooperate with other countries in order to exercise those rights and perform obligations
- to stop all local and global activities that violate the above-mentioned obligations
- to ensure compensation of ecological losses

An Ecological Code that is essentially different from the current Law on the Nature Preservation is particularly needed in Ukraine in view of the transition to a market economy, because many ecological mistakes were made under the centrally planned economy. The independence of Ukraine and its social and economic development depend to a considerable extent on finding solutions to the deep ecological and economic crises, which were inherited from the previous command and administrative system.

The principal causes of the ecological and economic crises are as follows: an unnatural economic system that by inertia still remains antiecological; technological backwardness in virtually every area of material production; imperfection of the national economy's structure; ecologically ungrounded distribution of productive forces; interference of the state in the sphere of production; predominance of the economy and ecological requirements by politics; excessive militarization of the economy; imperfection of economic and nature protection legislation; lack of integration with the European and world economic processes; and complete ecological illiteracy. However, nature protection alone, even if conducted perfectly, cannot solve the problems coming out of this ecological crisis because of the related economic crisis in Ukraine. Account must be taken of the causal relationship between the economy and the quality of the natural living environment. It is also necessary to redirect the entire economic system, however weak it may be, to integrating the criterion of ecological and economic efficiency, instead of the conventional direction toward the criterion of economic efficiency alone, which does not allow for accompanying (mainly separable) ecological effects of various production and economic activities. Only through complete ecologization of the economy is there a real way out of the deep crisis in Ukraine.

Transition to a market economy without properly taking into account ecological requirements creates a real threat of further worsening the ecological and economic crises. The most simple, cheap, and efficient way of solving the problem of introducing ecological requirements into the economic system of Ukraine would be to adapt the world experience—in particular of the American and West German systems of economic protection of the environment—to our conditions. These systems have been accommodated to market conditions for a long time. Help from the world society in solving ecological problems of Ukraine must be accompanied by demilitarization of the economy and ecologically grounded conversion of the defense industry.

The U.S. Environmental Protection Agency (EPA) has agreed to undertake a joint Ukrainian-American project entitled Economical Protection of the Natural Living Environment of Ukraine Under Market Conditions ("Eco-market-2000"). The government of the independent Ukraine should take this opportunity very seriously and do everything to realize it.

The concept of economic protection of the environment should be based on the principle of *ecological losses*, which is well grounded in scientific literature, as a component of necessary operating costs in every field of the economy, regardless of the form of ownership of means of production. Standard ecological losses should be included in costs of production (services), and losses above an agreed standard should be compensated for from companies' profits.

The government of Ukraine has recently directed the Ministry of Environmental Protection to prepare an experiment to introduce the American system of selling licenses for environmental pollution ("bubble principle") and other market mechanisms used in the area of environmental protection. This is the Ecomarket-2000 project. Companies taking part in the experiment should be granted tax and other benefits. Economic incentives should not be less important than economic sanctions.

A system of incentives and sanctions should be well grounded and clear for companies and local governing bodies to arouse their economic interest in introducing environmental quality control methods, which are primarily market methods and not administrative ones. Particularly dangerous pollutants, however, should not be subject to control by market methods. If there is a choice between ecologization of production (preventing pollution) and installation of purification works, the incentive for the first option should be much greater. Elements of the "bubble principle" (adapted to the Ukrainian conditions) should cover not only air pollution, but also pollution of water, soil, and other components of the environment.

The Ecomarket-2000 project should be implemented based on an appropriate resolution of the Council of Ministers of Ukraine and intergovernmental agreements between Ukraine and the U.S.A. (at the first stage), and Ukraine, U.S.A., Poland, Czech Republic, Slovakia, Hungary, and Germany (at the second stage).

These European countries, owing to their geographic location, similarity of ecological problems, and interrelationship of their radical solution, are interested in joint improvement of their systems for environmental protection and rational utilization of natural resources.

An unprecedented experiment on international sales of licenses (or shares), giving the right to pollute the environment in Central Europe, and coordinated measures on improving the use of natural resources would be of a great scientific and practical importance. Such an experiment could be conducted with the participation of the International Institute/Association for Regional Ecological Problems (IIAREP), which was founded at Lviv I. Franko State University in 1991 to consolidate the scientific expertise of universities, other establishments of higher education, and research institutions to solve complex territorial ecological problems in different branches of industry. Partners of IIAREP are universities and other educational and scientific and research institutions of Ukraine, Belarus, Poland, Czech Republic, Slovakia, Germany, France, Romania, Bulgaria, and the U.S.A.

IIAREP is a flexible scientific organization that, acting in accordance with its bylaws, creates temporary teams of highly qualified experts (production specialists from different branches of the economy, chemists, physicists, mathematicians, economists, lawyers, physicians, etc.) on a contract basis for carrying out specific assignments, which cannot be provided by any conventional scientific institution. For the purposes of research and for making expert conclusions, IIAREP uses, on a contract basis, equipment of educational and research institutions of Lviv and other cities, including equipment of partner organizations abroad. The program of IIAREP's activity includes theoretical (fundamental) research, applied research including approbation of results, and problems of ecological education and training.

In November 1991 IIAREP held the First International Regional Scientific and Educational Conference on Issues of Ecological Education and Training ("Ecoeducation-91") with the participation of representatives from Ukraine, Poland, Czech Republic, Slovakia, England, and the U.S.A. Proceedings of the conference are planned to be published. The first collection of scientific works of IIAREP is also being prepared for publication in English.

Two international projects are scheduled to begin in 1992: Economic Protection of the Natural Living Environment of Ukraine Under Market Conditions (Ecomarket-2000)—jointly with the Environmental Protection Agency of the United States; and An Alternative Concept of Power Supply for the City of Lviv ("Lviv-Ecopower-2000")—jointly with the Institute for Applied Ecology, Freiburg, Germany.

Returning to the issue of ecological federalism, it is necessary to point out that not every country of the world has acknowledged and included in its constitution the first principle of the Ecological Declaration, which was announced in 1972 by the UN Conference on the Environment: "Man has the fundamental right to freedom, equality, and adequate conditions of life, in an environment of a quality that permits a life of dignity and well-being."

Humankind is gradually, step by step, accepting the existence of close causal relationships between the condition of the environment and the real present and future economic development at both regional and global levels.

Today, conventional limits of ecological federalism as a form of the state system founded on the principles of federation (union) should be mandatory. Federations should become efficient tools for settling not only political, military, and economic questions, which have been the primary purpose of their creation, but also an organizational (legal) form for reaching common ecological goals.

Ecological federalism should be considered on at least on five levels: (1) the level of the idea of federalism and its moral, ethical, and philosophical comprehension; (2) the level of a political slogan that should be debated among diplomats, other state representatives, and in international organizations; (3) the level of theoretical and methodological and scientific and practical problems involving development of conceptual and methodological issues and conducting scientific and practical research; (4) the level of a specific legal science and practice that is supposed to produce grounded recommendations to create ecological federations and confederations of different hierarchical levels (state, interstate, world) as well as the drafting of legislative documents; (5) the level of assessment of the efficiency of ecofederations and international ecological laws.

The issue of ecological federalism as a tool for collectively solving acute environmental problems deserves close attention from representatives of legal and economic sciences. Today, this issue is gaining a special importance in the context of regional and world development, because development is impossible without a safe and healthy environment. The search for appropriate ecofederal regional and global structures will be exceptionally important for the social and economic development of society, for ensuring living conditions adequate for all human beings, and will contribute to the strengthening of peace and mutual understanding among all nations of our planet.

NOTES

1. V. I. Lenin, from *Complete Works*, Vol. 26 (Moscow: Foreign Language Publishers, 1960), 355.

2. *Our Common Future* (New York: Oxford University Press, 1987).

3. *Ibid*.

29

The Government Structure Over the U.S. Electric Industry: Federal–State Tensions

James E. Hickey, Jr.

There are about 3,500 separate electric systems in the United States that are owned by various government entities, by consumers (nonprofit cooperatives), and by shareholders (private companies). Most of the electricity in the U.S.A. is provided by private companies. The private electric companies are about 250 in number and they supply about 80% of the electricity in the United States. The private companies are tax-paying corporations that are financed by the sale of stocks and bonds and by the sale of electricity for profit. Most electric systems in the U.S.A. are connected to one another and there are connections with Canada and Mexico. Overall, the U.S. electric system provides a fairly reliable electric supply at a relatively reasonable price.

The government structure over the U.S. electric industry presently is divided between the federal government and the governments of the states. The tension created by this divided government structure has resulted in failures in the U.S. electric industry. Those failures include wasteful and expensive litigation over who has jurisdiction, the cancellation of needed power plants, unnecessarily high electric prices to consumers, a reduction of energy supply options, and harm to international relations. This paper briefly analyzes some of those failures in the U.S. system of dual government authority over electric markets. The paper suggests that other countries like the sovereign states of the former U.S.S.R. may provide, in certain respects, a viable alternative model for future government regulation of the electric industry than the U.S. structure.

GOVERNMENT REGULATION OF PRIVATE ELECTRIC COMPANIES

The present dual system of federal and state regulation of electricity in the

U.S.A. is somewhat an accident of history.

The electric industry in the U.S. began on September 4, 1882, when Thomas Edison, the inventor of the lightbulb, started the first private electric company for making electricity in New York City. At this time there was no government regulation. As electric use grew, electricity became an essential public service that was needed to operate factories and businesses and to provide light and heat for homes and offices. Because electricity became an essential public service, it began to be regulated by the states in order to assure reliable supply at a reasonable price.

State regulation of private electric companies was not based on competition. Rather, states granted companies exclusive rights to make and sell electricity in assigned geographic areas within the states. The states also set the price at which electricity could be sold at retail to consumers. For the most part, private electric companies welcomed state regulation because it prevented competition, wasteful duplication of facilities, and city governments from taking over profitable electric operations. The federal government began to regulate electricity transmitted across state borders and sales of electricity at wholesale in the 1930s. Thus, state authority over electric prices at present is confined to retail electric sales within a state (intrastate) and federal authority over electric prices is confined to interstate wholesale sales and interstate transmissions of electricity.

FAILURES IN THE FEDERAL-STATE REGULATORY STRUCTURE IN THE U.S.A.

The End of the U.S. Nuclear Power Industry

The end of the U.S. nuclear power industry is due, in large part, to conflicts between state and federal authorities over the construction and operation of nuclear power plants.

Commercial nuclear electric power development in the U.S.A. began in the 1950's. That development came within exclusive federal authority under laws passed by the Congress and signed by the president. The premises for exclusive federal government regulation were concerns about national security and health and safety. At that time, electricity made with nuclear power was thought by everyone to be the answer to unlimited electric supply to be sold at a very low price.

In the 1970s and 1980s, citizens in the states became very concerned about the safety of nuclear power plants and about the serious problem of where to dispose of nuclear power waste.

State and local governments, in response to those concerns expressed by their citizens, began to strongly oppose the building of nuclear power plants in their communities. The federal government, however, continued to encourage construction of new nuclear power plants as it was required to do by federal law. Each government entity attempted to assert jurisdiction. The result was tension and conflict between state and federal government entities that caused long and costly delays in issuing construction permits to build nuclear power plants and licenses to operate them. Resolution of the federalism tensions involved many lawsuits and administrative proceedings which, over time, made electricity generated by new nuclear power plants very expensive when compared to electricity made from power plants using coal, natural gas, and oil.

As a result, the commercial nuclear power industry is dead in the U.S.A. The nuclear electric plants that were built in the 1950s and 1960s are reaching the end of their productive lives. All nuclear power plants that were ordered since 1974 have been canceled (sometimes at the loss of billions of dollars of investment). No new nuclear power plants have been ordered since 1978 and there are no new orders coming in the future. This is an extraordinary situation for the U.S.A. because it comes at a time of great concern about global warming and acid rain caused by power plants fueled by oil and coal. It also comes at a time when the U.S.A. depends heavily on foreign petroleum, much of which is used in oil-fired and natural gas-fired electric power plants. This harms the U.S. trade balance, increases its national debt, and weakens its economy.

Federal-State Tensions Over Electric Prices

A long-standing tension exists between the exclusive power of states to regulate retail electric prices (the prices paid by consumers like factories and homeowners) and the exclusive power of the federal government to regulate interstate wholesale prices of electricity (like power sales between two utilities that sell electricity at retail). The tension comes when the federal government sets a wholesale price that the state authorities refuse to pass through to customers at retail. The federal government complains that the state by its refusal is preventing the wholesale price from having any effect and that the state is, in effect, requiring electric companies to swallow internally wholesale price increases granted by the federal government. The state government complains that if the state is required to pass along wholesale prices set by the federal government without question, then the federal government is wrongly interfering with the state's exclusive authority to set retail electric prices. This split in pricing authority is subject to constant, expensive litigation, which increases the price of electricity paid by everyone.

The Absence of a National Energy Supply Policy

In the U.S.A, the government does not directly regulate the private companies that supply the traditional fuels of oil, natural gas, and coal to electric companies. This means that those companies compete with one another for utility customers. As a result, coal companies oppose government policies favorable to the oil and natural gas industries and vice versa. And all three industries oppose government policies favorable to alternative, nontraditional sources of energy like solar power, geothermal power, or the making of fuel from corn (gasohol). This means that the U.S.A. has no coordinated national energy supply policy. The marketplace, with its wild swings in price, is primarily left to control supply and demand. At times, just as now, the U.S.A. is heavily dependent on foreign oil supply while, at the same time, it has enough domestic coal and natural gas reserves to meet all its electric fuel supply needs for the next 200 years (putting aside environmental concerns).

The Harm to International Relations

Federalism experts like Daniel Elazar have spoken about a "new species" of federalism. Perhaps one such "new species" of federalism may emerge in the form of central international authorities to address unique international electric production, supply, and sales problems among similarly situated states.

The reason that the United States and its neighbors (Mexico and Canada) may require such a "new federal" or "supernational" authority can be shown by the recent tension between the Province of Quebec and the State of New York. The tension is about using Quebec hydroelectricity to meet the energy needs of the population of Long Island, New York (6 million people). Long Islanders are at the limits of local electric supply because the Long Island communities and the State of New York successfully opposed federal government approval of a large nuclear power plant (800 megawatts) that was constructed on Long Island but has never opened (the Shoreham nuclear power plant). Long Island taxpayers have agreed to pay $5.5 billion in increased electric prices to tear down the plant as soon as possible or to convert it to burn natural gas.

Long Island has turned to Quebec (among other places and sources) to replace part of the electric power of that closed nuclear power plant. The Province of Quebec is building a huge hydroelectric project (the James Bay Project) that, if completed, will produce excess electricity that it wants to sell to Long Island. The problem is that New York State suddenly has decided not to contract with Quebec for that power. The reason for this decision is in part because the predictions about how much electricity New York will need in the future has changed and because New York objects to the environmental consequences in Canada that will be caused by the large-scale flooding that will take place to build the hydroelectric dams necessary to supply Long Island with power. New York State also objects, on human rights grounds, to the displacement of the Canadian Indian population (the Cree) when their land in Quebec is flooded by these hydroelectric dams.

As a result of New York's decision, the economy of Quebec is in serious danger. The Quebec government borrowed large sums of money from financial institutions, using as collateral the expectation of future electric sales by the province to Long Island. Quebec understandably objects that New York is controlling Canadian energy policy and the internal economy of Quebec on grounds that are totally a matter of Canadian sovereign authority. That is, Quebec says New York has no right to question the means of production of electricity inside Canada. New York may insist that it cannot contract for electricity made in Canada in a way that would violate New York law and international human rights law if that electricity were made in the same way in New York. This controversy has contributed to the tensions in international relations with Canada and may have profound implications for future relations of the U.S.A. with Mexico as well.

It is in this last example especially that the U.S.A. may have much to learn from government structures already in place to deal with electricity in the sovereign states of the former U.S.S.R. One solution that the U.S.A. appears likely to pursue to resolve these federalism tensions is to deregulate utilites at the federal level and to introduce competition among utilities at the state level. These trends, if pursued, do not resolve problems raised by integrating electric markets in Canada, Mexico, and the U.S.A. In the former U.S.S.R., all electricity assets presently are owned by the government and there are no immediate plans to privatize electric operations. In addition, electric coordination and supply among the new states continues to be handled, for the most part, in the same way it was handled in the U.S.S.R. This post-U.S.S.R. government structure, for the present, avoids the wasteful litigation, construction delays due to conflict, and the incoherent energy policy that exists in the U.S.A. In this area, it may well be the case that the West should learn from the sovereign states of the U.S.S.R. and that the states of the former U.S.S.R. should not rush to adopt federalism trends being pursued in the U.S.A. At a time when Mexico, the U.S.A., and Canada are searching for the appropriate structures to address the energy aspects of free trade and integration of markets, the states of the former U.S.S.R. already have such a structure to address the energy aspects of future economic relations. Such structures may prove useful in assuming economic and political sovereign equality in energy and electricity matters in the decades ahead.

30

The Influence of Local Authorities and the Public on Energy Policy in Ukraine

Victoria Yegorova

Pressing economic and social problems beset old industrial regions of Ukraine. The purpose of this paper is to find ways of confronting these problems that are compatible with both continuing economic growth in Ukraine and its transition toward a market economy. Regional policy must be considered in the development of a modern energy policy in Ukraine.

Changes in the system of management in the Ukrainian economy have resulted in a drastic growth in independence of the regions, which get increasing power to set up different policies, to stimulate specific sectors of activities, and to implement local forms of financial stimulations for industry. Up to now, these opportunities have not been used, but they must be used in a new economic system.

The paper concludes with recommendations about how to combine regional interests in the content of modern energy policy.

THE MODERN ENERGY POLICY IN UKRAINE

A modern energy policy in Ukraine must take into account two new features that have come up in the fuel-energy sector in the former U.S.S.R.: decentralization and nuclear power.

Decentralization

The first characteristic of the new directions of the energy sector in the former U.S.S.R. is a drastically increased independence of the regions in making decisions about locations of projects in general, and energy in particular. Desire to decrease output of fuel and energy arises primarily in regions with surplus production of energy resources because of the desire of local communities to improve their environmental situations.

Several decisions have already been made in response to the pressure of public organizations and local governments. They include the postponement of development of natural gas deposits on the Yamal peninsula, discontinuation of construction of a new coal surface mine in the Kuzbas, limitations placed on the development of coal reserves in Siberia, and wider use of natural gas in regions where reserves are located accompanied by reduction of the volume of gas, which is exported to the European part of the former U.S.S.R.

Nuclear Power

The second feature is a drastic reduction of the program of nuclear energy. When the details of the U.S.S.R.'s five-year plan (1986 to 1990) were published at the end of 1985 and the beginning of 1986, a goal was set for increasing electricity production in nuclear power plants (NPPs) five- to seven-fold between 1985 and 2000. Given an NPP capacity of 28 million kW in 1985 and production of 167 billion kWh of electricity, this would require increase in capacity to 140 to 200 million kW, and make possible an output of 850 to 1,200 billion kWh. Ukraine was to contribute 40 to 50 million kW and 240 to 300 billion kWh—approximately 25% of the total.

At the time, many specialists considered such a goal unrealistic. Following the Chernobyl tragedy it became clear that the goal would have to be drastically reduced. Despite the recognition, inertia has allowed the "big" nuclear program to be retained in many planning documents. However, information about the progress of construction of NPPs, the choice of new plant locations, and the attitude of the public and local authorities in various regions of the former U.S.S.R. lead to the following prognosis: the capacity of NPPs of the former U.S.S.R. in 2000 will not exceed 44–50 million kW and the production of electricity will be no greater than 300 billion kWh. In Ukraine, the capacity of NPPs would be less than 13 to 14 million kW and production of electricity less than 75–85 billion kWh.

One must also consider the possibility of keeping production of electricity in NPPs at the present level so that new capacity compensates for capacity taken out of operation. There also exists the possibility of the reduction of existing acting capacity, given that public organizations and even Supreme Soviets of the republics are faced with the task of prohibiting construction of new NPPs, stopping construction of new units in existing NPPs, and not putting into operation the energy units that are half finished. In light of the decision of the Supreme Soviet of Ukraine to take all three reactors of the Chernobyl NPP out of operation, the future of nuclear power in the republic is problematic indeed.

Under these circumstances, the Ukrainian energy sector will enter a new stage of development. This stage is a product of the transition of Ukraine from a centrally planned to a market economy, by the independence declarations of Ukraine and other republics, by unfavorable changes in the conditions of fuel and power production, and the corresponding pressure on resources that are required to provide an increase in production capacity of the Ukrainian energy sector.

The energy sector has a special influence upon the development of the Ukrainian economy. This sector has 5.4 million employees and it receives about 20% of all Ukrainian investments. A slowdown in the growth of the energy sector will impose a constraint on the growth of the economy. To mitigate this restraining effect, it is necessary to reduce demands for fuel and power resources, and to develop a strategy for energy supply that will be realized with a minimal allocation of national resources. It is also necessary to take into account that the energy sector is very capital-intensive and slow to change, and that a certain level of energy consumption is required to sustain operation of the economy.

Ukraine was for a long time a fuel, power, and metallurgical base of the former U.S.S.R. Ukrainian production was intended to satisfy all Union needs. Ukraine occupies less than 3% of the U.S.S.R. territory, but produces more than 17% of industrial output.

Because of its unbalanced economic structure, the one-sided dominance of the production of capital goods and the consequent neglect of consumer goods, the living conditions of the population have been held back. At present, 71.2% of the republic's industrial output is in capital goods, including 8.4% production of energy.

Most Ukrainian industries were built during the early five-year plan period shortly after World War II, and the technology is now out of date. In the electric power generating sector, physical depreciation amounts to 38% and, in the fuel sector, to 47% of the total value of capital assets. It is clear that the industrial potential of Ukraine requires a radical reconstruction and technical improvement.

The existing structure of the Ukrainian economy requires a high level of consumption of energy, which cannot be decreased significantly during the next 15 years (until 2005), even though energy-saving technology will be implemented. The scope for reducing energy requirements is estimated at only 1.5% per year during this period.

The Ukrainian economy is a complex system with a predominance of heavy industries. Extensive development of these industries was accompanied by intensive exploitation of natural resources without proper concern about the environment. As a result, the pressure on the environment in Ukraine exceeds six to seven times the average level for the former U.S.S.R.

During the next 15 years the development of the Ukrainian economy will be accompanied by increasing depletion of the most economic fossil fuels: oil and natural gas. Prior to 1980, Ukraine was self-sufficient in natural gas, exporting the surplus. However, even at its peak output in 1973, crude oil production met only 50% of Ukrainian domestic demand. In the mid-1970s, oil and natural gas output started to decrease, and by the end of 1980s had declined by one-third. Ukraine now meets only 10% of its oil and 25% of its natural gas needs. By 2010, oil output is expected to fall to 2.5 million tons as compared to 5.3 million tons in 1990, and natural gas production to 17 billion cubic meters as compared to 28.1 billion cubic meters in 1990 (see Table 1).

Table 1. Ukrainian Fuel Industry

Fuel	1990	1995	2000	2005	2010
Coal, million tons	164.8	170.0	172.0	175.0	178.0
Oil, million tons	5.3	4.4	3.8	3.0	2.5
Gas, billion cubic meters	28.1	15.6	17.0	17.0	17.0

Source: Ukrainian Ministry of Economy, 1991.

It is very difficult to predict the growth of consumption of electricity and heat in Ukraine because there are no reliable forecasts of future economic development. It is not clear how successful changes in the system of management and changes in economic structure will be. As a consequence, one must look to other countries for information that may be relevant to predictions of development of the Ukrainian economy. In Ukraine much is said of "foreign success" in reducing consumption of energy. In the countries where such success is alleged, national economies are supposedly so efficient that they have succeeded in stabilizing consumption of electricity.

Studies have shown that during the 10-year period from 1978 to 1988, global output of electricity grew, on the average, 3.8% per year (see Table 2). During the same period, annual growth of consumption in the former U.S.S.R. was 3.6%, and in Ukraine, 2.5%. It is important to note that during this period the rate of growth in several countries was considerably above the world average: in Brazil, India, China, and the Republic of South Africa, the rates of growth were from 7 to 10% per year. High rates of growth (about 5% per year) in comparison with Ukraine were also experienced in Canada, France, Sweden, and Australia. In some nations there were periods during which the output of electricity did not grow at all, or even declined. However, in the world as a whole, output grew more rapidly during the last five years.

Table 2. Dynamics of Electricity Output in the Countries that are the Largest Producers

Country	Output of Electricity, billion kWh		Average Annual Rates of Growth,%		
	1978	1988	Over 10 Years	Over First 5 Years	Over Second 5 Years
Whole World	7,512	10,950	3.8	3.0	4.6
U.S.A.	2,400	2,920	2.0	0.7	3.3
U.S.S.R.	1,202	1,705	3.6	3.4	3.8
Ukraine	208	266	2.5	2.3	2.6
Canada	316	495	4.6	4.8	4.4
Japan	554	740	2.9	1.1	4.6
China	256	543	7.8	6.5	9.1
Germany	345	415	1.9	0.6	3.0
Great Britain	288	305	0.6	0.8	2.0
France	226	380	5.3	5.0	5.7
Brazil	83	220	10.2	11.8	8.7
India	98	215	8.2	6.5	9.8
Italy	175	202	1.4	0.8	2.1
Republic of S. Africa	77	153	7.2	5.3	9.1
Sweden	91	148	5.0	2.4	7.7
Poland	116	144	2.2	1.7	2.7
Australia	83	134	4.9	5.3	4.6

Source: U.S.S.R.: Donbass is the base for electric power in Ukraine, 1991, J. Donetsk, V. B. Yegorova, V. V. Yershevish, A. A. Reshetniak.

The data in Table 2 allow us to draw some conclusions: first, overall world production of electricity continues to grow at rather high rates; and second, energy-saving technology in some countries reduced the growth of electricity production but did not affect the general upward trend.

In the Ukrainian economic plan (the General Project for Ukrainian Development to 2005) the necessary level of domestic consumption of electricity is set at 390 billion kWh. This is based on the assumption that consumption of electricity will grow 1.43 times from the 1990 level.

The problem of providing the Ukrainian economy with fuel and power for both the immediate future and to 2010 has become extremely acute because of the curtailment of further development of nuclear energy in the republic. The share of supply of fuel and power by the Ukrainian producers is expected to decline to 40–50% by 2005, as compared to 70% in 1990. No solution to this problem of energy deficiency appears to be available.

First, Ukraine cannot expect significant amounts of electricity to come from neighboring regions because all of them have been oriented to develop nuclear power plants, and they face energy shortages after discontinuation of the development of nuclear power projects in Belorussia and central regions of the European part of the Russian and North Caucasus.

Second, realization of plans to increase the supply of natural gas for Ukraine is problematic because of declining rates of growth of natural gas production in the republics of the former Soviet Union. The problem is accelerated by a trend toward increasing use of natural gas for nonenergy purposes, such as a raw material for the chemical industry in regions where natural gas reserves are located. A similar situation also exists with respect to coal from the Kuznetsk basin in Siberia, which otherwise would be a source of fuel for Ukraine.

Third, for all practical purposes, the potential for development of hydroenergy resources in Ukraine is fully exhausted. One can, however, visualize reconstruction or construction of locally significant small hydroelectric power plants on minor rivers. Less realistic—at least in the near future—is the possibility of constructing major hydroelectric plants in other republics that are designed to transmit electricity to Ukraine.

Fourth, the potential for substitution of nontraditional energy sources such as wind or solar energy for traditional fossil fuels such as coal, oil, and natural gas is not significant at the present time. As an illustration, to replace a thermal power generating unit of 800,000 kW such as the Slavianskaia thermal power station in the Donbass (Donbets), it would be necessary to operate no less than 8,000 wind powered units with a capacity of 100 kW each. There is no realistic possibility that such conversion to wind power could occur.

It is therefore clear that in the new conditions of economic development, providing Ukraine with adequate energy will require major planning and policy revisions. New patterns of development in the energy sector will have to emerge. It also follows that the role of the Donbass as Ukraine's fuel base will be much enhanced. Prudent policymaking requires reevaluation of the possibilities of the Donbass from the point of view of increasing the exploitation of Donbass coal. Such reevaluation must consider the economic and ecological impacts of increased use of Donbass coal reserves.

THE ROLE OF THE DONBASS COAL REGION IN THE ECONOMIC DEVELOPMENT OF UKRAINE

The Donbass is one of the most highly developed industrial regions of Ukraine. Its population of 8.2 million represents 22% of the republic's total. It has more than a quarter of all the industrial potential of the republic, and provides 80% of coal output.

Coal production in the Donbass has declined dramatically over the last 15 years from a maximum of 191.4 million tons in 1976 to 169.7 million tons in 1988. In 1989 the decline can be attributed to strikes. That year coal production decreased by almost 11 million tons. In 1990 another decline of more than 10 million tons occurred (see Table 3).

Table 3. Prospects of Coal Output in Ukraine, million tons

	1988	1989	1990	1995	2000	2005	2010
Ukraine	191.7	180.1	164.8	170.0	172.0	175.0	178.0
Ukrainian							
Donbass	169.7	157.5	145.0	150.0	154.3	158.2	164.5
Coal	73.2	66.7	64.4	71.8	76.1	77.5	81.7
Thermal	96.5	90.8	80.6	78.7	78.2	80.7	82.8

Source: Ukrainian Ministry of Economy, 1991.

The mining and geological conditions of the Donbass are challenging. As a result of the depth of mines and the difficult geological conditions, operating costs of coal production are considerable. More than half of the coal comes from mines with shafts that exceed 600 meters in depth, while 12% comes from mines that are more than 1,000 meters deep. The average thickness of seams is 1.12 meters, and extraction out of seams ranging 0.7–1.0 meters in depth accounts for 25.8% of production.

During the last 15 years the quality of coal has decreased dramatically because of changing mining technology. This technology change was not matched by a corresponding increase in the capacities of coal preparation plants. As a result, the ash content in coal for thermal electricity plants has increased from 29.5% in 1975 to 36.2% in 1988. It should be pointed out, however, that over 85% of coal used by thermal plants has no preparation. As a result, pollution has grown rapidly. The energy sector is responsible for 44% of the total amount of all pollution in Donbass. It is estimated that about 2 million tons of air pollutants are generated by the energy-generating sector. The coal industry alone is responsible for damage to 14,000 hectares of land.

Natural resources provide the base of the Donbass industrial potential, but the concentration of heavy industry has also led to environmental damage. The possibilities for the region's further development depend to a large extent on solutions to environmental problems being found. This represents a major negative constraint.

Unless effective and timely measures are taken, the level of Donbass coal production will continue to decline due to depletion of reserves at many operating mines. To stabilize production at its present level, it is necessary to compensate for depletion of reserves at existing mines by construction of new mines and expansion of existing ones where adequate reserves exist. Existing coal reserves make it possible to increase the present level of coal production, including output of coal used in thermal power plants. Within the Ukrainian part of the Donbass there are 72 proven locations for coal mining with a total capacity of 128 million tons per year. Of those, 43 sites are for new mines and 29 are for expansion of old mining facilities.

The expected production of coal in Ukraine by 2005 is estimated at about 175 million tons (see Table 3). That level of coal production will not be adequate to sustain current levels of electricity generation. Production of electricity will, thus, decrease the deficit amounting 60 billion kWh, and this deficit in electricity production will not be offset by other available fuel. Thus, the deficit for 2005 is estimated at approximately 20 million tons of coal.

The most realistic strategy for Ukraine from the present until the year 2005 is to solve the problem of domestic energy demand by increasing coal production in the Donbass. Coal is the primary energy resource available in Ukraine and the coal reserves of the Donbass provide the fuel base of Ukraine.

REGIONAL POLICY

Changes in the system of management in the Ukrainian economy have resulted in drastic growth in independence of regions. In the new economic system, local authorities and the public will play a larger role in choosing strategy for the development of the energy sector in the Donbass, including the solution of the social and environmental problems associated with such development.

To ascertain the attitude of the public and the local authorities toward energy sector development, the Institute of Industrial Economics of the Ukrainian Academy of Sciences launched a survey in the Donbass of the view of the city and regional Soviets of People's Deputies (elected city and regional councils), of environmental protection committees, of regional Soviets of Trade Unions, and of miners' strike committees. The survey examined approaches to solving economic, social, and environmental problems that would be followed in making decisions associated with transition of the Donbass economy to a market economy and the reconstruction of its industrial potential.

The local authorities and public underestimated the problems and the role that they will play in solving them. Analyses of the responses indicated that the attitude of the local authorities and public toward the problems were different. It was found that organizations that are in charge of particular aspects of Donbass development approached the problems one-sidedly—from their own particular positions—without viewing the problems in the full complexity.

The resource-producing regions that are dominated by large coal extraction enterprises seem to lack the resilience to renew themselves. Coal mining and its ancillary activities can contribute greatly to the growth of the regional economics. However, major projects can impose substantial changes on the economic and social character of small communities. Many communities that owe their existence to coal mining cease to be economically viable when mining ceases. Many areas of the Donbass derive most of their income from the coal industry and are particularly vulnerable. If the economically recoverable coal reserves ever run out, or if the governmental subsidies end, these areas will be faced with a limited ability to absorb such impacts.

In light of these complex interrelations, what priorities should be given to the various goals, and what policies should be implemented to encourage coal regions? It is possible to understand that if economic problems arise in the mining areas, communities of these areas cannot survive without government aid provided in direct and undirect ways.

Transition to a market economy will put into practice new styles of economic behavior by local coal producers and new forms of economic relations between coal enterprises and their consumers, government, local authorities, and the public.

At the beginning, the implementation of new economic relations requires a flexible and supportive role for government toward the coal industry. The objectives of government in this context are:

1. to provide a fair and balanced fiscal and regulatory framework;
2. to foster the development of the coal industry as a foundation for economic development;
3. to promote improved technological performance and increased efficiency in all facets of the industry;
4. to provide economic and scientific information required by the industry and the

general public;
5. to consider balanced and rational resources development that minimizes adverse environmental impacts of the production and utilization of coal;
6. to promote research and development as a means of identifying new users of coal;
7. to take a variety of measures to improve the investment environment, including accelerating infrastructure construction, perfecting economic legislation, training personnel, and so forth.

A regional policy for coal regions should aim to achieve a consensus among the many interests of a whole society and these separate regions. From this point of view the local authorities will need to carefully monitor development of the Donbass coal region and to fill gaps as they become evident, because the Donbass possesses many features of old industrialized regions characterized by a long history of industrial development.

Regional policy also must work to mobilize the growth potential of regions in order to improve the structure of the economy and to solve environmental and social problems. It involves a coordinated approach to regional problems and cooperation between different levels of government and between the public and industry. Through consensus-based decision making, regional policy should produce guidelines for implementing aid for coal regions based on the following elements:

1. technology and innovation, particularly the promotion of technology-oriented new enterprise formation and technology transfer;
2. planning to improve the coordination of industrial problems and environmental infrastructure;
3. culture and leisure infrastructure;
4. program for labor training.

Regional policy is considered to be a medium- to long-term strategy involving the removal of obstacles to regional development and structural change. The nature of the strategy is to provide "favorable conditions" for investment and to provide a limited amount of public finance for economically relevant infrastructure.

The move to a market economy means that Ukraine intends that its economic orientation be guided by market forces. This transition suggests a significant increase of power and obligations for local authorities that have rights to use economic market-oriented instruments to pursue their purposes in regional development. Local authorities can set up different policies to stimulate specific sectors of activities and to implement local forms of financial incentives for industry.

Rent collection is one of the major instruments of resource management. It gives the local government greater latitude to manage the resources they own. A regional economic strategy could establish a special fund to help maintain, strengthen, and diversify the regional economy, to develop a positive business climate, to provide a stable and progressive environment for investment and business development, and to upgrade Donbass resources into higher value-added products before leaving the region.

It is possible to consider royalties and maybe fuel or energy-use fees as a main source of regional funds to finance the creation, extension and restructuring of coal mines (and enterprises that use coal and by-products) to pay for conservation and pollution control, and to underwrite diversification of the regional economy.

Local government would be directly responsible for the allocation of investment in regional economy and for finding solutions to social and environmental problems. In this connection, it must provide incentives to the different kinds of investment projects through cost-sharing with coal enterprises and foreign companies, and assignment grants for starting small business. It is possible to implement regulations that could influence the behavior of coal producers and their consumers in a desirable direction. Creation of a regional stock exchange also would be very useful to stimulate economic public initiative and to support new businesses.

It is necessary to organize special market institutions or to adopt the function of existing institutions to pursue the objectives of new regulatory policy, because all exploration and development activities must receive government approval and must comply with established standards.

Environmental damage is widely viewed as a potential constraint on the revitalization of coal. It is important to emphasize that extraction and utilization of coal are largely based on technologies developed at a time when sensitivity to environmental impacts was minimal. Conflict exist between republican and regional interests. Therefore, the institutions for coal and the environment must take account of the needs of local communities, while at the same time ensuring that national and international standards are enforced.

Public hearings would provide an important opportunity for different points of view to be aired in an orderly semiformal forum. Hearings allow for an open, public testing of technical, environmental, social, and economic evidence from any party with the accompanying assurance that all relevant arguments, for and against, will be heard. Public hearings are an opportunity for the applicant (the company) and people who may be affected by a proposed development to explain their views, concerns, or objections in detail. Also, proposals to add new capacity could be reviewed by the regulatory commissions to verify that the new capacity is needed.

It is necessary to recommend that solving the problems of the energy sector's development in the Donbass requires the creation of a mechanism for joint participation between enterprises belonging to the energy sector, their consumers, local governments, and the public in the new planning and regulation of regional development (see Table 4).

Table 4. Functions of Various Levels of Government and Energy Sector in the Protection of the Environment in the Context of a Market Economy

State Government	Local Government	Energy Sector
1. Establish rules for economic activities and put them into practice.	1. Work out policy that achieves a consensus of the public interest and the interest of energy sector's enterprises.	1. Make decisions oriented toward achievement of goals provided by government's policies.
2. Act as arbitrator of disputes.	2. Control and assessment of the public use of natural resources.	2. Monitor ecological needs and improve production technology to reduce environmental damage.
3. Foster market relations between enterprises.	3. Maintain quality of environmental protection norms in the region	3. Strive for more efficient utilization of fuel and by-products.
4. Determine social and ecological priorities.	4. Support enterprises in making economical decisions and improving the environment.	4. Overcome accumulated balances in the use of natural resources.
5. Establish norms of of environmental quality for the future.	5. Provide feedbacks to achieve stable and effective development of the region.	
	6. Develop separate branch of activities to environment protection.	

Without adequate regulations to guide the operations of enterprises, there will not be enough incentives to restrain the environmentally damaging behavior of producers and users of energy resources. It should be the responsibility of the Ukrainian government to formulate general rules of economic activities, of local governments to work out the specific policies that achieve a consensus between public and energy producers' interests. These policies should provide support to enterprises in making economic decisions and improving the environment, as well as providing feedback to achieve stable and effective development of the region by using different fiscal and regulatory instruments.

CONCLUSIONS

1. In the new conditions of economic development, the concept of providing Ukraine with adequate energy has changed greatly. New patterns of development in the energy sector must emerge.

Providing reliable energy resources has been the Ukrainian energy sector's obligation for decades, but there is more to energy policy than making sure that fuel and power are available on demand. Needs evolve over time. Customers change, as do their concerns and priorities. These customer values must be factored into working out long-range energy policies that reflect the accepted decisions and implement the plans necessary to meet future requirements. These requirements are substantial, and without timely decisions on new demand and supply options, it will not be possible to achieve these objectives.

The objectives of government energy policy are to assure adequate, secure, and environmentally acceptable supplies of energy in the forms that people want and at the least costs practicable in the long term. It is possible to achieve these objectives by adopting new approaches for economic policies in the energy sector.

2. The Donbass is the most available Ukrainian fuel base and its role will be much enhanced. This requires a reevaluation of the possibilities of its development and of adverse economic and ecological impacts.

3. The system of management in the coal industry needs major structural reforms in a variety of areas to generate new economic relations and a healthy investment climate. The new economic environment requires a new response pattern. For this new phase of economic development of Ukraine, it is necessary to have appropriate behavior patterns for individuals, as well as for institutions and enterprises.

The Ukrainian economy is in transition to a market economy. In such a situation, with all participants in the economic system acting independently in different directions, unanticipated and dissonant consequences result. The economy cannot be self-organized without creation of adequate market mechanisms and institutions that meet the need for a new economic order. For these purposes a very important role of different levels of government is to provide appropriate policies to organize and maintain conditions that allow for the evolution of economic interactions based on competition.

4. A mechanism of financial and economic regulation of coal enterprises must be adequate to conform to the new economic relations. Taxes have to be the general form for interrelations between the government, local authorities, and the coal mining industry.

5. Regulatory policy for the coal mining industry can employ different economic instruments that are allowed to manage economic behavior of coal mines. The use of these instruments (such as investment tax credits, capital cost allowances, earned depletion allowances, resource allowances, flow-through

shares, limited partnerships, etc.) would support and maintain mining operations while reflecting the peculiar features of mining, including mineral depletion, uncertainty of exploration, and the importance of the industry to the Ukrainian economy.

6. In the present system, underground natural resources belong to the state, but once extracted, ownership is transferred without charge to the miners' collective of the mining enterprise. To eliminate this contradiction, a system of royalties should be implemented.

A royalty regime will give local communities an equitable share of profits from the development of regional mineral resources. Royalty regimes can be made sensitive to short-term changes in market prices. Furthermore, a coal royalty formula could be based on costs, revenue, and investment. The royalty would increase with the level of profits achieved. The flexible royalty rate could be increased from a minimum rate on small or marginally economic projects to higher levels on more profitable operations.

7. Royalty revenue from coal can be one of the main sources of special regional funds to finance the creation, extension, and restructuring of coal mines and enterprises that used coal and its by-products to finance conservation and pollution control, and to finance diversification of the regional economy. Donbass has many environmental problems, so it would be desirable to fix the fuel or energy-use fees that could be used as an additional source for regional funds to finance the restoration of damaged areas.

8. The government's interference in the economic activities of the energy sector and the coal industry, in particular, must be predictable. All policy instruments should be used on a long-term basis. Therefore, the approach to regulatory policy must establish a clear and consistent framework within which enterprises can operate.

The regulatory framework must embody policy objectives such as: economic energy efficiency, environmental protection, development infrastructure, introducing new technologies, and supporting research and development. To achieve desired effects, it is possible to use the regulatory and economic instruments that tend to focus on each of these specific areas. The aids to encourage the coal industry and coal consumers must be provided by granting economic incentives to attain the purposes considered above but not to cover the operating expenditures of coal mines.

9. A pricing system of coal products should be determined by their supply and demand, taking into account their quality from an ecological point of view. This means that a system of interrelations between mines and suppliers of materials and equipment, as well as consumers of coal products, must be reflected in market signals. Subsidies for mines in existing form must be reduced. Because of price control, energy consumption has been subsidized, but not conservation; this weakens incentives for domestic coal output and technological advance leading to supply imbalance. It is better in a transitional

period to provide granting subsidies to coal consumers on the basis that this would stimulate them to save and rationally use fuel and energy resources.

10. Local authorities would be directly responsible for allocation of investment in the regional economy and for finding solutions to social and environmental problems. The responsibility for the inherent regional problems must be shared between different levels of government and industry.

The aim of providing regional policy must be the mobilization of regional potential in order to improve the structure of economy.

11. Public opinion and the local authorities affect the development of the coal industry. Therefore, it is necessary to create a mechanism for interactions between the energy sector, local authorities, and the public, and to implement a public hearing procedure. This procedure would provide an important opportunity for different points of view to be aired which will assist in solving regional problems.

PART VII

ECONOMICS, FINANCE, AND BANKING

The U.S.S.R., before its decentralization and eventual breakup, had begun to try to reform its economic system, including banking practices and bank regulation and currency policy. The development of a viable financial system in the Russian Federation, as well as in other states of the former U.S.S.R., is a unique process with little applicable precedent in the modern world. The seven chapters in Part VII provide an overview of the early development of these financial systems.

Robert B. Charles' paper correctly observes that historic free market forces inside the former U.S.S.R. and the nature and pace of regional economic redevelopment will occur more rapidly in the absence of premature political reunion. Charles asserts four reasons why the former republics should be encouraged to develop independently: (1) cultural cohesion can be a positive economic force; (2) all-Union economies of scale are illusory; (3) pre-Soviet economic history reveals inherent entrepreneurial spirit; and (4) post-Soviet economic history confirms the Russian indigenous entrepreneurial spirit.

The paper by Jonah Otelsberg recognizes that the "marketing concept" of organizing economic activity is less appropriate in a society where the reigning reality is scarcity. The paper suggests that the former U.S.S.R. cannot create a market economy by copying the institutions and behaviors that now exist in the Western nations. Instead, Otelsberg stresses that the former Soviet Union must go through the stages that the Western countries have gone through in their transition from economies driven by limited demand.

Temiruz A. Beridze's paper addresses "economic sovereignty" during Russia's transitional period to a market economy. The paper concludes that political and economic sovereignty are both distinct and interconnected elements of a single whole. The paper stresses the need to improve the economy in order to improve the political sphere.

Olga Floroff's paper traces the development of Russia's corporate and joint-venture laws. The paper discusses the emergence of joint-stock companies in the former U.S.S.R. and the centralization of these companies through the Ministry of Finance of the RSFSR. Floroff concludes that while the new RSFSR laws encourage foreign investment, the instability of the region comprising the former U.S.S.R. slows down the pace of development of business relations between foreign business entities and soviet enterprises.

Nicholas N. Kozlov's paper traces the developments of Russia's financial system. It addresses early regulations in the sphere of foreign currency operations. The paper observes that the new regulations were an effort to simultaneously encourage the development of decentralized economic activity inside Russia on a ruble basis as well as to provide a source of hard currency for legitimate decentralized foreign trade. Kozlov argues forcefully that one of the most serious difficulties is to reform macroeconomic arrangements without first reforming the financial and fiscal institutions appropriate to cope with decentralized activity.

The paper by Sergei N. Gonchar and Tatiana U. Frolova examines early banking developments in the former republics of the Soviet Union. The paper addresses the unique characteristics of the "Soviet" commercial banks and stresses that the peculiarities of banking in the Russian Federation (as well as in other republics) should not be interpreted as an absence of conformity of the banking system to the demands of the market economy.

James W. Weller's paper explains the "dual" banking system in the United States and its evolution. It analyzes the benefits and costs of the U.S. system and examines recent congressional actions that attempt to narrow the authority of the states in the banking system. Weller explores the implications that the U.S. system may have for the developing banking system of the former U.S.S.R.

31

The Invisible Thread: Free Market Forces in Pre- and Post-Soviet Russia

Robert B. Charles

This paper presents a simple thesis:[1] Current and historic free market forces inside the former Soviet Union suggest that the region's economic redevelopment will occur more rapidly in the absence of near-term political reunion among the republics than in the presence of such a constraint.[2]

In October 1991, 12 republics reached a tentative accord on economic cooperation.[3] In December 1991 the Commonwealth of Independent States was declared.[4] During the same month, Gorbachev ceded the Union's nuclear arsenal to Boris Yeltsin's reconstituted Russia.[5] The significance of these events and their impact on countervailing republic and subrepublic claims to "economic sovereignty"[6] remain unclear. What is clear is this: Most former republics, and subrepublic nationalities, recognize a need for economic cooperation; at the same time, they maintain a strong "desire for national self-assertion,"[7] which threatens to destabilize any near-term political reunion.

This paper's thesis rests on three beliefs: (1) The former Soviet Union will require extensive foreign investments to redevelop.[8] (2) Foreign investment will be attracted only by stable economic conditions.[9] (3) Stable economic conditions will result more swiftly from decentralized, politically and economically sovereign, albeit cooperative, nation-states than from a premature political reunion.[10] The first two beliefs should not be controversial. The third requires some defending.

Four reasons explain why the former republics, or in some instances subrepublics, should be encouraged to develop independently: (1) cultural cohesion can be a positive economic force; (2) all-Union economies of scale are illusory; (3) pre-Soviet economic history reveals inherent entrepreneurial spirit; and (4) post-Soviet economic history confirms the Russian, and more generalized, indigenous entrepreneurial spirit.

CULTURAL COHESION CAN BE A POSITIVE ECONOMIC FORCE

The former Soviet Union contains nearly 200 ethnic groups or nationalities.[11] These ethnic groups, which differ markedly in their education, income, exposure to industrial development, geographic concentrations, historic traditions, and various indicia of culture, are not well integrated.

While 90% of the former Soviet population lives on one-eighth of the northern Eurasian land mass, most ethnic groups are concentrated. The Slavic peoples, for example, are found chiefly in the western portions of the former Union and Siberia; the Turkic peoples in Middle Asia, the Volga Valley, and Yakutia; the Mongol peoples in the Lower Volga and around Lake Baikal; races related to the Finns and Balts in the extreme northwest; and paleo-Asiatics and Tungus in the northeast.[12]

While the evils of nationalism are well known, and properly feared,[13] little attention has been paid, of late, to the hidden economic advantages in properly focused nationalism; cultural cohesion is one. Addressing this issue, Ludwig von Mises, F. A. Hayek's teacher, observed: "The dissolution of the multinational State gets rid of many superfluous complications because it separates territories from each other that are compactly inhabited by the members of one people."[14]

As Marshall Goldman points out, "the Central Asians and people of the Caucasus tend to hold on tenaciously to their native languages," a condition "likely to complicate communications in a rapidly integrated work force."[15] Von Mises goes a step further, linking national identity to the realization of economic aspirations.

> If only language questions . . . were the object of the national struggle, then one could think of paving the way for peace between peoples by special treatment of those questions. But the national struggle is not at all limited to schools and educational institutions, and to the official language of the courts and authorities. It embraces all of political life, even all that which . . . ties a unifying bond around the nations, the so-called economic aspect.[16]

Co-opting nationalism is not the only rationale for encouraging independent economic development. Other efficiencies result from encouraging an ethnically cohesive region to reflect its culture.

Before providing examples of positive differentiation, it should be noted that certain laws will have to be promulgated, explained, and enforced throughout the awakening post-Soviet Eurasian cultures. Equal treatment of minorities, privatization of property, and the development of a continental free trade zone head the list of important cross-cultural laws.[17] Having said this, some regions will likely value environmental protection over the rapid excavation of natural resources; others will favor the reverse approach. Some will promote economic growth based on services rather than manufacturing—for example, favoring tourism over production of heavy equipment; others will see great opportunity in reshaping the manufacturing sector. Some will see foreign investment as a boon, others as a bane. Some will, upon satisfying basic consumer needs, choose to move cautiously toward luxury items. Others will move swiftly to emulate the West. Finally, others may wish to rediscover their cultural roots, engaging in a bit of expurgation, after 70 years of Soviet trampling.

In short, acknowledging and accommodating the patchwork of nationalities spread over post-Soviet Eurasia is the fastest way to progress. The essential idea: secure each patch, then integrate these stable patches. Such a prescription does not controvert those who argue for coordinating agreements or for a continental free trade zone. Indeed, it provides the necessary stable participants for that process. With proper protection for minorities, independent, culturally cohesive nation-states should advance more rapidly than any alternative.

ALL-UNION ECONOMIES OF SCALE ARE ILLUSORY

No matter what the fate of the current Commonwealth of Independent States, a deep antipathy for centralized government will live in the hearts of those who were once counted Soviet citizens. In the near term, a basic fear of central authority will undercut what once seemed perfect economies of scale.

Two points need elaboration. One: Any attempt at continued central public control, even under Russian auspices, of formerly all-Union enterprises will be futile. These lingering vestiges of command decision making are dinosaurs—large, inefficient, and destined for extinction. Two: Once privatized, most all-Union enterprises will naturally disintegrate. Allocative ineffiiencies[18] and X-inefficiencies[19] will strongly encourage their breakup, once genuine competition begins. The reason for this is that crucial microeconomic questions will be more difficult to answer within any enterprise attempting to span the former Union. What product to produce, how to motivate culturally and geographically disparate workers, how to ferret out corruption, how to insure accountability, how to negotiate contracts with differing labor forces, how to coordinate input sourcing, marketing, and distribution are examples of issues much more readily addressed, particularly in a high-risk environment, by smaller enterprises.

An example: The U.S.S.R. rail system, although antiquated, was once integrated. Upon dissolution, independent republics began to seize the rolling stock.[20] To compound the disarray, manufacturers of rolling stock are spread throughout the former Union; for example, while "98 percent" of Ukraine's locomotives are produced in that republic, "the components for them are produced by 800 different factories which are situated all over the Soviet Union."[21] To continue such far-flung transcontinental production lines would not only be a waste of resources, it would now be impossible.

Likewise, the Soviet gas industry, under Gasprom, has long attempted to coordinate 50 enterprises Unionwide. While republic-level coordination may be required in the near term, former republics are likely to assert control and seek private developers as soon as direct sale of energy reserves becomes possible on the world market. Consider the Moscow Electrical Grid, which long served as the Union's coordinator of electrical energy; its continued existence will likely be premised on any benefits it offers those who supply energy and those who can afford it.

Similarly, the quixotic telecommunications system in the non-Baltic former Union no longer offers any advantage over the staged integration of modernized regional systems. As one expert stated in late 1991: "Expect to see, at the republic level, both regional and local attempts to rehabilitate the telephone system rather than any central effort."[22]

PRE-SOVIET ECONOMIC HISTORY REVEALS INHERENT ENTREPRENEURIAL SPIRIT

The myth of a pre-Soviet antientrepreneurial predisposition among Russians especially, and adjoining nationalities occasionally, should be dispelled once and for all.

First, pre-Soviet Russia, especially between 1890 and 1914, was tremendously inventive, creative, and productive.[23] After a slow start and the burdens inherent in shedding serfdom in 1861, it was on its way to becoming as industrialized and productive as the leading Western economies of the day.[24]

Scholars who are ready to blur the distinction between atheistic Soviet totalitarianism and Orthodox tsarist monarchy simply misread history. A more cerebral observer of the period, Dr. Nicholas S. Timasheff, noted:

> Beginning with the last decades of the nineteenth century, the Russian novel, Russian music, and the Russian theater, especially the Russian ballet, deeply influenced Western European art production. . . . As regards the standard of living, purely chronological comparisons are unfair. To judge correctly the state of the labor class in Russia late in the nineteenth century, one should rather compare it with that of England in the early nineteenth century, when capitalism was in the state of infancy in that country. Anyone who has read Engel's famous book will hardly assert that the Russian government and the Russian industrialists oppressed the lower class more than their British counterparts.[25]

In short, while tsarist Russia in the late nineteenth century lagged Western Europe's leading economies, it was advancing swiftly and also contributing enormously to the development of European civilization.[26]

The free market spirit of pre-Soviet Russia was both deliberate and well-known. As early as Peter the Great, "entrepreneurship was encouraged."[27] Even

Lenin knew about Russia's entrepreneurial roots. His short-lived New Economic Policy or "NEP" (1921–38) was an undisguised attempt to undo damage done by the civil war and the 1920 Nationalization Decree, by recourse to private enterprise. Until NEP was crushed by Soviet planners, it worked.[28]

Other examples of pre-Soviet entrepreneurialism abound. Petr Arkad'evich Stolypin's 1906 reforms allowed peasants to set up their own farms. The initiative was plainly successful. Some 70 years later, its remnants drew this observation from Hedrick Smith:

> Although the private plots constitute approximately 1 percent of the land under cultivation in the Soviet Union, the Communist press reported that 27% of the total value of agricultural output was generated by these plots in 1973. The productivity per acre on the private plots was approximately 40 times higher than that on the collectively farmed land.[29]

What Smith observed was the beleaguered, yet surviving, spirit of pre-Soviet Russian entrepreneurialism.

POST-SOVIET ECONOMIC HISTORY REVEALS THE RESILIENCE OF INDIGENOUS ENTREPRENEURIAL SPIRIT

There is much that is discouraging to be said about the former Soviet economy.[30] There is also the shadow of danger cast by rising popular discontent in post-Soviet Russia.[31] On the other hand, there is also dispassionate reason for hope. There are significant accomplishments and vast opportunities.

Commercial banks are being formed, such as the North Trad Bank (NTB) in St. Petersburg, founded in June 1991, valued at 30 million rubles, and boasting 8 offices and 60 employees.[32] Banks, with local depositors' faith, spur investment. NTB is a representative example; it has invested 60 percent of its assets in small businesses. Commercial banks are an important gateway of market entry for foreign firms. Thriving commercial banks located in Ukraine include Ukrinbank, Vidrodgennia (Renaissance), Ukrsotsbank (Head of the Board) in Kiev; AMB Bank in Odessa; Ugleprogressbank in Voroshilovgrad; and Transformatorbank in Zaporoshye.[33] Similarly, Uzbekistan is home to Naman-ganbank in Namangan, Shark in Samarkand, and Aviabank in Tashkent.[34] Other regions are undergoing parallel developments.

Securities and commodities exchanges, currently numbering some 300 across the former Union,[35] have been formed to facilitate free trade. Examples include the St. Petersburg Commodities Exchange, the Baltic Stock Exchange,[36] and the Moscow, St. Petersburg, and Tallinn Stock Exchanges.[37]

Independent television stations are popping up. NIKA, an independent Russian broadcasting corporation, licensed by Russia, has been active since 1988 in radio and television.[38]

Advanced state enterprises are being subdivided and privatized. Indigenous high-technology companies are emerging. Electronics and computers are among the industries with the steepest growth curves. For example, Syntex-Inforex (SI) is a Dubna company (65 miles north of Moscow) that has developed a computer network, produces its own modems, and is seeking to use satellite transmissions for business communications to North America and Europe.[39] Similarly, Elekton and Syjaskomputerservice, electronics and computer companies in the Tatar area, demonstrate that activity is not focused solely in Moscow.[40]

Elsewhere, laws on foreign investment, tailored to the fears and aspirations of the particular republic, are fresh off the presses.[41] Estonia's is a progressive example. In part, it reads: "a Foreign Investor shall have the same rights and obligations as legal persons and citizens, unless otherwise stipulated."[42] While regulation and licensing are in evidence, one need only consult an American law for evidence that free market forces can prevail despite substantial regulation and restriction.

Nor are the new laws going unnoticed. As early as November 1990, 200 joint ventures were registered in St. Petersburg, 39 of which were apparently active.[43] Established joint ventures, such as those involving McDonalds and Combustion Engineering,[44] are being joined by new market entrants. For example, IBM has opened offices in Moscow and St. Petersburg, with offices in Ukraine expected to follow.[45]

Nor should fresh opportunities be forgotten. Certain former state enterprises offer considerable potential. Puschino, a small town near Moscow, houses, for example, eight advanced biological research centers, none of which boasts any measurable business activity.[46]

Opportunities for investment in seemingly remote autonomous areas are too numerous to list. A few examples may suffice. The Tatar area offers undeveloped potential in oil, chemicals, laser processing, computers, electronics, medical instruments, and plastics, on top of more traditional heavy equipment manufacturing. The Baltics, while lacking raw materials, have well-developed economic structures. Georgia has a strong tradition of manufacturing. Belorussia, strong in basic textile, food, electrical, and agricultural equipment, has a particularly well-educated population. Kazakhstan is rich in oil, gas, and metals, as well as other minerals. Most of the other former republics offer considerable natural resources, it not also enthusiasm for market reform.

No one could possibly catalog the economic activity afoot in the former Union. This may, in deference to Adam Smith, turn out to be a good thing. In any event, pre-Soviet entrepreneurialism is, contrary to its long-time scholarly detractors,[47] certainly reawakening.

CONCLUSION: LATE 1991

Where once there crouched the Soviet Union, there now stands a towering question mark. No one can rule out the possibility that a reconstituted, pluralistic Union could permit stable economic growth. Nor can anyone rule out the possibility that a political reunion could facilitate reassertion of authoritarian control. However, the cultural diversity of the former republics, their past and present entrepreneurial spirit, and the absence of economically advantageous alternatives mitigate in favor of independent redevelopment. Western nations, businesses, and scholars should, in short, encourage cooperation among politically and economically sovereign nation-states in post-Soviet Eurasia. If we do, they will likely progress rapidly, with Adam Smith's "invisible hand" gently pulling an invisible thread between and among them.

EPILOGUE: LATE 1993

The foregoing was written in late 1991. In late 1993, we have seen a second coup attempt, watched the Russian Parliament dissolved and Constitution upended, seen the Russian Parliament building itself seized by communist hardliners and scorched in a firefight, and witnessed President Yeltsin's desperate reassertion of authority over the unwieldy process of fundamental change.

In fact, since late 1991, a great deal has transpired in Russia and its sister nation-states. New laws have been passed, many of them intended to encourage private investment. These laws include a variety of statutes and decrees on commercial issues, including foreign investment,[48] hard currency,[49] property,[50] exports and imports,[51] privatization,[52] and antitrust or anti-monopoly laws.[53] Other important Russian laws have also been promulgated since mid-1991.[54] Similarly, a flotilla of laws has been promulgated in the non-Russian former republics.[55]

Since mid-1991, Russia's debt has grown to approximately $69 billion, while its debt-service to export ratio has recovered to 38% (in 1992), simultaneously suggesting an ability to pay down this debt.

The Freedom Support Act[56] was enacted by the U.S. Congress and signed by President George Bush in October 1992. This law constituted "America's first comprehensive legislation for the support of economic and democratic development of the former Soviet Union."[57] At the 1993 Vancouver Summit, the U.S.A. committed to disbursement of $1.6 billion in additional aid to the former Soviet republics. The FY94 presidential budget forecast $1.1 billion in additional assistance for the former republics, and U.S. Treasury Secretary Lloyd Bentson pledged a further $1.8 billion in aid at the G-7 meeting in 1993.[58]

In 1992 the U.S. Overseas Private Investment Corporation (OPIC) began business in Russia, and the U.S. Trade and Development Agency (TDA) began offering grants to U.S. firms for conducting feasibility studies on Russian projects. Likewise, the European Bank for Reconstruction and Development (EBRD) authorized $300 million in aid to Russia, and to the other republics, of which the G-7 countries are committed to pay one-half.

Most recently, on September 28, 1993, the U.S. House of Representatives appropriated "$603,820,000 for assistance for the New Independent States of the former Soviet Union."[59] A substantial amount of this sum is dedicated to meeting America's commitment to EBRD; this appropriation should also provide benefits to other former republics, especially Ukraine and the Far East. That appropriation also effectively permits the Russian-American Enterprise Fund to "open its doors" for business.[60]

An air of discouragement that plainly hung low over a broken Union in late 1991 has lightened—to a degree. New storm clouds have, however, blown in. The great hopes of these infant nations, tied as they are to a belief in themselves, in capitalism, and in entrepreneurialism, have brought new uncertainties. Organized crime, disorganized and ineffective government, and violent nationalistic clashes are among the new uncertainties. Also hovering nearby is the threat that fragile and aspiring democracies could be suffocated under the yoke of authoritarianism.

Especially in Russia, there is a peculiar mixture of chaos and unquantifiable opportunity. The industries associated with oil, basic services, and various scientific disciplines show enormous promise. There is also a spiritual reawakening afoot, adding what appears to be a new stability to the tortoiselike transition from hopelessness to hope, even if that hope now seems at the rainbow's end. There is plainly a disorientation, and a sadness at the loss of much of Russia's rich pre-1917 culture. There are continuing signs of unfocused anxiety and of an all-too-understandable popular fear; people know that there will be pain in the longer-term transition.

At this writing, new parliamentary elections are scheduled for December 1993. If they occur, and the new Parliament is viewed as legitimate, the prevailing chaos may subside.

In the end, extreme uncertainty is probably a tunnel through which the former republics, each at its own speed, must pass. Beyond this tunnel lies the promise of independent, democratic, and largely free market societies. With stops and starts, international commerce is at least gaining a foothold in Russia; this fact, alone, is encouraging. Russia and other former republics are moving to accommodate such international commerce, and Western governments are contributing heartily to it. This is doubly encouraging.

Today as in 1991, it is still safe to say: "The cultural diversity of the former republics, their past and present entrepreneurial spirit, and the absence of economically advantageous alternatives . . . favor their independent redevelopment." And Smith's "invisible hand" continues "gently pulling an invisible thread between and among" them, and between these fledgling nation-states and the West.

NOTES

1. The body of this paper was written in late 1991; the epilogue was written in late 1993.

2. A "political reunion," for the purpose of this paper, means a political unit utilizing many or most of the following: a single currency, a single central bank, a single set of credit policies, a single commercial banking system, and a set of laws and regulations governing monetary or fiscal policy. For the purposes of this paper, political reunion need not, but probably would, imply a federal legislature, executive, judiciary, and military. At the time of this writing, the so-called Commonwealth of Independent States does not yet represent a "political reunion."

3. See, e.g., *The Economist*, October 5–11, 1992, at 51.

4. See, e.g., *The New York Times*, December 9, 1991, at 1.

5. See, e.g., *The Economist*, December 21, 1991–January 3, 1992, at 55–56.

6. "Economic sovereignty" may best be understood as the desire of a nation or people to autonomously decide the monetary, fiscal, and regulatory policies under which they will transact business. It necessarily implies a degree of "political sovereignty." See, e.g., "Will There Be a Ukraininan National Currency?" *Ukrainian Business Digest*, May 13, 1991; see also Rein Stamm, *U.S.S.R. Business Newsletter*, December 1990. Already, the republics have reserved broad economic powers to themselves, including control of their customs regimes, the right to negotiate freely on behalf of their populations, and the right to assert their own monetary and fiscal prerogatives. See, e.g., *The Economist*, August 3–9, 1991, at 45.

7. *The Economist*, August 3–9, 1991, at 45.

8. Grigorii Yavlinksy's May 1991 Plan, for example, sought $150 billion in Western aid for the U.S.S.R. over a five-year period. *Ukrainian Business Digest*, June 1991, at 6. As of mid-1991, the accumulated debt of the former Union stood at $65 billion. *The Economist*, August 3–9, 1991, at 45. In January 1992, *The Economist* declared: "The G-7 countries must turn up ready to offer massive financial aid to those states of the new Commonwealth that are moving forward with decisive programs of macroeconomic stabilization and market reform." *The Economist*, December 21, 1991–January 3, 1992, at 101.

9. See, e.g., James E. Alt and Alec K. Chrystal, *Political Economics* (Berkeley: University of California Press, 1983), at 71; James D. Gwartney and Richard Stroup, *Macroeconomics: Private and Public Choice* (New York: Academic Press, 1980), 71–72, 197–99, 264–65; *Ukrainian Business Digest*, June 1991, at 6.

10. There is a present predilection toward near-term political reunion, not just among former hardline communists, but also among many in the West. As one observer recently noted:

> Viewing the U.S.S.R. as a sort of "United States of Russia" is a subliminal parallel that, particularly for America, is easy to make. But the analogy quickly dissolves: the fifty states of the U.S. are arbitrarily

drawn political/administrative units, while the fifteen Soviet republics are discrete historic nations with indigenous cultures, languages, and, in most cases, distinctive political traditions.

Victor Rud, *Ukrainian Business Digest*, February 22, 1991, at 2.

11. See, e.g., George B. Cressey, *Soviet Potentials: A Geographic Appraisal* (Syracuse, NY: Syracuse University Press, 1962), at 26. These nationalities include Great Russians, Ukrainians, Belorussians, Uzbeks, Crimeans, Tatars, Kazan Tatars, Kazakhs, Azerbaizhans, Armenians, Georgians, Lithuanians, Jews, Moldavians, Germans, Chuvashes, Latuins, Iranians, Tajiks, Poles, Marduins, Turkmens, Bashkirs, Kirgiz, Estonians, Degestanians, Udmurts, Mari, Komi, Chechentsi, Ossetians, Greeks, Karelians, Karakalpaks, Koreans, Kabardianians, Finns, Kalmuks, and Bolgars. Cressey, *Soviet Potentials*, at 27, 313; see also George B. Cressey, *The Basis of Soviet Strength* (New York: Whittlesey House, 1945), at 43.

12. See Cressey, *Soviet Potentials*, at 36; see also Marshall I. Goldman, *U.S.S.R. in Crisis: The Failure of an Economic System* (New York: W. W. Norton, 1983), at 90–96.

13. Unmitigated nationalistic fervor has long been recognized, for example, as a source of war. Violent nationalism has also recently surfaced in Azerbaijan and Armenia, Uzbekistan, Tajikistan, and Kirgizia; Yugoslavia's current disintegration provides a vivid example of nationalism's darker side. *The New York Times*, November 11, 1991, at A7; *The Economist*, September 21–27, 1991, at 58–60.

14. Ludwig Von Mises, *Nation, State, and Economy* (New York: New York University Press, 1983), at 55.

15. Goldman, *U.S.S.R. in Crisis*, at 96.

16. Von Mises, *Nation, State, and Economy*, at 54.

17. See the "Epilogue" to this chapter for update on legal issues.

18. "Allocative inefficiency" is the use of an uneconomical combination of resources to produce goods or services for which there is not an intense demand relative to the opportunity costs of production. While this suggests that goods with a low elasticity of demand—that is, necessities such as food, soap, toilet paper, or medicine—could be produced by all-Union enterprises, the likelihood is that even these goods could be produced more economically by smaller enterprises. See, generally, Gwartney and Stroup, *Macroeconomics*, at 423; Richard G. Lipsey, *Positive Economics* (London: Weidenfeld and Nicolson, 1982), at 717.

19. "X-inefficiency" is the wasteful use of resources that results in a lower output level than was possible with the same resources. See, generally, Gwartney and Stroup, *Macroeconomics*, at 423; Lipsey, *Positive Economics*, at 717; Harvey Leibenstein, *Beyond Economic Man* (Cambridge, MA: Harvard University Press, 1976).

20. See Stamm, *U.S.S.R. Business Newsletter*, September 15, 1991.

21. Leonid Krawchuk, Interview in *Ukrainian Business Digest*, September 1991, at 3.

22. Stamm, *U.S.S.R. Business Newsletter*, September 1991.

23. "Between 1870 and 1914 [Russian industrial] output grew eightfold, about as fast as United States industrial output over the same period, and thus faster than output in Western Europe." Raymond Hutchins, *Soviet Economic Development* (New York: New York University Press), at 15. Marshall Goldman adds that "Russia in 1913 may have been economically superior to Japan and perhaps Italy." Marshall Goldman, *The Soviet Economy* (Englewood Cliffs, NJ: Prentice Hall, 1968), at 9. "By 1913, steel production was five times larger than in 1890. There was almost a tenfold increase in

the mining of coal. The railroad network almost tripled in size. . . . Comparable expansion in other sectors resulted in an average annual rate of industrial growth of about 8 percent in the 1890s." *Id.*, at 10. Other observers place the Russian growth rate even higher. See Alexander Gershenkron, *Economic Backwardness in Historical Perspective* (Cambridge, MA: Harvard University Press, 1962), at 219; Peter I. Lyashchenko, *History of the National Economy of Russia* (New York: Macmillan, 1949), at 525, 669. Recall also that prerevolutionary Russia offered to the Western world such literary titans as Pushkin, Gogol, Dostoevsky, and Tolstoy, not to mention the epic musical works of Tchaikovsky and Moussorgsky.

24. See, generally, Lyashchenko, *History of the National Economy of Russia*; Hutchins, *Soviet Economic Development*; Goldman, *The Soviet Economy*; Gershenkron, *Economic Backwardness in Historical Perspective.*

25. Nicholas S. Timasheff, *The Great Retreat: The Growth and Decline of Communism in Russia* (New York: E. P. Dutton, 1946), at 24–25.

26. See also note 22, *supra.*

27. Hutchins, *Soviet Economic Development*, at 14.

28. "Under NEP, signs of prosperity began to appear. Private enterprise flourished, especially in retail trade, which in 1923 was almost 80 percent in private hands." Hutchins, *Soviet Economic Development*, at 39.

29. Hedrick Smith, *The Russians* (New York: New York Times Book Co., 1976), at 199.

30. See, e.g., *The Wall Street Journal*, November 18, 1991, at A2, A12; *The Economist*, October 5–11, 1991, at 51–52; *The Economist*, November 21–27, 1991, at 58–60; *The Economist*, December 21, 1991–January 3, 1992, at 101–103.

31. See, e.g., *The Economist*, December 21, 1991–January 3, 1992, at 101. See also the "Epilogue" to this chapter.

32. Stamm, *U.S.S.R. Business Newsletter*, November 1991. (*Address*: NTB, Neckrasov Street 14, St. Petersburg, 191104, Russian Federation.)

33. See Stamm, *U.S.S.R. Business Newsletter*, November 1991. (*Addresses*: Ukrinbank, 19 Suvorova Street, Kiev, Ukraine, 251010; Vidrodgennia, 7a M. Kotsiubinskogo Street, Kiev, Ukraine; Ukrsotsbank, 9 Kovpaka Street, Kiev, Ukraine; AMB Bank, 6 Tserniakhovskogo Street, Odessa, Ukraine 270056; Ugleprogressbank, 83 Sovetskaya Street, Voroshilovgrad, Ukraine 358000; Transformatorbank, 3 Elektrozavodskaya Street, Zaporozhye, Ukraine 330660.)

34. Stamm, *U.S.S.R. Business Newsletter*, November 1991. (*Addresses*: Namanganbank, Ul. Tereshkovoi 19, Sovetsk District, Namangan, Uzbekistan 716026; Shark, Ul. Griboedova 20, Samarkand, Uzbekistan 703003; Aviabank, Ul. Pavla Poltaratskogo 736, Tashkent, Uzbekistan 700015.)

35. Stamm, *U.S.S.R. Business Newsletter*, August 1991.

36. Stamm, *U.S.S.R. Business Newsletter*, November 1991.

37. Stamm, *U.S.S.R. Business Newsletter*, November 1991. (*Addresses*: Moscow Stock Exchange, Department of Securities, Neglinnaya Street 12, Moscow 103016, Russian Federation; St. Petersburg Stock Exchange, Tschikovsky 62, St. Petersburg, Russian Federation; Tallinn Stock Exchange, Hillar Kala, Kuhlbarsi Street 1, Tallinn 200104, Estonia.)

38. Stamm, *U.S.S.R. Business Newsletter*, November 1991.

39. Stamm, *U.S.S.R. Business Newsletter*, November 1991. (*Address*: Syntex-Inforex, Sovetskaya 14, Dubna, Russian Federation.)

40. Stamm, *U.S.S.R. Business Newsletter*, November 1991. (*Addresses*: Elekton, Korolenko Street 58, Tatar Republic, Kazan 420057, Russian Federation; Syjaskomputerservice, Orenburghski, Tr. 10, Tartar Republic, Kazan 420059, Russian Federation.)

41. See, e.g., *Ukrainian Business Digest*, March 28, 1991, at 8; June 24, 1991, at 1; Stamm, *U.S.S.R. Business Newsletter*, November 1991. See also "Epilogue" for update on legal issues.

42. Stamm, *U.S.S.R. Business Newsletter*, November 1991.

43. Stamm, *U.S.S.R. Business Newsletter*, October 1991.

44. See *Ukrainian Business Digest*, January 22, 1991.

45. Stamm, *U.S.S.R. Business Newsletter*, November 1991.

46. Stamm, *U.S.S.R. Business Newsletter*, October 1991.

47. See, e.g., A. Inkeles and R. Bauer, *The Soviet Citizen* (Cambridge, MA: Harvard University Press, 1959), Stephen White, *Political Culture and Political Change in Communist States*, Archie Brown and Jack Gray, eds. (London: Macmillan, 1979).

48. New foreign investment laws include, for example, the Russian Soviet Federated Socialist Republic (RSFSR) law On Foreign Investment of July 4, 1991; RSFSR law On Investment Activity of June 26, 1991; the U.S.-Russian Treaty on the Encouragement and Reciprocal Protection of Investment of June 17, 1992; and the U.S.-Russian Agreement on Trade Relations of June 17, 1992.

49. A variety of hard current statutes and decrees have been promulgated, including the January 20, 1993 Russian Central Bank Instruction No. 11 On the Procedure for Sales of Goods to Citizens for Currency . . . ; the October 9, 1992 Russian Law No. 3615-1 On Hard-Currency Regulation . . . ; the October 27, 1992 Russian Presidential Decree No. 1306 On Sales to Citizens . . . of Products for Foreign Currency; the December 30, 1991 Presidential Decree On the Formation of the Russian Currency Reserve; the June 14, 1992 Presidential Decree No. 629 On Partial Changes in the Procedure of Mandatory Sale of Part of Hard-Currency Receipts and the Extraction of Export Duties; and Central Bank Instructions Nos. 02-104a and 7 in June 1992, No. 4 in April 1992, and No. 3 in January 1992.

50. Laws on property include the February 1992 law on Payments for Land; the August 1992 statute on State Monitoring of Land Use and Protection; and the May 29, 1992 RSFSR Law No. 443-1 On Liens.

51. Laws pertaining to customs—or exports and imports—include those on licenses and quotas, such as Russian Government Resolution No. 854 of November 1992 On the Licensing and Quotas of Exports and Imports, and the Presidential Decree No. 628 of June 14, 1992 On the Procedures for the Export of Strategically Important Raw Materials. Customs laws on tariffs and duties include Russian Government Resolution No. 91 of December 31, 1991 On the Introduction of Export Tariffs on Certain Goods Exported from Russia; Russian State Customs Order No. 603 of December 11, 1992 On the Export Tariff Rates in Effect from January 1, 1993; and Presidential Decrees No. 340 and No. 92 of March 15 and 20, 1993, respectively, On the Import Customs Tariff.

52. Basic Russian laws on privatization include the January 13, 1992 law on Basic Provisions of the 1992 Privatization Program; the RSFSR law of July 3, 1991 On the Privatization of State and Municipal Enterprises in the RSFSR; RSFSR law No. 2980-1 On Privatization of State-Owned and Municipal Enterprises (an amendment to the 1991

Law on Privatization); the law of March 1992 On Conversion of the Defense Industry . . . ; Regulation No. 631 of June 1992 Governing Land Sales; the Decree of July 1992 On Procedure for Implementing the Check System; the Russian statute of July 1992 On Commercialization of State Enterprises; the Decree No. 721 of July 1992 On Converting State Enterprises into Stock Companies; and the Decree of February 1992 On State Enterprise Privatization.

53. Russian antitrust or antimonopoly laws include RSFSR law of March 22, 1992 On Competition and Limiting Monopolistic Activity and Commodity Markets; and the Russian decree and statute of September 1992 On the State Committee for Anti-Monopoly Policy.

54. Other recent Russian laws of importance include various drafts of the Russian Constitution (now under revision once again); the June 1992 U.S.-Russian Treaty On Avoidance of Double Taxation; the February 1991 Russian Law on Banking; July 1991 laws on Privatization of Housing and Personal Privatization Accounts; the June 1992 Russian decrees on Supporting Bankrupt Enterprises; the March 1992 Russian Federation Arbitration Code (No. 2447-1); the statute of June 1992 on Procedure for Settling Disputes; the June 1992 Russian Decree No. 3118-1 on Changes in Law on the Arbitration Court; the provisional statute of the Court of Arbitration; the Decree of May 1992 (No. 2837-1) On Improving Economic Transactions; the August 1992 Decree On Creation of a Federal Contract System; the November 1991 Decree on Foreign Economic Activity; the September 1992 Russian Patent Law and May 1992 Law on Trademarks; the January 1992 Russian Pension Law Regulations and Resolution No. 73 on Minimum Wage and Social Security for the Underprivileged; the March 1992 labor law on Collective Contracts and Agreements; the law of February 1992 On Protection of Consumer Rights; the Russian Decree of 1992 No. 55 on Price Liberalization; Resolutions No. 547 of August 1992 on Joint Stock Shares Registration, No. 78 of December 1992 on Securities and their Circulation, and No. 23 of April 1992 on Certification for Securities Transactions; as well as the February 1992 law on Commodity Exchange Trading and various Russian tax laws, including the December 1992 laws on Fundamentals of the Tax System, Taxation of Corporate Profits, Taxation of Enterprises, Investment Tax Credits, Taxation of Persons Property, Value Added Tax, and Excise Tax.

55. For more information on laws in the non-Russian republics, especially commercial laws and regulations, consult the Office of General Counsel, U.S. Department of Commerce, or the National Technical Information Service, Springfield, MA 22161.

56. Public Law 102-511, 106 Stat 3320.

57. "What Russian Aid?" in *Butterworth's Central and East European Business Law Bulletin*, Vol. 3, No. 3 (June 1993), at 4.

58. *Id.*, at 6.

59. *Congressional Record-House*, H-7159, September 28, 1993, citing Conference Report on H.R. 2295.

60. The Russian-American Enterprise Fund was represented in 1993 by the law firm of Weil, Gotshal & Manges, at which the author of this chapter was an attorney.

32

Market Economy and Federalism

Jonah Otelsberg

This chapter examines the relationship between a new federal structure for the former Soviet Union and the creation of a market economy.

A market economy is an economic system in which the market determines the prices and quantities of goods and services produced. The regulating mechanism is the interaction between supply and demand.

The system that exists today in the so-called capitalist countries is based on the marketing concept, which puts the consumer and his or her needs at the center of all business activities. The marketing concept is appropriate for economically developed societies where the basic needs of the population are satisfied and where potential supply exceeds demand for products and services. This concept of organizing economic activity is less appropriate in a society where the reigning reality is scarcity. Thus, the former Soviet Union—where scarcity is endemic—cannot create a market economy by copying the institutions and behaviors that now exist in the West. It has to go through the stages that Western countries went through in their transition from economies driven by limited supply to economies driven by limited demand.

There is a close relationship between democracy and successful market economies. Both have as their foundation the importance of the individual who can choose leaders, activities to pursue, as well as the products to buy. Both the economic and political systems are rooted in the individual. The economic system exists to satisfy the needs of individuals, the political system exists to protect their rights. The political system's power comes from the rights given to it by individuals.

Such a system has to encourage private initiative as well as protect individuals from abuse. In short, it is a system built on the rights of individuals and committed to providing the greatest good to the largest number of people.

It is a system where political power is diffused and where the government plays a limited role in the economy. People are free to pursue their own activities without government interference or control, to the extent that their activities are legal, fair, and do not harm others.

The attempts to "restructure" the Soviet economy failed miserably in the years of Gorbachev's perestroika. A free market economy cannot be grafted onto a command economy. They are incompatible. A system created by force and the abuse of individuals cannot be reformed. It has to give place to a different system rooted in the rights of individuals.

The transition to some sort of federalism will help this process. The heavy hand of the center pressing on all aspects of life in the Union, controlling activities for the benefit of the center, will be replaced by local, regional, and republican authorities. These local authorities are much more likely to fashion laws and regulations suited to local needs and be responsive to public opinion.

Any new federation has to start from the bottom up: individuals banding into groups of common interest, groups uniting to promote their goals, forming local governments, which, in turn, may decide to create a confederation—a union of equals, created to solve local problems and satisfy mutual needs. Such a union—being a voluntary association—existing to solve real needs will be stable and, in time, prosperous.

In such an environment, business activity can flourish. Responding to local needs, using local resources, small businesses can grow and prosper. Eventually, if successful in the marketplace, they will grow throughout the confederation.

The new federal structures have to satisfy the needs of its participants. For example, there is the need to cooperate to assure fair value in transactions—a currency system that is stable whether there is one currency or several currencies convertible with ease into one another. There has to be agreement on other elements of the infrastructure: communication, transportation, banking, and so on.

On the basis of the new economic system there will grow political cooperation, which will help the development of each of its components. As Adam Smith said, individual vice—selfishness—will turn to public virtue —cooperation—as a basis for a better and safer life.

This paper will examine the relationship between a new federal structure for the Soviet Union and the creation of a market economy. Both are the goals of the Soviets and the hope of the outside world.

The Soviet Union has ceased to exist. Every day brings news of further disintegration and new claims of independence. Even the republics that have signed economic and political agreements are moving farther and farther away from the center and from each other. The Union and the economy are continuing their free fall toward disintegration.

Discussions of the state of the Soviet Union take as their assumption that a re-created political and economic union is necessary for economic problems to be properly addressed. That is not necessarily the case: political disintegration may be necessary for a market economy to take root.

Let us examine the components of a market economy. It is an economic system in which the market determines the prices and quantities of goods and services produced. The regulating mechanism is the interaction between supply and demand.

In his *Wealth of Nations*, Adam Smith described the "invisible hand" of the market as assuring a desirable societal result by converting "private vices" —such as selfishness—into "public virtues"—such as increased productivity. He recognized, however, that for this to be accomplished there has to exist an appropriate legal and institutional system that assures that not a single participant in the market has a direct effect on prices; prices are determined by aggregate supply and demand and each participant can buy or sell any quantity at this price.

The market economies of Western Europe evolved out of the ruins of feudalism, which limited personal freedoms, attached individuals to the land, and prescribed behavior to the minutest detail. The development of the capitalist system was preceded by the recognition of the individual as the source of rights and basic components of the economic system. The rapid development of trade was due to the ability of individuals to band together to form issue-oriented associations that allowed them to pool their resources and diminish the risk by sharing them among the participants. Joint-stock companies, first in Holland and then in England, became foundations for the prevailing form of economic entity in the West—the corporation. The system underwent many changes that accompanied technological developments and political realignments.

At the beginning of the industrial revolution there was scarcity. The demand for products exceeded the supply. This stimulated the development of industry to produce more and more goods and services. The greater production capacity resulting from technological innovations created demand for other services. Manufacturers were able to produce more than the local markets could absorb, and they needed effective means of transporting their goods to consumers outside their immediate markets. This stimulated development of auxiliary services such as banking, insurance, transportation, warehousing, as well as wholesaling and retailing. Eventually a buyer's market replaced the seller's market.

In such a system businesses have to start by learning about the consumers—their needs, their wants, beliefs, behaviors, lifestyles, and demographic characteristics. With that knowledge, businesses can plan their activities by designing products and services that satisfy the needs of the consumer.

The market economy in the United States and other Western countries flourished in societies that allowed the individuals the freedom to select their field of endeavor, their place of residence, their religious beliefs, their associations, and protected their right to own property.

One of the cornerstones of the market economy is freedom of expression and freedom of information. The 1990s are indeed the age of information explosion. This goes together with the marketing concept that demands knowledge and a wide information base for decision making. A market economy demands information to be available to both consumers and businesses. Consumers need information in order to make rational choices among the products and services that are available. Businesses need a free flow of information about the economy, political developments, changes in technology, their competitors' activities, and, most important, their potential consumers. The carriers of the information are various media (some traditional such as newspapers and journals, others the result of new technologies such as satellite television and computer networks).

The sources of information vary from private research organizations to trade associations and the government. The government is the main data collection agency; unlike data collected by private entities, government information is in the public domain and it is available to all.

While information is needed for the planning activities of both consumers and businesses in the system, there is a need for other infrastructures to allow the efficient allocation of resources and distribution of goods and services. These basic infrastructures include a stable currency, financial institutions, as well as an efficient transportation network.

There needs to be a stable unit of value that can be used by all sectors of society in the planning and execution of transactions. Such a unit is the local currency, whose value has to have some real relationship to its buying power within the economy. As most industrialized countries trade extensively with each other, the convertibility of the currency into other currencies is essential and its relationship with those currencies should be stable in order to allow efficient exchange of goods and services.

Financial institutions, such as banks, stock exchanges, venture capital suppliers, and so on, are essential. They ease access to the available financial resources and so stimulate investment. Stability cannot be assured unless there is a central bank to regulate the activities of the financial institutions. (In recent years in the United States the regulators of financial institutions were not successful in achieving these goals, but the system responds to realities and it is likely that a stronger system will evolve from the abuses of the 1980s.)

Along with the financial system, there is a need for a transportation system that will allow the efficient transfer of raw materials to factories, and of manufactured goods from factories to consumers. This means a network of roads, railroads, airplane routes, and such. In addition, other services associated with distribution have to be available such as warehousing, wholesaling, retailing, and insurance.

Above all, the system needs people who are free to buy what they want and to sell their skills where they want. The development of the system and its growth depends on risk takers, people who are wiling to take risks in the belief that they will have an opportunity to receive the benefit and keep it. The political system has to encourage private initiative, as well as protect the individuals from abuse.

How does the system created by 74 years of Soviet rule compare to the requirements of market economy? The system created was that of a command economy based on central planning. The plan was the sole guide to management decisions; resources were centrally allocated and output determined by the plan. The plans adopted by the various ministries were revised and coordinated by Gosplan, the Central Planning Agency.

Ever since the first five-year plan (1928–32), consumer goods were sacrificed to the accomplishment of the administrative goals of the command economy, with its emphasis on heavy industry and the military.

The state became a monopsony—the only buyer of goods and services produced—and a monopoly—the only seller of goods and services. The state also maintained its monopoly on information, values, education, culture, and other areas.

Private property was abolished, thus eliminating the motivation for risk taking among the populace.

The currency was controlled by the government. It did not perform its role as a unit of value as prices of goods, services, and labor were set by the government.

The banking system, limited as it was, was also a monopoly of the state and did not provide capital for economic expansion. Investment was for ideological or national security reasons. Other areas, such as industry, transportation, and housing, were neglected.

Individual mobility was highly restricted. One had to be registered in order to receive local services, including housing. Therefore, moving from city to city was extremely difficult, especially in those cities, such as Moscow, where opportunities were the greatest. Most people lived all their lives in the area where they were born, or where they were sent after graduation from college. It was almost impossible for an individual to initiate a change of location.

The Soviet economy was designed to be a single inter-dependent system, totally controlled by the center. The center, in its wisdom, decided what goods would be produced, where they would be produced, and where the resources needed for production would come from. These decisions were not based on any coherent economic rationale. Frequently, a factory's raw materials would come from a single supplier, who might be in another republic. It appears that the center created enterprises in far ends of the Union so as to assure that they could not easily communicate with each other, but by necessity had to go through the center via the various planning agencies and ministries. The bureaucracy created an economic system that could not function without it. Factories frequently had no idea where their raw materials came from, nor where their finished products were destined. That was not their concern. Their concern was to fulfill the plan, or at least appear to fulfill the plan.

Despite the high level of technology in many areas, the communication system is primitive—the telephones work erratically, letters take several weeks to be delivered.

One of the greatest weaknesses of the economic system is the total absence of a distribution system. As the government is the only buyer and seller, there are no intermediaries to provide storage and wholesaling services. This is most obvious in the agricultural sector, where a high percentage of the harvest either remains in the fields uncollected or rots in primitive storage facilities. Furthermore, the rail system is slow and overburdened and there is no transcontinental road network.

The command economy never worked well. It survived because of a political system that forcibly kept the population under tight control and ignorant about the rest of the world, while at the same time proclaiming its own superiority and commitment to its people. It was never able to provide for more than the bare necessities of life.

When Gorbachev initiated glasnost and perestroika he did not want to destroy the existing political or economic system; he intended to preserve the supremacy of the party and to adapt the system to new realities. He knew, unlike the U.S. Central Intelligence Agency, that the Soviet economy was falling apart and that the country could not continue to spend unlimited resources on the military. At the same time, he wanted to make only minimal changes in the economic order and distribution of power.

The relaxation of political and psychological control over the country had the unforeseen result that the economic controls no longer functioned. Economic patterns were disrupted, and the decline of the economy, which started under Brezhnev, continued at a faster rate. Problems became aggravated; the enterprises, given more freedom with regard to retention of their profits, refused to fulfill orders that they considered disadvantageous. Soviet enterprises adapted to the new conditions by ignoring the center and resorting to barter. The Soviet Union reverted from a socialist command economy to one where every enterprise and every household tried to be self sufficient and bartered what it had for what it needed.

The communist system has always ignored economic realities, and the debate over perestroika has continued to do so. This is true for the "democrats" as well as for the old line communists. Whatever tentative and hesitant steps were taken toward economic reform, they were inadequate to solve the serious economic and structural problems facing the Union. Furthermore, they were stifled and smothered by the communist bureaucracy. The nomenklatura were hostile to anything that approached or even hinted at a market economy. They feared—correctly—that any reform would dilute, if not end, their power and privileges.

Gorbachev's policies of glasnost and perestroika weakened the power of the Communist Party and its ability to impose its will throughout the vast Soviet Union. Its formal power was destroyed by the abortive putsch of August 1991. However, its members are still the dominant political and bureaucratic power within the country.

The greatest obstacles to reform toward a market economy are the remnants of the old command system: the expectation of receiving instructions from above and from the center; the large military enterprises that are overmanned, underfinanced, and a drain on resources; the lack of individual responsibility for the quality or usefulness of one's work; an unwieldy and unproductive bureaucracy, uncontrolled budget deficits, and an infrastructure inadequate for the needs of a dynamic economy.

A further obstacle is the lingering residue of fear and intimidation by a system that systematically repressed those who showed initiative, independence, and creativity. Only the party dogma was accepted as the route to success in society. Commercial activity by individuals was prohibited and those engaged in selling were labeled speculators—the most despised of criminal and antisocial activities. These practices instilled fear and limited and distorted the natural energy and creativity of the people.

As the formal system never fulfilled the desires of Soviet consumers, the people developed alternative means of satisfying their needs, including stealing from the workplace, bribing those in power, and networking. The imagination, creativity, and energy needed to develop such an informal system of self-supply instilled in many Soviet citizens the skills necessary for the development of a market economy.

The Soviet system is not salvageable. The sooner it completely falls apart the sooner the various Soviet peoples can start fashioning political and economic systems based on real needs. This will involve further disruption of the economic union imposed by force, a shrinking of internal trade, rising unemployment, and a falling standard of living. Humpty Dumpty cannot be put back together again. New systems have to be built. Some will succeed, some will not. Those that are successful will flourish and be a model for others.

Whatever replaces the Soviet Union will be burdened by the unresolved problems of a collapsed and moribund system. These are the structural problems of creating a sound and stable currency, and rebuilding the neglected infrastructure. There is also the social problem of a population whose lifestyle has been uprooted and discredited and is no longer sustainable. These problems cannot be solved overnight and can be resolved only within local or republican levels. Solutions planned at the center and imposed on the republics are no longer tenable.

In the final analysis, it is individuals who make an economy work. Once Soviet citizens have been freed of the excessive regulation and paternalism that restrict and interfere with their activities, they will start creating, out of their own needs and desires, a market economy. Once they try their wings, they may discover that they already know how to fly. Let them have the right to make choices and to benefit from the right decision as well as pay for the wrong ones.

The transition to some sort of federalism will help this process. The heavy hand of the center pressing on all aspects of life in the Union, controlling activities for the benefit of the center, can be replaced by local, regional, and republican authorities. These local authorities are much more likely to fashion laws and regulations suited to local needs.

No state-to-state help is going to create a market economy. Only individual efforts of small businesses and entrepreneurs can build an effective economy.

The Soviet people have many assets that should help them in this development. They are well educated—far better than their counterparts in the U.S.A. They already exercise a great deal of initiative on an individual level. What is holding them back is a legal and political system that does not guarantee their freedoms and makes entrepreneurial activity very difficult. As soon as this is abolished, the country may flourish as it did in the short period of NEP.

There is no possibility for the Soviet Union to jump over the stages of development of a market economy. They cannot start from a system dominated by the marketing concept. They have to start with small business that produce to satisfy local markets, and that will eventually grow into larger organizations. A market economy has to be a grassroots effort where individuals take risks and are provided resources with which to start up their ventures.

The basis for new federal structures is going to be the need to have some centralized functions for the benefit of all. There is the need to cooperate to assure fair value in their transactions—a currency system that is stable whether it is one currency or currencies convertible with ease into one another. They have to agree on other elements of the infrastructure: communication, transportation, and so on. Eventually they will evolve a system, not unlike that of Western Europe, of cooperation among independent sovereign parts.

REFERENCES

(all September 1990–August 1991)

Argumenty i Fakty
Business and Banks
Business Week
Business World
Consensus

Demokraticheskaya Rossiya
The Economist
Izvestia
Kommersant
Komsomolskaya Pravda
Kuranty
Moscow News
The New York Times
Niezavisimaya Gazeta
Novoye Vriemya
Ogoniok
Pravda
Rossiya
Rossiyskaya Gazeta
Sovietsakaya Rossiya
Viechernaya Moskva

33

Economic Sovereignty: New Aspects of Interaction Between Economics and Politics

Temiruz A. Beridze

Today in economic theory and practice there is no sensible alternative to successive transition to independence of economic links. Such logic of development could be explained not only by the fact that an economy is a multilevel system, and the producer is always limited in environment, but first and foremost by the fact that economic independence is an inevitable condition for realizing the economic interest of the producer. This interest is a fundamental motive of efficient economy and a necessary factor to shape and operate markets. This mostly concerns the republics of the former U.S.S.R., whose economic relative isolation is combined with the national state system. This combination makes the problems of economic sovereignty vividly political, and the problem of interaction of economics and politics within their framework becomes topical.

THE UNITY AND DIFFERENCE OF POLITICAL AND ECONOMIC SOVEREIGNTY

One of the most important problems that countries establishing their democratic political and economic systems are faced with, is to reach effective relations among central organizations, local powers, and subjects of an economy that shape market environment. This problem has become especially urgent with the disintegration of the U.S.S.R. and the emergence of the system of independent sovereign states. These sovereign units have had to deal with joint economic problems and growth as well as their own economic development—all under difficult conditions.

With independence, new states naturally invoke their new-found sovereignty with great frequency. Administrative-territorial formations, enterprises, and separate citizens are all called sovereign. However, such invocations of sovereignty often are disconnected, which initially introduces some confusion into the analysis of economy.

The concept of sovereignty is taken from the political lexicon of autonomy and power and does not have an adequate application in economics. There should be another approach to the problem of power in economy. It should not be understood in an absolute sense because there also exist certain economic and sociopolitical limitations.

Economic sovereignty is a relative notion ("economic independence" in a strict sense is unrealistic) because otherwise it assumes a closed (orientation on maximum self-sufficiency) and consequently inefficient economic system. The degree of relativity of economic sovereignty is more significant than in politics and stems from the very phenomena of market relations (satisfaction of material demands based on division of labor and exchange of its results). Market relations tend to cross national and state partitions. In this academic sense there arises the problem of the subject of sovereignty in economics—that is, the source of power in economics. In the latter case, the carrier of such power is a concrete producer.

A mere proclamation of an enterprise as a subject of sovereignty in economics is not enough. Though world economics was initially a market-oriented system of free entrepreneurship—that is, not the states, but separate companies, firms, and amalgamations were the subjects of economic relations—"national full-dress uniform" or "regional background" of this or that company has always played a certain role in locating economic priorities, in forming and providing competitive positions.

At present there appears to be no other choice than to give priority to enterprises. Such enterprises will tend to stabilize and grow economies and logically ought to naturally push the republics to economic unity and later on to certain forms of political unity. Bilateral movement, when economic and political decisions become mutual conditions for their realization, is necessary. That priority, of course, to be fruitful must take into consideration political-legal forms, contractual-constitutional conditions, and state-jurisdicial mechanisms.

THE PRINCIPAL BASES OF ECONOMIC SOVEREIGNTY

An economic system is not an isolated phenomenon or a thing in itself. It is determined not only by economic relations, but by social parameters of society as well, including its institutes of property and power and dominating values.

The first basis of economic sovereignty is the territory of the state, not only its geographic borders, but also its economic activities. Territory enables society to freely use its natural and human resources and lands. This function is realized through systems of national property allocation.

In a sovereign state it does not matter who handles these property resources, the state, separate individuals, corporations, communes, or physical or juridical persons. At bottom, the state has the right of territorial leadership—the supreme power within the state territory. The right of state territorial leadership should not be confused with the state's property, especially when there exists a variety of forms of property and a privatization process is under way.

The second basis of economic sovereignty is the system of means and instruments of economic policy and is related to territory. It is the arsenal of means and instruments that helps to protect national production from any unfavorable influence of foreign competition. However, in a regional or global economy, a single sovereign state cannot acquire its own sovereign isolated place. It must be open to the influx of commodities, capital, and hard currency from others.

The third basis of economic sovereignty is the state function of society. The basic line of development is determined by the role of the national state in economic affairs exerting an increasingly deep and comprehensive influence on the growth and development of the economy. The state acts as a significant player in the process of accumulating, mobilizing, and centralizing the savings of society for their future transfer into various spheres of the economy. Such economic-legal immunities as fiscal, customs, currency autonomy of the state, its control over the national budget, credit and banking systems are connected with this important function. Under present conditions of development, a number of these functions should become the subject of agreement between the republics of the former U.S.S.R. aimed at creating a single economic environment.

THE MECHANISM OF REALIZING ECONOMIC SOVEREIGNTY

The republic acts, first, as an economic environment, where market relations are being shaped. In this sense the whole economic activity within its territory is implemented according to the criterion of economic efficiency and economic expediency. Efficient functioning of the economy is estimated according to the criterion of satisfaction of a whole complex of needs (socioeconomic, demographic, ecological, cultural, etc.).

The republic constantly causes a certain contradiction between realization of the principle of territorial economy (specialization with an account of demands of a single economic environment) and national economic interest (a complex development in conformity with the internal criteria and demands). The solution to that contradiction is the realization of the principle of economic expediency of participation in the intra-Union division of labor, based on the equivalent exchange as one of the basic and natural demands of economic functioning. Equivalent exchange is assured by the formation of a single economic environment based on the principles of noninterference and sovereignty of each republic: complete self-dependence in solving resource problems.

In their territories, the republics have the right to establish forms of regulation, but in relations between the states, common rules of the game are fixed and with quite strict sanctions. Efficient management of the economy is possible only when "overlapping" of jurisdictions of different levels of power are minimized.

Realization of equality, of course, is always a difficulty in reaching efficiency. With the former republics we can speak only about the trend toward equal efficiency of different types of economics. That is why preservation of subsidies (as subventions) is necessary. For example, the European Community has the Fund of Regional Aid, which makes up for objective irregularities in the economic development of the Community among its members.

In some cases the transition to market equivalent exchange is at present impossible due to strictly-fixed and disproportionate technological economic structures.

There is also the existing system of prices, price policies, and price proportions among former republics that must be addressed. Liberalization of prices, transition to internal convertability of the ruble, and restructuring of pricing policies is needed among the republics. Transition to free prices on all types of production needs several stages. One-sided decisions of one republic on liberalization of prices place at a disadvantage those who lag behind. That is why a coordinated policy in liberalizing prices makes sense (especially regarding wholesale and purchase prices).

Economic trade among the republics at world prices in its turn raises a number of questions. First, there are many prices that are not competitive and that do not respond to the world market. What rate of exchange should be applied converting dollars, marks, and other currencies into rubles, when the ruble is nonconvertible? Will producers be able to produce at world prices? Even in the most developed countries, prices for many types of products on the internal market differ from those on the world market. At times states try to protect producers from unfavorable conditions caused by competition on the world market. Also, convertibility of currency, the breaking of cooperative ties, must not be allowed.

DEVELOPMENT OF ECONOMIC SOVEREIGNTY

Economic development is increasingly international and universal, phenomena without state borders and national partitions. However, in the former republics the real structures of society and social organisms find for themselves a most adequate form of self-realization and development in sovereign state systems. In periods of socioeconomic history of mankind, first the international, then the national side of social development comes to the forefront in certain countries. The advancement of international and national economic development remains largely an unrealized goal initially, and the content of sovereignty in economics reflects contradictory unity of processes of differentiation and integration of economic activities. Political and economic sovereignty are different, though interconnected, elements of a single whole. Infringement of one affects the other. Without improvement of the economy there cannot be improvement in other spheres, and vice versa: political agreement with an account of existing realities is a necessary condition for normal development of integration processes in the economy. Under these conditions, the dilemma of compatibility of political and economic reforms (decisions) disappears.

Today the danger is not in a probable loss of sovereignty within global civilization, but in strife for illusory independence that hinders the construction of the international mechanism that would protect the former republic. The emergence of a united world community will neither question nor repudiate state sovereignty.

34

Federal Aspects of the Development of the U.S.S.R. and RSFSR Economic Laws During Perestroika

Olga Floroff

It is a major fallacy that the Soviet Union has no previous experience in corporate and joint-venture laws. Soviet legal experience in these subjects did not start on January 13, 1987, when the Presidium of the U.S.S.R. Supreme Soviet adopted a Decree on Questions Concerning the Establishment in the Territory of the U.S.S.R. and Operation of Joint Ventures, International Amalgamations and Organizations with the Participation of Soviet and Foreign Organizations, Firms and Management Bodies."[1] It dates back to at least the 1920s.

The large complex of private partnerships existing in prerevolutionary Russia was destroyed by decrees of 1918–20. They were nationalized, confiscated, and monopolized by the state. Nevertheless, some, including trading houses, survived.

On July 27, 1918, the Russian Soviet of Peoples Commissars, the predecessor of the Council of Ministers, enacted a decree obligating all private joint-stock companies to register with the Department of Interior Trade of the Peoples Commissariat of Trade and Industry. At this time, the Soviet Union had not yet been formed. And even the first postrevolutionary constitution for Russia was promulgated only 17 days prior to this date.[2]

In the spring of 1921, the New Economic Policy was inaugurated. Its implementation was necessary to give the country's economy an opportunity to recover. Private enterprise in small industry and retail trade was allowed. A limited use of hired labor in agriculture and restricted land leasing was permitted.[3] At the end of 1921, the 9th Congress of Soviets allowed the creation of "mixed joint-stock companies" with participation of state capital and foreign capital. The purpose of these companies was to prepare and market export commodities and to import food to Russia. The participation of the

Peoples Commissariat of Foreign Trade in these joint-stock companies was mandatory. These were the first joint ventures in postrevolutionary Russia.

In March 1922 the Commission on Creation of Mixed Joint-stock Companies was convened. Most of the companies were formed with state capital and some were formed with participation of private capital.[4] The Civil Code of the Russian Federation came into force January 1, 1923, and provided the legal framework for the creation and operation of joint-stock companies.[5] Unfortunately for the Russian economy, the New Economic Policy lasted only five years until October 1, 1928, when the first of Stalin's Five-Year Plans went into operation. Joint-stock companies, with the very few exceptions not involving private capital (like Intourist), were eliminated.

For about 60 years corporate law was nonexistent in the U.S.S.R. The first outlines of corporate law appeared in Soviet jurisprudence on January 13, 1987, when the Joint Venture Decree and the Resolution of the U.S.S.R. Council of Ministers No. 49 on the Establishment in the Territory of the U.S.S.R. and Operation of Joint Ventures with Participation of Soviet Organizations and Firms from Capitalist and Developing Countries were promulgated.[6]

Since the adoption of the Joint Venture Decree and Resolution No. 49, the legal environment in the U.S.S.R. has changed dramatically and at great speed. At the time of the adoption of the Joint Venture Decree and Resolution No. 49, the only types of Soviet enterprises operating in the territory of the Soviet Union were state-owned enterprises. It should be noted that these state-owned enterprises had much less self-determination than they have now because legislation defining their independence, the Law on State-owned Enterprises,[7] was adopted June 30, 1987, approximately six months later.

No republican laws governing the creation and operation of joint ventures had been adopted after 1987, so the republics followed the Joint Venture Decree and the Resolution No. 49.

Under Article 73, paragraph (4) of the U.S.S.R. Constitution[8]—in force at the time—the highest legislative body of the U.S.S.R. (Congress of Peoples' Deputies and the Supreme Soviet of the U.S.S.R.) promulgates fundamental legislation for the U.S.S.R. and union republics.[9] Each of the fifteen union republics in turn adopted its own laws (codes of union republics) consistent with the main principles stipulated in the fundamentals, and the "war of laws" was in full swing.

Even before the coup d'état was attempted and successfully suppressed, the union republics stopped being obedient servants of the central government. Russia was one of these, though not the most disobedient republic. On June 12, 1990, the first Congress of People's Deputies of the RSFSR declared political independence for Russia and proclaimed "the full authority of the RSFSR in resolution of all questions with the exception of those that were voluntarily transferred to the U.S.S.R. authorities."[10] The declaration also proclaimed superiority of the RSFSR Constitution and RSFSR laws on the territory of the

RSFSR and all-Union laws in contradiction of the sovereign rights of the RSFSR were suspended.[11] These republic covenants contradicted the main provisions of the U.S.S.R. Constitution and were *at least in appearance* disregarded by central authorities. Two months later, on August 12, 1990, again in contradiction to the U.S.S.R. Constitution, the Presidium of the Supreme Soviet of the RSFSR enacted a Resolution on Protection of the Economic Base of RSFSR Sovereignty.[12] This resolution stated that the transformation of state-owned enterprises on RSFSR territory into joint-stock companies and the transformation of state property into other forms of property would be performed in accordance with and within the terms stipulated by RSFSR laws.[13]

On October 24, 1990, the U.S.S.R. Parliament adopted the Law on Assurance of Application of the U.S.S.R. Statutes and other U.S.S.R. Legislative Acts."[14] The law stipulated that if the statute of the republic differs from the U.S.S.R. statute, the U.S.S.R. statute prevails up to the time of signing of the All-Union Treaty.[15] If a U.S.S.R. law or any other legislative act or act of the U.S.S.R. executive body, in the opinion of the republic, violated republic sovereign rights, the matter was resolved by the Committee on Constitutional Control of the U.S.S.R. in accordance with the provisions of Article 124 of the U.S.S.R. Constitution.[16]

Also on October 24, 1990, the Russian Parliament adopted the Law on Application of Acts of U.S.S.R. Agencies on the Territory of the RSFSR[17] as a challenge to the U.S.S.R. Law on Assurance of Application of the U.S.S.R. Statutes and Other U.S.S.R. Legislative Acts. Under this law, all U.S.S.R. laws and the U.S.S.R. Presidents' Decrees, to be applicable in the RSFSR, must be ratified by the RSFSR Supreme Soviet. Similarly, all acts issued by the representatives of the executive power of the U.S.S.R., to be applicable in the RSFSR, must be confirmed by the RSFSR Council of Ministers.[18] All previously enacted U.S.S.R. acts remain valid in the RSFSR only if they are not suspended by the RSFSR Supreme Soviet or Council of Ministers.[19] One month later, the validity of the U.S.S.R. Law on Enterprises in the U.S.S.R. was abrogated (see *infra*).[20]

On January 22, Russia challenged the central authorities once again. The Council of Ministers of the RSFSR enacted Regulations on the Order of Transfer of Enterprises and Organizations Under All-Union Authority, Located on the Territory of RSFSR to RSFSR Governmental Agency Authority."[21]

Within a two-year period beginning in late 1989, a significant number of all-Union laws bearing direct relation to economic activity of enterprises in the USSR were adopted. The most important of them included the following:

1. Fundamental Legislation of the U.S.S.R. and the Union Republics on Leasehold[22]
2. Fundamental Legislation of the U.S.S.R. and the Union Republics on Land Ownership[23]

3. Law of the Union of Soviet Socialist Republics on Property in the U.S.S.R.[24]
4. Law of the Union of Soviet Socialist Republics on Enterprises[25]
5. Fundamental Legislation of the U.S.S.R. and the Union Republics in Investment in the U.S.S.R.[26]
6. Fundamental Legislation of the U.S.S.R. and the Union Republics on Foreign Investment in the U.S.S.R.[27]

The Fundamental Legislation of the U.S.S.R. and Union Republics on Leasing was the first law to provide for the creation of various types of enterprises "based on collective ownership such as collective enterprises (specific types of corporations whose shares belong to its employees), cooperatives, joint stock companies," and so on.[28] The Law on Enterprises developed this idea and gave a broad description of creation, operation, and termination of enterprises. It did not define each specific type of enterprise permitted to exist under the guidance of this law.

Half a year later, on December 25, 1990, the Parliament of the RSFSR adopted the RSFSR Law on Enterprises and Entrepreneurial Activity,[29]which addresses the creation, operation, and termination of specific enterprises with different legal and organizational status, including state-owned enterprises, enterprises owned by municipal authorities, private (family) businesses, partnerships, mixed (limited) partnerships, limited liability partnerships (closed joint-stock companies), and joint-stock companies.[30] The classification provided by RSFSR law differs from the classification provided by the all-Union laws.

Both sets of laws refer to joint-stock companies. The emergence of joint-stock companies in the U.S.S.R. and the republics was an expected result of economic changes in the country. Joint-stock and Limited Liability Companies Regulations enacted by the U.S.S.R. Council of Ministers[31] and Joint-stock Company Regulations enacted by the RSFSR Council of Ministers[32] were enacted by executive authority rather than by a legislative body. Strictly speaking they are legislative enactments rather than statutes. The U.S.S.R. Regulations were a temporary measure. The RSFSR Joint-stock Company Regulations were expressly made a "temporary measure" until adoption of the RSFSR Law on Joint-stock Companies."[33]

After the failed coup, all republics, even those seriously considering the possibility of signing the new version of the Union Treaty, claimed more economic independence and are certain to adopt and follow their own joint-stock companies law. The Russian Federation Council of Ministers, in its Resolution No. 601 on Enactment of Joint-stock Companies Regulations, rejected the application of the all-Union regulations and instructed all joint-stock companies registered before the enactment of the Russian Joint-stock Companies Regulations to reregister with the Ministry of Finance of the RSFSR.[34]

The issue of registration (incorporation) of joint-stock companies in the

RSFSR is very confusing, because it produces contradictions between the all-Union Regulations and the RSFSR Regulations and within the body of RSFSR law itself.

RSFSR Joint-stock Companies Regulations provide for joint-stock company registration in the Ministry of Finance of the RSFSR. Such centralization is hardly reasonable in a country as big as Russia and may cause significant delays and unnecessary violations of the provision of Article 32 of the RSFSR Joint-stock Companies Regulations, which requires registration of a joint-stock company to be executed within 30 days after filing the foundation documents. Centralization is even more unreasonable considering that several rather large autonomous republics within Russia also demand some degree of independence. This provision also expressly contradicts the RSFSR Law on Enterprises and Entrepreneurial Activity,[35] which provides for registration of *all* enterprises in local Soviets of Peoples Deputies where the enterprise is located.[36] This provision shows the immaturity of Soviet legislators in corporate matters. In accordance with the RSFSR Constitution,[37] local Soviets represent legislative power and perform their duties at sessions held at least three times a year.[38] Between sessions, the authority of Soviets is represented by the presidiums, which are prohibited from interfering in the day-to-day activity of the executive committees of the local Soviets.[39] Registration of enterprises is not a legislative activity; it is within the authority of governmental agencies. In the United States, Articles of Incorporation are filed with the secretary of a particular state, which represents the executive power. It seems that the provision of the U.S.S.R. regulations requiring registration with an executive committee of the local Soviet within whose constituency the company is located is the most reasonable course of action.[40]

It is safe to presume that RSFSR laws require double registration, which is not unusual for registration procedures stipulated by RSFSR laws. The RSFSR Law on Foreign Investment in the RSFSR[41] requires all foreign investors to register with the RSFSR Ministry of Finances[42] in accordance with the RSFSR Law on Enterprises and Entrepreneurial Activity.[43]

RSFSR Joint-stock Companies Regulations expressly allow foreign legal entities and foreign citizens to become founders of the joint-stock companies.[44] The Law on Foreign Investments in the RSFSR allows foreign investors to create and operate foreign investment enterprises (joint ventures or fully owned enterprises) and their affiliates in the form of joint-stock companies and other economic units and partnerships.[45] Enterprises with foreign investments may be created by charter and registration or by share acquisition in an already existing enterprises.[46]

In the United States, each state has an incorporation statute that governs the creation and activity of the corporation. The most favorable state statute is the Delaware law, and most American corporations are incorporated there. By contrast, all joint-stock companies created in Russia are governed by the

RSFSR (not other republics) Regulations on Joint-stock Companies.[47]

In the U.S.A. the process of incorporation consists of filing Articles of Incorporation, signed and acknowledged by incorporators, with the secretary of state. The new corporation must hold an organizational meeting to adopt the bylaws and authorize the issuance of the first share of stock.

The U.S.S.R. and the RSFSR regulations have different, and sometimes contradictory, provisions. The procedure stipulated by the U.S.S.R. Regulations on Joint-stock and Limited Liability Companies requires the following documents to be filed for registration: (1) the agreement among the founders;[48] (2) the agreement between the founders and shareholders;[49] and (3) the bylaws approved by the foundation meeting.[50] For a corporation to be created, two kinds of agreements must be signed, shares should be subscribed to and partially paid for,[51] and bylaws have to be approved at the foundation meeting.[52] In the Russian Federation, the procedure is different, but also unusual for American lawyers.

In the Russian Federation, a joint-stock company is registered by filing the following: (1) application for registration, which is a formal agreement among the company founders;[53] (2) bylaws approved at the foundation meeting and filed within 30 days;[54] and (3) a protocol of the foundation meeting.[55]

Once the joint-stock company is properly registered, it is issued a temporary certificate of registration.[56] Within 30 days after the registration, 50% of statutory capital has to be received and then the official certificate of registration is issued, otherwise registration is considered null and void.[57]

The subscription to shares in the U.S.A. is regulated by the Federal Securities Act of 1933. It applies broadly to the interstate sale of securities. The main objective of the Securities Act is to provide full disclosure of information to the investor and to prevent fraud and misrepresentation. It would behoove Russia to promulgate a law with similar objectives for two reasons: (1) Russia is a very large country with several republics; and (2) the development of joint-stock companies in the former republics will inevitably result in interrepublican sale of securities.

There are discrepancies as to the type and kind of shares that may be issued by a company in Russia. The U.S.S.R. Joint-stock Companies Regulations provide for bearer shares and registered shares with the restriction that citizens may own only registered shares of stock.[58] RSFSR regulations are more strict in that they provide only for registered shares.[59] This provision is not unreasonable given the contemporary tendency to regulate movement of various kinds of securities and the immaturity of dealings with securities in the RSFSR.

A rather disturbing aspect of the RSFSR Regulations on Joint-stock Companies is the inability of stockholders to dismiss a member of the board of directors prior to expiration of his or her term.[60] The U.S.S.R. Regulations contain the right of stockholders to dismiss members of the supervisory board and the board of directors or the management body of the joint-stock company, though it is not specified whether they may be dismissed with or without cause.[61]

A special problem is the transformation of old state-owned enterprises into joint-stock companies. The RSFSR Law on Privatization of State- and Municipal-owned Enterprises,[62] which developed the legal frame of privatization of state-owned enterprises in the Russian Republic was adopted only three days after the U.S.S.R. Law on Basic Principles of De-stateization and Privatization of Enterprises. The U.S.S.R. Regulations on Joint-Stock and Limited Liability Companies contain a specific provision stipulating that a state-owned enterprise has the right to convert to a joint-stock company by issuance of shares for the full value of its assets.[63] To convert, the joint decision of a labor collective and "appropriately empowered state authority" is required. At the time that the U.S.S.R. Regulations on Joint-stock and Limited Liability Companies were enacted, functions of the "appropriately empowered state authority" were performed by the ministries. On July 1, 1991, the U.S.S.R. Law on Basic Principles of De-stateization and Privatization of Enterprises[64] created the U.S.S.R. State Property Fund,[65] which makes decisions on privatization of enterprises.[66] If the labor collective initiates the procedure and the U.S.S.R. State Property Fund disagrees with it, the disagreement falls under the jurisdiction of the Supreme Arbitration Tribunal of the U.S.S.R.[67]

The U.S.S.R. Law on Basic Principles of De-stateization and Privatization of Enterprises reflects the desire of the central authority to continue to control the republics. However, it also reflects the reluctant acknowledgment of the central authorities that the republics are not going to surrender their independence and will regulate their own economy. Article 2 of the U.S.S.R. Law on Basic Principles of De-stateization and Privatization defines the terms and the order of privatization of enterprises owned by the U.S.S.R., and lays out only *the general provisions* of privatization of enterprises owned by the republics and their administrative units.

In accordance with RSFSR Regulations on Joint-stock Companies, the decision to convert a state-owned enterprise into a joint-stock company has to be adopted by the "empowered state authority."[68] Such an authority was created by Regulations on State Committee on Management of State Property, which provides for the creation and operation of the RSFSR State Committee on Management of State Property.[69] The Committee makes decisions on conversion of state-owned enterprises into joint-stock companies[70] and it is an independent governmental agency that is accountable to the RSFSR Council of Ministers.[71]

U.S.S.R. government agencies are barely mentioned in Russian Conversion documents because the Russian Council of Ministers also provided for transfer of the U.S.S.R. owned enterprises to the RSFSR.[72] Those resolutions were not just empty threats. On May 7, 1991, the RSFSR Council of Ministers adopted a Resolution On Transfer of Several Enterprises in the Coal Industry, Located on

RSFSR Territory, to the Authority of RSFSR Governmental Agencies.[73] The initiative for transfer came from the labor collectives of these enterprises.

The transfer procedure has several elements: (1) enterprises within U.S.S.R. authority express their desire to be owned by RSFSR governmental agencies;[74] (2) if there are no objections from the U.S.S.R. governmental agencies, the RSFSR State Committee on Management of State Property adopts the decision to accept this enterprise into the RSFSR governmental agencies' jurisdiction;[75] (3) if the U.S.S.R. agencies object, the RSFSR State Committee on Management of State Property files a motion to the U.S.S.R. governmental agencies on transfer of the enterprise; (4) if this motion is denied, the RSFSR State Committee on Management of State Property makes a decision and *notifies* the U.S.S.R. government agencies of the decision;[76] (5) within the period of transfer from one authority to another, the enterprise has to be registered in accordance with the RSFSR Law on Enterprises and Entrepreneurial Activity; (6) the decision to convert the state-owned enterprise into a joint-stock company may be adopted simultaneously;[77] (7) all transfers are free of charge.[78]

Absence of political stability, lack of clarity of future economic development of the country as a union (whether political or economic), the elimination of major economic and financial structures that followed the failure of the August 19, 1991, coup, and chaos in relations between the all-Union and republican legislatures create significant problems for foreign investors, who in general are very much attracted by the enormous wealth and scope of the country. And even though new RSFSR laws are mostly encouraging and favorable to foreign investors, instability of the central-republican relations slows down the pace of development of business relations between foreign business entities and soviet enterprises.

NOTES

1. Decree of the Presidium of the U.S.S.R. Supreme Soviet on Questions Concerning the Establishment in the Territory of the U.S.S.R. and Operation of Joint Ventures, International Amalgamations, and Organizations with the Participation of Soviet and Foreign Organizations, Firms, and Management Bodies, (adopted January 13, 1987), published in *Vedomosti of the Supreme Soviet of the U.S.S.R.* (hereafter *Vedomosti*) No. 2, St. 35 (hereafter referred to as Joint Venture Decree).

2. The first Russian Soviet Federated Socialist Republic Constitution was promulgated July 10, 1918.

3. See I. Braude, "Joint-stock companies and partnerships in trade and industry" (Moscow, 1923).

4. See J. Izraelit, "Joint-stock Companies"(Moscow, 1928).

5. Civil Code of Russian Soviet Federated Socialist Republic (adopted November 15, 1922), Articles 322–326.

6. Resolution of the U.S.S.R. Council of Ministers No. 49 on the Establishment in the Territory of the U.S.S.R. and Operation of Joint Ventures with Participation of Soviet Organizations and Firms from Capitalist and Developing Countries (enacted January 13, 1987), published in *Vedomosti*, No. 2, St. 40 (hereafter referred to as Resolution No. 49).

7. The U.S.S.R. Law on State-owned Enterprises (enacted June 30, 1987), published in *Izvestia*, July 1, 1987.

8. The Constitution (The Supreme Law of the Land) of the Union of Soviet Socialist Republics, with changes and amendments, related to the improvement of the system of government management, as amended by U.S.S.R. Law as of December 26, 1990, published in *Vedomosti*, 1991, No. 1, St. 4.

9. Constitution of the Union of Soviet Socialist Republics, Article 73, para. 4.

10. Declaration on State Sovereignty of the Russian Soviet Federated Socialist Republic (promulgated June 12, 1990), published in *Vedomosti*, No. 2, St. 22, Article 5, para. 2.

11. *Id.*, Article 5, para. 3.

12. Resolution of the Presidium of the Supreme Soviet of the RSFSR On Protection of Economic Basis of the RSFSR Sovereignty (enacted August 9, 1990), published in *Vedomosti*, No. 10, St. 133.

13. *Id.*, Article 4.

14. The U.S.S.R. Law on Assurance of Application of the U.S.S.R. Statutes and other U.S.S.R. Legislative Acts (promulgated October 24, 1990), published in *Vedomosti*, No. 44, St. 918.

15. *Id.*, Article 1.

16. *Id.*, Article 2.

17. On Application of Acts of the U.S.S.R. Agencies on the Territory of the RSFSR (enacted October 24, 1990), published in *New Laws of Russia* (Moscow, 1991).

18. *Id.*, Article 2.

19. *Id.*, Article 4.

20. Resolution of the Supreme Soviet of the RSFSR on Enactment of the RSFSR Law on Enterprises and Entrepreneurial Activity (adopted December 25, 1990), published in *Vedomosti*, No. 30, Article 2.

21. Regulations on Order of Transfer of Enterprises and Organizations Under All-Union Authority, Located on the Territory of RSFSR to RSFSR Governmental Agency Authority (enacted January 22, 1991), published in *Law and Economics*, No. 3, 1991, *Postfactum* (Moscow).

22. The Fundamental Legislation of the Union of Soviet Socialist Republics and the Union Republics on Leasehold, St. No. 481 (enacted November 23, 1989), published in *Vedomosti*, No. 25.

23. The Fundamental Legislation of the Union of Soviet Socialist Republics and the Union Republics on Land Ownership, St. No. 129 (enacted February 28, 1990), published in *Vedomosti*, No. 10.

24. Law of the Union of Soviet Socialist Republics on Property in the U.S.S.R., St. No. 164 (enacted March 6, 1990), published in *Vedomosti*, No. 11.

25. Law of the Union of Soviet Socialist Republics on Enterprises (enacted June 4, 1990), published in *Izvestia*, June 12, 1990.

26. The Fundamental Legislation of the Union of Soviet Socialist Republics and the

Union Republics in Investment in the U.S.S.R., St. No. 1109 (enacted December 10, 1990), published in *Vedomosti*, No. 51.

27. The Fundamental Legislation of the Union of Soviet Socialist Republics and the Union Republics on Foreign Investment in the U.S.S.R. (enacted July 2, 1991), published in *Izvestia*, July 16, 1991.

28. The Fundamental Legislation of the U.S.S.R. and the Union Republics on Leasehold, Article 10.

29. The Law of the RSFSR on Enterprises and Entrepreneurial Activity (enacted December 25, 1990), published in *Vedomosti*, No. 30.

30. *Id.*, Articles 6–12.

31. Regulations on Joint-stock and Limited Liabilities Companies (enacted by Resolution of the U.S.S.R. Council of Ministers No. 590, June 19, 1990), published in *Bulletin of Legal Regulations of the U.S.S.R. Ministries and Departments*, No. 2, July 1990.

32. Regulations on Joint-stock Companies in the RSFSR (enacted by Resolution No. 601, December 25, 1990), published in *New Laws on Enterprises* (Moscow, 1991), p. 183.

33. Resolution of the RSFSR Council of Ministers No. 601, Article 1.

34. *Id.*, Article 7.

35. The Law of the RSFSR on Enterprise and Entrepreneurial Activity, *supra* note 29.

36. The RSFSR Law on Enterprises and Entrepreneurial Activity, Article 34.

37. Constitution of Russian Soviet Federated Socialist Republic (adopted April 12, 1978, with changes and amendments inserted by the RSFSR Laws enacted October 27, 1989, May 31, 1990, June 16, 1990, and December 15, 1990), *Sovetskaya Rossiya* (Moscow, 1991).

38. *Id.*, Article 141.

39. The RSFSR Law on Relations Between Soviets of Peoples' Deputies and Their Executive Committees During the Period of Economic Reforms (enacted October 10, 1990), published in *New Laws of Russia* (Moscow, 1991), p. 168.

40. Regulations on Joint-stock and Limited Liability Companies in the USSR, Article 9.

41. The RSFSR Law on Foreign Investments in the RSFSR (enacted June 4, 1991), published in *The Most Important Documents of the Month* (July 1991).

42. *Id.*, Article 13.

43. *Id.*, Article 16.

44. Regulations on Joint-stock Companies in the RSFSR, Article 11.

45. The RSFSR Law on Foreign Investments in the RSFSR, Article 12.

46. *Id.*, Article 13.

47. On Enactment of Joint-stock Companies Regulations, Resolution of RSFSR Council of Ministers No. 601, Article 8.

48. Regulations on Joint-stock and Limited Liability Companies in the U.S.S.R., Article 38., para. 3.

49. *Id.*, Article 39.

50. *Id.*, Article 7, Article 47, para. 3a.

51. *Id.*, Article 42, para. 3.

52. *Id.*, Article 47, para 3a.

53. Regulations on Joint-stock Companies in the RSFSR, Articles 14, 16 and 25.

54. *Id.*, Articles 14, 19 and 25.

55. *Id.*, Article 14 and 25.

56. Regulations on Joint-stock Companies in the RSFSR, Article 33.

57. *Id.*, Articles 27, 33.

58. Regulations on Joint-stock and Limited Liability Companies in the U.S.S.R., Article 34.

59. Regulations on Joint-stock Companies in the RSFSR, Article 46.

60. *Id.*, Article 113.

61. Regulations on Joint-stock and Limited Liability Companies in the U.S.S.R., Article 49.

62. The RSFSR Law on Privatization of State- and Municipal-owned Enterprises in the RSFSR (enacted July 3, 1991), published in *The Most Important Documents of the Month*, July, 1991.

63. *Id.*, Article 46.

64. The Law on Basic Principles of De-stateization and Privatization of Enterprises (enacted July 1, 1991), published in *Izvestia*, August 8, 1991.

65. *Id.*, Article 7.

66. *Id.*, Article 9, para. 2.

67. *Id.*

68. RSFSR Regulations on Joint-stock Companies, Article 12.

69. Regulations on State Committee on Management of State Property (enacted by the Resolution of the RSFSR Council of Ministers No. 35, January, 21, 1991), published in *Law and Economics*, No. 3, 1991, *Postfactum* (Moscow).

70. Regulations on State Committee on Management of State Property, Part III, Article 7.

71. *Id.*, Part I, Article 1.

72. Regulations on Order of Transfer of Enterprises and Organizations Under All-Union Authority, *supra* note 21.

73. Resolution of the RSFSR Council of Ministers on Transfer of Several Enterprises in the Coal Industry Located on RSFSR Territory to the Authority of RSFSR Governmental Agencies (enacted May 7, 1991), published in *Law and Economics*, No. 9, 1991, *Postfactum* (Moscow).

74. *Id.*, Article 1.

75. *Id.*, Article 5.

76. *Id.*, Article 6.

77. *Id.*, Article 7.

78. *Id.*, Article 2.

35

Financial Reform in the Former U.S.S.R.

Nicholas N. Kozlov

Since August 1991, the pace of change in the Soviet-Russian financial system has matched the flow of political developments, particularly in the wake of the very fluid situation induced by the collapse of central authority. During the week (December 1, 1991) that this chapter was written, the assets of Gosbank S.S.S.R. and Vneshekonombank S.S.S.R. were sequestered by the Central Bank of Russia,[1] the Russian republican government took upon itself the funding of the Union government budget, and the overwhelming passage of the Ukrainian independence referendum was accompanied by strong indications that several republics (states), including Russia, would begin issuing their own currencies.[2] The December 8 declaration of the formation of a Commonwealth of Independent States envisioned that a single currency unit would be maintained, but this is increasingly unlikely, given the intentions expressed by Ukraine and Moldavia.

The current predilection for the "microfoundations of macro" within the economics profession has led most Western observers of perestroika to focus primarily on decentralization and price liberalization, with very little thought given to the establishment of macroinstitutions necessary to support decentralized economic activity or to the appropriate sequencing of reforms in the transition from an administered economy to a market economy.[3] Macro "policy" suggestions from most Western advisers are limited to sermons on the imperative of fiscal and monetary austerity. Unfortunately, Soviet policymakers have followed this lead, and reforms such as the devolution of decision-making authority to the enterprise level (the July 1987 Law on State Enterprise [Association]), introduction of novel property relations (the 1988 Law on Cooperatives), and decentralization of foreign trade (beginning January 1987) all preceded the implementation of comprehensive measures to establish commercial financial and (systematic) public fiscal structures appropriate to decentralized economic activity. (Indeed, such structures are still absent as the virtually total decontrol of prices is under way.) This neglect of "macro-foundations of micro" has clearly come home to roost, as the decentralization measures adopted since 1988 have promoted unplanned growth of the money supply and the appearance of a massive government budget deficit.[4] The central point is simple: there exist *no* microeconomic institutional arrangements—either administered or market in nature—that can function in conditions of macroeconomic imbalance.

BANKING AND FINANCE IN THE ADMINISTERED ECONOMY

Traditional Soviet financial structures are well-enough known to require only a brief introduction. Gosbank S.S.S.R. (State Bank of the U.S.S.R.) has been the ubiquitous Soviet financial institution, serving as a universal settlements bank, short-term creditor to industrial enterprises, recipient of government budget revenues, and center of currency emission. Long-term financing of major investment expenditures and financing of foreign trade were carried out by Gosbank's subordinate Stroibank (Bank for Financing Capital Investments) and Vneshtorgbank (Bank for Foreign Trade). The public was able to hold savings deposits, but not transactions deposits, at Gostrudsberkassy (State Labor Savings Bank) branches. The latter institution engaged in virtually no credit operations of its own, and historically has been essentially a department of the Ministry of Finance (prior to the 1960s) or Gosbank S.S.S.R.

Soviet economists and policymakers, and most Western observers, have generally emphasized the strict demarcation between cash money (*nalichnye den'gi*) and scriptural money (*beznalichnye den'gi*) in the traditional Soviet setting. Use of the former has been confined to the consumer and collective sector, where it served as a means of circulation, while the latter has been utilized only in the state (industry, transport, state agriculture, etc.) sector, where it served as means of payment. With some minor exceptions, consumer purchases were exclusively on a cash basis, whereas interenterprise and enterprise-government transactions were conducted entirely in scriptural money—that is, transfers of funds among Gosbank accounts. Except for those few enterprises that directly engaged in retail activity (receipts from which were promptly deposited with Gosbank), the only instance in which an enterprise would "touch" cash would be upon withdrawal of the wage packet from Gosbank on payday, prior to distribution to the workforce. At the retail level, Soviet cash money was an "active" claim on resources and, assuming a particular item was available, it could be acquired upon the presentation of rubles.

Scriptural money, however, played a "passive" role in the traditional Soviet setting. For an enterprise to acquire inputs, for example, having scriptural money on account at Gosbank was insufficient. Even more necessary than a bank account with a positive balance was the active claim on resources afforded by physical allocation certificates distributed by the planning network in accordance with the economic plan. Although such allocated resources had to be paid for, flows of funds were only a reflection of the physical plan-allocation process, and performed only a monitoring and control function (albeit an important one) in the evaluation of plan fulfillment. Enterprise accounts at Gosbank were accessible only for those specific purposes spelled out by the plan, funds for planned activities were routinely made available, and the bulk of enterprise profit was siphoned off to the state budget. All of these arrangements were well-suited to the nature of the administratively planned economy.

Nevertheless, as Marie Lavigne has shown, it was never the case that an impermeable firewall separated the circulation of passive scriptural money from the circulation of active cash money.[5] Even prior to the 1988 relaxation of wage norms, changes in scriptural flows would "leak" into the cash sector via wage disbursements. This process simply became more pronounced after 1988.[6] The logic of decentralization would suggest integration of the two types of money and the transition to an active money and credit system with macroeconomic controls. Strangely, however, even the final version of the "official" (i.e., emanating from the last Union Council of Ministers) economic reform strategy called only for fortifying the cash-scriptural distinction to stem the rising leakage into cash.[7]

REFORMS PRIOR TO AUGUST 1988

The principal intent of bank reforms decreed in 1987 (implemented January 1, 1988) was the separation of the government budgetary process from the financing of commercial activity, and the introduction of some measure of decentralization and commercial criteria in lending. The reform called for Gosbank to cease financing industry and commerce, and for such financing to be taken up by a new system of functionally specialized banks. After the reform, the principal Soviet financial institutions included Gosbank S.S.S.R., Promstroibank S.S.S.R. (Industrial-Construction Bank of the U.S.S.R.), Agroprombank S.S.S.R. (Agricultural-Industrial Bank of the U.S.S.R.), Zhilsotsbank S.S.S.R. (Bank for Housing-Communal Economy and Social Development of the U.S.S.R.), Vneshekonombank S.S.S.R. (Bank for Foreign Economic Activity of the U.S.S.R.), and Sberbank S.S.S.R. (Bank for Labor Savings and Credit to the Public of the U.S.S.R.).[8] The latter two were basically the restructured Vneshtorgbank and Gostrudsberkassy, respectively. Sberbank remained independent for only a year, and in 1990 was again subordinated to Gosbank. Banking activity in the U.S.S.R. has traditionally generated considerable profits, but, as was also the case with profits of industrial enterprises, these accrued to the government budget. The 1988 reform allowed banks to retain a much larger portion of their profits, and placed them on full *khozraschet* (self-support) and self-financing.

A Council of Banks of the U.S.S.R. was established to coordinate and oversee the activity of Gosbank and the specialized banks. The Council consisted of the chairs of the respective banks and other (unspecified) Union departments. The Council itself was headed by the chair of Gosbank. Each of the specialized Union banks was directed to establish republic-level (and, if necessary, regional and urban) departments. The functional specialization of the new independent banks was to be ensured by their subordination to the relevant branch ministries, which maintained the right to appoint the chair of the bank. Enterprises were permitted to deal with only one bank, and credit terms continued to be established administratively via interest rate controls (by Gosbank), imposition of credit limitations for the specialized banks (by Gosplan), and ministerial supervision of lending. The administered interest rate structure was differentiated according to the intended use of the credits (i.e., for planned uses, above-planned activities, or unforseen circumstances). Moreover, bank officials were given the right to make modifications, within limits, of the established interest rate structure. In case of default, the decree allowed for the possibility of liquidation or reorganization, but the procedure for this remained unspecified.

Agroprombank and Promstroibank were easily the largest of the specialized banks in terms of credits outstanding, together accounting for just over 80 percent of the total. Neither of these two banks, nor Zhilsotsbank, independently attracted the entirety of their lendable resources. Rather, they were to a greater or lesser degree funded by Gosbank. On the other hand, Sberbank, although the largest deposit-taker in the system, was the smallest in terms of credits outstanding—about 2% of the total.[9]

THE FINANCIAL SYSTEM AFTER 1988

The institutional arrangements outlined in the preceding section proved to be unstable and transitory. In the second half of 1988, the implementation of the Law on Cooperatives and the appearance of a Gosbank decree (August) authorizing the formation of independent commercial banks rapidly altered the nature of the Soviet financial system.[10] By September, some 150 such (cooperative and commercial) banks had been established, a year later there were 400, and by September 1, 1991, 1,535 were in operation. The average commercial bank in September 1991 had capital of 10.63 million rubles, deposits of 72.5 million rubles, and loans outstanding (short- and long-term) of 121.85 million rubles.[11]

From the moment (March 1988) of the first appearance of the draft Law on

Cooperatives, it was envisioned (Article 21) to permit the formation of cooperative banks, primarily because of the expectation that the specialized state banks would be less than enthusiastic about financing cooperative economic activity. A bank established by a cooperative (or a consortium of cooperatives) was given the right to underwrite securities issued by the cooperative, to accept deposits from citizens or state enterprises, and to receive credits from the specialized banks.

Commercial banks were authorized to accept deposits and engage in short- and long-term lending. Generally, the commercial banks are established by a state enterprise or group of enterprises (state farms have also organized banks)[12] and are not so much financial intermediaries as pools of finance organized by the banks' founders and large institutional depositors. The commercial Interbank appears to be representative.[13] Interbank was registered with the Central Bank of the RSFSR in November 1990, with an initial capitalization of 70 million rubles and $1 million. The 16 founders of the bank include industrial enterprises, educational societies, a Soviet-Spanish joint venture, a state bank, and government agencies.[14] The bank's principal depositors are large institutions: the Association of Inter-Branch Scientific-Technical Complexes and the Moscow Metals Exchange. As apparently is often the case, Interbank was founded largely to accommodate the credit requirements of its founders, especially in those instances when the specialized banks are unwilling or unable to do so. These sorts of arrangements obviously raise some very interesting issues.

The state specialized banks, very soon after their establishment, began to be converted into joint-stock companies. The shareholders generally include the Ministry of Finance, industrial ministries, regional or city governments, and enterprises. This process is moving most rapidly with Zhilsotsbank; the commercial bank Mosbiznesbank is essentially the former Moscow city Zhilsotsbank.[15]

Soviet/Russian commercial banking, from the August 1988 Gosbank decree to the present time, is a relatively unregulated activity. So long as they adhere to several prudential balance sheet requirements, commercial banks are by and large free to take deposits, to make short- and long-term loans, to pursue equity investments, and to purchase real estate. Banks are prohibited from engaging in material production. Prior to the formal regulatory legislation passed in December 1990, such regulations as did exist were established by ad hoc decrees of Gosbank or the government.

In December 1990, legislation on the central bank and banks and banking activity was passed, separately, by the U.S.S.R. and RSFSR Supreme Soviets. Although the Union and Russian laws were in many respects contradictory, and expressed conflicting jurisdictional claims, events since December 8, 1991, have rendered these issues moot. The following discussion is confined to the RSFSR legislation.[16]

The Central Bank of the Russian Federation (or Bank of Russia) is owned by the state (the government of the Russian Federation), and while independent of executive authority, is subordinate to the Supreme Soviet of the Russian Federation. The chair of the Central Bank is appointed for a five-year term by the Supreme Soviet, and is subject to removal from office at the discretion of the Supreme Soviet. Members of the Board of Directors are chosen by the chair of the Central Bank, subject to approval by the Presidium of the Supreme Soviet. The Bank is expected to be self-financing. Among the tasks specifically enumerated for the Bank are regulation of the circulation of money, stabilization of the ruble, formulation of a unified monetary and credit policy, organization of a payments system, protection of the interests of depositors, monitoring the activity of commercial banks, and carrying out international currency operations.

It is expected that the Bank will accomplish these objectives using the standard tools of money supply management, as well as by enforcing the following regulatory standards: minimum levels of founding capital (currently 100 million rubles for a commercial bank, but apt to soon go higher given the rapid pace of inflation), minimum capital-liability ratios (1:20 for a commercial and 1:12 for a cooperative bank), minimum reserve requirements (10%), several indicators of balance sheet liquidity, ceilings on the amount of credit (in relation to capital) that can be extended to one borrower, and ceilings on the use of liabilities for equity purchases. Limitations on the government debt are established by the Supreme Soviet, and the Bank of Russia is permitted (within these limits) to extend credits to the Ministry of Finance.

Banks are defined as institutions having the status of juridical persons, which attract financial resources from other juridical or physical persons and then distribute them according to commercial criteria. "Other" financial institutions may engage in less than the full range of banking activity. Deposit taking and loan granting, organizing payments, underwriting and dealing in securities, foreign exchange operations, dealing in precious metals, managing trust accounts, and offering brokerage or other consulting services are all treated by the legislation as permissible banking activities. The only explicit prohibitions are manufacture (production) or the trading of manufactures, and insurance services in areas other than insurance against financial risk.

Since the December 1990 legislation was introduced, there have been substantial modifications in the sphere of foreign currency operations. As of April 1991, the regulation of transactions involving foreign currency became considerably more restrictive than envisioned earlier.[17] At the same time, exchanges at which hard currency can be purchased for rubles (at market rates) have been established, supplanting the ad hoc occasional hard currrency auctions previously conducted by Vneshekonombank. This was partly a response to the emergence of hard currency debt repayment problems. But even more so, the restriction of hard currency transactions on Soviet territory was necessary to counter the parallel dollar economy that appeared following the dismantling of central planning and the decentralization of foreign trade. A characteristic scenario: the director of a Soviet plywood producing enterprise approaches his regular lumber supplier to arrange deliveries for the coming year. The supplier requests payment in hard currency, which is impossible for the plywood producer because their output is sold entirely inside the U.S.S.R. for rubles. The response of the lumber supplier is that deregulation of foreign trade has allowed him to sell lumber abroad, and mandatory (planned) allocations of materials have been suspended. Since there is demand on the world market for his lumber, it will be sold abroad and the plywood producer will have to look elsewhere for supplies.[18] The new regulations are thus an effort simultaneously to encourage the development of decentralized economic activity inside Russia on a ruble basis, as well as provide a source of hard currency for legitimate decentralized foreign trade.

The May 1991 hard currency regulations require enterprises to sell 40 percent of their hard currency earnings to Gosbank at the very overvalued commercial exchange rate (the earnings of joint ventures with more than 30 percent foreign participation are exempt). At the same time, they prohibit (with some exceptions) Russian enterprises or joint ventures from selling on the Russian market for hard currency. There are restrictions on hard currency payments to Russian citizens for work or services performed in Russia. Both Russian and foreign enterprises are permitted to hold ruble and hard currency accounts with Russian banks, although only a limited number of banks at the present time can offer the full range of foreign currency transactions. The hard currency exchange established by the legislation does not permit foreign enterprises to sell hard currency for rubles (as a means of escaping the unfavorable commercial exchange rate), and buyers of hard currency must declare the purpose to which the currency will be applied and must utilize the currency within two months of the purchase.

CURRENT DEVELOPMENTS

Contrary to the frequently voiced opinion that the principal contradiction was between the old "center" and (unspecified, yet supposedly univocal) "independence minded" entities, and that removal of the center would immediately relax all obstacles to progress, the collapse of central authority considerably complicates the situation. Political conflict at the intrarepublican level is pronounced and will escalate. President Boris Yeltsin and Vice-President Aleksandr Rutskoi are sharply at odds over the conduct of economic reform, to the extent that Rutskoi was recently scheduled to address a rally demanding the overthrow of the government he serves as vice-president! (Rutskoi failed to appear.) Yeltsin has also split with his former supporter

Gavril Popov, mayor of Moscow.

Likewise, turf disputes over more narrow economic questions will not abate with the collapse of the center. There are complaints that the Central Bank of Russia is even more inclined to "petty tutelage" than the former Gosbank S.S.S.R..[19] The commercial banks are displeased that the former specialized banks, even though they have been reorganized as commercial institutions, continue to receive favorable treatment from republican authorities and the central bank.[20] Care has to be taken in the organization of simple conferences not to involve too formally representatives of both the Central Bank of Russia and the Association of Commercial Bankers, for fear that the conference will be boycotted by one or the other party.[21]

The most serious difficulties will arise from the macroeconomic problem alluded to at the beginning of this chapter: reform of microeconomic arrangements (decontrol of prices, privatization) plunges ahead in conditions of uncontrolled macroimbalance, and without the financial and fiscal institutions appropriate to decentralized activity in place. President Yeltsin's absorption of the Union government bureaucracy into the Russian, besides not solving the problem of a bloated bureaucratic structure, means that Russia has inherited the Union's budget deficit. Yeltsin purchased the cooperation of the military by offering to pay double, and this debt will come due as well. Under such macroeconomic conditions, microinstitutional reform seems at least as misguided as the austerity "shock therapy" approach adopted in Poland or the former German Democratic Republic. Indeed, the current course of Russian policy may provoke a "shock therapy" response when inflation becomes intolerable, with results that will prove devastating to Russian industry.

NOTES

1. Postanovlenie Verkhovnogo Soveta RSFSR, "O finansovo-kreditnom obespechenii ekonomicheskoi reformy i reorganizatsii bankovskoi sistemy RSFSR." *Ekonomika i Zhizn'*, No. 50 (8379), December 1991.

2. There was even some indication prior to the Gosbank action and the Ukrainian referendum that Russia might proceed with the issue of a new "Russian ruble." V. Kozlov (head of department, U.S.S.R. Ministry of Finance), "Ruble with a Tri-Color Stripe," *Ekonomika i Zhizn'*, No. 47 (8376), November 1991.

3. The late Ed Hewett managed to write a lengthy book on the Soviet economic reform, the index to which carries no reference whatsoever to money, and has one listing for reform of the banking system, which refers the reader to a one paragraph discussion. Ed A. Hewett, *Reforming the Soviet Economy* (Washington, DC: Brookings Institution, 1988).

4. "It has apparently been decided by the leadership to effect the transition from an administered to a commodity economy by the single, simple expedient of ceasing to administer." Iu. M. Kolochkov, deputy head of department, Ministry of Economics and Forecasting of the U.S.S.R., November 25, 1991. The problematic fiscal situation of the

Soviet Union has been nicely analyzed by Ronald I. McKinnon, in his *The Order of Economic Liberalization* (Baltimore: Johns Hopkins University Press, 1991). Official data on the money supply only began to be published in September 1991. See McKinnon's Table 1.

5. Marie Lavigne, "The Creation of Money by the State Bank of the U.S.S.R.," *Economy and Society*, Vol. 7, No. 1 (February 1978). See also S. M. Ignat'ev, "Bankovskaia sistema: Puti reformy," *Ekonomika i organizatsiia promyshlenogo proizvodstva*, No. 8, 1988.

6. The ratio of the growth rate of money wages to the growth rate of labor productivity:

1986	1.2
1987	1.5
1988	1.6
1989	4.1

In 1990, money wages rose by 12.5 percent while labor productivity declined by 3 percent. *Narodnoe Khoziastvo S.S.S.R.*. (Moscow: Finansyi i statistika, 1989), and *Ekonomika i Zhizn'*, various 1991 issues.

7. N. I. Ryzhkov (then prime minister), "Effektivnost', konsolidatsiia, reforma—put' k zdorovoi ekonomike," Report to the Second U.S.S.R. Congress of Peoples' Deputies, *Pravda*, No. 348 (26066), December 14, 1989. See also the Decree of the U.S.S.R. Congress of Peoples' Deputies "O merakh po ozdorovleniu ekonomiki, etapakh ekonomicheskoi reformy i printsipial'nykh podkhodakh k razrabotke trinadtsatago piatiletnego plana," *Pravda*, No. 356 (26074), December 22, 1989.

8. The new arrangements were spelled out in a July 1987 decree (No. 821) issued jointly by the Central Committee of the CPSU and the Council of Ministers, "O sovershenstvovanii sistemy bankov v strane i uselenii ikh vozdeistviia na povyshenie effektivnosti ekonomiki," *O korennoi perestroike upravleniia ekonomikoi. Sbornik dokumentov* (Moscow: Politizdat, 1987).

9. Data compiled from Gosbank statistics.

10. "Proekt Zakona S.S.S.R. "O kooperatsii v S.S.S.R.," *Izvestia*, March 5, 1988. Also Vladimir P. Okhlopkov, chair of the board, Commercial Bank, "Business Russia," July 30, 1991.

11. Okhlopkov, in *ibid.*; N. Garetovskii, "Vedomstvennost' v bankovskoi sisteme?" *Ekonomicheskaia Gazeta*, No. 37, September 1989; and V. Zakharov, "Est'li garmonia v bankovskoi sfere?" *Ekonomika i Zhizn'* No. 44 (8373), October 1991.

12. The well-known sovkhoz "Balaia Dacha," in the Moscow suburbs, participated in the founding of a commercial bank in order to escape the tutelage of the Central Bank of Russia. Mark Meerovich Nakhmanovich, vice-director on economic questions, Sovkhoz "Belaia Dacha," August 18, 1991.

13. Aleksandr Molchanov, formerly a staff worker for the Central Committee of the CPSU, is Chair of the Board of Interbank.

14. The founders of Interbank are: the Association Intertraining, Gosstrakh S.S.S.R., Gostrakh RSFSR, Sberbank S.S.S.R., the industrial enterprise Vek, the Institute of Senior Management Personnel of the Academy of National Economy, the editorial collective of *Izvestia*, the Moscow Institute for Upgrading the Qualifications of Workers in the Chemical Industry, the Society Znanie, the all-Union Center for Juridical

Education of the Society Znanie, the Moscow Scientific-Production Union Astra, the industrial enterprise Kvant, the Scientific-Production Union Elma, the multisectoral association Avtoelektronsistema, the Soviet-Spanish joint venture Interslav, and the joint-stock company Birzha Metallov.

15. Irina Evgeneva, Information Department, "Mosbiznesbank," January 15, 1991.

16. Zakon RSFSR "O Tsentral'nom banke RSFSR (Banke Rossii)," and Zakon RSFSR "O bankakh i bankovskoi deiatel' nosti" (both dated December 2, 1990), *Pravovye Osnovy Deiatel'nosti Bankov, Ikh Kreditnykh i Raschetnykh Otnoshenii* (Moscow: AO Fakt, 1991).

17. Zakon SSSR "O valiutnom regulirovanii." Also, the Gosbank decrees "O regulirovanii valiutnykh operatsii na territorii S.S.S.R. (Osnovnye polozheniia)," in *Ekonomika i Zhizn'*, No. 22 (8351), May 1991; "Pravila osuschestvleniia operatsii v Tsentre provedeniia mezhbankovskikh valiutnykh operatsii (Valiutnaia birzha) Gosudarstvennogo banka S.S.S.R.," in *Ekonomika i Zhizn'*, No. 25 (8354), June 1991; and "Regulirovanie valiutnykh operatsii," in *Ekonomika i Zhizn'*, No. 33 (8362), August 1991.

18. This tale was related to the author by a Soviet plywood producer from Vladivostok in November 1990, at Hofstra University.

19. Nakhmanovich, Sovkhoz "Belaiz Dacha."

20. S. Berezin, "'Voina' bankov: konkurentsiia ili konfrontatsiia?" *Ekonomika i Zhizn'*, No. 37 (8366), September 1991.

21. Peter Barenboim, scientific coordinator, International Center for Draft-Legislative Expertise (Moscow), November 28, 1991.

36

Some Aspects of the Banking System in Russia

Sergei N. Gonchar and Tatiana U. Frolova

The development of banks in the Russian Federation, as well as in other states that constituted the former Soviet Union, has been an original evolutionary process that has left behind the development of economies of the newly formed states on the territory of the former U.S.S.R. This chapter tries to reveal some aspects of the banking sphere development in the former U.S.S.R. republics. Specifically, it discusses the State Bank of the U.S.S.R. as of September 1, 1991.

In U.S.S.R. enterprises and their associations, a gap existed and was regularly maintained between the processes of material production and financial reproduction. There was little economic correlation between material reproduction (production output, industrial capacities, industrial resources) and financial reproduction (financial resources). This position was in full conformity with the existing mechanism of the economy. The banking system of the U.S.S.R., which did not pursue its own commercial goals, was one of the main supports of the existing order. Changes in the state system of the country, the collapse of the territorial division of labor, and liquidation of the "vertical" system of administration put the enterprises to the task of reaching unity between the processes of material and financial reproduction, and the new commercial banks have become an instrument in this process.

Commercial banks in the former U.S.S.R. do not correspond in many respects to those in the countries with market economies. They have several notable characteristics:

- They offer banking services of an economic branch character, irrespective of the financial position of a given client where granting credits plays the major role. The provision of accounting services plays a secondary role and is aimed at the task of forming credit resourses (at the expense of clients accounts in the banks).

- The location of commercial banks on the territory of the country is irrespective of the intensity of economic activities in different regions (again, this reflects existing schemes of branch administration). This feature is supplemented by strict regulation of the foundation of ownership capital of commercial banks. Therefore, the banks pay much more attention to the problem of forming their capital than to the problems of forming a certain circle of clients.
- Usually the rate of dividends does not mean much to the shareholders of the banks. Often, shareholders are attracted by receiving a wide range of banking services (first of all credits) in their "own" bank.
- In many cases banks must deal with clients who have heavy overdue indebtedness from former state banks and are not ready to pay it off.

Commercial banks with those characteristics regularly buy large amounts of resources in state banks at a comparatively low interest rate. Thus they are able to provide that debt with finance sources. At the same time, the state banks receive an opportunity to influence the work of the commercial banks by determining conditions of granting credits, levels of interest rate, and by attempts to regulate relations among commercial banks (for example, it is prohibited for the bank that borrowed resources from the state bank to grant loans to other commercial banks). These peculiarities of banking in the Russian Federation (as well as in other republics) should not be interpreted as a failure to conform the banking system to the demands of the market economy because commercial banks are actively participating in the radical changes of the economic mechanisms in the former U.S.S.R. In order of formation, regulations and norms of banking operations are the same for all the banks. But they differ by their origin, by the interests they represent.

The so-called branch banks play an especially significant role in the transition from a planned to a market economy. The circle of banks of this kind is wide enough and has assembled considerable financial resources. Commercial banks created on the branch principle play an important role by granting credit, which provides enterprises with an opportunity to achieve a correlation between the needs of material production and financial resources. They also promote breakup of the branch system of administration, because branch enterprises receive access to financing in accordance with volume, cost, and terms.

In addition to branch banks, there are three more types of banks that should be mentioned: old banks, new regional banks, and high activity banks.

Old banks is a conventional and a widely used name for commercial banks that were created by transforming branches of the state specialized banks (Promotroybank, Agroprombank, Zhilsotsbank). These banks faced few problems of formation of their capital, had stable financial ties, a good basis upon which to accumulate credit resources, and a certain circle of clients.

Old banks have two serious problems. First, old banks have old clients in the form of state enterprises with heavy overdue indebtedness. The short-term loans granted to state enterprises several years ago for the needs of current activities have now become long-term debt. For many years the short-term credit has been a hidden form of inventory replenishment of these enterprises (a centrally planned target on the level of branch administration and central financial bodies). Resources of the State Bank of the U.S.S.R. provided allocation of such loans. Demand for these credits was usually caused by withdrawal of part of the net profit of state enterprises to centralized funds. During the period of transformation of the branches of the specialized State Banks into independent commercial banks, nothing was done to do away with the debt of this kind.

Second, the old banks had no opportunity to choose clients and were to provide this indebtedness in the full amount. The perspective of paying debts off remains very uncertain because in many cases the financial plans of the debtors simply do not envisage payment. In addition, banks do not stop crediting state enterprises because this will affect the system of their accounts and will lead to further destabilization of production ties.

The *new regional banks* are a completely new type of bank, and they have a large role in the banking system. They tend to concentrate in the industrial centers but are located throughout the country. Their formation was not connected with the structures of the State Bank. On their own, they have solved problems of accumulation of the ownership of capital and have formed their own circles of clients. They base their work on commercial principles and receive almost no support from the State Bank. The emergence of these regional banks is very original indeed and is also connected with the process of radical changes embracing branches of economy.

As a rule, the shareholders of this type of bank receive modest interest rates paid out of capital, but they highly value the efficiency and activity of banks in solving different questions (especially of granting credit). Decisions regarding granting loans to clients that are not shareholders of the bank are made taking into account the possibilities of clients as producers of goods and services and their utility for the shareholders of the bank (supplies of commodities, raw materials, and services are a serious problem).

The volume of their banking operations remains small, although they have the ability and potential for increasing them according to the norms of banking regulations of the Central Bank of Russia and national banks of republics.

Regional banks have high liquidity and are very careful about risky projects. They usually grant short-term and middle-term loans. Long-term credits are granted taking into consideration interests of shareholders and often connected with shares in the results of production. They are organized as limited companies. They generally do not seek transformation into open-type shareholder societies to avoid strengthening "alien" influences on their activity. At the same time, they admit new shareholders from other regions and with nonstate types of ownership. The inflow of such shareholders has increased.

These banks quickly assimilate new types of banking services, show a readiness to participate in stock exchange operations with stock and securities, and actively achieve the right to take part in foreign currency transactions. Though their interests are concentrated mainly in the region of their location, they show vivid interest in interregional and interrepublican ties. Absence of restrictions of credit exchange between the banks in different regions, creation of their image, advertisement, setting of production ties between shareholders of various banks, and so on, are incentives to establish interregional ties. Regional banks actively establish their branches and representative offices in different parts of the former U.S.S.R. and are ready to set direct correspondence ties; this is new for commercial banks. These banks are not well-known by the population, because they have just begun to render services to people. In the future, they can play a major role in the process of privatization of state enterprises.

High activity banks are another type of new bank. This type of bank most fully corresponds to the idea of the bank in the market economy and they have gained popularity in the country. They deal with commercial structures and their main task is to maximize profits. They have every reason to be considered pioneers in the development of new farms and methods of business. At present, the capital of these banks is sufficient due to their active work in issuing and selling their shares.

Naturally, banks of this type are more independent in their credit policy—in choosing their clients. Their business is connected with structural changes in the economy and development of the so-called alternative economy. They are free from obligations to render services to reproductional processes of previous years, but some complications are connected with this too (enterprises of commercial orientation created on the basis of productional capacities, which are apportioned from the structures of state enterprises and which could, without regret and losses, be transferred or sold to commercial bodies). The high activity banks aimed at the accumulation of financial resources for providing qualitative and structural changes using the high effective activity of the alternative economy.

High activity banks tend to be independent from the State Bank's policy. The exercise of independence has been inhibited by high inflation. In Russia high activity banks began to make every effort to receive free access to the credit resources of the Central Bank of Russia and began to struggle against protective trends in its activities. The antagonism between the Central Bank and the high activity banks reached its critical point in the second half of 1991, when high activity banks tried to form under their auspices an opposition to the Central Bank structures.

The limits of this chapter do not allow for a more detailed characterization of the present banking system in the Russian Federation and other republics. In spite of the banks' heterogeneity, the banking system in Russia functions stably, as confirmed by the work of the commercial banks during the two last months of 1991. At this time, nearly all the clients held back debts because they actively prepared for liberalization of prices. Enterprises did not hasten to sell their production and actively supplied their stocks in order to realize them the next year when the prices got higher.

The increase of interest rates during November and December was 2–3% but that was not too sharp, taking into account the circumstances of that moment.

It was not accidental that the Central Bank of Russia rose to the question about "credit intervention" by the commercial banks and took measures to ease it. But credit intervention is caused by two reasons: first is absence of a clear concept of the banking style development in Russia; second is the constant inflow of monetary mass and increasing credit activity of the banks.

Prospects of further evolution of the banking system are closely connected with putting into life the privatization program. Today, this program in the Russian Federation has not acquired a clear form. It will bring demand in long-term credits, although with rapid inflation, it will be a rather difficult task for commercial banks. Then there will be the need to create an interregional credit market, which is practically nil today.

Rendering services by the banks to the personnel of the state enterprises during the process of redeeming the state property will further widen the span of banking activities. Finally, the banks will have to assume the credit practice opposing the apparent trends of stagnation.

In spite of all the changes, the evolution of commercial banks in the different states of the former U.S.S.R. will have one model, meeting the demands of the market economy in spite of the specific features of each region in accordance with the development of this country's economy and taking into consideration competition among banks.

37

Designing a Bank Regulation System for the Former U.S.S.R.: Federalism Issues Under the U.S. Dual Banking System

James W. Weller

While the Soviet Union no longer exists, what will ultimately take its place appears uncertain. At the time of the writing of this paper, a Commonwealth of Independent States, made up of some of the member states of the former Union, had moved to fill this void. But the exact framework in which this Commonwealth is to function remains murky, at best. Previously, the Soviet Union had been groping toward reform of its entire economic system, including banking, currency, and bank regulation, and it is assumed that such reforms may be pursued in the developing Commonwealth.[1] The establishment of a system of banking regulation is the subject of this paper.

In the United States, bank regulation takes place on two levels. Federal authorities regulate banking, while regulatory authority is also concurrently exercised by the individual states. The interplay of regulatory authority, providing what has been termed the dual banking system in the United States, has generated a host of federalism issues.

Banking regulation in the Commonwealth developing in Eastern Europe may be established in an analogous framework. The individual states may regulate banking, while ceding some of their power to a central authority also regulating banking. By focusing on how some of the problems of regulation have been resolved in the United States and the balance that has been struck between federal and state regulatory control, a fuller understanding of the advantages and disadvantages of such a banking regulation system can be analyzed, understood, and dealt with in designing a system for the Commonwealth of Independent states.

This paper will begin with a discussion of how the dual regulatory system operates in the United States, and how it evolved to its present state. Discussion will touch on some of the benefits and drawbacks of the U.S. system. Next, focus will shift to recent changes in the system, and recent action by which Congress is attempting to narrow the authority of the states in the system. Evidence of this can be seen in recent efforts in Congress to enlarge federal regulation of bank branching. Some suggest that the very dual system of regulation is threatened by this. Finally, this paper will offer some tentative conclusions as to the continued vitality of the U.S. dual banking system, and the implications this holds for a system based on it in the Commonwealth of Independent States.

THE OPERATION OF THE U.S. DUAL BANKING SYSTEM

Current System of Regulation

Analysis of banking regulation must begin with the state and federal institutions responsible for such regulation. It has been said that bank regulation in the United States occurs on two levels, only one of which in the true sense is dual.[2] The first level involves chartering of banks. All banks in the United States must be chartered by either the state in which the bank is situated or by federal authorities. State chartering results in the bank being subjected to regulation by state regulators applying state law, which includes monitoring and regular examination of a bank's books and records, to determine compliance with state laws and to evaluate the bank's performance.[3] Alternatively, banks chartered by federal authorities are subject to review by federal regulators—the Office of the Comptroller of the Currency (OCC)—applying federal law.[4]

Superimposed over chartering authority (and its attendant powers), is a second system of regulation, exclusively federal, which is primarily administered through the Federal Reserve Board (FRB) and the Federal Deposit Insurance Corporation (FDIC). All national banks (chartered by the OCC) are, and must be, members of the Federal Reserve System, which is administered by the FRB (whose job is also to manage the nation's money supply).[5] State banks may choose to become members of the Federal Reserve System (state member banks), but are not required to do so.[6] Membership in the Federal Reserve System subjects a bank to federal regulation through regular inspection in a broad range of matters, including minimum reserve requirements and review of proposed changes in bank structure, such as mergers and branching.[7]

In addition, the FDIC, which insures all deposits in national banks, exercises supervisory functions over national banks and state member banks (both of which are required to maintain FDIC insurance), and any nonmember state bank that holds FDIC insurance. (In most states, all banks are required to be FDIC insured.) The FDIC benefits state banks by offering deposit insurance below the market rate,[8] in return for regular FDIC inspection and regulations.[9]

A defining characteristic of the dual federal-state regulatory system is the ability of a bank to choose the system by which it is to be regulated. Thus, a bank is free to choose state or federal chartering, and membership in the Federal Reserve System. Once having made that choice the bank may change its charter.[10] Thus, a state-chartered bank may trade in its charter for a federal one, and vice versa. Commentators have often lauded this feature of the American system, which promotes competition between regulators, each eager to have the bank under its regulatory control.

> [T]he historic value of dual banking lies in its ability to provide an escape valve from arbitrary or discriminatory chartering and regulatory policies at either the state or Federal level. . . . [O]ne of the historic objectives of dual banking has been to provide alternative supervisory frameworks under which commercial banks may choose to operate, thereby safeguarding against the extension of harsh, oppressive, and discriminatory supervision to institutions without recourse to alternative arrangements.[11]

Assuming that banks are rational regulatory consumers, discrepancies in regulations in the two systems should result in a shift toward or away from one regulatory system.[12] In fact, the evidence indicates that a fluid dynamic does exist. Banks do perceive differences in regulation and will change charters.[13]

Has This Created The Best System?

A question that often arises is whether state and federal dual regulators and regulations (and a bank's ability to choose between them) produces the best scheme for regulation. Advocates of the dual system argue that the competitive environment created by the dual banking system results in innovation and new products.[14] They point to one of the fundamental justifications for the system of federalism in the United States: the individual states are permitted to serve as "laboratories for change."[15] In this vein, it has been said that federal and state regulatory agencies "can be viewed as [corporate] firms producing different brands of regulation and engaged in a species of competition for market shares,"[16] since banks are free to switch from a more restrictive to a less restrictive regulator.

Indeed, innovation by state regulators, which was then ultimately adopted by federal regulators, has been quite copious. Examples of this include free banking laws, checking accounts, branch banking, real estate lending, trust services, reserve requirements, and deposit insurance.[17] In addition, states led the way in providing for interstate electronic funds transfer systems through the use of automated teller machines, they developed the use of negotiable order of withdrawal (NOW) accounts,[18] they originated interstate acquisition of banks through bank holding companies,[19] and they are continuing to expand the powers of state banks to engage in securities, insurance, and real estate dealing.[20] Innovations on the state level stand in contrast with proposals for change on the federal level to expand bank powers, which since 1982 have largely been unsuccessful.[21]

Critics contend, however, that competition resulting from the dual banking system results in a dangerous "competition in laxity," which encourages regulators to enact the most permissive legislation so as to attract banks to their jurisdiction.[22] A twist on this is the contention that dangerous competition is furthered though FDIC insurance (which most banks must have), since bank failures are borne throughout the country, not simply by a state that is lax in its regulations. Thus, states have an incentive to be lax since they reap many benefits but only suffer part of any regulatory damages.[23] However, some empirical data demonstrate that state banks, on the whole, maintain higher capital ratios, have more favorable financial results, and have lower failure rates than national banks.[24]

The Evolution of the Dual Banking System and Branch Banking

For many years Congress repeatedly rejected attempts to erode the dual system by curtailing the power of the states to regulate banks. This has begun to change. One area in which a shift in regulatory authority may be occurring is regulation governing bank branching: the laws that govern the ability of a bank to establish one or more branches.[25] The McFadden Act, which was adopted by Congress in 1927 and amended in 1933, provides that national banks can establish branches only within their home state and only to the extent expressly permitted by state law.[26] McFadden was designed to provide a decentralized banking system. As recently noted by the Supreme Court:

> It is significant . . . that Congress rejected attempts to allow national banks to branch without regard to state law. . . . There are many expressions of concern about the effects of branching among those who supported the McFadden Act, as well as among its opponents. Allusion was made to the danger that national banks might obtain monopoly control over credit and money if permitted to branch. The sponsor of the Act himself stated that "[t]his bill is much more an antibranch-banking bill than a branch-banking bill." . . . In short, Congress was concerned not only with equalizing the status of state and federal banks, but also with preventing the perceived danger of unlimited branching (*Clark v. Securities Indus. Ass'n.*, 479 U.S. 388, 403 [1987]).

In passing, and later amending, McFadden, Congress rejected proposals that would have allowed national banks to establish branches across state lines.[27]

But the tension between state and federal regulation of banking has never disappeared, and proposals to curtail state regulation are being considered on a regular basis, particularly in the area of bank branching. Most recently, Congress passed legislation encroaching on state regulation over bank branching, and has considered even more expansive legislation, which would altogether repeal McFadden.[28] Consideration of those two developments, described below, points up the ongoing struggle between regulatory authorities engendered by the dual banking system.

FIRREA

In August 1989 Congress enacted the Financial Institutions Reform, Recovery, and Enforcement Act of 1989 (FIRREA). FIRREA was enacted in response to the large number of failing thrift institutions[29] in the United States and was designed to restructure regulation of such savings institutions.[30] Most significantly, FIRREA established the Resolution Trust Corporation (RTC), a new government agency (under the management of the FDIC) whose job is to manage and resolve failed savings associations by taking over the operation of such associations when in receivership or conservatorship.

Typically, the assets of the failed association are liquidated at auction. It is not unusual for the buyer to be a national bank that wishes to use the purchased assets—such as a now-defunct office—as a branch. Such sales occur despite the fact that, in many instances, state branch banking laws would not otherwise allow the purchasing bank to operate the purchased office as a branch, because pursuant to FIRREA, the RTC is authorized to override such state laws.[31] The RTC's authority to do this, however, appears to conflict with the McFadden Act and—it is no surprise—federalism concerns raised by FIRREA have been at the forefront of the few cases that have addressed the propriety of the RTC's sale of failed thrift assets where the RTC overrides state bank branching laws.

State of Colorado ex rel. Colorado State Banking Board v. Resolution Trust Corporation,[32] arose from the sale of the assets of two failed thrifts to two national banks in, respectively, New Mexico and Colorado. In each case, the prospective purchasing national bank made its bid contingent on operating the offices of the defunct thrift as a branch office. Relevant New Mexico and Colorado state bank branching laws would not have otherwise permitted the acquiring national banks to operate branches at these locations.[33] The proposed sales were challenged by groups representing the interests of state commercial banks, and, in Colorado, by the Colorado State Banking Board.

At issue was a provision of FIRREA, 12 U.S.C. §1823(k)(1), which provides, in relevant part:

(k) Emergency Acquisitions
  (1) In general
    (A) Acquisitions authorized
      (i) Transactions described
        Notwithstanding any provisions of State law, upon determining that severe financial conditions threaten the stability of a significant number of

savings associations, or of savings associations possessing significant financial resources; *the Corporation, in its discretion* and if it determines such authorization would lessen the risk to the Corporation, *may authorize*:

(I) *a savings association* that is eligible for assistance pursuant to subsection (c) of this section *to merge or consolidate with, or to transfer its assets and liabilities to,* any other savings association or any insured bank,

(II) any other savings association to acquire control of such savings association, or

(III) any company to acquire control of such savings association or to acquire the assets or assume the liabilities thereof.

The Corporation may not authorize any transaction under this subsection unless the Corporation determines that the authorization will not present a substantial risk to the safety or soundness of the savings association to be acquired or any acquiring entity.

(ii) Terms of transactions

Mergers, consolidations, transfers, and acquisitions under this subsection shall be on such terms as the Corporation shall provide.

. . . .

(vi) Continued applicability of certain state restrictions.

Nothing in this subsection overrides or supersedes State laws restricting or limiting the activities of a savings association on behalf of another entity.[34]

The Court began, and swiftly concluded (by a narrow 2-1 finding), its analysis by observing that this section grants the RTC broad discretionary authority to override state law. "Subsection (K)(1) . . . expresses clear congressional authorization for the RTC to override state branch banking law."[35] Continuing, the Court recognized that "state branch banking laws impede emergency acquisitions,"[36] and so can be overridden. In so finding, short shrift was made of arguments that 1823(k)(1) simply authorizes *acquisition* of a failed thrift, but does not govern postacquisition operation. As a result, the majority rejected the argument that no impediment to a sale arises if the acquired thrift offices are not operated as a branch, but are instead operated in another manner, such as a separate bank.

In the course of its analysis, the Court examined the McFadden Act and concluded, perhaps amazingly, that its decision was not only consistent with, but actually supported McFadden. The Court reasoned that pursuant to McFadden, "Congress intended to place national and state banks on a basis of 'competitive equality' insofar as branch banking was concerned."[37] This objective was upheld in the present case because "if a regulation is applied in a particular state, both state and national banks may acquire and operate existing thrift offices. And neither state nor national banks may create new branches in violation of state law. The regulation provides their competitive equality."[38]

But the majority's reasoning, and in particular its concern with promoting "competitive equality," is troubling and does not appear consistent with either the letter or spirit of McFadden. As the dissent notes, the same court had previously held that the McFadden Act guarantees states the right to determine "when, where and how, a national bank may branch, *if indeed it may branch at all*."[39] To say that "competitive equality" is promoted ignores the fact that the *states' authority* to make banking decisions is being usurped.

Moreover, as the dissent also argues, it is *not* state law that is overridden by the majority's reading of FIRREA, but federal law: the McFadden Act.

> The McFadden Act incorporates by reference state branch banking laws *governing state banks*. Therefore, it is the McFadden Act that requires uniformity between the way federal and state banks may operate insofar as branching is concerned.[40]

The dissent continued its attack upon the majority's easy dismissal of McFadden by observing that

> the RTC seeks to rely primarily on the general language of §1823(k)(1) to override the very specific language of the McFadden Act, which unequivocally and directly prohibits federal branch banking in states where state branch banking is not allowed. I do not believe that it is too much to ask that when and if Congress decides to amend a fundamental sixty-three-year-old banking statute that it should do so explicitly.[41]

Since the decision in *Colorado*, the RTC has continued to administer and dispose of failed thrifts,[42] but the issues raised by *Colorado* regarding the interaction of FIRREA and McFadden, and whether FIRREA represents a substantial amendment of McFadden, as posed by the dissent, have not received further judicial attention.[43] However, developments have occurred on the legislative front.

Proposals to Repeal McFadden

Recent proposed legislation has generated additional debate over the dual banking system and its necessity, through proposals to repeal McFadden and permit widespread, interstate branching of banks.[44] While such proposed legislation has not been enacted, the lengthy debate on the issue suggests the constant evolution of regulatory authority in the United States, and that a further shift is developing away from the right of states to regulate.

As with enactment of FIRREA, heightened interest by Congress with bank regulation appears to be a product of the thrift crises, and the concomitant concern this has generated that the banking industry, like the thrift industry, might be threatened with widespread failures. A legislative movement was kicked off by President George Bush on February 5, 1991, with the release of a blueprint for reform, developed by the Treasury Department. This plan would have provided for the immediate branching by a national bank into any state, through the vehicle of a bank holding company, wherein such a holding company could already buy a bank.[45] The Treasury plan also proposed full nationwide interstate branching after three years, *regardless* of whether such branching was state authorized.[46]

In short, Treasury was proposing wholesale repeal of McFadden, which in the minds of numerous commentators would have the effect of substantially abrogating the dual banking system.[47] Essentially, the states would lose all control over branching. State lobbying groups responded immediately.[48] Opposing the Treasury Department proposal, Professor Arthur Wilmarth, Jr., a leading authority on banking and advocate of the dual banking system, noted that the deference to state control spelled out in McFadden

> has enabled our banking system to remain free from monopolistic or oligopolistic control, and has ensured that banks are responsive to the needs of their local communities for credit and other financial services. . . . It is doubtful whether a viable dual banking system could long survive if Congress preempted state control over bank structure under the McFadden Act and the Douglas Amendment. . . . [The National Bank Charter would have] a large and potentially decisive advantage over the state option.[49]

Debate in Congress was heated, and as a result the bill that eventually reached the floor of the Senate, almost ten months after being proposed, had significantly evolved from that proposed by the president. Rather than eliminating all barriers to interstate branching, as originally proposed, the modified bill would have permitted each state to opt out of the branching provisions, but only if the state legislature did so within three years after passage of the bill.[50] The chairman of the Senate Banking Committee, Senator Donald Riegle, stated the case for limiting state control over interstate branching as follows:

> First, these reforms are good public policy. Branch banks, banks with geographically diversified portfolios of assets and liabilities, are less likely to fail. That is a statistical fact. And, therefore, they pose less of a risk to the deposit insurance system and ultimately the taxpayers.
>
> Second, interstate branching is more efficient than interstate banking because branch networks entail less duplication of administrative expenses than do bank networks. More efficient banks are more profitable and less likely to fail, and in turn, become a taxpayer liability. Interstate branches will also be more convenient for consumers.
>
> Third, interstate banking and branching is already happening. Thirty-four of the fifty States already permit nationwide interstate banking, and 14 of the remaining 16 States permit some form of interstate banking. So this is a matter that has already developed very fully on its own prior to this bill coming to the floor.[51]

Senator Riegle's comments, whose substance was echoed by numerous others,[52] are of particular interest for two reasons. First, they demonstrate the mind-set of Congress: fear of the possible collapse of the banking industry, and a sense that whatever legislation is necessary to avoid that result should be passed, perhaps regardless of other considerations. Second, they show little concern for the effect such legislation would have on state regulatory authority.

This seeming lack of concern with protection of state's rights was seized upon by opponents. Typical were the comments of Senator Wendell H. Ford, who stated:

> Let me summarize briefly my original concerns with the Senate bill. First, I believe it fails to adequately consider States' rights. It fails to let States continue to set reasonable restrictions on the terms and conditions of entry of out-of-State banks into their States.
>
> Second, the Senate bill fails to take into account the legitimate franchise interests of small community banks throughout this country. Most States attempt to recognize these legitimate interests. . . .
>
> Third, I believe the current Senate provisions undermine our dual banking system. In many parts of this country, many feel the dual banking system is something to be maintained. State regulators regulate State chartered banks. The Comptroller of the Currency regulates national banks. And consumers get the benefits of a varied and competitive system. The Senate bill, however, imposes a uniform set of rules on all States regarding interstate banking and branching that is simply not necessary.
>
> The Senate bill imposes a phased-in transition to interstate banking and branching which leaves very little discretion to States. . . .
>
> Mr. President, interstate banking is a growing trend. I agree that we should allow it on a nationwide basis. But should we take all rights away from States to regulate this activity? We know that interstate affiliations have increased in recent years. Thirty-four States currently allow some form of nationwide interstate banking. Fourteen States allow interstate banking on a regional basis. Only two States do not allow interstate banking at all. But there are reasonable restrictions in the 48 States allowing interstate banking. There is no need to force a single set of rules upon the States.[53]

Perhaps the most disturbing aspect of the proposal to abrogate states' rights over branching is the premise that without such legislation the banking system might collapse. But, as established by Professor Wilmarth, the conclusion that state banks were, and are, in immediate threat of collapse seems without any statistical basis. Among other things, unlike the situation in the thrift industry, state banks maintain a higher average capital ratio than thrifts.[54] As also noted by former FDIC Chairman William Seidman, in recent years the banking system has proved quite stable and, in fact, state banks have actually been *making money*.[55]

Ultimately, the states' lobbying efforts bore fruit; in the final Senate-House committee conference, the bill was stripped of all proposed banking industry reforms and, in particular, the proposals to permit interstate banking and branching, through repeal or modification of McFadden.[56]

It may be that Congress' rejection of the proposed repeal of McFadden indicates an acceptance of the act as fundamental to the dual banking system; but the fact that a lengthy debate occurred suggests continued congressional fascination with curtailing states' rights and that the balance between federal and state regulation of banking may in the future swing further against the states. Indeed, in his State of the Union address on January 28, 1992, President Bush once again called for passage of legislation to reform the banking system.[57]

CONCLUSION

The dual regulatory system has endured in the United States for a considerable period of time. Its record of innovation is clear and, accordingly, the system recommends itself to a federation, or confederation of states, considering how to regulate banking. It is therefore unfortunate that recent events demonstrate that federal authorities in the United States have diminished, and have sought to diminish further, the ability of states to continue to serve as "laboratories for change" in banking regulation.

NOTES

1. For instance, on October 5, 1991, the Soviet Union signed an agreement with the International Monetary Fund (IMF) by which it will receive, *inter alia*, advice on setting up a Western-style banking system. See *The New York Times*, October 6, 1991 at A12.

2. The existence of the dual banking system is largely the product of a historical accident. Prior to 1863, regulation of banks was essentially left to the states. While the federal government had chartered two banks, all other bank charters, and the attendant regulatory framework accompanying chartering, were exclusively the domain of the several states. Arthur Wilmarth, Jr., "The Expansion of State Bank Powers, the Federal Response, and the Case for Preserving the Dual Banking System," 58 *Fordham Law Review* 1133, 1153 (1990). The minimal federal overview of the banking industry was a product of the early republic's distrust of concentrated power, both political and financial.

In 1863 Congress legislated a system of national banks providing for federal chartering and regulation of bank members of the system. When instituted, the intent was not to provide an alternative system of regulation to the state system, but to provide a reliable system of currency to replace the system of notes then issued by state banks, and to establish an easily accessible market for federal bonds then being issued to finance the Civil War. Henry N. Butler and Jonathan R. Macey, "The Myth of Competition in the Dual Banking System," 73 *Cornell Law Review* 677, 681 (1988). It was anticipated by Congress that state banks would quickly convert to national charters and that, as a result, the dual system would soon be phased out. When this did not occur, Congress enacted a prohibitive tax on state bank-issued notes, so as to compel conversion to national charters. Stephen K. Huber, "The Dual Banking System: Interaction of Federal and State Law in the Regulation of Banking," 25 *Consumer Finance Law Quarterly Report* 51, 52 (1988). (State charters were generally viewed as more favorable because of lower capital requirements, easier reserve requirements, and less regulation.) However, Congress was foiled by the ability of state-chartered banks to shift from note-based operations (which Congress now controlled) to deposit-based, by pioneering the use of checking accounts. In short, the origin of the present dual banking system lies in the early attempt by Congress to usurp the authority of state regulators, and reap the associated benefits by being the sole regulating authority.

3. Kenneth E. Scott, "The Dual Banking System: A Model of Competition in Regulation," 30 *Stanford Law Review* 1, 5–6 (1977). A number of activities are typically regulated, including reserve requirements, interest rates, restrictions on the size of loans to one individual, trading in securities and real estate, and branching within the state. Even a bank chartered by federal authorities (and subject to federal monitoring) would still be subject to certain state local laws, such as zoning, usury, and unclaimed property laws. See, e.g., Huber, *supra* note 2, at 53.

4. See, e.g., 12 C.F.R. §4 (1991) defining the authority of the Comptroller of the Currency.

5. The FRB controls the nation's money supply by, *inter alia*, buying and selling U.S. securities on the open market. To join the Federal Reserve System, a bank must place a certain amount of required reserves in one of the twelve federal reserve district banks. 12 U.S.C. §323 (1990).

6. By joining the system, state banks enjoy numerous benefits, including check clearing and wire transfer services performed by system banks. State member banks can also borrow money from a federal regional reserve bank at a lower discount rate. See, e.g., 12 U.S.C. §357 (1990).

7. Scott, *supra* note 4, at 6.

8. S. Buser, A. Caen, and E. Kane, "Federal Deposit Insurance, Regulatory Policy and Optimal Bank Capital," *Journal of Finance*, March 1981, at 51.

9. Scott, *supra* note 4, at 6.

10. This is subject to the caveat that the bank gain approval from the system it is seeking to enter. See Scott, *supra* note 4, at 9. See also, Butler and Macey, *supra* note 2, at 685, who note that obtaining a charter is a long, drawn out, expensive affair, and therefore switching regulators is not an easy process.

11. William James Brown, *The Dual Banking System in the United States*, (New York: American Bankers Association, 1968), 59, 64–65.

12. Such discrepancies may simply be the product of differences between federal and state statutes. A classic example of this is statutory provisions on reserve requirements—pursuant to which banks must retain assets as safe and liquid. These requirements are generally equal to a percentage of the bank's deposit liabilities, and vary widely from state to state and, accordingly, vary when compared with those imposed by federal regulators through the Federal Revenue System. See generally, Scott, *supra* note 3, at 18–20. Another example is regulations governing the maximum amount that may be loaned by a bank to a single borrower. Such limits are generally defined in terms of a percentage of the bank's net worth. Again, these limits vary from jurisdiction to jurisdiction. See generally, *id.*

Discrepancies may also result from differences in agency enforcement. While regulations governing banking may be set down in black and white, authorities typically have the discretion to determine how, when, and if the regulation is to be applied in each situation. Enforcement will vary from jurisdiction to jurisdiction—even where the regulations are identical. See generally, Scott, *supra* note 3, at 20–22.

13. In his seminal work, Professor Scott describes the pattern of conversions from one authority to another in the period 1950–74. He opines that these shifts result in changes by the authority suffering losses. See Scott, *supra* note 3, at 25–35.

14. See, e.g., *Independent Bankers Ass'n. v. Smith*, 534 F. 2d 917, 921 (D.C. Cir. 1973), *cert. denied*, 429 U.S. 862 (1976) (acknowledging the benefits of competition to banking, though incorrectly crediting Congress with purposely establishing the dual system); see generally, Wilmarth, *supra* note 2, at 1155–59.

For a discussion of the support the dual banking system has generally received, see generally, Wilmarth, *supra* note 2, at 1155; Brown, *supra* note 11, at 33–38, 59–66; Tamar Frankel, "The Dual State-Federal Regulation of Financial Institutions—A Proposal," 53 *Brooklyn Law Review* 53, 54–56 (1987).

15. *New State Ice Co. v. Liebman*, 285 U.S. 262, 311 (1932) (Brandeis, J.)

16. Scott, *supra* note 3, at 32.

17. See Wilmarth, *supra* note 2, at 1156.

18. NOW accounts are savings accounts that allow the use of withdrawal by checks. In a sense, they are checking accounts that bear interest. Congress gave nationwide authorization for NOW accounts only after the states demonstrated their utility. Wilmarth, *supra* note 2, at 1157.

19. *Id.*; see, e.g., New York Banking Law §142-b (McKinney 1990). A bank holding company is a company that owns or controls one or more banking institutions. See, e.g., New York Banking Law §141(3) (McKinney 1990).

20. See Wilmarth *supra* note 2, at 1177–81. As discussed below, proposals in 1991 to expand the ability of national banks to engage in securities, insurance, and real estate dealing were rejected by Congress.

21. A significant exception has been federal efforts to expand the intrastate branching abilities of national banks beyond those permitted by state regulators of state banks; this has been accomplished despite the restrictions seemingly imposed by the McFadden Act, see *infra* note 27, which only permits a national bank to branch within a state to the extent a state bank can do so. For instance, it was recently held that certain off-premises facilities operated by national banks are not "branches" (prohibited by state law, and made applicable to national banks by McFadden), and so do not come within the ambit of the McFadden Act. See Wilmarth, *supra* note 2, at 1159 (citing *Clarke v. Securities Indus. Ass'n*, 479 U.S. 388, 404–409 [1987]); *Independent Bankers Ass'n of New York State, Inc., v. Marine Midland Bank*, 757 F.2d 453 (2d Cir. 1985); *Independent Bankers Ass'n of Am. v. Heimann*, 627 F.2d 486 (D.C. Cir. 1980). This innovation on the federal plane was followed by liberalization of statewide branching laws by many state regulators, so as to maintain parity with natinal banks. See Wilmarth, *supra* note 2, at 1157–59, for a discussion of other federal innovations, subsequently adopted by the states.

While such innovation on the federal level may result in increased efficiency, the question arises as to whether such top-down innovation, which states feel compelled to adopt to stay competitive, effectively usurp state regulatory power.

22. See generally, Address by Arthur Burns, Chairman of the Board of Governors of the Federal Reserve System, October 21, 1974, cited in Scott *supra* note 3, at 13;

Melainie L. Fein, "The Fragmented Depository Institutions System: A Case for Verification," 29 *American University Law Review* 633, 675–76, 698–700 (1986). Another criticism is the inefficiency generated by requiring banks to be aware of and to comply with both state and federal rules, rather than a single set of regulations. Huber, *supra* note 2, at 54.

23. Butler and Macey, *supra* note 2, at 680, 696, 713–13. For a fuller discussion of the competition in laxity argument, see, e.g., Daniel R. Fischel, Andrew M. Rosenfield, and Robert S. Stillman, "The Regulation of Banks and Bank Holding Companies," 73 *Virginia Law Review* 301, 306–13 (1987); Frankel, *supra* note 14, at 58–61.

Contrarily, others argue that public officials and regulators cannot throw caution to the winds, even with FDIC insurance, because of the possible political ramifications of numerous bank failures. Wilmarth, *supra* note 2, at 1242. Interestingly, the competition in laxity argument has also been advanced, and rejected, with respect to corporate chartering. Wilmarth, *supra* note 2, at 1248. Here, investor discipline, which may be analogous to bank holding companies that "invest" in a bank in another state through purchase, provides a disincentive to excessive laxity.

24. Wilmarth, *supra* note 2, at 1243–44.

25. See Stephen A. Rhoades, "Interstate Banking and Product Line Expansion: Implications from Available Evidence," 18 *Loyola of Los Angeles Law Review* 1115, 1117 (1985). Mr. Rhoades, a member of the Federal Reserve Board, notes that by 1985, already interstate banking, through bank holding companies, had become a pressing policy issue.

26. McFadden Act of 1927, 12 U.S.C. §36(c) (1988). The act states, in relevant part:

(c) A national banking association may, with the approval of the Comptroller of the Currency, establish and operate new branches: (1) Within the limits of the city, town or village in which said association is situated, if such establishment and operation are at the time expressly authorized to State banks by the law of the State in question; and (2) at any point within the State in which said association is situated, if such establishment and operation are at the time authorized to State banks by the statute law of the State in question by language specifically granting such authority affirmatively and not merely by implication or recognition, and subject to the restrictions as to location imposed by the law of the State on State banks. In any State in which State banks are permitted by statute law to maintain branches within county or greater limits, if no bank is located and doing business in the place where the proposed agency is to be located, any national banking association situated in such State may, with the approval of the Comptroller of the Currency, establish and operate, without regard to the capital requirements of this section, a seasonal agency in any resort community within the limits of the county in which the main office of such association is located, for the purpose of receiving and paying out deposits, issuing and cashing checks and drafts, and doing business incident thereto: Provided, That any permit issued under this sentence shall be revoked upon the opening of a State or national bank in such community. Except as provided in the immediately preceding sentence, no such association shall establish a branch outside of the city, town, or village in which it is situated unless it has a combined capital stock and surplus, equal to the combined amount of capital stock and surplus, if any, required by the law of the State in which such association is situated for the establishment of such branches by State banks, or, if the law of such State requires only a minimum capital stock for the establishment of such branches by State banks, unless such association has not less than an equal amount of capital stock.

The Douglas Amendment, 12 U.S.C. §1842(d), passed in 1956, prohibits bank holding companies from acquiring a bank outside the state where its principal operations are located, unless specifically authorized by the state law of the state in which the bank to be acquired is located. Again, this legislation reflected Congressional recognition of the usefulness of the dual banking system. Wilmarth, *supra* note 2, at 1154.

27. Wilmarth, *supra* note 2, at 1154.

28. This is to be contrasted with the expansion of bank branching rights through changes on the *state* level. During the 1970s and 1980s, a number of states expanded the ability of a bank to branch intrastate. See Dean F. Amel and Michael J. Jacowski, "Trends in Banking Structure Since the Mid-1970s," 75 *Federal Reserve Bulletin* 120, 121–22 (1989). This was accomplished while generally retaining restrictions on branching across state lines. Most states have also authorized the acquisition of local banks by out-of-state bank holding companies. See Wilmarth, *supra* note 2, at 1144–45.

29. "Thrifts" are to be distinguished from banks. A number of institutions can be classified as "thrifts," including building and loan associations and savings and loan associations. Such institutions were originally small concerns, established to encourage savings and home building, among local constituent members. Members of the association received shares in the association and, thereafter, made regular payments toward the value of such shares. Members could obtain loans based on the par value of such shares, before such shares were fully paid for. Those familiar with the film *It's a Wonderful Life* will recall the "Bailey Building and Loan" as typical of the early breed.

While savings and loans possess many characteristics similar to those of a savings *bank*, they issue no capital stock. They have members, rather than depositors, who hold shares issued by the association, and make dues or share payments, rather than deposits. Unlike depositors in a savings bank, members of a savings and loan enjoy certain voting rights in the association's operations.

Historically, thrifts have served as a vital source for mortgage lending for single-family dwellings. It has been estimated that by 1989 half of the nation's mortgage funding for one- to four-family dwellings was provided by thrift institutions. See e.g., Gregory Pulles, Robert Whitlock, and James Hogg, *FIRREA, A Legislative History and Section-By-Section Analysis*, §§1–2 (1990).

30. Prior to FIRREA's enactment in 1989, losses in the thrift industry had reached record heights, in 1988 alone $12.1 billion was lost. See Nathaniel C. Nash, "Savings Loss Put at 2.3 Billion," *The New York Times*, March 22, 1989 at B1. See also, Amel and Jacowski, *supra* note 28, at 124 (stating total number of FDIC-insured bank failures for the years 1977–88). Losses in the thrift industry were due to several factors. The 1970s and 1980s witnessed a rapid increase in interest rates paid by banks on depositor's accounts. In order to allow thrifts to compete more agressively for deposits (by raising interest rates paid still higher), in 1980 Congress passed the Depository Deregulation and Monetary Control Act, which phased out interest rate caps. Thrifts, now effectively forced to pay even higher interest rates, found themselves losing money, since a substantial portion of their assets were locked into long-term mortgages, issued at lower rates than that which they were paying. In search of a way to fund the higher interest rates they were paying, a number of thrifts pursued risky investments, including junk bonds. Relaxed state supervision, which permitted such risky investing, also resulted in rampant fraud and insider abuse of thrifts. By 1989 such practices had led to extensive failures in the thrift industry and insolvency in the Federal Savings and Loan Insurance Corportion (FSLIC), which insured thrift depositor funds (much like the FDIC insures bank depositor funds). See, e.g., Pulles et al., *supra* note 29 at §2.

31. While FIRREA was enacted principally to resolve problems and curb certain abusive practices in the thrift industry, by enhancing federal supervision (at the expense

of state regulation), FIRREA's enhancement of federal supervision and regulation also applies to the banking industry.

32. 926 F. 2d 931 (10th Cir. 1991).

33. New Mexico limits bank branching to within the same county. N.M. Stat. Ann. §58-5-3 (1986 Repl.). Branching into an adjoining county or within 120 miles is permissible only if no competing banks are located at the proposed limits. Colorado law permits branching only in extremely limited cases, none of which were applicable to this case. Colo. Rev. Stat. §11-6-101 (1987 Repl.).

34. 12 U.S.C. §1823(k)(1)(A)(i), (ii), (vi) (emphasis added).

35. 926 F.2d at 936.

36. 926 F.2d at 928.

37. 926 F. 2d at 946 (*quoting First Nat'l Bank of Logan v. Walker Bank & Trust Co.*, 385 U.S. 252, *reh'g denied*, 385 U.S. 1032 (1968).

38. 926 F.2d at 946. Professor Scott has vigorously attacked the "competitive equality" doctrine as being a *force majeure* in the dual banking system. Instead, "the very core of the dual banking system is the simultaneous existence of different regulatory options that are *not* alike in terms of statutory provisions, regulatory implementation and administrative policy; there is no 'principle' whatever of initial identity." Scott, *supra* note 3, at 41. As also noted by Scott: "federal law permits a national bank to establish a branch in a particular location only if under state law such a branch would be authorized for state banks 'expressly' or 'affirmatively' and not by implication." *Id.* "Although seductively simple, the competitive equality slogan does not describe accurately the dual banking system in either its whole or its parts, and by giving the slogan their allegiance the courts will merely be led astray." *Id.*

39. 926 F.2d at 952 (*quoting State of Utah ex rel., Department of Financial Institutions v. Zions First National Bank of Ogden, Utah*, 615 F.2d 903, 906 (10th Cir. 1980) (emphasis added).

40. 926 F.2d at 951 (emphasis in original).

41. 926 F.2d at 950. In addition, noting that §1823 (k)(1) permits the RTC to override any state statute *prohibiting* mergers or which *materially disadvantages* the merged entity, the dissent found fault with the majority's result, since its findings—overriding state banking laws—would promote a *competitive advantage* over *all* other banks in Colorado and New Mexico. Thus, unlike any other bank in either state, the successful bidder for the failed thrift's assets can branch.

The dissent also reasoned that a state law prohibiting a bank from operating the acquired assets as a branch, such as the Colorado and New Mexico statutes, does not *ipso facto* work a divesture so as to make purchase of the assets of the thrift prohibitively unattractive; the acquired office simply cannot be operated as a branch. Each such newly acquired location could be operated as a separate bank. 926 F.2d at 952.

In this vein, the dissent noted that the ability to operate the facility as a branch was not an asset the facility had to begin with, so the value of the asset is not diminished. Contrarily, the majority reading would result in an *enhancement* of value when the facility could be operated as a branch. Taking the majority's position to the extreme the dissent opined: "What if the RTC decides that a savings and loan will have more value as a merger candidate if it can bestow immunity to its merger partner for state zoning laws, or pollution laws, or Sunday closure laws? May the RTC abrogate those state laws too?" 926 F.2d at 953. The only response by the majority on this point was to note that the state law sought to be overcome must work a "material disadvantage" on the ability of the RTC to dispose of the assets of the failed association. Apparently, branching laws work such a "material disadvantage," but could not the same be said with respect to at least some of the dissent's examples?

42. In addition to failed thrifts, the FDIC recently projected 239 bank failures in 1992 alone, involving $118 billion in assets. See October 23, 1991, letter from Andrew C. Hove, acting chairman, FDIC, to Donald Riegle, chairman of Senate Banking Committee, 137 *Congressional Record* S16585 (daily ed. November 13, 1991). It thus appears that the FDIC and RTC will be busy with disposing of such failed institutions for some time to come, and the issues raised above will continue to receive attention.

43. Previously, in *Arkansas State Bank Com'r v. Resolution Trust Corp.*, 955 F.2d 16 (8th Cir. 1990), the majority (2-1) also approved an RTC sale that had the effect of repudiating the bank branching laws of Arkansas. As in *Colorado*, the dissent there found the RTC's actions in direct conflict with McFadden, wherein "Congress acknowledged the preeminence of state authority to authorize the limit of branch banking authority." *Id.* at 176.

44. Earlier, President Jimmy Carter issued a report advocating a retreat from the McFadden Act by the removal of restrictions on interstate branching by national banks and by allowing interstate acquisitions of banks through bank holding companies. But these wide sweeping proposals were largely rejected. See Wilmarth, *supra* note 2, at 1154.

45. Other important proposals included repealing long-standing restrictions on commercial bank activities so as to permit diversification into such areas as securities, insurance, and real estate dealing.

46. See "State Bank Supervisors Formally Publish Their Proposal for Interstate Branching," *BNA's Banking Report News*, April 8, 1991.

47. Treasury argued that interstate branching would strengthen banks and avoid failures, by allowing for greater geographic diversity. See "Treasury Official Rejects Compromise on Interstate Branching By Rep. Vento," *BNA's Branching Report News*, May 20, 1991.

48. See *id*. For example, the National Conference of State Legislatures (a powerful trade and lobbying group), adopted a resolution supporting preservation of the dual banking system, which they contended was threatened by the Treasury Department proposals on interstate branching. See "NCSL Opposes Federal Interstate Branching, Suggests Strengthening of CRA," *BNA's Banking Report News*, May 13, 1991.

49. "State Bank Supervisors Formally Publish their Proposals for Interstate Branching," *BNA's Banking Report News*, April 8, 1991. Professor Wilmarth proposed legislation that would allow states to pass laws explicitly permitting out-of-state banks to come in through branches, while giving the states leeway to impose a number of conditions. This proposal won wide support from various state and community bankers' associations and lobbying groups. See *id.*; "CSBS Denounces Treasury Reform Proposal as Death Knell for State Regulatory Rules," *BNA's Banking Report News*, April 29, 1991 (Conference of State Bank Supervisors opposing repeal of McFadden, as it would destroy dual banking, and endorsing Professor Wilmarth's proposal).

50. See 137 *Congressional Record* S16698 (daily ed. November 14, 1991). Even this proposal appears less than satisfying since it would still have required affirmative action by individual states rejecting interstate branching.

51. 137 *Congressional Record* S16697 (daily ed. November 14, 1991).

52. See, e.g., Testimony of Lowell C. Bryor of McKinsey & Co., 137 *Congressional Record* S16699 (daily ed. November 14, 1991) (calling McFadden an anachronism); Comments of Senator Chafee, 137 *Congressional Record* S16601 (daily ed. November 13, 1991).

53. Remarks of Senator Wendell H. Ford, 137 *Congressional Record* S16697 (daily ed. November 14, 1991). See Comments of Senator Dale Bumpers, 137 *Congressional Record* S16702-04 (daily ed. November 14, 1991). See also, Comments of Senator William V. Roth, Jr., 137 *Congressional Record* S18625 (daily ed. November 27, 1991) (noting that "the dual banking system is nothing more than the doctrine of federalism in operation in the area of banking. The genesis of federalism is that individual states can serve as the laboratory for investors without the risk of a national experiment").

54. See Wilmarth, *supra* note 2, at 1243–48; "Congress Sends President Bill to Rescue Bank Insurance Fund," *BNA's Banking Report News*, December 2, 1991.

55. See "CSBS Denounces Treasury Reform Proposal as Death Knell For State Regulatory Rule," *BNA's Banking Report News*, April 29, 1991.

56. See *BNA's Banking Report News*, *supra* note 55.

57. See *The New York Times*, January 29, 1992 at A16–17.

PART VIII

INDIVIDUAL AND COLLECTIVE HUMAN RIGHTS

Part VIII addresses governmental structures that have an impact on a diverse range of human rights issues.

The notion that all sovereign governments have a legal obligation to respect the human rights of individuals and groups of individuals has emerged only after World War II with the adoption of the Universal Declaration on Human Rights[1] and the subsequent international treaties forming the international bill of human rights.[2] The dominant impediment to enforcement of those human rights is state sovereignty, which in its most unbridled form bars any inquiry by the international community about what takes place inside a state's territory. Despite that impediment, international human rights law undeniably is influencing the local and federal laws of states in regard to the rights of citizens. In addition, international human rights instruments such as the Helsinki Accords[3] adopted in 1975 by the former U.S.S.R., among others, provided at least a quasi-legal basis for the assertions of the right of self-determination that led to the breakup of the former U.S.S.R. and the movement toward democratically elected governments in Eastern Europe.

William Rich addresses human rights from the perspective of morality and federalism in the United States. He suggests compellingly that the allocation of power between the states and the federal government ought to be guided by fairness toward individuals and minority groups, by government responsibility to assure the basic necessities of life for the least advantaged citizens, and by protecting the moral standards of local communities. In this sense, Mr. Rich is certainly correct that federalism is not a "neutral" principle employed antiseptically to separate state and local power from federal or national government power.

Boris A. Tsepov's paper examines the development of human rights in the former U.S.S.R. and the Russian Federation. It observes that, during the time of Mikhail Gorbachev prior to the breakup of the U.S.S.R., the initial primary movement toward meaningful human rights progress was in foreign relations rather than in domestic reform. Of course, the acceptance internationally by the U.S.S.R. of international human rights obligations also led to changes in the domestic content and application of individual and collective human rights law to conform with the international obligations. Inside Russia this is reflected in the 1991 Declaration of the Rights and Freedoms of Man and Citizen.

Boris Sergeevich Krylov's paper deals with federalism and the human right of self-determination in the former U.S.S.R. It properly distinguishes the territorial-based federal systems of the U.S.A, Australia, Austria, Switzerland, and even to a certain extent the then Czechoslovakia from the federations based on identifiable nationalities like the U.S.S.R., the Russian Federation, and the then Yugoslavia. In nationality-based federal systems the contours of the right of self-determination may be seriously affected by immigration and emigration policies. Krylov's paper observes that the combination of federalism issues and heightened appreciation of self-determination rights helps to explain the confederative or commonwealth form taken by the CIS.

Zulfia M. Mirshakar's paper analyzes the language aspect of the human right to culture in the former U.S.S.R. With the breakup of the U.S.S.R., the legal predicate for the dominance of the Russian language was removed and an emotional tendency arose to replace Russian with other ethnic languages. The paper contains a fascinating examination of the struggles that regional and state governments have had in dealing with the status of the Russian language in relation to ethnic or other state languages. Formally and informally, important functions exist for the Russian language, especially in international affairs.

Norman I. Silber's paper analyzes the rights of humans as consumers. The federalism problem here is to decide to what extent federal or national governments should preempt local laws in order to better protect consumers without destroying valuable economic markets, goods, and services. The paper focuses on the preemption problems in the United States on such timely topics as food labeling, cigarette warnings, and automobile airbags.

Finally, the paper by Vern R. Walker considers the important functions and duties of government when humans are injured by accidents in the home, the workplace, hospitals, and in transportation (land, sea, and air). The problems in governmental terms involve the obligations of local or national government to prevent accidents and to treat and compensate victims when accidents do occur. Governments must also decide which members of society will bear how much of the financial and resource burdens of accident prevention and accident victims and compensation.

NOTES

1. Universal Declaration of Human Rights, adopted by the UN General Assembly, December 10, 1948, UNGA Res. 217A (III), UN Doc. A/810, at 71 (1948).

2. In addition to the Universal Declaration, the International Bill of Human Rights consists of the International Covenant on Civil and Political Rights, International Covenant on Civil and Political Rights done at New York, December 16, 1966, entered into force, March 23, 1976, UNGA Res. 2200 (XXI), 21 UN GAOR, Supp. (No. 16) 52, UN Doc. A/6316 (1967), reprinted in 6 *International Legal Materials* 368 (1967); the

Optional Protocol to the International Covenant in Civil and Political Rights, done at New York, December 16, 1966, entered into force, March 23, 1976, UNGA Res. 2200 (XXI), 21 UN GAOR, Supp. (No. 16) 59, UN Doc. A/6316 (1967), reprinted in 6 *International Legal Materials* 383 (1967); and the International Covenant on Economic, Social, and Cultural Rights, done at New York, December 16, 1966, entered into force, January 3, 1976, UNGA Res. 2200 (XXI), 21 UN GAOR, Supp. (No. 16) 49, UN Doc. A/6316 (1967), reprinted in 6 *International Legal Materials* 360 (1967).

3. Final Act of the Conference on Security and Co-Operation in Europe, adopted by the Conference on Security and Co-operation in Europe at Helsinki, August 1, 1975, Department of State Publication No. 8826 (General Foreign Service 298), reprinted in 14 *International Legal Materials* 1292 (1975).

38

Moral Dimensions of Federalism

William Rich

A constitution establishes a structure for the government and identifies fundamental principles that guide relationships within that structure. Framers of the federal structure of the United States Constitution intended to disperse power, safeguard liberty, and foster leadership by those motivated by a "love of justice" and a heightened sense of the "public good."[1] A system that limited self-interested factions from abusing power at society's expense also protected fundamental moral standards. In the words of Justice William Brennan: "Federalism is a device for realizing the concepts of decency and fairness which are among the fundamental principles of liberty and justice lying at the base of all our civil and political institutions."[2]

Successive generations of Americans have engaged in virtually constant debate regarding the purpose, merits, and constitutional stature of federalism. We question whether local or central governments will best foster economic growth, advance social welfare, or protect against tyranny. Behind the façade of these debates, however, issues of morality often hang in the balance. By focusing on federalism, generations of Americans have avoided responsibility for issues ranging from slavery to the death penalty.

The discussion that follows begins with an historical view of this relationship between morality and federalism. It challenges the concept of federalism as a "neutral" principle that separates state and national authority, and seeks to demonstrate that federalism has a moral dimension that may weigh on the side of either state or federal responsibility, depending upon the context of the debate. It also proposes a framework for resolving these issues within the constitutional structure of the United States. The goal is to reassess the use of federalism arguments so that issues of morality will not be hidden or sacrificed because of expressed concerns for specific structural values.

The term "morality" will be addressed in three different contexts. The first focuses primarily on the question of fairness toward fundamental individual or minority interests.[3] The second addresses questions about social responsibility for basic necessities of life.[4] The third involves the moral concerns of a majority within contemporary communities.[5] A description of these contexts will be combined with an analysis of their relationship to a federal structure.

MORAL "RIGHTS" OF INDIVIDUALS AND MINORITY GROUPS

As delegates gathered for the Constitutional Convention, attention quickly focused on the issue of how power should be shared between central and state governments. Initially, delegates from large states appeared to unite around the plan proposed by the Virginia delegation that favored a relatively strong central government. Small states, worried about losing power to a central government dominated by their larger neighbors, supported proposals for a more limited central authority. Within the first few weeks of the Convention, however, large southern states switched their allegiance out of concern that a strong central government would control issues of slavery. Support for a new central government with increased power was only reached following the compromise that protected state authority over slaves.

Decades later the United States Supreme Court concluded in *Dred Scott v. Sandford*[6] that the Constitution stood in the way of congressional efforts to limit slavery. In his opinion for the Court, Chief Justice Roger Taney concluded that principles of federalism made moral issues irrelevant; the federal government lacked the power to free slaves taken into the territories that it governed.[7]

The constitutional amendments that followed the Civil War ostensibly erased the curse of the Constitutional Convention while establishing national responsibility for enforcing norms of liberty and equality. The Compromise of 1877, however, ended the era of "reconstruction" and restored racist state governments in return for Republican control of the presidency.[8] In essence, that compromise assured that Congress would not use its power to enforce principles of freedom and equality. Six years later the U.S. Supreme Court enshrined that position, again citing principles of federalism, by blocking congressional power to prohibit private acts of racial discrimination.[9]

In the twentieth century, issues of racial discrimination continued to be addressed in terms of federalism. Arguments regarding school segregation in the case of *Brown v. Board of Education*, and subsequent debates regarding civil rights legislation in the 1950s and 1960s, were often framed in terms of "states' rights" rather than as disagreements regarding the morality of racial discrimination. Assertions of federal power to end racial discrimination were compared to acts of Adolf Hitler and Benito Mussolini.[10] A majority in Congress and a unanimous Supreme Court[11] rejected such arguments and established the priority of a principle that prohibited invidious racial discrimination.

Recent efforts to eliminate racial disparities, however, have been frustrated because of a reassertion of federalism arguments that favor deference to the states. Repeatedly, efforts in this country to establish conditions of racial equality have been met and eventually frustrated by "principles of federalism."

Slavery and racial discrimination exemplify a broader range of moral issues that involve protection of the minority from majoritarian excesses. Principles of criminal procedure embedded in the Fourth, Fifth, Sixth, and Eighth Amendments have an analogous moral stature, and have been subjected to similar federalism arguments. Justice Sandra Day O'Connor opened a recent opinion for the U.S. Supreme Court by stating: "This is a case about Federalism."[12] Justice Harry Blackmun reacted angrily to the majority's opinion, which he described as a methodical review of "federalism, comity, state sovereignty and preservation of state resources" in which one "searches . . . in vain for any mention of [the petitioner's] right to a criminal proceeding free from constitutional defect or his interest in finding a forum for his constitutional challenge to his conviction and sentence of death."[13]

Tolerance of political and religious minorities has also been eroded as a result of comparable deference to state authority.[14] Even speech that is objectionable primarily because it involves criticism of the government has been afforded reduced judicial protection because of the Supreme Court's decisions to defer to local decision makers.[15] Federalism arguments of this nature, which result in reduced judicial scrutiny, undermine the substantive principles embedded in the Constitution.[16]

PROTECTING THE LEAST ADVANTAGED

A second moral issue that often intersects with federalism debates involves the government's obligation to secure and protect basic necessities of life for the least advantaged of its citizens. Sixteenth-century Elizabethan poor laws[17] established secular responsibility for public welfare. Colonial governments recognized provision of public welfare as a responsibility of local government.[18] That perspective was coupled with an understanding that the local community was responsible only for "their own" and remained free to exclude those who suffered from the "moral pestilence" of poverty.[19] Although welfare claims lack the constitutional stature of the claims to fairness and equality discussed above,[20] a government role in protecting the poor has been consistently accepted in this country. Many states explicitly provide for such protection within their constitutions.[21]

Federalism arguments, however, continue to restrict central government responsibility for assisting those with special needs: children, the disabled, those unable to meet their health care needs, the elderly, the unemployable, and the working poor. Opponents of welfare assistance often framed their opposition in terms of deference to state decision making. The less popular the needy group, the more likely that assistance will be relegated to state or local communities.[22]

Arguments that state responsibility for welfare assistance will produce efficiency, autonomy, or state experimentation do not withstand careful scrutiny.[23] Few would claim that autonomy of welfare recipients was advanced by federal decisions to avoid establishing or raising benefit levels.[24] Asserted advantages of federalism, however, apply with a particularly cruel twist to recipients of state welfare programs. Thus, one of the arguments most frequently made for state autonomy is based on a marketplace analogy. States are expected to compete with each other to offer attractive environments for both people and capital. In the welfare context, however, stereotypes portray people attracted by generous welfare benefits as undesirable and likely to remain dependent upon the state for support. Opponents also view the cost of substantial welfare programs as a barrier to capital investment. As a result, despite assertions of benign neutrality, the marketplace inhibits state or local programs that support dependent citizens. Destructive competition among states victimizes this vulnerable and unpopular group.[25] To make matters worse, the poorest states have the greatest problems and are in the worst position to address them;[26] recession generates demands for "welfare reform," which becomes a code for cutbacks in assistance.

Competition among the states cannot be relied upon to protect nonproductive members of a society. The unemployable will be protected only by a sense of social morality; that moral sense should not be obscured by arguments for federalism.

This position does not support a broader conclusion that total responsibility for providing public welfare assistance should be in the hands of the federal government. The value of dispersing power was demonstrated in the 1980s: a federal administration hostile toward interests of the disabled poor was blocked in part by state protection from federal abuse.[27] The key, however, is to disperse power in a manner that eliminates the destructive aspects of federalism, and also to expose illegitimate references to federalism that are made to disguise arguments for reduced standards. In the absence of such safeguards, the U.S. brand of federalism will continue to foster the lowest standards of health and welfare protection for the poor of any developed nation.[28]

POLICE POWERS AND COMMUNITY STANDARDS

A third category of issues that could be described in moral terms, but that involves different considerations of federalism, has to do with ongoing regulation of community moral standards through positive law. This category includes local formulation and enforcement of criminal law, as well as laws regulating property, contracts, torts, marital relationships, and so on. The term "police power" has generally been used as a catchall to represent state and local authority to regulate these issues. By exercising their police power, state and local governments establish and protect the conventional moral standards of their communities.

It is in this context that principles of federalism point toward maximum deference to the states. Different treatment of these issues is not a function of relative levels of political support. Even when it may be appropriate to speak in terms of a national moral consensus, federal action should still be constrained when the moral principles involved are adequately protected through local participation.[29] By definition, the contemporary majority should address these issues; local control can protect nuances of community morality, and legitimate pluralist values should be allowed to flourish in the context of local autonomy. State control over issues within this context, however, must also be understood in terms of its relationship to the individual, minority group, and welfare interests included in the first two categories. Those national interests should not necessarily prevail whenever they conflict with police power concerns. When such instances of moral conflict occur, however, federalism concerns point in both directions, and simple references to "federalism" should not be used as the basis for a reflexive deference to local control.

An example of this intersection can be seen in the distinctions between criminal law and criminal procedure. When states decide that those who commit assault or battery should be prosecuted, they are exercising their authority to regulate community moral standards. National interests in protecting the minority are based on underlying concepts of liberty and respect that would not extend protection to the act of an assault by one person on another. The national interest, however, should protect individuals *charged* with assault to assure that the majority's disregard for criminals is not translated into abusive procedures.[30] National interests should also extend to the conditions under which those convicted of crimes are held.[31]

SUMMARY AND CONCLUSION

The question of whether the principle of federalism should lead to deference to the central government or to local authorities will vary depending upon the substantive moral issue that is at stake. Issues involving core constitutional values as well as those involving "destructive" competition among the states warrant national protection. Issues of conventional morality that do not implicate other constitutional concerns should be resolved at the state or local levels. Experience in the United States illustrates the significance of this moral framework for analysis of federalism.

The immoral institution of slavery, followed by a century of enforced segregation, reflected inappropriate deference to the states under the guise of federalism. That history teaches us that values that have core constitutional stature should receive increased national protection. State interests may need to be considered in an analysis of these issues, but they should be identified and directly weighed, not hidden behind general references to federalism. Entrenched values that warrant constraints on majoritarian impulses have become the special province of judicial protection. Federalism arguments that weaken that protection are incompatible with the basic moral principles on which the federal structure of this government was premised.

Inappropriate deference to local decision makers has also undercut protection for citizens who are necessarily dependent upon the state for their basic welfare. In this context the destructive competition of federalism actually undermines moral values; competitive pressure causes states to avoid responsibility for unemployable poor or disabled citizens. There are legitimate debates regarding the extent to which the government should assist those in need. Those who oppose such assistance on substantive grounds, however, should not be permitted to hide their opposition behind the mask of federalism, since federalism itself is a source of the problem. While it may be appropriate to rely upon the moral sense of the contemporary majority to protect the poor and the disabled, it is not reasonable to use the federal structure as a basis for undermining that moral sense.

The first two categories of moral discourse that affect law and legislation may be contrasted with a third. Deference to local authorities is appropriate for articulation and implementation of a conventional morality that does not infringe upon individual or minority rights, and does not involve the destructive competition of protective programs. In this context, values of pluralism and participatory democracy can be strengthened without the need for national consensus. Local autonomy may be respected as a valuable constraint on the central accumulation of power. As a result, in this third context the federal government should act with care to avoid encroaching upon traditional spheres of state responsibility. Because deference to the states in this context helps to preserve our republican ideals, national authority should not be asserted unless justified by factors that go beyond mere majoritarian support.

The moral dimensions of "our federalism"[32] serve as a guide to the division of power between state and national governments. Ignoring these issues, or suggesting that the term federalism implies deference to the states regardless of the moral context in which a dispute arises, will lead us to repeat past abuses of individual and minority rights. A federal structure that embraces this distinction, however, will protect our fundamental principles and our civic virtue.

NOTES

1. Federalist 10 (Madison) in Clinton Rossiter, ed, *The Federalist Papers* 82 (London: Mentor, 1961).

2. William Brennan, "Federal Habeas Corpus and State Prisoners: An Exercise in Federalism," 7 *Utah Law Review* 423, 442 (1961), quoted in *Coleman v. Thompson*, U.S., 111 S.Ct. 2546, 2570 (1991) (Blackmun, J., dissenting).

3. This category may be generally equated with those "'basic values' implicit in the concept of ordered liberty." *Poe v. Ullman*, 367 U.S. 497 (1961) (Harlan, J., dissenting); *Palko v. Connecticut*, 302 U.S. 319 (1937). Alternatively, it could be defined in relationship to the issues warranting increased judicial scrutiny as identified by Justice Harlan Stone in footnote four of *United States v. Carolene Products Co.*, 304 U.S., 152, n.4 (1938), or in terms of the doctrine of rights discussed by Ronald Dworkin in *Takings Rights Seriously* (Cambridge, MA: Harvard University Press, 1977). The moral authority of these principles could be traced to Immanuel Kant or to a range of other philosophers. See Dworkin at 198. The debate regarding the appropriate origin or scope of these rights, however, is left for other forums.

4. The moral obligation of society to assure that no one is denied basic necessities of life has ancient roots. As a government obligation, it can be traced to the Elizabethan poor laws. See 43 Eliz., ch. 2 (1601). Colonial counterparts reflect a common moral obligation recognized prior to formation of the United States. See Stefan A. Riesenfeld, "The Formative Era of American Public Assistance Law," 43 *California Law Review* 175 (1955). A link between this second category and the first may be identified in the terms of John Rawls, who addressed the relationship between Kantian moral values and the "difference principle," which constrains redistribution of wealth in light of an obligation to improve the welfare of the least advantaged. See John Rawls, *A Theory of Justice* at 75–83, 251–257 (Cambridge, MA: Belknap Press of Harvard University Press, 1971). It may be assumed for purposes of this discussion that this second category has been consistently recognized in American law, even though its specific content has varied over time and is not mandated by constitutional principles. But see William Rich, "Equal Protection for the Poor: Fair Distribution to Meet Brutal Needs," 24 *San Diego Law Review* 1117 (1987); William H. Simon, "Rights and Redistribution in the Welfare System," 38 *Stanford Law Review* 1431 (1986).

5. This context is generally consistent with the concept of conventional morality or, in other words, the moral standards of a contemporary majority. These standards can be thought of in terms of current statutory law. By definition, these majoritarian standards should also be understood as limited by the "fundamental principles" identified in terms of category one.

6. 60 U.S. (19 How.) 393 (1857). The only prior case in which the Supreme Court had invalidated an act of Congress was *Marbury v. Madison*, 5 U.S. (1 Cranch) 137 (1803). *Dred Scott* was the first case in which the principle of federal deference to state authority was cited as the basis for overturning a congressional act.

7. 60 U.S. at 452.

8. C. Vann Woodward, *The Strange Career of Jim Crow* (New York: Oxford University Press, 3d ed. 1975).

9. The Civil Rights Cases, 109 U.S. 3 (1883). The Court decided that the Fourteenth Amendment only gave Congress power to address racial discrimination

committed by the states. *Id.* at 14.

10. Bernard Schwartz, ed., *Statutory History of the United States, Civil Rights* (New York: Chelsea House, 1970), at 1302. For a comparable comparison of national power under the Civil Rights Act of 1964 to Soviet, as well as German and Italian, fascism, see the comments of Senators Sparkman and Talmadge. *Id.* at 1167.

11. *Heart of Atlanta Motel v. United States*, 379 U.S. 241 (1964).

12. *Coleman v. Thompson*, 501 U.S. 722, 111 S.Ct. 2546, 2552 (1991).

13. *Id.* at 2569. For further discussion of the *Coleman* case, see *infra* at notes 24–30 and accompanying text.

14. See, eg., *Employment Division, Department of Human Resources v. Smith*, 110 S.Ct. 1595, 1606 (1990), in which the Supreme Court rejected use of a "compelling state interest test" to analyze sacramental use of peyote by the Native American Church:

> It may fairly be said that leaving accommodation to the political process will place at a relative disadvantage those religious practices that are not widely engaged in; but that unavoidable consequence of democratic government must be preferred to a system in which each conscience is a law unto itself or in which judges weigh the social importance of all laws against the centrality of all religious beliefs.

Id. at 890.

15. See, e.g., *Gentile v. State Bar of Nevada*, U.S., 111 S.Ct. 2720 (1991) in which a majority adopted a reduced standard for reviewing state regulation of lawyers who speak to the news media regarding pending cases. Justice Anthony M. Kennedy's dissent noted that "this case involves pure speech in the political forum . . . and should, therefore, be accorded protection which "approximated the clear and present danger test." *Id.* at 2724, 2725. See also *Connick v. Meyers*, 461 U.S. 138 (1983) (reduced scrutiny applied to review limits on speech activities of public employees); *Cornelius v. NAACP Legal Defense & Education Fund*, 473 U.S. 788 (1985) (limiting scrutiny of subject matter constraints on charitable fund-raising from federal employees).

16. Nothing in this account would suggest that states should not be free to interpret and even expand upon the values of respect for minority concerns identified above. The point is rather that principles developed by the central government, either Congress or the courts, should not be weakened because of such concerns. For those inclined to support affirmative efforts to redress problems of societal and institutionalized discrimination, the Supreme Court deference to Congress and restraint on local communities in the context of "affirmative action" was particularly perverse. See *City of Richmond v. J. A. Croson*, U.S., 109 S.Ct. 706 (1989).

17. See Riesenfeld, *supra* note 4.

18. *Id.*

19. See *New York v. Miln*, 36 U.S. 102 (1837); *Edwards v. California*, 314 U.S. 160 (1941).

20. Numerous arguments have been advanced that suggest a basis for protecting the poor under the U.S. Constitution. See Frank Michelman, "The Supreme Court, 1968 Term–Forward: On Protecting the Poor through the Fourteenth Amendment," 83 *Harvard Law Review* 7 (1969); Rich, *supra* note 4, at 1117. The Supreme Court, however, has commonly marginalized the status of welfare claims. See, e.g., *Edelman v. Jordan*, 415 U.S. 651 (1974).

It should be noted that the international community has generally recognized the constitutional significance of the principle that governments have the responsibility to assure that the least advantaged of their citizens will be assured basic necessities of life. See, e.g., International Covenant on Economic, Social and Cultural Rights, UN Doc. A/6316 (1966), 993 UNTS 3, entered into force on January 3, 1976; European Convention for the Protection of Human Rights and Fundamental Freedoms, November 4, 1950, 213 UNTS 222 (1953).

21. At least 16 states have express constitutional provisions for aid to the poor. Adam S. Cohen, "More Myths of Parity: State Court Forums and Constitutional Actions for the Right to Shelter," 38 *Emory Law Journal* 615, 634 (1989).

22. Thus, the federal welfare system might be described in terms of a popular hierarchy with the elderly or disabled on top, dependent children someplace in the middle, and dependent adults at the lowest rung of the ladder. The federal government funds and administers the first group, provides some funds but no administration for the second, and disavows any responsibility for the third. See generally, Joel F. Handler, *Reforming the Poor: Welfare Policy, Federalism, and Morality* (New York: Basic Books, 1972).

23. Deborah Maranville, "Welfare and Federalism," 36 *Loyola Law Review* 1, 5–10 (1990).

24. *Id.* at 6.

25. *Id.* at 33. Maranville discusses this problem in terms of "market failure." She also discusses the possibility that employment oriented welfare programs could be perceived as "developmental" rather than as "redistributive," and as a result could be seen as a source for attracting capital. *Id.* at 46–52. Disabled or truly marginalized citizens, however, are unlikely to be perceived in such terms.

26. *Id.* at 42. Note in this context the especially brutal brand of federalism currently practiced by the U.S. government. While federal funds have been reduced, federal mandates have increased. As a result, states may not be able to compete with each other by lowering standards. They are, however, seeking reductions in those standards because of the enormous financial pressures that they have been forced to live with.

27. The Social Security Administration had eliminated thousands of disabled individuals from the Social Security Insurance program. Responses from state officials and others led to reversal of that policy. Separation of power between the legislative, executive, and judicial branches was also seen as an important check on the administration in that case. See Maranville, *supra* note 23, at 30.

28. See Margaret S. Gordon, *Social Security Policies in Industrial Countries* (Cambridge: Cambridge University Press, 1988), at 14; Robert Morris, *Testing the Limits of Social Welfare* (Hanover, NH: pub. for Brandeis University Press by University Press of New England, 1988), at 3.

29. Federal responsibility for such issues may even undermine the national government's ability to address more basic concerns. Thus, the Judicial Conference, the Federal Bar Association, and the American Judges Association have all opposed congressional moves to "federalize" prosecution of homicide cases in which firearms are used. Chief Justice William Rehnquist wrote on behalf of the Judicial Conference that "[s]uch expansion of federal jurisdiction would be inconsistent with long-accepted concepts of federalism. . . . Not only will bona fide federal criminal prosecutions suffer . . . but federal courts . . . will be unable to carry out their vital responsibilities to provide timely forums for civil cases." "Groups Oppose Federalization of Homicide Cases," *The Third Branch*, October 1991, at 5.

30. Considerations of federalism should, therefore, not have been a factor in

Coleman v. Thompson, *supra*. note 2. Justice Harry Blackmun made this point in his dissenting opinion: "Federal habeas review of state court judgments, respectfully employed to safeguard federal rights, is no invasion of State sovereignty. . . . [T]he considered exercise by federal courts—in vindication of fundamental constitutional rights—of the habeas jurisdiction conferred on them by Congress exemplifies the full expression of this Nation's federalism." 111 S.Ct. at 2570.

31. See, e.g., *Wilson v. Seiter*, U.S., 111 S.Ct. 2321 (1991).

32. See *Younger v. Harris*, 401 U.S. 37 (1971); Hon. Harry T. Edwards, "The Changing Notion of 'Our Federalism,'" 33 *Wayne Law Review* 1015 (1987).

39

Protection and Promotion of Human Rights: Power Allocation Among Central, Regional, and Local Governments in the Russian Federation

Boris A. Tsepov

Alexander Hamilton affirmed in 1775 that the sacred rights of mankind were written as with a sunbeam in the whole volume of human nature and could never be erased or obscured by mortal power. This philosophical maxim presents the very essence of democracy and of a democratic state. It denies the superiority of any power over human rights and proclaims the absolute character of human rights. On the other hand, that denial itself confirms the inevitability of attempts of power to limit human rights in any way available.

An organization in all its forms, including a state as an organization of human society, is always based on certain limitations of the rights of its elements or, in case of a state organization, its subjects. The core of the problem is the level, scope, and volume of such limitations. Any state, which pretends to be a democracy, should provide the lowest possible level of limitations of the rights of its subjects to keep a delicate but sustainable balance of interests of those who govern and who are governed.

Accepting that all human beings are born free and equal in dignity and rights without distinction and discrimination of any kind, a democratic state assumes the responsibility for their effective exercise. To this end a democratic state establishes corresponding legal mechanisms and procedures. The effectiveness of those mechanisms and procedures seems to be a matter of crucial importance for democracy because of numerous collisions of interests that frequently accompany man-to-power and citizen-to-state relations, which, at least theoretically, should be maintained on the basis of mutually acceptable compromises. It seems very important that citizens, seeking in their turn the limitation of state powers, would not deprive a state of its essential prerogatives that enable it to act as a governing authority.

One of the most important means to provide a balance of interests is the organization of state power itself in its "horizontal" and "vertical" dimensions. The "horizontal" dimensions of state power involve the distribution and separation of power in a state among its executive, legislative, and judicial branches. The competitive character of their interrelationship should not impede their cooperation, and, at the same time, should assure that no one branch gets superiority or concentrates all the powers of a state in one branch's hands. The "vertical" dimension of power distribution, especially in federal systems, means the allocation of powers and responsibilities, including those in the field of human rights, among federal, regional, and local authorities of a state.

It is well-known that the United States, through difficult and lengthy processes, succeeded in reaching a very high degree of decentralization and deconcentration of state power. Nevertheless, the state stays strong and in all respects is capable of governing the country while at the same time protecting civil and political human rights. The U.S.S.R. and the Russian Federation are less perfect in the protection of certain human rights than the United States. The Soviet Union was a state with an extremely high level of centralization and concentration of power, which was almost entirely monopolized by the Communist Party elite and the party apparatus. The state power was seized by the party, which ignored the very notion of "human rights" and substituted it with such quasi-democratic inven-tions as "communists' code of morality" and "rights and responsibilities of the party members." In fact, human rights have never been a popular subject in constitutional instruments in the U.S.S.R. From the first Soviet Constitution, the list of human rights became shorter and the human rights substance weaker and weaker. Only the so-called Brezhnev Constitution might be considered as an exception because it did contain a special accent on citizens' (not human) rights. However, most of the 30 articles of the Brezhnev Constitution that ad-dressed Soviet citizens' rights were designed primarily to meet the challenges of international politics in the 1970s. They did not bring substantial changes in human rights domestically, because those rights could not be implemented.

The situation in the constituent republics of the former U.S.S.R. has been no better. The republics' constitutions were worked out along the lines of their "big sister"—the U.S.S.R. Constitution—and carefully reproduced its inapplicable norms and principles, including those on human rights. Legislation in the republics in turn adapted the basics from the all-Union legislation to each republic's needs. As a result, there is a high degree of legislative uniformity in the republics that, in trying to please the so-called center (the federal authorities of the Union) and demonstrate loyalty to the federal state power, sometimes has imposed additional limitations on their citizens' rights.

Public interest in the problem of human rights greatly increased after Mikhail Gorbachev came to office. Unfortunately, there were more ardent speeches than practical deeds during that time. The main accent (as a result of political pressure from the West) was placed on the search for possible solutions to so-called weak points in the Soviet human rights record (free emigration, political prisoners, repressive psychiatry, etc.). During that period, a number of new democratically oriented laws (on press freedom, on religion and religious associations, etc.) were passed. However, these laws were largely ineffective because the allocation of state power, both horizontal and vertical, remained unchanged. Even modest attempts of the federal authorities in Moscow to strengthen and protect human rights at the republic and local levels died before producing any effect.

During the first years of perestroika, many democratic reforms initiated by the federal authorities had a sad end in the silence of offices of various republic and local leaders. It soon became obvious that human rights could not be adequately protected in the country unless the state itself underwent serious reform. Unfortunately, the federal authorities hesitated to begin necessary reforms because of the danger that substantial, noncosmetic reforms of the state power structures, including the distribution and reallocation of powers, would break the political status quo and lead to the end of the Soviet federal state. In any event, the Soviet Union collapsed due in large part to the efforts of the constituent republics where, under the influence of democratic and nationalist forces, the old party guard began to lose the command.

The infamous "war of the laws" took place, during which Russia, as well as Ukraine and Belarus and other republics, one after another, proclaimed the superiority of their constitutions and legislations over those of the U.S.S.R. The laws dealing with human rights that had been passed in the republics of the former Soviet Union during the period known as the period of "sovereignization" were too weak and had almost no means of enforcement to change significantly the human rights situation for the better. Their main utility was to be the arm in the political struggle of the republics against the dominance of the center, the federal authorities.

During that time the center could not take a decisive step on the way to reform the Soviet federation. Instead, the center's main efforts concentrated on foreign policy, where, admittedly, a number of substantial goals, including the development of international cooperation in the field of human rights, were achieved. The Soviet government opened an active dialogue with the West, and especially the United States, on a number of delicate human rights problems that were considered to be particularly sensitive for the U.S.S.R. Domestically, that dialogue led to one of the most important directions for the government policy: the adjustment of the U.S.S.R. legislation on human rights with the responsibilities of the U.S.S.R. under the international instruments, including those of the United Nations and CSCE.

During those years the U.S.S.R. began preparations that finally led to the recognition of the competence of international mechanisms on verification of a status of human rights in various nations, and to the consideration of communications, including those from individuals on violation of their rights by a state. The U.S.S.R. revoked its earlier reservations on six international human rights conventions (on torture, on the elimination of all forms of racial discrimination, and others) and agreed to recognize the competence of the International Court of Justice to consider any disputes between state parties with respect to the interpretation or application of those conventions. This significantly helped to raise the international human rights standing of the U.S.S.R. and served to encourage the future democratic development of Soviet human rights legislation. However, it unfortunately did not change the everyday life of the citizens of the Soviet Federation.

The aborted coup in August 1991 put an end to the efforts of the center to retain the Soviet federation, and it ceased to exist as a geopolitical reality before the end of that year.

In November 1991, on the wave of democratic euphoria and aspirations of the rule of law, the Supreme Soviet of the Russian Federation adopted the Declaration of Rights and Freedoms of Man and Citizen. The Russian Declaration is similar to the Universal Declaration of Human Rights adopted by the United Nations in 1948 and it has constitutional law status. It contains new and very important provisions, such as the recognition that all human beings are born free and equal in dignity and rights, freedom of emigration, and freedom of information. It also imposed on the state a duty not to conceal from the public information on facts endangering the health and life of people (e.g., the Chernobyl case). For the first time in Russian history, constitutional law establishes the Parliament's authority to fulfill and protect human rights and creates the post of ombudsman, an institution well-known in many West European democracies.

At the same time, the Declaration is far from perfect. For example, Article 39 of the Declaration permits the state to temporarily limit the rights and freedoms of people in time of public emergency. However, the number and nature of these limitations are not specified and remain unclear. In addition, the meaning of Article I of the Declaration is uncertain. Article I both recognizes that international human rights norms and standards are superior to the norms of the legislation of the Russian Federation, and determines that the rights of the Russian citizens derive *directly* from the international legal instruments.

Finally, the human rights provisions of the new Federal Treaty of the Russian Federation has been signed by almost all the constituencies of the Federation (except Tatarstan and Chechnia) and approved by the Congress of People's Deputies in Moscow. According to the treaty, the protection of human rights is mainly the prerogative of the federal authorities and partly is considered as the matter of joint responsibility of federal, republic, region, and district powers. The very fact that the local authorities, as well as federal ones, will take part in strengthening human rights is a clear sign of a more democratic allocation of power in the Russian Federation. However, it remains unclear the degree to which cooperation among federal and local authorities will be realized under the treaty. Under the treaty, federal authority is exclusive with regard to questions of criminal, criminal procedural, and penal legislation, as well as civil and civil procedure covering the great bulk of norms directly affecting human rights. Only administrative, labor, housing law problems, and the corresponding procedures are determined as an area of *joint responsibility* of the federal and local authorities. Such joint responsibility could be considered as just and nondiscriminatory only if the treaty text includes a special article to deal with power sharing conflicts by impartial and objective determination by the Constitutional Court.

The new Constitution of the Russian Federation is now before the participants of the Congress of People's Deputies, and comments on the Constitution are premature. After all, there was in the United States a period of years between independence and adoption of the Constitution. In Russia, it might also be useful not to rush to work out the new Constitution.

40

Concept of Federalism in Light of the Rights of Nations to Self-Determination

Boris Sergeevich Krylov

The problem of the dependence of a state system on its national composition began attracting the attention of political figures and scientists as long ago as the Versailles Peace Treaty. It became especially acute by the end of the World War II, when many new states appeared on the world map. The populations of those states either represented certain national communities or strived to become such. For a variety of reasons, those strivings were not always a success.

This problem has never been so acute as nowadays. This is confirmed by the developments in the former Yugoslavia and in the former Soviet Union. Both states were federations based on a community of basically unitary states, each of which might be considered as mononational. However, in both federations member-states lacked a national main body, though they were proclaimed to have one. Thus, a ruinous contradiction arose: one part of the society strove to strengthen national origins, while another part, which did not belong to the nation that gave the name to the state, opposed arising nationalism.

This contradiction led to confrontation which was aggravated by nationalistic manifestations both at the state level and in everyday life. In the U.S.S.R. this confrontation has gone through different stages. Before the 1930s the central authorities of the Soviet Union strove to support all national cultures, as a result of which many peoples, who even had had no written languages before, were granted rights to primary and then secondary education in their native languages and could enter universities. National literatures had appeared and started developing with a measure of success.

This process ended with the adoption and implemention of the policy of integrating natural cultures by strengthening their ties with the culture of the people whose language was that of international communication—that is, the language and culture of the Russian people. This policy was implemented by purely administrative, rather than scientific, methods. The policy was aimed at accelerating the process of political hegemonism, rather than resulting from certain prevailing theoretical views. This circumstance was of a predominant significance for the development and subsequent collapse of federalism in the Soviet Union.

For decades federalism had been regarded as a successful solution to the national question in uniting different peoples within the borders of a single state. The essence of a federation is to strictly distribute competence between the federation and the member-states, where distribution is based on the rights of the state that became a member of the federation rather than on the will of the center or the federation. This arrangement increases the distance between the federal center and bodies of the member-states because each relies upon an independent state structure and constituent voters. The independence in obtaining mandates lays the foundation for the relations between the federation and its member-states and independent states on the other.

The possibility of such a federal structure depends on the development of democracy in both each member-state and the federation as a whole. It also depends on the situation in the world community. Up to recent decades the center of power in federations was shifting toward federal government. However, today a reverse process seems to be taking place, in part, because many state functions previously executed by federal governments are increasingly now guided by international law, especially international human rights law. One need only refer to the UN Charter and to some documents of the 1975 Helsinki Accords, which set forth a number of rules that states may not ignore.

The development of human rights in the Universal Declaration of Human Rights, international treaties, and other instruments has had a strong effect on the activity of human beings in the social sphere to politicize populations.

However, while being politicized, people strive to communicate their national manifestations of human personality. One would think that federation features should be similarly manifested in federations with subjects based on the territorial principles, for instance, in the United States of America, Australia, Austria, and in those formed by national states as the subjects, such as Switzerland, the former Czechoslovakia, Yugoslavia, and the Soviet Union. The main feature of federations based on the national principle is that virtually all problems in relations between the federal government and the governments of the member-states acquire national color and are regarded also as a relationship between individual and federation sovereignties. The relations between the federation and its members are international relations, while the actions of the federation authorities that cause discontent in member-states are also considered encroachments on the sovereignty of the member-state people. Even reasonable and quite justified actions of the federal bodies to achieve common goals may lead to friction stimulated by the national features and differences of the members.

This phenomenon is aggravated by the atmosphere of exaggeration of the national characteristics of man. However, today's migration of populations has reached such a level that sometimes whole population groups of different nations come in contact with one another, and such groups are difficult to assimilate. Individuals often prefer to stay within a group of persons of the same nationality, rather than assimilate into a common mass identity. This occurs most frequently when an individual or migrated group is part of a people with vivid national characteristics. For example, in the former Soviet Union representatives of the Caucasian nationalities—especially Armenians, Chechens, and Ossetians—preserve their national features irrespective of their place of living, and form stable national communities. It seems that the U.S.A. cannot be called a "melting pot" for different nationalities any longer: Spanish- and Italian-speaking enclaves have formed there, it has Chinatowns, and so on.

This has given rise to problems of providing education in other languages, creating mass media for the people who speak other languages, and so on. While acknowledging the difficulties encountered by the U.S.A., we should recognize that overcoming them is far from impossible, since English-speaking people constitute the major and overwhelming part of the U.S. population.

A different situation has evolved in the Soviet Union. It is inhabited by over a hundred nationalities that ignore the borders of their national states. For example, the 1989 population census reveals that Russians amounted to only 51% of the total population of the Soviet Union, and that only slightly more than 80% of Russians live within the borders of the Russian Federation. Only 66% of Armenians living in the U.S.S.R. reside in Armenia.

In addition, the populations of the so-called autonomous republics (which were part of the constituent republics of the Soviet Union and now are the members of the Commonwealth of Independent States) are heterogeneous in composition. For example, the Bashkir Republic included in the Russian Federation has only 22% Bashkirs (Tartars comprise 28% of the population and Russians 39%). About 40% of the Bashkir population of the country resides outside the republic. And in 1923, when the Buryat Republic was formed, the Buryat-Mongols made up 236,700 people, or 48.9% of the population. By the time of the 1989 census, the population of the republic increased to 1,038,000 people, but the Buryat population increased just slightly, to 249,000 people. In addition, 178,000 Buryats live outside the republic and Buryats in the Buryat Republic now amounts to only 24% of the population. Such a situation is also characteristic of other republics within the Russian Federation. Yakuts comprise 33% in the Yakut Republic, Karelians 10.1% in the Karelian Republic, and Kalmyks 45.4% in Kalmykia.

For many reasons, in particular migration of the population to sites of huge industrial projects, it has turned out that the peoples who gave names to the republics were represented by insignificant minorities in them and the threat of losing the natural culture and language became very real. The problem of protecting the indigenous population from desolving in the mass of "new-comers" with their own culture evolved even in the national republics. Two principal ways seem to exist for protecting a people: first, to create conditions that will limit migration; second, to provide real guarantees for preservation of language, culture, history, and habitat of peoples without infringing the rights of others. Both ways are used quite broadly all over the world, including the U.S.S.R.

Every state has the right to control immigration and emigration. For exampe, Sweden and Finland take measures to keep out immigrants. However, it is illegitimate to limit migrations in a way that discriminates against a segment of the state population, such as is occurring in the new Baltic republics. From the viewpoint of law and morality, human rights of any person must not be infringed because of the nation they belong to. Restricting human rights to the choice of residence on national backgrounds is absolutely un-acceptable because those restrictions will inevitably lead to the violation of human rights.

Ensuring equal rights to all citizens irrespective of nationality is addressed in the Declaration of Human Rights and Freedoms that has been recently adopted by the Congress of People's Deputies of the U.S.S.R. The provisions of the Declaration are compulsory for execution by all state bodies, officials, public organizations, and citizens. The Declaration states that all citizens are equal before the law and have equal rights to be protected by the law, irrespective of national origin, language, and other circumstances. The right to the use of native languages, education in the native languages, and preservation and development of the national cultures is secured for everyone. Direct or indirect limitation of rights and any racial or national preferences are prohibited.

The regeneration of national statehood is unobjectionable provided it actually excludes any violations of human rights. The present trend toward regeneration of national statehood is to a considerable extent the reaction to the years when the Soviet Union was essentially a unitary state with explicit aspirations to level national features of peoples without sufficient attention to national cultures. The regeneration of national statehood is also affected by economic reasons and from ungrounded hope that difficulties could be more easily overcome after loosening ties with other states. Obviously, the policy of self-reliance cannot lead to success.

Regeneration of national statehood may also neglect other nationalities. In the autumn of 1991, certain circles in the Chechen-Ingush Republic of Russia (integrating two peoples who are very close in their language and culture) began to seek separation of Chechnia from the Russian Federation to form an independent state. Similar movements are underway in the Kabardian-Balkar

Republic.

These independence movements have relevance to the complex and long process of transformation of the Soviet Union into the Commonwealth of Independent States. Initially, the Soviet Union was to be replaced by a new union of states, also a federation, but not one close to a unitary state. All its member-states would enjoy real and comprehensive rights but it also would have strong Union (federal) bodies. Such a union would have been something new as compared with the former Union, which existed before perestroika (i.e., before April 1985). This form of union was reflected in a draft of the new Union Treaty published late in December 1991. Many republics were becoming certain that the preserved Union bodies would in fact never waive their powers and would remain independent in their decisions, even if contrary to the interests of the federation member-states. Under those particular conditions the federative form effectively opposed sovereignty for the member-states.

The draft of the treaty, on the one hand, stipulated that each member-republic of the treaty was an independent state, and the resulting Union of sovereign states was really a confederation that would execute its powers within the limits voluntarily bestowed upon it by the sovereign members of the treaty. On the other hand, the treaty also created a new state, a subject of international law. Apart from being the subject of international law, the new single state would be an organizer of the united armed forces. This, however, was such a departure from a classic confederation that it gave rise to fears that the new Union would preserve too many features of the old one. As it turned out, not a single republic accepted the initial treaty.

On December 8, 1991, the leaders of three major states of the former Soviet Union signed the Commonwealth Agreement, which was based on radically new principles. They proclaimed their intent to build democratic legal states and to develop their relations on the basis of mutual recognition and respect of national sovereignty, principles of equality and noninterference in the internal affairs of one another, and in a belief that further development of friendship and mutually beneficial cooperation would conform to the vital interests of their nations and would serve the course of peace and security.

The founding states undertook obligations that were common for all civilized states of the modern world. They voluntarily decided jointly to coordinate foreign policy, to form and develop common economic space, to participate in European and Asian markets, to accept uniform customs and migration policies, to expand transportation and communication systems, to protect the environment and ecological safety, and to fight against organized crime.

They also agreed to preserve the joint command of the common military-strategic space, and to maintain centralized control over nuclear arms. The nuclear arms reduction process is proceeding very successfully, and Belorussia and Ukraine have spoken out in favor of becoming nuclear-free states.

The leaders of 11 independent states gathered in Alma-Ata, the capital of Kazakhstan, on December 21. They declared that Azerbaijan, Armenia, Belarus, Kazakhstan, Kirghizia, Moldova, Russian Federation, Tajikistan, Turkmenistan, Uzbekistan, and Ukraine would form the Commonwealth of Independent States (CIS). The Alma-Ata Declaration provides that the participants will interact on the principles of equality through coordinating institutions that shall be formed on a parity basis and shall act in compliance with the procedures determined by the agreement among the members of the CIS, which will be neither a state nor a state superstructure.

The CIS members subscribed to all generally recognized rules of international law. They concluded the agreement for joint measures to ensure comprehensive control over nuclear weapons and adequate nuclear safety.

With the formation of the CIS, the U.S.S.R. ceased to exist. The creation of the CIS on the territory of the former Soviet Union reflects a radically new political reality that is emerging. Viewed optimistically, the CIS has put an end to disintegration that resulted mainly from a disbelief that the former state structures of the U.S.S.R. could be used for the democratic renewal of the society and formation of the economy based on market relations.

The independent states are showing some signs of rapprochement. This will allow them to use more effectively the potential of each state in mutual interests. Institutions are being formed to coordinate activities of the Commonwealth states where their interests are mutual.

Obviously, this is only the beginning. However, when considering the present situation we should bear in mind that over the past five years, all the states of the former Soviet Union and their peoples have acquired the feeling of self-respect. And this is the foundation for building a society that would provide for the development of each person and of the institutions created by everyone. Of course, there is a long way ahead. But, as a saying goes, the first step is the hardest. And we are ready for it. New social relations are formed step by step in each independent state. They are not always positive, but the process as a whole is obviously progressive.

The formation of the new CIS is by no means a federation or even a confederation. It is actually a "commonwealth of independent states," interconnected by a myriad of economic and cultural ties (despite religious differences). They are interconnected by a mutual past and by millions of family ties. In addition, the CIS members have many global obligations that can be met only by acting together.

There is only one conclusion to be reached: The CIS will be able to develop successfully only if the common ties mentioned above are preserved and multiplied. The states may remain independent, but they will be interconnected and, in the final analysis, interdependent states. In my opinion this will determine the ways of their development. If they follow the principles of democracy in their relations, if the freedom of an individual and the freedom of each state formation are secured, mutual confidence will increase. Then the laws of rational organization of society will come into effect. The form of integration adopted today will become different and tighter. We will not rush to name it. This is for the future. And it will come.

41

Language Problems of Federalism in Tajikistan

Zulfia M. Mirshakar

Language is one of the most important elements of culture and reflects the historical, social, and spiritual development of the people. It often is the monument of a national culture, and the culture of society and social environment is displayed through the relation of culture toward language.

Ethnic diversity defines the language situation in the former U.S.S.R. The people speak more than 130 languages, which belong to many different systems and families (East Slavic, Baltic, Finno-Ugric, Turkic, Iranian, Caucasian, Paleoasian, etc.). The speakers differ in number (from millions up to hundreds of millions) and in the character and volume of duties performed (from serving the needs of the state, the republics, and autonomies to the everyday necessities in the family).

Tajikistan has Russian as its common language, which for a long time was considered the language of international intercourse. The Russian language also serves the state needs (government of the state, central press, radio and television, transport, the armed forces, foreign relations, modern large-scale industry, some branches of fundamental science, cosmonautics, and mail communication). The Russian language acquired its common language function from the former Russian Empire before the 1917 October Revolution, and the subsequent Soviet society inherited the Russian language as its common language. The Languages of Nations of the U.S.S.R. Law, adopted not long ago, has consolidated the state status of the Russian language. It has determined the sphere of its use in the country. The Law also reserves to the Russian language the important function of international intercourse.

In the course of historical development, the language situation in the U.S.S.R. has suffered profound changes. From the very beginning of its existence, the Soviet state adopted, on November 15, 1917, the Declaration of

Rights of Russian Nations, in which the question about the national languages of peoples of the country was settled. Under the Declaration, free development of all national minorities and their languages was proclaimed side by side with national equality and sovereignty.

During the intensive state-building decades of the 1920s and 1930s, illiteracy was overcome, individual nations found autonomy, and written language and literature were introduced for more than 50 languages ignorant of letters. Schools to teach mother tongues were established, and manuals, dictionaries, and other educational literature were published. Language vocabularies were enriched, their functions were enlarged, and they began to be used in the spheres of social and state activity, education, mass communication, science, and culture. As bilingualism and polylingualism were further developed, the Russian language was voluntarily chosen as the language of international intercourse.

After the late 1930s the national and language situation in the U.S.S.R. changed abruptly. Autonomics were abolished, individual nationalities were deported beyond the borders of their motherland, and the newly created written languages were abolished as if they had not been used. In general, less attention was paid to the development of national languages. This change had an especially a negative effect on languages of less populated nationalities. However, the defense of "small" nations' languages, and especially striving to keep the mother tongue and culture, were called the display of nationalism and purism. In addition, social functions of national languages began being reduced, the quality of mother tongue education was also lowered, and active assimilation of smaller nations and ethnic groups was undertaken.

Policies of spiritual life centralization of the Soviet society, of "internationalization and natural assimilation," and of complete merging of languages, cultures, and nations restrained and reduced development of languages not only artificially, restricting the sphere of their usage further on, but they objectively led to the general polylingualism in the majority of the republics. These policies adversely affected the number of national schools and kindergartens. Instructors taught using mainly the Russian language in the higher educational institutions. Theses in national languages were not taken into consideration, and all this led to degeneration and assimilation of national languages.

The institution of perestroika has inspired the national and language policy of our country by putting language into the center of social attention as the basis of national culture and as one of the most important means of expressing and keeping national originality.

The problem of national and language relations has overwhelmed all the regions of our multinational federation where, within one territorial and administrative unit, two, three, or even more languages function and interact. The importance of local languages for national cultures became more prominent. Efforts were made to raise the status of local languages by more thorough study of their structure, by enriching their vocabulary, and by enlarging their functional and communicative possibilities. In the course of all these changes, language laws were adopted in all republics in 1989 and 1990. These laws stressed the development of national languages. Languages of all republics were elevated to state language status. Having secured the status of the state language to the language of aboriginal nationality, each republic wanted to enhance the prestige of the republican languages and to secure legal guarantees for their free functioning.

Each republic determined the legal status of the Russian languages in its law in its own way. In most republics (like Ukraine, Belorussia, Azerbaijan, Moldova, Latvia, Armenia, Kirgizia, Uzbekistan, and Tajikistan), the Russian language is the language of international intercourse. However, the status of Russian as the international intercourse language varies from republic to republic. In Turkmenia and Kazakhastan, Russian is considered the language that functions freely. In Georgia and Estonia, the status of the Russian language is not determined at all. In Lithuania, Russian is the language of international intercourse, but only outside Lithuania. With the recent secession of the Baltic republics and the situation in Georgia, the Russian language has an unfavorable status. Finally, in some autonomous republics, Russian has been replaced by national languages as the state language.

In addition, the Russian-speaking population of the country and nationalities and ethnic groups that either have autonomy or are not in the structure of the republics and subject to the language law (about 60 million persons or 43% of the non-Russian population of the country) came out against the state status of national languages, forseeing infringement of their civil rights and restriction of speaking Russian and their native language. All this has created a complicated language situation in the country.

On April 24, 1990, the Third Session of the Supreme Soviet of the U.S.S.R. adopted the Law of Languages of Nations of the U.S.S.R. that offered to guarantee the constitutional equality, freedom of development, and valuable use of all national languages of the country within their ethnic existence. The question about languages was being considered at an all-Union legislative level for the first time during the existence of the Soviet power.

A commission on the problems of development of language, culture, national and international traditions, and historical heritage protection was instructed to work out the draft law. Outstanding linguists, lawyers, sociologists, and representatives of the creative intelligentsia took part in the preparation of the draft law. Lively discussions all over the country were provoked by the press, by radio and television. Letters and appeals urgently demanded that the Russian language become the state language. The task of the Commission was to establish general principles to guide language policy in the U.S.S.R., to guarantee the free development and use of national languages of the U.S.S.R. within a legal language regime, and to assure the rights of the citizens to use national languages.

The status of the Union republics' languages and the official language of the U.S.S.R., as well as other national languages of the U.S.S.R., was stated in 25 articles of the language law. The decisive step has been taken in legally securing the free development and use of all national languages of our country. The Union and autonomous republics are given the right to determine the legal status of their languages at their discretion, up to declaring them as the state ones. At the same time, other national units have broad rights in language adjustment and use. Local government bodies in places where the population speaking another language is large enough are given the right to settle the problems of using either language independently.

The Russian language, as one of the official and working UN Organization languages, is declared by law the official language of the Union, keeping for itself the function of the international intercourse language. As the official language, Russian is used by all-Union control systems (i.e., transport, power systems, etc.), by the armed forces of the U.S.S.R., and by the railway forces of the U.S.S.R. As the language of international intercourse, Russian is used in international relations, in the activities of diplomatic representatives of the U.S.S.R., in foreign cooperation, and in the official registration of international documents.

Article 25 of the Law is aimed at defense of the national languages of the Soviet Union against "propaganda of animosity and scorn," against putting "obstacles and restrictions in their use," and against "violation of the Soviet legislation, Union and Autonomous Language Laws."

Adoption of Union and republican language laws has opened wide prospects for the development of languages and cultures of smaller nations of our country. For example, the language life of the Gorno-Badakhshan Autonomous Region (GBAR) is a component of the language life in Tajikistan, and, in turn, the language situation in Tajikistan and the GBAR serves as a model of ethno-language processes occurring all over the country. The GBAR is an autonomous region of the Tajik Republic formed on January 2, 1925. It is situated in the southeast of the republic in the Pamir Mountains. The region is multinational and multilingual. It occupies a territory of 63,700 sq. km. According to the all-Union census of population in 1989, 164,000 persons live in the GBAR, including Tajiks (144,000), Kirghizes (2,000), Russians (3,100), Ukranians (2,000), Belorussians (500), Kazakhs (400), Tatars (300), Uzbeks (200), and other nationalities (160). Thus, the Tajiks are about 90 percent of the total regional population, whereas other nationalities are about 10 percent. However, the data of the all-Union census do not disclose the true demographic picture of this region.

Under the label "the Tajiks" there are a great number of ethnic communities that live in the region. There are the Tajik-speaking populations living in the

Vanch and Kalaikhum regions who speak the Darvazi and Vancki dialects of the Tajik language. There is the Pamiri-speaking population (the basic population of the region), who speak 14 languages and dialects (Shugnani, Rushani, Vakhani, Ishkashimi, Bartangi, Khufi, Roshorvi, Yazgulami, Bajuvi, and Shakhdari).

Under the Pamiri languages, there are a number of purely oral languages in the Pripamirs, which belong to the East Iranian group of the Indo-European family of languages (the Shugnano-Rushani language group, Vakhani, Ishkashimi, and Yazgulami languages). All the languages, exclusive of Sarikoli, are represented on the territory of the GBAR along the Pyanj, Gund, Shakh-Dar, and Bartang Rivers. Shugnani and Rushani are also spoken in the southern part of Badakhshan province in Afghanistan. The Sarikoli language extends over the Sinkiang-Uigur Autonomous Region in China and in Sarikol. The Vakhani language extends over the Upper Pyanj and is spoken both in Afghanistan and in the GBAR. It is also spoken in contiguous regions of China, India, and Pakistan. On the territory of the (former) Soviet Union, the Ishkashimi language is represented by one village—Ryn—which extends mainly over the northern part of Badakhshan province in Afghanistan. The Yazgulami language extends over the River Yazgulam—the right tributary of the Pyanj—and outside the GBAR as well, in the Vakhsh Valley among settlers. Among all Pamiri languages, the Shugnano-Rushani is spoken by the greatest number of people in GBAR (about 80,000 persons). By contrast, the Ishkashimi language is spoken by the least in number of people (about 600 inhabitants of the village Ryn). The total number of people speaking Yazgulami is approximately 2,000–3,000. People speaking the Vakhani language are about 9,000–10,000 in number.

Unfortunately, the data on the number of people speaking those varied languages is only approximate for two reasons. First, there is a lack of hard statistical data on the extent of the aboriginal population in the Pamiri region. Second, the all-Union censuses from 1959 up to the census of 1989 recorded the Pamiri nations of the GBAR as Tajiks without distinguishing their native language, as if whole ethnic groups had disappeared. However, the census of 1926 recorded 194 nationalities in Tajikistan, while the census data in 1939 indicated 99 nationalities, and the census of 1959 tabulated 109 ethnicons.

Nations in other republics have suffered the same fate in the compilation of statistical data and language characteristics. The Kurds who live in Turkmenia have been ranked among the Turkmens, and the Turkmen language has been stated as their mother tongue. The Avars, Lezghins, Kryzes, and some other Daghestan nations in Azerbaijan have been ranked among the Azerbaijanians, and the Azerbaijanian language has been listed as their mother tongue. The Central Asian Arabs have been ranked among the Tajiks, Uzbeks, the Dungans in the Ferghan valley, the Uigurs in the Andijan region, and the Persians in the Samarkand region in Uzbekistan. The Tajiks who comprise the majority of the population in the large cities of Samarkand and Bukhara, which in the 1920s became Uzbek, were recorded in the documents as Uzbeks. The Batsbians, speaking the "one village" language in Georgia, have considered the Georgian language as their mother tongue.

Pamiri nations that live in the Tajik republic use a more developed literary Tajik language in all spheres of their social life. Beyond a shadow of a doubt, the Tajik language has played a progressive part in the life of the Pamiri. In Badakhshan, where many languages and dialects have no written language function, the influence of the Tajik language—literary, cognate, and widely spread—is indisputable. The Tajik language is accepted on the territory of Badakhshan as the main means of oral and written communication among the Pamiri-speaking nations, and it has historical and social roots. Its dissemination in the Pamir region is closely connected with the name of the great thinker of the eleventh century, Nosir Khisrov—the missionary who devoted his last years to enlightenment in the Pamirs. The Tajik language's wider functions and richer vocabulary spread as the language of religion and worship. It also became the langauge of interethnic intercourse, promoted consolidation of Pamiri nations, and helped to establish contacts with neighboring nations. The lack of native written languages facilitated the use of the Tajik language by the Pamiri as both the literary language and the language of official intercourse.

At the end of the last century, in the 1880–90s, Russian officers, topographers, geographers, botanists, and geologists began to explore the Pamirs. The Pamirs attracted the Russian Empire not only by its exotic character and resoures, but it was also of great strategic importance. The first Russian reconnoiter detachment was headed by Colonel Ionof, who not only "mopped up" the Pamirs from strangers but corrected the English geography of the Pamirs and made English diplomats accept the borders in the Pamirs that exist to date. The Pamirs were voluntarily annexed to Russia in 1892, which enlarged the political and cultural links between Russia and the local nations and contributed to the development of a new type of bilingualism, with Russian as the second language. The Russian language became the language of education of local nations, beginning in 1909 with the opening of a four-year Russian-native school in Khorog.

Among the present aboriginal population of the region, bilingualism and polylingualism (i.e., good knowledge of the Tajik and Russian languages side by side with the mother tongue having no written language) are widespread. Both the Tajik and Russian languages facilitate the same function as the Pamiri written languages—intercourse, administration, and communication. In formal contacts—in family, in everyday life, in the streets, in transport, in schools, at the primary stage of teaching for explaining a subject to a child who can hear and understand his native speech—high and low mother tongues function in the Pamiri-speaking part of the Gorno-Badakhshan Region.

In the period of intensive language building in Tajikistan in the 1930s, the written language using the Latin alphabet was founded for the Shugnani language because most people spoke it. Primary school teaching was done in the Shugnani language. For this purpose, teachers were trained and books were translated and published in the Shugnani language.

However, this first experience of development of one of the mountainous region languages came to grief in 1938, when the Shugnani written language was abolished. The abolition of the Shugnani alphabet gave rise to statements about assimilation of the Pamiri nations with the Tajik nationality in scientific literature. However, it is still premature to speak about assimilation of the small Pamiri nations with the Tajik one.

With the growth of national consciousness that covered all the regions of Tajikistan, the problem of national language and cultural rebirth arose keenly with the Pamiri nations as well. The third article of the language law of Tajikistan is aimed at defense of oral languages on the territory of the republic. It provides: "The Tajik republic ensures conditions for free development and use of the Gorno-Badakhshani (the Pamiri) languages and preservation of the Yagnobi language." (In Central Tajikistan, high in the Fann Mountains, on the almost inaccessible banks of the Yagnob River, which can be reached only by helicopter or walking across the pass, the Yagnobi live in several villages called kishlaks.) The Yagnobi are very much like the Pamiri in appearance. They have preserved the spoken language of the ancient Sogdii. The Yagnobi language belongs to the Eastern subgroup of Iranian languages. In the 1970s, the number of people speaking the language was approximately 2,000–5,000 persons. Today, it is very difficult to hear it spoken because the Yagnobi were often deported to a distance of a thousand kilometers into the valleys. During recent years some Yagnobi have returned to their native land, but many of them have lost their mother tongue and they speak only Tajik. It is estimated that there were only 200–300 persons in Yagnob in 1990.

The specially organized regional commission in the GBAR has carried out legislative enactments aimed at observance and execution of the third article within the language law. The language building program in the region is aimed at establishing favorable conditions both to further develop use of the Pamiri nations' mother tongues and to spread bilingualism and polylingualism with the Tajik and Russian languages in the region to avoid national self-isolation.

Recently, a single language alphabet was compiled for all the Pamiri nations based on the Cyrillic alphabet. With creation of the written language and alphabet books for all languages, a real opportunity will appear to organize teaching in both the Pamiri and Tajik languages at primary schools. In addition, teaching of the Pamiri languages as special subjects is now planned at secondary schools. In the columns of the regional press, you can read stories and verses of local authors in the Pamiri languages. By manufacture of printing equipment, printing presses, and printing machines, they are planning to publish separate newspapers in the Pamiri languages, to issue a periodical fiction magazine, and to develop book printing in languages of the Pamiri nations.

A large group of Palmiri languages linguists, under the aegis of the Tajik Academy of Sciences, is engaged in scientifically investigating the history and modern grammar of the languages. A Pamiri base of the Tajik Academy of Sciences has been established in the regional center of the GBAR. Scientific-research institutes will function attached to it and will become centers of studying the Pamirs.

You can now hear songs in the mother tongues on both local and republican radio and television. During the last two years mass performances of "Shomi Badakhshan" ("The Evening of Badakhshan") were held in Dushanbe. Representatives of the Pamiri nations recite verses, sing songs, and narrate funny stories in the mother tongues. They also dance and perform scenes of everyday life within "The Evenings." In the town of Khorog—the center of the GBAR—for the first time the regional theater has staged the play "The Golden Kishlak" (village) by the national poet of Tajikistan, Mirsaid Mirshakar, written in the Shugnani language and based on local material. You can hear songs in the Pamiri languages sung by young singers in the concert halls of the region.

The languages of the Pamiri nations have been developing and gaining strength.

BIBLIOGRAPHY

Aitmatof, Ch. 1989. "Live Yourself and Let Others Live: Apropos of the Draft of Languages of the Nations of the U.S.S.R. Law." *Literaturnaya Gazeta*, November 22.

Baskakof, A. N. 1991. "Some Remarks Apropos of Language Laws," in *The Russian Language in the U.S.S.R.*., 4.

Demographic Yearbook of the U.S.S.R.: 1990. Moscow: Finansi i Statistika.

Gavriluk, A., and V. Yaroshenko. 1987. *The Pamirs*. Moscow.

Isaef, M. I. 1990. "Language and Law," in *The Russian Language at National School*, 7.

Karamshoef, D. 1991. "Shall We Have the Alphabet?" in *Badakh-shoni Soveti*, May 30.

Modern Ethnic Processes in the U.S.S.R., 2. 1977. Moscow.

National and Language Relations in the U.S.S.R.: Situation and Prospects. 1989. Moscow: Nauka.

Oranskii, I. M. 1979. *The Iranian Languages in the Historical Interpretation*. Moscow: Nauka.

Shambezoda, Kh. 1989. "Influence of Languages with Different Social Status upon the Shugnani Language Having No Written Language," Thesis, Candidate of Philological Sciences, Moscow.

The Social and Economic Progress and the Flowering of Spiritual Life of Nations in Central Asia and Kazakhstan under Conditions of Socialism. 1986. Dushanbe.

Solntsef, V. M. 1991. "The Language Problem in Multinational Countries and the Language Situation in the U.S.S.R," in *The Russian Language in the U.S.S.R.*, 4.
Zeimal, E. 1989. "Nations and Their Languages under Socialism." *Communist*, 15.

42

Consumer Protection Laws of the States: How Much Diversity Should the Central Government Discourage? Where Desirable, How Should Uniformity Be Promoted?

Norman I. Silber

THE PARADOX OF THE "EMPIRE WITHIN AN EMPIRE"

At the core of American federalism lies the paradox of *Imperium in Imperio*, or an "empire within an empire."[1] It has been said that without the exercise of relatively autonomous political power by legislative bodies on at least two planes of government, there would be no federal system. Without such a concept, political power would be either centralized or else dispersed in a confederal fashion. The framers of the Constitution most feared usurpation of power, not by the federal government, but by the states. James Madison, for example, expressed the common opinion, based on the experience with the Articles of Confederation, that

> there was less danger of encroachment from the General (federal) government than from the state government; that the mischief from encroachments would be less fatal if made by the former than if made by the latter. All the examples of other confederacies prove the greater tendency in such systems to anarchy than to tyranny; to a disobedience of the members than to usurpations of the federal head.[2]

At the core of the American federal system are concurrent powers that belong to the states, and that are beyond the ability of the federal government to curtail or displace through preemption. These include the power to tax in the absence of evidence that a state has imposed a burden on commerce among the several states; the power to regulate the impact of businesses and individuals on localities; and the power of state courts to enforce common law rules.

Historically, the states have taken on a first-line role in policing the local marketplace for signs of fraud and abuse. In recent years, and especially after the Republican election victory of 1980, states aggressively have pursued the enforcement of consumer rights in areas where federal agencies also have authority. One reason for this state assertiveness is that many federal agencies no longer have the resources to carry out their responsibilities by themselves. Another is that states may have stronger laws at their disposal than the federal government. And the deregulation of health and safety programs, which was aggressively pursued during the Reagan and Bush administrations, was a goal not shared by many segments of society, well-reflected in many state political bodies. Not surprisingly, state agencies often decided to take actions that might have been taken by previous federal regimes. These trends have been reflected in increasingly divergent attitudes toward consumer protection taken by state and federal court systems.

While there has been a trend in favor of increasingly aggressive consumer protection by the states, there also has been a countervailing trend at work: a sharp increase in federal preemptive action. Many recently enacted federal laws express provisions for "total," or "complete," federal preemption (although there are many kinds of "totality").

Political scientists and legal scholars have identified various types of "complete" federal preemption.[3] These types include (1) laws that repudiate state financial or administrative assistance to the federal government in implementing a regulatory regime but depend on interpretations and legal definitions in significant respects; (2) laws that forbid states from establishing economic regulations; (3) laws that forbid individuals from discriminating on particular grounds but that reserve the right to discriminate to government entities; (4) federal laws incorporating state and local assistance; (5) laws that preempt the states from regulating but that allow states to regulate their own activities; (6) limited regulatory turnbacks that allow federal authorities to delegate certain authorities to the states; (7) mandates to states to enact parallel state laws; and (8) requirements that states must comply with federal laws in the enactment of state laws.

Let me provide a few examples of such preemptive rules. The Flammable Fabrics Act stipulates that "this Act is intended to supersede any law of any State or political subdivision thereof inconsistent with its provisions."[4] Similarly, the U.S. Grain Standards Act[5] forbids states or political subdivisions to require "inspection or description in accordance with any standards of kind, class, quality, condition or other characteristics of grain as a condition of shipment, or sale, of such grain in interstate or foreign commerce, or require any license for, or impose any other restrictions upon, the performance of any official's inspection function under the Act by official inspection personnel."[6] The Federal Food, Drug, and Cosmetic Act[7] forbids state and local governments "to establish . . . any standard which is applicable to the same aspect of the performance of such product and which is not identical to the federal standard."[8] At the state level, laws continue to be passed that serve local needs, but whose subjects touch on federally regulated fields.[9]

And so the state "empires" are being confined by federal action. The increasingly aggressive consumer protection activities of the states have been confronted, and increassingly thwarted, by preemptive provisions of federal laws. Challenges based on explicit preemption provisions, and on doctrines that assert preemption by implication, are being levied against state consumer protection laws and state common law causes of action. In fact, as indicated below, states are now being encouraged to express the inclination to be preempted by federal laws within their own state regulations and administrative decrees.[10] It falls to the courts to determine where the appropriate limits of federal preemption are to be drawn to determine how far each empire may extend.

Consider, in this context, several illustrations of the development of case law with respect to the preemption of state law and state common law rights of action.

PREEMPTION OF STATE AND LOCAL LAWS BY FEDERAL LAWS AND FEDERAL REGULATIONS: FOOD LABELING

There exist, and have existed for a long time, extensive federal regulations affecting the marketing of food and food products. Some of the federal statutes that regulate food labeling contain specific preemption language—principally the Federal Meat Inspection Act (FMIA),[11] the Poultry Products Inspection Act,[12] and the Fair Packaging and Labeling Act.[13] Others, such as the Food, Drug, and Cosmetic Act (FDCA),[14] contain no specific language. Nevertheless, the states have continued to legislate in the area of food packaging and food labeling.

The touchstone case for any discussion of preemption in the food labeling area is *Jones v. Rath Packing Co.*[15] In *Jones*, a meatpacker sought to prevent a California county director of weights and measures from removing from stores packages of bacon that the California director declared to be underweight.[16] The Supreme Court held that, as applied to packaged bacon that was subject to the labeling requirements of the FMIA, a state's weight labeling statute and duly promulgated regulations were preempted by federal law. The Court began its analysis by observing that, when the area sought to be preempted has been "traditionally occupied by the states, we start with the assumption that the historic police powers of the States were not to be superseded by the Federal Act."[17] For preemption to occur, the Court held, such a result must have been "the clear and manifest purpose of Congress."[18] This assumption was intended to assure that "'the federal-state balance' will not be disturbed unintentionally by Congress or unnecessarily by the courts."[19] Thus, Congress must *intend*, either explicitly or impliedly, that federal legislation preempt conflicting state law.

When there is no clear expression of Congress' intent to preempt, preemption may still occur if Congress has impliedly expressed an intent to preempt state law. Such an intent may be implied if Congress (1) occupies the field of law, leaving no room for state law to coexist, or (2) by creating an actual conflict between state and federal law. The latter is accomplished when (a) Congress makes compliance with both the state and federal laws impossible, or (b) state law stands as an obstacle to the accomplishment or execution of the full purposes and objectives of Congress under the federal law.[20]

The Court in *Rath Packing Co.* held that state statutes and regulations that did not allow for reasonable variations from stated weight, resulting from loss of moisture during the course of good distribution practices, were in actual conflict with the federal FMIA.[21] The Court explained that FMIA, in defining when meat or a meat product was misbranded, provided that "reasonable variations" between the actual weight and the weight stated on the label could be permitted by regulations prescribed by the Secretary of Agriculture, and the Secretary's *regulations* did, in fact, permit "[r]easonable variations caused by loss or gain of moisture during the course of good distribution practices or by unavoidable deviations in good manufacturing practice[s]."[22] The federal law prohibited the states from imposing labeling or packaging requirements "different than" those imposed under the act.[23] The Court noted that the state law implicitly allowed for variations from the stated weight caused by unavoidable deviations in the manufacturing process by its use of a statistical sampling process. Nevertheless, the state law failed to allow for moisture loss and so was "different than" the federal requirement, thus, falling within the scope of the federal preemption provision.

In 1985 a grocery manufacturers' association brought an action against the enforcement of a New York regulatory scheme.[24] The state scheme required anyone who sold prepared foods containing cheese "alternatives," whether for carry-out or for consumption on the premises, to display a sign that disclosed, in three-inch letters, those foods that contained "imitation cheese," and other specific packaging labels. Nowhere in the FMIA or the FDCA was the word "imitation" defined. The Department of Agriculture contended that a nutritionally *superior* food substitute would be misbranded under the state law because of an FDCA regulation,[25] which provided that the word "imitation" must only be used with respect to a nutritionally *inferior* substitute. The court found that there was actual conflict between the New York labeling scheme and its federal counterpart. Since including the term "imitation" on the label of a nutritionally superior alternative cheese in order to comply with New York law would render the product misbranded under federal law (FDCA), actual conflict existed between the two regulatory schemes.[26] The court stressed that, in concurrent enforcement of a law, a state will not be permitted to prevent the distribution in commerce of any article that conformed to the definition and standard of identity or composition set by the federal act. The court, thus, by summary judgment, concluded that the Poultry Products Inspection Act[27] preempted New York laws.

The congressionally declared goal of the Fair Packaging and Labeling Act[28] is that packages and their labels should allow consumers to obtain accurate information about the quantity and the contents of goods and facilitate comparisons of value.[29] Section 1461 of the act provides that it is the express intent of Congress to supersede less stringent state laws relating to the net quantity of contents of consumer commodities, as well as those that require different information from the requirements of the act. In *L & L Started Pullets, Inc. v. Gourdine*,[30] the court held that city and state regulations involving the labeling of egg weights and measures were not preempted by the Fair Packaging and Labeling Act or other laws because that was not Congress' intent. The court relied on the "presumption" against finding congressional intent to preempt where the specific subject of regulation has traditionally been delegated to the states "as within their legitimate police powers."[31]

On the other hand, consider the recent case of *Lever Bros. Co. v. Maurer*,[32] in which a manufacturer of dairy products successfully enjoined the enforcement of a state statute that prohibited the use in a product label of the word "BUTTER." The court held that since federal law required that a product label must include the ingredients contained in a product, it would be impossible to comply with both state and federal laws. Again the state law was preempted by federal laws under the supremacy clause.[33]

The increasing success of federal preemption claims diminishes the range and intensity of state protective activity without ensuring that the federal activity will replace that state activity which had been foregone. Recent conflicts between the state and federal levels of government over food labeling, in particular, show signs of further reducing the realm of state activities. After more than a decade in which the federal government has been inactive with respect to the establishment of labeling requirements, the Environmental Protection Agency, the Food and Drug Administration, and the Federal Trade Commission have begun to develop new regulations that would dramatically change nutritional labeling requirements for many foods. These regulations would also regulate the marketing of environmental marketing claims—by providing minimum standards, for example, for such words as "recyclable" or "biodegradable."[34] This federal activity may be attributed, at least in part, to the fact that manufacturers have expressed some dismay at the profusion of state and local laws that provide different definitions for these and other terms. This suggests a sensible desire to increase marketing predictability and uniformity of regulating laws. It also threatens to cut back on state policing initiatives, however, since most of the proposals for these regulations would involve strong preemption provisions that would have the federal regulations supersede state and local laws.[35]

THE IMPLICIT PREEMPTION OF COMMON LAW TORT REMEDIES: CIGARETTES AND AIRBAGS

Cigarettes

A great deal of attention has attended the tort claims brought by smokers against cigarette manufacturers. The most publicized claim was that of Rose and Antonio Cipollone, who charged three cigarette manufacturers with failing to adequately warn them of the risks of smoking and with producing an unreasonably dangerous product.[36] The Cipollones' claim was opposed by cigarette manufacturers, who claimed that the 1965 federal Cigarette Act,[37] which prescribed uniform warning labels for cigarette packages and advertisements, preempted any state tort law claims relating to smoking and health that would seek to challenge the adequacy of those warning labels.[38] Initially, the content and sufficiency of cigarette warning labels were left to the individual states to define. However, after the states passed numerous different warning labels that were to be placed on cigarettes sold within each of their different jurisdictions, Congress created a single federal warning label scheme with its enactment of the 1965 Cigarette Act. Through the Cigarette Act, Congress dictated the specific wording of a cigarette label intended to warn consumers of the product's health hazards and created a uniform standard. The act included this congressional declaration of policy and purpose:

> It is the policy of the Congress, and the purpose of this chapter, to establish a comprehensive Federal Program to deal with cigarette labeling and advertising with respect to any relationship between smoking and health, whereby (1) the public may be adequately informed that cigarette smoking may be hazardous to health by inclusion of a warning to that effect on each package of cigarettes; and (2) commerce and the national economy may be (A) protected to the maximum extent consistent with this declared policy and (B) not impeded by diverse, nonuniform, and confusing labeling and advertising regulations with respect to any relationship between smoking and health.[39]

Nowhere does the Cigarette Act state specifically that state court actions are barred.[40] The Cigarette Act also contains a preemption provision that states:

> (a) No statement relating to smoking and health, other than the statement required by section 1333 of this title, shall be required on any cigarette package.
> (b) No requirement or prohibition based on smoking and health shall be imposed under State law with respect to the advertising or promotion of any cigarettes the packages of which are labeled in conformity with the provisions of this chapter.[41]

Despite the absence of express preemption language, the courts in cigarette preemption cases have taken the view that, under an "implied preemption" analysis, which asks whether state law stands as an obstacle to the accomplishment of the full purposes of Congress,[42] by "disrupting excessively" the balance of interests established by Congress. That is, that the suits against the cigarette manufacturers and distributors upset the Cigarette Act's balance between the protection of health and the protection of trade and the national economy.[43] This position was first assumed in 1986 by the Third Circuit Court of Appeals[44] and subsequently upheld by at least three other courts of appeal and two state appellate courts.[45]

Airbags

The question of whether common law tort actions can be preempted by federal laws in the absence of explicit preemption language has expanded from cigarette litigation to airbag litigation. Recent circuit court decisions suggest that manufacturers are successfully raising the preemption defense in other types of product liability, design defect actions, related to the absence of airbags in cars.[46] Safety standards adopted pursuant to the National Traffic and Motor Vehicle Safety Act of 1966,[47] as subsequently amended, provide manufacturers with options for complying with occupant crash protection standards, of which airbags in conjunction with seatbelts is only one.[48] The issue is whether a manufacturer who chooses one of these options and meets all of its requirements thereby is free from tort liability.[49] The inquiry in these cases has been whether Congress intended to prevent all further state action concerning safety restraints in automobiles by giving manufacturers these options; in essence, whether Congress intended to preempt state tort law claims.

In 1968 the Eighth Circuit decided that Congress intended the National Traffic and Motor Vehicle Safety Act to be an addition to the common law of negligence and product liability and not a replacement for it.[50] Therefore, plaintiffs could maintain state tort actions under the 1966 law.[51] Several recent court decisions, however, have held that the National Traffic and Motor Vehicle Safety Act preempts a consumer's ability to maintain a state common law design action against an automobile manufacturer for failing to install an airbag in its products.[52] As the First Circuit viewed it,

> Congress believed that for the federal standards to be effective, they had to be uniform throughout the country. . . . A state regulation requiring passive restraints would be expressly preempted because it would destroy the uniformity of the federal standard. . . . By the same token, a defective design action which, if successful, effectively would likewise destroy the national uniformity of the federal standard and exceed the state's authority.[53]

The opposing view, expressed recently in *Garret v. Ford Motor Co.*,[54] relies on cases such as *Silkwood v. Kerr-McGee Corp.*[55] to support the proposition that a jury award of damages is not a form of state regulation, that damage awards for failure to install airbags are not a form of state regulation, and that "damage suits will tend to encourage safety, not countervail it." From this perspective, state tort law claims should not be preempted because, while they do not encourage uniformity, they do achieve Congress' goals of more safely designed cars.

PREEMPTION BY STATE INVITATION: CONSUMER BANKING SERVICES

Suppose you are a state legislator presented with the latest version of Revised Articles III and IV by the National Conference of Commissioners on Uniform State Laws and the America Law Institute, which is concerned with negotiable instruments and bank collections.[56] Among the earliest sections you encounter is Section 3-102(c),[57] which delineates the following relationship between federal and state law: "Regulations of the Board of Governors of the Federal Reserve System and operating circulars of the Federal Reserve Banks supersede any inconsistent provisions of this Article to the extent of the inconsistency."[58]

This preemption language sounds familiar enough and, indeed, similar preemption clauses exist in many federal banking enactments. Perhaps the only unusual aspect of the language itself lies in its inclusion of "operating circulars," in addition to regulations, as administrative declarations that preempt state law. Regulations of the Federal Reserve Board have the effect of statutory law and, as we have already seen, may preempt inconsistent state law.[59]

Operating circulars, however, are not developed and promulgated according to the administrative processes and procedures that normally lend legitimacy to federal regulations.[60] Federal Reserve Banks develop operating circulars pursuant to authority either granted by the Federal Reserve Act or delegated through a Federal Reserve regulation.[61] When operating circulars are uniform for all Reserve Banks, as are the majority, the individual Reserve Banks themselves draft the language of the operating circular, which is then submitted to the Federal Reserve Board, which adopts the operating circular, presumably in the same way it would a regulation.[62] The same procedural standards, including procedures for public notice and comment, which are met by the Federal Reserve Board when it promulgates regulations, apparently are not met when operating circulars are developed.[63]

It is not only the language of the preemption provision that is unusual; it is also the plane of government at which the provision has been located. This particular preemption provision is located within a body of state law. Why should a state legislator adopt a state law that reifies federal preemption of essentially the same subject matter—negotiable instruments law—that has not previously been wholly occupied by federal law? It is possible that, since the drafters' goal is to create uniformity and predictability in commercial transactions, and since banking law has become increasingly national in scope, a state would contain within it interest groups that would welcome one uniform rule in preference to nonuniform state rules, however advantageous particular divergent rules otherwise might be. Any such intent is not compellingly expressed in the statute or indicated by its comments—and if it were so expressed might generate controversy.

Explicit preemption provisions contained within federal legislation and regulations provide courts and regulators with valuable guidance about legislative or administrative intentions to preempt. What incentive is there, however, for a state to issue a written declaration and "invitation" to a federal regulatory body to exercise a maximum level of federal supersession over a broad area of law that is "traditionally the province" of the states? It might be argued that after a state has adopted such a preemption provision, preemption determinations will still be made under the same traditional preemption analysis outlined above. The very fact that the state has adopted such a preemption provision, however, will be strong evidence of the states' *intent* to be preempted.

The problem I refer to will arise when courts are asked to address the preemption by a federal regulation or operating circular of a state law related to Article III. A court so challenged reasonably may assume that the state intended to be preempted because, in adopting the Uniform Commercial Code (UCC), the state could have chosen not to adopt any such preemption provision. A court might conclude, in its choice of a preemption provision, that the state adopted a highly restrictive provision.[64] Beyond the effect on courts that determine preemption under a standard analysis, consider the "chilling" effect such a provision may have on state consumer initiatives. Adopting such a provision may well provide a disincentive to states contemplating the adoption of their own legislation in areas where the provision might intrude.[65]

THE CORROSIVE EFFECT OF "COMPLETE" PREEMPTION

The doctrine of preemption is complex and unsettled. What does appear, however, is a trend toward the inclusion of explicit federal preemption provisions that confine areas of governance in domains formerly the traditional province of the states. Although there have been instances in which states have invited preemption, driven by a presumable need for uniformity, those situations are exceptional. On the whole, state governors and activists have resisted the preemption of what had previously been exclusively state activities.

This resistance to preemption has been especially vigorous with respect to consumer protection laws. Local consumer groups often have lobbied for their own states to better protect consumer interests and have obtained significant consumer protection measures or won higher consumer protection thresholds through court decisions. In the cases considered here, however, it has been just when local consumer groups have made these substantial gains that local companies and businesses have lobbied Congress to obtain complete preemption by enacting a "uniform" standard.[66]

If and when such uniform standards are adopted through a total preemption approach, state interests may be damaged. The vitality of the state governments may be diminished, individual state innovation may be stifled, and popular resentment may be sparked by local consumer groups. The tension between federal and state governments, furthermore, creates conflicts that serve to corrode federalism and that, in turn, erodes political safeguards that federalism, at least in theory, seeks to protect and to maintain.

As demonstrated above, uniformity appears to be the chief benefit out of such a "complete preemption" arrangement—and the advantages to uniformity, both for businesses and consumers, should not be minimized. However, if uniformity sufficient to achieve national goals can be accomplished without total preemption of state consumer protection laws, much would be gained. It appears to me that there are several uniformity-promoting solutions, short of total preemption provisions, that should be considered. Here I will mention two. Interstate compacts and regional agreements can be used to foster uniformity without federal involvement. And perhaps the most notably successful American approach to achieving uniformity without federalization, which began almost a century ago, has been the encouragement of model legislation proposed for adoption in each state: Model Rules, and Uniform State Laws.

INTERSTATE COMPACTS, MODEL LAWS, AND UNIFORM CODES: MINIMIZING THE STATE-FEDERAL CONFLICT

Professor Jonathan R. Macey recently observed that, in the abstract, the concept of federalism is a "revered sacred cow"—politicians shout the virtues of state autonomy whenever deference to the states happens to serve their political needs, yet "are quick to wield the power of the supremacy clause whenever a single national rule in a particular area furthers their political interests."[67] Politically, the incentives for federal lawmakers and state lawmakers to desire either to defer to, or preempt, legislation promulgated at another level are continually shifting as the political landscape changes. On occasions, the states have attempted to forestall federal preemptive action by promoting the adoption of uniform state laws and entering into interstate compacts, creating agencies with powers to solve problems. An example of the unsuccessful effort of the latter nature is the Mid-Atlantic States Air Pollution Control Compact, which was entered into by Connecticut, New Jersey, and New York in 1967 subsequent to President Lyndon B. Johnson's message to Congress on air pollution, recommending federal preemption no responsibility for air pollution abatement. Congress did not grant its consent to the use of the interstate compact.

One way that the states have preserved their autonomy while achieving a degree of uniformity not otherwise obtainable has been through two institutions: the National Conference of Commissioners on Uniform State Laws established in 1891, and the American Law Institute established in 1923. These two groups are responsible for the development and promulgation of model rules and uniform state laws. The UCC is prepared by the American Law Institute (ALI) in cooperation with the National Conference of Commissioners on Uniform State Laws. The initial drafting of the uniform laws is accomplished by practicing lawyers and legal teachers in the particular field or area of law, under the supervision of the ALI and the commissioners.

Model rules (for example, the Model Penal Code) and uniform legislation (for example, the Uniform Commercial Code) have approached the goal of a uniform interpretation of the law without resort to federal legislation. Where the goals of uniformity arise from concern that an individual state's legislation can be defeated through the application of conflict of law rules in federal litigation, or when the interest in an essentially uniform national law is great, it may be sufficient to adopt such an approach instead of adopting a federal rule.

The Uniform Commercial Code provides an excellent example of uniform laws approach; the Model Penal Code provides an example of the model law approach. Model laws may serve other, seemingly secondary, functions as well as providing uniformity. The Model Penal Code (MPC), for example, is far more complete than any state legislation. In this instance, model laws serve a notice-giving function; what is a crime in one state would be a crime in any other state that had adopted the MPC.[68]

CONCLUDING THOUGHTS

I am not familiar with the law of the Soviet Union. It would appear, however, that the problems of the "empire within an empire" are particularly troublesome at this moment in history. The very idea of "total preemption" by the central authority may be out of the realm of possibility. In such an environment, the use of a model law or a uniform law approach may prove to be worth considering.

NOTES

1. See Joseph Francis Zimmerman, *Federal Preemption, The Silent Revolution*, 83–107 (1991).

2. James Madison, *Notes of Debates in the Federal Convention of 1787*, 164–65 (Koch, ed., 1987).

3. See Zimmerman, *supra* note 1, at 83–107.

4. 15 U.S.C.A. §§ 1191 et. seq. (West, 1992).

5. 7 U.S.C.A. § 71 et. seq. (West, 1992).

6. 7 U.S.C.A. § 87g (West, 1992).

7. 21 U.S.C.A. §§ 301 et. seq. (West, 1992).

8. 21 U.S.C.A. § 360ss (West, 1992).

9. See e.g., *Ingersoll-Rand Co. v. McClendon*, 498 U.S. 133 (1990) (federal ERISA preempting employee's Texas state law claim for wrongful discharge); *California v. Federal Energy Regulatory Comm'n.*, 495 U.S. 490 (1990) (Federal Power Act preempting more stringent California state statutes relating to minimum stream flow requirements for river on which a federally licensed hydroelectric project was located); *Felder v. Casey*, 487 U.S. 131 (1988) (federal civil rights actions brought in state court preempting Wisconsin notice-of-claim statute); *Mackey v. Lanier Collections Agency & Svce.*, 486 U.S. 825 (1988) (federal ERISA preempting Georgia state statutes singling out ERISA welfare plan benefits for protective treatment under state garnishment procedures); *City of New York v. FCC*, 486 U.S. 57 (1988) (FCC regulations preempting state and local technical standards governing cable television); *Schneidewind v. ANR Pipeline Co.*, 485 U.S. 293 (1988) (Natural Gas Act preempting Michigan state utility company regulations).

10. See, e.g., Revised Uniform Commercial Code § 3–102 (West, 1991).

11. 21 U.S.C.A. §§ 601–691 (West, 1992).

12. 21 U.S.C.A. §§ 451–469 (West, 1992).

13. 15 U.S.C.A. §§ 1451–1461 (West, 1992).

14. 21 U.S.C.A. §§ 301–392 (West, 1992).

15. *Jones v. Rath Packing Co.*, 430 U.S. 519 (1977).

16. *Id.*, at 523–24.

17. *Id.* at 525.

18. *Id.*

19. *Id.*

20. *Rice v. Santa Fe Elevator Corp.*, 331 U.S. 218, 230 (1947).

21. *Jones*, *supra* note 15, at 526–28.

22. *Id.*, at 529–30.

23. *Id.*, at 530.

24. *Grocery Mfrs. of America, Inc. v. Gerace*, 755 F.2d 993 (2d Cir. 1985).

25. The discussion, up to this point, has been whether federal *statutes* preempt state law. However, as has long been the case, federal *regulations* have "no less preemptive effect than federal statutes." *De La Cuesta*, 458 U.S. at 153. See also *Capital Cities Cable, Inc. v. Crisp*, 467 U.S. 691 (1984). The Court in *De La Cuesta* held that "[w]here Congress has directed an administrator to exercise his discretion, his judgments are subject to judicial review only to determine whether he has exceeded his statutory authority or acted arbitrarily." *De La Cuesta*, 458 U.S. at 153–54 (citing

United States v. Shimer, 367 U.S. 374, 381–82 [1961]). Thus, federal regulations are given the same preemptive effect as federal statutes if those regulations are a valid exercise of validly delegated congressional authority.

26. The federal FDCA regulation provided that if the substitute product contained less of any essential nutrient present to a measurable degree in the food for which it was substituted, the substitute must be labeled with the word "imitation."

27. 21 U.S.C.A. §§ 451–469 (West, 1992) (the federal regulatory scheme at issue in that case).

28. 15 U.S.C.A. §§ 1451–1461 (West, 1992).

29. *Id.*

30. 592 F. Supp. 367 (S.D.N.Y. 1984), *aff'd*, 762 F.2d 1 (2d Cir. 1984).

31. *Id.* at 372. The court found that "protection of the public against false weights and measures or misleading statements about them is one of the oldest exercises of governmental regulatory power." *Id.* (quoting *Swift & Co. v. Wickham*, 230 F. Supp., 151, 153 [S.D.N.Y. 1974, *aff'd mem.*, 508 F.2d 836 (2d Cir. 1975)]).

32. 712 F. Supp. 645 (S.D. Ohio 1989).

33. U.S. Const. art. VI, cl. 2. "The preemption doctrine . . . has its roots in the Supremacy Clause." *De La Cuesta*, 458 U.S. at 152.

34. Eric T. Greenberg, "Green Issues Are Ripe: The Regulation of Environmental Marketing Claims," 3 *Loyola Consumer Law Reporter* 80 (1991).

35. See Robert J. Del Tufo, "How Federal and State Governments Can Share Consumer Protection Power," 43 *Administrative Law Review* 495 (1991).

36. *Cipollone v. Liggett Group, Inc.*, 789 F.2d 181 (3d Cir. 1986), *cert. denied*, 479 U.S. 1043 (1987).

37. P.L. 89-92, 79 Stat. 282 (1965).

38. *Cipollone, supra* note 36, at 183–84.

39. 15 U.S.C.A. § 1331 (West, 1992).

40. But see Paul G. Christ and John M. Majoras, "The 'New' Wave in Smoking and Health Litigation," 54 *Tennessee Law Review* 551 (1987)(arguing express preemption of state court actions).

41. 15 U.S.C.A § 1334 (West, 1992).

42. Mary Ann K. Bosack, "Cigarette Act Preemption—Refining the Analysis," 66 *New York University Law Review* 756, 774 (1991).

43. See *Palmer v. Liggett Group, Inc.*, 825 F.2d 620, 626 (1st Cir. 1987).

44. *Cipollone, supra* note 36, at 187.

45. *Palmer v. Liggett Group, Inc.*, 825 F.2d 620 (1st Cir. 1987); *Stephen v. American Brands, Inc.*, 825 F.2d 312 (11th Cir. 1987); *Roysdon v. R. J. Reynolds Tobacco Co.*, 849 F.2d 230 (6th Cir. 1988); *Forster v. R. J. Reynolds Tobacco Co.*, 437 N.W.2d 655 (Minn. 1989); but see *Dewey v. Brown & Williamson Tobacco Corp.*, 225 N.J. Super 375, 542 A.2d 919, *rev'd*, 121 N.J. 69, 577 A.2d 1239 (1990). See also Note, "The Liability of Cigarette Manufacturers for Lung Cancer: An Analysis of the Federal Cigarette Labeling and Advertising Act and Preemption of Strict Liability in Tort Against Cigarette Act Preemption—Refining the Analysis," 66 *New York University Law Review* 756 (1991).

46. *Wood v. General Motors Corp.*, 865 F.2d 395 (1st Cir. 1988); *Taylor v. General Motors Corp.*, 875 F.2d 816 (11th Cir. 1989).

47. 15 U.S.C.A. §§ 1381–1420 (West, 1982 & Supp., 1992) [hereinafter NTMVSA].

48. See 49 C.F.R. §§ 571.208 S4.1.2.1, .2, .3 (1987).

49. The manufacturers have consistently chosen their third option, providing a lap and shoulder belt with a warning system. See Frank Waters, "Air Bag Litigation: Plaintiffs, Start Your Engines," 13 *Pepperdine Law Review* 1063, 1068 n. 39 (1986).

50. *Larsen v. General Motors Corp.*, 391 F.2d 495 (8th Cir. 1968).

51. The act, on its face, dealt with both the preemption of state laws and state common law actions. Section 1392(d) clearly seems to preempt any state safety standard on a subject that is addressed by a comparable federal standard:

> Whenever a Federal motor vehicle safety standard established under this subchapter is in effect, no State or political subdivision of a State shall have any authority either to establish, or to continue in effect, with respect to any motor vehicle or item of motor vehicle equipment any safety standard applicable to the same aspect of performance of such vehicle or item of equipment which is not identical to the Federal standard.

Section 1397(k), however, states that "[c]ompliance with any Federal motor vehicle safety standard issued under this subchapter does not exempt any person from any liability under common law." This language would appear to clear the way for common law suits; and yet, some courts have held that these suits are preempted despite the language in this savings clause, see, e.g., *Heftel v. General Motors Corp.*, No. 85-1713 (D.D.C. February 23, 1988); *Hughes v. Ford Motor Co.*, 677 F. Supp. 76 (D. Conn. 1987); *Cox v. Baltimore County*, 646 F. 761 (D.Md.1986); *Wood v. General Motors Corp.*, 673 F. Supp. 1108 (D.Mass 1987) (Wood I), *rev'd*, 865 F.2d 395 (1st Cir. 1988) (Wood II), *appeal pending*, 110 S.Ct. 41 (1989).

52. *Wood v. General Motors Corp.*, *supra* note 51. See, e.g., *Heftel v. General Motors Corp.*, No. 85-1713, *Hughes v. Ford Motor Co.*, *Cox v. Baltimore County*, *Wood v. General Motors Corp.*—all *supra* note 51.

53. *Wood*, 865 F.2d at 412.

54. 684 F. Supp. 407 (D.Md. 1987).

55. 464 U.S. 238 (1984).

56. See generally Revised Uniform Commercial Code, Articles 3 and 4 (West, 1991) [hereinafter UCC].

57. Revised UCC § 3–102(c) (West, 1991).

58. *Id.*

59. Most federal regulations, including those of the Federal Reserve, are promulgated by authority of congressional enactments, thus the requirement that a regulation, to preempt state law, must be a valid exercise of validly delegated authority to the agency by Congress. The supremacy clause of the Constitution provides that federal law shall displace or preempt state laws in the event of conflicts. Norman Silber, "Why the UCC Should Not Subordinate Itself to Federal Authority," 55 *University of Pittsburgh Law Review* 441, 1994.

60. See the Administrative Procedures Act, 5 U.S.C. §551 et seq.; see also Peter Strauss, *An Introduction to Administrative Justice in the United States*, 155–84 (1989).

61. Federal Reserve Act §§ 4, 13, 14(e), and 16 (codified, in part, at 12 U.S.C.A. §§ 248, 301, 341, 342, 343, 358). See, e.g., 12 C.F.R. §§ 210.25(c), 210.3(a) (1991).

62. Telephone interview with Federal Reserve Bank of New York.

63. For example, it is still not clear whether the Board provides for the same notice and comment periods required by the Administrative Procedure Act. "In some instances,

the operating circulars are issued pursuant to a Federal Reserve Board regulation. In other cases, the Reserve Bank issues the operating circular under its own authority under the Federal Reserve Act, subject to *review* by the Federal Reserve Board." Official Comment #3, Revised UCC § 3–102 (West, 1991). See also *General Motors Corp. v. Abrams*, 897 F.2d 34 (2d Cir. 1990) (holding that consent orders issued by the Federal Trade Commission could preempt state law if all conditions were met under the traditional preemption analysis).

64. Less absolute preemption provisions are well known to banking law. See e.g., Consumer Credit Protection Act § 919, 15 U.S.C.A. § 1693q (West, 1991) ("A State law is not inconsistent with this subchapter if the protection such law affords any consumer is greater than the protection afforded by this subchapter"); Uniform Commercial Code § 4–103 (West, 1991), which provides that "Federal Reserve regulations and operating circulars . . . have the affect of agreements . . . whether or not specifically assented to by all parties interested in items handled," UCC § 4–103(b). Comment 3 states that "[t]his Article recognizes that 'operating circulars' issued pursuant to the regulations and concerned with operating details *as appropriate* may, within their proper sphere, vary the effect of the Article." *Id.*

65. State legislatures would be forced to steer far clear of the area covered by the preemption provision. Federal statutes and regulations are promulgated as a result of a well-defined, well-publicized procedure. Operating circulars, however, may be revised at will by the Federal Reserve Banks. See Federal Reserve Bank of New York Operating Circular #4, Para. 78 (Revised 1988). Additionally, it is unclear what procedural safeguards are provided for in the adoption, much less the revision of operating circulars. See Silber, *supra* note 59, at 463–69. Thus, state legislators will never be certain of whether new state legislation will be preempted by an operating circular.

66. Zimmerman states that manufacturing industries became concerned with individual state laws prescribing standards that varied from state to state, thereby necessitating the manufacture of different models to meet standards in particular states. The automobile industry, for instance, lobbied Congress to preempt, totally, responsibility for establishing emission standards for new motor vehicles. One representative wrote that "a single standard, though tough, is likely to be better than fifty standards, some loose, some very tough. Another governor wrote that "industry can function more efficiently when state to state differences in product regulation are eliminated." Zimmerman, *supra* note 1.

67. "Federal Deference to Local Regulators and the Economic Theory of Regulation: Toward a Public-Choice Explanation of Federalism," 76 *Virginia Law Review* 265 (1990).

68. See Model Penal Code and Commentaries (ALI, 1985).

43

Federalism and Compensation for Accidental Injuries

Vern R. Walker

This chapter discusses federalism considerations in the design and implementation of compensation systems for accidental injuries to persons. By "accidental injuries" I mean the wide range of unintended injuries that occur to people in the course of daily life. These injuries include such common events as accidents in the household, health care injuries (such as side effects from drugs or unintended accidents during hospitalization), and accidents resulting from the use of consumer products. The term also includes transportation accidents, whether in private automobiles or public transportation (on land or sea, or in air travel). Workplace accidents are also included, as are widespread public health disasters such as nuclear accidents and earthquakes.

Total dollar costs of such accidents are difficult to estimate reasonably, let alone confirm. What is clear, however, is that the cost of such accidents can be a very substantial percentage of a nation's gross domestic product. For example, a recent governmental study estimates that the costs of injuries and property damage in motor vehicle accidents alone in the United States in 1988 were $280 billion.[1] The National Safety Council estimates that the cost of workplace accidents in the United States in 1989 was $48.5 billion, with some 1.7 million people being injured.[2]

Estimates of the costs of the Chernobyl nuclear accident have ranged as high as 200 billion rubles, according to reports published in 1990, not counting the loss of productivity of the hundreds of thousands of people in the fallout zone.[3] Such societal losses are real, regardless of how federal, state, and local governments choose to deal with them.

Although many losses due to accidents can be measured in economic terms, many cannot. Accident losses include:

1. direct expenses resulting from the accident, such as health care expenses and

rehabilitation expenses;

2. economic costs that are not direct expenses, such as the lost earnings to the accident victim and the lost productivity to the economy; and
3. psychological injuries, such as the pain and suffering of the victim, the embarrassment of disfigurement, the struggle of living with a disability, and a personal sense of injustice if a wrong goes unredressed.

Again, all such losses are real, whether or not they can be measured in dollars, and whether or not complete compensation is ever possible.

As we examine federalism considerations in designing compensation systems to deal with accidental injury, I will be referring continually to a set of objectives for any compensation system. While I do not have time to justify each of these objectives this morning, I trust that you will find them sufficiently intuitive for our purposes. I count as major social objectives the following:[4]

Deterrence: An adequate compensation system should also work to reduce the incidence of accidents (the rate of occurrence), as well as reduce the severity of the accidents that do occur. Accident deterrence not only makes economic sense, but deterrence is necessary in order to avoid those losses that are not completely compensable (such as psychological injuries).

Burden Sharing: An adequate system should try to minimize the burden of the accidents that do in fact occur, principally by shifting at least some of the costs away from the unfortunate victims and spreading those costs among parties who are in a better position to absorb them. This is a primary function of insurance, through which people spread the costs of their accidents among a large number of persons. Modern governments recognize burden sharing as a matter of economic good sense as well as distributive justice—as when national governments provide disaster relief to an earthquake area.

Achieving Justice: An adequate compensation system should seek to achieve justice by determining social responsibility for causing an accident, by fairly allocating liability for paying for the losses caused by the accident, and by punishing those accident causers who are deserving of punishment.

Minimizing Transaction Costs: Finally, the compensation system designed to achieve the above objectives should not itself be so costly to run that those costs of running the system substantially increase the total societal losses due to accidents. In other words, there can be substantial costs associated with running the social system for managing accident costs.

Now I will use these four objectives as criteria for evaluating the following systems of achieving compensation. As you will recognize, I have selected for discussion five approaches that place the focus on federalism alternatives:

1. Let the *free market* handle accident losses, and have no governmental system to address compensation.
2. Provide *governmental insurance* only, or provide only governmental health care.
3. Adjudicate liability for accidents through private lawsuits, brought in *local courts*

that apply *local liability laws.*
4. Adjudicate liability in *state-level tribunals* and use *state-level liability laws* to determine liability.
5. Adjudicate liability in *federal tribunals*, using *federal liability laws.*

These five approaches are not the only possibilities, but they are representative of systems that are tried. In the United States, for example, we have examples of all five approaches. In the end, I will suggest that "hybrid approaches," combining the strengths provided by different elements of each of several approaches, are probably the best. But let us first quickly look at each approach independently, considering them as exclusive of each other.

FREE MARKET (NO GOVERNMENTAL INVOLVEMENT)

Governments often take this approach, providing no socially imposed liability laws, and leaving individuals to take care of themselves—for example, through their savings or their private insurance, if they can afford it. In the United States, this is largely the approach when people suffer psychological or economic injuries only, without physical injury. It is also largely the approach when the parties are commercial entities, and we leave liability to the law of contracts.

One major advantage of not holding a business liable to pay for an accident that it has caused is that the business does not suffer a drain on the capital it has raised—it can put its capital to work producing products and jobs, and not paying for injuries. Another major advantage is that such a system has very low transaction costs. Since there is no government bureaucracy at all, the transaction costs are largely those associated with acquiring private insurance.

When judged against our four objectives, however, this approach does not receive very high marks. Such a system does very little to deter accidents from happening, since no one is held liable. Such a system does nothing to produce burden sharing among the population, although those who can afford private insurance often, in fact, spread the costs of their own covered accidents among the members of the insurance risk pool. Nor does such a "hands-off" system do anything to redress the community's sense of injustice against accident causers. The only objective, in fact, that such a system achieves is keeping transaction costs low.

GOVERNMENTAL INSURANCE OR HEALTH CARE ONLY

Another approach is for the government to provide insurance or health care services funded out of general taxes. Examples of this approach are governmental disability pensions, or a governmental health care system.[5] Under this approach, however, no liability is imposed on accident causers. It is basically the same approach as the free market approach, except that insurance or health care is provided for all citizens.

The obvious major advantage of this approach is that all citizens receive at least minimal health care and perhaps subsistence income. With respect to at least those accident losses, the government creates a large, mandatory risk pool and spreads the costs of accidents to all taxpayers. Meanwhile, businesses that in fact cause the accidents do not experience an additional drain (over general taxes) to pay for the injuries they cause.

When the governmental insurance only system is evaluated against the four objectives, I conclude that the system still does little or nothing to deter accidents from happening. While there is a definite success in burden sharing, this is limited in practice by the level of benefits provided. Because comprehensive health care or truly adequate disability income, for example, are very expensive, such systems often provide limited benefits in practice. Also, such systems still leave largely unaddressed the sense of injustice that those who cause accidents go unpunished. As for transaction costs, I am unsure how to classify such systems. The bureaucracy needed to implement them is clearly costly, but so is a private system of health care. So I have decided to assign a "neutral score" on this objective.

PRIVATE, LOCAL LITIGATION AND LOCAL LIABILITY LAWS

The oldest governmental approach in the United States (which continues to be the only governmental approach for many localities and for many kinds of injuries) is the "common law" of torts. Under this system, wide discretion is given to local juries, usually made up of a few citizens from the community where the accident happened, to decide whether the defendant caused the accident, whether the defendant should be liable for the accident, and, if liable, how much the defendant should pay in damages to the accident victim.

Major advantages include responsiveness of the law to the sense of justice of the local community, and the lack of need for a centralized bureaucracy other than the court system.

The deterrent effect of such a system is clear. In fact, if the defendant can be hauled into a local court and forced by a local group of citizens to pay whatever amount of damages they deem appropriate (within bounds), the deterrent effect may be so great that no company wants to do business in that community.

I am also ambivalent about how well such a system achieves the other objectives. While some burden sharing occurs whenever the jury awards damages to the accident victim, the whims of the juries may tend to produce haphazard results—sometimes awarding large sums for one accident, sometimes little or no compensation for a very similar accident. Moreover, although accident victims are often vindicated and justice is served, some accident victims inevitably go uncompensated, and they then feel cheated by the government as well as by the defendant; and defendants often feel that the local juries are merely taking their money unjustly. Finally, the experience in the United States is that the transaction costs of such a system can be very high indeed, due mainly to the litigation costs (attorneys' fees, the cost of generating evidence, and so forth).[6]

STATE-LEVEL TRIBUNALS AND STATE-LEVEL LIABILITY LAWS

The U.S. experience provides two sorts of examples here. There are specialized insurance pools (such as Workers Compensation Systems), and there are specialized liability statutes (such as product liability statutes). To take the example of specialized insurance pools, businesses covered under a Workers Compensation System typically pay insurance premiums based on a percentage of their payroll—a percentage based on average risks associated with the type of employment, and perhaps adjusted for safety inspections of the employer's facilities and past safety experience.[7] Workers receive benefits from the insurance fund for personal injuries resulting from an accident that arose out of and in the course of employment.[8] The major advantages of such a system are that there is a statewide, uniform, and predictable payout schedule for workplace accidents that applies to all covered employees; there are reduced litigation costs in the streamlined claims system; and there is a relatively low time-to-compensation for the injured worker.

Such state-level systems can have a deterrent effect, to the extent that liability damages or increased premiums are tied to responsibility for accident causation. There is also burden sharing within the covered sector—the liability damages or increased premiums paid by employers or product manufacturers are usually paid ultimately by the customer, who pays a higher price for the goods or services produced. Such systems have the potential to achieve justice through holding employers or product manufacturers accountable for at least avoidable accidents. While transaction costs may be substantial, they might not be as high as either governmental insurance only or private local litigation.

FEDERAL TRIBUNALS AND FEDERAL LAWS

Examples in the United States include a national statute setting up a quasi-insurance trust fund for certain side effects due to childhood vaccinations—the National Childhood Vaccine Injury Act of 1986[9]—and the recurring proposals for federal product liability legislation.[10] The federal approach to accident compensation has been used sparingly in the United States, and has generally been used in situations requiring uniformity of liability laws (for example, in such areas as maritime injuries);[11] those types of rare accidents that require larger insurance pools (such as the fortunately rare reactions to childhood vaccinations);[12] and accidents requiring large-scale adjudication (nuclear incidents, for example).[13]

It is useful to compare the federal approach to the state-level approach, both for the cases of accidents in general and for the special situations I have just enumerated. I would suggest the following scores on the four objectives. First, with respect to deterrence, I doubt whether you see much difference between federal systems and state-level systems, whether in general or in those special situations. Second, while in general federal systems produce no better burden sharing compared to state-level systems, in those special situations (for example, widespread accidents or very rare accidents) a federal approach can be a more efficient spreading mechanism. Third, as for achieving justice, I think that in general people have more confidence in tribunals and laws originating closer to home, and hence federal systems are worse than state-level systems. But in those special situations, especially where defendants are foreign parties (such as in cases involving imported products or in maritime collision cases), a federal system can achieve justice on a par with (and probably better than) a multitude of state-level systems. Finally, while central, federal bureaucracies are often more costly to run in general, in special situations (such as widespread accidents) economies of scale can make them the more efficient alternative.

CONCLUSION

What do I conclude from all of this? Let me suggest the following for your consideration.

1. A free market, hands-off approach is rarely the best approach, although it can occasionally be justified.
2. A system in which the government provides only insurance or health care provides broad (if limited) coverage to all citizens, but it by itself is a very inefficient and costly system, when evaluated on the basis of all four objectives.
3. In general, state-level systems have the potential to be the most effective and the most efficient means of achieving the four objectives.
4. A hybrid of a state-level system with some local elements (such as some limited powers for local courts to add limited punitive damages) might produce a more just system than a state-level system only.
5. In selected situations, but *only* in those selected situations, a federal system can be more effective and more efficient than a multitude of state-level systems.

NOTES

1. Robert D. Bischoff, "Accidents: Who Wins, Who Loses, Who Pays," *National Underwriters Property & Casualty*, February 4, 1991, at 25 (describing results of study by the National Highway Traffic and Safety Administration and the Centers for Disease Control). The University of Michigan's Transportation Research Institute estimates that the costs (including medical costs, pain and suffering, loss of productivity, and property damage) associated with motor vehicle accidents in Michigan alone in 1988 totaled $7.1 billion. Paul E. Eisenstein, "Police May Have to Get Tough Before More Folks Buckle Up," *Washington Times*, July 20, 1990, at G10.

2. Glenn Coleman, "A Message from a Nation's Nanny; We're Safer, But Council Keeps Guard Up," *Crain's Chicago Business*, October 29, 1990, at 3.

3. See, e.g., Y. Koryakin, "Chernobyl's Price is 200 Billion," reported in *Soviert Press Digest*, October 1990.

4. See, e.g., the work of Dean Guido Calabresi, *The Costs of Accidents: A Legal and Economic Analysis* (1970), 24–33. For other lead writings on the goals of an accident compensation system, see, e.g., George P. Fletcher, "Fairness and Utility in Tort Theory," 85 *Harvard Law Review* 537 (1972); Richard A. Epstein, "A Theory of Strict Liability," 2 *Journal of Legal Studies* 151 (1973).

5. An example in the United States is provided by disability benefits under the national Social Security System, 42 U.S.C. §§ 401 *et seq.*, 423, 424a.

6. A 1988 RAND Corporation study estimates that in automobile tort litigation, the net compensation to plaintiffs is only 52% of total expenditures, with plaintiffs' legal expenses accounting for 24% and defendants' legal expenses, 13%. In nonautomobile torts, the plaintiffs' net compensation dropped to 43%, and in asbestos injury cases, the figure was only 37%. Hugh J. Moore, Jr., "New RAND Study Demystifies Conflicting Statistics Regarding Tort Litigation," *Litigation News*, August 1988, at 1, 7.

7. Arthur Larson, *The Law of Workmen's Compensation* (1990), § 92.60; Marc A. Franklin and Robert L. Rabin, *Cases and Materials on Tort Law and Alternatives* (4th ed., 1987), 691.

8. See generally James Robert Chelius, *Workplace Safety and Health: The Role of Workers' Compensation* (1977), 20–28 (reprinted in Franklin and Rabin, *supra* note 7, at 684–91); Paul C. Weiler, "Workers' Compensation and Product Liability: The Interaction of a Tort and Non-Tort Regime," 50 *Ohio State Law Journal* 825 (1989) (reprinted in 39 *Defense Law Journal* 415 [1990]).

9. 42 U.S.C. § 300aa-1 *et seq.* Congress enacted a manufacturer's excise tax on vaccines, created a vaccine injury compensation trust fund with the tax revenues, and established a no-fault system through which compensation is payable if a child experiences certain symptoms within specified time periods after vaccination (if the government cannot prove that the symptoms were not caused by the vaccine). Peter Barton Hutt and Richard A. Merrill, *Food and Drug Law: Cases and Materials* (1991), 718–19.

10. E.g., Senate Bill S. 1400 in the 101st Congress, entitled the Product Liability Reform Act, was approved (13–7) in May 1990 by the Senate Committee on Commerce, Science, and Transportation, but was not acted on by the Senate. A bill with identical provisions, but with the title Product Liability Fairness Act, S. 640, was introduced in the 102d Congress (1991). "Product Liability 'Fairness' Bill Introduced; Proponents

Predict Passage in This Congress," *Product Safety and Liability Reporter*, BNA, March 15, 1991, at 288. In the fall of 1991, the Senate Committee on Commerce, Science, and Transportation approved the bill (by a 13–7 vote), and it was sent to the Senate Judiciary Committee for review. "New Product Liability Bills," *ABA Journal*, March 1992, at 89.

11. E.g., the Jones Act, 46 U.S.C. § 688, makes the provisions of the Federal Employers' Liability Act, 45 U.S.C. §§ 51–60, applicable to members of a ship's crew. "A complex combination of fault, strict liability and compensation systems comes into play when maritime injuries occur." Franklin and Rabin, *supra* note 7, at 703.

12. It is reported that recently the trust fund established by the National Childhood Vaccine Injury Act had pending against it more than 4,000 claims for a total of $2 billion, compared to the $80 million annual budget authorized by Congress. "U.S. Immunization Campaign Struggles; Problems Include High Vaccine Costs, Poor Access and Parental Indifference," *Washington Post*, October 22, 1991, at 35.

13. See the Atomic Energy Act of 1954, as amended, 42 U.S.C. §§ 2011 *et seq.*

Index

About the Editors and Contributors

TEMIRUZ A. BERIDZE is Chair of the Microeconomics Department of the Institute of Economics of the Georgian Academy of Sciences in Tbilisi, Georgia. He has authored or co-authored over sixty publications and was awarded the medal of the Georgian Academy of Sciences for his work on *The Efficiency of Regional Economy.*

LEE P. BRECKINRIDGE is Professor of Law at Northeastern University School of Law, where she specializes in environmental and natural resources law. Her publications address the role of local communities and intermediary organizations in ecosystem management and biodiversity protection under domestic and international law.

RICHARD BRIFFAULT is Professor of Law and Director of the Legislative Drafting and Research Fund at the Columbia University School of Law. He has published numerous law review articles on state-local relations, federalism, voting rights, and the law of the political process.

ROBERT B. CHARLES is Chief-of-Staff and Chief Counsel to the National Security, International Affairs, and Criminal Justice Subcommittee, Government Reform and Oversight Committee, of the U.S. House of Representatives. Charles is a life member of the Council on Foreign Relations, and has written extensively on constitutional law and international affairs.

GENNADII N. CHEBOTAREV is Dean of the School of Law at Tyumen State University, Tyumen, Russia. He is the author of many scholarly articles and monographs.

CATHERINE THÉRÈSE CLARKE is an S.J.D. candidate at Harvard Law School, where she is researching and writing in the area of comparative criminal procedure; specifically, issues related to policing the police and confession law under democratic principles. She teaches and writes in the areas of Constitution Law and Criminal Law and Procedure.

ROBERT V. DANIELS is Professor Emeritus of History at the University of Vermont. He is a specialist on the history of the Soviet Union and post-Communist Russia, and has directed two USIA exchange programs between Vermont and the Karelian Republic. His most recent books include *The End of the Communist Revolution*; *Soviet Communism from Reform to Collapse*; and a revised edition of *A Documentary History of Communism*.

MARTHA A. FIELD is a Professor of Law at Harvard Law School who teaches constitutional law and family law, among other subjects, and writes and lectures extensively concerning constitutional and legal rights of people who have disabilities. She has argued before the United States Supreme Court for a broad construction of special education provisions.

OLGA FLOROFF is a solo practitioner in immigration law, business law, and international business law. She is Vice-chairman of the Committee of Soviet and Eastern European Law of the New York State Bar Association.

TATIANA U. FROLOVA is Head Economist at Electrobank, Commercial Bank for the Development of the Power Industry in Moscow, Russia. She worked before in the same capacity at the Moscow Commercial Bank for the Development of the Social Sphere in Moscow.

SERGEI N. GONCHAR was Financial Analyst and Economist at the Glavnostroibank in Moscow, Russia.

PHILIP J. GROSSMAN is Assistant Professor of Economics at Wayne State University in Detroit. His principal research efforts have been in intergovernmental relations and the size and growth of government.

JOHN N. HAZARD was Professor of Law at Columbia University from 1946 until 1995. He authored *Communists and Their Law*, *The Soviet System of Government*, *Settling Disputes in Society*, *Law and Social Change in the U.S.S.R.*, *Managing Change in the U.S.S.R.*, and *The Soviet Legal System* (with Butler and Maggs).

THOMAS W. HAZLETT teaches economics and public policy at the University of California, Davis, where he is an associate professor of agricultural and resource economics and Director of the Program on Telecommunications Policy at the Institute of Governmental Affairs.

STEPHEN HESS is Senior Fellow in Governmental Studies at the Brookings Institution. His major research work has been in the fields of the presidency and the media, and his publications include *Organizing the Presidency, The Presidential Campaign, The Washington Reporters, The Government/Press Connection*, and, most recently, *International News and Foreign Correspondents.*

JAMES E. HICKEY, JR., Codirector of the 1992 Conference on Government Structures in the U.S.A. and the Sovereign States of the Former U.S.S.R., is Professor of Law at Hofstra University School of Law. He teaches, writes, and practices in international and domestic energy and natural resources law. He is coauthor of *Energy Law and Policy* and coeditor of *The Environment: Global Problems, Local Solutions* (Greenwood, 1994).

ERIK P. HOFFMANN is Professor of Political Science at the State University of New York at Albany and an Associate of Columbia University's Harriman Institute. He is coeditor of *Post-Communist Studies and Political Science: Methodology and Empirical Theory in Sovietology.*

ALEXEI I. IVANDAEV is Rector and President of Tyumen State University, Tyumen, Russia.

BARBARA JANCAR-WEBSTER is Professor of Political Science at the State University of New York at Brockport. In 1989, she was the recipient of the Harold and Margaret Sprout Award of the International Studies Association for the best book on international environmental affairs for her monograph, *Management in the Soviet Union and Yugoslavia.* Most of her publications address the politics of the environment in Central and Eastern Europe and the former Soviet Union.

OLEG S. KOLBASOV is an official in the Ministry of the Ecology and Natural Resources of the Russian Federation in Moscow, Russia. He has lectured and published widely in the field of ecological security.

NICHOLAS N. KOZLOV is Assistant Professor of Economics at Hofstra University. His principal research interest is finance, privatization, and monetary policy in the former socialist countries, particularly Russia. His work has been published in the U.S.A. and Russia.

SVETLANA N. KRAVCHENKO is Associate Professor of Law at L'viv State University, L'viv, Ukraine. Her publications include *Intercourse with Nature: Ecological, Moral, and Legal Norms* (1984); *Social and Psychological Aspects of Legal Environmental Protection* (1988); and *Realization of Ecological Legislation* (1990).

BORIS SERGEEVICH KRYLOV is Chair, Department of International Relations, Institute of Legislation and Comparative Legal Studies at the Supreme Soviet of the Russian Federation, Moscow, Russia. He is the author of *The U.S.A.: Federation, States, and Local Government; The Parliament of the Bourgeois State;* and many other publications.

SARAH F. LIEBSCHUTZ is Distinguished Service Professor and Chair of the Political Science Department at the State University of New York at Brockport. Her most recent book is *Bargaining Under Federalism: Contemporary New York* (1991).

HANS A. LINDE is Senior Judge, Oregon Supreme Court, and lecturer at Willamette University College of Law at Salem, Oregon. He is the coauthor (with George Bunn) of *Legislative and Administrative Process* (1976), and is a Fellow of the American Academy of Arts and Sciences.

MIKHAIL MARCHENKO is Vice Rector of Moscow State University. He teaches law and writes in constitutional law and theory. He is author of six books and more than 100 articles, and is also a coauthor and editor of the textbook, *The Theory of the State and Law*.

ZULFIA M. MIRSHAKAR is Lecturer in the Department of Russian at the Tadzhik State Institute of the Arts, Dushanbe, Tadzhikistan. Her research interests include lexicology and etymology of the Pamir languages. She has published widely in her field.

RICHARD P. NATHAN is Distinguished Professor of Political Science and Public Policy, State University of New York at Albany, and Director of the Nelson A. Rockefeller Institute of Government and provost of the Rockefeller College of Public Affairs and Policy. His books include *Turning Promises into Performance* (1993), *The Administrative Presidency* (1983), *Reagan and the States* (1987), and *Social Science in Government* (1988).

HELEN OSTROVIDOVA is Staff Researcher, Department of Political Studies, Institute for International Economic and Political Studies, Moscow. Her primary publications include *Yugoslavia* (1984), *The Church and Its Role in Eastern Europe* (1987), and *The Current Political Situation in Yugoslavia* (1991).

JONAH OTELSBERG is a Professor of Business Administration and Marketing at York College, the City University of New York. She has had several articles published both in Russia and the United States, and has presented papers at various conferences in the United States.

THOMAS EARL PORTER is Assistant Professor of History at North Carolina Agricultural and Technical State University in Greensboro. He is coauthor of "Public Initiative in Late Imperial Russia" (with William Gleason), as well as the author of a monograph entitled "The Zemstvo and the Emergence of Civil Society in Late Imperial Russia, 1864–1917."

PRIYA RAJAGOPALAN is an Instructor of Economics at Purdue University and graduate student in economics at Wayne State University in Detroit.

WILLIAM RICH is a Professor at Washburn University School of Law, where he has also served as associate dean and acting dean of the law faculty. He has written on comparative constitutional law and is coauthoring a new edition of *Modern Constitutional Law*.

MARAT A. SARSEMBAYEV is Chair, Department of International Law, at Kazakh State University, Alma-Ata, Kazakhstan. He is senior lecturer in international law and the legal regulation of external economic activities.

VLADIMIR A. SAVELIEV is Chair and Senior Research Fellow in the Study Group on Foreign Policy Decision Making, Institute of the U.S. and Canada, Russian Academy of Sciences, Moscow. He has published in the fields of American politics, labor and Constitutional law, and Soviet-American relations, among others.

YURII S. SHEMSHUCHENKO is Director of the Institute of State and Law, Academy of Sciences of Ukraine, Kiev, where he is a corresponding member and lecturer with professorial rank. His primary research concentrates on problems of constitutional and state law.

NORMAN I. SILBER is Professor of Law at Hofstra University, where he teaches commercial law, consumer law, and legal history. He is the author of many publications, including *Test and Protest: The Influence of Consumers Union*.

LYUDMILA M. SIMONOVA is Assistant Professor and Assistant Chair of the Economics Department of Tyumen State University, Tyumen, Russia.

SUSAN W. TIEFENBRUN is Administrative Director of both the Center for the Study of Communications Law, Information, and Technology and the International Law Programs at Hofstra University School of Law.

BORIS A. TSEPOV is with the Foreign Ministry of the Russian Federation, Moscow. Until 1993, Dr. Tsepov was Senior Legal Councilor in the Russian Federation Permanent Mission to the United Nations in New York.

YURI TUNITSIA is Executive Director of the International Institute and Association for Regional Ecological Problems at L'viv State University in L'viv, Ukraine. He is also Chair of the Department of Nature-Usage and Nature-Protection. He is the author of over 100 books, monographs, and periodical articles, some of which have been published in the United States.

ALEXEJ UGRINSKY is Adjunct Associate Professor of German and Director of Documentation, Finance, and Planning at the Hofstra Cultural Center. He served as coordinator of the 1992 Conference on Government Structures in the U.S.A. and the Sovereign States of the Former U.S.S.R., Dr. Ugrinsky's published works include *Gerald R. Ford and the Politics of Post-Watergate America* (Greenwood, 1993); *The Presidency and Domestic Policies of Jimmy Carter* (Greenwood, 1994); and *Jimmy Carter—Foreign Policy and Post-Presidential Years* (Greenwood, 1994).

W. GARY VAUSE is Associate Dean and Director of the Center for Dispute Resolution at Stetson University College of Law, where he teaches International Business Transactions. He has published extensively on legal developments in non-market and transitional economies, and frequently lectures and consults abroad on the role of law in emerging market economies.

IRINA A. VEKSHINA is Assistant Professor in the Department of State and Administrative Law, Kemerov State University School of Law, Kemerov, Russia. She also is Scientific Advisor to the Kemerov Council of State Deputies. She is a member of the Advisory Council to the Committee of the Supreme Soviet of the Russian Federation.

VERN R. WALKER is Professor of Law at the Hofstra University School of Law and was previously a Partner in the law firm of Swidler & Berlin in Washington, D.C. He is a coauthor of *Product Risk Reduction in the Chemical Industry* (1985), and has written numerous articles on the use of scientific information in legal decision-making.

JAMES W. WELLER is an attorney with the law firm of Rivkin, Radler & Kremer, in Uniondale, New York. He is also an adjunct professor at the State University of New York at Stony Brook teaching constitutional interpretation.

GORDON S. WOOD is University Professor and Professor of History at Brown University. His principal research interests are in the history of the American Revolution and its aftermath. His books include *The Creation of the American Republic, 1776–1787* and *The Radicalism of the American Revolution*.

VICTORIA YEGOROVA is Associate Professor in Economics at the Institute of Industrial Economics at the Ukrainian Academy of Sciences, Donetsk, Ukraine.

Hofstra University's Cultural and Intercultural Studies
Coordinating Editor, Alexej Ugrinsky

James Joyce and His Contemporaries
(Editors: Diana A. Ben-Merre and Maureen Murphy)

The World of George Sand
(Editors: Natalie Datlof, Jeanne Fuchs, and David A. Powell)

Richard M. Nixon: Politician, President, Administrator
(Editors: Leon Friedman and William F. Levantrosser)

Watergate and Afterward: The Legacy of Richard M. Nixon
(Editors: Leon Friedman and William F. Levantrosser)

Immigration and Ethnicity: American Society—"Melting Pot" or "Salad Bowl"?
(Editors: Michael D'Innocenzo and Josef P. Sirefman)

Johann Sebastian: A Tercentenary Celebration
(Editor: Seymour L. Benstock)

Cold War Patriot and Statesman: Richard M. Nixon
(Editors: Leon Friedman and William F. Levantrosser)

Jimmy Carter: Foreign Policy and Post-Presidential Years
(Editors: Herbert D. Rosenbaum and Alexej Ugrinsky)

The Presidency and Domestic Policies of Jimmy Carter
(Editors: Herbert D. Rosenbaum and Alexej Ugrinsky

Money: Lure, Lore, and Literature
(Editor: John Louis DiGaetani)

Games and Great Ideas: A Guide for Elementary School Physical Educators and Classroom Teachers
(Editor: Rhonda L. Clements)

Contested Terrain: Power, Politics, and Participation in Suburbia
(Editors: Marc L. Silver and Martin Melkonian)

Van Gogh 100
(Editor: Joseph D. Masheck)

www.ingramcontent.com/pod-product-compliance
Ingram Content Group UK Ltd.
Pitfield, Milton Keynes, MK11 3LW, UK
UKHW020906190926
475560UK00010B/318

9 780313 296536